The Chronological

Life
of
Christ
Volume 1

The Chronological
Life of Christ

Volume 1
From Glory to Galilee

Mark E. Moore

COLLEGE PRESS
PUBLISHING COMPANY
Joplin, Missouri

Cover Design: Mark A. Cole

Library of Congress Cataloging-in-Publication Data

Moore, Mark E. (Mark Edward), 1963–
    The chronological life of Christ / Mark E. Moore.
        p.   cm.
    Includes text from: The NIV harmony of the Gospels / Robert L. Thomas,
    editor and Stanley N. Gundry, associate editor.
    Includes bibliographical references and index.
    Contents: v. 1. From glory to Galilee.
    ISBN 0-89900-751–1 (pbk.)
    1. Jesus Christ—Biography.   2. Jesus Christ—Chronology.   3. Bible. N.T.
    Gospels—Harmonies, English.   I. Bible. N.T. Gospels. English. New
    International. 1996.   II. Title.
    BT301.2.M58 1996
    226'.1077—dc20   96-12594
                                                          CIP

DEDICATED
TO
SETH WILSON

There are still giants in the land.

ABBREVIATIONS

ABW	Archaeology in the Biblical World
AL	Alliance Life
Ant	Antiquities of the Jews
ATJ	Asbury Theological Journal
ATR	Anglican Theological Review
AUSS	Andrews University Seminary Studies
BA	Biblical Archaeologist
BAR	Biblical Archaeology Review
BETS	Bulletin of the Evangelical Theological Society
BibSac	Bibliotheca Sacra
BibT	Bible Today
BJRL	Bulletin of the John Rylands University Library of Manchester
BR	Bible Review
BT	Bible Translator
BW	Biblical World
CBQ	Catholic Biblical Quarterly
ChHist	Church History
ChicSt	Chicago Studies
ChrCen	Christian Century
CJ	Concordia Journal
CQ	Covenant Quarterly
CS	Christian Standard
CSR	Christian Scholar's Review
CT	Christianity Today
CTJ	Calvin Theological Journal
CTM	Concordia Theological Monthly
CTR	Criswell Theological Review
CurTM	Currents in Theology and Mission
DJ	Discipleship Journal
EvQ	Evangelical Quarterly
ExpT	Expository Times
GR	Gordon Review
GTJ	Grace Theological Journal
GWPA	Gospel Witness and Protestant Advocate
HeyJ	Heythrop Journal
HibJ	Hibbert Journal
HTR	Harvard Theological Review
IEJ	Israel Exploration Journal
Int	Interpretation
ITQ	Irish Theological Quarterly
JAMA	Journal of the American Medical Association
JBL	Journal of Biblical Literature
JES	Journal of Ecumenical Studies
JETS	Journal of the Evangelical Theological Society
JHLT	Journal of Hispanic/Latino Theology
JJS	Journal of Jewish Studies
JPSP	Journal of Personality and Social Psychology
JPST	Journal of Psychology and Theology
JQR	Jewish Quarterly Review
JSNT	Journal for the Study of the New Testament
JTS	Journal of Theological Studies
JTSA	Journal of Theology Southern Africa
LexTQ	Lexington Theological Quarterly
LXX	Septuagint

MT	Masoretic Text	*SwJT*	Southwestern Journal of Theology
NovT	Novum Testamentum	*TB*	Tyndale Bulletin
NT	New Testament	*TheolEd*	Theological Educator
NTS	New Testament Studies	*TrinJ*	Trinity Journal
OT	Old Testament	*TS*	Theological Studies
PEQ	Palestine Exploration Quarterly	*VE*	Vox Evangelica
Pres	Presbyterion	*War*	Jewish Wars
PRS	Perspectives in Religious Studies	*WTJ*	Westminster Theological Journal
RB	Revue Biblique	*ZNW*	*Zeitschrift für die neutestamentliche Wissenschaft und die Kunde der ältern Kirche*
RestQ	Restoration Quarterly		
RevExp	Review & Expositor		
SJT	Scottish Journal of Theology		
ST	Studia Theologica		

Note: not all of these are cited in Vol. 1.

Key to Marginal Icons

 Parables

 Prayer (major teachings about/examples of)

 Fulfilled Prophecies

 Deity of Christ (claims of/witnesses to)

 End-time Teachings

 Healings and other Miracles

 The Kingdom/Church

TABLE OF CONTENTS

INTRODUCTION

Jesus of Nazareth, the incomparable Christ, was unique in the extreme. This is his story as told by four witnesses. Their names are Matthew, Mark, Luke and John. In this volume, we have woven their testimonies together to get the "big picture" so to speak. Granted, there is a danger in doing that. Namely, each of the Gospel writers has carefully crafted their books. Each has a unique literary flavor. By blending them, we risk losing the uniqueness of each. At least that's the criticism currently leveled against harmonistic studies in the life of Christ.

However, there are good reasons to harmonize the four Gospels into a composite whole:

(1) Each Gospel has a unique flavor. We don't "taste" it merely by looking at each book individually. Sometimes the best way to observe Matthew's themes, for example, is by comparing his presentation to Luke's and Mark's. In other words, harmony studies can actually highlight each Gospel's uniqueness rather than neglect them.

(2) The Gospels are not just literary products. What we have here are true historical records. Therefore, we have treated them much like we would treat witnesses in a court of law. By combining all the witnesses, we get a fuller, more detailed account of Jesus Christ.

(3) The study of individual Gospels highlights each Evangelist's theology. On the other hand, the study of all four together highlights the chronology of Jesus' life. That is, it allows us to see the development and the "ebb and flow" of his ministry. By looking at Jesus through all four lenses, we see him in a way that we never could by using just one. Perhaps that's why God gave us all four.

(4) Studying the Gospels harmonistically is nothing new. Preachers, commentators and students who study the Gospels almost invariably take a peek at parallel passages in the other Evangelists. The fact that "everyone is doing it anyway" may justify a more purposeful harmony such as this one. In addition, harmony studies stand in a long and noble

line of tradition. From R.C. Foster's *Studies in the Life of Christ*, to J.W. McGarvey's *The Four-fold Gospel*, clear on back to Tatian's *Diatessaron*, Bible students have compared these four majestic portraits of Jesus. In fact, one might even make a case that Luke and perhaps also John, wrote with an eye on the other Gospels.

UNIQUE FEATURES:

What we have here is **a companion to the NIV harmony** by Thomas and Gundry.[1] Of course, the harmony prints the Gospel text in four columns. We have squeezed it into one and added brief exegetical comments. The purpose of these comments is twofold. Obviously, they are intended to clarify the meaning of the text. But beyond that, these comments are designed to draw you into the scene. We hope to paint such a realistic picture that you find Palestinian dust between your toes from having walked with Jesus.

The texts of all four Gospels have been combined and printed in a different typeface to read as a single "story line." By simply using the superscripted letters [MT,MK,LK,JN] to represent Matthew, Mark, Luke and John respectively, the reader can quickly identify which Evangelist said what. This will allow you to read all four Gospels at once. Now, we are not suggesting that this combination of words is a more accurate account of what Jesus actually said (i.e., Jesus' *Ipsissima Verba*). Rather, we are suggesting that this allows us to see all the major details of each incident as told by the four witnesses. All four Gospels tell the truth sufficiently. But by comparing and combining their testimony we can reconstruct the scene with fuller and more colorful detail.

There is one other feature of this book worth mentioning. That is the **footnotes**. The big stuff is all covered in the middle of the page. But there are a number of scholarly discussions and references in which more advanced students might be interested. We've tucked that information into footnotes at the bottom of the page for more advanced study.

Now I must let you in on my secret. It was God's gift to me to study the life of his Son, Jesus. This delightful labor has changed the contours of my heart. What you now hold in your hand is his product more than my own. It is my meager gift back to God. If it blesses you along the way, I will be supremely satisfied.

Mark E. Moore

---

[1]HarperSanFrancisco, Division of HarperCollins, 1988. With permission, we have followed their section numbers with a few minor variations.

PART ONE
BEGINNINGS

§ 1
Luke's
Introduction to
His Gospel
(Lk 1:1-4)

¹Many have undertaken to draw up an account of the things that have been fulfilled[a] among us, ²just as they were handed down to us by those who from the first were eyewitnesses and servants of the word. ³Therefore, since I myself have carefully investigated everything from the beginning, it seemed good also to me to write an orderly account for you, most excellent Theophilus, ⁴so that you may know the certainty of the things you have been taught.

[a]1 Or *been surely believed*

Of the four Gospels, Luke alone states his purpose in an introductory paragraph. So, we will begin with him. These first four verses make up one long, carefully constructed sentence in Greek. In fact, some think that it is the finest Greek sentence in all the NT. That is interesting since the rest of chapters 1-2 are filled with Aramaic-type phrases and are not "pure" Greek. What we have then is a formal introduction in verses one to four where Luke "struts his stuff." However, he then uses idioms appropriate to his subject matter in the material that follows. He is a literary genius. We discover right away in Luke that our intellects are in for a treat!

While this is a fancy introduction, it was not out of the ordinary. It was customary among Greek and Hellenistic historians to use this kind of introduction.[1] They sought to assure the reader of their capability, thorough research and reliability. Luke will describe his motivation (vv. 1-2), his credentials (v. 3) and his specific purpose (v. 4).[2]

The word which begins Luke's Gospel [*epeidepēr*] is translated as "therefore" in the NIV, and placed at verse three for the sake of English

---

[1]There are ample examples of this type of introduction in Herodotus, Dionysius, Polybius, Hippocrates, Josephus, etc. See T. Callan, "The Preface of Luke-Acts and Historiography," *NTS* 31 (1985): 576-581; H.J. Cadbury, "Commentary on the Preface of Luke-Acts." In *Beginnings*, ed. F.J. Foakes-Jackson and K. Lake, 2:489-510.

[2]See. D.J. Sneen, "An Exegesis of Luke 1:1-4 with Special Regard to Luke's Purpose as a Historian," *ExpT* 83 (1971): 40-43.

style. It is a classical word which sets the stage for Luke's formal introduction.

Luke is motivated to write by the "many" who have gone before him. The fact that they have written about Jesus sets the precedent for Luke's own rendition. Furthermore, Vincent (*Word Studies in the NT*, I:251) says that this word [*epicheireō*, lit. "set their hand to"], implies that their previous attempts were unsuccessful (see also Johnson, pp. 27-28). Although this is not a necessary implication, Luke obviously sees something lacking. This caused him to undertake this extensive project which resulted in his two-volume work, Luke and Acts. These books would begin with the birth of John the Baptist and follow the gospel clear to Rome. In other words, Luke begins farther back and continues far beyond the narrative of the other three Evangelists.

Luke uses three sources for his research.[3] First, he uses events that he and/or his audience participated in — **things that have been fulfilled**. This translation doesn't do full justice to the verb tense Luke uses. We might say, "Things that have come to fruition among us." As a historian, Luke doesn't just tell us what happened. Rather, there is a theological meaning and a sovereign design behind each of the events he records. Second, Luke uses the previously **written materials**. As verse one states, there were many who had already "drawn up an account" of Jesus' life. This may even include the writings of Matthew and Mark. Third, there was **oral testimony** of eyewitnesses. This should not be taken lightly. Luke stresses that their witness goes clear back to the beginning of the story. They are well-informed and highly credible. Any theory of gospel origins that does not take into account all three sources that Luke lists is destined to be seriously flawed. Furthermore, Luke's veracity can be verified by the fact that he admits, up-front, that he, himself, was **not** an eyewitness. This is not the work of a fanciful storyteller, but an honest, reliable researcher.

Luke uses a fascinating word for *investigate*. Etymologically, it means to follow alongside. It pictures the pesky reporter with his note pad and pen incessantly asking questions. Luke did careful and detailed research which he describes here with four words:

1) *Everything*. Luke is the longest and most complete of the four Gospels. And combined with Acts it makes up 27% of the NT. We read more from the pen of Luke than we do from Peter or John or even Paul. From Luke we get a full understanding of the beginnings of the Christian Church.

---

[3]Cf. R.H. Stein, "Luke 1:1-4 and *Traditionsgeschichte*," *JETS* 26/4 (Dec 1983): 421-430.

2) *From the beginning.* Luke is the only Gospel writer who gives us a fully detailed account of the birth of Jesus and John.

3) *Carefully.* Better, "Accurately." His investigation was careful, precise and accurate. There have been many who criticized Luke as a historian, but never with great success or the support of archaeology.

4) *Orderly Account.* It was not just that Luke's account was orderly, but it was in order. This word seems to indicate a chronological procession (cf. Lk 8:1; Acts 3:24; 11:4; and 18:23). This is not to say that Luke never deviates from a strict chronology for a thematic arrangement or theological purpose, but he is the only Gospel writer to claim to be chronological in his arrangement. We ought to keep this in mind when harmonizing the four Gospels.

Luke's book is addressed to the **most excellent Theophilus**. The title "Most excellent" was often given to those of the equestrian order, (i.e., the cavalry) or to governors (as referring to Felix, Acts 23:26; 24:3 and to Festus, Acts 26:25). The name "Theophilus" means "Friend of God." Some believe him to be a fictitious representation of all those who love God, yet this specific title of honor, "Most excellent," argues against that. It seems likely that he was an associate or acquaintance whom Luke wants to convert or strengthen in his faith. It is also possible that he is a Roman official whom Luke would like to convince that Christianity is a legal religion (perhaps even Paul's defense attorney in Rome, cf. Acts 28). Another strong possibility is that Theophilus is the patron or publisher of the book.[4] It was, after all, not uncommon for a writer to dedicate his book to the fellow footing the bill. This much is certain, however, Luke did not produce these two volumes for Theophilus alone. While it is addressed to this individual, it is meant for the broader Christian community.

Finally, we come to the theme of the book in verse 4: "To provide evidence so that you should know with certainty the things you were taught" (cf. Jn 20:31). Theophilus (and the broader Christian community) obviously had some instruction about Jesus. This dual treatise, Luke/Acts, intends to bring it to fruition. It will seek to "make certain" the facts about Jesus. This word [*asphaleian*], in both its verb and noun forms, most often refers to securing a person in prison (Mt 27:64-66; Acts 5:23; 16:24). It is a word which describes the surest of conviction. This book tells about Jesus. It is both convincing and compelling.

---

[4]Cf. E.T. Goodspeed, "Some Greek Notes: I. Was Theophilus Luke's Publisher?" *JBL* 73 (1954): 84.

**§2
John's
Introduction to
Jesus**
(Jn 1:1-18)

Luke's introduction reflects the Greek Historical literature that he was so familiar with. John's introduction, on the other hand, reflects the Jewish wisdom literature[5] of his culture. For example, he uses Hebrew poetic parallelism[6] and recurring key words which are clues to the dominant theme(s) of the text.[7]

In fact, a number of scholars believe this prologue was not only a poem, but an early Christian hymn[8] which sets the tone or even the outline for the rest of the book. Staley says it this way: "Just as the first strophe of the prologue sets the tone for the symmetrical, rhythmic shape of the entire prologue, so also the symmetrical shape of the prologue sets the tone for the structure of the narrative to follow" (p. 242).[9]

This prologue is complex, not only rhetorically, but also theologically. Some of John's concepts are quite deep. But even the simplest reader can't miss John's main point: Jesus is affiliated with God.

Jn 1:1-2

[1]In the beginning was the Word, and the Word was with God, and the Word was God. [2]He was with God in the beginning.

"In the beginning" ties together at least three books: Genesis, John and 1 John. All three open with this thought. Both Genesis and John

---

[5]Thomas Tobin, "The Prologue of John and Hellenistic Jewish Speculation" *CBQ* 52 (Apr 1990): 252-269, compares John with Philo. He suggests that they both use an anagogical hermeneutic, only John reflects Palestinian Midrash while Philo comes from the Hellenistic tradition of Alexandria.

[6]Mathias Rissi offers an in-depth analysis of the poetry of this section ("John 1:1-18," *Int*, 31 [Oct 1977]): 394-401).

[7]Jeff Staley, "The Structure of John's Prologue: Its Implication for the Gospel's Narrative Structure," *CBQ* 48: 241-264, calls this rhetorical device *Leitwort*. He suggests that *phōs* and *ginomai* are two such words. He observes that *ginomai*, for example, "occurs at least once in each section of the prologue's chiastic structure, and so it becomes a major unifying component of the prologue" (p. 249).

[8]E.g., Barclay Newman, "Some observations regarding a Poetic Restructuring of John 1:1-18," *BT*, 29 (Apr 1978): 206-212; Thomas Tobin, "The Prologue of John and Hellenistic Jewish Speculation," *CBQ* 52 (Apr 1990): 252-269. However, most attempts at analyzing the structure of John's prologue fall prey to two errors. First, they tend to assume radical redaction, viewing vv. 6-8, 13, 15 as later editorial comments and intrusions into the original hymn (cf. Charles Giblin, "Two Complementary Literary Structures in John 1:1-18," *JBL* 104/1 [1985]: 87-103). Second, they often suggest what seems to be a "forced" chiasm on the text. Indeed, John does use the typical Jewish device of repetition (e.g., v. 1; vv. 6-8 & 15), but it is not clearly identifiable chiasm (as can be seen by the variety of chiastic structures suggested by scholars).

[9]Jeff Staley, "The Structure of John's Prologue: Its Implications for the Gospel's Narrative Structure," *CBQ* 48: 241-264. He divides the book into five sections, each one larger than the last (1:1-18; 1:19-3:36; 4:1-6:71; 7:1-10:42; 11:1-21:25). Furthermore, in a chart on p. 264, he suggests that each element of the prologue is repeated in each of the five following sections.

speak specifically of creation. Both John and 1 John speak specifically of the incarnation (Jn 1:14; 1 Jn 1:1-2). Thus, Jesus, the incarnate Logos, was fully existent, fully operational from the beginning of creation.

In these first five verses, John makes four startling assertions about Jesus: He is the Logos; he is God; he is the creator of life; and he is the light.

JESUS IS THE LOGOS

When we read that Jesus is "The Word," we naturally think about the word of God — the Bible. We kind of spirtualize it to mean that Jesus was the incarnational message of God. That's not bad, it's just not complete. This word *logos* was thick with meaning for both Greek philosophers and Hebrew theologians.

For example, Socrates and Plato used *logos* to refer to ideas which resided in the "Divine Mind." In other words, *logos* was not merely a grammatical unit of human speech, but the very thoughts of the gods that somehow filtered down to man. The Stoics, under a guy named Zeno (300 B.C.), took it a step further. *Logos* was not just a divine idea, but a divine command. That is, what the gods think and say takes actual physical form in space and time. It's like what we read in Genesis 1: God said . . . and it was so. Thus the *logos* of the gods had creative force (which was called *logos spermatikos*). The Mystery cults went one step further. They added to *logos* the idea of communication with the gods. *If a god spoke with man, logos = revelation. If man spoke with a god, logos = prayer.* Both, however, were considered mysterious and sacred. And Hermes was supposedly the messenger which delivered the *logos* for both parties. So much for Greek philosophy.

Along comes Philo. He was a Hebrew theologian who loved Greek philosophy. So he used the Greeks' definition of *logos* and applied it to the OT. He talked about *logos* in terms of a bridge between the transcendent God and the physical world. It was a kind of semi-god force that moved back and forth between heaven and earth. Thus, in Jewish Theology, *logos* came to mean "an active force from God — that which caused a certain result": (1) Creation, Genesis 1:3; (2) Healing, Psalms 107:20; 147:15,18; or (3) Revelation.

For the Greek, *logos* was the "filtered" ideas of a god in Human Philosophy. For the Hebrews it represented the spoken word of God which became concrete human reality. John adapts both ideas. For him, *logos* was the incarnation of both the wisdom of God and the active agent of God — Jesus Christ. The difference for John, however, is that nothing was lost when *logos* descended to earth. This *logos* doesn't merely represent God's thoughts, he is God incarnate. Thus, the mind of God invades human history.

JESUS IS GOD

This concept of *logos* allows us to understand a bit more about Jesus. Prior to Jesus' incarnation, he existed as God in this "*logos*" state. Not only do John and Paul claim preexistence for Jesus; Jesus himself makes that claim (Jn 6:38; 8:42; 16:27; 17:5) in the presence of both friend and foe. He was with God at the beginning of creation (Jn 1:1-3, 18; 1 Cor 8:6; Col 1:16; 1 Jn 1:1) and shared in God's ministry to the Israelites (1 Cor 10:3-4). Although he was equal with the Father in glory, power, and riches (Jn 17:5; 2 Cor 8:9; Phil 2:6), he was in submission to God and thus sent from God as his representative from heaven (Jn 6:38, 51; 8:42; 13:3; 16:27, 30; Rom 8:3; Gal 4:4; 1 Jn 4:9-10). In this obedient act of incarnation he stripped himself in order to accomplish his Father's will. He was humbled by taking the form of a human being (Rom 8:3; Phil 2:7-8), and dying as the embodiment of sin (2 Cor 5:21).

Now, if the *logos* was equal to Jehovah, why do some say that he was merely "a god" or "god-like"? The Greek text of verse 1 has no definite article ("the") in the phrase "And the Word was God." Therefore, some religious groups are tempted to add the indefinite article ("a"), which the Greek language does not have. Sometimes that is an appropriate translation, but not always. The definite article in Greek specifies a particular object (person, place or thing). It is as if one pointed his finger and said, "that one." An anarthrous Greek noun (a noun without an article), on the other hand, signifies the quality or characteristic of the specified noun. Thus, the phrase, "And the Word was God" describes the Word as having "God-quality/character." Instead of saying that Jesus was merely "a god" or "god-like," this verse is an explicit claim to the deity of Jesus.[10] [Note: this same grammatical structure is found also in v. 12 and 18 where it would be clearly inappropriate to add an indefinite article. See especially John 4:24 "God is spirit."][11]

---

[10]E.L. Miller, "The Logos was God," *EvQ* 53/2 (1981): 65-77 comes to several significant conclusions about this phrase: (1) "Divine" should be rejected as too weak a rendering for *theos*. (2) The general and immediate contexts of the phrase suggest a definite, not qualitative or adjectival, meaning for *theos*. (3) The absence of the article suggests that John avoids a full equation of the *logos* and *theos*, as does 1:1b. (4) But along with 1:2, it does suggest the concept of the Christian (Triune) God.

[11]For a more detailed discussion of Greek anarthrous nouns see C.H. Dodd, "New Testament Translation Problems II," *BT* 28/1 (Jan 1977): 101-104 and P.B. Harner, "Qualitative Anarthrous Predicate Nouns: Mark 15:39 and John 1:1," *JBL* 92 (1973): 75ff.

Admittedly, it is difficult to swallow this claim that Jesus, the man, was God incarnate. If John was the only one to make such a claim we might dismiss him as a lunatic or a poet. But he is accompanied by both Peter and Paul who equate Jesus with Jehovah in their letters (Rom 9:5; 2 Thess 1:12; Titus 2:13; 2 Pet 1:1; 1 Jn 5:20). Furthermore, both Jesus' friends (Jn 1:18; Mt 14:33; 16:16-19; Lk 7:13-16; 23:39-43) and foes (Mk 3:11; 27:54; Mk 15:39; Lk 4:41; Jn 3:1-2) allude to his divine nature. More than that, Jesus claims it himself. He accepts worship as God (Mt 16:16-17; 26:6-13; Lk 5:8-9; 7:36-50; 19:35-40; Jn 20:27-29). He performs works unique to God (Mt 28:18; Mk 2:10; Jn 5:24-30; 14:6; Rom 3:21-26; 5:5-17; 1 Cor 15:16-19, 35-58; Phil 3:21; Col 1:16-17; 2:3; Heb 1:3). In addition, he makes specific claims to his deity (Mt 10:32-33; 16:13-18; 28:18; Mk 2:10; 9:41; 14:62; Jn 5:30-40; 8:23-24, 58; 9:37; 10:30, 36; 14:9; 17:1-3). This doesn't even include all Jesus' "I AM" statements in John (6:35, 41, 48, 51; 8:12, 58; 9:5; 10:7, 9, 11, 14, 36; 11:25; 14:6; 15:1, 5; Rev. 1:8, 17; 22:16). The bottom line is that we have all four Evangelists, Peter, Paul, and Jesus himself reaffirming John 1:1 — Jesus is *logos* — God incarnate.

Jn 1:3-5

³Through him all things were made; without him nothing was made that has been made. ⁴In him was life, and that life was the light of men. ⁵The light shines in the darkness, but the darkness has not understood³ it.

³5 Or *darkness, and the darkness has not overcome*

JESUS IS THE CREATOR OF LIFE

Aside from this verse (Jn 1:3), there are two other clear claims in the NT that Jesus created the world — 1 Corinthians 8:6 and Colossians 1:16. From these three passages we learn (1) Jesus was under the authority of the Father and (2) Jesus was the active agent which carried out the will of the Father in creation. This idea of Jesus the *logos* can easily be read into the Genesis account. First, we remember that God created by the force of his Word — "God said . . . and it was so." Second, we recall God's words of Genesis 1:26, "Let us make man in our image, in our likeness." There was a plurality of God's personality at creation. Christian theologians have inferred from this the idea of the Trinity. Indeed, John clearly implies that Jesus was the active agent carrying out God's creative will.

Since Jesus, the *logos*, was responsible for creation, John can say that "In him was life." There are actually three Greek words for life: *bios*, *psychē* and *zoē*. *Bios* (from which we get biology) indicates "here and now" kind of life — the duration of life. *Psychē* (lit. soul), indicates

(1) the individual life — the personality of the person, and (2) the breath of the person. The third word (*zoē*), which John uses here, is the intensive life (as opposed to the *bios* — extensive life). It is what we might call "being alive."

In fact, when John talks about "eternal life" he only uses this word *zoē* (Jn 3:15-16, 36; 4:14, 36; 5:24, 39; 6:27, 40, 47, 54, 68; 10:28; 12:25, 50; 17:2-3; 1 Jn 1:2; 2:25; 3:15; 5:11, 13, 20). Therefore, the life Jesus gives us is not a quantity of life, but quality of life. One does not enter "eternal life" upon his death. One obtains eternal life through a relationship with the living Christ (Jn 5:40; 1 Jn 5:11-12). As we encounter Jesus through the word (Jn 5:24, 39; 6:63, 68), and place our faith in him (3:15-16, 36; 6:40, 47; 20:31; 1 Jn 5:13), we receive life because he gives it to us as a gift (Jn 10:28; 17:2-3).

Jesus himself is life (1 Jn 1:1-2)! When we have a relationship with him we too become fully alive (cf. Rom 8:10-11). Surely there is a future aspect to this eternal life, that is, it lasts forever. More significantly, it begins in the present (Jn 10:10; 1 Jn 3:14-15; 5:11-13). The bottom line is this: Jesus saves me from my sins. That is eternal life (Jn 6:51). I have a personal relationship with the Son of God, beginning today, and lasting through eternity.

JESUS IS THE LIGHT

Jesus is not only the life but also the light. This is a strong theme for John. Of the 72 times *phōs* is used in the NT, 33 belong to John's writings. Except for the prophetic utterances of Matthew 4:16 and Luke 2:32, John is the only Gospel writer to use the term "light" to refer to Jesus. The other writers use it to refer to the people of the kingdom of God in our relationship with the world. John, however, pulls together the two great themes of light and life — both of which are personified in Jesus (1:9-14; 8:12; 9:5; 12:35-36, 46). John is also more marked in his portrayal of the battle between light and darkness (Jn 1:5; 3:19-20; 1 Jn 2:8; cf. 2 Cor 6:14). The ethical comparison of light and darkness was not original with Christian theology, however, but was previously used in Greek philosophy. The gods, in fact, were pictured as dwelling in a realm of light. The OT, as well as the Gnostics and Essenes, employed this same metaphor. Yet here, the fact that the Father is called the light (1 Jn 1:5), demonstrates again that John portrays Jesus as God.

The main function of light in John's writings is to expose the reality of that which surrounds us. Those who walk in the light, then, are innocent (Jn 3:19-21; 1 Jn 1:7; 2:9; cf. Rom 13:12), because they are able to see (ethically) and respond properly to their surroundings. On the other hand, those that walk in the darkness are prone to stumbling (Jn 11:10; 12:35; 1 Jn 2:11). There is also the freedom to choose exposure to the light or the secrecy of darkness. Eschatologically, the fate of the wicked is pictured as darkness while that of the righteous is pictured as light, especially God's own light, which is provided for the New Jerusalem (Rev 21:23; 22:5).

All this talk about the "light" raises a practical question: What does John mean, "The darkness has not understood it"? This Greek word, *katalambanō*, is a compound word from "down" and "to take/receive." Thus, etymologically it indicates a "holding down" in some way or another. There are two directions that this word can go. First, it can indicate an intellectual holding down (i.e., understanding, comprehending, apprehending; cf. Acts 25:25; Eph 3:18). We use the same idiom when we say, "I get it." Second, its primary meaning is physically holding something down (i.e., overcoming, subduing, extinguishing; cf. Jn 8:3; 12:35; 1 Cor 9:24; 1 Thess 5:4). These two thrusts are seen in the various translations: KJV & NASB = "Comprehend"; RSV & Modern = "Overcome"; Living = "Extinguish"; ASV = "Apprehend." It is important to understand that the Greek word can, at one and the same time, carry both connotations. However, since we do not have an equivalent English word, we have to settle for "either/or."

Therefore, this verse carries two primary connotations. First, the darkness has not overcome the light. That is to say, when you walk in a room and flip on a light, the darkness does not squelch it. When Jesus, the light, came into the dark world, he conquered, not vice versa. This may seem strange considering that the light was nailed to a cross, but then again, the story ends with a resurrection. The second emphasis states that the darkness did not apprehend the truth/reality of the light. Jesus was indeed the most misunderstood figure in human history.[12]

Jn 1:6-9   [6]There came a man who was sent from God; his name was John. [7]He came as a witness to testify concerning that light, so that through him all men might believe. [8]He himself was not the light; he came only as a witness to the light. [9]The true light that gives light to every man was coming into the world.[a]

[a]9 Or *This was the true light that gives light to every man who comes into the world*

John the Baptist has an interesting biography. He was the prophesied forerunner of Jesus (Isa 40:3-4; Mal 3:1; 4:5). It was his job to clear the way for Jesus by preparing people's hearts through preaching. He entered

---

[12]Plato's cave is a good illustration of how the darkness does not understand the light (*Republic*, VII).

the world through the priestly line. His father, Zechariah, was from the course of Abijah (1 Chr 24:10) and his mother descended from Aaron (Lk 1:5). Their barren state and miraculous pregnancy is described in Luke 1 and Matthew 1. Jesus and John were related in some way (probably cousins), and John was his elder by about six months (Lk 1:36). He was circumcised on the eighth day and set apart as a Nazirite (Lk 1:15). All else we know about John's early life is found in Luke 1:80.

John began his prophetic ministry in A.D. 25 — the 15th year of Tiberias Caesar (Lk 3:1). He attracted large crowds (Mt 3:5) as he preached and baptized in Bethany on the other side of the Jordan (Jn 1:28). His preaching is summarized in the phrase, "The kingdom of God is coming" and his ministry by immersion of repentance for the forgiveness of sins (Mk 1:4). So forceful was his preaching that many took him to be the reincarnation of Elijah, Jeremiah or another prophet (Mt 16:14). Jesus says that he was the greatest person ever born of a woman (Mt 11:11). An interesting fact, however, is that John never performed a miracle (Jn 10:41). His greatest act, perhaps, was his baptism of Jesus. With that act his ministry wound its way to a conclusion. Although he continued to baptize (Jn 3:23; 4:1), he recognized that he had accomplished that which was set before him to do (Jn 3:30).

Herod's antics and the vindictiveness of his evil wife, Herodias, caused the death of the last OT prophet. John was beheaded at the castle of Machaerus on the Dead Sea. Although he died through treachery, he successfully completed his God-given task. He prepared for and pointed out Jesus, the true light.

How is it true that Jesus gives light to every man (v. 9)? There are a number of passages that seem to make Jesus a universal savior (Jn 1:9, 29; 4:42; 12:32; Rom 5:18; 11:32; 1 Tim 2:6; 4:10; 1 Jn 2:2). Obviously not all men are Christians, so these passages can't mean that Jesus saved all men and made everything bright and cheery. In fact, John has just said the darkness rejects the light (v. 5). There are at least three valid explanations of these verses. First, Jesus did, in fact, impact human history more than any other single figure. The world is a better, wiser, more humane place because of his 33-year stint. Second, his influence continues to be felt through the church he left behind. If it were not for Jesus' followers, the world would be centuries behind where it is now in science, education, politics and medicine. Third, because he made light available, he opened the possibility for each person to be enlightened.

Jn 1:10-13   [10]He was in the world, and though the world was made through him, the world did not recognize him. [11]He came to that which was his own, but his own did not receive him. [12]Yet to all who received him, to those who believed in his name, he gave the right to become children of God — [13]children born not of natural descent,[a] nor of human decision or a husband's will, but born of God.

[a]*13 Greek of bloods*

Several introductory comments are appropriate here: (1) We have the extraordinary right, through Jesus, to become children of God. The word (*exousia*) literally means "power" or "authority." (2) By nature we must be adopted into his family; we are not natural children (Rom 8:14-17). (3) The transaction is made when we respond to Jesus and by faith receive his name (cf. Gal 3:26) and we are led by his Spirit (Rom 8:14). (4) Jesus, himself, promised this to the peacemakers (Mt 5:9).

Aside from the two enigmatic references in Genesis 6:2, 4, this is a NT concept. A brief survey of the NT reveals how we recognize the children of God and what kind of benefits they can expect. First, children of God are known by their actions: (1) They stop sinning (1 Jn 3:9-10; 5:18). (2) They love each other (1 Jn 4:7). (3) They believe in Jesus (1 Jn 5:1). (4) They love God and keep his commands (1 Jn 5:2). Second, children of God can expect certain blessings: (1) We have victory over the world (1 Jn 5:4). (2) We have an intimacy with the Father by which we can call him "Abba" (Rom 8:15; Gal 4:6). (3) We become fellow heirs with Christ (Rom 8:17). (4) We await future blessings when Jesus returns (Rom 8:19-21; 1 Jn 3:1-2).

These children of God are oddities. Verse 13 gives three peculiar descriptions of them. First, the NIV "Natural descent" is simply the Greek word for "blood." Second, "Human decision" would probably be more accurately rendered "the will/passions of the flesh." And third, the "husband's decision" would indicate the desire of a man for offspring. All three of these underscore the physical, sensual, and biological relationship of reproduction. This is not what John means by children of God. Although current Greek mythology spoke frequently about sexual union between the gods and humans, John stresses that the children of God are associated at the spiritual rather than the physical level.

Jn 1:14

[14]The Word became flesh and made his dwelling among us. We have seen his glory, the glory of the One and Only,[a] who came from the Father, full of grace and truth.

[a]*14,18 Or the Only Begotten*

The incarnation is perhaps the most wonderful truth of history. Its implications are deep and wide. It tells us that God desires to communicate himself to us and because of our diminutive nature, was only able to do that by speaking at our level and becoming one of us. It tells us that God truly understands our nature and sufferings (Heb 2:17-18). It tells us of the seriousness of our sins, because Christ came to die for them. It tells us of God's love for man — he is involved in human history. In fact, he is a major player. It tells us that the bridge between divinity and humanity is crossable. We therefore have the hope of future fellowship in God's presence.

Isaiah 9:6-7 predicts the incarnation. Truly, God indwelling a human body is most difficult to imagine. So much so that the incarnation has become a trademark of Christian impiety in Jewish and Muslim circles. Yet this truth, which borders on the mythological, is the greatest hope and comfort for those who can accept it. Indeed we have the surest evidence of the incarnation: prophecy, character and miracles of Christ, and the logical necessity of God communicating with us on our level. Simply put, because we could not reach up to God, he came down to us.

If we are going to accept the incarnation, is it not fair to expect some evidence to back up such a wild claim? Is it not fair to ask, "Did Jesus act like God? Did he do the things God alone is able to do?" The answer to these questions is a resounding "YES!"

1. He was prophesied (Isa 9:6-7)
2. He performed miracles (Jn 10:25)
3. He taught with authority (Mt 7:28-29)
4. He had supernatural knowledge (Mt 21:1-3; 24:1-2; 26:17-35; Mk 2:6-8; Jn 1:47-49; 2:23-25; 4:16-19, 28-30; 11:4, 11-15; 14:29; 16:4; 18:4; 21:5-6, 18-19).
5. He was sinless (Jn 8:46; 2 Cor 5:21; Heb 4:15; 1 Pet 2:22)
6. He was one with the Father (Jn 1:1-5, 18; 3:35-36; 10:25-30; 14:1-11)
7. He accepted worship (Mt 16:16-17; 26:6-13; Lk 5:8-9; 7:36-50; 19:35-40; Jn 20:27-29)

Through the incarnation, the logos took the form of God's "One and Only" (*monogenēs*) Son. The Greek word is a compound of "one" and "beget." Thus some translations render it, "only begotten." The problem is that this gives the impression Jesus was somehow conceived (aside from his incarnation). The word, indeed, can mean "only child" (Lk 7:12; 8:42; 9:38). It would be more accurate to render it as "unique." In fact, every use in John (5 of its 9 uses), would be accurately rendered by "unique" (Jn 1:14, 18; 3:16, 18; 1 Jn 4:9). It is not so much the begetting that is stressed as the unique nature of the object or person. (Certainly, when the word is used of God in v. 18 it does not mean begotten.) It is as if to say, "This is the only one in its class" (cf. Heb 11:17).

Jn 1:15-18

¹⁵John testifies concerning him. He cries out, saying, "This was he of whom I said, 'He who comes after me has surpassed me because he was before me.'" ¹⁶From the fullness of his grace we have all received one blessing after another.

[17]For the law was given through Moses; grace and truth came through Jesus Christ. [18]No one has ever seen God, but God the One and Only,[a] who is at the Father's side, has made him known.

[a]*14,18* Or *the Only Begotten*

We are certainly glad to read that we all receive "one blessing after another" (v. 16). [Literally "grace upon grace" or "grace instead/in place of grace."] But what in the world does that mean, exactly? Before we can decipher the meaning, we must first determine who is speaking here: John the Apostle or John the Baptist. If it is John the Apostle, writing about A.D. 95, then he probably means something like this: "The Grace of our Lord Jesus Christ superseded and replaced the gift of the Law given through Moses."[13] The NIV ends John the Baptist's words at v. 15. But we could just as easily place the end of the quotation at v. 16, 17 or even 18. Do these words contain "too mature a theology" for John the Baptist? (Cf. Jn 1:23, 29, 33). If, then, we view these words as the Baptist's, they probably mean something like this: "God has blessed his people time and again. And now, in Jesus, we receive his greatest gift."[14]

No matter which view we adopt, v. 17 serves as an explanation for v. 16. The blessing of Jesus is contrasted to the blessing of the law of Moses. Most likely Exodus 33-34 serves as a background for this idea, and perhaps more specifically Exodus 33:13 or 34:6.[15] What Israel longed for, what we all need so desperately, John announces as having come. "For what the law was powerless to do in that it was weakened by the sinful nature, God did by sending his own Son in the likeness of sinful man to be a sin offering" (Rom 8:3).

Along with salvation come many other blessings: the Holy Spirit, peace, victory, spiritual gifts, fellowship in the church, the promise of heaven, physical healing, purpose in life. Truly, in Jesus, we receive one blessing after another.

One of the greatest blessings Jesus gives us is a glimpse of God. Moses asked God for the privilege of seeing him (Exod 33:18). God allowed him to see only his back — the remnant of glory which was left

---

[13]For this view see W.J. Dumbrell, "Law and Grace: The Nature of the Contrast in John 1:17," *EvQ* 58 (Jan 1986): 25-37. He reads *anti* as contrast. Therefore he suggests that this marks the beginning of a new community ("Children of God" v. 12), and a new law (i.e., Grace).

[14]For this view see Z.C. Hodges, "Grace after Grace — John 1:16," *BibSac* 135 (Jan 1978): 34-45.

[15]For conflicting views see L.J. Kuyper, "Grace and Truth: An Old Testament Description of God, and Its Use in the Johannine Gospel," *Int* 18 (1964): 3; and A. Hanson, "John 1:14-18 and Exodus 34," *NTS* 23 (1976): 90-95.

after God had departed. God explained that no human was able to look on him without dying (Exod 33:20).

What, then, do we make of passages such as Genesis 3:8, God walking with Adam in the Garden or Genesis 18:1, the Lord appearing to Abraham near the oaks of Mamre? We must conclude that these were theophanies — mere appearances of God in another bodily form. Cottrell (*God the Creator*, p. 230) suggests that these bodies were created *ex nihilo* for the duration of the appearance and then vanished again into nothingness. He goes on to say, "Just as God is naturally invisible to the material realm because he is spirit, so also is he naturally invisible to the spiritual realm because he is uncreated and transcendent" (p. 231).

But Jesus, in a way that we could understand, in a form that we could survive, showed us what God was like. When we look at him, we see the actions and the character of God, cloaked in the form of a man. Verse 18 not only describes one of our greatest blessings in Jesus; it makes one of the boldest claims for his deity.

§ 3
The Genealogy
of Jesus
(Mt 1:1-17; Lk 3:23b-38)

Luke's introduction looks like good Greek history. John's reminds us of Jewish Wisdom Literature. Matthew's resembles a Jewish legal/religious document. Furthermore, the Hebrew OT begins and ends with a record of genealogies. The Hebrew OT ended with 1 & 2 Chronicles. Genesis uses the title "These are the generations of . . ." as a major divider of the book (Gen 6:9; 10:1; 11:10, 27; 25:12, 19; 36:1, 9; 37:2). Matthew also starts with "A record of the genealogy" (*biblos geneseōs*). It also seems significant that the word "birth" (lit. genesis) is used in verse 18 just after the genealogical record. Thus, this theme continues throughout the book.

Genealogies had three essential functions: (1) To show the character of a particular line. In other words, a man's descendants supposedly acted like him. Such is the case when Seth's line is contrasted to Cain's (Gen 4:25ff). (2) To demonstrate God's working in history with a particular people. This helped establish a corporate identity. And, (3) to prove biological succession.

This third purpose was important for legal and political transactions:

(1) Property was distributed based on family affiliation.

(2) The Aaronic priesthood demanded biological affiliation. In fact, in Ezra's day, priests who could not prove their ancestry were considered unclean (Neh 7:61-64). This was of critical importance after the Babylonian captivity and the prevalence of intermarriage (Ezra 2:59-63; 10:9-44; Neh 13:23-28).

(3) Genealogies were a way of keeping the lines "clean" (Deut 7:1-4; 23:1-8). This was especially important after the days of Hellenization.

(4) Jewish military arrangement was by tribes (Num 1:2-4), even when they were camping in the wilderness (Num 2:2, 17; 10:1-28).

(5) Taxes and offerings in the temple were made according to genealogical lines (Num 7:11-89).

(6) The Davidic kingdom of Judah always relied on direct succession. This became even more important when it was connected to Messianic fulfillment (Isa 11:1-5).

Mt 1:1-17

¹A record of the genealogy of Jesus Christ the son of David, the son of Abraham: ²Abraham was the father of Isaac, Isaac the father of Jacob, Jacob the father of Judah and his brothers, ³Judah the father of Perez and Zerah, whose mother was Tamar, Perez the father of Hezron, Hezron the father of Ram, ⁴Ram the father of Amminadab, Amminadab the father of Nahshon, Nahshon the father of Salmon, ⁵Salmon the father of Boaz, whose mother was Rahab, Boaz the father of Obed, whose mother was Ruth, Obed the father of Jesse, ⁶and Jesse the father of King David. David was the father of Solomon, whose mother had been Uriah's wife, ⁷Solomon the father of Rehoboam, Rehoboam the father of Abijah, Abijah the father of Asa, ⁸Asa the father of Jehoshaphat, Jehoshaphat the father of Jehoram, Jehoram the father of Uzziah, ⁹Uzziah the father of Jotham, Jotham the father of Ahaz, Ahaz the father of Hezekiah, ¹⁰Hezekiah the father of Manasseh, Manasseh the father of Amon, Amon the father of Josiah, ¹¹and Josiah the father of Jeconiah[a] and his brothers at the time of the exile to Babylon. ¹²After the exile to Babylon: Jeconiah was the father of Shealtiel, Shealtiel the father of Zerubbabel, ¹³Zerubbabel the father of Abiud, Abiud the father of Eliakim, Eliakim the father of Azor, ¹⁴Azor the father of Zadok, Zadok the father of Akim, Akim the father of Eliud, ¹⁵Eliud the father of Eleazar, Eleazar the father of Matthan, Matthan the father of Jacob, ¹⁶and Jacob the father of Joseph, the husband of Mary, of whom was born Jesus, who is called Christ. ¹⁷Thus there were fourteen generations in all from Abraham to David, fourteen from David to the exile to Babylon, and fourteen from the exile to the Christ.[b]

[a]*11 That is, Jehoiachin; also in verse 12*   [b]*17 Or Messiah. "The Christ" (Greek) and "the Messiah" (Hebrew) both mean "the Anointed One."*

Matthew arranges his genealogy into three sets of 14 names (v. 17), each representing a major period of Israel's history: Abraham, David, Exile. He intends to show that Jesus is the fulfillment of all Jewish history. The problem is that the second set of names only includes 13 generations. Did Matthew miscount? The likelihood of a professional tax collector miscounting a genealogy is not great. What further confounds the issue is Matthew omits four names in v. 9 (Ahaziah, Joash, Amaziah, and Jehoiakim), which are found in the 1 Chronicles genealogy. In other words, Matthew could have listed 14/17/14 names but drops four of them, resulting in 14/13/14.

Now, one must realize that the Jews were not interested in "complete" lists (this is primarily a Western expectation). They were interested in establishing the fact of descent. Persons were often omitted from a genealogy who were seen as insignificant or unflattering to the family. Furthermore, the words "Father," "Son," and "Beget" can be used to establish a relationship between a man and his grandfather/grandson or even further down the biological line. These words simply connect two people within a family, they do not always state scientifically their biological relationship. Thus, even if a few names are left out of the genealogy, we can still speak accurately of a great-grandfather "begetting" a progenitor.

Some have suggested these omissions were a result of scribal error. The first three names are from 1 Chronicles 3:11-12. It is possible that the scribe's eye would pass from Ahaziah straight to Azariah, thereby leaving out three persons. Also, the omission of Jehoiakim may be explained by its similarity to his son, Jehoiachin (1 Chron 3:16). The bottom line is that Matthew is accused of making a clerical error.

A more likely explanation, however, is that Matthew purposely arranges the genealogy into 3 divisions of fourteen generations each. In other words, he purposely leaves out four kings in order to retain his structural arrangement. The question is, "Why would Matthew want fourteen names in each list and why would he only list 13 names in the central section?" The answer to both questions is: David.[16]

We notice in verse 1 that Matthew purposefully places David before Abraham, abandoning the chronological order of the rest of the genealogy. Why does he place David first? For emphasis. In fact, David's prominence in verse one is a key to the whole book. Matthew's unique emphasis is that Jesus is the king of the Jews, the promised progenitor of David. With this understanding we move now to verse 6 and give David a "double portion." In other words, by counting David twice, our list suddenly becomes 14/14/14. What is more striking is that the letters of David's name have a numeric value in Hebrew of 14. While this type of "numeric interpretation" (*gematria*) is quite foreign to us, it was a common rabbinic method of interpretation. The Hebrew language uses its alphabet as its numbering system as well. Therefore, children would learn arithmetic with the letters of their names, making this kind of "numerology" more common and more easily recognized. Matthew, like

---

[16]Aside from making this genealogy easier to remember, the number 14 was used in Apocalyptic literature (e.g., 2 Baruch 53-74) to indicate the fullness of time and the ushering in of the Messianic era. See H.C. Waetjen, "The Genealogy as the Key to the Gospel According to Matthew." *JBL*, 95/2 (1976): 205-230.

Luke and John, introduces his book with a style marvelously appropriate to his audience.[17]

Another striking feature of Matthew's genealogy is his inclusion of women. It was pretty uncommon to include women in genealogies, but not unheard of (cf. 1 Chron 1:32; 2:17-21, 24, 26). However, you would expect them to be exemplary. The inclusion of these particular women is simply scandalous. Tamar was guilty of prostitution and incest (Gen 38:6-30). Rahab was apparently a foreign harlot (Josh 2:1,3; 6:17, 23, 25; Heb 11:31). Ruth was a foreigner. And, Bathsheba was an adulteress (2 Sam 12:24), and perhaps considered a foreigner by her marriage to a Hittite.[18]

These gals did not belong in the lineage of the Messiah! Yet, there they are, as a neon reminder of the grace of God. When Mary was accused of being raped (or worse)[19] and ostracized by her family and friends, each of these women could have stood next to her and said, "Honey, I know how you feel."

At the same time, Matthew describes Mary differently than the others. All five women give birth to a son in the lineage of David. The first four use an identical linguistic structure — "Out of" (*ek tēs*). With Mary, however, the structure changes to "Out of whom was begotten" (*ex hēs egennēthē*). It would appear that Matthew is making a subtle statement about the virgin birth of Jesus.

Before moving on to Luke's genealogy, there is a curious theological thorn we must deal with. In 2 Sam 7:12-17, God promises David that through Solomon's line there would always be a descendant to sit on his throne. However, Jeremiah 22:30 says, "Record this man as if childless, a man who will not prosper in his lifetime, for none of his offspring will prosper, none will sit on the throne of David or rule anymore in Judah." How is it that God can keep both promises?

Since Jesus was the adopted son of Joseph, he becomes legal heir to Joseph's lineage. At the same time Matthew makes it clear he was not Joseph's physical son, not only in 18-25, but even in v. 16. Thirty-nine times in vv. 2-16, Matthew uses the verb *egennēsen* = "He became the father of." Then suddenly in v. 16, he breaks the pattern when he comes to Joseph who is only said to be the husband of Mary. Also, the words "of whom," which are ambiguous in English, are feminine in Greek.

---

[17]For a more detailed description of this "numerology" see B.M. Newman, "Matthew 1:1-18: Some Comments and a Suggested Restructuring," *BT* 27/2 (Apr 1976): 209-212.

[18]Cf. T. H. Graves, "Matthew 1:1-17," *Rev Exp*, 86 (1989): 595-600.

[19]Ancient Jewish opinions of Mary were not flattering. Some considered her to be raped by Joseph or a Roman soldier. Others portrayed her simply as being a fornicator.

Matthew subtly, but clearly states that Jesus was the adopted son of Joseph (and legal heir to the throne of David), and the natural son of Mary. Thus, both 2 Samuel 7:12-17 and Jeremiah 22:30 are fulfilled.

Lk 3:23-38

[23]Now Jesus himself was about thirty years old when he began his ministry. He was the son, so it was thought, of Joseph, the son of Heli, [24]the son of Matthat, the son of Levi, the son of Melki, the son of Jannai, the son of Joseph, [25]the son of Mattathias, the son of Amos, the son of Nahum, the son of Esli, the son of Naggai, [26]the son of Maath, the son of Mattathias, the son of Semein, the son of Josech, the son of Joda, [27]the son of Joanan, the son of Rhesa, the son of Zerubbabel, the son of Shealtiel, the son of Neri, [28]the son of Melki, the son of Addi, the son of Cosam, the son of Elmadam, the son of Er, [29]the son of Joshua, the son of Eliezer, the son of Jorim, the son of Matthat, the son of Levi, [30]the son of Simeon, the son of Judah, the son of Joseph, the son of Jonam, the son of Eliakim, [31]the son of Melea, the son of Menna, the son of Mattatha, the son of Nathan, the son of David, [32]the son of Jesse, the son of Obed, the son of Boaz, the son of Salmon,[a] the son of Nahshon, [33]the son of Amminadab, the son of Ram,[b] the son of Hezron, the son of Perez, the son of Judah, [34]the son of Jacob, the son of Isaac, the son of Abraham, the son of Terah, the son of Nahor, [35]the son of Serug, the son of Reu, the son of Peleg, the son of Eber, the son of Shelah, [36]the son of Cainan, the son of Arphaxad, the son of Shem, the son of Noah, the son of Lamech, [37]the son of Methuselah, the son of Enoch, the son of Jared, the son of Mahalalel, the son of Kenan, [38]the son of Enosh, the son of Seth, the son of Adam, the son of God.

[a]*32 Some early manuscripts *Sala*   [b]*33 Some manuscripts *Amminadab, the son of Admin, the son of Arni*; other manuscripts vary widely.

There are three main differences between Matthew's genealogy and Luke's.

(A) Matthew begins with Abraham and moves forward toward Jesus whereas Luke begins with Jesus and moves backward all the way to Adam.

(B) If Luke's list is inverted and placed beside Matthew's list, the portion between Abraham and David is virtually identical. However, between David and Joseph, the two are obviously two distinct lists. The only names which appear in both lists in the same order are Shealtiel and Zerubbabel (Mt 1:12; Lk 3:27).

(C) Luke's list contains forty progenitors between David and Christ; Matthew's only has twenty-six.

How can we account for these differences? It appears that we have two distinct lists. So, who do they belong to? There have been a number of different theories suggested.[20] The first theory was proposed by Julius

[20]Cf. R. Thomas & S. Gundry, *A Harmony of the Gospels* (Chicago: Moody), pp. 313-319.

Africanus (d. A.D. 240). He suggested that Matthew gives the genealogy of Joseph's biological father whereas Luke gives the genealogy of Joseph's legal father. According to the laws of Levirate marriage, if a man died childless, it was his brother's responsibility to foster a child for him. In such a case, the dead man would still be the legal father for the purpose of inheritance, and the live man the biological father. This theory is based on the assumption that Joseph's legal father died childless. Although it is a distinct possibility, there is nothing in the text to suggest that this was the case.

A second theory, advocated first by J. Gresham Machen in *The Virgin Birth of Christ*, states that Matthew gives the *legal* descent of Joseph, whereas Luke gives the *physical* descent. The difference is, Matthew's account traces the legal heir to the Davidic throne, which would have come down to Joseph. In such an account, because the line failed at Jeconiah (Jer 22:30), it "skipped a beat" biologically and passed over to the next legal heir to the throne (e.g., Shealtiel, Mt 1:12, cf. Lk 3:27). Therefore, Matthew "changes tracks" from the biological line to the collateral line. If this is the case, Matthew asks the question, "Who is the heir of David?" whereas Luke asks, "Who is Joseph's father?" This view is based on the assumption that Matthew's account jumps to the collateral line. Again, this is certainly possible, but nothing in the text would necessitate or even suggest such.[21]

A third theory suggests that Luke's record does not belong to Joseph at all but, in fact, lists Mary's family. Assuming that there was no male heir and that she was the oldest child, she would become the heiress (Num 27:1-11; 36:1-12). If this were the case, when she married Joseph, he, in practicality, would become the heir to this line as well. Hence, Joseph is listed in place of Mary in Luke's account.

A fourth theory, like the third, suggests that Mary's line is given in Luke. Joseph, however, is not a part of the genealogy but merely a parenthetical comment of Luke 3:23, which should read, "Jesus . . . being the son (as was supposed of Joseph) of Heli . . ." The Greek would allow such a punctuation and even suggest it from the fact that of all the names in this list, Joseph alone lacks an article. In addition, "Son" could certainly apply to Heli as Jesus' grandfather. Furthermore, Luke likely omits Mary's name since women were seldom included in genealogical lists. Although Matthew included four women in his list, Luke has no women in his.

---

[21]R.P. Nettelhorst offers an interesting twist on these first two theories. He proposes that both genealogies are Joseph's, but Matthew traces his mother's line while Luke traces his father's line. See "Genealogy of Jesus," *JETS* 31 (June 1988): 169-172.

This last theory would allow Matthew's genealogy to speak of biological, rather than legal or collateral descent. Thus, Matthew's use of the word "begat" would retain its normal usage rather than figurative. Besides, Matthew's interest in Jesus' relationship with the OT would be more strongly supported if his genealogy was Joseph's real descent (as well as legal descent), giving Jesus legal claim to the Davidic throne. Luke's genealogy of Jesus through a biological parent would fit his emphasis on the humanity of Jesus.

Beyond these sticky issues, there are a number of valuable lessons to be learned from the genealogical records. First, God is interested in people. He loves us, names us, accounts us, and expects us to live in obedience to him. Second, God can use unknown and fallen people to accomplish his purposes. God's plans and means are greater than our fallible efforts. Third, God is sovereign. His designs will be accomplished! He ordains and directs history through human participants. Fourth, these two genealogies give us a glimpse of Jesus' identity. Humanly, he was Mary's son; legally, he was Joseph's son; fundamentally, he was God's Son.

PART TWO
TWO DIVINE BIRTHS

This particular section of Luke (chs. 1-2) weaves back and forth between the birth narratives comparing Jesus and John, giving somewhat of a "soap opera" effect. Birth narratives like these are common in Greco-Roman biographies of famous people. Their purpose is to answer this single question: How do we account for such a life as this? At the same time, Luke 1-2 is filled with Hebraic thoughts and phrases. It consistently echoes the themes and theology of the OT (esp. Judg 13:2-7; 1 Sam 1-3; Gen 18:11ff). Hence, we have a classic Greco-Roman form, immersed into a Hebrew setting. Luke has carefully and skillfully reflected the culture of the characters in this narrative.

Furthermore, there are many details which one would expect only from an eyewitness account (e.g., the angel standing at the *right* hand of the altar, v. 11). These colorful little tidbits remind us that Luke was, indeed, using the firsthand information he had gleaned from the eyewitnesses (cf. 1:1-4). And while Luke is a wonderfully careful historian, this stuff isn't about the past. Luke is laying a foundation here for the life of Jesus. These events point prophetically to the future. They help us predict what we are about to encounter in the life and ministry of Jesus.

§ 4
John's Birth
Revealed to
Zechariah
(Lk 1:5-25)

⁵In the time of Herod king of Judea there was a priest named Zechariah, who belonged to the priestly division of Abijah; his wife Elizabeth was also a descendant of Aaron. ⁶Both of them were upright in the sight of God, observing all the Lord's commandments and regulations blamelessly. ⁷But they had no children, because Elizabeth was barren; and they were both well along in years.

Herod the Great was a shrewd politician, a failure with his family, a voracious builder, and a passionate lover. He was appointed by Rome as the king of the Jews after they could not settle their own civil disputes. He reigned from 37 B.C. to 4 B.C.

During this time there were twenty-four divisions of priests with approximately 900 in each for a grand total of 21,600 (Josephus *Against Apion*, 2. 108 — estimates the total at 20,000). Each division would serve one week every six months. On the Sabbath, all the men of the division, who were 24 years and older would serve. On the other six days, only 50 or so would serve, being chosen by lot. On the great feasts of Passover, Pentecost and Tabernacles, all 24 divisions served. The rest of the time they lived in their homes which were scattered about Judea. Not only was Zechariah a priest, but he was married to the daughter of the priest — this was a double honor. They were a sweet old couple, who lived model lives of purity and piety.

Sadly, they lived under the "curse" of barrenness. Children were viewed as a blessing from the Lord (Exod 23:26; Deut 7:14), the antithesis being that barrenness was a curse from the Lord (Job 15:34). When a woman's barrenness was reversed, it was seen as an indication of God's blessing and vice versa (1 Sam 2:5; Isa 54:1; Gal 4:27).

Barrenness was a curse because a woman without a child would have no one to support and protect her after her husband died (Job 24:21). Moreover, she became the object of scorn from other women (Gen 11:30, Sarai; Gen 25:21; 29:31, Rachel).

Due to their age, Zechariah and Elizabeth have no hope of God removing their "curse" of barrenness. Luke's verbs here are colorful. He combines the imperfect verb "to be" with the perfect participle "to advance." By this Luke indicates that they were in the present state of having grown old. Furthermore, day by day, they were growing older. We have here the sad picture of a barren Jewish couple. They had strong hopes for a child. As they grew older, and continued to do so, their dreams slipped away into the distance like a ship lost from port. These hopes were now but a vague memory.

As for their exact age, one guess is probably about as good as another, although a Jew was not considered old until 60. Hence, one might guess that they were about 80 years old.

Lk 1:8-17

[8]Once when Zechariah's division was on duty and he was serving as priest before God, [9]he was chosen by lot, according to the custom of the priesthood, to go into the temple of the Lord and burn incense. [10]And when the time for the burning of incense came, all the assembled worshipers were praying outside.

[11]Then an angel of the Lord appeared to him, standing at the right side of the altar of incense. [12]When Zechariah saw him, he was startled and was gripped with fear. [13]But the angel said to him: "Do not be afraid, Zechariah; your prayer has been heard. Your wife Elizabeth will bear you a son, and you are to give him the name John. [14]He will be a joy and delight to you, and many will rejoice because of his birth, [15]for he will be great in the sight of the Lord. He is never to take wine or other fermented drink, and he will be filled with the Holy Spirit even

from birth.[a] [16]Many of the people of Israel will he bring back to the Lord their God. [17]And he will go on before the Lord, in the spirit and power of Elijah, to turn the hearts of the fathers to their children and the disobedient to the wisdom of the righteous — to make ready a people prepared for the Lord."

[a]*15* Or *from his mother's womb*

A priest's day began by cleaning up the temple precincts before dawn. Early in the morning at least three lots would be cast to determine the following duties: (1) Rekindling the fire on the altar and servicing with the morning sacrifice. (2) The officiating priest of the day. (3) Trimming the golden candlestick and preparing incense within the Holy Place. This third duty was the most sacred service of the day. The incense symbolized the ascending prayers of the saints (Ps 141:2; Rev 5:8; 8:3,4). It was prepared both morning and evening so that it burned perpetually before the Lord (Exod 30:8). This is likely the afternoon sacrifice, in conjunction with the hour of prayer (3 p.m.). Only once in a lifetime was a priest allowed to perform this duty. He was fortunate indeed if he got to do it at all.

Zechariah would choose two friends or relatives to help him in the sacred duty of burning the incense. One would clean the altar from the previous evening's offering. While worshiping he would move backwards out of the Holy Place. The second would then come forward and spread live coals from the altar of sacrifice to the outer edges of the altar of incense. He also worships and exits the Holy Place backwards, leaving Zechariah alone to perform his sacred duty. The inner sanctuary was dimly lit by the seven-branched candlestick on the south. To the north was the table of shewbread; to the west, nearest the Holy of Holies, was the altar of incense.

At just the right time, he would spread the incense on the altar. The priests and people outside, seeing the offering rise to God would bow in reverent worship and prayer. Many people from all over the city came to the temple at this hour for prayer. Most priests completed their duties rather quickly, fearing the wrath of God if they tarried. Thus, Zechariah's delay was unusual.

After Zechariah's helpers leave, he is there all alone . . . he thinks. An angel has slipped in on him. The way Luke phrases it, it looks like Gabriel had been standing there for awhile between the altar of incense and the golden lampstand, unnoticed by Zechariah who is absorbed in his duties. When he finally notices the angel, he is petrified. That is the normal reaction to angelic visitations. But compound that with his sacred solo duties in the Holy Place, and Zechariah has just cause for alarm. Gabriel, with a classic angelic line, tries to calm and comfort him:

"Don't be afraid," [lit. *stop being afraid*]." (Probably easier said than done).

Then Gabriel adds this: "Your prayer has been heard. Your wife Elizabeth will bear you a son." But that prayer was a *very* old one. Besides, you know that "old man" Zechariah, in the Holy Place of God, performing a once-in-a-lifetime religious duty, was NOT praying about procreation. Needless to say, the promise of a son seemed quite out of place and impossible to Zechariah.

But there is another surprise to come. This was no ordinary son. They were to name him John, meaning "the Lord is gracious." He was to have a special diet (v. 15). This appears to be a description of a lifetime Nazirite vow (e.g., Samson, Judges 13:4,5; Samuel, 1 Sam. 1:11). He would be precious to his parents (v. 14). He would call many Israelites back to God (v. 16-17), and he would be God's man, with Elijah's power, preparing people for the coming of the Lord (Isa 40:3-5; Mal 3:1-5; 4:5-6). At long last, the 400 years of prophetic silence is broken.

Lk 1:18-20

[18]Zechariah asked the angel, "How can I be sure of this? I am an old man and my wife is well along in years." [19]The angel answered, "I am Gabriel. I stand in the presence of God, and I have been sent to speak to you and to tell you this good news. [20]And now you will be silent and not able to speak until the day this happens, because you did not believe my words, which will come true at their proper time."

This is all too much for Zechariah to take in. He just can't believe it. So he asks for proof. While that sounds reasonable to us, it must have seemed pretty shallow to Gabriel.[1] After all, he hung around the throne of God. He was in the know. And his sources were pretty reliable.

But since Zechariah wanted a sign, Gabriel gave him one! He would "live in silence" until John was born. Anderson suggests that this should be understood as being *deaf* not *dumb*.[2] He says that "this special punishment was inflicted on Zechariah because he had not believed what he had *heard* . . . that is, he would not henceforth *hear ANY words* until the angel's words were fulfilled" (pp. 23-24). In Luke 1:62, when John is

---

[1]Aside from Gabriel, meaning "God is Great," (Dan 8:16; 9:21; Lk 1:19, 26), Michael the Archangel is the only other angel mentioned by name (Jude 9: Rev 12:7; Dan 10:13, 21; 12:1). Furthermore, the last time Gabriel spoke (Dan 9-10), it was about the coming of the Messiah. It would be natural, then, for Zechariah (and us), to listen to his words with Messianic/ prophetic expectation.

[2]J.G. Anderson, "A New Translation of Luke 1:20," *BT* 20 (Jan 1969): 21-24. He bases this on the following evidence: (1) The use of this phrase in the LXX, (2) Etymology of *siōpaō*, (3) the periphrastic structure of *esē siōpōn* = "You will live in silence," and (4) context.

born, the neighbors used sign language to communicate with Zechariah. He then answers their question by writing, not speaking. That would indicate that he was both deaf and dumb. Perhaps then, the conclusion should be that this word silent [*siōpaō*] can include both problems — deaf and dumb.

Although the text does not say that Zechariah's dumbness was punishment for seeking a sign, it appears to be both the rebuke and the sign itself. After all, Jesus criticizes those who sought signs after sufficient evidence has already been given (Mt 12:38-39; Lk 11:29; Jn 6:30).

However, both Gideon (Judg 6:38-39) and Hezekiah (2 Kgs 20:8) asked for a sign and were given one without any kind of criticism or punishment. Ahaz was told to ask for a sign but would not (Isa 7:11). Why the apparent contradiction between the OT sign seeking and the NT criticism of such? Notice that Hezekiah and Ahaz were dealing with human messengers whereas the NT passages deal with divine messengers (i.e., Gabriel and Jesus). Furthermore, Jesus, through his miracles, and Gabriel, through his presence in the Holy Place, already offered sufficient evidence of their credibility. Hence, an additional sign should not have been necessary.

Lk 1:21-25

[21]Meanwhile, the people were waiting for Zechariah and wondering why he stayed so long in the temple. [22]When he came out, he could not speak to them. They realized he had seen a vision in the temple, for he kept making signs to them but remained unable to speak. [23]When his time of service was completed, he returned home. [24]After this his wife Elizabeth became pregnant and for five months remained in seclusion. [25]"The Lord has done this for me," she said. "In these days he has shown his favor and taken away my disgrace among the people."

Just outside the temple, the worshipers watch the smoke ascend to heaven. They begin their prayers. But then they realize that Zechariah has not come out. The longer he takes, the more nervous they get. Perhaps he has been struck by God! Suddenly, out he comes with the strangest look. He can't say a word. But through certain charades he is finally able to tell them what happened.

When the week was over, he returned home to his wife, Elizabeth. And sure enough, she became pregnant. Now that must have been quite a spectacle. It sent her into five months of seclusion. In holy privacy, she kept to herself until God's blessing was evident. When she came out, glory to God!, she was FULL of joy. God had removed from her the curse of barrenness.

§ 5
Jesus' Birth Revealed to Mary
(Lk 1:26-38)

What we have here is a classic "birth announcement." It was a common literary device in ancient biographies of famous people (e.g., Suetonius, "Augustus," 94, in *Lives of the Twelve Caesars*). It was designed to answer this important question: "How do we explain such an extraordinary life?" Talbert says, "All of the canonical Gospels wrestle with the same issue. Mark explains Jesus' unique life as due to his being the bearer of the Spirit . . . at his baptism (Mk 1:9-11). John's explanation is that the preexistent Word became flesh and dwelt among us (Jn 1:14)."[3] Both Matthew and Luke explain Jesus' uniqueness through the virgin birth.

Lk 1:26-29

[26]In the sixth month, God sent the angel Gabriel to Nazareth, a town in Galilee, [27]to a virgin pledged to be married to a man named Joseph, a descendant of David. The virgin's name was Mary. [28]The angel went to her and said, "Greetings, you who are highly favored! The Lord is with you." [29]Mary was greatly troubled at his words and wondered what kind of greeting this might be.

When Elizabeth was six months pregnant,[4] God sent Gabriel on another mission. This time to Nazareth, not Jerusalem. This time to a young girl, not an old man. Both messages were similar: You're going to have a baby. Both times Gabriel had to allay their fear through God's promise. And while both Mary and Zechariah wonder about the possibility of this announcement, Mary has complete faith and commitment to the angelic message.

Shortly after a girl hit her teens, she would be betrothed, that is, engaged. The parents of the prospective couple would make the arrangements and, in fact, choose the partner. Although this does not meet *our* cultural mores, it remains, to this day, an effective means of marriage. Once a young man saved a dowry, he would choose a mediator (possibly a friend). The mediator would go, with the young man's parents, to the house of the prospective bride. Her parents would meet them and offer a drink. The party would refuse the drink until the price of the dowry had been set and consent of the bride given. Her parents would then choose a mediator for their side and the negotiations would begin. Once the matter was settled, refreshments were brought out and everyone celebrated the agreement. Betrothal would probably last no longer than a year before the wedding. This contract was legally binding, and could only be broken by death or divorce. In case of the former, the woman

---

[3]CH. Talbert, "Luke 1:26-31," *Int* 39 (July 1985): 288-291.

[4]If Edersheim (I:135) is correct, that the course of Abijah served the 1st week of October, then we are now near the month of April. Hence, Jesus would be born in late December or early January.

was considered a widow. Yet sexual relations were not permitted until after the wedding ceremony. According to Jewish custom, Mary was probably about fifteen years old.[5]

This must be a wonderful time in Mary's life. She is young, she is a virgin, she is engaged. All is normal, all is well. Gabriel enters the scene with this remarkable greeting: "Greetings, you who are highly favored." From this passage comes the famed "Ave Maria." Although these words frightened her, they got her attention and set a positive tone for the message to come.

Lk 1:30-33

[30]But the angel said to her, "Do not be afraid, Mary, you have found favor with God. [31]You will be with child and give birth to a son, and you are to give him the name Jesus. [32]He will be great and will be called the Son of the Most High. The Lord God will give him the throne of his father David, [33]and he will reign over the house of Jacob forever; his kingdom will never end."

Zechariah was afraid at the *sight* of Gabriel. Mary is troubled by his *message*. Fear is the normal reaction to an angelic visitation. In addition, the angels usually say, "Don't be afraid," (cf. Gen 15:1; 26:24; Dan 10:19; Mt 28:5; Lk 1:13, 30; 2:10; Acts 18:9; Rev 1:17). Angels are often harbingers of judgment and/or agents of destruction, but not this time. Mary shouldn't fear but rejoice. She will have a son and she is to name him Jesus.

"Jesus" comes from the Hebrew name "Joshua" meaning "Jehovah saves." Joshua was a type of Christ, in that he led God's people into the promised land, conquering their enemies. It should also be noted that "Christ" is not Jesus' last name but his official title. "Christ" is the Greek word equivalent to the Hebrew "Messiah." They both mean, "The anointed one." Other names and titles for Jesus are: Son of Man, Son of God, Son of David, God, Lord, Word, Servant, Savior, Lamb of God, High Priest, Mediator, Last Adam, Prophet, Priest, King.

Gabriel's description of Jesus is astounding in light of OT prophecy. "Son of the Most High" is an exalted title for God. Thus, Jesus is called the Son of the Very God. Interestingly, Jesus is only called "Son of the Most High" by the Gerasene Demoniac (Mk 5:7; Lk 8:28). Even more startling is the fact that Jesus said that we too could become sons of the Most High (Lk 6:35). We are adopted through the blood of Jesus (Jn 1:12; Rom 8:14-17; 1 Jn 3:1-2).

"Throne of David" designates the royal lineage of the kingdom of

---

[5]Cf. D. Robinson, "The Incredible Announcement," *His* 35 (Dec 1974): 2-4. He says, "Legends about Joseph being an old man have no shred of biblical basis," and suggests that Joseph was about 18 years old.

the Jews. David became the archetype of the king of God's people. 2 Samuel 7:16 (cf. 1 Chr 17:11-15) made this promise: "Your house and your kingdom will endure forever before me; *your throne will be established forever*." However, the bottom fell out of that kingdom in the days of Jehoiachin, of whom God said, "He will have no one to sit on the throne of David." As was discussed before in relation to Jesus' genealogy, both promises were fulfilled when Jesus, who was not of Jehoiachin's line, but was of David's line, became the king of the Jews.

Mary was familiar with the Scriptures. In her "Magnificat" she used at least thirty words or phrases from the OT. This talk about David's throne would likely have brought Isaiah 7:14 and 9:6-7 to her mind — a child born of a virgin who would sit forever on David's throne. These messianic prophecies would have added to her knowledge of her son's identity.

"House of Jacob" symbolized all of Israel, since Jacob, the father of the twelve patriarchs, was seen as the father of the entire Jewish nation. It is often used this way in prophetic literature (Isa 2:5-6; 8:17; 10:20; 14:1; 29:22; 46:3; 48:1; 58:1; Jer 2:4; 5:20; Ezek 20:5; Amos 3:13; 9:8; Obad 1:17-18; Micah 2:7; 3:9).

Lk 1:34-38

[34]"How will this be," Mary asked the angel, "since I am a virgin?" [35]The angel answered, "The Holy Spirit will come upon you, and the power of the Most High will overshadow you. So the holy one to be born will be called[a] the Son of God. [36]Even Elizabeth your relative is going to have a child in her old age, and she who was said to be barren is in her sixth month. [37]For nothing is impossible with God." [38]"I am the Lord's servant," Mary answered. "May it be to me as you have said." Then the angel left her.

[a]*35* Or *So the child to be born will be called holy,*

Many have struggled with the miracle of a virgin birth.[6] Indeed, both the Greek word *parthenos* and the Hebrew word *alma* can be translated "young woman."[7] However, in this context, it *must* mean "virgin" since Mary claims to have "never known a man." The bottom line is: Do we choose to believe what Luke and Matthew claim? Or to put it another way: Is God able to perform a creative miracle such as this? It will do no good to say that Matthew and Luke's audiences were pre-scientific, hence they could believe such stories. You don't need to be "modern" to

---

[6]Cf. R.E. Brown, "The Problem of Virginal Conception," *TS* 33 (1972): 3-34.

[7]Cf. C.H. Dodd, "New Testament Translation Problems I," *BT*, 27/3 (July 1976): 301-305. However, cf. J. Carmignac, "The Meaning of *parthenos* in Lk 1:27 — A Reply to C.H. Dodd," *BT* 28 (1977): 327-330.

understand where babies come from.[8] And Luke, as a physician, would not have accepted this lightly. The bottom line is that if God was able to create life in Eden, he can create life in a womb.[9]

One may have an irreverent and sensual curiosity about the mechanics of Mary's conception. The fact is, we just do not know how it happened. Verse 35 says that the Holy Spirit "came upon" Mary. In the OT that phrase indicated Holy Spirit empowerment, not physical contact. Although pagan mythology speaks of cohabitation between the gods and humans, there is no grammatical, contextual or theological basis for reading into this passage any kind of a sexual encounter between Mary and the Holy Spirit.

All this would be difficult and frightening for Mary to believe. It would be difficult, because she knew she was a virgin. Hence, Gabriel gives her a sign. Her aged and barren relative Elizabeth was pregnant. If God can do for Elizabeth what he promised, then he will be faithful to Mary as well. Although we don't know just how Mary and Elizabeth were related, we do know that Elizabeth was old enough to be Mary's grandmother.

Not only was this difficult to believe; it was also frightening. First, an adulteress was to be stoned (Lev 20:10). Even if she was not killed, she would almost certainly lose the man she loved (and, in fact, would have had Gabriel not intervened). Furthermore, who wants to marry a "used" woman. In addition, single women in that culture didn't have a lot of job opportunities. And, of course, living in a small community, everyone would know what was going on. It would not take the grapevine long to label Mary with the scarlet letter. This precious and pure young thing would shock everyone with her "impropriety."

Even understanding the consequences, Mary's faith in God drove her to say, "May it be to me as you have said." The Greek text uses an optative, an unusual verb form which expresses a wish or a desire. There are two extremes to be avoided here. One is the worship of Mary (i.e., Mariolatry, often observed in Catholicism). She is great but she is not God(ess). The other side of this same dingy coin is the Protestant neglect of this incredible young woman. Compared to Abraham, Sarah, and

---

[8]D.M. Smith, "Luke 1:26-38," *Int,* 29 (Oct 1975): 411-417, goes so far as to say, "We know, as people of antiquity did not, that virgins do not conceive and bear sons." Such chronological snobbery is certainly misguided.

[9]J. Nolland (p. 57-58) rightly notes, "The origin for this tradition of a virginal conception cannot be found in any of the pagan myths of divine paternity. They move in a totally different world of thought. . . . The best explanation is finally the historical one: Jesus was born without the intervention of a human father."

Zechariah, Mary's faith shines above them all. She had more to lose. Yet, without wavering, she invites the will of God to prevail in her life.

**§ 6
Mary's Visit
with Elizabeth**
(Lk 1:39-45)

[39]At that time Mary got ready and hurried to a town in the hill country of Judea, [40]where she entered Zechariah's home and greeted Elizabeth. [41]When Elizabeth heard Mary's greeting, the baby leaped in her womb, and Elizabeth was filled with the Holy Spirit. [42]In a loud voice she exclaimed: "Blessed are you among women, and blessed is the child you will bear! [43]But why am I so favored, that the mother of my Lord should come to me? [44]As soon as the sound of your greeting reached my ears, the baby in my womb leaped for joy. [45]Blessed is she who has believed that what the Lord has said to her will be accomplished!"

It would take Mary 3-4 days to travel from Nazareth to the hill country of Judea. Since no town is specified we can only narrow the trip to 50-70 miles. She quickly packs a few necessities and takes off, probably within a day or two of Gabriel's announcement. (We can't help but wonder what her parents thought.) When Mary arrives at Elizabeth's doorstep, she is less than a week pregnant.

It was a logical place for Mary to go for the necessary seclusion during the first months of her pregnancy. Elizabeth would offer her evidence of God's mighty work. In fact, if anyone would be supportive and believing, it would be Elizabeth. Plus, Mary would be a help to Elizabeth cleaning and cooking during the last trimester of her pregnancy — especially during the hot summer months of Judea.

As soon as Mary greeted Elizabeth, John leaped in her womb. The word Luke uses could also be translated as "skipped." It is normally associated with a leap of joy, sometimes in relation to the Messiah (e.g., Mal 4:2). The word "baby" [*brephos*], specifies an unborn child. This is a rather odd bit of divine evidence. First, the baby leaped while Mary was greeting Elizabeth. It appears that John's jump, not Mary's words, told of the secret in her womb. Second, how would the fetus, John, know when to jump for joy except by the prompting of the Holy Spirit?

What would the neighbors think of this pregnant woman, over 60, shouting about her teenage relative? Elizabeth's response is as prophetic as her son's. Filled with the Spirit,[10] she identified both Mary and Jesus as God's blessed instruments. "Blessed are you among women" is the way the Hebrews said, "You are most blessed of all women." In other words, Mary is "Queen of the Hill" in terms of God's blessing. This bud-

---

[10]The Spirit's two most important jobs are performed here: (1) Testifying to the truth of Jesus (Jn 15:26), and (2) Guiding our thinking and speaking out through us for Jesus (Mt 10:19-20).

ding life in Mary's womb, this mere blastula, why this was Elizabeth's Lord! Elizabeth recognized the Lordship of Christ *in utero*.

§ 7
The Magnificat
(Lk 1:46-56)

⁴⁶And Mary said:
"My soul glorifies the Lord
⁴⁷   and my spirit rejoices in God my Savior,
⁴⁸for he has been mindful
    of the humble state of his servant.
From now on all generations will call me blessed,
⁴⁹   for the Mighty One has done great things for me —
    holy is his name.
⁵⁰His mercy extends to those who fear him,
    from generation to generation.
⁵¹He has performed mighty deeds with his arm;
    he has scattered those who are proud in their inmost thoughts.
⁵²He has brought down rulers from their thrones
    but has lifted up the humble.
⁵³He has filled the hungry with good things
    but has sent the rich away empty.
⁵⁴He has helped his servant Israel,
    remembering to be merciful
⁵⁵to Abraham and his descendants forever,
    even as he said to our fathers."
⁵⁶Mary stayed with Elizabeth for about three months and then returned home.

Although Mary is a simple peasant girl, her poem is anything but simple.[11] It is as skillfully crafted as any Hebrew poem in the OT even though it is recorded in classy Greek. Its rich Hebrew theology is as fine as its form. It alludes to a great number of OT phrases and ideas.[12] But it is most similar to Hannah's prayer (1 Sam 2:1-10), although Hannah's situation was actually much more similar to Elizabeth's than to Mary's.[13] The poem has been named "The Magnificat," which is the Latin word for "magnify."

We are not told, of course, how this poem was preserved. It seems unlikely that Elizabeth transcribed as Mary uttered these words. Also, it is not likely that either woman would remember verbatim what rolled off Mary's lips. Nor does it seem likely that a poem of this depth and clarity

---

[11]R.C. Tannenhill, "The Magnificat as Poem," *JBL* 93 (1974): 263-275, analyzes the complexity of Mary's poem.

[12]J. Koontz, "Mary's Magnificat," *BibSac* 116 (Oct 1959): 336-349, lists OT references alluded to by each phrase of the poem (p. 339), which include references from each of the three Hebrew divisions of the OT.

[13]Some early MSS, in fact, do ascribe this poem to Elizabeth (see S. Benko, "The Magnificat: A History of the Controversy," *JBL* 86 [1967]: 263-275).

is the product of an instantaneous expression of praise. But this by no means indicates that Luke made it up or even edited it (although he likely translated it from Aramaic into Greek). There are better explanations. For instance, Mary may have composed this poem *en route* to Judea or even during her three month stay with Elizabeth. While the text doesn't say that Mary was inspired by the Holy Spirit to speak this poem, the Holy Spirit has just come upon her in a powerful way to generate new life in her womb. Hence, he may also have been involved in its composition.

The poem is divided into three parts: God's favor toward (1) Mary, 46-49; (2) the humble, 50-53; and (3) Israel, 54-55. Mary highlights the sovereignty of God both in the OT and in her own life. Her character shines through her words. She is a humble Hebrew girl, well versed in the OT, and filled with faith and devotion to God.

Her interest here is in the way God reverses the states of men. God takes a humble maid and exalts her among all women (vv. 48-50). (In v. 48, Mary apparently recognizes the importance of her impending birth.) God takes the exalted and humbles them (vv. 51-52). He feeds the hungry (v. 53), and he lifts up Israel as a nation (vv. 54-55). The whole theme of this song is reversal (cf. Mt 19:30-20:16; James 4:10; 1 Pet 5:6; Phil 2:5-11).

Verses 51-55 describe things God "did." However, this is probably a poetic way of describing what God "always does."[14] Now, how does God scatter the proud (v. 51)? The NIV translation renders this phrase, "in the thoughts of their hearts." However, this may be rendered, "with the thoughts of their hearts." In other words, God may scatter them through their own warped ideas.

We are not told that Mary stayed until John was born. But this three months (v. 56) would put her right at the normal time of delivery. It seems most natural that Mary would stay until John was born and then return home. At this point, Mary returns to Nazareth. Joseph then learns of her condition (Mt 1:18-25).

---

§ 8a
John's Birth
(Lk 1:57-66)

[57]When it was time for Elizabeth to have her baby, she gave birth to a son. [58]Her neighbors and relatives heard that the Lord had shown her great mercy, and they shared her joy. [59]On the eighth day they came to circumcise the child, and they were going to name him after his father Zechariah, [60]but his mother spoke up and said, "No! He is to be called John." [61]They said to her, "There is no one among your relatives who has that name."

---

[14]This literary device is called the "gnomic aorist."

The birth of John became a community event. There was great curiosity because of the angelic announcement and Zechariah's dumb/mute condition. Of course, there would also be great concern for Elizabeth's safety. After all, a woman of her age ought not to be giving birth. But when child and mother were both healthy, all the neighbors celebrated with them.

Like other Jewish boys, on the eighth day, Elizabeth brings him out to have him circumcised according to the law. Circumcision was first commanded of Abraham (Gen 17:9-14), as a sign of his special covenant with God. Along with Sabbath keeping, this became the identifying mark of God's people.

After eight days, the neighbors get their first good gawk at the boy and start calling him by the wrong name. They assumed that he would be named Zechariah, after his father. That, after all, was the normal Jewish custom. Elizabeth puts an immediate halt to it. Gabriel's instructions were to name him John. So she has been calling him John for the full eight days now.

Lk 1:62-66

⁶²Then they made signs to his father, to find out what he would like to name the child. ⁶³He asked for a writing tablet, and to everyone's astonishment he wrote, "His name is John." ⁶⁴Immediately his mouth was opened and his tongue was loosed, and he began to speak, praising God. ⁶⁵The neighbors were all filled with awe, and throughout the hill country of Judea people were talking about all these things. ⁶⁶Everyone who heard this wondered about it, asking, "What then is this child going to be?" For the Lord's hand was with him.

The neighbors refuse to listen to Elizabeth. They turn to her husband to settle the argument. Zechariah is apparently still deaf as well as dumb (this is a legitimate use of the word, cf. Lk 7:22), so they communicate through "sign language." He pulls out a writing tablet. This was probably a small wooden board covered with a reusable wax film which could be inscribed. He settles the argument by writing, "His name is John." This was shocking! The rumor mill started spinning through the hill country. It was obvious to all that God's hand was involved in this child of destiny. They wondered what would come of all this.

**§ 8b
Zechariah's
Song**
(Lk 1:67-79)

⁶⁷His father Zechariah was filled with the Holy Spirit and prophesied:
.⁶⁸"Praise be to the Lord, the God of Israel,
    because he has come and has redeemed his people.
⁶⁹He has raised up a horn⁸ of salvation for us
    in the house of his servant David
⁷⁰(as he said through his holy prophets of long ago),
⁷¹salvation from our enemies

and from the hand of all who hate us —
[72]to show mercy to our fathers
   and to remember his holy covenant,
[73]   the oath he swore to our father Abraham:
[74]to rescue us from the hand of our enemies,
   and to enable us to serve him without fear
[75]   in holiness and righteousness before him all our days.
[76]And you, my child, will be called a prophet of the Most High;
   for you will go on before the Lord to prepare the way for him,
[77]to give his people the knowledge of salvation
   through the forgiveness of their sins,
[78]because of the tender mercy of our God,
   by which the rising sun will come to us from heaven
[79]to shine on those living in darkness
      and in the shadow of death,
   to guide our feet into the path of peace."

[a]*69 Horn* here symbolizes strength

Zechariah's tongue was untied. The Holy Spirit came upon him just like one of the prophets of old. This utterance, which has been called the "Benedictus," is both poetic and prophetic. Like the Magnificat, it is pregnant with Hebraisms and OT allusions. It sketches several prophecies which were fulfilled by the coming of Jesus and John:

   a. Redemption of Israel, v. 68.
   b. Horn of Salvation from the house of David, v. 69.
   c. Salvation from our enemies, v. 71.
   d. Completion of the promises made to the fathers, vv. 72-74.
   e. We would be able to serve God without fear, vv. 74-75.
   f. The forerunner of the Messiah, v. 76.
   g. Bring forgiveness of sins, v. 77.
   h. The light of God will shine on those in darkness, v. 78-79.

The poem opens with a celebration of redemption. The word literally means "payment" or "ransom." In the OT, it referred primarily to the Exodus. Presently, the Jews hoped for a similar "release" from the bondage of Rome (Lk 24:21). From our angle, we see that the redemption Jesus offered was not through a military campaign but through the cross. Jesus offered the only acceptable payment for our sins — his own blood. The cross *was* redemption.

In verse 69, this Messiah is described as our "horn of salvation." Because of the great strength of the horned animals in the Near East, the horn became a symbol of power. Every other use of "horn" in the NT is confined to the book of Revelation. There, it refers to three entities: Jesus, as the Lamb; the altar of God; and alternately, the Dragon and the Beast. There is a mighty battle being fought for our salvation between great, but unequal, cosmic powers. Revelation makes it clear that this is really not a great contest for God, even though the power of both sides is staggering to us.

This prophetic utterance breaks the 400-year silence since Malachi. The specific quote of v. 71 can be found in Psalm 106:10. The concept, however, can be found in nearly every prophetic book. It is clear that Zechariah has in mind here a physical deliverance as did his contemporaries. However, the rest of the Gospel will reveal the spiritual nature of its fulfillment.

Zechariah was acutely aware that his son, John, would announce the coming of the Messiah (v. 76). He even describes how John would announce the forgiveness of sins (v. 77). Surely he is familiar with the OT job description of this "forerunner" (cf. Mal 3:1; 4:5; Isa 40:3; Mt 3:3).

John would prepare the way and the Messiah would "rise" behind him. The term "rising" in the OT, especially in the context of "branch" had a strong Messianic implication which must be kept in mind here. The coming of Jesus is being compared to a sunrise which dispels the dark of night (cf. Mt 4:16; Lk 2:32; Jn 1:4-9; 3:20-21; 8:12). There is a new day rising with hope of salvation for God's people.

§ 8c
Growth and
Emergence of
John
(Lk 1:80)

[80]And the child grew and became strong in spirit; and he lived in the desert until he appeared publicly to Israel.

This verse spans 30 years. The word "appeared" could be translated by "commissioned," "pointed out," "shown forth," or even "inaugurated." It was used of a public announcement of an official nomination. In other words, this describes John's "inauguration."

It is believed by some that John was a member of the Qumran community. If his parents, being old, died in his youth, he might have been adopted by that community. It was, after all, a good way for a celibate community to reproduce itself. We must keep in mind, however, that there is not a shred of historical data to support this view besides the fact that John, like the Qumranites, was an ascetic who lived in the desert.

PART THREE
THE EARLY YEARS OF JESUS CHRIST

§ 9
Joseph Learns of Jesus
(Mt 1:18-25)

The first chapter of Matthew is designed to answer a single question: Who is Jesus? There are two answers. The first is given in verses 1-17. He is the *Son of David* through his adopted father Joseph. In fact, Joseph is the only person in the Gospels, other than Jesus, to be called "the Son of David," (v. 20). The second answer is this: Jesus is the *Son of God* by an immaculate conception (vv. 18-25), and is thus to be called *Immanuel — God with us* (cf. Isa 8:10). Both answers are tied together with the word *genesis* (v. 1, 18). They describe what we call the *incarnation*. God robed himself in human flesh and dwelt among men (cf. Mt 17:17; 18:20; 26:29; 28:20).

Mt 1:18-21

[18]This is how the birth of Jesus Christ came about: His mother Mary was pledged to be married to Joseph, but before they came together, she was found to be with child through the Holy Spirit. [19]Because Joseph her husband was a righteous man and did not want to expose her to public disgrace, he had in mind to divorce her quietly. [20]But after he had considered this, an angel of the Lord appeared to him in a dream and said, "Joseph son of David, do not be afraid to take Mary home as your wife, because what is conceived in her is from the Holy Spirit. [21]She will give birth to a son, and you are to give him the name Jesus,[a] because he will save his people from their sins."

[a]*21 Jesus is the Greek form of Joshua, which means the Lord saves.*

This event apparently took place after Mary's three-month visit with Elizabeth. Mary is now beginning to show, even under the loose Palestinian garb. Something has to be done. In order for Joseph to deny his own involvement he needs to make some kind of statement.

There are two options available to Joseph. He can make a public and humiliating trial of her which could potentially end in stoning. Or he can give her a certificate of divorce in the presence of two witnesses. In the eyes of the community she is defiled.

Joseph was about to take the second option and spare Mary public humiliation. While both kind and reasonable, it is not God's will. An angel intervenes through a dream. While that sounds odd to us it was common for Jews to view dreams as messages from God. In fact, there were twelve different men in the OT to whom God spoke through dreams (Gen 20:3; 28:12; 31:10; 31:24; 37:5; 40:9; 40:16; 41:1, Judg 7:13, 1 Kgs 3:5, Dan 2:3; 7:1). Furthermore, Joel 2:28 says that dreams will be one of the signs of the Messianic age. Moreover, there are five dreams recorded in the NT, all in Matthew, and three of the five are to Joseph (Mt 1:20; 2:12-13, 19, 22; 27:19).

The dream tells Joseph three things. First, Mary is not defiled. Her pregnancy is due to the Holy Spirit, not fornication. Therefore, take her as your wife. Second, she is going to have a baby boy. As his "adopted" father, you are to name him "Jesus" (i.e., "Jehovah saves"). Third, this is going to be a special child. He will "save his people from their sins."

This phrase carries a very "spiritual" implication to the Christian reader. To the Jew, however, it was more practical and political. The sins of Israel often led to national punishment through a foreign nation. This is exactly what the Jews were experiencing under the occupation of Rome. Joseph, no doubt, shared the current popular expectation of a political liberator Messiah who would free the Jews from the *result* or *punishment* for their sins. However, the true meaning of this prophecy is not found in a cavalry but in Calvary.

Mt 1:22-25

²²All this took place to fulfill what the Lord had said through the prophet: ²³"The virgin will be with child and will give birth to a son, and they will call him Immanuel"ᵃ — which means, "God with us." ²⁴When Joseph woke up, he did what the angel of the Lord had commanded him and took Mary home as his wife. ²⁵But he had no union with her until she gave birth to a son. And he gave him the name Jesus.

ᵃ23 Isaiah 7:14

This prophecy is from Isaiah 7:14. There a word is used [*alma*] which may mean either virgin or young maiden. When the prophecy was first fulfilled about 732 B.C., the word meant "maiden." God offered Ahaz a sign for the coming judgment upon Judah through Egypt and Assyria (Isa 7:11-19). A little boy would be born to a young woman. God said, "He will eat curds and honey at the time he knows enough to refuse evil and choose good. For before the boy will know enough to refuse evil and choose good, the land whose two kings you dread will be forsaken" (vv. 15-16). This has obvious meaning for Ahaz's day. Some propose that this son is Hezekiah or some other member of the royal line. Others suggest it to be Judean boys in general. But the best contextual suggestion seems to be Maher-Shalal-Hash-Baz (Isa 8:3). With all of these suggestions, however, none will suggest the necessity of a virgin birth.

This prophecy saw its greater fulfillment in the birth of Jesus, as is suggested from the context of the prophecy (Isa 8:17-18; 9:1-2, 6-7), as well as its inspired interpretation (Mt 1:23). Here, as well as in Luke, we are obviously talking about a virgin. Gabriel told Joseph that the life in Mary's womb came from the Holy Spirit, not sexual union with a man.

This virgin-born child would be called "Immanuel," "God with us." The implication is that the transcendent God would dwell among men. The Israelites had seen a type of that in the Holy of Holies. But even then, only one man could speak with him and only once a year. There was also the picture of Adam walking with God in the cool of the day. Then there was this "human-looking" Son of Man in the clouds of heaven (Dan 7:13). However, God incarnate, in the person of Jesus, was beyond the wildest dreams of any Jew at that time.

When Joseph woke up, he knew that God had spoken to him in a dream. But how would Joseph have been able to distinguish this angelic message from a normal dream? The answer is quite simple — he could not and would not. The fact is that dreams were generally viewed by the Jews of the first century as divine communication, that is, as favorable omens from God. They were so common that the Talmud (*Ber 55 b*) says, "If any one sleeps seven days without dreaming (or rather, remembering his dream for interpretation), call him wicked" (as unremembered of God), (Edersheim, I:155). Consequently Joseph, in obedience to the dream, was willing to accept Mary as his wife.

Beyond the elaborate and legal betrothal, nothing was left but the wedding ceremony. After the ceremony, the woman would move in with her husband. We're not told what kind of a ceremony they had. But once Joseph brought Mary to live with him, they were considered husband and wife. Still, Joseph doesn't have sexual relations with her until after the birth of Jesus. This is not because sex is evil, but so that no one could deny the uniqueness and holiness of Jesus' birth.[1]

§ 10
The Birth of
Jesus
(Lk 2:1-7)

[1]In those days Caesar Augustus issued a decree that a census should be taken of the entire Roman world. [2](This was the first census that took place while Quirinius was governor of Syria.) [3]And everyone went to his own town to register.

---

[1]Verse 25, as well as Mary's children, seems to argue against any theory of her perpetual virginity. The idea originates from the apocryphal book, *Protevangelium of James* 14:15-19, which goes so far as to suggest that Mary's hymen was not broken even during delivery.

The Caesar of the day was Gaius Octavius. He was born September 23, 63 B.C. He was adopted by his great uncle, Julius Caesar, who was assassinated on March 15, 44 B.C. He was only 19 at the time but was a shrewd politician. He became one of the three most powerful men of the empire. At the battle of Actium, September 2, 31 B.C., after defeating Mark Antony, he conquered all rivals. By refusing such titles as "king" and "dictator" he showed, ostensibly, that he did not want to be emperor. Practically, however, that is exactly what he became. It was Octavius who claimed the title of Caesar which would eventually claim divinity. He ruled until his death in A.D. 14.

During the later part of his reign, he began to take a census of the entire Roman empire so that they could collect taxes more efficiently.[2] He could not, of course, do it all at once. Rather, he ordered different provinces to enroll at different times. Because the Roman empire was so vast and diverse, the method of enrolling people had to be suitable for each particular people group and geographical area.

When it came to the Jews, they would register by tribe, clan and family. In order to do that they would need to travel to their ancestral city. This was probably where the genealogical records were kept. Joseph, being a descendent of David, would obviously go to Bethlehem (cf. 1 Sam 16:1; 17:58).

The most famous census of Quirinius was in A.D. 6 while he was governor of Syria. It was remembered because of the riots it spawned (Acts 5:37; Josephus, *Ant.* 18. 26). Yet this is ten years too late for the birth of Christ. Is Luke off by a decade? There are two possible solutions. First, Quirinius was a military leader in Syria (8-4 B.C.), before he became the actual governor of Syria in A.D. 6-7. The word translated "governor" could be understood as "leader." Hence, Luke would be saying that this was the first census taken during Quirinius' military leadership, not the second census taken during his governorship. A second, and perhaps simpler, solution is to translate the word *protē* as "before" rather than "first." Hence, Luke is saying that this was not the famous census during the reign of Quirinius, but the one before that.[3]

Luke was well aware of the census taken in A.D. 6 for he mentions it in Acts 5:37. Furthermore, the mention of Quirinius is not essential to the narrative. Therefore, we might want to give Luke the benefit of the doubt

---

[2]Cf. Tacitus, *Ann.* 1.11; Dio Cassius 53.30.2.

[3]See W. Brindle, "The Census and Quirinius: Luke 2:2," *JETS* 27/1 (Mar 1984): 43-52 and J. Nolland, *Luke*, in Word Biblical Commentary, Vol 35a (Dallas: Word, 1989), p. 101.

since he is careful not to include doubtful and superficial information. It would seem, then, that the mention of Quirinius was intended to distinguish between the earlier and later census. In light of Luke's reliable research, it seems prudent to accept the accuracy of his account, admitting he probably knew the historical details of which we are ignorant.

Lk 2:4-7

⁴So Joseph also went up from the town of Nazareth in Galilee to Judea, to Bethlehem the town of David, because he belonged to the house and line of David. ⁵He went there to register with Mary, who was pledged to be married to him and was expecting a child. ⁶While they were there, the time came for the baby to be born, ⁷and she gave birth to her firstborn, a son. She wrapped him in cloths and placed him in a manger, because there was no room for them in the inn.

Joseph took Mary and traveled nearly 70 miles from Nazareth to Bethlehem. This "House of Bread" lay five miles south of Jerusalem. It was here that the "Bread of Life" was born (around December 5 B.C. or January 4 B.C.). This fulfilled Micah's prophecy (5:2). In this humble village, the Messiah made his grand appearance on earth.

Luke correctly says that Joseph and Mary "had been" pledged to be married. They are actually husband and wife (cf. Mt 1:24), except, of course, they are abstaining from coitus. They arrive at the village and look for a place to stay. Our traditional nativity scenes picture Mary and Joseph put out in a barn by an insensitive or at least overbooked innkeeper. Bailey argues, however, that this is hardly possible.[4] First, Palestinian hospitality is great. Certainly someone would have made room for the couple, especially since she is about to burst and this was his ancestral city! Second, inns were more a Roman conception than Jewish. Since Bethlehem is not a major city nor on any trade routes, it is not likely that they would have had much more than a "flophouse." The fact is, this word is better translated "guest room" (cf. Lk 22:11). The normal word for "inn" is *pandocheion* (cf. Lk 10:34) not *katalyma*. Hence, we suggest that Jesus was born in a private home, not in a barn.[5]

Why then would there be a manger (i.e., an animal feed trough) inside a home? Bailey explains that Palestinian homes often have an entry way below the family living area (cf. Lk 13:15). The animals are brought in at night to keep them from being stolen, to "guard" the house and to heat the house during winter. There would, of course, be feed

---

[4]K.E. Bailey, "The Manger and the Inn," *Bible & Spade* 10 (Sum-Aut 1981): 74-85.

[5]Ancient tradition pictures Jesus as born in a cave (Justin Martyr, *Dialogue with Trypho*, 79; *Protevangelion of James*, 7.14). However, a number of Palestinian homes were built out of caves.

troughs either attached to the wall or between the entryway and the raised family living area. The bottom line is that it is common to find mangers in Palestinian homes. Therefore, we suggest this reading of verses 6-7: "Some time after[6] Mary and Joseph came to Bethlehem Mary gave birth. Since the guest room was already filled, she delivered in the main living area of the house and used the manger as a crib." In typical Hebrew fashion, she binds the baby's legs for warmth and protection.

Jesus is called the "firstborn." Primarily this indicates his legal status under the Mosaic law (Exod 13:2; Deut 21:15-17), but it also shows that Mary apparently had other children. At least six are mentioned: James, Joses, Judas and Simon (Matt 13:55), and at least two sisters. The simplest reading of the text is that Jesus had several younger half-brothers and half-sisters.

**§ 11
The Worship of
the Shepherds**
(Lk 2:8-20)

[8]And there were shepherds living out in the fields nearby, keeping watch over their flocks at night. [9]An angel of the Lord appeared to them, and the glory of the Lord shone around them, and they were terrified. [10]But the angel said to them, "Do not be afraid. I bring you good news of great joy that will be for all the people. [11]Today in the town of David a Savior has been born to you; he is Christ[a] the Lord. [12]This will be a sign to you: You will find a baby wrapped in cloths and lying in a manger." [13]Suddenly a great company of the heavenly host appeared with the angel, praising God and saying, [14]"Glory to God in the highest, and on earth peace to men on whom his favor rests."

[a]11 Or *Messiah*. "The Christ" (Greek) and "the Messiah" (Hebrew) both mean "the Anointed One"; also in verse 26.

Shepherding was among the lowliest of occupations. It was scorned because the work made it next to impossible to strictly observe the regulations of the law. We see then, from the beginning, God extends his mercy to social outcasts.

It should also be recognized that the shepherd is a symbol of those who care for God's people. This symbolism extends from David, the shepherd boy, to Jesus the Great Shepherd, from the Elders of Israel to the Elders of the church (Ps 23:1; Isa 40:11; Jer 23:1-4; Heb 13:20; 1 Pet 2:25; 5:2).

These lowly shepherds may well have been keeping watch over the sacrificial lambs. In other words, when they get big enough, they will be shipped up to Jerusalem and slain for the sins of Israel. They are about to get a glimpse of the Lamb of God, who will die for the sins of the world

---

[6]Verse 6 seems to presuppose some time between their arrival in Bethlehem and the birth of Jesus.

(Jn 1:29). We have a double symbolism. The shepherds will meet the one true shepherd who is, paradoxically, also the one true lamb.

It does seem odd that the shepherds are out with the sheep at night rather than putting them up in pens. However, supposing that there was a sudden surge of visitors to Jerusalem for the census, this would be a dandy time to make a sacrifice. Perhaps all the pens are full. Even in December and January, the nights in Palestine don't get cold enough to endanger the shepherds or the sheep in the fields. As Longeneker notes, however, this says little or nothing about the date of Jesus' birth:

> The traditional date for the Nativity was set, long after the event, to coincide with a pagan festival, thus demonstrating that the "Sol Invictus," the "Unconquerable Sun," had indeed been conquered. December 25 was widely celebrated as the date of Jesus' birth by the end of the fourth century. January 6 was also an important date in the early church, held by many as the occasion of the arrival of the wise men and known as Epiphany. (p. 845)

The shepherds are frightened at the sight of the angels. Who wouldn't be? So far, Zechariah, Mary and Joseph have seen an angel and all have been frightened. In addition to the angel, these shepherds saw the glory of the Lord shining around them. It is no small wonder they were struck with great fear.

They are instructed to look for a sign in the "City of David." This phrase is used forty-three times in the NIV. Almost all references are to Jerusalem. However, it can also refer to Bethlehem since David was born there (1 Sam 17:12). The sign would be a newborn infant who had been wrapped in strips of cloth and laid in a manger. This "wrapping" was a normal part of post-natal care. The distinctive part of this sign, however, is the manger. It would not be normal to use a feeding trough as a crib.

We notice that with each of the three angelic announcements, God's people are given a sign to support their faith. Zechariah was deaf and dumb. Mary witnessed the miraculous conception in Elizabeth's barren old age. And now, these shepherds will find Jesus exactly as described by the angels. There is a lesson in this. God does not expect us to believe blindly. He gives us the necessary information and then backs it up with signs to validate his message. That, in fact, is the purpose of miracles. Faith means, "Taking God at his word."

About that time, a whole flock of angels appear (lit. "a heavenly army"), a multitude of angelic warriors, announcing peace, not war. A textual variant has led to a difference in readings in the KJV text and the modern translations. The KJV reads, "On earth peace, goodwill toward men." "Goodwill" [*eudokia*] is in the nominative case, which makes it part of the subject of the sentence along with "peace." However, in the most ancient manuscripts, which were found after the translation of the KJV, an "s" is added to *eudokia*, which makes it genitive, describing "men." Thus, it is rendered in the modern versions, "Men of goodwill" or NIV, "Men with whom he is pleased."

Furthermore, both Mueller and Dodd suggest that *eudokias* expresses will/choice rather than emotion.[7] In other words, it is not that God is happy with men and therefore grants salvation in Jesus. Rather, he has chosen to bestow this wonderful gift of Jesus. The bottom line: The gift of Jesus is based on God's sovereign choice, not men's pleasant character.

Lk 2:15-20

[15]When the angels had left them and gone into heaven, the shepherds said to one another, "Let's go to Bethlehem and see this thing that has happened, which the Lord has told us about." [16]So they hurried off and found Mary and Joseph, and the baby, who was lying in the manger. [17]When they had seen him, they spread the word concerning what had been told them about this child, [18]and all who heard it were amazed at what the shepherds said to them. [19]But Mary treasured up all these things and pondered them in her heart. [20]The shepherds returned, glorifying and praising God for all the things they had heard and seen, which were just as they had been told.

The shepherds make a beeline to Bethlehem. (They probably left the sheep in the care of one poor shepherd who drew the short straw). Sure enough, they find exactly what the angels had announced. They spread the word around town and predictably, it amazes everyone. This is pretty big stuff for a sleepy little village like Bethlehem.

Mary did not miss a lick! Consider all she now knows. She's heard from Gabriel, the dream of Joseph, the words of Elizabeth, the prophecy of Zechariah, the revelation of the shepherds and all the Messianic prophecies. Yet to come is the revelation of Simeon and Anna the Prophetess.[8]

---

[7]C.H. Dodd, "New Testament Translation Problems II," *BT* 28/1 (Jan 1977): 104-110 and T. Mueller, "Observations on Some New Testament Texts Based on Generative-Transformational Grammar," *BT* 29 (Jan 1978): 117-120.

[8]Consider all that Mary now knows about Jesus:
  I. **From Gabriel** (Lk 1:31-35): (1) Great, (2) Son of the Most High, (3) he would sit on the throne of David (cf. Isa 9:6-7); (4) he will reign over the house of Jacob forever; (5) his kingdom will have no end; (6) the holy one, (7) Son of God.
  II. **From Elizabeth** (Lk 1:43): (8) "Mother of my Lord."
  III. **Magnificat** (Lk 1:48-55): (9) "All generations will count me blessed;" (10) he will help Israel and Abraham's offspring.
  IV. **From Joseph** (Mt 1:20-23): (11) Conceived of Holy Spirit; (12) he would save the people from their sins; (13) Immanuel ("God with us") from Isa 7:14.

Mary has a lot to "think about." This word, "pondered," etymologically, could be rendered, "to cast about within." She is mulling over all these thoughts within her brain. You can just see them rolling around in there being churned over and over. Mary is still trying to put all this into perspective.

§ 12
Circumcision
of Jesus
(Lk 2:21)

[21]On the eighth day, when it was time to circumcise him, he was named Jesus, the name the angel had given him before he had been conceived.

Luke continues to compare and contrast the birth of John and Jesus. As with John, Jesus was: (1) circumcised on the eighth day, (2) named at the time of his circumcision, and (3) given a name before conception from an angelic encounter.

Truly Jesus was born "under the law" (Gal 4:4). He was kosher from his sandals to his sideburns. This narrative traces that heritage.

§ 13
Jesus
Presented in
the Temple
(Lk 2:22-38)

When Jesus' parents take him to the temple for purification (cf. 1 Sam 1:24, 28), they meet two significant people: Simeon and Anna. Both of them are old and both are influenced by the Holy Spirit. They have waited all their lives to see this child and now that they have, their lives are complete. Furthermore, Simeon's prophetic utterance, "Nunc Dimittis," is parallel to Zechariah's "Benedictus." Both proclamations explain the role of the newborn child.

Lk 2:22-24

[22]When the time of their purification according to the Law of Moses had been completed, Joseph and Mary took him to Jerusalem to present him to the Lord [23](as it is written in the Law of the Lord, "Every firstborn male is to be consecrated to the Lord"[a]), [24]and to offer a sacrifice in keeping with what is said in the Law of the Lord: "a pair of doves or two young pigeons."[b]

[a]*23* Exodus 13:2,12   [b]*24* Lev. 12:8

Leviticus 12:1-8 outlines the days of purification for the woman after childbirth. If it was a girl, the woman would be unclean for fourteen days, and remain in "blood of purification for sixty-six days." After the birth of a boy, she was unclean for seven days, the eighth would be

---

V. **From the Shepherds** (Lk 2:11): (14) Savior.
VI. **From Simeon** (Lk 2:26-35): (15) The Christ = Messiah; (16) Salvation; Light of revelation to the Gentiles (cf. Isa 42:6 & 49:6); (17) Rise and fall of many in Israel; (18) Sword will pierce even Mary's own soul.
VII. **From the Prophets** (Lk 2:38): (19) He is the redemption of Israel.

the day for his circumcision, and she would remain in her "blood of purification for thirty-three days." After such a time (forty days for a son and eighty for a daughter), she would go to the temple and offer two sacrifices. The first sacrifice was a lamb for a burnt offering, the second was a pigeon or turtledove as a sin offering. If she were poor, instead of offering a lamb, she could offer a turtledove or a young pigeon. The price of both birds would be less than a quarter. By doing this, Mary and Joseph revealed they were of the poorer class. In the court of the women, there were thirteen trumpet-shaped chests into which offerings were dropped. The third "trumpet," as they were called, was reserved for the offerings of the poor which paid for their sacrificial animals.

This purification ceremony had two purposes. First, it emphasized the corruption of humanity and the purity of God. We should not, however, read into this that sexual relations, becoming pregnant or giving birth is sinful. Second, it was just plain sanitary. The mother and child would have forty days of privacy, rest and quarantine.

Exodus 13:2-12 describes the consecration of the firstborn male. God demands the firstborn male to be given to him whether man or beast. They could then be redeemed from the Lord at a set price. The cost would be roughly equivalent to five or ten dollars. We must understand, this follows on the heels of the tenth plague of Egypt, the death of every firstborn. It was by this plague that the Israelites were freed. The consecration of the firstborn was intended as a sign. It was a reminder of how God freed Israel from Egypt.

Lk 2:25-32

²⁵Now there was a man in Jerusalem called Simeon, who was righteous and devout. He was waiting for the consolation of Israel, and the Holy Spirit was upon him. ²⁶It had been revealed to him by the Holy Spirit that he would not die before he had seen the Lord's Christ. ²⁷Moved by the Spirit, he went into the temple courts. When the parents brought in the child Jesus to do for him what the custom of the Law required, ²⁸Simeon took him in his arms and praised God, saying:

²⁹"Sovereign Lord, as you have promised,
    you now dismissᵃ your servant in peace.
³⁰For my eyes have seen your salvation,
³¹   which you have prepared in the sight of all people,
³²a light for revelation to the Gentiles
    and for glory to your people Israel."

ᵃ29 Or promised, / now dismiss

Simeon is apparently a priest. After all, he takes the child in his arms and blesses him at the time of "presentation." That was the job of a priest. But he is more than a priest. Due to his purity and patient hope for Messiah, God allowed him to become a prophet. The Holy Spirit came upon him like the prophets of old and revealed to him that Messiah would come in his own lifetime. The Holy Spirit even directed his steps into the temple to be at the right place at the right time so that when Mary and Joseph brought their baby boy in, he was the first priest they met.

Simeon took Jesus in his arms and praised God for the coming of the "consolation of Israel" (Isa 40:1; 49:13; 51:3; 52:9; 54:11; 61:2; 66:13; Jer 31:13). But more than a consolation to the Jews, Jesus was the light to the Gentiles. This was a foreign concept to the Jews of Simeon's day. Although the Old Testament frequently speaks of salvation to the Gentiles (Gen 12:3; Ps 67:2; Isa 2:2; 42:6; 49:6; Joel 2:28; Amos 9:11-12; etc.), the Jews consistently rejected any idea of Gentile inclusion. Even the early church struggled with this. There was no greater fight in the book of Acts than over the Gentiles being part of the church (cf. chapters 10-11, 15; verse 28:28).

Lk 2:33-35

[33]The child's father and mother marveled at what was said about him. [34]Then Simeon blessed them and said to Mary, his mother: "This child is destined to cause the falling and rising of many in Israel, and to be a sign that will be spoken against, [35]so that the thoughts of many hearts will be revealed. And a sword will pierce your own soul too."

Although Simeon had some wonderful and encouraging things to say about Jesus, it was not all positive. He would cause many in Israel to rise. To others he would be a stumbling block — to those who rejected him (Isa 8:14; Mt 21:42, 44; Acts 4:11; Rom 9:33; 1 Cor 1:23). To those who accept him, he is the resurrection and the life (Jn 11:25; Rom 6:4,9; Eph 2:6).

He would also be a "pain" to Mary, as well as the whole nation. A sword would pierce her soul. This is not the short, quick Roman sword [*machaira*]. This is the long, broad sword, [*romphaia*], associated with great injury and pain. We believe this to refer to the crucifixion of her Son. This event would be devastating to Mary. Not only would she lose her Son, she would also, temporarily, lose her hope in the redemption of Israel.

Lk 2:36-38

[36]There was also a prophetess, Anna, the daughter of Phanuel, of the tribe of Asher. She was very old; she had lived with her husband seven years after her marriage, [37]and then was a widow until she was eighty-four.[a] She never left the temple but worshiped night and day, fasting and praying. [38]Coming up to them at that very moment, she gave thanks to God and spoke about the child to all who were looking forward to the redemption of Jerusalem.

[a]37 Or *widow for eighty-four years*

Simeon's counterpart comes onto the scene. Her name is Anna. She was one of several prophetesses mentioned in the Bible (Exod 15:20; Judg 4:4; 2 Kgs 22:14; Neh 6:14; Isa 8:3; Acts 2:17; 21:9; 1 Cor 11:5). She is also an elderly widow, now eighty-four years old.[9] She was married for seven years. Assuming she was married at about seventeen years old, she has been a widow for some sixty years. She is a well-established figure around the temple.

She had watched God preparing the political times for the Messiah.[10] She has seen Julius Caesar rise to power and knew of his assassination. She watched the steady and sad decline of the illustrious Maccabean rule which gave freedom to her people for the first time since Ezra and Nehemiah two hundred years before. She was a young woman when Pompey, a Roman general, conquered the Mid-East for Rome. She watched as the hated Idumeans (Edomites) of the Herod family were placed in power over Palestine. She witnessed the rise of two opposing religious parties (the Pharisees and Sadducees). She had lived under Rome's heavy taxation and under the Jewish heavy religious legalism. The times were ripe for Christ . . . She watched, and waited and hoped.

Anna had worshipped, or rather "served" in the temple for nearly sixty years. Praying and fasting are not verbs but nouns (dative). They indicate the means by which she served. Being a woman, not even from the tribe of Levi, she would never be able to offer sacrifices or do any other priestly duties. She serves in the only way she can, prayer and fasting.

These were times of great Messianic expectation. Jerusalem was occupied by Rome. Herod, a corrupt Idumean, was the king of the Jews. The Maccabean revolt of some one hundred fifty years earlier was now just a memory. Yet the Scriptures echo across the years that the Jews are God's chosen people. Through them would come the deliverer. Unfortunately, the materialistic culture of the Greeks, foisted upon them by the Hellenists, blinded them from spiritual hopes and left them searching for a military/political messiah.

---

[9]The NIV's translation (in the main text) leads us to believe that Anna was 84 years old. But v. 37 could also be translated, "She was a widow for 84 years," as in the NIV footnote. Thus she would be well over 100 years old. M.P. John, "Luke 2:36-37: How Old Was Anna," *BT* 26 (Apr 1975): 247, verifies that it would have been possible, but not likely for her to live that long (cf. Judith 16:22-23).

[10]Noland (p. 125) suggests that Anna's age is symbolic, not literal. He says that "84" may represent 7 X 12 = the completion of waiting for the Messiah.

§ 14
The Magi Visit Jesus
(Mt 2:1-12)

This is kind of an odd text. Whereas, Luke, the Evangelist to the Gentiles, presents Jesus in the temple, Matthew, the Evangelist to the Jews, presents the adoration of the Gentiles (Edersheim, I:202). On the heels of Simeon's prophecy, we get the first glimpse of its fulfillment: Jesus is a light to the Gentiles. Already we have seen the seeds of the gospel touch women, social outcasts (shepherds), and Gentiles (Magi) in a significant way.

Mt 2:1-6

[1]After Jesus was born in Bethlehem in Judea, during the time of King Herod, Magi[a] from the east came to Jerusalem [2]and asked, "Where is the one who has been born king of the Jews? We saw his star in the east[b] and have come to worship him."

[3]When King Herod heard this he was disturbed, and all Jerusalem with him. [4]When he had called together all the people's chief priests and teachers of the law, he asked them where the Christ[c] was to be born. [5]"In Bethlehem in Judea," they replied, "for this is what the prophet has written:

[6]"But you, Bethlehem, in the land of Judah,
    are by no means least among the rulers of Judah;
for out of you will come a ruler
    who will be the shepherd of my people Israel.'"[d]

[a]1 Traditionally *Wise Men*   [b]2 Or *star when it rose*   [c]4 Or *Messiah*   [d]6 Micah 5:2

These Magi were apparently "religious" teachers of the Medes and Persians. Our word "magic" comes from this word. Although the Magi were not untouched by superstition and cultic arts, they were primarily the scholars of the day. Not only were they involved in astrology, they also studied astronomy, medicine, math, and natural science. Likely they became interested in the sacred literature of the Jews and the wisdom it offered during the Babylonian Captivity. They are mentioned in the LXX, Philo, Josephus, and several other secular writers.

These Magi saw some kind of astral phenomenon in Babylon which led them to believe that a new king of the Jews was coming. There have been a number of guesses as to what that phenomenon was.[11] Astronomers, with the help of computers, have sought to determine the alignment of the natural celestial bodies which would have been visible from Mesopotamia about 6 B.C. There did seem to be an alignment of Jupiter and Saturn in the constellation of Pisces about 6 B.C. This usually happens only once every eight hundred years, but took place three times (May, October and December) near the time of Jesus' birth. A year later the planet Mars joined them. However, none of the naturalistic theories adequately account for verse 9 when the star moved before them and

---

[11]S. Begley, "The Christmas Star — Or Was it Planets?" *Newsweek* (Dec 30, 1991): 54-55.

rested over the place where Jesus was. The Magi gave much importance to astrological signs as portents of things to come. It would be natural for them to interpret this stellar alignment as a divine message (Edersheim, I:209-216).

They came to Jerusalem not to find Jesus, but to find direction. They were going to Herod, the King of the Jews. It was natural enough to go to the head of a nation with an event of this magnitude. Besides that, Jerusalem was the religious capital of the Jews. Their wise men should be able to answer a question like this.

This whole encounter troubled Herod. Throughout Herod's political career he had been plagued with seditions and trouble primarily from his own family. He killed several of his own sons, as well as his wife Mariamne (Josephus, *Ant.* 7. 61-145), and his mother-in-law, fearing that they would take over his kingdom (which was a strong possibility).

Furthermore, Herod was now near his deathbed. It was a period of his life in which he suffered mental disorder. His body was ulcerated and putrefied. He was a very sick, paranoid, and savage man at this point in his life. It is little wonder that Herod was troubled when he discovered this infant competition. All Jerusalem was troubled with Herod, not out of sympathy for him, but out of fear of how he would respond. They knew all too well his reputation.

Although Herod is deathly ill, he is still quite cunning. In verse four Herod calls together the chief priests and scribes. From these he learns *where* the Messiah is to be born. In verse seven he secretly called together the Magi. From these he learns *when* the child is born. Thus it appears that Herod alone had the "full scoop." He fakes a desire to worship the Christ-Child. Thus, he plans to glean all the information about the child that he can. Fortunately, God warned both the Magi (v. 12) and Joseph (v. 13) of Herod's plot and both escaped his schemes.

The temple administrators (chief priests) and the main teachers (scribes) conclude that the Messiah was to be born in Bethlehem. That was the current interpretation of Micah 5:2 (cf. Jer. Ber. ii. 4). But verse six changes a number of words from the Micah 5:2 passage.[12] In other words, it is not an exact quote but an "interpretive translation." Matthew's Jewish readers would understand that he was not "tampering" with the text, but expounding on its true meaning. This was a common Jewish mode of teaching, somewhat like paraphrasing a text in a sermon.

---

[12]For specifics see A.J. Petrotta, "A Closer Look at Matt 2:6 and Its Old Testament Sources," *JETS* 28/1 (Mar 1985): 47-52 and G. Archer & G. Chirichigno, *O.T. Quotations in the N.T.* (Chicago: Moody, 1983), p. 157.

Heater suggests that Matthew is really combining three verses (Gen 49:10; 2 Sam 5:2; Mic 5:2), and showing how they all fit together to predict the birth of the Messiah in Bethlehem.[13]

Mt 2:7-12

[7]Then Herod called the Magi secretly and found out from them the exact time the star had appeared. [8]He sent them to Bethlehem and said, "Go and make a careful search for the child. As soon as you find him, report to me, so that I too may go and worship him."

[9]After they had heard the king, they went on their way, and the star they had seen in the east[a] went ahead of them until it stopped over the place where the child was. [10]When they saw the star, they were overjoyed. [11]On coming to the house, they saw the child with his mother Mary, and they bowed down and worshiped him. Then they opened their treasures and presented him with gifts of gold and of incense and of myrrh. [12]And having been warned in a dream not to go back to Herod, they returned to their country by another route.

[a]9 Or *seen when it rose*

Mary and Joseph have apparently taken up residence in Bethlehem, perhaps even in their own home. We are not told why they chose to stay in Bethlehem. But it would be much more comfortable than returning to Nazareth where they and their child would be scorned for the apparent fornication. Plus, Joseph is a carpenter; surely he could get as much business in Bethlehem as in Nazareth.

The Magi follow the star to the very house of Joseph and Mary. This obviously took place much later than the visit of the shepherds. After all, Herod wanted to kill the baby boys up to two years of age. (Our Christmas plays are somewhat condensed, apocryphal versions.) When they finally see the child, they are overjoyed. Bowing in worship, they present him with lavish offerings. These gifts represent the riches of their far-off country.[14] It is their way of paying homage to a king. And it is God's way of validating his Son. Although Jesus' birth is shrouded with suspicion in Nazareth, the heavens themselves declare his divinity. Furthermore, the Magi represent Jesus' first acceptance by Gentiles. This pictures things to come.

§ 15
**Jesus' Passage
Through Egypt**
(Mt 2:13-18)

[13]When they had gone, an angel of the Lord appeared to Joseph in a dream. "Get up," he said, "take the child and his mother and escape to Egypt. Stay there until I tell you, for Herod is going to search for the child to kill him."

[13]H. Heater, "Matthew 2:6 and its O.T. Sources," *JETS* 26 (Dec 1983): 395-397.

[14]The fact that there were three gifts does not necessarily imply that there were three wise men. Nonetheless, they have traditionally been ascribed the names Gaspar, Melchior, and Balthasar.

15where he stayed until the death of Herod. And so was fulfilled what the Lord had said through the prophet: "Out of Egypt I called my son."a

a15 Hosea 11:1

Herod died a most gruesome death in 4 B.C. (Josephus, *Ant.* 17. 146-192), with an ulcerated and putrefied body. He knew that the Jews hated him and couldn't wait for him to die. So just prior to his death he rounded up all the nobles of Judea and had them held in the Hippodrome. He commanded that upon his death they all be killed so that his own death would not be without mourning. Fortunately, when he died his sister ordered the release of the Jewish noblemen. Paradoxically, Herod received an honorable burial by the people of Jerusalem.

This historical background sets the stage for what happens here. Herod, on his deathbed, was insane, brutal, and paranoid. This Christ-Child posed a significant threat to his rule, at least in Herod's twisted mind. He had to eliminate the child. When the angel warned Joseph through a dream, he escaped under the cover of darkness and led his little family down to Egypt.

The border of Egypt was only seventy-five miles away, although tradition has them travel to Motorea, the sight of the Egyptian Jewish temple built in 150 B.C. At this time there were nearly a million Jews in Egypt. Many of its communities, especially Alexandria, were favorable to Jews. They could easily have found a community of Jews to take them in.

Matthew says that this event fulfilled Hosea 11:1, "Out of Egypt I called my son." The only problem is that Hosea 11:1 is *clearly* about the nation of Israel, not the Messiah. In fact, Hosea 11:2 says, "But the more I called Israel, the further they went from me. They sacrificed to the Baals and they burned incense to images." Did Matthew rip this verse out of context and apply it to Jesus inappropriately? No! Matthew is not treating Hosea 11:1 as predictive prophecy. He is NOT saying that Hosea is predicting the Messiah. Rather, he is saying that Jesus represents the nation of Israel and there were certain similarities between the two that are certainly more than coincidence. As Matthew compared the life of Jesus to the life of Israel he noticed that both of them were oppressed and both were called by God out of Egypt. In other words, Matthew is not looking forward from Hosea and seeing Jesus. He is starting with Jesus and looking back to parallel events in the life of Israel. Matthew never denies the literal, historic meaning of Hosea 11:1.[15]

---

[15]See the excellent explanation by T.L. Howard, "The Use of Hosea 11:1 in Matthew 2:15: An Alternative Solution," *BibSac* 143 (Oct 1986): 314-328.

Mt 2:16-18

¹⁶When Herod realized that he had been outwitted by the Magi, he was furious, and he gave orders to kill all the boys in Bethlehem and its vicinity who were two years old and under, in accordance with the time he had learned from the Magi. ¹⁷Then what was said through the prophet Jeremiah was fulfilled: ¹⁸"A voice is heard in Ramah, weeping and great mourning, Rachel weeping for her children and refusing to be comforted, because they are no more."

An angel warned Joseph in a dream to escape to Egypt. An angel also warned the Magi not to pass back through Jerusalem on their way back home. Herod was one of the most powerful men in the world at that time. And he was both insane and savage. When these magi never returned, Herod realized he had been outwitted. So he sends his soldiers to slay the little baby boys of Bethlehem and its surrounding area. It was a brutal and gruesome command these soldiers were called to carry out. But we probably should not think in terms of hundreds of children being massacred. In fact, considering the population of Bethlehem and its vicinity, Herod could have scarcely killed more than 20 children.

Josephus is silent about this whole incident. As strange as that may seem, this horrid deed was mild compared to some of the outrageous deeds of Herod, especially during his last days, in which he seemed to lose his sanity. For instance, he killed several of his own sons, fearing that they would take his kingdom. He even had his own wife, Mariamne, put to death. So many died at this man's hands that a few infants is only moderately noteworthy. Besides, Josephus tends to avoid information pertaining to Christianity unless it is critical to his storyline. He is writing to a Roman audience that is hardly interested in this new sect of the Jews. Accordingly, it's not so surprising that Josephus doesn't record this incident.

Again Matthew supports his text with prophecy. He sees the slaughter of the Bethlehem infants in Jeremiah 31:15, "A voice is heard in Ramah . . . Rachel weeping for her children." Ramah is a little village five miles to the north of Jerusalem. Rachel's children were Ephraim, Manasseh and Benjamin. These three tribes composed the geographic area of North Judah and Samaria.

Originally this referred to the Babylonian captivity (586 B.C.), after the destruction of Jerusalem. As the people of Judah were marched from Jerusalem, through Samaria and on into Babylon, there was weeping heard in Ramah, the first town they passed through. Symbolically then it refers to the weeping for the loss of children. Thus, it applies here. Bethlehem, in the same general vicinity, also experiences the loss of her children. Matthew is not saying that Jeremiah 31:15 prophesied this event in the life of Jesus but that it mirrored it.

Matthew is following common rabbinic rules of interpretation. Although these interpretations seem somewhat unnatural to us, they were common and acceptable among the Jews. Furthermore, one must not discount the influence of the Holy Spirit to guide Matthew in understanding OT prophecy. In addition, Jesus himself may have explained some of these passages to his disciples (cf. Lk 24:27). Finally, Jesus, as the antitype of Israel, indeed represents the deeper/fuller understanding of these texts.

**§ 16
Return to
Nazareth**
(Mt 2:19-23;
Lk 2:39)

Mt 2:19-23

Matthew describes Jesus' "sojourn" in Egypt. Luke, however, simply says that the holy family returned to Nazareth right after his presentation in the temple. It is not that he disagrees with Matthew, but that he merely compresses the narrative by leaving out this detail of Jesus' life.

¹⁹After Herod died, an angel of the Lord appeared in a dream to Joseph in Egypt ²⁰and said, "Get up, take the child and his mother and go to the land of Israel, for those who were trying to take the child's life are dead." ²¹So he got up, took the child and his mother and went to the land of Israel. ²²But when he heard that Archelaus was reigning in Judea in place of his father Herod, he was afraid to go there. Having been warned in a dream, he withdrew to the district of Galilee, ²³and he went and lived in a town called Nazareth. So was fulfilled what was said through the prophets: "He will be called a Nazarene."

Herod died in March-April of 4 B.C. Josephus describes the gruesome details of his death (*Ant.* 17. 168-192). It was a fitting end of a life so filled with violence. Herod's will stated that Archelaus was to rule in Galilee and Perea (Josephus, *Ant.* 17. 146). But on his deathbed, in his deranged state (and probably under the providence of God), Herod changes his will. He gave Archelaus control of Judea, and Herod Antipas was switched over to Galilee and Perea (Josephus, *Ant.* 17. 188-189). This was a very significant move. You see, Archelaus was a vicious and power-hungry man. Even while his father was alive he made several attempts to steal his throne. Right after he took office in Jerusalem he slaughtered 3,000 men in the temple who contested his leadership (Josephus, *Ant.* 17. 213-218). It would be dangerous for Joseph to lead his family back into Archelaus' territory. So God moved Archelaus out of Galilee, into Jerusalem. This "forced" Joseph to return to Nazareth, which Matthew sees as a fulfillment of the prophets.

Nazareth was a rustic place filled with people of the soil. They had frequent interaction with Gentiles from the commercial world. This little town is eighteen miles due west of the southern tip of the Sea of Galilee. It sits, unseen, in a basin surrounded by the fifteen hills of Galilee. From the crest around the perimeter one can see as far as thirty miles on a clear day.

There was much prejudice against the Galileans. Compared to Jerusalem, Nazareth is an insignificant place. Nathaniel expressed the customary disdain for Nazareth (Jn 1:46). They had a tendency to "swallow" their guttural vowels, thus their speech sounded hillbilly-ish. Galilee was also a hotbed of political activity, especially through the Zealots. This also contributed to the prejudice they felt from Jerusalem. In addition, because they were surrounded by Gentiles, their observance of the law, especially the oral law, was not as meticulous as the Jerusalem Jews. The point is, you would not expect the Jewish Messiah to come from such an insignificant and questionable place. In fact, the Jerusalem Jews said that no prophet came from Galilee (Jn 7:52). That simply was not true. Jonah and probably Nahum were born in Galilee and Elijah and Elisha both had considerable ministries there. Thus, the Messiah could potentially come from there.

Matthew takes all this a step further. He records this move to Nazareth as a fulfillment of prophecy: "He will be called a Nazarene." Try as you will, you cannot find those exact words in the OT. Therefore, we conclude that Matthew is not quoting prophecy but alluding to "the prophets." In fact, only here does Matthew use the plural "prophets" to introduce a "citation." The bottom line is this: Matthew is not giving a direct quote but referring to a common theme of the OT prophets.[16] He is probably using a play on the word "Nazareth" to refer to the Messiah. The word Nazareth comes from the Hebrew word meaning "branch" [*nezer*]. It is one of the metaphors for the Messiah (Isa 11:1). Another word meaning branch is *zemach*. It carries even stronger Messianic implications (Jer 23:5; 33:15; Zech 3:8; 6:12). Through this wordplay, Matthew suggests that the Branch of David (i.e., the Messiah), grew up in Nazareth ("The Branch"). Matthew is suggesting that although Nazareth is a surprising place for the Messiah to be raised, it is not unwarranted for the prophets to have forseen this event.

§ 17-19
Growth of
Jesus
(Lk 2:40-52)

Except for this account, we have nothing describing the youth of Jesus. There are a few apocryphal myths, most of which portray Jesus as abusing his miraculous power (e.g., *Mary, Protevangelion, Infancy*). These fit neither the purpose of the Gospel nor the character of our Lord.

---

[16]W.B. Tatum, "Matthew 2:23: Wordplay and Misleading Translations," *BT* 27/1 (Jan 1976): 135-138.

In this simple narrative we read of dignity and wisdom in the young life of Jesus. We also see clearly that by the time of his bar mitzvah he understood his divine heritage and messianic purpose.

Verse 49 is the key verse for this passage. We should keep an eye on the three themes revolving around that verse. First, Jesus is the Son of God (cf. Lk 1:32, 35; 3:22; 4:3, 9, 41; 8:28; 9:35; 10:22; 20:13; 22:70). Mary calls Joseph his father (v. 48). But Jesus reminds her that God is his true Father (v. 49). Second, Mary and Joseph are amazed and confused by Jesus' response (v. 50). Jesus will continue to amaze and confuse people (Lk 4:22, 32, 36; 5:26; 8:25, 56; 9:7, 43; 11:14; 24:22, 41). Third, Jesus is under divine directives. He says it was necessary (*dei*), that he be in his Father's house. Throughout his ministry, Jesus will be directed by divine compulsion (Lk 4:43; 9:22; 13:33; 17:25; 19:5; 22:37, 42; 24:7). At the same time, Jesus submitted to the parental authority of Joseph and Mary (v. 51).

Lk 2:40

⁴⁰And the child grew and became strong; he was filled with wisdom, and the grace of God was upon him.

The story of Jesus in the temple at age twelve does not stand alone. It is sandwiched between two statements about his physical, social, and spiritual growth (vv. 40 & 52). Through Luke alone we get a brief glimpse into Jesus' otherwise silent thirty years. This incident is well chosen. It comes at a critical time in Jesus' life.[17] He is making the transition from childhood to adulthood. There was never a time in Jesus' life where his identity was not clear. His parents were told at his birth. And he understood it as he entered his teenage years.

This event reflects many of the major themes of Luke's book. For example, the book both begins and ends in Jerusalem. It frequently includes major elements of this story: "passover," "three days," and "seeking" Jesus in the wrong place, which may point to Luke's larger context.[18] In other words, Jesus' adult years were consistent with his childhood years. The message is the same; the person is the same.

Lk 2:41-45

⁴¹Every year his parents went to Jerusalem for the Feast of the Passover. ⁴²When he was twelve years old, they went up to the Feast, according to the

---

[17]Nolland and Johnson both note that age 12 was an important age for heroes in Greco-Roman literature. It was common to describe some great exploit or impression they made at that age when they made the transition from childhood to adulthood. For examples, see Xenophon, *Cyropaedia* 1.2.8; Josephus, *Ant.* 5, 348; Philo, *Life of Moses*, 1:21. A more complete list is given by de Jong, "Sonship, Wisdom, Infancy: Luke 2:41-51a," *NTS* 24 (1977-78): 317-354.

[18]J.F. Jansen, "Luke 2:41-52," *Int* 30 (Oct 1976): 400-404.

custom. [43]After the Feast was over, while his parents were returning home, the boy Jesus stayed behind in Jerusalem, but they were unaware of it. [44]Thinking he was in their company, they traveled on for a day. Then they began looking for him among their relatives and friends. [45]When they did not find him, they went back to Jerusalem to look for him.

This feast was likely a yearly trek for the poor family. It was the height of the religious calendar. Every year they would take the time and money to celebrate this feast in Jerusalem. There were three feasts that each Jew was expected to celebrate in Jerusalem annually (Exod 34:22-23): Passover, Pentecost, and Tabernacles. For many this was practically impossible. Jesus' parents at least attended Passover.

On the way to Jerusalem, this line of worshipers sang the Psalms of ascent as they approached Jerusalem (Ps 120-134). As they arrive in Jerusalem the local citizens would invite them into their homes. The residents were generous, the pilgrim's needs were simple, and the provisions of the feast were abundant.

When Jesus was twelve years old, his family took their annual trip to the Passover. That was a special one for Jesus because he was passing into "adulthood." At age twelve a Jewish boy became a man. Today, it is celebrated with the bar mitzvah (meaning "son of the covenant"). We notice that Luke changes words now referring to Jesus. He had been calling him a *paidion*, v. 40. He now refers to him as *pais*, v. 43, which means "servant" or "child." At this age a Jewish boy is expected to keep the law, learn a trade and attend the great Jewish feasts. This would be Jesus' first appearance in the temple. In a crowd of up to 210,000, Jesus would see for the first time the sacrifices, washings, milling priests, animals and money changers. It was an awesome edifice, especially for a child from the little town in Galilee.

Verse 43 says that the family took off "after the feast was over." But Luke literally says, "When the days had been completed." The feast, in fact, might not have been over. It lasted a full seven days, but the people were only required to stay for the first three. They would have already eaten the Paschal supper, offered their offerings, and taken part in the major ceremonies of the feast. Edersheim (II:248-249) suggests that it was not yet over. He states that the teachers came out and taught in the courts during the feast but would not have been available afterward. Thus, Jesus would have had to meet them in the temple courts during the feast, apparently on the third through the fifth day. After the first three days of the feast, when the "good stuff" was already over, many folks would head back home. People from Galilee generally traveled in a large group of friends and family. It is not so surprising that a mature twelve year old would not need constant watch among a caravan of friends and family. At this intermediate age, it could be assumed that he would be with either the women or with the men and older boys. Both Mary and Joseph may have assumed Jesus to be with the other.

When the caravan stopped for the night, Mary and Joseph would look for their son (v. 44). This is a strong word. It indicates that they *kept looking all around*. Luke describes them searching for their boy intensely and continually.

Lk 2:46-50

⁴⁶After three days they found him in the temple courts, sitting among the teachers, listening to them and asking them questions. ⁴⁷Everyone who heard him was amazed at his understanding and his answers. ⁴⁸When his parents saw him, they were astonished. His mother said to him, "Son, why have you treated us like this? Your father and I have been anxiously searching for you."

⁴⁹"Why were you searching for me?" he asked. "Didn't you know I had to be in my Father's house?" ⁵⁰But they did not understand what he was saying to them.

It took them three days to find Jesus. The first day was their journey away from Jerusalem. The second day was on their way back. The third day they found Jesus in the temple. In the Jewish terms this would constitute, "after three days."

Talk about a precocious child. Jesus was not only asking mature questions and listening to the answers. He was giving answers to their questions. Of course, question/answer was a normal Jewish form of education. But still, Jesus was clearly a brilliant child. At this time Annas was the high priest, the very man who would try Jesus some twenty-one years later. We can't help but wonder if he also took part in this educational encounter with Christ. In addition, Hillel was supposedly born c. 112 B.C. and according to tradition, lived one hundred twenty years. This event probably took place in A.D. 8. Thus, there is a remote possibility that Hillel also was in the audience. Almost certainly his grandson, Gamaliel, would have been.

No doubt some of the questions revolved around the Passover and its true meaning as fulfilled in the Messiah. Perhaps they even discussed such passages as Isaiah 53, the lamb of God, or Psalm 22, the nature of the execution of the Messiah.

Can you think of a more human reaction than verse 48? What mother has not felt the same panic at a lost child? What mother has not then both embraced and scolded the child? We get a hint of that here with Mary. The word "anxiously" (v. 48) comes from a word often associated with acute pain. Joseph and Mary were hurting while they looked for Jesus. Thus Mary says, "We painfully searched . . . !"

Jesus said that they should have known that he was "in his Father's house." Other translations say, "About my Father's business." The word house is not actually used. The Greek phrase can be rendered either way. But since Mary was addressing Jesus' location, it seems reasonable that Jesus' reply would also.[19]

This is really an incredible account. Through Luke, we hear the first recorded words of Jesus and we get a glimpse of his first "messianic consciousness." Even at the age of twelve he knew who his real "Dad" was. He also knew what his primary obligations were.

We do not know if Joseph ever understood. He was brave and humble to even step into this role. Mary, however, learns step by step through the life and ministry of Jesus. Yet even she did not fully comprehend until after the resurrection. We can't be sure that anyone did.

Lk 2:51-52

⁵¹Then he went down to Nazareth with them and was obedient to them. But his mother treasured all these things in her heart. ⁵²And Jesus grew in wisdom and stature, and in favor with God and men.

After affirming Jesus' divinity, his humanity is highlighted. Jesus, in perfect humility, submitted to imperfect parents. His human nature is clearly seen in his obedience. Jesus understood God-ordained authority. We cannot obey God if we do not obey his properly ordained authority.

Again we see Mary storing up all these things in her heart (cf. Lk 2:19). She is an incredibly perceptive and reflective young lady.

We see normal and positive growth in the young man, Jesus (cf. 1 Sam 2:26 and Prov 3:4). This concludes the childhood narratives of Jesus. It is clear that he was outwardly a very normal Jewish boy, under pious parents. Yet both he and Mary understood that he was the Messiah. As he grew, they waited for the call of God to bring him from the obscurity of Nazareth to his national ministry.

---

[19]Also the preposition *en* generally refers to location.

PART FOUR
MINISTRY OF JOHN THE BAPTIST

§ 20
Setting the Stage
(Mk 1:1;
Lk 3:1-2)

[MK 1:]¹The beginning of the gospel about Jesus Christ, the Son of God.ᵃ

ᵃ1 Some manuscripts do not have *the Son of God*

Unlike the other Evangelists, Mark has no formal introduction. His opening line grabs our attention like a trumpet blast. Its effect on Mark's original readers might have been something like this: "Hey, there's good news in Jesus!"

Mark then quickly jumps right in the middle of the plot. He opens with a series of vignettes which immediately set the stage for Jesus' ministry: An OT quotation, the preaching of John, and the baptism and temptation of Jesus.

Lk 3:1-2

¹In the fifteenth year of the reign of Tiberius Caesar — when Pontius Pilate was governor of Judea, Herod tetrarch of Galilee, his brother Philip tetrarch of Iturea and Traconitis, and Lysanias tetrarch of Abilene — ²during the high priesthood of Annas and Caiaphas, the word of God came to John son of Zechariah in the desert.

Luke doesn't write "Once upon a time." He nails this narrative into history with specific leaders (vv. 1-2). And this time he really outdoes himself. He lists no less than seven rulers in this "chronological drumroll":

1. Tiberius Caesar — His predecessor, Augustus, died on August 19, A.D. 14. If Tiberius immediately took power, this would place this narrative between A.D. 28 and 29 according to the normal Roman method of reckoning.
2. Herod — Herod Antipas was the son of Herod the Great. He ruled Galilee and Perea from 4 B.C. to A.D. 39 (cf. Lk 3:19-20; 13:31; 23:7).
3. Philip — Like Herod Antipas, he was a son of Herod the Great. He ruled Iturea and Traconitis, northeast of Palestine from 4 B.C. to

A.D. 33/34. A Tetrarch was one who ruled over part of Palestine which was then divided into four parts.

4. Lysanias — no significant historical reference.
5. Pilate — This is Pontius Pilate who ruled as governor from A.D. 26-36.
6. Annas — "The official high priesthood of Annas had ended in A.D. 15, but his influence was so great, especially during the high priesthood of his son-in-law Caiaphas (A.D. 18-36) (cf. Jn 18:13), that his name is naturally mentioned along with that of Caiaphas" (Liefeld, p. 854). It appears that Annas, according to the Jewish law, was high priest for life (cf. Jn 11:49; 18:13; Acts 4:6).
7. Caiaphas — He was the officially designated high priest by the Roman government (A.D. 18-36). He was the fourth to be appointed after Annas. The government finally found a pawn they could manipulate, although the people would still look to Annas for leadership.

§ 21
The Ministry of John the Baptist
(Mt 3:1-6;
Mk 1:2-6;
Lk 3:3-6; cf.
John 1:19-23)

[MT 3:]1In those days John the Baptist came, preaching in the Desert of Judea.

[LK 3:]3He went into all the country around the Jordan, preaching a baptism of repentance for the forgiveness of sins,

[MT 3:]2saying, "Repent, for the kingdom of heaven is near."

With the coming of John, Messianic prophecies begin to fall into place like the tumblers of a lock, releasing the mystery of God — the Good News of Jesus Christ. It was John's job to introduce the Messiah. He did this through an itinerant ministry along the banks of the Jordan River near Bethany (Jn 1:28; 10:40). People from all over Palestine flooded to hear him.

His message was simple, yet profound: The kingdom of God is coming. In order to personally prepare for this coming kingdom, they must repent and be baptized. John's baptism is a precursor for Christian baptism. Both are baptisms "of repentance for the forgiveness of sins" (cf. Acts 2:38). The Scriptures teach that John's baptism, as well as Old Testament sacrifices, actually accomplished forgiveness of sins, even before the cross. Like us, they were "justified by faith" (cf. Rom 4:1-25; Gal 3:1ff). The only difference is that we look backward to the cross and they looked forward to it. But all are saved by faith, that is, by trusting God's promise.

Some have suggested that John's baptism was borrowed from Jewish proselyte baptism, Essenes' ritual cleansing or even Zoroastrian initiation rites. While there are some similarities, the differences are greater.

(1) These other groups baptized themselves rather than being baptized. (2) These other baptisms were for ritual cleansing (common in the OT, Lev 14:9; Num 19:19; 8:7). But John's baptism dealt with repentance. John dealt with the inner man, these others only dealt with the outer man. (3) John's baptism was not for initiates or neophytes, it was for the Jews who considered themselves already pure. And (4) John's baptism dealt with sin rather than conformity to religious ritual. Josephus misunderstands John's baptism, placing it on the level of contemporary baptisms:

> He was a good man and commanded the Jews to exercise virtue, both as justice toward one another and piety toward God, and so to come to baptism; for baptism would be acceptable to God, if they made use of it; not in order to expiate some sin, but for the purification of the body, provided that the soul was thoroughly purified beforehand by righteousness (*Ant.* 18. 117).

Indeed, the forms are the same, but the meaning is entirely different. John's baptism forms a bridge between Jewish cultus and Christian sacrament.

Lk 3:4-6 *with*
Mk 1:2-3

[LK 3:]4As is written in the book of the words of Isaiah the prophet:

[MK 1:]2"I will send my messenger ahead of you,
    who will prepare your way"a —
3a voice of one calling in the desert,
'Prepare the way for the Lord,
    make straight paths for him.'"b

[LK 3:]5Every valley shall be filled in,
    every mountain and hill made low.
The crooked roads shall become straight,
    the rough ways smooth.
6And all mankind will see God's salvation."c

a*[Mk 1:]2* Mal. 3:1   b*3* Isaiah 40:3   c*[Lk 3:]6* Isaiah 40:3-5

All three Synoptics quote from Isaiah 40:3. Luke also includes Isaiah 4-5 (omitting 5a). Mark prefaces Isaiah's words with a quote from Malachi 3:1 (and Exod 23:20), predicting the coming of Elijah. The Jewish people expected Elijah to return before the Messiah. After all, he never really died (2 Kgs 2:11). Malachi 4:5 predicts his return in preparation for the coming of the Messiah. Jesus applies these very passages to John (Mt 11:14).

This is figurative language that describes the preparation made for the coming of a king or some other dignitary. When it was known that a king was coming, "construction crews" would literally go out and prepare the road. They would clear the rocks, straighten the curves and fill in the potholes. John did this for Jesus through his preaching. He introduced many Messianic concepts as well as a baptism of repentance which would prepare the hearts and minds of the people to follow Jesus.

The Synoptics use the LXX for this quotation, which has a couple of minor changes from the Hebrew text. First, "Make *his* paths straight" in the Hebrew is literally, "Our God." Also in Matthew 3:3, the word "Lord" is a translation from the Hebrew of Jehovah. The bottom line is that both of these changes intimate that Jesus is Jehovah, God.

Mt 3:4-6

⁴John's clothes were made of camel's hair, and he had a leather belt around his waist. His food was locusts and wild honey. ⁵People went out to him from Jerusalem and all Judea and the whole region of the Jordan. ⁶Confessing their sins, they were baptized by him in the Jordan River.

Both Matthew and Mark paint a portrait of John. He is an odd-looking ascetic. He has a camel-hair coat, cinched up by a leather belt. And his diet of wild honey and locusts sounds less than acceptable. However, he is probably stranger in appearance to us than to people of his day. Other prophets had worn such garb (2 Kgs 1:8 [cf. Mal 4:5]; Zech 13:4). Locusts were clean food (Lev 11:22), and still commonly eaten by the poor in the Middle East and Orient. Often they would be seasoned with milk or wild honey. John's demeanor may be rustic and course, but not unheard of. In our culture we might refer to him as a mountain man.

§ 22
The Preaching
of John the
Baptist
(Mt 3:7-10;
Lk 3:7-14)

[LK3:]7John said to the crowds {many of the Pharisees and Sadducees^MT} coming out to be baptized by him, "You brood of vipers! Who warned you to flee from the coming wrath? ⁸Produce fruit in keeping with repentance. And do not begin to say to yourselves, 'We have Abraham as our father.' For I tell you that out of these stones God can raise up children for Abraham. ⁹The ax is already at the root of the trees, and every tree that does not produce good fruit will be cut down and thrown into the fire."

John's preaching is both practical and penetrating. Matthew (3:7) indicates that John was speaking specifically to the scribes and Pharisees who had come out to him. This makes his words all the more poignant. He goes so far as to call them a brood of vipers, a figure Jesus also used to refer to the Pharisees (Mt 23:33). John's boldness is characteristic of the OT prophets.

We know that the crowds came out to be baptized by John. But did the Pharisees and Sadducees also come out to be baptized by him? Matthew describes the Pharisees and Sadducees coming "on [*epi ton*] John's baptism." This might mean that they came "in order to be baptized." But elsewhere in Matthew *epi ton* never means "in order to." It can, however, mean "on account of" (cf. Mt 15:32; 22:34). Thus, the likely understanding is that the Pharisees came out to John *on account of* his baptism.

It may be something like this: They went out to interrogate John concerning his authority to baptize (Jn 1:24-25). Some of them may have been sincere, but most of the Pharisees and Sadducees only feigned sincerity for the sake of the crowds. John saw right through their thin veneer and called them down (Lk 3:7-9). So the Pharisees and Sadducees, or at least the greatest majority of them, refused to submit to John's baptism (Lk 7:30; Mt 21:23-27).

The Pharisees and Sadducees were right in coming out to be baptized by John, but their motives were clearly wrong. What they needed was repentance which produced appropriate fruit. The word "repentance" literally means "a change of mind." This, however, may mislead the English reader. The Greek concept of "mind" included the will as well as the thoughts. Thus, the mind controlled both the thoughts and the behavior of a person. Just as faith without works is dead, so repentance, without appropriate changes in behavior, is meaningless (cf. Acts 17:30-31; 26:20). This is not to say that you have to be sinless or you have not really repented. The issue is not the level of a person's holiness, but his direction. Are we moving toward the nature of God, or away from it?

These factions were convinced that their Jewish heritage assured them a position with God. John, though, warns them about trusting their heritage above true repentance. True enough, they were progenitors of Abraham. This did not necessarily make them "sons" of Abraham. In Jewish culture, the son was to represent the character of the father (cf. Mt 23:29-32). The thought of the Pharisees was that their lineage and position gave them favor with God. It is the old adage "It's not what you know but who you know." John corrected that misunderstanding before they could even get it out of their mouths. We are justified before God because of our relationship with him, not with our ancestors. True children of Abraham come not from the flesh but from faith in the promise of God (Rom 9:6-9; Gal 6:16).

Repentance is all the more urgent in light of the imminent judgment. John says that the ax is in place and ready for action. It will chop down any tree that does not produce appropriate fruit. Jesus later echoes John's warning (Lk 6:43-45; Jn 15:1-6). Furthermore, the verbs "cut down" and "thrown" are in the present tense, not future, indicating the immediacy of the action. Not only will there be individual future judgment but it appears that there is a present judgment on the whole Jewish system.

Lk 3:10-14

¹⁰"What should we do then?" the crowd asked.

¹¹John answered, "The man with two tunics should share with him who has none, and the one who has food should do the same."

¹²Tax collectors also came to be baptized. "Teacher," they asked, "what should we do?"

¹³"Don't collect any more than you are required to," he told them.

¹⁴Then some soldiers asked him, "And what should we do?"

He replied, "Don't extort money and don't accuse people falsely — be content with your pay."

What then should we do to repent? Three groups come to John asking this same question (Lk 3:10-14): The Jewish crowd, the tax collectors, and the soldiers. This sounds similar to Acts 2:36-37.

First John responds to the question of the crowd. The tunic was the "undergarment" worn inside the cloak, or outer garment. Everyone really needed one, but you could get along all right without an extra. Therefore, if we have more than we need, we should share with a person who has less than (s)he needs. John is not suggesting a communal life such as was found in Qumran; he is simply talking about basic benevolence. Food and clothes are necessities. How can we be lovers of God if we sit idly by as our fellowman lacks the basic needs of life? (cf. 2 Cor 8:13-15; James 2:15-17; 1 John 3:17).

Next John talks to the tax collectors. Along with harlots and murderers, these people were the most despised in Israel. They were considered apostates. Even the "Greeks regarded the word 'publican' as synonymous with 'plunderer'" (McGarvey, p. 76). Under the Roman system of taxation, a particular province was sold to the highest bidder. These were the chief tax collectors, like Zacchaeus (Lk 19:2). They promised the emperor that they would collect so much tax from a certain area. Then, they hired their underlings to actually collect the taxes from individuals. The chief tax collectors made their living by collecting more than they had to send to Rome. The more they collected the more they gained. The excess was all profit. Likewise, the underlings made their living by collecting more than the chief tax collector asked. Thus, the more abusive you were, the richer you got. In addition, their work often rendered them ceremonially unclean. They were not only hated, they were excluded from Jewish society.

The crowds must have been mildly disappointed that John did not suggest any social reform or even a rebellion. Repentance merely demands justice. Even the tax collectors deserve to make a living, but not exorbitantly.

Finally, the *soldiers* [lit. "those serving as subordinates"] are told not to rob people. It is possible that these are temple guards, which were

Jewish. But from John's advice, it seems more likely that they were the hated Roman soldiers. Because of their position, Roman soldiers could, and did, extort money by threatening people. John's final phrase is telling: "Be satisfied with your wages." The wage of a Roman soldier was about two hundred and twenty-five denarii per year. A denarius was day's wage for a common laborer. Also, the soldier's food, clothing and arms were deducted form their salary. Even though they received Roman citizenship upon their retirement, their paycheck was pretty slim. It is understandable they would be unsatisfied with their wages. But, as John says, that is no excuse to rob someone else.

§ 23
Baptism of
Spirit and Fire
(Mt 3:11-12;
Mk 1:7-8;
Lk 3:15-18)

The contrast and comparison between Jesus and John continues. When the people look to John as the Messiah, he appropriately points to another. He was merely the forerunner. And as wonderful as his baptism was, the Messiah's would be much more powerful.

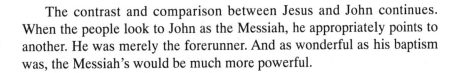

[LK 3:]15The people were waiting expectantly and were all wondering in their hearts if John might possibly be the Christ.a 16John answered them all, "I baptize you withb water {for repentanceMT}. But {after meMT,MK} one more powerful than I will come, the thongs of whose sandals I am not worthy to {stoop down andMK} untie {carryMT}. He will baptize you with the Holy Spirit and with fire. 17His winnowing fork is in his hand to clear his threshing floor and to gather the wheat into his barn, but he will burn up the chaff with unquenchable fire." 18And with many other words John exhorted the people and preached the good news to them.

a15 Or *Messiah*   b16 Or *in*

The people were not just wondering if John was the Messiah; they were wishing he was.[1] The expectation of the Messiah had reached an all-time high. Considering the Roman occupation, they were hoping for a militaristic Messiah (Ps 2; Isa 9:6-7) who would be king (Ps 110). John's popularity had the potential of causing such an uprising. Considering the four hundred years of prophetic silence, they were expecting a Messiah who would be a prophet (Deut 18:15, 18). John certainly fit the bill. Considering the poor social conditions and the wealth of the Herods, they were hoping for a Messiah who would bring financial prosperity (Amos 9:13-15). John's ascetic lifestyle didn't seem to fit this, but hey, two out of three ain't bad.

John wasn't the Christ. In fact, he didn't even feel worthy to untie his shoe. In other words, John didn't feel fit to serve Jesus in the most menial task of a slave. John knew he wasn't the Messiah and his baptism

---

[1]The *optative* verb tense Luke uses in 3:15 indicates a wish or a desire.

proved it. He could only baptize with water. The Messiah's baptism would be with the Holy Spirit and fire. While this may represent a single baptism of purification (Guelich, pp. 27-28), it seems more likely that these are actually two separate baptisms. First, we have the baptism of the Holy Spirit. It was identified twice in the NT, on the day of Pentecost (Acts 1:5; 2:1-4) and in the house of Cornelius (Acts 11:15-17). Both times it was at the birth of a new church (Jewish and Gentile). Both times it proved that God had accepted these people. And both times it was accompanied by the gift of tongues.

Is the baptism of the Holy Spirit the same as Christian immersion in water? Granted, Paul uses the same kind of language to describe Christian baptism (1 Cor 12:13; Eph 4:5). John the Baptist seemed to indicate that Jesus would baptize all of them in the Holy Spirit (Mt 3:11; Mk 1:8; Lk 3:16; Jn 1:33). Nevertheless, there are some significant differences between the baptism of the Holy Spirit and Christian baptism. (1) The two times baptism of the Holy Spirit is identified (Acts 2, 10), it was not for repentance but for evidence. (2) It was identified by the gift of tongues, which is never connected with Christian Baptism.[2] And (3) there was no water immersion involved in either case of the Baptism of the Holy Spirit. Our conclusion then, is that the *indwelling* of the Holy Spirit is clearly promised through Christian Baptism (Acts 2:38; 19:1-6; cf. Jn 3:5; 7:38-39; Titus 3:5). This Holy Spirit baptism was a unique evidence of God's acceptance of two new churches (Acts 2; 10). It may be possible that "Holy Spirit baptism" can refer to both the supernatural experience of Acts 2 & 10 as well as water immersion, but the two are clearly different.

The second baptism of Jesus was with fire. Because the Holy Spirit descended on the Apostles in Acts 2:3 in a form that looked like tongues of fire, some have interpreted the baptism of fire and the Spirit as a single event. They are not. The baptism of the Holy Spirit is a good thing. The baptism of fire is a bad thing. Essentially, it is judgment. The context describes it as a farmer winnowing wheat and then burning off the worthless chaff. That is not an event that Christians look forward to.

Luke reminds us (v. 18) that we have here only a synopsis of John's preaching. But the crux of his message is repentance in light of the coming kingdom, and the greatness of the coming Christ.

---

[2]In Acts 19:1-7, the speaking in tongues was not connected with baptism but with the laying on of the Apostle Paul's hands.

PART FIVE
TRANSITION FROM JOHN TO JESUS

§ 24
Jesus' Baptism
(Mt 3:13-17;
Mk 1:9-11;
Lk 3:21-23a)

Jesus' baptism has two functions. First, it announces the inauguration of Jesus' public ministry. The Spirit descends and John steps into the background. Jesus is now center-stage. Second, his baptism identifies Jesus. In fact, Luke connects Jesus' baptism with his genealogy. In relation to John, he is far superior. In relation to the crowd, he is Christ. (Three separate signs from heaven will validate Jesus as Messiah.) In relation to God, he is both the beloved Son and the suffering servant, an unexpected paradox for Jesus' contemporaries.

Mt 3:13-15

[13]Then Jesus came from {Nazareth in[MK]} Galilee to the Jordan to be baptized by John. [14]But John tried to deter him, saying, "I need to be baptized by you, and do you come to me?"
[15]Jesus replied, "Let it be so now; it is proper for us to do this to fulfill all righteousness." Then John consented.

Jesus was not baptized because he heard John's preaching. He traveled all the way from Nazareth to Bethany in order to be baptized by John (Mt 3:13). Why was Jesus baptized? Certainly he had no sin that needed remission. Jesus himself gives the reason: Matthew 3:15, "It is proper for us to do this to fulfill all righteousness." It might be an insignificant observation, but we notice that Jesus said "it is proper for *us* to do this." John also participated in fulfilling all righteousness. So the question becomes, "How did Jesus (and John) fulfill all righteousness by being baptized?" First, John's baptism was God-ordained through his prophet (Jn 1:33). Thus Jesus demonstrates submission to God's authority. Second, this was the divinely appointed method by which Jesus would be revealed as the Son of God (Jn 1:31-34). Third, this was Jesus' inauguration into ministry through which he fulfilled the law. Fourth, Jesus gives us an example to follow. And fifth, it appears that Jesus is acting as the personification of all Israel. Through his baptism, a new community of God's people is created.[1]

---

[1]C.G. Dennison, "How is Jesus the Son of God?: Luke's Baptism Narrative and Christology," *CTJ* 17 (Apr 1982): 6-25.

Lk 3:21-23 *with*
Mk 1:10, Mt 3:16

²¹When all the people were being baptized, Jesus was baptized too. And as {Jesus was coming up out of the water,ᴹᴷ} he was praying. {At that momentᴹᵀ} heaven was {tornᴹᴷ} opened ²²and the Holy Spirit descended on him in bodily form like a dove. And a voice came from heaven: "You are my Son, whom I love; with you I am well pleased."

²³Now Jesus himself was about thirty years old when he began his ministry.

Jesus' prayers were powerful. In Luke especially, they preceded significant events. For instance, he prayed all night before naming the Twelve apostles (Lk 6:12). Prayer introduced his first self-revelation (Lk 9:18). It was while Jesus was praying on the mountain that his transfiguration took place (Lk 9:29). And before his arrest and crucifixion we find him prostrate in Gethsemane (Lk 22:41-44). This was the source of power for Jesus. We're not too terribly surprised then, that right after Jesus prays (Lk 3:21), the heavens were ripped open (Mk). This was the first sign.

This symbolized a vision of Deity (Ezek 1:1; Acts 7:56; 10:11). Mark uses a vivid word [*schizomenous*, 1:10], meaning the sky was "torn asunder." From this "rift" the Holy Spirit came down from heaven just as Jesus was coming up from the water. All four Gospel writers describe the Holy Spirit as a dove. The theological implications of the second sign are somewhat vague. It may simply be that the movement of the Spirit resembled that of a dove. He is also compared to fire (Acts 2:3) and "hovering" (Gen 1:2). Likely more is implied. The dove is a symbol of purity, gentleness and peace. But Luke clarifies that it was more than a symbol, but, in fact, a "bodily form."

John saw this "manifestation" of the Holy Spirit and the crowds probably did as well. This would afford great evidence that Jesus was the one John had promised. This would help the crowds make the transition from John to Jesus (cf. Jn 1:32-34).

The third sign was the voice that came from heaven. God validated Jesus three times with a voice from heaven (Lk 3:22; 9:35; Jn 12:28). The Evangelists suggest that our confession of Jesus must be nothing less than God's. The three parts of God's declaration of Jesus, find their background in the OT. "You are my son² . . . with you I am well pleased" is based on Psalm 2:7 and Isaiah 42:1. God's deep love for his Son may be an allusion to Genesis 22.³ Nothing here is new. But all is rich and

---

²"Adoptionism" is the idea that Jesus *became* the Son of God at baptism. But none of the Synoptics support that. All three of them declare Jesus *was* the Son of God already. In addition, the birth narratives of Matthew and Luke speak clearly that Jesus was God's Son at conception. And both John and Paul would add that Jesus was God before he ever became a man.

³W. Stegner, "The Baptism of Jesus: A Story Modeled on the Binding of Isaac," *BR* 1

deeply rooted in the Old Testament prophecy of the Messiah. Further-more, all three of these signs at Jesus' baptism (the heavens opened, the voice of God and the Spirit descending), were Jewish expectations of the inauguration of the Messiah.[4] In the *Testaments of the Twelve Patriarchs*, in reference to the Messiah, *T. Levi* (18:6-8) says,

> The heavens will be opened, and from the temple of glory sanctification will come upon him with a fatherly voice, as from Abraham to Isaac.
> And the glory of the Most High shall burst forth upon him.
> And the spirit of understanding and sanctification shall rest upon him [in the water.]
> For he shall give the majesty of the Lord to those who are his sons in truth forever.

Again, *T. Jud.* (24:3) says, "And the heavens will be opened upon him to pour out the spirit as a blessing of the Holy Father. And he will pour the spirit of grace on you." The first century Jews would therefore interpret all three of these signs as evidence of the Messiah. Thus, Jesus' public ministry is inaugurated and the entire Trinity is involved: The transcendent Father, the incarnate Son, and the descending Spirit. Typical of Luke, he puts a chronological "P.S." on the text, noting that Jesus was about thirty years old.

**§ 25
Jesus'
Temptation**
(Mt 4:1-11;
Mk 1:12-13;
Lk 4:1-13)

The account of Jesus' baptism teaches us that Jesus is the Christ. Therefore, the question is no longer whether Jesus is the Messiah, but "What kind of Messiah is he?" Jesus' contemporaries hoped he would be a political hero. That is not the kind of Messiah we find here. Jesus is the personification of Israel, reliving their wilderness experience (cf. Deut 6-8). Israel's lasted forty years, Jesus' lasted forty days. Jesus is the second Adam,[5] who resisted the temptation of acting like God even though he had every right to do so (Phil 2:6-7). And Jesus is the new Moses, the liberator of God's people (Deut 34:1-8; cf. Deut 18:15, 18).

The battle is on. As Jesus steps into his role as Messiah, Satan

---

(Fall 1985): 36-46. He suggests that the later Jewish targums of Genesis 22 serve as background material for Jesus' baptism. If true, this would connect Jesus' baptism with the cross; cf. Mark 10:38; 15:37-38.

[4]J.R. Edwards, "The Baptism of Jesus According to the Gospel of Mark," *JETS* 34/1 (Mar 1991): 43-57.

[5]As early as Justin Martyr (*Dialogue with Trypho* 103), the temptation of Christ has been connected with Adam in the garden. Rom 5:12-21 and 1 Cor 15:45-49 continue this comparison as do the apocalyptic portraits of Adam.

assumes his role as adversary.[6] Jesus goes from the baptistry to the "frying pan." With each temptation Satan offered Jesus an easier route to his Messianic ministry. But each of these shortcuts would also "short-circuit" God's plan. To our delight, Jesus rejected them all. Furthermore, Jesus was tempted "in all ways like we are." Therefore, he understands our struggles. He offers us a model for overcoming temptations through the Word of God.

Mt 4:1-4 *with*
Mk 1:12-13,
Lk 4:1-2

¹Then Jesus {full of the Holy Spirit,[LK]} was led {at once[MK]} by the Spirit into the desert to be tempted by the devil. ²After fasting forty days and forty nights, he was hungry. {He was with the wild animals.[MK]} ³The tempter {Satan,[MK]} {the devil,[LK]} came to him and said, "If you are the Son of God, tell these stones to become bread."

⁴Jesus answered, "It is written: 'Man does not live on bread alone, but on every word that comes from the mouth of God.'"[a]

ᵃ4 Deut 8:3

Jesus, full of the Holy Spirit (Lk 4:1), was led into the desert. Mark's language is more picturesque. Literally, he says Jesus was "thrown out" or "thrust" into the desert. Here Jesus has a face-off with Satan. Luke uses the Greek word "devil" (*diabolos*, meaning "the slanderer," or "one who falsely accuses"). Matthew uses both the Greek word "devil" as well as its Hebrew counterpart, "Satan" (*satanos*, "adversary"). Satan is a powerful angel (2 Cor 11:14; 2 Thess 2:9; Jude 6; Rev 13:13-14) who apparently was ousted from heaven because of his great pride (Job 1-2; Isa 14:12; Lk 10:18; 1 Tim 3:6). He rules the dark forces of this world (2 Pet 2:4; Jude 6; cf. 2 Cor 4:4) and seeks to destroy God's church (1 Pet 5:8; Rev 12:13-17). Yet he is still under God's control (Job 1:12; 2:6; Mt 12:29).

This is not a fair fight. Jesus is weakened by forty days of total fasting. Even so, Satan is still at a severe disadvantage. Some have questioned whether Jesus could have actually fasted for forty days. But he was not the first to do it (cf. Moses, Exod 34:28; and Elijah, 1 Kgs 19:4-8); nor has he been the last. A number of modern fasts lasting at least forty days have put to rest undue doubt. Mark adds an interesting tidbit: "And he was with the wild animals." In other words, Jesus was all alone and very hungry. Physically he was empty, but spiritually he was full. Too often our experience is the reverse.

---

[6]P. Pokorny, "The Temptation Stories and their Intention," *NTS* 20 (1973-1974): 115-127. He observes that in the history of religions, initiation and temptation often go hand in hand. Many Christians have had similar experiences. Right after a "mountaintop" experience, we often face our most severe trials.

Several observations should be made about these three temptations before each is examined separately. First, each of these three temptations starts with an "if." The first two use the conditional clause: "If you are the Son of God." There is a conspicuous lack of an article. Thus it could be rendered, "If you are A son of God." Furthermore, it is an ambiguous statement. It could be real or alleged. Satan is taunting Jesus. In essence he says, "Prove yourself."

Second, the three temptations parallel what is written in 1 John 2:15-17:

> Do not love the world or anything in the world. If anyone loves the world, the love of the Father is not in him. For everything in the world — the cravings of sinful man, the lust of his eyes and the boasting of what he has and does — comes not from the Father but from the world. The world and its desires pass away, but the man who does the will of God lives forever.

This also describes the three ways in which Eve was tempted in Genesis 3:6: "When the woman saw that the fruit of the tree was good for food and pleasing to the eye, and also desirable for gaining wisdom, she took some and ate it. She also gave some to her husband, who was with her, and he ate it." This leads us to believe that there are only three ways in which Satan can tempt you: through lust of the eyes, lust of the flesh and the boastful pride of life.

Third, although Satan is the tempter, if we sin, we are accountable. James 1:14 says, "But each one is tempted when, by his own evil desire, he is dragged away and enticed." It is no good saying, "The devil made me do it." Furthermore, some may say, "O sure, Jesus did not sin because he was the Son of God." We must keep in mind, however, that the second Adam was as capable of sinning as the first Adam was of being sinless.

Fourth, it is noteworthy that Jesus resists each of these temptations by quoting Scripture. We should do no less. (All of these Scripture quotations are quite literal to both the Hebrew and LXX except for Jesus' last quote from Deuteronomy 6:13 which is somewhat of an interpretive paraphrase.) If we are dogged by a besetting sin, the answer lies in memorizing the Word of God and submitting to the Holy Spirit's leading in our lives, rather than in mustering enough self-control to conquer it. We are dangerously foolish if we imagine that we can go nose to nose with Satan. This text shows that he is clever, articulate, and Biblically literate.

Finally, Matthew and Luke give the second and third temptation in opposite order. The reason for this is that both arrange their narratives to end in a climax. Luke's version climaxes with Satan taking Jesus to the temple (the focal point of Luke) and (mis)quoting Scripture. Matthew's, however, climaxes with (a) the heinously blasphemous request for Jesus to bow down and worship Satan, and (b) Jesus' command that Satan "begone" (v. 10).

TEMPTATION #1: Lust of the Flesh

Jesus is called to feed himself through miraculous means. On first sight, this does not seem to be sinful. The general populace would have loved it. After all, they expected the Messiah to perform just such wonders for the prosperity of his people (cf. 2 Baruch 29:3-8). But it would have been a misuse of his divine power. If Jesus starts using his power for selfish ends at the beginning of his ministry, there is no way that he could have completed his march through Gethsemane. Furthermore, it would take him out of the realm of human existence. It could no longer be said that he suffered like we do (Heb 4:15-16), in that he used a miraculous means of escape and we can't.

In Deuteronomy 8:3, Moses is reminding Israel to humble themselves and rely on God and not in themselves. He reminds them of God's provision of manna in the desert. Thus, Jesus' temptation is compared with the Israelites in the wilderness. There are several parallels at this level: forty days compared with forty years; being led by the Spirit; and testing in the desert.

Mt 4:5-7 *with*
Lk 4:9-10

⁵Then the devil took him to the holy city {Jerusalem^LK} and had him stand on the highest point of the temple. ⁶"If you are the Son of God," he said, "throw yourself down. For it is written:
"'He will command his angels concerning you, {to guard you carefully;^LK}
    and they will lift you up in their hands,
    so that you will not strike your foot against a stone.'ᵃ"
⁷Jesus answered him, "It is also written: 'Do not put the Lord your God to the test.'ᵇ"

ᵃ6 Psalm 91:11,12   ᵇ7 Deut. 6:16

TEMPTATION #2: Boastful Pride of Life

We are not certain where the highest point of the temple was. There are three possibilities: (1) Apex of the sanctuary, (2) top of Solomon's porch, (3) top of the royal portico (see Josephus, *Ant.* 15. 412-413). It was Jewish tradition that the Messiah would miraculously and spectacularly appear on top of the temple. Thus, Jesus would have been immediately hailed as the popular Messiah. It would have saved a lot of time and a lot of "messy" ministry. The problem is that he would have been completely misunderstood and God's plans would have been thwarted.

Satan now gets into the Scripture quoting act, and he does it with his usual deceit. He quotes Psalm 91:11, but leaves out the last phrase: "In all your ways." This could have been intentionally omitted. All God's ways certainly would not include self-seeking pride. To this extent, however, Satan is correct — God sends help and protection through "guardian" angels (cf. Job 1:10; 2 Kgs 6:8-17; Ps 34:7; Jude 9).

Lk 4:5-8,13 *with*
Mt 4:10-11,
Mk 1:13b

⁵The devil led him up to a high place and showed him in an instant all the kingdoms of the world. ⁶And he said to him, "I will give you all their authority and splendor, for it has been given to me, and I can give it to anyone I want to. ⁷So if you worship me, it will all be yours."

⁸Jesus answered, "{Away from me, Satan!ᴹᵀ} It is written: 'Worship the Lord your God and serve him only.'ᵃ"

¹³When the devil had finished all this tempting, he left him until an opportune time {and angels came and attended himᴹᵀ·ᴹᴷ}.

ᵃ8 Deut. 6:13

TEMPTATION #3: Lust of the Eyes

Satan took him to a very high hill (Mt) and showed him in an instant (Lk) all the kingdoms of the world. This would seem to indicate a miraculous vision. However, if Shepherd (p. 73) is right, Jesus would have been able to see an impressive panoramic view of Palestine from the top of Mt. Quarantiania, and the roads leading to all the major kingdoms of the then known world — Rome, Greece, Egypt, Persia and Assyria.

Satan claims to have dominion over the earth. Essentially, but temporarily, this is true. It must be kept in mind, however, that Satan's control is limited. He is on a leash. Anything beyond that leash is out of his domain (cf. Jn 12:31; 14:30; 16:11; 2 Cor 4:4; Eph 2:2; 1 John 4:4; 5:19). Concerning this, McGarvey says,

> It was true that Satan and his emissaries had, by usurpation, gained an apparent possession of the world, but Jesus had right to it as the heir of God (Mt 21:33-43). Being stronger than Satan, he had come to regain his kingdom, not by treaty, but by conquest (Lk 11:19-22). Moreover, he would obtain it as a spiritual and not as a carnal kingdom (p. 98).

Satan's request for worship is absolutely outrageous! However, he is subtle in his request. This verb is an aorist subjunctive which indicates a single action. Satan is not asking Jesus to continually give him allegiance . . . just this once.

At the end of his temptations, Jesus commands Satan to leave. And, of course, he must obey the master. Luke records that he left him until an opportune time. Quoting Scripture will send Satan running (cf. James 4:7). He will be back, as he was with Jesus, the first chance he gets. But the Word of God is the key to conquering the tempter.

At this point Mark jumps back in the narrative alongside Matthew and tells us that angels came and ministered to Jesus. The next time we read something like this will be in the garden of Gethsemane, another watershed moment of Jesus' life (Lk 22:43).

**§ 26
Questions about John's Identity**
(Jn 1:19-28)

[19]Now this was John's testimony when the Jews of Jerusalem sent priests and Levites to ask him who he was. [20]He did not fail to confess, but confessed freely, "I am not the Christ."[a]

[21]They asked him, "Then who are you? Are you Elijah?"

He said, "I am not."

"Are you the Prophet?"

He answered, "No."

[22]Finally they said, "Who are you? Give us an answer to take back to those who sent us. What do you say about yourself?"

[23]John replied in the words of Isaiah the prophet, "I am the voice of one calling in the desert, 'Make straight the way for the Lord.'[b]"

[a]20 Or *Messiah*. "The Christ" (Greek) and "the Messiah" (Hebrew) both mean "the Anointed one"; also in verse 25   [b]23 Isaiah 40:3

John created quite a stir. At least three distinct groups come out to meet John: The populace (Lk 3:15), the Sadducees (Jn 1:19-23) and the Pharisees (Jn 1:24-27). Each comes out with a question: "Are you the Messiah?" When John says, "No!" they ask a second question: "Then who are you and why do you act the way you do?"

In John 1:19-23 a second group comes with their questions, the priests and their compatriots, the Levites. For the most part they aligned with the political views of the Sadducees. They did not even believe in a literal Messiah! They come neither to learn from John nor to repent of their sins. They are protecting their territory as the religious leaders of Israel. When their services were empty, they began to ask where everyone was. They come out to see for themselves who this "self-proclaimed prophet" might be.

John freely admitted that he was not the Christ. "Christ" is the Greek translation of the Hebrew, "Messiah," meaning "the anointed one." In the OT three positions were anointed, all of which the Messiah was to fulfill: the Prophet (Deut 18:15,18), the Priest (Ps 110:4) and the King (Ps 2; Isa 2:1-4; 9:6-7).

"Are you Elijah?" they asked. John said, "No." Why would they think that John was Elijah? Popular Jewish theology expected Elijah to return. After all, he had not died. And Malachi predicted his return (Mal

3:1; 4:5). Now, there was some confusion about the role Elijah was to play when he returned. Would he be (a) the Messiah, (b) the forerunner of the Messiah (Mal 3:1), or (c) a harbinger of judgment (Mal 4:5)?

Jesus said that John was, in fact, the "Elijah who was to come" (Mt 11:14), and he quoted Malachi 3:1 as evidence (Mt 11:10). John, however, denies that he is Elijah. How can we reconcile this difference? (1) Perhaps John did not fully understand his role. This, however, is unlikely considering that he is about to quote Isaiah 40:3 as a description of his own identity. (2) Perhaps there is a difference between Malachi 3:1 and 4:5. If the Sadducees were asking whether he fulfilled Malachi 4:5 and if that text refers to a witness yet to come (e.g., Rev 11:3, as some have proposed), then John correctly answered that he was not that person. (3) Most likely, the popular misconception was that Elijah was, indeed, the Messiah to come. The Sadducees' three questions do not seem to make a distinction between the Messiah, Elijah, and THE prophet (cf. Deut 18:15, 18). Thus, John correctly answers that he is not the person they think Elijah is.

Since they were obviously off track, they finally say, "Well then you tell us who you are" (Jn 1:22). John phrased his response with the words of Isaiah the Prophet, "I am the voice of one calling in the desert, 'Make straight the way for the Lord'" (Isa 40:3).

Jn 1:24-28

²⁴Now some Pharisees who had been sent ²⁵questioned him, "Why then do you baptize if you are not the Christ, nor Elijah, nor the Prophet?"

²⁶"I baptize with[a] water," John replied, "but among you stands one you do not know. ²⁷He is the one who comes after me, the thongs of whose sandals I am not worthy to untie."

²⁸This all happened at Bethany on the other side of the Jordan, where John was baptizing.

[a]26 Or in; also in verses 31 and 33

The third group, the Pharisees, now come to question John's identity (Jn 1:24-27). They have been listening to him deny that he is the Messiah. And yet his activity asserts a certain level of authority. They ask, "All right, if you are not the Messiah, or Elijah, or the Prophet, then why do you baptize?"

John's answer to this third question is quite similar to his answer to the Sadducees' question: "I am preparatory to the Messiah; my baptism is preparatory to his baptism." He then reiterates that Jesus is, by far, his superior. John's audience had heard these words earlier, before Jesus was baptized. [See comments on sec. 23; Mt 3:11; Mk 1:7; Lk 3:16]. But earlier John said, "He is coming." Now he says, "He is right among you!"

§ 27
John Identifies Jesus
(Jn 1:29-34)

²⁹The next day John saw Jesus coming toward him and said, "Look, the Lamb of God, who takes away the sin of the world! ³⁰This is the one I meant when I said, 'A man who comes after me has surpassed me because he was before me.' ³¹I myself did not know him, but the reason I came baptizing with water was that he might be revealed to Israel."

The day after John was questioned about his identity and pointed to someone greater (Jn 1:19-27), he saw Jesus walking toward him. He cried out, "Behold, the Lamb of God, who takes away the sin of the world." How could he have identified Jesus so quickly? Well, this is not the first time that these two have met. Forty days earlier John baptized Jesus (cf. v. 32). They are not strangers. There was a deep affinity between their families when they were infants. This relationship has likely been kept up through the years. The least we could say is that the stories about their infancies have been passed along through the families.

This identification of the "Lamb of God" is rich with symbolic meaning. The first use of the word "lamb" in the Bible is Genesis 22:7-8 when Isaac asks Abraham where the lamb is for sacrifice and he responds prophetically, "God will provide." The next major use is in Exodus (12:3-4ff.), where the Passover Lamb is a substitute sacrifice for the firstborn. And of course, all through Leviticus and Numbers (thirty-four times), it is used to refer to the Sin offering, a year old lamb without blemish. Isaiah uses the symbol of a Lamb to refer to God's suffering servant (53:7), and so he is called in 1 Corinthians 5:7, the Passover Lamb. Two things are striking about this Lamb. First, Jesus fits this type/antitype of the Bible. He suffered in our place as the sin offering. He provided the release of the firstborn as the Passover lamb. He is the fulfillment of Isaiah 53:7 and Genesis 22:8, the Lamb provided by God himself as our substitution. It is staggering that from the outset of Jesus' ministry his purpose is identified so clearly. How could any in John's audience miss the meaning of the Lamb of God? More striking still is the twenty-six uses of the word "lamb" in Revelation. This silent, slain sacrifice becomes the victorious, supreme sovereign.

Jn 1:32-34

³²Then John gave this testimony: "I saw the Spirit come down from heaven as a dove and remain on him. ³³I would not have known him, except that the one who sent me to baptize with water told me, 'The man on whom you see the Spirit come down and remain is he who will baptize with the Holy Spirit.' ³⁴I have seen and I testify that this is the Son of God."

John could not have missed Jesus. The Holy Spirit, in the form of a dove, was God's divinely ordained identification of the Messiah. John has now been meditating on that for forty days.

§ 28
Jesus' First
Disciples
(Jn 1:35-51)

This is the third of four consecutive days described here in the first chapter of John (cf. vv. 29, 35, 43). Edersheim (I:345) says that the normal Jewish custom was for widows to be married on Thursday and for young women to be married on Wednesday. In John 2:1-11 we will be at a wedding. Its festivities make it appear to be a Wednesday wedding of a maiden. If this is true, we can work backwards and come up with the following chronology: (1) Thursday, the interview with John and members from the Sanhedrin, vv. 19-28. (2) Friday, Jesus returns from the wilderness, vv. 29-34. (3) Saturday, for the second day in a row, John lays his eyes on Jesus and identifies him as the Lamb of God (vv. 35-42). John apparently only has two disciples with him. Perhaps the rest have taken the Sabbath off. Nevertheless, these two are the first to follow Jesus. And according to our Gospel records, this is the last time that John sees Jesus, as he marches off with two of John's finer students. (4) Sunday, Jesus meets Nathanael, via Philip, and his small entourage of disciples (Andrew, John, Peter, James, Philip, and Nathanael) pack their bags and return with Jesus to Galilee (vv. 43-51). Three days later they will find themselves in Cana at a wedding (Jn 2:1).

Jn 1:35-40

³⁵The next day John was there again with two of his disciples. ³⁶When he saw Jesus passing by, he said, "Look, the Lamb of God!"

³⁷When the two disciples heard him say this, they followed Jesus. ³⁸Turning around, Jesus saw them following and asked, "What do you want?"

They said, "Rabbi" (which means Teacher), "where are you staying?"

³⁹"Come," he replied, "and you will see."

So they went and saw where he was staying, and spent that day with him. It was about the tenth hour.

⁴⁰Andrew, Simon Peter's brother, was one of the two who heard what John had said and who had followed Jesus.

THE CALL OF ANDREW AND JOHN:

The scene, with its curt details, is almost humorous. Jesus turns and says, "What do you seek?" The real question is, "*Who* do you seek?" The disciple of Jesus does not seek a "thing," but a person. It seems as if they are taken off guard by Jesus' abruptness. It is like they stammer for a moment and then ask this inane question, "Uhhh, where are you staying?" Jesus' response is again short: "Come and you will see," or "If you will just follow me you will see for yourself!"

About four in the afternoon (i.e., the tenth hour, counting from sunrise),[7] Jesus calls Andrew (vv. 39-40). His unnamed partner is likely

---

[7]Hendriksen (pp. 104-105) and Westcott (Vol. 2, pp. 324-326) argue that John uses a Roman-civil timing which begins counting the hours of a day from midnight. That would

John. John tends to leave his own name out of the narrative (Jn 13:23; 19:26, 35; 21:7, 20, 24). Besides, John mentions the exact hour during which they followed Jesus. This little eyewitness detail demonstrates how memorable the event was to John. He was so deeply impacted by the moment of his first call he even remembers the hands of his watch. From this point on, John gives eyewitness details. If this was not John's call to discipleship, he is silent on the matter.

Jn. 1:41-42

⁴¹The first thing Andrew did was to find his brother Simon and tell him, "We have found the Messiah" (that is, the Christ). ⁴²And he brought him to Jesus.

Jesus looked at him and said, "You are Simon son of John. You will be called Cephas" (which, when translated, is Peterª).

ª42 Both *Cephas* (Aramaic) and *Peter* (Greek) mean *rock*.

THE CALL OF PETER AND JAMES:

Andrew goes and tells his brother Peter, "We have found the Messiah." (John translates "Messiah" from Hebrew into its Greek equivalent "Christ.") As was his custom, Andrew brought Peter to Jesus (cf. Jn 6:8; 12:22).

Literally, v. 41 states that "he found first his own brother Simon." We are not told that Andrew found anyone else. It is likely that John is intimating that Andrew was the first to go get his brother *while John was the second to go get his brother*. In other words, Andrew got his brother, Peter; and John got his brother, James. The first four disciples of Jesus were Peter, Andrew, James and John. This would help explain the later call of these four fishermen (Mt 4:18-22; Lk 5:1-11), as well as the inner circle of Jesus' disciples.

When Jesus meets Peter he gives him a new nickname, "Cephas," which means "rock." He would truly not earn his name until after the resurrection, when he was transformed from a deserter to a powerful preacher. The name seems to fit Peter well enough.

---

mean that this event took place at 10 a.m. rather than 4 p.m. This method of reckoning time is also the most comfortable explanation of John's other passages in which he mentions specific hours of the day (Jn 4:6; 4:52 and especially 19:14). The problem is, the primary support for a Roman-civil method of timing is virtually nonexistent. True enough, Pliny (*Natural History*, 2.79.188) said that the Roman priests reckoned a *civil day* as lasting from midnight to midnight for the purposes of legal leases. However, in the previous sentence he said that "the common people everywhere" count the *hours of a day* from dawn until dark. Indeed, Roman sundials, without exception, reflect this practice. The middle of the day is "VI" not "XII." In Jewish circles, the hours of a day could be counted from either dawn or dusk. But there is no example of the hours of a day ever being counted from midnight (R. T. Beckwith, "The Day, Its Divisions and Its Limits, In Biblical Thought," *EvQ* 43 [1971]: 218-227).

Jn 1:43-51

[43]The next day Jesus decided to leave for Galilee. Finding Philip, he said to him, "Follow me."

[44]Philip, like Andrew and Peter, was from the town of Bethsaida. [45]Philip found Nathanael and told him, "We have found the one Moses wrote about in the Law, and about whom the prophets also wrote — Jesus of Nazareth, the son of Joseph."

[46]"Nazareth! Can anything good come from there?" Nathanael asked. "Come and see," said Philip.

[47]When Jesus saw Nathanael approaching, he said of him, "Here is a true Israelite, in whom there is nothing false."

[48]"How do you know me?" Nathanael asked.

Jesus answered, "I saw you while you were still under the fig tree before Philip called you."

[49]Then Nathanael declared, "Rabbi, you are the Son of God; you are the King of Israel."

[50]Jesus said, "You believe[a] because I told you I saw you under the fig tree. You shall see greater things than that." [51]He then added, "I tell you[b] the truth, you[b] shall see heaven open, and the angels of God ascending and descending on the Son of Man."

[a]50 Or Do you believe . . . ?   [b]51 The Greek is plural

THE CALL OF PHILIP AND NATHANAEL:

Philip is likely a friend of the four fishermen (Peter, Andrew, James and John), who took up following Jesus the day before. He too was from this small fishing village of Bethsaida. On his way back to Galilee, Jesus calls Philip also. It is interesting that of all the Apostles, only Philip and Andrew have Greek names (Hendriksen, p. 108). This might explain why the Greeks of John 12:20-22 sought out these two in order to gain a hearing with Jesus.[8]

Apparently Jesus was not exactly on his way out of town when he called Philip. After all, Philip has time enough to go get Nathanael.[9] Philip tries to lure him with an intriguing proposition. He suggests that they have found the Messiah Moses wrote about. Philip's sentence is couched in such a way so as to maximize excitement and minimize offense. That is, the first word of his sentence is "Messiah" and the last is "Nazareth." But the fact that Jesus was from Nazareth does not slip by Nathanael. He can't believe anything good would come from there. Perhaps he is expressing some popular prejudice against this small town

---

[8]Aside from the lists of Apostles (Mt 10:3; Mk 3:18; Lk 6:14; and Acts 1:13), Philip is mentioned in three other incidents in John 1:43-48; 6:5, 7; 12:21-22 and 14:8-9.

[9]Nathanael is probably the same person that the Synoptics call Bartholomew. There are four evidences for this. (1) Nathanael is his family name, thus it is likely that he would have had another name. (2) John never uses the name Bartholomew and the Synoptics

in the hill country of Galilee. There is nothing to prove that the Galileans disdain Nazareth. Although Nathanael is without guile (v. 47), he still may be expressing a colloquial rivalry between Nazareth and his home-town of Cana (Jn 21:2), just a few miles to the north. Philip finally entices Nathanael to meet Jesus with the simple challenge, "Come see for yourself!"[10]

Nathanael's interaction with Jesus is interesting. If we listen with Jewish ears we hear echoes of Jacob in the OT. As Nathanael approaches, Jesus calls him a guileless Israelite. Trudinger says,

> Jacob, in the traditional story of Jacob and Esau, had become virtually a synonym for "deceit." In Genesis 27:36, Esau laments: "Has he not rightly been called Jacob, because he has cheated me these two times?" This very same deceitful Jacob, however, is a key figure in God's plan for humankind's salvation and later in the story is re-named "Israel" by God. Jesus' greeting could thus be expressed, "Look, Israel without a trace of Jacob left in him!" It is *this* that startles Nathanael.[11]

Nathanael is deeply impressed that Jesus knew him. Then Jesus says, in so many words, "Oh that was nothin', watch this: I saw you sitting under the fig tree!" This so impressed Nathanael that he confesses that Jesus is the Messiah of God. He was the first to do so without a revelation by God or an angel. But what's the big deal? So Jesus saw him sitting under a fig tree? The dense leaves of the fig made it a favorite resting place of Palestinians. It therefore became a place for meditation and the study of the Torah (*Ecclesiastes Rabbah* 5:15). In addition, the fig tree was a symbol of Israel and the Messiah (Micah 4:4; Mt 24:32; Lk 13:6-9). We can only guess, but it seems like there is more to Jesus' words than first meets the eye. Perhaps Jesus knew that Nathanael had been studying the Bible and contemplating the Messiah, perhaps even from the story of Jacob. But this much seems clear: Jesus saw Nathanael's heartfelt longing for the Messiah. Jesus got inside Nathanael's mind and this caused Nathanael to believe in Jesus and take up following him.

Jesus again takes Philip and Nathanael back to Jacob. He says *they* will see angels ascending and descending. If we look for a literal fulfill-

---

never use Nathanael. (3) In the synoptic lists of the Apostles, Bartholomew stands next to Philip. (4) All other disciples in this chapter become Apostles.

[10]Just as Matthew and Luke describe Jesus' humble beginnings in Bethlehem, so John describes his humble beginnings in Nazareth.

[11]L.P. Trudinger, "An Israelite in whom there is no Guile: An Interpretive Note on John 1:45-51," *EvQ* 54 (Apr 1982): 117-120.

ment of this in Jesus' ministry we will come up empty. However, the allusion to Jacob's ladder is rich. We must look to Genesis 28 for the context. During the midst of Jacob's dream, God pronounces a blessing on him that climaxes with these words, "And in thy seed shall all the families of the earth be blessed." Jesus is the fulfillment of this 2,000 year old vision. And, in a sense, this is Nathanael's "Bethel" (cf. Gen 28:19).

In this passage Jesus is called, "The Lamb of God," "the Son of God," "the Messiah," and "the King of Israel." Yet Jesus refers to himself as, "Son of Man." This title comes from Daniel 7:13-14. Jesus uses it of himself some 76 times. "Son of Man" highlights Jesus' affinity with humanity. Thus, from John 1:1 to John 1:51 we see the full descent of God incarnated into human flesh.

§ 29
Wedding at
Cana
(Jn 2:1-11)

Jn 2:1-5

This scene, in a way, leaves us up in the air. There are many unanswered questions: What was Mary's role? What was Nathanael's relationship to the couple? Who was this couple? Did Jesus know them previously? How? etc. As an eyewitness, John could have answered all these questions. But he chooses to emphasize Jesus. He is the main character of this wedding feast, the only one that really matters.

¹On the third day a wedding took place at Cana in Galilee. Jesus' mother was there, ²and Jesus and his disciples had also been invited to the wedding. ³When the wine was gone, Jesus' mother said to him, "They have no more wine."

⁴"Dear woman, why do you involve me?" Jesus replied. "My time has not yet come." ⁵His mother said to the servants, "Do whatever he tells you."

What could be more delightful than a wedding feast? And what better place for Jesus' first miracle? If Edersheim (I:345) is correct, this is a Wednesday wedding of a young maiden. The feast began at twilight and often lasted up to seven days (Gen 29:27; Judg 14:12). Jesus shows up with his first six disciples after three days of traveling from the Jordan to Cana.[12] Several sites have been designated as Cana, ranging from four to eighteen miles north of Nazareth. Any of them were close enough that Mary could have been called on to participate in the organization of the wedding. Furthermore, Jesus would have plenty of time to stop by Nazareth on his way to Cana.

Jesus was invited to the feast along with his disciples. It could be that Nathanael, who was from Cana, invited them. He may have even been a relative or close friend of the couple. Or perhaps Jesus learned of

---

[12]Just as John gives the last week of Christ's ministry in some detail (Jn 12:1), so here he enumerates the first week of Christ's ministry (Jn 1:29, 35, 43, 2:1).

the wedding when he stopped in at Nazareth (if, indeed, he did).

When the wedding wine gave out, Mary informed Jesus of the embarrassing predicament, which could even have resulted in a possible lawsuit.[13] Likely, Mary was involved in the administration of the banquet, so she knew about the wine.[14] And perhaps Jesus' extra guests were partially responsible for the wine running out. Without actually asking Jesus to do anything, she suggests that he could. For thirty years now she has pondered the prophecies and angelic announcements about Jesus. Now he has been baptized, initiated in the wilderness and has returned home with his first humble following. It is only natural that Mary would expect him to miraculously reveal himself.

Jesus obviously does not refuse Mary's "request." He does, however, scrutinize her motives and expectations. His brief response to Mary has three parts. First, he addresses her as "dear woman" rather than "Mom." It was a polite title, like "Ma'am," (cf. Jn 19:26), and yet a definite statement about their relationship. She now must submit to him as Christ rather than leading him as "son." Then Jesus says, "Why do you involve me?" [lit. "what to me to you"]. This is a common Hebrew idiom, roughly meaning, "What business is that of mine?" Essentially, Jesus is asking Mary to carefully consider their relationship. Finally, he said his hour has not yet come. In other words, "Mary, don't expect a public proclamation just yet" (cf. Jn 7:6, 9). Jesus' life was predestined. The events of his incarnation (Gal 4:4) and ministry were meticulously planned AND TIMED so as to lead to Calvary at the right moment. John's use of the words "hour" and "time" indicate God's plan for Jesus (cf. Jn 2:4; 7:6, 8, 30; 8:20; 12:23, 27; 13:1; 17:1), especially in his death.

Mary's response indicates that she still expects Jesus to move to meet the need. Perhaps the tone of his voice, or a wink, or some other words to which we are not privy, indicate that Jesus would help. Nonetheless, this is the only command we know that Mary ever gave, "Whatever he says to you, do it." That is not bad advice!

Jn 2:6-10   [6]Nearby stood six stone water jars, the kind used by the Jews for ceremonial washing, each holding from twenty to thirty gallons.[a]

[7]Jesus said to the servants, "Fill the jars with water"; so they filled them to the brim.

---

[13]K.T. Cooper, "The Best Wine: John 2:1-11," *WTJ* 41 (Spr 1979): 364-380.

[14]Joseph is not mentioned in the narrative, even though the rest of the family is there (Jn 2:12), perhaps assisting their mother with the details of the wedding. This may indicate that Joseph is deceased.

[8]Then he told them, "Now draw some out and take it to the master of the banquet."

They did so, [9]and the master of the banquet tasted the water that had been turned into wine. He did not realize where it had come from, though the servants who had drawn the water knew. Then he called the bridegroom aside [10]and said, "Everyone brings out the choice wine first and then the cheaper wine after the guests have had too much to drink; but you have saved the best till now."

[a]6 Greek *two to three metretes* (probably about 75 to 115 liters)

Jesus pointed to six stone waterpots used for ritual washing. They could each hold twenty to thirty gallons. That would total one hundred twenty to one hundred fifty gallons of wine. Aside from meeting the needs of the banquet, this would make a pretty fair wedding gift. Jesus commands that they be filled with water to the brim. This will indicate (1) a great quantity, and (2) nothing else was "slipped into the punch," (3) as purification jars, they contained water, not wine. Therefore, there wouldn't even be any residue of wine in them.

Some of the "water" was drawn out of the pots and taken to the "headwaiter" who was responsible for three things: (1) Tasting all food and wine to see that it was acceptable, (2) keeping order in the party (he would break a glass if someone got unruly), and (3) officiating over the banquet. This fellow was not privy to Jesus' assistance. When he drank the water/wine he found it delicious. Its "goodness" was not found in its intoxicating ability but in its taste. In fact, Palestinian wine was significantly watered down. Although a person could become drunk with it, there were far more effective liqueurs. Wine was the normal table drink which accompanied meals. So good was this wine that the "headwaiter" called the bridegroom and complimented him on his fare. Normally the best is served first, not last.

Jn 2:11

[11]This, the first of his miraculous signs, Jesus performed at Cana in Galilee. He thus revealed his glory, and his disciples put their faith in him.

Jesus performed many signs and wonders. This is the first of seven that John chooses to record (v. 11). And it was pretty much a private display for the disciples, as are the other six. John's seven "signs" are not intended to showcase Jesus' power but to validate his position as God's Son.

These signs do more than simply validate Jesus or describe some event in his life. If Blomberg is correct, Jesus' miracles, like his parables, are metaphors for the kingdom. They are, so to speak, enacted parables.[15] This is not to say that they are not historically true. Recent

---

[15]C.L. Blomberg, "New Testament Miracles and Higher Criticism: Climbing up the Slippery Slope," *JETS* 27/4 (Dec 1984): 425-438.

scholars have shown that an antisupernatural bias is scientifically and philosophically indefensible. What it does say is that John chose to describe only certain miracles of Jesus because they pictured what his Messianic ministry was really all about.

Therefore, we must ask, "What does this sign point to?" Toussaint makes a couple of helpful suggestions.[16] First, the new wine at the wedding feast points to the coming kingdom. In the OT, it was likened to wine (Isa 25:6; 55:1; Joel 3:18; Amos 9:13). In the NT, it is pictured as a banquet, especially at a wedding (Mt 8:11; 22:1-14; Lk 13:29; 14:15-24; Rev 19:7-9). It would be new and different from the old kingdom (cf. Mk 2:21-22). Second, Jesus goes overboard. He provides much more wine than could possibly be needed. This super-abundance is also characteristic of the kingdom of God (Phil 4:7; Rom 5:20; 1 Pet 1:8; cf. Amos 9:13ff.). Thus, at Mary's prompting, Jesus inaugurates his miracle working ministry, not publicly, but privately to his disciples. In doing so, he pictured what the coming kingdom was going to be like.

**§ 30
Jesus & Co.
Visit
Capernaum
(Jn 2:12)**

[12]After this he went down to Capernaum with his mother and brothers and his disciples. There they stayed for a few days.

Jesus moves from the hill country of Cana to the shores of the Sea of Galilee, the stomping ground of the six disciples who follow him. Along with the six are Jesus' four brothers and his mother. The fact that their sisters are not present may indicate that they are married and consequently saddled with domestic responsibilities.

Nine times the brothers of the Lord are mentioned. Six times they are directly connected with Mary (Mt 12:46; 13:55; Mk 3:32; 6:3; Lk 8:19-20; Jn 2:12); three times they are not (Jn 7:3, 5, 10; 1 Cor 9:5; Gal 1:19). This is a good indication that these boys are natural sons of Mary rather than nephews or Joseph's sons by a previous marriage. The fact that Jesus entrusts the care of Mary to John from the cross (Jn 19:25-27), may indicate nothing more than his brothers' rejection of him or the fact that being younger brothers, they were not as committed to her care as John.

As McGarvey notes (p. 120), this brief visit to Capernaum suggests several things: (1) It shows how the nobleman, who sought Jesus at Cana, could have become acquainted with him (Jn 4:46-54). (2) It shows Jesus' movement away from Nazareth to Capernaum, which would

---

[16]S.D. Toussaint, "The Significance of the First Sign in John's Gospel," *BibSac* 134 (Jan 1977): 45-51.

become his "base of operations" (Mt 4:13; 9:1; Mk 2:1). This further suggests a certain dynamic in the relationship between the Nazarene and his Capernaum disciples as well as Jesus' subsequent visit to Nazareth. And (3) it shows that Jesus did not just cut off his natural family ties, at least not until after the upcoming Passover.

**§ 31
The First
Cleansing of
the Temple
(Jn 2:13-22)**

Like Josiah and Hezekiah of old, Jesus purifies God's temple. This is a gutsy move, which may suggest that Jesus is the Messiah (cf. Mal 2:2-3).[17] The focus of this incident is not on the temple and its corruption so much as it is on Jesus and his person. Read in conjunction with the wedding at Cana, we get a glimpse of both sides of Jesus' ministry. On the one hand, he is the great Messiah of the new kingdom with all its lavish and delightful provisions. On the other hand, he is a suffering servant, rejected and destroyed by the Jewish leaders, only to be raised again on the third day.

All four Gospels record the cleansing of the temple. But the Synoptics place it at the end of Jesus' ministry (Mt 21:12-13; Mk 11:15-17; Lk 19:45-46), not the beginning, like John. It is possible that there was only one cleansing and that John places it here for theological emphasis rather than chronological precision. After all, there are striking similarities (e.g., same place, animals and money changers), for obvious reasons. There are also considerable differences. For example, only John mentions the whip, the prophecy from Psalm 69:9, and the prediction about destroying the temple. The Synoptics also add the prophecies of Isaiah 56:7 and Jeremiah 7:11-14, as well as Mark's comment about Jesus halting traffic through the temple. This leads us to conclude that Jesus did, in fact, cleanse the temple twice. This bold action serves both to open and to close his public ministry.

John alone allows us to date Jesus' ministry based on the various feasts he attended: (1) First Passover (2:13); (2) Second Passover (supposedly), (5:1); (3) Third Passover (6:4); (4) Tabernacles (7:2); (5) Dedication (10:22); (6) Fourth Passover (11:55). Furthermore, John the Baptist's ministry can be dated in A.D. 26 (Lk 3:1), probably in the fall. Jesus was likely baptized that winter. He spent forty days in the wilderness (Mt 4:2); seven days gaining his first disciples and going to the wedding at Cana (Jn 1:29, 35, 43; 2:1). He visits Capernaum for a few days (Jn 2:12) and then hot-foots it to Jerusalem for the Passover

---

[17]R.H. Hiers, "Purification of the Temple: Preparation for the Kingdom of God," *JBL* 90 (1971): 82-90.

which would take place on the 15th of Nisan (approximately April), A.D. 27. This is further confirmed by verse 20, since Herod began rebuilding his temple in 19 B.C., forty-six years would place Jesus in A.D. 27.

Jn 2:13-17

¹³When it was almost time for the Jewish Passover, Jesus went up to Jerusalem. ¹⁴In the temple courts he found men selling cattle, sheep and doves, and others sitting at tables exchanging money. ¹⁵So he made a whip out of cords, and drove all from the temple area, both sheep and cattle; he scattered the coins of the money changers and overturned their tables. ¹⁶To those who sold doves he said, "Get these out of here! How dare you turn my Father's house into a market!"

¹⁷His disciples remembered that it is written: "Zeal for your house will consume me."ᵃ

ᵃ*17* Psalm 69:9

In a sense, this is Jesus' inaugural address. About a month before the feast construction crews would go out and repair the roads and bridges. Sepulchres would be painted in order to protect travelers from defiling themselves by accidently stepping on one (Edersheim, I:367). Jesus & Co. would join the joyous procession as they climbed from Capernaum, at about six hundred feet below sea level, to Jerusalem, about 2,550 feet above sea level. As they moved upward toward the Holy City they would sing the Hallel Psalms (120-134).

THE CORRUPTION

As Jesus walked into the temple it looked and smelled like a hybrid stockyard/circus. There would be blood spattered about the altar, oxen and sheep lowing, birds cooing, squawking, and flitting about when they were manhandled. The people were cosmopolitan (as well as neapolitan), from all over the Roman world. They brought with them vacation money in a desire to make a sacrifice to their God. For the wealthy pious, this was an annual affair. For the poorer class it may be a once-in-a-lifetime experience. How disappointing for them this scene must have been.

The whole spectacle came to be known as the "Bazaar of Annas."[18] He was the Jewish high priest. His power was only exceeded by his avarice and greed. He was revered and feared. He had set up quite a profitable venture for himself in the courts of the sacred temple. It worked something like this (cf. Edersheim, I:369): If a worshiper brought in an animal to be sacrificed the officiating priest [*mumcheh*] would undoubtedly find something wrong with it and offer to buy it off him at a devalued price. The animal would then be taken back to the

---

[18]J. MacArthur, *Matthew*, Vol. 3 (Chicago: Moody, 1988), p. 268.

pens of the priests, blessed and sold to another worshiper for an inflated price. The original worshiper then had to purchase a "kosher" animal at an exorbitant price, sometimes four or five times its actual value. When he pulled his money out of his pocket, if it was not Palestinian coinage, he would have to visit the money changer to get the proper currency. When he did, he was charged a fifteen to twenty percent fee for the exchange. It was quite a scam.

In addition to the sacrifices, every Jew was required to submit a half-shekel temple tax annually (Exod 30:13; Mt 17:24). Jews from other areas (e.g., Persia, Tyre, Syria, Egypt, Greece, and Rome), who used different coinage, would also have to pay the exchange fee. Hamilton observes that the temple in Jerusalem, like the pagan religious temples of the day, served as the central bank of the area (cf. 2 Macc. 3:6-15).[19] There were a lot of financial moguls running around taking advantage of these pious pilgrims.

All this made the visitors bitter. But they had no other choice if they wanted to fulfill their pious inclinations. To make matters worse there were no set fees for the animals. It was all up for grabs. Thus there was constant and heated haggling going on over prices. Faces were red, fists were clenched, and voices were raised . . . all for the worship of God.

THE CLEANSING

When Jesus enters the temple, he is immediately enraged. He begins weaving a whip out of some rope. There would certainly have been plenty laying around with all those animals. He skillfully and forcefully implements his instrument and clears out the barn. When verse 15 says, "He drove them all," it refers, no doubt, to the money changers (its nearest antecedent). The animals are innocent; it's these deviant humans that need discipline.

How is it that Jesus got away with this when he is so totally outnumbered? There may be several explanations: (1) Even in his incarnate state, Jesus' purity and passion were divine. That, in itself, is intimidating. (2) The money changers are hirelings. They run in the face of danger. Besides, some of them likely have a deep sense of guilt about what they are doing — they know it is not right. (3) The people must have been cheering as Jesus turned over tables and spilled change all over the floor. It was a popular move and in his angry zeal the people would no doubt support him. (4) There is a Roman garrison watching the proceedings of the feast from the Tower of Antonia. Jesus has already

---

[19]N.Q. Hamilton, "Temple Cleansing and Temple Bank," *JBL* 83 (1964): 356-372.

captured their attention. The last thing the Sadducees want to do is to fan it into flame. They could lose their positions and possibly even their lives. These are perilous times. People are looking for a savior and are willing to fight if they find one.

He says to them "Stop making my Father's house a house of commerce."[20] John weaves into the narrative his own commentary in v. 17. The disciples remember Psalm 69:9a, "Zeal for thy house will consume me." That is an interesting quotation for several reasons. First, Psalm 69 is Messianic (cf. v. 21). This is part of their very early understanding of Jesus. Second, the word "consume" is literally "eaten up." This verse does not merely mean to suggest that Jesus had a driving passion for the temple. In its original context it is a cry of pain and desperation. Like David, Jesus' passion for God is going to get him into trouble. Third, the verb tense of this word "consume" has been changed from the past in the LXX to the future here in John. Historically, as David wrote Psalm 69, he had already experienced suffering because of his zeal for God. Jesus, however, was looking for it in the future. Even now, he was challenging the authority of both the High Priest and the Procurator, both of whom claimed control of the central bank of the temple.

Jn 2:18-22

[18]Then the Jews demanded of him, "What miraculous sign can you show us to prove your authority to do all this?"

[19]Jesus answered them, "Destroy this temple, and I will raise it again in three days."

[20]The Jews replied, "It has taken forty-six years to build this temple, and you are going to raise it in three days?" [21]But the temple he had spoken of was his body. [22]After he was raised from the dead, his disciples recalled what he had said. Then they believed the Scripture and the words that Jesus had spoken.

The Jews[21] (i.e., Sadducean priests) were in a pickle. They were about to lose a bunch of money, which was one of their greatest loves. On the other hand, they were about to get beat up if they oppose this Jesus. They address him with cautious cordiality. They do not deny his identity but they do ask for proof of it. They ask for a sign. According to

---

[20]*mē* with the present imperative indicates to cease whatever action is already in progress.

[21]In John, the term *"the Jews,"* sometimes refers to Jewish people in general, Jewish customs, or even to Judeans. Usually, however, it is a "hostile" term, referring to unbelieving Jewish authorities. R.A. Culpepper, "The Gospel of John and the Jews," Rev & Exp 84 (Spr 1987): 273-288, suggests that the farther into the book we go, the more hostile *hoi Ioudaioi* becomes. Furthermore, John's original audience (c. A.D. 90) was being ousted from the synagogue. Thus, this negative presentation of the Jewish authorities (aside from being historically accurate), would serve as a reminder to Christians that faithfulness to Christ is not the same as faithfulness to the synagogue. Even Jesus was ostracized by the religious hierarchy of his day.

popular Jewish expectations the Messiah would come with great signs and wonders. Thus, these Sadducees, who did not even believe in a literal Messiah, were coddling to the crowd.

Jesus doesn't want to play their game. The only sign Jesus offers is the resurrection. They misunderstand him because they take his words literally (cf. Jn 3:3-4; 4:14-15; 4:32-33; 6:51-52; 7:34-35; 8:51-52; 11:11-12; 14:4-5). They can't see how Jesus could rebuild an edifice in three days that it took construction crews forty-six years to build. This will come up again at Jesus' trial (Mt 26:61; Mk 14:58) as well as at Stephen's (Acts 6:14), when they are charged with threatening to destroy the temple. And yet it would appear that the Pharisees understood what Jesus intended when they put guards at the tomb (Mt 27:62-66).

It is significant that the word "temple" [*hieron*] of v. 14, is changed to *naos* in v. 19-21. This latter word, strictly speaking, is the "shrine" where a god dwells. It is used in 1 Corinthians 3:16-17 and 6:19 to refer to the body of the Christian. Obviously, Jesus was speaking about his own body as the dwelling place of God. The disciples later remembered this very discussion and it sparked in them even greater faith in Jesus.

This incident is not about the temple edifice, but the person of Jesus. Nevertheless, Jesus' death did, in fact, make the temple obsolete. The final sacrifice had been made and the veil was torn in two. God was no longer in the Holy of Holies. Instead, God dwells in the hearts of men through the Holy Spirit (1 Cor 6:19). Furthermore, God's judgment fell upon the Jews and their temple for killing Jesus. It would be destroyed in A.D. 70. To this day OT worship in the temple has not been restored.

§ 32a
Early
Response to
Jesus' Miracles
(Jn 2:23-25)

[23]Now while he was in Jerusalem at the Passover Feast, many people saw the miraculous signs he was doing and believed in his name.[a] [24]But Jesus would not entrust himself to them, for he knew all men. [25]He did not need man's testimony about man, for he knew what was in a man.

[a]23 Or *and believed in him*

The crowds believe in Jesus because of his signs (v. 23). But really Jesus has not done any signs, save the cleansing of the temple (cf. Mal 3:1-3) and responding to the Sadducees, neither of which were really miraculous. What, then, were these signs? Jesus will spend upwards of eight to nine months in Judea (Jn 4:35). It is likely that he did many miracles in the area. However, John seems to indicate that they believe on him here and now, during the feast. So perhaps there were miracles during the Passover that we are not specifically told about.

Even though the crowds believe in Jesus, he refuses to entrust himself to them. He knows their hearts (cf. Jn 1:42, 47-48; 3:3; 4:29; 6:61, 64; 13:11; 21:17). They do appear to be true believers. That is, John says they "believed in his name" just like other true believers (cf. 1:12-13; 3:18, etc.).[22] But even "believers" can be fickle and unreliable. Jesus allows them to trust in him; but he will not entrust himself to them.

§ 32b
Nicodemus
Meets Jesus
(Jn 3:1-21)

Jesus' interview with Nicodemus illustrates the last two verses (Jn 2:24-25). Here comes one of those "believers," to whom Jesus would not entrust himself. Nicodemus is tentative, afraid and confused. Yet he represents the cream of the crop! This chapter will move us from insufficient faith (vv. 1-9) to sterling faith (vv. 31-36).

The movement of this chapter will take us from report (2:23-25) to dialogue (3:1-12) to monologue (3:17-21) with Jesus. And then again from report (3:22-24) to dialogue (3:25-30) to monologue (3:31-36) with John.

Jn 3:1-2

[1]Now there was a man of the Pharisees named Nicodemus, a member of the Jewish ruling council. [2]He came to Jesus at night and said, "Rabbi, we know you are a teacher who has come from God. For no one could perform the miraculous signs you are doing if God were not with him."

Nicodemus runs in the fast lane. As a member of the Sanhedrin, he has clout dripping off him. He is also an insider in the swelling debate caused by Jesus cleansing the temple (Jn 2:12-25). Perhaps night time is the only available opportunity for such a busy fellow to talk with Jesus. This, however, is doubtful considering his clout and the centrality of Jesus in the religious arena of the day. This IS the business of a religious leader like Nicodemus. So why come to Jesus at night? Perhaps the cover of darkness is a welcome attendant of his interview with Jesus. Or perhaps it is the only time he could get with Jesus for a private interview. But the symbolism of "night" seems significant.[23]

Nicodemus addresses Jesus respectfully. He obviously isn't the only Sanhedrin member with pro-Jesus leanings. A number of the "big boys" are aware of Jesus' power, position, and origin.[24] Jesus' signs are undeni-

---

[22]Z.C. Hodges, "Untrustworthy Believers — John 2:23-25," *BibSac* 135 (Apr-Jun 1978): 139-152.

[23]F.P. Cotterell, "The Nicodemus Conversation: A Fresh Appraisal," *ExpT*, 96 (May 1985): 237-242, suggests four possible understandings of "night": (1) a simple chronological marker, (2) Nicodemus' desire for anonymity, (3) symbolism, as in 1:8-9; 3:19-20; 9:4; 11:10; 13:30, (4) rabbis often engaged in theological discussion at night.

[24]Nicodemus may well have had disciples of his own following him to interview Jesus. Hence, the plural "we know" would refer to his students, not necessarily other Sanhedrin members. It may also refer back to the general believers of John 2:23.

able, both their existence and their evidence of God's blessing on Jesus' life. There are other Jewish "teachers" who claim to perform miracles, but there is a world of difference between Jesus and the others.

Although he does not become an open follower of Jesus, Nicodemus shows deep respect and commitment to him.[25] In John 7:50-52, he defends Jesus' right to a fair trial. And in John 19:38-39 he brings spices for his burial. Before we accuse him of cowardice, we should remember that Nicodemus was the only Pharisee who ever came to Jesus in such obvious sincerity.

What we have here is apparently only a brief summary of the interaction between these two men. It is almost as if we get to read John's notes that he scribbled while listening off to one side. Yet, they are thorough enough to follow the main ideas and even emotions of the meeting. The text comes at us in three volleys: vv. 3-8; 9-15; 16-21.

Jn 3:3-8

[3]In reply Jesus declared, "I tell you the truth, no one can see the kingdom of God unless he is born again."[a]

[4]"How can a man be born when he is old?" Nicodemus asked. "Surely he cannot enter a second time into his mother's womb to be born!"

[5]Jesus answered, "I tell you the truth, no one can enter the kingdom of God unless he is born of water and the Spirit. [6]Flesh gives birth to flesh, but the Spirit[b] gives birth to spirit. [7]You should not be surprised at my saying, 'You[c] must be born again.' [8]The wind blows wherever it pleases. You hear its sound, but you cannot tell where it comes from or where it is going. So it is with everyone born of the Spirit."

[a]3 Or *born from above*; also in verse 7   [b]6 Or *but spirit*   [c]7 The Greek is plural

Jesus replies in verse 3, not to what Nicodemus has spoken, but to his deepest need and perhaps his hidden desire. Perhaps more than any miracle Jesus has performed, his ability to read Nicodemus' heart would draw this man into the kingdom.

Entrance into the kingdom of God requires new birth. The Greek word [*anōthen*], might be better translated "from above" as it is elsewhere (cf. Jn 3:3, 7, 31; 19:11, 23). It is not just new in time but new in nature — it is a *heavenly* birth. Nicodemus knows that you can't literally be born again, especially when he is so old.[26] But Jesus says, "You're right, this is not a physical rebirth but a spiritual rebirth."

The phrase "born of water and the Spirit," has been the source of

---

[25]J.M. Bassler, "Mixed Signals: Nicodemus in the Fourth Gospel," *JBL* 108/4 (1989): 635-646, observes that Nicodemus provides neither a positive example nor a negative one. This may allow a vacillating reader to identify with this character.

[26]Nicodemus uses an interesting word when he asks, "How can a man be born when he is *old*." Pythagoras defines this word "old" [*gerōn*], as one who is between 60-80 years old.

much debate. Various suggestions have been offered as to the meaning of the water which fall into three categories. First, "water" might refer to the water associated with physical birth, such as amniotic fluid,[27] or semen.[28] However, there are no clear examples in Jewish literature of birth being associated with either of these types of "water."

Second, water might refer to purification. Some suggest that Jesus was calling Nicodemus to submit to John's baptism, which has just been mentioned (Jn 1:23, 26; 3:23). Aside from the fact that John's baptism was not associated with the Spirit, John himself has started pointing people away from himself and toward Jesus. Perhaps the cleansing is not a ritual washing but a symbolic reference to the Holy Spirit.[29] After all, the OT often associates the Holy Spirit with both wind and water (Gen 1:2; Joel 2:28-29; Isa 44:3; Ezek 36:25-27), especially in terms of bringing people to life (Isa 32:15-17; 55:1-3; Jer 2:13; 17:13; Zech 14:8). In addition, the word "spirit" is also translated "wind." Thus, Jesus may be saying that in order to be born from above one must be birthed through wind and water. Both metaphors describe the Holy Spirit, both come from heaven, and both are symbols of cleansing in the OT.

Third, the water may refer to baptism.[30] We support this third option for the following reasons:

(1) Both nouns (water and spirit) are governed by a single preposition. Thus, Jesus refers to one birth, not two.
(2) The words "water" and "Spirit" are linked in Ezekiel 36:25-27 where the author looks forward to an eschatalogical cleansing which afford its recipients a new heart and a new spirit. This appropriately pictures the sacrament of baptism.
(3) The concept of baptism has already been introduced by John. Thus we are not surprised to encounter both water and spirit baptism (Jn 1:25-26, 28, 31-33).
(4) Water and Spirit are connected in other baptism passages (Mt 28:19; Acts 2:38; 19:1-7; Titus 3:5).

If, indeed this is a reflection on Nicodemus himself, we have a hint that he was an elderly statesman.

[27]For advocates of this view see R. Fowler, "Born of water and the Spirit (Jn 3:5)," *ExpT* 82 (1971): 159; and D.G. Spriggs, "Meaning of Water in John 3:5," *ExpT* 85 (1974): 150.

[28]See Leon Morris, *Expository Reflections on the Gospel of John*, (Grand Rapids: Baker, 1986), 90-91.

[29]See Z.C. Hodges, "Water and Spirit — John 3:5," *BibSac* 135 (July 1978): 206-220.

[30]See L.L. Belleville, "'Born of Water and Spirit': John 3:5," *TrinJ* 1 (1980): 125-140.

(5) The Greek and Latin Fathers interpret this verse unanimously as immersion.

(6) In the very next pericope we find Jesus baptizing (Jn 3:22).

(7) John's original readers could hardly have read this combination (water & Spirit), and not thought of baptism.[31]

Indeed, Christian baptism is anachronistic here. Jesus could hardly have rebuked Nicodemus (v. 10) for not submitting to Christian baptism which has not yet even been instituted. But John's baptism (Jn 1:26) will give way to Jesus' baptism (Jn 1:33; 3:22) which will become Christian baptism (Mt 28:19).

It was pretty demeaning for Jesus to expect Nicodemus to be reborn. That would be like asking the President to take a Jr. High civics class. Academically and professionally this fellow had arrived. Now Jesus was calling him to total resignation of his achievements. This might be appropriate for proselytes or even children, but NOT a Doctor of the Law.

This first volley turns on the word Spirit/Wind. In both Hebrew and Greek it is the same word. It paints a powerful picture. You cannot grab the Holy Spirit in a headlock and squeeze some power out of him any more than you can grab some wind and keep it in your pocket for later. The important question for a Kingdom citizen is not, "Do you possess the Holy Spirit?" but "Does the Holy Spirit possess you?" Notice also in verse 8 that the "freewheeling" individual is not just the Holy Spirit, but all who are born of the Spirit. Such a one cannot be confined, predicted or restricted. Nothing exists that is as free as the wind.

Jn 3:9-15

[9]"How can this be?" Nicodemus asked.

[10]"You are Israel's teacher," said Jesus, "and do you not understand these things? [11]I tell you the truth, we speak of what we know, and we testify to what we have seen, but still you people do not accept our testimony. [12]I have spoken to you of earthly things and you do not believe; how then will you believe if I speak of heavenly things? [13]No one has ever gone into heaven except the one who came from heaven — the Son of Man.[a] [14]Just as Moses lifted up the snake in the desert, so the Son of Man must be lifted up, [15]that everyone who believes in him may have eternal life.[b]

[a]13 Some manuscripts *Man, who is in heaven*   [b]15 Or *believes may have eternal life in him*

In the first volley, Nicodemus asks two questions. Now he is only allowed one, "How can this be?" Again, because Nicodemus is steeped

---

[31]In a similar way, John's readers would naturally think of communion when reading Jn 6:53-54 and the indwelling of the Holy Spirit when reading Jn 7:38-39.

in rabbinic ideas and religious politics, he is unable to understand the basic truths of the kingdom. The lesson to be learned is this (v. 13): In order to truly understand the heart of God, we must listen and submit to the person of Jesus. He alone has carved a path from heaven to earth and he alone knows the way back.

In verse 10, Jesus is not gentle. By using the article with both *Israel* and *teacher*, Jesus is on the verge of mocking Nicodemus with emphasis. It might have sounded to him something like this: "You mean to tell me that you are such a famous teacher of Israel and yet you can't grasp these basics." At this point the dialogue becomes monologue.

Jesus says that he had been speaking of earthly things. That is to say, such rebirth is a spiritual act which is played out through earthly symbols. But what is to come (Jn 3:16), originates in heaven. How much more difficult *God's love* will be to understand than *regeneration*.

Jesus is like the snake of Moses (Num 21:8-9). Because of Israel's constant grumbling, God lost his patience and began to destroy them with vipers. The result was fairly predictable — instant repentance. But it was not that easy. Healing came from looking at the bronze snake that Moses made and hoisted on top of a pole. In like manner, Jesus would be hoisted up (on the cross).[32] And all who look to him (in faith), will be saved from their snake bite (the punishment of sin). This is the third symbolic reference that John has made to Jesus' death (cf. 1:29; 2:19).

Jn 3:16-21

¹⁶"For God so loved[33] the world that he gave his one and only Son,ᵃ that whoever believes in him shall not perish but have eternal life. ¹⁷For God did not send his Son into the world to condemn the world, but to save the world through him. ¹⁸Whoever believes in him is not condemned, but whoever does not believe stands condemned already because he has not believed in the name of God's one and only Son.ᵇ ¹⁹This is the verdict: Light has come into the world, but men loved darkness instead of light because their deeds were evil. ²⁰Everyone who does evil hates the light, and will not come into the light for fear that his deeds will be exposed. ²¹But whoever lives by the truth comes into the light, so that it may be seen plainly that what he has done has been done through God."ᶜ

ᵃ*16* Or *his only begotten Son*   ᵇ*18* Or *God's only begotten Son*   ᶜ*21* Some interpreters end the quotation after verse 15.

It is difficult to know if vv. 16-21 are Jesus' words or John's. At any

---

[32]When John speaks of Jesus' exaltation/lifting up he includes the crucifixion, resurrection and ascension all in one.

[33]The words so loved [Gk. *houtōs*] indicate the *quality* rather than the *quantity* of God's love. H.K. Moulton, "John 3:15 — God So Loved the World," *BT* 27/2 (Apr 1976): 242, suggests the following translation: "This is how God loved the world: He sent his only Son . . ."

event, this is the gospel in a capsule (3:16-18) — it is the crowning jewel of the New Testament. Nowhere else has theology been so simplified and yet reached such sublime heights. We almost need to read the text with an exclamation point behind each word.

McGarvey (p. 131), says this about John 3:16:

> It is a lesson as to God's love: 1. Its magnitude — he gave his only begotten Son. 2. Its reach — he gave to a sinful world (Rom 5:8). 3. Its impartiality — he gives to whomsoever; that is, to all alike (Mt 5:45; Rev 22:17). 4. Its beneficial richness — it blesses with life eternal. 5. Its limitation — it is nowhere said that God so loves that he will save unbelievers.

Jesus has come to save, not to judge. It is his desire to bring eternal life — not just a quantity of life but a divine quality of life. Yet, because his words are those of God, response to Jesus becomes the anvil on which all are tested.

Jesus is good in the extreme (3:19-21). But he is not tame. He is demanding; he is painfully incisive; he is vindictive of sin and intolerant of unbelief; he is light that ruthlessly exposes[34] our wickedness. If a man is not ready to be stripped bare and clothed only in Christ, he has no other option but to cower in the darkness.

§ 33
From John to Jesus
(Jn 3:22-36)

John alone bears witness to Jesus' early Judean ministry which lasted 8-9 months. In the Synoptics we have no hint of this period which took place between Matthew 4:11 and 12 (cf. Mk 1:13-14; Lk 4:13-14). Jesus came to Jerusalem for the Passover (Jn 2:13, about April) and stayed until four months before harvest (Jn 4:35). During this time Jesus cleansed the temple (Jn 2:13-22), performed many miracles (Jn 2:23; 3:2), and baptized disciples (Jn 3:23). But we have very meager details of his actual words and deeds.

During these days, John's popularity was falling off as quickly as Jesus' was growing. That is, in fact, exactly what John desired. But in their fraternal competition, John's disciples saw this as a real setback. This is the impetus behind our text.

Jn 3:22-26

²²After this, Jesus and his disciples went out into the Judean countryside, where he spent some time with them, and baptized. ²³Now John also was baptizing at Aenon near Salim, because there was plenty of water, and people were constantly coming to be baptized. ²⁴(This was before John was put in prison.)

---

[34]The word John uses [*elenchō*], not only means "to bring to light" but also includes the idea of "convict" which leads to "reprove" which culminates in "punishment."

[25]An argument developed between some of John's disciples and a certain Jew[a] over the matter of ceremonial washing. [26]They came to John and said to him, "Rabbi, that man who was with you on the other side of the Jordan — the one you testified about — well, he is baptizing, and everyone is going to him."

[a]*25 Some manuscripts and certain Jews*

Jesus continues and extends John's work and baptism. Meanwhile, John is plugging away in Aenon near Salim. The word "Salim" means "springs." McGarvey says this "perennial stream, with copious springs all along its course, furnishes, even in the longest, driest summers, the 'much water' required for baptism" (p. 134).

John has about another eight months of freedom (Mt 4:12; Mk 1:14). Some unnamed Jew confronts John's disciples with the issue of purification (v. 25). This triggers their interview with John in v. 26. Why? Likely the debate over purification centered around the nature of John's baptism and the forgiveness of sin. This would naturally lead into Jesus' baptism, which took the same form. And yet John promised a new type of baptism — in the Holy Spirit and fire. From our vantage point, we can see that Jesus' Spirit baptism was not yet. But this Jew likely would have expected it immediately and would have wanted to know several things: (1) Why does Jesus' baptism look like John's — what is the difference? (2) How is Jesus' baptism with the Holy Spirit and fire? (3) How is water immersion effective for the forgiveness of sins?

Their jealous comment in v. 26 carries a subtle rebuke to John aligning with Jesus. These hard-core disciples of John are hanging on. No doubt they hold John in honor, but mistakenly so. John will once again, not so gently, send them over to Jesus. He is having a difficult time weaning these pups.

Jn 3:27-30

[27]To this John replied, "A man can receive only what is given him from heaven. [28]You yourselves can testify that I said, 'I am not the Christ[a] but am sent ahead of him.' [29]The bride belongs to the bridegroom. The friend who attends the bridegroom waits and listens for him, and is full of joy when he hears the bridegroom's voice. That joy is mine, and it is now complete. [30]He must become greater; I must become less.

[a]*28 Or Messiah*

These are the last recorded words of John the Baptist. They show John's dignity and Jesus' superiority. His first statement, "A man can receive nothing, unless it has been given him from heaven," can apply either to himself or to Jesus. If he means Jesus, he would be saying, "Jesus received his ministry from God, therefore, I am pleased that he has so many disciples." But if John is talking about himself, he may be saying, "My ministry I received from God. Therefore, I have no right to promote myself or exceed the bound of my purpose." This makes a lot of sense, especially in the context of vv. 28-30.

John's picture from verse 29 was a joyous and common one in his day (cf. Jer 7:34; 25:10; 33:11). The friend of the bridegroom would announce his coming, ask for the hand of the bride, and prepare the arrangements for the reception. But his joy was in promoting his friend, not himself. Likewise, John's joy is in Jesus' advancement, not in his own. Never were more noble words spoken from a disciple than these of John, "He must increase, but I must decrease."

Jn 3:31-36

31"The one who comes from above is above all; the one who is from the earth belongs to the earth, and speaks as one from the earth. The one who comes from heaven is above all. 32He testifies to what he has seen and heard, but no one accepts his testimony. 33The man who has accepted it has certified that God is truthful. 34For the one whom God has sent speaks the words of God, for God[a] gives the Spirit without limit. 35The Father loves the Son and has placed everything in his hands. 36Whoever believes in the Son has eternal life, but whoever rejects the Son will not see life, for God's wrath remains on him."[b]

[a]*34* Greek *he*   [b]*36* Some interpreters end the quotation after verse 30.

Once again, John's theology[35] of Jesus astounds us (vv. 31-36). Here we have a fully developed understanding of Jesus' divinity and sonship, as well as obedient faith in response to him. The NIV's interpretive translation of "rejects" (v. 36) leaves a bit to be desired. The word is more accurately rendered "disobey" [*apeitheō*]. Elsewhere it is translated, "not persuaded." Like its companion word "faith," it deals with a belief that leads to action (cf. James 2:20).

§ 34
Jesus Leaves
Judea for
Galilee
(Mt 4:12;
Mk 1:14a;
Lk 3:19-20;
4:14a; Jn 4:1-4)

This brief section is transitional. It bridges two of Jesus' earliest encounters — Nicodemus, the mature, educated, respected leader; and the Samaritan woman, the sinful, uneducated, foreign outsider. In the midst of such great contrast, Jesus is the golden thread that holds them together. They both needed him most of all. Moreover, this brief text moves the entire gospel narrative: (a) From emphasis on John to Jesus, (b) from ministry in Judea to Galilee, (c) from opposition of John to opposition to Jesus, (d) from Jesus' nascent ministry to his full popularity. It is a pivotal text. It is so significant that it marks the beginning of Jesus' major ministry (Lk 23:5; Acts 10:37).

Lk 3:19-20

19But when John rebuked Herod the tetrarch because of Herodias, his

---

[35]That is assuming that these are the words of John the Baptist and not John the author.

brother's wife, and all the other evil things he had done, [20]Herod added this to them all: he locked John up in prison.

Mt 4:12 *with*
Lk 4:14a

[12]When Jesus heard that John had been put in prison, he returned to Galilee {in the power of the Spirit[LK]}.

Jesus has to move from Judea to Galilee for a number of reasons. First, *John's arrest* closes his public ministry which is estimated at fourteen to eighteen months. But it also creates a danger for Jesus because of his close association with John. They are relatives, a mere six months apart in age. John has identified Jesus as the reason for his ministry. They have close "professional" ties. Furthermore, they are both practicing immersion of the same nature and preaching the same doctrine — repentance and the kingdom of God. They are two peas in a pod. Thus, Jesus flees in order to avoid a premature arrest by Herod (which later proved to be a very real danger, cf. Lk 13:31-32). But there is more to it than this. John is preaching in Salim and Aenon. Although neither site can be identified with precision, they were somewhere on the border of Samaria and Galilee. Thus, Jesus is working in southern Palestine while John concentrates on middle/upper Palestine. When John is arrested he leaves a spiritual vacuum in the area which was most open to the preaching of the kingdom. Jesus would more than fill the void left by John.

Second, Jesus was apparently *guided by the Holy Spirit*. Luke 4:14 says that "Jesus returned *in the power of the Spirit*." He understands the divine timing involved in his ministry (Jn 10:18; 13:1; 14:31). He is also aware that he is fulfilling God's predetermined plan (Jn 2:4; 7:30; 8:20; 12:23). We also remember that Galilee had been prophetically identified as the place of Jesus' ministry (Isa 9:1-2; Mt 4:14-16).

Jn 4:1-4

[1]The Pharisees heard that Jesus was gaining and baptizing more disciples than John, [2]although in fact it was not Jesus who baptized, but his disciples. [3]When the Lord learned of this, he left Judea and went back once more to Galilee.
[4]Now he had to go through Samaria.

Here is a third reason Jesus made the move from Judea to Galilee. He is likely avoiding an imminent confrontation with the Pharisees. Jesus' popularity is swelling (John 3:26). The crowds are growing, even more than they had for John. This irritated the competitive, jealous spirits of the Pharisees (cf. Mt 27:18). "The influence of the Pharisees was far greater in Judea than in Galilee, and the Sanhedrin would readily have arrested Jesus had he remained in Judea (Jn 7:1; 10:39)" (McGarvey, p. 140). Furthermore, with the arrest of John (Mt 4:12; Mk 1:14), Jesus is the sole target both of the Pharisees' aggression and the disciples' devotion.

Meanwhile, Jesus is practicing immersion. This is obviously not Christian baptism since Jesus has neither died nor risen again (cf. Rom 6:1-6). It is simply the continuation of John's baptism for remission of sins (Mk 1:4) as the entrance into the kingdom (Jn 3:5). It would later be replaced by Christian baptism as the initiation rite of the Kingdom (Mt 28:18-20; Acts 2:38; Col 2:11-12). But for now, it marks those who are willing to become like children (Lk 18:16-17) and be born again (Jn 3:5).

In a typical parenthetical comment (cf. Jn 3:24; 4:8,9b), we learn that Jesus delegates the baptismal act to his disciples (Jn 4:2). This would avoid the very controversy which later embroiled Paul in 1 Corinthians 1:14-17.

§ 35a
Jesus and the
Woman of
Samaria
(Jn 4:5-26)

In many ways, the encounter with this woman stands in comparison/contrast with Jesus' interview with Nicodemus. She was an outsider, he was an insider. He was prestigious, she was an outcast. She was ignoble, he was held in honor. The similarity of both, however, is their eager expectation of the coming Messiah. In the remainder of this chapter, John will lay out three important themes: Living Water, True Worship, and Gentile Inclusion. All three of these find their fulfillment in the person of Jesus.

We would also do well to pay attention to the "water" talk thus far in John. In chapter 1 John used water for baptism of repentance as entrance into the kingdom. In chapter 2 Jesus turned the water in the purification jars into wine, a potential foreshadowing of the new kingdom he was inaugurating. In chapter three Jesus told Nicodemus that he must be born again of water and the Holy Spirit. And now, at the well of Samaria, Jesus offers himself, the living water, to this Samaritan woman.

John has just stated in v. 4 that it was necessary [*edei*], for Jesus to pass through Samaria. Most Jews chose to return to Galilee through Perea, by crossing over the Jordan. It was longer, but it avoided the potential ceremonial defilement of the Samaritans and the very real possibility of violence because of racial tensions. Jesus, however, chooses this more direct route. He may be in a hurry to get back to Galilee (although he does tarry two days in the region, v. 40). Or he may want to avoid the Jewish crowds in Perea or Herod himself, since Perea was part of his jurisdiction. A third possibility is that Jesus senses a divine appointment with this woman and is constrained to pass through Samaria, not by political pressure but predestination.

Jn 4:5-9

[5]So he came to a town in Samaria called Sychar, near the plot of ground Jacob had given to his son Joseph. [6]Jacob's well was there, and Jesus, tired as he was from the journey, sat down by the well. It was about the sixth hour.

[7]When a Samaritan woman came to draw water, Jesus said to her, "Will you give me a drink?" [8](His disciples had gone into the town to buy food.)

[9]The Samaritan woman said to him, "You are a Jew and I am a Samaritan woman. How can you ask me for a drink?" (For Jews do not associate with Samaritans.[a])

[a]9 Or *do not use dishes Samaritans have used*

Sychar is a village (here generously called a city), about a quarter mile from Jacob's well. It is approximately thirty miles north of Jerusalem. Jesus and his crew arrive about noon. Jesus sends them into town while he rests on the well. (This is the only place we can be sure of where Jesus stood within a six foot radius.) The well is now seventy-five feet deep and only contains water in it during wet winters. It has been filled with rocks and debris. During Jesus' day it was probably over one hundred feet deep.

Jesus is all alone at the well; the disciples have run off into town to buy food. In their absence this Samaritan woman comes to draw water. Jesus asks her to get some for him. This is a shocking request because she is a woman and more than that, she is a Samaritan.[36] Men in those days did not talk to women in public, not even their wives. Furthermore, as John puts it, "Jews have no dealings with Samaritans." The verb literally means, "use together with." It often has reference to vessels. Thus, a Jew would not normally drink from the same glass as a Samaritan, which is essentially what Jesus is requesting (Hendricksen, p. 161). The fact that Jews did have some interaction with Samaritans (e.g., buying and selling,) is obvious from v. 8. Elsewhere Jesus also shows a desire to overcome prejudice (Lk 9:54-55; 10:25-37; 17:11-19), although he did class Samaritans with Gentiles (Mt 10:5), and labeled them as strangers and aliens (Lk 17:18).

Jn 4:10-15

[10]Jesus answered her, "If you knew the gift of God and who it is that asks you for a drink, you would have asked him and he would have given you living water."

[11]"Sir," the woman said, "you have nothing to draw with and the well is deep. Where can you get this living water? [12]Are you greater than our father Jacob, who gave us the well and drank from it himself, as did also his sons and his flocks and herds?"

[13]Jesus answered, "Everyone who drinks this water will be thirsty again, [14]but whoever drinks the water I give him will never thirst. Indeed, the water I give him

---

[36]J.D.M. Derrett, "The Samaritan Woman's Purity (John 4:4-52)," *EvQ* 60/4 (1988): 291-298.

will become in him a spring of water welling up to eternal life." ¹⁵The woman said to him, "Sir, give me this water so that I won't get thirsty and have to keep coming here to draw water."

Jesus now really grabs her attention with a couple of hypothetical subjunctives, "If you really knew who I was you would ask me for living water." This phrase, "living water," was used of springs, creeks and rivers. It signified water that ran rather than just stood in a cistern or a well (Gen 26:19; Lev 14:5). She takes Jesus literally. "You have nothing to draw with and the well is deep," she replied. It is obvious that Jesus could not get living water for her out of this well. However, there were a number of springs in the area. Perhaps she thought this newcomer knew of an especially delicious source of water. From our vantage point, we realize that Jesus was speaking of spiritual things, especially relating to the Holy Spirit (Jn 7:37-39).

Jacob, the great Jewish patriarch, worked hard to dig this deep well. It went through rock and tapped into a natural spring deep in the ground. It was a great source of pure, cool water. Surely this stranger is no match for Jacob (v. 12)! But Jesus audaciously claims that he can do better. His water permanently quenches your thirst. Furthermore, this living water becomes an internal spring. The fountain it produces is none other than eternal life. Obviously, their conversation began at Jacob's well but is quickly scaling the heights of heaven.

Unfortunately, she is not ready for such sublime refreshment. She would be satisfied if she didn't have to lug a water jar in and out of town day after day. She says, "Give me this water so that I may not get thirsty nor have to *keep coming* so far" [present subjunctive]. It was only about a ten minute walk but pretty wearisome with a full jug of water day in and day out. We can almost read into her comment the words, "All right buddy, prove yourself!" So he does, and it is more than she bargained for.

Jn 4:16-18

¹⁶He told her, "Go, call your husband and come back."
¹⁷"I have no husband," she replied.
Jesus said to her, "You are right when you say you have no husband. ¹⁸The fact is, you have had five husbands, and the man you now have is not your husband. What you have just said is quite true."

Why would Jesus now ask her to go call her husband? Is Jesus calling her to submit to her husband's spiritual leadership? Is he calling her to repent of her sinfulness? Is he allowing the reader to understand his love for the sinful? Is he seizing the opportunity to demonstrate his omniscience? Whatever his motives [we understand here the tenuous nature of psychoanalyzing a historical figure], Jesus effectively grabs her attention and draws her to himself. Because Jesus knew her previous life, she was convinced that he could deliver on this living water stuff.

> Very abrupt is the woman's answer. She, who has been so very talkative (note 4:11, 12, 15), suddenly becomes close-mouthed. It is interesting to count the number of words in her various replies: according to the Greek in verse nine she uses 11 words . . . in verse fifteen, 13 words . . . in verses eleven and twelve, 42 words . . . but in verse seventeen, only 3 words: "not I-have husband" (Hendriksen, p. 164).

Jesus apparently hit a sensitive button. Then he calls further attention to it by placing the word "husband" at the beginning of the sentence, giving it an extra punch.

It is not so surprising that she has had five husbands. Divorce was especially common among the Romans of the day who generally kept a wife at home and a mistress for social events. Even the Jews, following the liberal teachings of Hillel, divorced their wives with alarming regularity. Hillel even permitted divorce "if she burnt his dinner while cooking." The Samaritan ethic of marriage was likely somewhere in between that of the Romans and that of the Jews.

Jn 4:19-26

[19]"Sir," the woman said, "I can see that you are a prophet. [20]Our fathers worshiped on this mountain, but you Jews claim that the place where we must worship is in Jerusalem."

[21]Jesus declared, "Believe me, woman, a time is coming when you will worship the Father neither on this mountain nor in Jerusalem. [22]You Samaritans worship what you do not know; we worship what we do know, for salvation is from the Jews. [23]Yet a time is coming and has now come when the true worshipers will worship the Father in spirit and truth, for they are the kind of worshipers the Father seeks. [24]God is spirit, and his worshipers must worship in spirit and in truth."

[25]The woman said, "I know that Messiah" (called Christ) "is coming. When he comes, he will explain everything to us."

[26]Then Jesus declared, "I who speak to you am he."

Jesus peers into her private past. She quickly confesses Jesus is a prophet. This much is obvious. But she now diverts the conversation from her sinful life to a raging theological debate — the proper place of worship. Some have accused her of just wanting to hide from her sin. But her motives may be deeper than that. Suppose you met a prophet who could tell all the secrets of your life. What kind of questions would you ask? It seems entirely appropriate that this Samaritan questions Jesus about this most controversial issue between the Jews and her people.

The question is all the more provocative when we realize that they were standing at the base of Mt. Gerizim, 1050' below the site of the old temple. With a sweep of her hand, she could actually point to the rubble of the ancient Samaritan temple which had been destroyed in 127 B.C. by another Jerusalem Jew, John Hyrcanus.[37] This was a "hot-button" for her people.

According to the Jews, Jerusalem was the only God-ordained place of worship (Deut 12:5-11; 1 Kgs 9:3; 2 Chr 3:1). According to the Samaritans it was Gerizim.[38]

Both Jews and Samaritans erred in thinking that worship was a specific deed done with the body at a certain locale rather than a heart bent on knowing and loving God. Jesus now introduces a new relationship with God (Jer 31:31-34; Heb 8:8-12), where the Spirit of God and the spirit of man commingle (1 Cor 2:10-14; 6:19).

Indeed, salvation is from the Jews: Psalm 147:19-20; Isaiah 2:3; Amos 3:2; Micah 4:1-2; Romans 3:1-2; 9:3-5, 18. A time is coming quickly, however, when the temple veil will be torn asunder (Mt 27:51), and salvation will be for all peoples (Acts 10:34-35). The emphasis will shift from the place to a person. The people of God will realize that God does not need a temple built with human hands (Acts 7:48; 17:24).

"God is Spirit."[39] Theology flows from the lips of Jesus in simple chunks that children can get a hold of but that theologians cannot fathom. Such is this little nugget of truth. It answers so many questions about the nature of God and yet leads us to just as many more.

She doesn't know how to respond to Jesus. He has her pinned. So she just blows it off saying, "Well, the Messiah will make it all clear to us." So Jesus said: "Lady, I am the Messiah." It would be another two years before Jesus is this clear again about his identity (Mt 16:16-18).

---

[37]R.J. Bull, "Archaeological Context for Understanding John 4:20," *BA* 38 (May 1975): 54-60.

[38]McGarvey (p. 147) enumerates the reasons the Samaritans put forth for Gerizim being the proper place of worship: "(1) Here God appeared to Abraham for the first time after his entering Canaan (Gen 7:6-7). (2) Here Jacob first dwelt (Gen 33:18). (3) Here Joseph came seeking his brethren (Gen 37:12-13). (4) Here was a city of refuge (Josh 20:7-9). (5) Here Joshua read the blessings and cursings (Josh 8:33). (6) Here also he gave his last address (Josh 24:1). (7) Here were buried the bones of Joseph (Josh 24:32). And (8) the neighborhood was prominent at the time of the division of the ten tribes (1 Kgs 12:1, 25)." In addition, modern Samaritan tradition also attributes to Gerizim: Paradise on its summit, the dust from which Adam was formed, first altar built by Adam, Seth and Noah; the resting place of the Ark, and the only place the flood did not cover and thus the only place not defiled by dead bodies; the place where Abraham met Melchizedek and later offered up Isaac, and the true locale of Bethel (McGarvey, p. 147-148).

[39]God is also described as light (1 John 1:5); love (1 John 4:8, 16); and fire (Heb 12:29).

He knows the Samaritans are not going to force him to be a political Messiah (cf. Jn 6:15). Furthermore, since he is only going to be there for two days he is able to be a bit more forward. The Samaritans did, indeed, have a high Messianic expectation (Acts 8:9; Josephus, *Ant.* 18. 85), as is evidenced by their response.

§ 35b
The Harvest is
Ripe
(Jn 4:27-38)

[27]Just then his disciples returned and were surprised to find him talking with a woman. But no one asked, "What do you want?" or "Why are you talking with her?"

[28]Then, leaving her water jar, the woman went back to the town and said to the people, [29]"Come, see a man who told me everything I ever did. Could this be the Christ[a]?" [30]They came out of the town and made their way toward him.

[a]*29* Or *Messiah*

The disciples return with supper. They are amazed, naturally, that Jesus is talking to this woman. But no one says anything. In the past nine to ten months, they have learned that Jesus knows what he is doing. Although he is acting oddly, they trust his decision. Or else they don't have the guts to confront him about it.

There is much speculation about why the woman left her water pot. Most say that she was just so enraptured in the discussion with Jesus, that she forgot it. However, it is possible that she has drawn the water and left it there with the Messiah, giving him the drink he asked her for (v. 7).

She runs into town with natural exuberance (which is the normal response to meeting Jesus). Knowing that a woman in her culture, especially one of her reputation, will not be very convincing, she opens with a winsome comment: "Come see a man who told me all the things that I have done." Now that would generate a good deal of interest. Why, a woman of her reputation must have done some "juicy" things worth hearing about.

As far as we know, Jesus had not actually told her *everything* she had done. But he did cover the entire span of her adult life. That was enough to convince her that he knew her thoroughly. She then asks the crowd, "This is not the Christ, is it?" She phrases it in such a way as to expect a negative answer. She really knows how to grab a man's attention (which might be concluded by her marital experience). They left the town in droves to see Jesus. But notice, too, this woman's progressive awareness of who Jesus is: Verse 9 — "Jew;" 11 — "Sir [Lord];" 19 — "Prophet;" 29 — "Christ."

Jn 4:31-38

[31]Meanwhile his disciples urged him, "Rabbi, eat something."
[32]But he said to them, "I have food to eat that you know nothing about."

[33]Then his disciples said to each other, "Could someone have brought him food?"

[34]"My food," said Jesus, "is to do the will of him who sent me and to finish his work. [35]Do you not say, 'Four months more and then the harvest'? I tell you, open your eyes and look at the fields! They are ripe for harvest. [36]Even now the reaper draws his wages, even now he harvests the crop for eternal life, so that the sower and the reaper may be glad together. [37]Thus the saying 'One sows and another reaps' is true. [38]I sent you to reap what you have not worked for. Others have done the hard work, and you have reaped the benefits of their labor."

Meanwhile the disciples offer Jesus some food, which he refuses. It is likely that Jesus' natural hunger is overcome by his excitement at his first clear declaration of his Messiahship. The disciples, thinking in terms of the flesh, misunderstand Jesus. The woman got confused about spiritual water; these fellows get confused about spiritual food. Jesus starts to teach them about spiritual food, but there just isn't enough time. Here comes the crowd.

It was December (or early January), and the spring harvest was still four months away.[40] But Jesus says "Look, the fields are white." As they did, perhaps they saw the white cloaked Samaritans marching across the green fields to meet this potential Messiah. The harvest indeed was plentiful (cf. Mt 9:37-38; Lk 10:2).

"He who sows and he who reaps may rejoice together" is an allusion to Amos 9:13. This passage describes the joy of the Messianic era when the harvest is so fruitful and so sudden that the sower and the reaper work alongside one another.[41] "One sows, and another reaps." Jesus is clearly calling the disciples to reap, but who have been the sowers? Answer: Moses, Prophets, John the Baptist, Jesus, and even the Samaritan woman.

§ 35c
Sychar
Submits to
Christ
(Jn 4:39-42)

[39]Many of the Samaritans from that town believed in him because of the woman's testimony, "He told me everything I ever did." [40]So when the Samaritans came to him, they urged him to stay with them, and he stayed two days. [41]And because of his words many more became believers. [42]They said to the woman, "We no longer believe just because of what you said; now we have heard for ourselves, and we know that this man really is the Savior of the world."

---

[40]A.W. Argyle, "A Note on John 4:35," *ExpT* 82 (1971): 247-248, suggests that John 4:35 is "a perfect iambic line" and thus proverbial poetry. Jesus may have been quoting a common proverb from some unknown Greek source. But it is also perfectly possible that Jesus, familiar with Greek verse, composed it himself.

[41]Amos 9:11-12 is clearly applied to the Christian era in Acts 15:16-17. It seems logical to assume that Amos 9:13-14 are in a similar context of the nascent Church, especially in light of Jesus' words here.

Because of the testimony of this woman, many in Sychar believe in Jesus. They prevail on him to stay another two days. During this time even more people believe in him.

We don't know just how deep and how mature their faith is, but they do call him the "Savior of the world" (cf. Mt 1:21; Lk 2:11; Acts 5:31; 13:23; Phil 3:20; Eph 5:23; Titus 1:4; 2:13; 3:6; 2 Tim 1:10; 2 Peter 1:1, 11; 2:20; 3:2, 18). There will be others who apprehend the Christ in such a short period of time. When your heart is open, it does not take long to see Jesus for who he is (Mt 8:5-13; Mk 15:39; Lk 1:42; Jn 1:49; Acts 16:31-34).

McGarvey notes that this text breaks down three formidable walls: (1) Racial prejudice; (2) Gender — Jesus endorses this woman's fitness to receive spiritual instruction and even her suitability to announce his presence and position; (3) Moral rectitude. Jesus has indeed come to save the least and the lost.

PART SIX
GALILEAN MINISTRY
December, A.D. 27—April, A.D. 29

Jesus only spent two days in Samaria but reaped a great harvest. His converts in Galilee will not come so easily but they are still more receptive than the crowd in Judea.

When we think of Jesus' life and deeds, we mostly remember what he did in Galilee (Mt 4:12-15:20; Mk 1:14-7:23; Lk 4:14-9:17; Jn 4:46-54; 6:1-71). This is the classic Jesus. Here in this multi-ethnic, rugged, rural area Jesus will call eleven of his twelve disciples, preach the Sermon on the Mount, do most of his famous miracles, feed the thousands, walk on water, set up "home-base" in Capernaum, and many other wondrous works. The country of Galilee is only surpassed in beauty and productivity by the Lord who ministered there. It has been more than a year since Jesus left Galilee to be baptized by John (Mt 3:13; Mk 1:9). Now, after eight to nine months of ministry in Judea, Jesus returns once more to his homeland.

§ 36
Jesus Returns
to Galilee
(Jn 4:43-45)

[43]After the two days he left for Galilee. [44](Now Jesus himself had pointed out that a prophet has no honor in his own country.) [45]When he arrived in Galilee, the Galileans welcomed him. They had seen all that he had done in Jerusalem at the Passover Feast, for they also had been there.

Since "A prophet has no honor in his own country" (Lk 4:24), Jesus first gained fame in Judea (Jn 2:23; 3:26; 4:1), not only by cleansing the temple (Jn 2:13-22), but also by performing many miracles (Jn 2:23). Many of these Galileans were no doubt at the feast when Jesus went nose to nose with Annas' power block . . . and won! He would be the local hero. Small town boy goes to the big city and beats up the big-wigs. The Galileans certainly would have been among the earliest believers mentioned by John (2:23). Now that he comes to Galilee with a little fame under his belt, his own people are willing to receive him. [NOTE: Jesus was known as a Galilean — Jn 1:46; 7:41-52; Lk 23:5-7.]

Jesus is still not ready, however, to tackle his hometown of Nazareth (Mt 13:58; Lk 4:22-31). In fact, both times Jesus has returned to Galilee, he ministers first in Cana: At the wedding (Jn 2:1-11) and the healing of the nobleman's son (Jn 4:46-54). Luke 4:15 also hints at an itinerant ministry of Jesus in Galilee prior to his return to Nazareth (4:16-31). We will notice a shift in Jesus' Galilean ministry from Cana (Jn 4:45-54), to Nazareth (Lk 4:16-30), to Capernaum (Mt 4:13-17; Lk 4:31).

§ 37
The Nature of
Jesus' Galilean
Ministry
(Mk 1:14b-15
with Mt 4:17;
Lk 4:14b-15)

{¹⁷From that time on Jesus began to preach,ᴹᵀ} ¹⁴. . . proclaiming the good news of God, ¹⁵"The time has come," he said. "The kingdom of God {heavenᴹᵀ} is near. Repent and believe the good news."

¹⁴. . . and news about him spread through the whole countryside. ¹⁵He taught in their synagogues, and everyone praised him.

From section 34 we learned that Jesus left Judea for three reasons: (1) Political pressure of the Pharisees (Jn 4:1); (2) John the Baptist was thrown in prison by Herod (Mt 4:12; Mk 1:14; Lk 3:19-20); and (3) Jesus was influenced by the Holy Spirit (Lk 4:14). John adds to the Synoptics two important encounters at this point: The Samaritan woman (Jn 4:5-42) and the nobleman's son (Jn 4:46-54). These episodes show us that Jesus, as he moves into Galilee, ministers to all kinds of people, not just the religious "right."

Jesus' ministry was on a divine timetable. Jesus recognized that it was the right time for him to make this move to Galilee (Mk 1:15), not merely because of the volatile socio-political climate of Judea, but perhaps also in fulfillment of prophecy. Daniel 9:24-27 predicts that the Messiah would be revealed at the beginning of the seventieth week. Most commentators agree that each day is to be reckoned as a full year. Thus the seventy weeks equals four hundred and ninety years. Hence, the Messiah was to be revealed four hundred and eighty-three years after the prophecy was given, which was likely B.C. 457 (cf. Ezra 7). This would put the inauguration of the Messianic ministry at A.D. 26 — right on schedule. This is another one of many Messianic prophecies that point precisely to Jesus of Nazareth.

Two things strike us about Jesus' early preaching. First, his message was identical to John the Baptist's: "Repent for the kingdom of heaven is at hand." It was a simple message and it was a joyous announcement. It was the "good news" (Gk = gospel) that the reign of God was invading the realm of men. Second, we are struck with the eager reception of Jesus. The Galileans *loved* him. In synagogue after synagogue, the excitement of Jesus emanated out to the rural communities.

§ 38
Jesus in Cana
Heals the
Nobleman's
Son at
Capernaum
(Jn 4:46-54)

Jesus now performs his second identified miracle. Again, it is in Cana of Galilee, the hometown of Nathanael. Many commentators have compared this miracle to the healing of the centurion's servant (Mt 8:1, 5-13; Lk 7:1-10).[1] There are several similarities: (1) Jesus is entreated to heal a beloved son/servant. (2) Jesus performs the healing from a distance. (3) The city of Capernaum is involved. There are several significant differences here, however: (1) Jesus was in Cana as opposed to Capernaum (Lk 7:1). (2) The nobleman asked Jesus to come to his house, the centurion discouraged it. (3) Jewish elders entreated Jesus on behalf of the centurion, a Gentile. (4) Jesus commends the centurion's faith but rebukes the nobleman for seeking a sign. Although the narratives may look similar, their general tone, time, and purpose are different. The point of the centurion narrative is to demonstrate his great faith in Jesus. The point of the nobleman narrative is to demonstrate Jesus' rising popularity and the faith which his miracles generated.

Jn 4:46-48

[46]Once more he visited Cana in Galilee, where he had turned the water into wine. And there was a certain royal official whose son lay sick at Capernaum. [47]When this man heard that Jesus had arrived in Galilee from Judea, he went to him and begged him to come and heal his son, who was close to death.
[48]"Unless you people see miraculous signs and wonders," Jesus told him, "you will never believe."

This royal official is quite possibly a servant of Herod Antipas. At least Josephus uses this same word some six hundred times to designate a servant of Herod. We find other noble servants of Herod in the NT such as Cuza (Lk 8:3) and Manaen (Acts 12:1), who are, perhaps, co-laborers with this man. "It is possible that the official was a Gentile. If so, the three persons Jesus interviewed in this early ministry represented the Jews, the Samaritans, and the Gentiles — in short, the world he came to save" (Tenney, p. 60). Whoever he is, he is acting within the cultural belief that this famed rabbi has powerful prayers. We note, however, that the nobleman's faith goes beyond asking for prayer for healing. He asks Jesus to come down to his house and act as a miracle-worker.

In response to his request, Jesus rebukes him and the crowd (note the plural), for seeking a sign. This won't be the last time Jesus shows disdain for miracle-mongers (cf. Mt 11:20-24). Jesus wants us to believe in him for who he is, not just for what he does (Jn 10:38; 14:11; 15:22-24; 20:29). Miracles are evidence of Jesus' identity. They were even used to bolster the faith of John the Baptist (Mt 11:4-5), but they will

---

[1]Even such great commentators as Origen, Chrysostom, Irenaeus and Eusebius have at least partially represented these two narratives as one and the same event.

never satisfy the insatiable curiosity of thrill-seekers, nor will they force faith on those who refuse to submit to Jesus (Mt 12:38-45). How disappointing this must be for Jesus to come down from Sychar of Samaria, where they flocked to him because of his words alone, unto Galilee, his own people, who demand a circus show.

Why does Jesus rebuke this poor man for a lack of faith? Isn't that a bit harsh? After all, his son is on his deathbed and he comes to Jesus begging for some divine help. But his faith falls short in two ways. First, he assumes that Jesus has to come to his house to heal the boy. Second, he only believes that Jesus can heal the boy, not raise him from the dead. We must also remember that Jesus does not rebuke this man alone, but the entire crowd. Perhaps something in their expressions reveals their delight that Jesus would do yet another sign. Before we get too critical of Jesus, we should note that he did, in fact, heal the boy!

Jn 4:49-54

[49]The royal official said, "Sir, come down before my child dies."

[50]Jesus replied, "You may go. Your son will live."

The man took Jesus at his word and departed. [51]While he was still on the way, his servants met him with the news that his boy was living. [52]When he inquired as to the time when his son got better, they said to him, "The fever left him yesterday at the seventh hour."

[53]Then the father realized that this was the exact time at which Jesus had said to him, "Your son will live." So he and all his household believed.

[54]This was the second miraculous sign that Jesus performed, having come from Judea to Galilee.

This nobleman is urgent. He pleads for help. Jesus responds to this urgent father. He heals the child from about twenty miles away. Likewise, the nobleman responds to Jesus. He takes Jesus at his word and starts off toward Capernaum.

The boy's fever broke about 1 p.m. The servants keep a close eye on him through the night. By morning it's obvious that the lad is going to be all right. These servants are so excited, they can't wait for their master's return. They run out to meet him halfway. Meanwhile, the nobleman has spent the night somewhere along the twenty mile trek from Cana to Capernaum.[2] Sometime the next morning he meets his happy band of servants. They've got good news! His child is healed. The father naturally verified the time at which the fever broke. It coincided precisely with the

---

[2]Since it is only 1 p.m. and twenty miles from Capernaum, we wonder why this father didn't make it home the same day his son was healed. Perhaps he was so confident in Jesus' power that he takes his time returning. Perhaps the servants do meet him that same evening along the road but since the sun has already set they consider it a new day. Most likely, however, the nobleman just got delayed along the way somehow.

time at which Jesus gave the declaration that the child was healed.

There is no way for this to be psychosomatic, nor much likelihood of coincidence. Not only does he believe, but so does his entire household. (For other household conversions cf. Acts 10:23-26; 16:14-15, 34; 18:8).

§ 39
Jesus' Rejection
at Nazareth
(Luke 4:16-31a)

Jesus has been away from Nazareth for almost a year now. He has been baptized by John, spent forty days and nights in the desert being tempted by Satan, attracted his first few followers, performed a miracle in Cana, cleansed the temple during the Passover, performed a number of miracles, and spent eight to nine months gaining disciples and baptizing in Judea. He now returns to his home county, but not his home. His preaching tour takes him through several cities and synagogues, including Cana where he heals the nobleman's son. Preaching was popular, and a popular preacher was followed. Such is the case with Jesus. His intrigue is spreading throughout the region.

He now returns to the town where he was "brought up" (v. 16), or better, "nurtured" [Gk. perfect participle]. Not only did Jesus grow up here, but here he was nourished, nurtured and matured. Here he went to school, learned a trade, competed in sports, etc. He was the hometown boy, making it big.

Lk 4:16-21

¹⁶He went to Nazareth, where he had been brought up, and on the Sabbath day he went into the synagogue, as was his custom. And he stood up to read. ¹⁷The scroll of the prophet Isaiah was handed to him. Unrolling it, he found the place where it is written:
¹⁸"The Spirit of the Lord is on me,
    because he has anointed me
    to preach good news to the poor.
He has sent me to proclaim freedom for the prisoners
    and recovery of sight for the blind,
to release the oppressed,
¹⁹   to proclaim the year of the Lord's favor."[a]
²⁰Then he rolled up the scroll, gave it back to the attendant and sat down. The eyes of everyone in the synagogue were fastened on him, ²¹and he began by saying to them, "Today this scripture is fulfilled in your hearing."

[a]*19* Isaiah 61:1,2

Jesus made a practice of being at the synagogue worship each week. When he returns to his home turf, we are not surprised to see him in the synagogue. All eyes were on him. We can just imagine the elders reminiscing about what a fine student Jesus was in Sabbath School. Naturally, Jesus is the guest preacher for the day.

From a Jewish standpoint all this is very normal. The preacher would stand up to read the Scripture and then sit down to teach the people. That is exactly what Jesus does (vv. 16, 20; cf. Mt 5:1; Mk 4:1; Jn 8:2). Furthermore, each synagogue service consisted of two parts: Liturgy and Teaching. The liturgy was a series of prayers and recitations, followed by the teaching. The teaching consisted of a series of seven readings, each no less than three verses, followed by a sermon. The readings from the Law apparently followed a three year cycle. The selection from the prophets was likely up to the preacher (Nolland, p. 194). Hence, Jesus turns to his own chosen sermon text.

The sermon was expected to be Biblically accurate, precise, and somewhat interesting from a literary point of view. Afterward the congregation was allowed to ask questions of the speaker. The sermon was normally given by a trained rabbi, but a prominent visitor, such as Jesus, might also be asked to speak.

Jesus selects a passage from Isaiah 61:1-2. It clearly describes the ministry of the Messiah. In fact the word "anoint" was originally the root of the word "Messiah." Jesus' audience can hardly miss that.

His ministry is described in several ways:

(1) Led by/Filled with the Spirit
(2) Release the Oppressed — literally "those who have been broken in pieces." Jesus releases shattered lives from the oppression they have experienced. He is gentle and kind for those who are hurting. Isaiah 61:2 adds, "To comfort all who mourn."
(3) Miracle Working — healing the blind
(4) Proclaiming Lord's Favor — literally "the acceptable year of the Lord." This infers the year of Jubilee, Leviticus 25:8-17, when all things were returned or released to their original owners. The year of Jubilee, every fiftieth year, is a picture of what Jesus did for us at Calvary. The Jubilee is the Messianic reign.

All eyes were *fastened* on him (v. 20). This word, in its other uses, carries extreme emotion. People loved good preaching. And Jesus, in the few short months that he had been away, had gained quite a reputation as a preacher. Rumors were beginning to spread about him being the Messiah. What is he going to say? In the crowd are feelings of anticipation, pride, jealousy, friendship, and superiority. Watch closely as Jesus meets their expectations head-on.

Jesus hands the scroll back to the attendant,[3] and begins to teach. **"Today this scripture has been fulfilled in your hearing (v. 21)"** This

---

[3]This person, called the *chazzan*, was paid staff of the synagogue. He was somewhere between our minister and janitor. He had charge over all the sacred duties and articles, including the scrolls.

verb, "fulfilled," is in the perfect tense, indicating completed past action. This prophecy was not fulfilled as they watched, but it had already been fulfilled and they were looking at it in the person of Jesus. We can hardly understand how audacious this claim must have appeared to these simple folks of Nazareth. This is only the first sentence of his sermon. The rest was regretably left unrecorded.

Lk 4:22-27

²²All spoke well of him and were amazed at the gracious words that came from his lips. "Isn't this Joseph's son?" they asked.

²³Jesus said to them, "Surely you will quote this proverb to me: 'Physician, heal yourself! Do here in your hometown what we have heard that you did in Capernaum.'"

²⁴"I tell you the truth," he continued, "no prophet is accepted in his hometown. ²⁵I assure you that there were many widows in Israel in Elijah's time, when the sky was shut for three and a half years and there was a severe famine throughout the land. ²⁶Yet Elijah was not sent to any of them, but to a widow in Zarephath in the region of Sidon. ²⁷And there were many in Israel with leprosy[a] in the time of Elisha the prophet, yet not one of them was cleansed — only Naaman the Syrian."

[a]27 The Greek word was used for various diseases affecting the skin—not necessarily leprosy.

The NIV translates v. 22 interpretively, "All spoke well of him." Luke literally says, "They testified about him." The word "witness" [*martyreō*] does not necessarily mean "to approve of" but merely to "attest to." This is especially true since it is connected with "amaze" [*thaumazō*], which always falls short of genuine faith.[4] The bottom line is that these people are talking *about* Jesus but they were not committed *to* Jesus. They are impressed with his preaching ability, but infuriated by the message he brings. That explains how their "testimony" can so quickly turn to hostility (vv. 28-29).

"Isn't this Joseph's son?" Of course it is; everyone knew that! They know this guy. He sure sounds good. Where did all that wisdom come from all of a sudden? This may even be a reflection of the plain simple nature of his stepfather.

Jesus now reminds them of this famous proverb, "Physician heal thyself" (v. 23). Jesus had apparently already done several miracles in Capernaum and the locals want a repeat performance. It is common for a plumber to have leaky faucets and a mechanic to have a car that will

---

[4]John Nolland, "Impressed Unbelievers as Witnesses to Christ," *JBL* 98/2 (1979): 219-229. He also demonstrates that Luke frequently cites testimony about Jesus from those who do not believe (p. 226). Rhetorically, they serve as "unbiased" witnesses to Jesus' powerful preaching.

barely run. They practice their trades very well . . . elsewhere. This is basically the idea of this parable. Jesus predicts that his people will say, "You did all these wonderful miracles in other cities, why not here in your hometown?" The answer is given the next and final time that Jesus returns to Nazareth: He did no mighty miracles there because of their unbelief (Mk 6:5-6).

This reminds us of the jeering mob at the foot of the cross. They said, "He saved others; let him save himself if he is the Christ of God, the Chosen One" (Lk 23:35). The soldiers also, and even the criminal hung next to him, made similar remarks (Lk 23:36-39). All this was prophesied in Psalm 22:8.

Jesus counters their saying with his own (v. 24): No prophet is welcome in his own country. The truth of his parable demonstrates the falsehood of theirs. They claim that charity begins at home. But the fact is, Jesus offers "charity" but it is refused. How many times was Jesus rejected by his own people? "He came to that which was his own, but his own did not receive him" (Jn 1:11). John has already used this parable to explain why Jesus did not immediately return to Nazareth (Jn 4:43-45). Not only does Jesus make this claim but he is about to illustrate the truth with events from the lives of two prominent prophets (vv. 25-27): Elijah and Elisha.

This sets up a pattern that will continue throughout the early years of the church. Jesus goes to his own, they reject him, he turns to others. We see him extolling the faith of the Gentile centurion (Lk 7:1-10); we see him leaving Nazareth for Capernaum (Mt 4:13); we see him on the brow of the hill overlooking Jerusalem, lamenting their rejection of their Messiah (Mt 23:37). Time and time again, Jesus was rejected and thus he turned away. In like manner, the book of Acts records the Apostles taking Jesus to the Jews, being rejected and then turning to the Gentiles. This was especially true of Paul's journeys. In every town he entered he first went to the synagogue and preached Jesus. When he was rejected there, he turned to the Gentiles. Charity would have begun in Nazareth had they accepted Jesus.[5]

The story of Elijah and the widow can be read in 1 Kings 17:1-16. The point is this: Because the Jews rejected Elijah the prophet, he was sent to help a Gentile widow. The story of Elisha and Naaman can be read in 2 Kings 5:1-14. The point is this: The Jews rejected Elisha the prophet, and he healed a Gentile leper and not a Jewish one. Likewise,

---

[5]L.C. Crockett, "Luke 4:25-27 and Jewish-Gentile Relations in Luke-Acts, *JBL* 88 (1969): 177-183, suggests that the emphasis of this passage is not the rejection of the Jews but the inclusion of the Gentiles (cf. Acts 13:46), and the future reconciliation of Jews and Gentiles in the church.

Jesus is being rejected by his own people, and he also is going to go and minister to foreign fields.

Lk 4:28-31a

[28]All the people in the synagogue were furious when they heard this. [29]They got up, drove him out of the town, and took him to the brow of the hill on which the town was built, in order to throw him down the cliff. [30]But he walked right through the crowd and went on his way.
[31]Then he went down to Capernaum, a town in Galilee.

The crowd is furious. This seems to be the typical reaction when the Jews heard anything nice about the Gentiles. They had been raised believing that God created Gentiles to fuel the flames of hell. Paul got in trouble for the same thing (Acts 22:21).

It would be interesting to know the choreography of the event that followed (vv. 29-30). Did they force Jesus up the hill? Or did he go willingly? Was it a miracle that he passed through their midst? Or did his righteousness keep them from touching him? If it was a miracle, did he just disappear or did he overpower them or did they become paralyzed?

This much we do know, no one takes the life of the Son of Man. He lays it down. It was not yet time for him to die. There would be other times when they would try to lay their hands on him (Jn 7:30; 10:39), even violently (Jn 8:59; 10:31). No one would touch him until the time had come and he submitted to it.

**§ 40
Jesus Moves
to Capernaum**
(Mt 4:13-16)

[13]Leaving Nazareth, he went and lived in Capernaum, which was by the lake in the area of Zebulun and Naphtali — [14]to fulfill what was said through the prophet Isaiah:
[15]"Land of Zebulun and land of Naphtali,
    the way to the sea, along the Jordan,
Galilee of the Gentiles —
[16]the people living in darkness
    have seen a great light;
on those living in the land of the shadow of death
    a light has dawned."[a]

[a]*16* Isaiah 9:1,2

This is a significant move for Jesus. Capernaum, being a larger city, offers Jesus more visibility and opportunity to preach. His move also demonstrates the thorough rejection of Jesus in Nazareth. For the next year or more, Capernaum will be the "headquarters" of Jesus' campaigns. It is located on the northwest corner of the sea of Galilee and provides a multicultural commercial center for Jesus' preaching.

Prior to the Assyrian captivity of 722 B.C., this area was allotted to the tribes of Zebulun and Naphtali. It was taken over by foreigners after

Israel was deported. Even in Jesus' day it was up to 50% Gentile (Blomberg, p. 88). McGarvey says that it was "called Galilee of the Gentiles because it was, according to Strabo and others, inhabited by Egyptians, Arabians, and Phoenicians, as well as by Hebrews" (p. 160). Isaiah 9:1-2 predicts Galilee's future blessing.[6] Into a culture of darkness comes Jesus, the light of the world (Jn 1:4-5, 9; 3:19; 7:52).

§ 41
Jesus Calls
Four Fisherman
(Mt 4:18-22;
Mk 1:16-20;
Lk 5:1-11)[7]

This is obviously a significant event for the disciples, but it was also a significant event for the early church. Their experience of following Jesus is mirrored in these four fisherman. For many Christians, Jesus' call to become "fishers of men," mixed with fear and worship, is all very familiar.

Furthermore, this incident shows that Jesus not only fraternized with the working class, but used them significantly in the propagation of the kingdom. While their "doctrinal faith" leaves much to be desired, their "practical faith" is exemplary. In other words, what they believe about Jesus turns out to be wrong; but their trust *in* Jesus is right on!

From this event comes the Christian acrostic of the fish. The Greek word for fish is *ichthys*. Each of the five Greek letters stand for the beginning of the following words: Jesus, Christ, God, Son, Savior. It was the secret password for the catacomb worship services. Christian theology is summarized in this symbol.

Mt 4:18 *with*
Lk 5:1a

{One day[LK]} [18]As Jesus was walking beside the Sea of Galilee he saw two brothers, Simon called Peter and his brother Andrew. They were casting a net into the lake, for they were fishermen.

Lk 5:1b-3

[1]. . . as Jesus was standing by the Lake of Gennesaret,[a] with the people crowding around him and listening to the word of God, [2]he saw at the water's edge two boats, left there by the fishermen, who were washing their nets. [3]He got into one of the boats, the one belonging to Simon, and asked him to put out a little from shore. Then he sat down and taught the people from the boat.

[a]*1* That is, Sea of Galilee

---

[6] This is one of the few places where the NT quote is closer to the Masoretic Text than to the LXX (see Archer & Chirichigno, *O.T. Quotations in the N.T.*, p. 98).

[7]There are significant differences between Luke's rendition of the call of the fishermen and that of Matthew and Mark. This has led many harmonists to view them as two separate events. However, we will place them together here since their details can be adequately harmonized and since it would not be likely that Jesus twice calls Peter to leave his vocation. However, this is one of the few places where we take Luke out of order. We should observe that Luke places this incident after Jesus' ministry in Capernaum (4:31-37), healing Peter's mother-in-law (4:38-41), and the first Galilean tour (4:42-44).

Jesus calls these four men — two pairs of brothers, all aligned with their fishing business — Peter, Andrew, James and John. They worked on what is generally called the Sea of Galilee (also called Gennesaret, Chinneroth, or the Sea of Tiberias). But it is actually a lake, not a sea. It is shaped like a pear, twelve miles from north to south and seven miles across at its widest. Oddly, it sits in a basin six hundred and eighty-two feet below sea level, surrounded by a perimeter of one-thousand-foot hills, and it is teeming with fish.

Fishing was one of the three great industries of Palestine along with agriculture and shepherding. It was a lucrative business on this lake. A typically rabbinic exaggeration states that there were three hundred different kinds of fish in the Sea of Galilee. Edersheim describes several such rabbinic teachings about fish, including how to prepare them (I:473). Certainly, fishing was big business in Palestine. Even one of the gates of Jerusalem was called the "Fish Gate" (Neh 3:3).

As Jesus walks along the shore, the fishermen are cleaning their nets after working unproductively all night (Lk 5:5). This was the bane of their work — meticulously cleaning out the pebbles, grasses and sand which had tangled themselves in their nets and repairing the torn strands after heavy use all night.

Simon and Andrew are the first Jesus encounters. They are casting their nets into the lake. This is the only time this kind of net [*amphiblēstron*], is mentioned in the Bible. This was a relatively small net which was cast into the water and sunk whatever was below it. It would then be drawn up and whatever was in its "bell" would be taken in. The second kind of net mentioned in the Bible was the *sagēnē* — a drag net that was pulled behind the boat (only used in Mt 13:47). The most common net was the *diktya*, also mentioned twice in our passage. It was the normal casting net. These larger nets are being cleaned while one of these guys is fooling around in the shallows with the *amphiblēstron*, trying to redeem their night of catching nothing.

The crowds press in on Jesus. He is already so popular that he cannot move about freely. Mobbed like a movie star, Jesus employs Peter's empty fishing boat as a pulpit and uses the shore as an amphitheater.

Lk 5:4-7

⁴When he had finished speaking, he said to Simon, "Put out into deep water, and let down[a] the nets for a catch."

⁵Simon answered, "Master, we've worked hard all night and haven't caught anything. But because you say so, I will let down the nets."

⁶When they had done so, they caught such a large number of fish that their nets began to break. ⁷So they signaled their partners in the other boat to come and help them, and they came and filled both boats so full that they began to sink.

ᵃ4 The Greek verb is plural.

Jesus asks Peter to push off a short distance from the shore in order to teach. But when he is finished he directs Peter to "cast off" into the deep and let down his net. This is a passionate scene. Peter is tired and frustrated. They have worked all night dropping and hoisting their nets and caught nothing. We must remember, this was not a fishing vacation with a little rod and reel. These are heavy boats, large nets, and their major means of support. Furthermore, Peter has just finished cleaning the nets. Now Jesus is asking him to dirty them up again. This landlubber does not even know that it is the wrong time to fish. In addition, the best fishing is usually near the shore, not in the deep of the lake.

Peter says, "But Master, because you say so, I'll do it." This unusual word "master" [*epistata*] is used only by Luke and always in reference to Jesus. This is a momentous phrase. Peter is a professional fisherman. He knows the sea and he knows the odds of going out there and catching a fish. Nevertheless, he has seen Jesus in action before. More than a year ago, as he followed John the Baptist, he saw Jesus baptized. He watched Jesus cleanse the temple, he was there in Samaria after Jesus talked to the woman at the well. He witnessed the healings in Judea and the miraculous transformation of water into wine in Cana. After nearly nine months of following Jesus, Peter went back to his family fishing business at the lake, while Jesus preached in his own hometown. Now they are reunited. Jesus makes this simple, although absurd, request. But because of Peter's respect and trust in Jesus, he obeys.

As Peter pulls up the nets, his muscles flex, his eyes bug out, and an involuntary smile breaks out all over his face. It is such a large number of fish, in fact, that their nets begin to tear and their boat begins to sink. The smile turns to a grimace. He knows that he needs some help. Luke uses a word that means "to beckon with a nod." That makes sense. His hands are full of net, he could hardly wave to his partners, and he certainly can't let go. Besides that, he is too far out to shout effectively and too busy to have a friendly chat with his partners.

The second boat of their family business comes out to help, manned by James and John. They pass on the other side of the net and begin to pull up so that the net is between the two boats. As they pull up, fish begin to spill over into the boat. So many, in fact, that both boats sink deeper and deeper into the water in threat of going under. This was about all the blessing they could handle! They were shut out the night before with nearly nine months of bills to catch up on since following Jesus. But today, in one beautiful moment, the Lord takes care of their electricity bill and even provides enough extra for a new dress for Peter's wife.

Lk 5:8-10a

⁸When Simon Peter saw this, he fell at Jesus' knees and said, "Go away from me, Lord; I am a sinful man!" ⁹For he and all his companions were astonished at the catch of fish they had taken, ¹⁰and so were James and John, the sons of Zebedee, Simon's partners.

You would think that Peter would kind of like having Jesus around. After all, he is good for business. After they got their boats steadied and their hearts stopped pounding, Peter falls to his knees on a slimy pile of fish. He had just seen Jesus, really seen him, for who he is. He says, "Depart from me, Lord, for I am a sinful man." A couple things ought to be observed. (1) Peter is thinking correctly. He, unlike the crowds, is not selfishly seeking a miracle. He is thinking about what it really meant to be in the presence of perfect purity. Jesus' purity demands obedience and ushers in judgment. (2) Peter is responding out of fear of the presence of God himself. It was a fearful miracle to him. The people on the banks are no doubt laughing and cheering and selling souvenir T-shirts, but they were not in the boats that almost sank. They were not so personally touched by this miracle as Peter and Co. Besides, this is one professional fisherman who understands the power of the lake and majesty of this miracle. As Jesus saw through the waters to the fish, so he saw through Peter into the depths of his heart.

Lk 5:10b-11
with Mt 4:19-20,
Mk 1:17-18

Then Jesus said to Simon, "Don't be afraid; {follow me^MT,MK} from now on you will catch men." ¹¹So {at once^MT,MK} they pulled their boats up on shore, left everything and followed him.

Mt 4:21-22
with Mk 1:20

²¹Going on from there, he saw two other brothers, James son of Zebedee and his brother John. They were in a boat with their father Zebedee, preparing their nets. {Without delay^MK} Jesus called them, ²²and immediately they left the boat and their father {in the boat with the hired men^MK} and followed him.

Once the disciples are back on the shore the crowds would gather and start to count the fish as they were sorted. Peter's employees (Mk 1:20), would no doubt start cleaning their nets (again). It is at this time that Jesus uses their present occupation to call them in a way that they can visualize — Fishers of Men. Like other analogies, not all points of comparison are applicable. Jesus is not asking them to trap or capture men, but simply to collect them into the kingdom of God. Peter and Andrew respond to Jesus' call.

Luke departs here from the other synoptic writers. Matthew and Mark both say, "I will make you fishers of men." The word Luke uses does not mean to fish but to take live captives. It is used only one other time (2 Tim 2:26). There it describes how we rescue from Satan those whom he has caught alive. This call is one of battle. We tread behind enemy lines to free the captives whom Satan has seized.

The three men walk a short distance farther and encounter their partners, James and John. They are sitting with their father, Zebedee, in their stout fishing boat, also cleaning their nets and repairing the torn spots from this massive catch. Jesus also calls them and they likewise respond, leaving their father in the boat with the hired servants (Mk 1:20).[8] Of these latter two, we observe that James was the first Apostolic martyr whose death is recorded in Acts 12. And John was the last surviving Apostle as he writes Revelation about A.D. 95, and according to tradition, the only Apostle who died a natural death.

I don't suppose that Zebedee was any too happy to be left to clean up by himself. Of course, their business was big enough to have hired servants to do most of the dirty work. It may seem unkind for these two sons to leave their father with the family business, but such is the nature of discipleship (cf. Mt 10:37).

This call may seem too sudden to merit such a response. But we must remember that these four have already traveled with Jesus for about a year now (cf. Jn 1:35-51), and have just witnessed a miraculous catch of fish. Jesus enters into their domain and proves his power. He now calls them into *his* domain to be empowered to fish for men. What else is there to do when such a one as Jesus calls you to his vocation?

Jesus' call of these men is unique: (1) There is already antagonism against Jesus in Jerusalem. They know there will be danger in following this man. (2) He calls them to abandon their occupations, which are lucrative, popular, and steady. This is a tremendous step of faith for them. (3) Jesus calls them, not to a new doctrine but to a new direction. The contemporary rabbis considered it a sacred duty to gather students about them. Jesus, however, doesn't ask them to come and learn, but to come and do, or rather to come and be. The flicker of the kingdom begins to flair.

§ 42
Teaching in the
Synagogue &
Casting Out a
Demon
(Mk 1:21-28; Lk
4:31b-37)

These next two events (§ 42-43) take place on a single Sabbath.[9] Here, we get a glimpse of Jesus' ministry in its pristine state. There are no meddling Pharisees from Jerusalem. Jesus, the great physician, meets

[8]Mark adds this tidbit of information about the servants, which he likely gleaned from Peter's preaching. Otherwise, the accounts of this call in Matthew and Mark are virtually identical.

[9]Luke presents two back-to-back episodes in a synagogue. In the first, Jesus is despised and cast out of his hometown synagogue (4:16-31). In the second, Jesus is honored after casting out a demon in the Capernaum synagogue (4:32-37). In both, Jesus amazes the crowd with his powerful teaching.

the needs of the people who yet adore him. In humility and divinity he touches the crowds. The prophecy Jesus quoted in the synagogue at Nazareth begins to be fulfilled (Lk 4:18-19; Isa 61:1-2). There is no conflict, no complication . . . yet. We would prefer this simple purity if it were not for the fact that Jesus' self-revelation cannot exist in such a state. By the nature of Jesus' miracles and identity, he is going to attract attention, devotion, and controversy.

Mk 1:21-22

²¹They went to Capernaum, and when the Sabbath came, Jesus went into the synagogue and began to teach. ²²The people were amazed at his teaching, because he taught them as one who had authority, not as the teachers of the law.

Luke says that Jesus taught on the Sabbaths (plural), potentially leaving room for several weeks of teaching as well as the call of the four fishermen (Lk 5:1-11). Jesus taught with authority. There was a marked difference between him and the scribes. The common mode of teaching for the scribes was to quote a long list of other scribal authorities. This supposedly gave credibility to their teaching. Jesus, in contrast, simply said, "But I say." Furthermore, the truth of his words were their own authority. The people needed no "professional stamp of approval" for them to recognize truth as truth. As usual, the crowd was amazed (cf. Mt 7:28; 13:54; 19:25; 22:33; Mk 1:22; 6:2; 7:37; 10:26; 11:18; Lk 2:48; 4:32; 9:43; Acts 13:12).

Lk 4:33-35
with Mk 1:26

³³In the synagogue there was a man possessed by a demon, an evil[a] spirit. He cried out at the top of his voice, ³⁴"Ha! What do you want with us, Jesus of Nazareth? Have you come to destroy us? I know who you are — the Holy One of God!"
³⁵"Be quiet!" Jesus said sternly. "Come out of him!" Then the demon threw the man down before them all and {shook him violently and[MK]} came out {of him with a shriek[MK]} without injuring him.

[a]*33* Greek *unclean*; also in verse 36

This is the first of several times that Jesus will confront a demon,[10] or, as Luke calls it "a spirit of an unclean demon." His culture was riddled with superstitions about demons (cf. Edersheim, Appendix XVI).[11]

---

[10]Appropriately, this is the first miracle recorded by Mark. Jesus' power over demons epitomized both his miraculous ability as well as the inauguration of the Kingdom of God. The point of the story is this: "Here comes the King!" Furthermore, this is the first miracle shared by Mark and Luke. It is quite uncommon for Mark and Luke to tell about an incident where Matthew is silent.

[11]For example, P.T. Butler (p. 76), cites the following: "Exorcists of that day believed the air was populated by evil spirits, and that on certain occasions they entered into men through food and drink. . . . Some of the rabbis believed that since demons were invisible

In fact, the Jews had a large body of literature dealing with demons. It dealt primarily with two things: (1) demons being the disembodied spirits of wicked people, and (2) exorcism by magical incantations. Jewish superstitions, however, do not mean that demons don't exist. Jesus does not deal with superstitions but with realities.

Edersheim (I:480), notices how Jesus dealt with demons as a reality and not merely as superstition or psychosis: (1) He commissioned his disciples to cast them out (Mt 10:8). (2) He thanked God when they were cast out (Lk 10:17-18). (3) He reproved his disciples when they could not cast them out (Mt 17:17). Either Jesus was duped by the superstitions of his day, or he pretended they were real in order to gain a hearing among the crowds, or demons were, in fact, a reality.

Demons were real then as they are today.[12] We may not see as much manifestation of demons in one culture as we do in others. However, this does not mean they do not exist. Satan is wise in which tools he uses. As a carpenter knows which tool to use in any given situation, so also Satan knows which instruments of evil are effective in a given place and time.

While it would be a mistake to deny the reality of demonic activity, so also is it a mistake to overemphasize it. Ours is a day of morbid curiosity in the occult, even in Christian circles with our "power encounters." Here are several truths that should be reflected in our theology and experience of demons:

1. Satan is neither omnipotent nor omniscient. To claim to be tempted by Satan may be a bit boastful — he probably has bigger fish to fry.
2. There is no indication that demons "specialize" in certain activities such as cancer, anger, selfishness, pride, stealing, etc. In other words, although demons appear to have personalities (Mk 5:8; 9:25), there is no indication that a certain affliction is caused by a certain demon and therefore needs to be identified before it can be exorcised.
3. The idea that you must obtain a demon's name or you will be unable

---

if one put sifted ashes on the threshold of the house, their footprints might be seen in the morning, prints like those that a chicken might leave. One rabbi, in order to protect himself against demons, always took a lamb with him every time he went to the bathroom since they attacked animals as well as human beings."

[12]Although this is the prevailing opinion among Evangelical Christians, not all would admit the reality of demons today. For instance, Edersheim believes that it was a phenomenon restricted to the ministry of Jesus. He bases this belief on the fact that demon possession is not mentioned in either the OT, the Apocrypha or the Mishnah (I:481). Furthermore, some have attempted to consign all reports of demon possession to hysteria, schizophrenia, epilepsy and other psychological or physiological phenomenon (cf. J.K. Howard, "New Testament Exorcism and its Significance Today," *ExpT* 96 [Jan 1985]: 105-109). But these diagnoses are too vague to account for all the facts (cf. John Montgomery [Ed.], *Demon Possession*, Minneapolis: Bethany Fellowship, 1976).

to exorcise it has its roots more in Greek and Jewish magic practices than in Scripture.

4. That we are in spiritual warfare is undeniable. However, it is false and faithless to view this battle as dualistic — fairly equivalent powers of darkness and light and one will barely win over the other. The Holy Spirit is infinitely more powerful than the created, fallen, evil spirits. There is simply no contest.

5. There is no indication that the victory of good angels is contingent upon the prayers of the saints. It is pure fiction that humans empower angelic spirits with their supplications.

6. Demons are not illnesses. In the Gospels sickness and disease are identified as separate from demons. Sickness is a natural part of our fallen world. Demons are a spiritual part of a "heavenly fall."

After Jesus had taught in the synagogue, this demon-possessed man pipes up, "Ha! What do you want with us?" Luke's little added expletive "Ha" carries with it extreme emotion. It can indicate fear, hate, and anger all at the same time. The second part of this phrase "What do you want with us?" can also be translated, "What do we have to do with each other?" or even "Why this interference?"

The demons then ask Jesus if he is going to destroy them. This is Jesus' first confrontation of demons. They give up before the fight even started. Jesus so totally overpowers them that they resign themselves to defeat. We who are filled with the Spirit of Christ have nothing to fear from demons.

The startling thing is that these demons were more aware of Jesus' true identity than the other attenders of the synagogue, including Jesus' own disciples. The demoniac said, "I know who you are — the Holy one of God." We are reminded of James 2:19, "Even the demons believe, and shudder."

But Jesus forbids them to speak. Why? Because: (1) Jesus has not yet had time to teach and display the true nature of his Messiahship. A mistaken notion of Messiah may do more harm than good. (2) It's pretty bad publicity to have demons praise you. (3) Works are louder than words. Jesus wanted his actions to speak for themselves.

So Jesus "muzzled" them by ordering [*epetimēsen*] their silence. This word demands attention. Jesus will use it again in the next pericope (Lk 4:39, 41), when healing Peter's mother-in-law. It is a key word in understanding the purpose of this section. Kee gives the following definition to *epitimaō*: "The word of command by which God's agent defeats his enemies, thus preparing for the coming of God's kingdom."[13] He

---

[13]H.C. Kee, "The Terminology of Mark's Exorcism Stories," *NTS* 14 (1967-8): 232-246.

traces its use in broader Jewish literature, and finds that it describes God's cosmic struggle against the forces of darkness, evident in both sickness and demon possession. Therefore, it shows that this one event is but a part of a long-standing battle. Furthermore, this demonstrates the in-breaking of the Kingdom of God which marks the beginning of the end for Satan's dominion.

The demon reluctantly gives up his prey. As a spoiled child who can't get his way, he throws the man down. This pathetic, yellow-bellied demon takes one last pot-shot at the man. This cowardly act of defiance is the last pleasure of attack he will know on this man. Luke, the physician, makes a note that the demon did not injure the man. He dare not in the presence of the God/Man.

This was **not** an exorcism. There was no magical incantation or formula. Actually, this was more like a healing.[14] Jesus, simply on the authority of his word, commanded this demon to leave and he did. The point of the story is not demonology but the authority of Jesus.

Let's remove the false superstition about the undue power of demons. They are real, they are active, and they are in submission to the word of Christ. We who are possessed by the Holy Spirit have nothing to fear from an unholy spirit. "Greater is he who is in you than he who is in the world" (1 Jn 4:4). Jesus came to "destroy the works of the Devil" (1 Jn 3:8), and will, on the last day, destroy all his workers (Mt 25:41).

Mk 1:27-28

[27]The people were all so amazed that they asked each other, "What is this? A new teaching — and with authority! He even gives orders to evil spirits and they obey him." [28]News about him spread quickly over the whole region of Galilee.

The crowd is shocked, not by Jesus' deed, but by the power of his words. The deed serves to validate the word, not the other way around. The powerful word of Jesus is exalted, both his ability to teach and his ability to command demons.

§ 43
Healing Peter's
Mother-in-Law
(Mt 8:14-17;
Mk 1:29-34;
Lk 4:38-41)

[MK 1:]29As soon as they left the synagogue, they went with James and John to the home of Simon and Andrew. [30]Simon's mother-in-law was in bed with a {high[LK]} fever, and they told Jesus about her. [31]So he went to her, {bent over her and rebuked the fever, and[LK]} took her hand and helped her up. The fever left her and she began to wait on them.

Jesus leaves the synagogue and goes immediately to the home of Peter and Andrew. Either the two have moved to Capernaum from

---

[14]Cf. J.K. Howard, "New Testament Exorcism and its Significance Today," *ExpT* 96 (Jan 1985): 105-109.

Bethsaida (Jn 1:44, lit. "House of Fish"), or Bethsaida was actually a suburb of Capernaum.

Peter is caring for his wife's mother (cf. 1 Cor 9:5). She is in bed with a "great fever." The physicians of the day categorized fevers into "great" and "small." A small fever was any minor ailment. The "great fever" might include malaria or some other serious sickness.[15] Peter's mother-in-law is seriously ill and may have been for some time.

All three accounts offer different details about this healing. Luke says he stood over her; Matthew adds that he touched her hand; and Mark says he took her by the hand and lifted her up. At the same time Jesus "rebuked the fever." This is the same word used to describe how Jesus rebuked the demon in the synagogue (Lk 4:35). This has led some to speculate that Jesus saw demonic activity behind this and other illnesses. But verses 40 and 41 make a clear distinction between sicknesses and demons. We cannot blame all sicknesses and mental ills on demons. They are a natural part of our fallen world. However, the fact that Jesus rebukes both demons and diseases shows that he came to destroy all the works of the Devil. The coming of the kingdom marks the beginning of the end for Satan's dominion through demons as well as the curse of Eden through diseases and death.

Peter's mother-in-law is so thoroughly healed that she gets up immediately and "began to wait on them." This phrase is captured in one Greek word. It is the same word from which we get "deacon" [*diakoneō*]. In its simplest form, it means to wait on tables, (not in the sense of a restaurant, but in the home). It is an amazing thing that she was able to do this. Even when a person is healed by natural means from a fever, they still have a loss of energy from which it takes a while to recover. When Jesus heals, he heals so completely that this woman is even released from the aftermath of the fever fatigue.

Lk 4:40-41 *with*
Mk 1:32; Mt 8:16

[40]When {after[MK]} the sun was setting, the people brought to Jesus all who had various kinds of sickness, and laying his hands on each one, he healed them. [41]Moreover, {he drove out the spirits with a word, and[MT]} demons came out of many people, shouting, "You are the Son of God!" But he rebuked them and would not allow them to speak, because they knew he was the Christ.[a]

---

[15]Edersheim offers this interesting note about the fever: "The Talmud gives this disease precisely the same name (*Eshatha Tsemirta*), 'burning fever,' and prescribes for it a magical remedy, of which the principal part is to tie a knife wholly of iron by a braid of hair to a thornbush, and to repeat on successive days Exod. iii. 2, 3, then ver. 4, and finally v. 5, after which the bush is to be cut down, while a certain magical formula is pronounced" [Shabb. 37 a], (I:486).

Mt 8:17

¹⁷This was to fulfill what was spoken through the prophet Isaiah:
"He took up our infirmities
    and carried our diseases."ᵇ

ᵃLk 4:41 or *Messiah*   ᵇMt 8:17 Isaiah 53:4

The sun is setting. The whole city comes out to Jesus. Remembering that this is a Sabbath day, and that the holy day runs from sundown Friday to sundown Saturday, these people are coming to Jesus at the first possible legal time. This is one of the most touching scenes of all the Bible. As dusk gives way to early evening, and as stars begin to appear one by one, cots and stretchers line the streets all around Peter's house. Without opposition or antagonism, the master walks by each sick person, surrounded by their families, and touches them individually [*heni hekastō*]. Each one is healed; each face has a smile, surely including our Lord's. Tears of joy flow through the streets. Laughter is heard from corner to corner in Capernaum. We can't imagine this crowd disassembling until the early morning hours. And up early the next morning they would be in search of the healer.

The demons, as is their custom, are confessing that Jesus was the Son of God. Jesus, as is his custom, will not allow them to speak. It is not yet time for Jesus to be revealed as the Christ. The people are expectant for the Messiah, but in no way ready to receive him. They desperately want a Messiah, but only on their terms, to meet their expectations. Jesus is different than their dream . . . better, but different. Therefore, this announcement by the demons would do more damage than good. Let us not imagine for even a moment that a demon is going to do something to progress the work of the kingdom of God.

Both Mark and Luke use an interesting verb tense. When it says, "They knew he was the Christ," it indicates that they "had known." It was no new revelation to the demons. They had known it for quite some time.

At this point, Matthew introduces the fulfillment of Isaiah 53:4, "Surely he took up our infirmities and carried our sorrows, yet we considered him stricken by God, smitten by him and afflicted." This has obvious reference, especially considering the context, to the crucifixion. At the same time, Matthew attributes its fulfillment to this event. This has several important implications: (1) Prophecy may have two valid applications; in this case, one physical and one spiritual. (2) Jesus not only heals us spiritually (1 Pet. 2:24), but also physically. (3) Isaiah 53 is a description of Jesus that is as true today as when it was written. This being the case, Jesus must still be healing today. His method is obviously different, since he is not here physically to personally touch us. But he is still the Great Physician of both body and spirit.

**§ 44
The First Tour
of Galilee**
(Mt 4:23-25;
Mk 1:35-39;
Lk 4:42-44)

Jesus is having great success. His sermons and healings are attracting great crowds. This is just the kind of achievement for which the disciples hope. In the midst of such growing fame, however, Jesus jumps ship. The disciples want to crowd him into the spotlight. Jesus demonstrates different priorities.

Mk 1:35-37
with Lk 4:42

[35]Very early in the morning, while it was still dark, Jesus got up, left the house and went off to a solitary place, where he prayed. [36]Simon and his companions went to look for him, [37]and when they found him, they exclaimed: "Everyone is looking for you!" {They tried to keep him from leaving them.[LK]}

Lk 4:43

[43]But he said, "I must preach the good news of the kingdom of God to the other towns also, because that is why I was sent."

After healing long into the night, Jesus puts the disciples to bed. They likely fall asleep with a smile on their faces. Jesus also retires, perhaps not sleeping at all. After a few short hours he is up again. He dresses and slips quietly out of the house long before the sun rises. For Jesus, solitary prayer is more essential than sleep. In the morning when Jesus' bed is found empty, Simon (note Mark's interest in Peter) leads the crowd in a search for him.

When the gang finds Jesus, Peter says, "Everyone is looking for you." The rest of them chime in and try to keep Jesus from leaving Capernaum. But Jesus operates on his Father's agenda rather than playing for the crowds. He's not so parochial as to preach to only one city. This kingdom is much broader than these disciples ever suspected.

Mt 4:23-25
with Lk 4:44

[23]Jesus went throughout Galilee {Judea[LK]}[a], teaching in their synagogues, preaching the good news of the kingdom, and healing every disease and sickness among the people. [24]News about him spread all over Syria, and people brought to him all who were ill with various diseases, those suffering severe pain, the demon-possessed, those having seizures, and the paralyzed, and he healed them. [25]Large crowds from Galilee, the Decapolis,[b] Jerusalem, Judea and the region across the Jordan followed him.

[a]*Lk 4:44* Or *the land of the Jews*; some manuscripts *Galilee*   [b]*Mt 4:25* That is, the Ten Cities

Against the will of the crowds, Jesus embarks on his first Galilean tour. Luke differs from Matthew and Mark. He says that Jesus preaches in the synagogues of Judea. There is a weak textual variant, retained in the KJV which reads "Galilee." In all likelihood, "Judea" was what Luke wrote. However, the chronology and movement of the ministry of Jesus, as well as the parallel passages, indicates that Jesus' tour is indeed in Galilee. Thus we come to this conclusion: What Luke means to indicate is not "synagogues of Judea" but rather "Synagogues of the [land of the] Jews" which would, of course, include Galilee (cf. Lk 1:5; 6:17; 7:17;

23:5). In other words, Luke is not talking merely about geography but ethnicity.

Jesus' fame spreads like wildfire. Matthew goes out of his way to say that Jesus can heal anything, from demon-possession, to paralysis, to epilepsy.[16] His reputation as a healer extends to the farthest borders of Israel and then some. From Syria in the north to Judea in the south, from the elite in Jerusalem to the borderline of Decapolis, people brought their patients and loved ones to Jesus. None were disappointed. There was nothing he couldn't fix and no one he wouldn't touch.

§ 45
A Leper
Cleansed
(Mt 8:2-4;
Mk 1:40-45;
Lk 5:12-16)

This is one of the most touching scenes of the Bible. No disease carried with it the same stigma and social ostracism as leprosy. This outcast throws himself at the mercy of Jesus. Jesus touches him. Instead of Jesus becoming unclean, this leper becomes clean.

[LK 5:]12While Jesus was in one of the towns, a man came along who was covered with leprosy.ᵃ When he saw Jesus, he fell {on his knees^MT,MK} with his face to the ground and begged him, "Lord, if you are willing, you can make me clean."

[MK 1:]41Filled with compassion, Jesus reached out his hand and touched the man. "I am willing," he said. "Be clean!" 42Immediately the leprosy left him and he was cured.

ᵃ12 The Greek word was used for various diseases affecting the skin—not necessarily leprosy.

Jesus sets out for his first Galilean tour and is accosted by a leper.[17] The word "leprosy" comes from "lepo" meaning to "Peel off like scales." It is described only two times (Num 12:10; 2 Kgs 5:27), and in both instances it is "white as snow." Thus, many modern commentators have identified it with psoriasis and elephantiasis. However, neither of these conditions compare to the detailed description of leprosy in Leviticus 13.[18]

---

[16]This word "epilepsy" [*selēniazomai*] is difficult to translate. Etymologically it means "moonstruck." It may indicate epilepsy, a physical ailment, or insanity, a psychological ailment, both of which were associated with the moon in Jesus' day. The translation difficulties of this word in Mt 4:24 are explained by J.M. Ross, "Epileptic or Moonstruck?" *BT* 29 (Jan 1978): 126-128.

[17]Matthew makes it look like this leper accosted Jesus as he came down from the mountain after the Sermon on the Mount. However, when placed beside Mark and Luke, we see that it is a topical arrangement, not a chronological one.

[18]Cf. R. Cochrane, "No Wonder You're Confused about Leprosy," *Eternity* (September 1965): 12-14; K.P. Gramberg, "Leprosy and the Bible," *BT* (Jan 1960): 10-23; and J.L. Swellengrebel, "Leprosy and the Bible," *BT* (April 1960): 69-81.

The leper came up to Jesus, knelt before him and then fell on his face. This action was illegal since a leper was required to keep away from people.

> Wrapped in mourner's garb the leper passed by, his cry "Unclean!" was to incite others to pray for him — but also to avoid him. No one was even to salute him; his bed was to be low, inclining towards the ground. If he even put his head into a place, it became unclean. No less a distance than four cubits (six feet) must be kept from a leper; or if the wind came from that direction, a hundred were scarcely sufficient. Rabbi Meir would not eat an egg purchased in a street where there was a leper. Another Rabbi boasted, that he always threw stones at them to keep them far off, while others hid themselves or ran away (Edersheim, p. 495).

Normally, if someone approached them they were to call out the warning, "Unclean, Unclean!" (Lev 13:45-46). Instead, this leper begged of Jesus, "Lord, if you are willing, you can make me clean." There is no precedent for this man's request. He would have run from any other rabbi whose sometimes violent ostracism could cause him injury, to say nothing of humiliation.[19] Furthermore, there is no OT example of this kind of cleansing from leprosy. In the only case of leper cleansing in the OT, Elijah and Naaman (2 Kgs 5:1-19), there was no physical touch and Naaman was not a Jew. There is precious little reason for this leper to be so confident that Jesus could or would heal him. Along this line, it is of interest that there was never a case of leprosy healed outside the direct agency of God.

Jesus, "moved with pity,"[20] reached out and grabbed [*hapto*] the guy. Touching a leper would have defiled any other man. But instead of Jesus becoming unclean, this man became clean. Certainly, Jesus could have healed the man by his word. After all, he healed the nobleman's son at a

---

[19]As Edersheim notes (p. 493), "Once declared leprous, the sufferer was soon made to feel the utter heartlessness of Rabbinism. To banish him outside walled towns may have been a necessity, which, perhaps, required to be enforced by the threatened penalty of forty stripes save one." However, C.R. Kazmierski, "Evangelist and Leper: A Socio-Cultural Study of Mark 1:40-45," *NTS* 38 (1992): 37-50, suggests that these regulations were not strictly kept in smaller villages, especially the further one got away from Jerusalem.

[20]C.H. Cave, "The Leper: Mark 1:40-45," *NTS* 25 (1979): 245-250, contends for the weak textual variant of "he was angry" [*orgistheis*] rather than "he felt compassion" [*splanchnistheis*]. This would turn this story of healing into one of controversy. This would account for (1) Jesus' command to be silent and sending him away, (2) the use of the word "strong warning" [*embrimesamenos*], and (3) the context of other controversy stories. However, this textual variant is too weak to follow and the categories of form criticism have proven to be less than reliable. So we accept the text as it is in the NIV.

distance of 20 miles (Jn 4:45-54). Why does Jesus not do that here? He realized that this man had several needs: (1) He needed to be cleansed of leprosy. (2) He needed to feel the touch of another human hand. He had lived in isolation and rejection and now needs to be brought back into society. (3) He needs to be delivered from the social stigma of having had leprosy. Thus, his cleansing had three parts: Physical, emotional, and social. Jesus deals with the physical need by cleansing the leprosy. He deals with the emotional by touching him. And he deals with the social by having him go to the temple and offer the appropriate sacrifice.

Mk 1:43-45 *with*
Lk 5:15-16

[43]Jesus sent him away at once with a strong warning: [44]"See that you don't tell this to anyone. But go, show yourself to the priest and offer the sacrifices that Moses commanded for your cleansing, as a testimony to them." [45]Instead he went out and began to talk freely, spreading the news. As a result, Jesus could no longer enter a town openly but stayed outside in lonely places. Yet the people still came to him from everywhere. {Crowds of people came to hear him and to be healed of their sicknesses. [16]But Jesus often withdrew to lonely places and prayed.[LK]}

Moses designated an offering as evidence for cleansing of leprosy (Lev 14-15). Because the leper was a total outcast in Israel, even after cleansing had taken place, there may still be a stigma hovering over the leper. The sacrifice was a public sign of acceptance by the priests and thus by God of the cleansing of the leper. Thus, the person could be brought back into society without further rejection or alienation.

Why does Jesus command him to keep silent about this? First, as prejudice against Jesus rises, this leper's chances of being declared clean by a priest would diminish due to his connection with Jesus. Thus, it was for the leper's benefit. Second, it was for Jesus' benefit. His popularity is rising at such an alarming rate that he is already mobbed by the crowds. Jesus is trying to avoid the very thing that happened (Mk 1:45) — the leper blabs it all over and the crowds swelled so that Jesus can no longer enter any city but has to stay in the country.[21] Furthermore, as is indicated by Luke 5:15, Jesus' presence creates excitement for the wrong reasons. The crowds want physical healing and a circus show. This makes it all the more difficult to teach his true identity. Finally, the tensions have begun to rise between Jesus and the religious hierarchy. There is no need for a premature, nasty confrontation.

---

[21]C.R. Kazmierski, "Evangelist and Leper: A Socio-Cultural Study of Mark 1:40-45," *NTS* 38 (1992): 37-50, suggests that it is the leper, not Jesus, who could no longer enter a city freely (Mk 1:45b). However, while "Jesus" is not in the Greek text, the parallel in Lk 5:15-16 clearly speaks of Jesus, not the leper, being mobbed.

In the midst of all this popularity, Jesus frequently[22] withdrew into the wilderness to pray (Lk 5:16). When Jesus got the busiest, he prayed the most. That is a lesson we would do well to learn. We cannot afford to be without the power and perspective that prayer offers, *especially* when our schedules get tight.

§ 46
Healing and
Forgiving a
Paralytic
(Mt 9:1-8;[23]
Mk 2:1-12;
Lk 5:17-26).

As Jesus draws his first Galilean tour to a close we find him again in Capernaum, most likely in Simon Peter's house (Mk 1:29). The healing of the leper (the only incident we are given from his first tour), and the healing of this paralytic, are representative of Jesus' work and have several things in common: (1) Jesus shows concern for more than their physical well-being. (2) These healings are unprecedented. Nothing like it had ever been done (cf. Mk 2:12). (3) The healing demonstrates divine power. (4) Jesus acts in ways quite contrary to contemporary rabbis.

In our present narrative, we will see, for the first time, official opposition to Jesus from the religious hierarchy. Soon they will object to Jesus at four levels (McGarvey, p. 183): (1) Blasphemy, (2) interaction with tax collectors and sinners, (3) neglect of ascetic duties (washings, fasting, etc.), and (4) Sabbath violations.

Mt 9:1-2

[1]A few days later, when Jesus again entered Capernaum, the people heard that he had come home. [2]So many gathered that there was no room left, not even outside the door, and he preached the word to them.

Lk 5:17-21 *with*
Mk 2:3-4, Mt 9:2

[17]Pharisees and teachers of the law, who had come from every village of Galilee and from Judea and Jerusalem, were sitting there. And the power of the Lord was present for him to heal the sick. [18]Some {four[MK]} men came carrying a paralytic on a mat and tried to take him into the house to lay him before Jesus. [19]When they could not find a way to do this because of the crowd, they went up on the roof and {made an opening in the roof above Jesus and, after digging through it[MK]} lowered him on his mat through the tiles into the middle of the crowd, right in front of Jesus.

[20]When Jesus saw their faith, he said, "Friend {take heart, son[MT]}, your sins are forgiven."

[21]The Pharisees and the teachers of the law began thinking to themselves, "Who is this fellow who speaks blasphemy? Who can forgive sins but God alone?"

Jesus somehow manages to enter the city unnoticed and takes the opportunity to lay low for a few days. As soon as the rumor spread that

---

[22]Notice the present participle [*hypochōrōn*].

[23]Again, we understand that Matthew offers a topical arrangement rather than chronological. Thus, his introduction (9:1), about crossing the Sea of Galilee, is for literary flow rather than actual movement.

Jesus is back, the crowds again assemble at Peter's front door. Jesus begins to teach the crowds day after day. The Pharisees and teachers of the law hear that his classes are in session and stream to him from the villages scattered across Galilee, Judea and Jerusalem. The house is soon packed.[24]

As near as we can tell, Peter lived in an upper-middle-class home. It would have consisted of a square courtyard with rooms all around it. At one corner of the court would be a door leading to the street. It likely could have been two story with an open rooftop surrounded by a parapet for safety. All around the courtyard would have been an awning which allowed the occupants of the house to move from room to room outside, but still sheltered from the sun and rain. We picture Jesus standing outside his quarters teaching the thronging crowd that pressed into the courtyard. There is a line outside the front gate trying to press their way in.

Luke (5:17) notices what will soon be evident to the entire crowd, that "the power of the Lord was present for him to perform healing." Four men carry in this paralytic on a "bed" which we would call a "cot" or a "stretcher." It was probably nothing more than some animal skin and some supporting boards. This poor fellow is used to being carried around. We would like to know a bit more about his condition. Is he paralyzed from birth? Is it a neck injury later in life? Is he married with a family to support? We are simply not told. But this much we can ascertain from Jewish culture — the only job he could hold was to get some friends to lay him by a busy gate where he might beg for alms. It is likely that these same four men carried him everyday to a public place so that he could lay there, looking pathetic, and be gawked at all day, hoping that someone would throw a few pennies at him.

We don't know whose idea it is to carry the paralytic to Jesus. But it is a cumbersome process. The crowd outside the door won't budge. A child, perhaps, could squeeze between their legs, but not four grown men with a stretcher. Thus, they climb up on the roof. It is possible that there was an outdoor staircase to the roof, but this is unlikely since it would only invite robbers. It is more likely that they get in the neighbor's house, go up on their roof and then hop over to Peter's. The houses were often close enough together to make this possible, but it could not have been done without attracting attention. But then, they have only begun to do that! Why are they so intense about getting this fellow to Jesus TODAY? Answer: Jesus is unpredictable — here today, gone tomorrow. This may, in fact, be their only chance.

---

[24]Luke uses a perfect verb tense to indicated that the Pharisees "were in the present state of having been there." In other words, they've been hanging around for a few days. Thus, this is not the first time they have heard Jesus speak.

They climb down onto the awning above where Jesus stood. They cannot see him, but they can tell where he is by the direction the crowd faces. These awnings were made out of thatched tile pieces. Thus, Mark (2:4) says that these four "dug" through the roof. They pull out some of the grass, mud and sticks until they could finally dismantle a large tile section and lower their friend down.[25] The people standing in front of Jesus in the open courtyard can see what was going on. Jesus, no doubt, notices that the crowd is somewhat distracted. Soon bits of grass and dirt and twigs begin to fall around him as he preaches. Suddenly the sunlight streams through the awning and a shadowy figure on a pallet is lowered down. Now don't you wonder if the fellow on the pallet had an impish little grin on his face as he lay there in front of Jesus? Surely he is just a little embarrassed about breaking up the sermon?

Jesus, respecting the faith of the four men, declares this paralytic forgiven of his sins (cf. Lk 7:48; 23:43). They come to Jesus for a healing (perhaps so that they won't have to carry their friend around anymore). But what they get is an absolution. That has to be mildly disappointing for the four. But it was extremely infuriating to the Pharisees. You see, Jesus is acting like God!

The Pharisees sit piously in their seats of honor listening to Jesus' sermon. But when they hear this, they come unglued. They huddle together in a brief conference and unanimously conclude that Jesus had just blasphemed. "Who can forgive sins," they asked, "but God alone?" Their basic logic is correct: Only God has the moral authority to forgive sins (cf. Isa 43:25). Their theology is correct, but they are badly mistaken in their evaluation of Jesus.

Blasphemy is essentially "reviling" or "insulting" (cf. Titus 3:2; 2 Pet 2:2; Jude 8). One could blaspheme God by (1) insulting him, (2) by refusing to give him due praise, or (3) by raising yourself to the level of God with the result that you bring God down to your level. It was this third form of "blasphemy" that caused the Pharisees to balk at Jesus' claim. The fact that blasphemy was punishable by death in Jewish law explains their ferocity against Jesus.

---

[25]Luke uses the word *keramōn* for the roof, indicating "clay." Thus, some commentators (cf. McGarvey, p. 184) would place Jesus actually inside the house and have these four men dig through the solid roof. Such vandalism seems a bit extreme. Although this is a possibility, our present reconstruction seems more likely. J. Vonnorsdall, "Mark 2:1-12," *Int* 36 (Jan 1982): 58-63, playfully suggests that "If experience as a parish pastor holds the clue," perhaps Jesus employed his own carpentry skills to patch the roof after the crowds dispersed.

Mk 2:8-12 *with*
Mt 9:4

[8]Immediately Jesus knew in his spirit that this was what they were thinking in their hearts, and he said to them, "Why are you thinking these {evil[MT]} things? [9]Which is easier: to say to the paralytic, 'Your sins are forgiven,' or to say, 'Get up, take your mat and walk'? [10]But that you may know that the Son of Man has authority on earth to forgive sins. . . ." He said to the paralytic, [11]"I tell you, get up, take your mat and go home."

Lk 5:25-26 *with*
Mt 9:8

[25]Immediately he stood up in front of them, took what he had been lying on and went home praising God. [26]Everyone was amazed and gave praise to God {who had given such authority to men[MT]}. They were filled with awe and said, "We have seen remarkable things today."

Jesus again perceives their thoughts "in his spirit" and even evaluates them as "evil." Jesus responds, not with mere argumentation, but with undeniable evidence. He asks, "Which is easier to say, 'Your sins are forgiven' or to say, 'Rise, take up your pallet and walk?'" The fact is, they are both easy to say but quite impossible to do. Furthermore, anyone could *say* your sins are forgiven and there is no way to *prove* whether they are or not. But if someone should say, "Rise, take up your bed and walk," that is immediately verifiable.

And so we come to the center of the text: "But that you may know that the Son of Man has authority on earth to forgive sins. . . ."[26] Jesus breaks off his sentence midstream (Mk 2:10), turns to the paralytic and says, "Take up your bed and go home." It is as if Jesus says, "Just watch this!"

By proving he could heal the paralytic, he also proves that he has forgiven the man's sin. The Jews, of course, would believe the physical problem is caused by the spiritual problem (cf. Jn 9:2). Thus, Jesus not only releases the man from paralysis but also the social stigma of being a sinner.

Immediately the man obeys Jesus, taking up his stretcher and going home. The crowd that would not let him in, now easily parts to let him through. Wouldn't you? The paralytic exits, praising God. The crowd is flabbergasted. The Pharisees are silent. What could they say in the face of the people's assessment? "We have seen remarkable things today. We have never seen anything like this." The crowd is not responding primarily to the healing. They have seen this kind of thing before in this very

---

[26]Some scholars have attacked this text. Because it so clearly identifies the purpose and person of Jesus, they say that it must have been added later to this healing story (cf. L.S. Hay, "The Son of Man in Mark 2:10 and 2:28," *JBL* 89 (1970): 69-75). However, R.T. Mead, "The Healing of the Paralytic — A Unit?" *JBL* 80 (1960): 348-354, has persuasively shown that in spite of the supposed difficulties inherent in this text, the healing of the paralytic makes little sense divorced from the pronouncement of the Son of Man (Mk 2:5b-10).

house. What they have never seen before is a man with divine authority to forgive sins. Thus, Jesus' miracle has three parts: (1) Forgiveness of sins, (2) reading minds, (3) healing paralysis. All three are stunning.

§ 47a
The Call of
Levi/Matthew
(Mt 9:9;
Mk 2:13-14;
Lk 5:27-28)

Like the previous episode, Jesus again deals with forgiveness of sins. We don't necessarily need to read these events as if one followed immediately upon the other. They are placed here together because of their similar content.

We can scarcely appreciate how radical Jesus' concept of forgiveness is. Judaism, like all other world religions, only allows a person to come to God after they have been cleansed (i.e., made worthy). But this is just not possible. Jesus, on the other hand, first invites us to God, and then through our relationship with him, we are cleansed. This is so much more reasonable and gentle.

Mk 2:13-14 *with*
Mt 9:9, Lk 5:28

¹³Once again Jesus went out beside the lake. A large crowd came to him, and he began to teach them. ¹⁴As he walked along, he saw Levi {Matthew^MT} son of Alphaeus sitting at the tax collector's booth. "Follow me," Jesus told him, and Levi got up, {left everything^LK} and followed him.

Again we find Jesus in one of his favorite haunts doing what he does best — teaching the people. The Sea of Galilee is buzzing with people. Anytime Jesus shows up, he has a ready crowd. Even the lake itself seems eager to provide a natural amphitheater for the Master.

At the conclusion of the day's lesson, Jesus passes a tax collector sitting at his booth. It is either located on the shore itself, collecting revenues from goods transported across the lake, or on the road leading to Capernaum. Either spot would provide a lucrative income for this employee of the Roman Government.

Luke and Mark call him by a purely Jewish name — Levi. He calls himself Matthew (Aramaic), meaning "gift of God."

As far as the Apostles go, he was the most unlikely candidate. As a tax collector, he would have been violently opposed by orthodox Judaism. In fact, the Hebrew word for tax collector [*mokhes*], seems to have as its root meaning "oppression" and "injustice." The Jews simply hated this oppressive system of Roman taxation. They hated the high percentage of taxes. They hated the sheer number of different taxes: Polls, bridges, roads, harbors, income, town, grain, wine, fish, fruit, etc. They hated how their money was spent on immoral and idolatrous activities. But most of all, they hated what Roman taxation represented: Roman domination of the people of God.

Consequently, any Jew who worked for the Roman "IRS" was viewed as a traitor of the worst sort. Matthew is therefore ostracized from all forms of Jewish life, especially their synagogue services. "His money was considered tainted and defiled anyone who accepted it. He could not serve as a witness. The rabbis had no word of help for the publican, because they expected him by external conformity to the law to be justified before God" (Shepard, p. 143).

As the writer of the first Gospel, we learn more from Matthew about OT prophecies and Jewish traditions than from any other writer. Reading his book we would think that he was a Jew's Jew. What are we to make of this? Perhaps Matthew longed for his Jewish roots and yet was hard-pressed by his job security. Likely in solitude he studied the Scriptures, coming to independent conclusions and an individual hope of the Messiah. (It is difficult to believe that Matthew only studied the OT under Jesus.) We should learn from Matthew that those on the sidelines who look so antagonistic might just be the greatest converts.

As Jesus passes by, he looks at Levi. Most people try to ignore him; some try to sneak by him. Jesus was different. He meets Levi eyeball-to-eyeball and calls him to immediate discipleship.

Matthew responds immediately and radically. Likely Levi is familiar with Jesus. The Sea of Galilee, especially this shore near Capernaum, is Jesus' "headquarters." Undoubtedly he had heard Jesus preach. He may even have witnessed Jesus' call to the four fisherman. Certainly he had collected plenty of taxes from them, especially after that great miraculous catch. Furthermore, the brevity of the text makes it look like Levi just up and left his tax table for the scrambling crowds to pillage his coins. That is not necessary. He likely closed up shop and then settled accounts with the Roman authorities over him. To do less would have been irresponsible and even dangerous, thus jeopardizing the ministry of Jesus.

We have seen four fishermen leave their private business in the hands of their father. However, they always have the option to return. In fact, after the resurrection, the Apostles return to Galilee and spend their time fishing as they wait for Jesus. Levi is different — he has no other options. When he steps out of that tax collector's booth it is for the last time. He is a small member of a large corporate structure. There are eager young publicans itching to sit in his lucrative seat. When he leaves, he leaves for good.

§ 47b
A Banquet at
Matthew's
House
(Mt 9:10-13;
Mk 2:15-17;
Lk 5:29-32)

[LK 5:]29Then Levi held a great banquet for Jesus at his house, and a large crowd of tax collectors and others {"sinners"MT,MK} were eating with them, {for there were many who followed him.MK} 30But the Pharisees and the teachers of the law who belonged to their sect complained to his disciples, "Why do you {your teacherMT} eat and drink with tax collectors and 'sinners'?"

[MK 2:]17On hearing this, Jesus said to them, "It is not the healthy who need a doctor, but the sick. I have not come to call the righteous, but sinners."

[MT 9:]13But go and learn what this means: 'I desire mercy, not sacrifice.'a For I have not come to call the righteous, but sinners."

a13 Hosea 6:6

Matthew takes Jesus home and does for him what seemed most honorable — throws him a party, not just for Jesus but for all his disciples (Mk 2:15). Who is he going to invite? The same people we all would — our friends. The only problem is that Matthew's friends are all sinners and tax collectors like him (cf. Mt 11:19; 18:17; 21:31-32; Lk 15:1).[27] This is typical evangelism. When sinners meet Jesus, get ready for a flood, because they want all their friends to know the same joy they have just found.

Just as Matthew's response is typical of sinners, so the response of the Pharisees and their scribes is typical of the religious community. They oppose Jesus because of the misapplication of the proverb: "Birds of a feather flock together." Furthermore, they are shifty in the way they do it. They don't oppose Jesus to his face, but grumble against his disciples (Lk 5:30). It would be nearly impossible for these disciples to be unmoved by the Pharisees intimidating complaint. All their lives they have revered these men. Now they find themselves on the other side of the fence from them.

In addition, they would have been a bit squeamish about eating with Matthew in the first place. These are local boys. They have observed the ostracism Matthew had to endure. Perhaps they even flung some of the gossip themselves that was constantly thrown in Levi's direction. Undoubtedly they would have had second thoughts about following Jesus into Levi's house. In fact, this may have tempted them to abandon ship altogether.

Jesus overhears the surreptitious sabotage and brings it to a quick end with his beautiful proverb. Jesus, the great physician, is unconcerned with men's opinions of him. And as a physician, he has never been concerned about getting big bucks. He is driven by a compassion for the

---

[27]Luke, in his typical compassion for the least and the lost, simply says "others" in place of "sinners."

sick. "Where Pharisaic interest stops at assessment, Jesus' concern moves on to treatment: The sinners are sick and need to be helped, not contaminated and deserving to be spurned" (Nolland, p. 250).

We talk a lot about loving sinners and wanting to win the world, but we expect them to wipe their feet before they come into church. We get angry when they smoke in the church bathroom. We don't understand when they say, "Right on" instead of "Amen." And wait till you hear the silence in the crowded fellowship hall when one of them uses a dirty word. The church must learn that she is not a Hotel for Saints but a Hospital for Sinners.

Matthew alone (and typically) adds the quote from Hosea 6:6, "Go and learn what this means, 'I desire mercy and not sacrifice.'" "Go and learn" was a typical phrase a rabbi would use with a student who had not "done his homework." Jesus is treating these Ph.D.'s as novices. They are deeply insulted. But they deserve to be for their mixed up priorities. They are more concerned about religious piety than people. Thus, Hosea 6:6 is poignantly applicable. The Semitic idiom "this, not that," is understood as "more of this than that." It was not that God did not want their sacrifices, but more than sacrifices God wanted mercy. The middle-class church still stumbles over Jesus at this point as Blomberg points out:

> Many of us, like the Pharisees, at best ignore the outcasts of our society and at worst continue to discriminate against them. We do well to consider substantially increasing our spiritual, evangelistic, and social outreach to minorities, the homeless, prostitutes, addicts and pushers, gays and lesbians, AIDS victims, and the like, as well as to the more hidden outcasts such as divorcees, single parents, the elderly, white-collar alcoholics, and so on. . . We dare not join with sinners in their sinning, but we may well have to go places with them and encounter the world's wickedness in ways that the contemporary Pharisees in our churches will decry" (p. 157).

§ 48
Feasting vs.
Fasting;
Old vs. New
(Mt 9:14-17;
Mk 2:18-22;
Lk 5:33-39)

Matthew's banquet fostered not one, but two complaints against Jesus: (1) Fraternizing with sinners and (2) feasting instead of fasting. This narrative is "part 2" of Matthew's party, and stands out as the centerpiece of Luke's controversy stories (Lk 5:1-6:16). The bottom line is that the gospel of Jesus "cannot be reduced to being a patch repairing the 'old' (v. 36) and which may not be constrained within the bounds of the 'old' (vv. 37-38)" (Nolland, p. 250).

Mk 2:18-20 *with*
Lk 5:33,
Mt 9:14-15

¹⁸Now John's disciples and the Pharisees were fasting. Some people {John's disciples^{MT}} came and asked Jesus, "How is it that John's disciples and the disciples of the Pharisees {often fast and pray^{LK}} are fasting, but yours are not? {[They] go on eating and drinking^{LK}}"

¹⁹Jesus answered, "How can the guests of the bridegroom fast {mourn^{MT}} while he is with them? They cannot, so long as they have him with them. ²⁰But the time will come when the bridegroom will be taken from them, and on that day they will fast.

According to the Law, there was only one commanded fast per year, the Day of Atonement. But the Pharisees fasted each Monday and Thursday as a demonstration of their extreme piety. Likely, then, Matthew's party fell on one of these days when the "really religious" people weren't eating.

It is somewhat curious that John's disciples align with the Pharisees rather than with Jesus. After all, John consistently pointed to Jesus as the Messiah while rebuking the Pharisees as a brood of vipers. On the other hand, John is now in prison and these die-hard disciples (who for some reason or another never switched over to following Jesus), may feel that Jesus is not doing all he could to help John out. It may also be important to remember that Jesus and John have different modes of operation (Mt 11:18-19). John was thoroughly ascetic while Jesus was much more "liberal." This must have been confusing and a bit offensive to John's disciples.

Jesus' response is insightful and logical. When the bridegroom is around, it's time to celebrate! So Jesus asks, "Do people fast during the bridegroom's wedding banquet?" We notice a couple things about this question. First, it is phrased in Greek so as to expect a negative answer — "Of course not!" Second, Jesus uses for himself one of the very titles John used to describe him — bridegroom. Thus, Jesus reminds them of the teaching of their own master (Jn 3:29).

The point is, you don't fast/mourn at a wedding. Jesus' ministry was a time for joy and celebration. That was kind of odd since Jesus, like John, preached repentance, which was appropriately accompanied by fasting. Soon enough, however, Jesus' disciples would grieve over the loss of their Lord. The word "taken away" [*aparthē*], indicates a somewhat violent removal. Already Jesus is alluding to the cross. For three days there would be much mourning from his followers. Even now, between his ascension and return, his followers are saddened by his absence. It is now time for mourning/fasting. We are comforted by the presence of his Spirit. This still leaves us with a mixed blessing — the Kingdom of God *now* but *not yet*.

Lk 5:36-39 *with*
Mt 9:16, Mk 2:21

³⁶He told them this parable: "No one tears a patch from a new garment and sews it on an old one. If he does, he will have torn the new garment, {the new

piece will pull away from the old, making the tear worse,^{MTMK}} and the patch from the new will not match the old. ³⁷And no one pours new wine into old wineskins. If he does, the new wine will burst the skins, the wine will run out and the wineskins will be ruined. ³⁸No, new wine must be poured into new wineskins. ³⁹And no one after drinking old wine wants the new, for he says, 'The old is better.'"

The first parable Jesus tells is about cloth and the second is about wine. The main lesson in both is that it is inappropriate for the disciples to fast while Jesus is with them. It is a time for rejoicing, not a time for fasting. Furthermore, both illustrations show that inappropriate actions can cause a great deal of destruction.

A secondary lesson is about the old and the new. The new does not fit into the old. You cannot take the regime of Jesus and cram it into the old legalistic code and cultus, especially as outlined by the Pharisees. Both will be ruined.

Luke alone adds this keen observation (5:39) that people tend to prefer the old to the new. Jesus is merely citing this proverb, not approving it. It is generally true that old wine is better. But this is where the metaphor stops. With the kingdom, the new (gospel) is better than the old (law). Yet the same principle applies: People like the old better. People get used to old ways and want to continue in them. Such is the nature of ritual.

We are not just talking about chronology, for today, the gospel is also quite old. People still tend to feel more comfortable with law than with grace. Even though law damns us, it at least tells us in black and white what is expected. Jesus simply calls us to follow him with no assurance of where we might end up. Who knows when he is going to lead us unto the likes of Matthew and his sinner friend! The code of the law may be dark, but its paths are certain; the gospel, although liberating, frightens us with its infinite expectations.

§ 49a
A Lame Man
Healed at the
Pool of
Bethesda on
the Sabbath
(Jn 5:1-9)

This is the second paralytic that Jesus heals (cf. § 53; Mt 9:1-8; Mk 2:1-12; Lk 5:17-26). Edersheim observes four points of similarity between the two incidents: (1) Jesus uses identical wording: "Rise, take up your bed and walk" (Mk 2:9; Jn 5:8). (2) Jesus is, without words, accused of blasphemy for forgiving sins (Jn 5:18). As a result, the religious hierarchy wants to kill him. (3) In both instances the real issue is Jesus' authority (Jn 5:27). And (4) in both cases, Jesus appeals to his works as evidence of his authority (Mk 2:10; Jn 5:36).

Jn 5:1-5

¹Some time later, Jesus went up to Jerusalem for a feast of the Jews. ²Now there is in Jerusalem near the Sheep Gate a pool, which in Aramaic is called

Bethesda[a] and which is surrounded by five covered colonnades. [3]Here a great number of disabled people used to lie — the blind, the lame, the paralyzed.[b] [5]One who was there had been an invalid for thirty-eight years.

[a]2 Some manuscripts Bethzatha; other manuscripts Bethsaida [b]3 Some less important manuscripts paralyzed—and they waited for the moving of the waters. [4]From time to time an angel of the Lord would come down and stir up the waters. The first one into the pool after each such disturbance would be cured of whatever disease he had.

Jesus' Galilean ministry is punctuated with a visit to Jerusalem during one of the feasts. We really can't know which one it was, but Hendricksen builds a strong case for Passover (pp. 188-189). If that is true, then this marks the beginning of Jesus' second year of ministry.

Jesus went to this public water hole, which was surrounded by five covered porches. The pool was called Bethesda, "house of mercy." It was near the Sheep Gate, probably named after the sacrificial lambs which were led through it into the temple.[28] It looked like some kind of a sick ward. For some reason, people gathered there hoping for a healing.

Verses 3b-4 explain why, "They waited for the moving of the waters. From time to time an angel of the Lord would come down and stir up the waters. The first one into the pool after each such disturbance would be cured of whatever disease he had." But these words are not included in the NIV main text because they are not found in any manuscript before the fourth century.[29] How then did they become part of the KJV text? This is only guesswork, but it seems reasonable to assume that early in the second century,[30] some scribe wrote a note in the margin explaining verse 7, which later was adopted as part of the text itself. This addition

---

[28]There have been no less than six locations suggested for this pool. The most likely, according to Wieand, is the twin pools by the church of St. Anne. Furthermore, the text of v. 2 is difficult. First, the word "gate" is not in the Greek text but is supplied. Therefore, we may be talking about the "Sheep pool" rather than the "Sheep gate." Second, there are several strong textual variants for Bethesda including *Bethsaida*, *Bezatha, Bethzatha*, etc. Each of these difficulties are analyzed by D.J. Wieand, "John 5:2 and the Pool of Bethesda," *NTS* 12 (1966): 392-404. However, neither the historicity of this event, nor the theological message of the passage are affected by these questions.

Based on the present tense of verse 2, "there is in Jerusalem . . . ," D.B. Wallace argues that John may have written his gospel prior to A.D. 70 since the colonnades of this pool would have been destroyed ("John 5:2 and the Date of the Fourth Gospel," *Biblica* 71 [1990]: 177-205).

[29]However, Zane Hodges gives a lengthy defense of their inclusion, "The Angel at Bethesda," *BibSac* 136 (1979): 25-39, contra Bruce Metzger, *A Textual Commentary on the Greek New Testament* (London: UBS, 1971), p. 209.

[30]Tertullian (c. 145-220 A.D.), was familiar with this passage. He says, "An angel, by his intervention, was wont to stir the pool at Bethsaida. They who were complaining of ill health used to watch for him; for whoever was the first to descend into these waters, after his washing ceased to complain" (*On Baptism* V).

likely represents the popular perception at the time of Jesus. We do not need to assume, however, that John (or even the scribe who inserted this note), accepted the truth of the statement; only that the populace did. In fact, it is unreasonable to assume that God would act in such a whimsical manner. Furthermore, it seems a bit unfair that those who needed healing the least would have the greatest chance of obtaining it by beating everyone else to the pool. We have no other example of God healing in such a manner. Thus we (1) reject vv. 3b and 4 as part of the original text,[31] (2) reject the truth of the statement, but (3) accept that it accurately describes the popular belief of Jesus' day.

One of the invalids at the pool had suffered some sort of paralysis for thirty-eight years. There is no need to assume that he was at the pool for thirty-eight years, just sick for that long. Here we have a room full of sick people; Jesus selects only one and heals him. He could just as easily have waved his hand and healed them all. But he chooses only one. Why? Jesus is obviously not performing this miracle out of compassion (alone). In fact, it would appear that Jesus wants to start a fight with the religious leaders over this Sabbath controversy. It was a dandy!

Jn 5:6-9

[6]When Jesus saw him lying there and learned that he had been in this condition for a long time, he asked him, "Do you want to get well?"

[7]"Sir," the invalid replied, "I have no one to help me into the pool when the water is stirred. While I am trying to get in, someone else goes down ahead of me."

[8]Then Jesus said to him, "Get up! Pick up your mat and walk." [9]At once the man was cured; he picked up his mat and walked.

The day on which this took place was a Sabbath,

In verse 6 Jesus asks an odd, almost silly, question, "Do you wish to get well?" His presence at the pool should make that obvious enough. Who would NOT want to get well after thirty-eight years of sickness? Paradoxically, there are people who would rather be sick than well, for a number of reasons. Others, especially after years of sickness, lose the will to be well.

The man's problem is obvious; he has no help getting into the pool. The other not-so-sick people beat him to the punch, so Jesus helps him out. He deliberately heals this fellow on the Sabbath. To make matters worse, Jesus orders him to pick up his mat and leave. The man slips out in silence, but the fireworks are about to begin.

The Sabbath, along with circumcision and dietary regulations, set

---

[31]We agree here with G.D. Fee who evaluates the arguments of Metzger and Hodges and argues for the exclusion of John 5:3b-4, "On the Inauthenticity of John 5:3b-4" *EvQ* 54 (Oct 1982): 207-218.

the Jews apart from the other cultures that surrounded them. This was a critical part of their heritage and they took it seriously. Rabbinic Judaism had surrounded the Sabbath with literally hundreds of peripheral rules to insure that their disciples did not break God's simple command to rest on the Sabbath. Within this vast body of oral traditions were precise regulations about healing. You could save a person's life on the Sabbath, but healing merely to help someone would have to wait until the next day. Jesus knew precisely what he was doing by healing this man and ordering him to carry his cot. He was confronting the institutional authorities of Judaism over this very serious matter of Sabbath keeping.

§ 49b
Controversy
over the
Sabbath
Healing
(Jn 5:10-18)

¹⁰and so the Jews said to the man who had been healed, "It is the Sabbath; the law forbids you to carry your mat."
¹¹But he replied, "The man who made me well said to me, 'Pick up your mat and walk.'"
¹²So they asked him, "Who is this fellow who told you to pick it up and walk?"
¹³The man who was healed had no idea who it was, for Jesus had slipped away into the crowd that was there.

Although the Sabbath Law (Exod 20:10), is pretty open-ended, it was clear that a person was not to carry heavy loads (cf. Jer 17:19-27; Neh 13:15). The oral traditions surrounding the Sabbath, however, added unbelievable specification as to just what a "burden" might entail. They are intricate to the point of being ludicrous. (See Edersheim, Appendix 17, II:777). Furthermore, it is amazing that these oral traditions had so thoroughly supplanted the Word of God. It should be observed here that Jesus NEVER broke a single God-given Sabbath regulation. But he constantly challenged and disregarded the Pharisaic codes surrounding Sabbath observance (cf. § 50, 51, 110). In our present narrative, Jesus did so blatantly and purposefully.

This poor lame man's joy is soon mixed with fear and rejection. He is just doing what he has been told to do. But the Pharisees are furious when they catch him carrying his cot. Seeking to justify himself, he blames it on Jesus who had ordered him to do so. Certainly if someone heals you after thirty-eight years of paralysis, you do what he says! From our perspective, however, we're a bit put out with the little fink. Yet who would not do the same thing in the face of such imposing opposition?

Notice that the Jews[32] do not ask the man, "Who healed you," but

---

[32]Again, in John's usage, this term "Jews" almost invariably refers to the antagonistic religious leaders (i.e., the Pharisees and Sadducees, cf. 1:19; 7:17; 9:22; 18:12, 14), except when describing "Jewish" things (e.g., feasts or customs).

"Who is the man who said to you, 'Take up your pallet and walk'?" They refuse to admit, or at least to stress, the miracle. They prefer to concentrate on the offense of breaking one of their traditions. Now the poor fellow can't even come up with an alibi because Jesus slipped away too soon (v. 13).

Jn 5:14-18

¹⁴Later Jesus found him at the temple and said to him, "See, you are well again. Stop sinning or something worse may happen to you." ¹⁵The man went away and told the Jews that it was Jesus who had made him well.

¹⁶So, because Jesus was doing these things on the Sabbath, the Jews persecuted him. ¹⁷Jesus said to them, "My Father is always at his work to this very day, and I, too, am working." ¹⁸For this reason the Jews tried all the harder to kill him; not only was he breaking the Sabbath, but he was even calling God his own Father, making himself equal with God.

Sometime later Jesus finds him in the temple. This may have been the first time in his life that he is able to enter that edifice and worship God since cripples weren't allowed to participate. Jesus warns him that if he keeps on sinning he might encounter a fate worse than paralysis.

The current thought of Jesus' day was that sickness was caused by sin. Hence, the man's paralysis would have been attributed to God's punishment for some evil deed he did. If this fellow doesn't straighten up, God will smite him even more severely. Apparently Jesus doesn't buy into that illogic (cf. Jn 9:1-4). So what *is* Jesus saying? What is this "worse thing"? It seems reasonable to interpret Jesus' statement as judgment. This certainly fits the context of this chapter (vv. 27-30). In other words, if his new found health is used for evil, he may wind up in hell. But even beyond that, the context would suggest that his sin was NOT some fleshly avarice, but simply unbelief. He didn't expect a miracle, he tattled on Jesus, and will now go turn him over to the officials.

It may be unfair to accuse this man of evil motives, but how could he not have known that his "snitching" would get Jesus in trouble? Perhaps the Jews ordered him to tell them if he learned who the healer was. We just cannot know. But we do know the result. Jesus was harassed by the officials for violating the Sabbath regulations.

Under normal circumstances, a blue-collar worker from Galilee would buckle under the pressure of the Jerusalem hierarchy. But Jesus counters their accusation with a bold acclamation: "My Father is working until now, and I Myself am working." In other words, "Like father, like son." Such a claim was sure to ruffle a few feathers.

It is certainly true that God rested on the seventh day (Gen 2:3). But every moment of every day God sustains his creation. Jesus, like his Father, continues to work at all times, every day. Now the Jews are *really* mad. Not only did Jesus defy their traditions, but even blasphemed, according to their way of thinking. By claiming to be God's Son, Jesus is putting himself on par with God. They have correctly interpreted his words but they don't believe them for even a minute. Such blatant blasphemy requires death! So they set out with a vengeance to get the job done.

§ 49c
A Sermon on Jesus' Deity and Credentials
(Jn 5:19-47)

This sermon is one of the clearest declarations of Jesus' deity and credentials. But it is couched in Jewish idioms so that to fully understand it one must think like a Jew. Its real meaning is not merely discerned through understanding the words themselves, but by observing current Jewish culture and the reaction of Jesus' audience. It can be divided into three sections: (1) A comparison between Jesus and the Father (vv. 19-23), (2) resurrection unto life and unto judgment (vv. 24-30), and (3) various witnesses to Jesus (vv. 31-47).

Jn 5:19-23

[19]Jesus gave them this answer: "I tell you the truth, the Son can do nothing by himself; he can do only what he sees his Father doing, because whatever the Father does the Son also does. [20]For the Father loves the Son and shows him all he does. Yes, to your amazement he will show him even greater things than these. [21]For just as the Father raises the dead and gives them life, even so the Son gives life to whom he is pleased to give it. [22]Moreover, the Father judges no one, but has entrusted all judgment to the Son, [23]that all may honor the Son just as they honor the Father. He who does not honor the Son does not honor the Father, who sent him."

Jesus first establishes his relationship to the Father by making four comparisons in verses 19-23:
1. Jesus does the same things, in the same way the Father does (v. 19). He thus claims to understand God's plans and priorities.
2. Because the Father loves the Son, he reveals his work to him, and the best is yet to come (v. 20). Certainly there would be more miracles. But the greatest work of Jesus would be in things like: (a) showing us what God is like and preparing a way for us to come to him, (b) redeeming man from sin, (c) giving us hope beyond the grave, (d) sending the Holy Spirit, (e) establishing and perfecting (eschatologically) his kingdom. We are, by nature, enthralled with the miraculous. But Jesus' greatest work is much richer and deeper than this.
3. As the Father raises the dead, so also does the Son (v. 21).
4. The Father has given judgment over to the Son (v. 22; cf. 3:18-19; Mt 25:31ff.), in order that the Son may be honored "even as" the Father is honored.

The implications of this are astounding! Jesus has the ability and the authority of the Father. If this premise is accepted then Jesus is the end of man's search for God. He will lead us to the Father (Jn 14:6). Furthermore, if we reject Jesus, we have rejected the Father. This sets the stage for the rest of Jesus' sermon.

Jn 5:24-30

²⁴"I tell you the truth, whoever hears my word and believes him who sent me has eternal life and will not be condemned; he has crossed over from death to life. ²⁵I tell you the truth, a time is coming and has now come when the dead will hear the voice of the Son of God and those who hear will live. ²⁶For as the Father has life in himself, so he has granted the Son to have life in himself. ²⁷And he has given him authority to judge because he is the Son of Man.

²⁸"Do not be amazed at this, for a time is coming when all who are in their graves will hear his voice ²⁹and come out — those who have done good will rise to live, and those who have done evil will rise to be condemned. ³⁰By myself I can do nothing; I judge only as I hear, and my judgment is just, for I seek not to please myself but him who sent me."

Verses 21-23 launch Jesus into his present discussion: Resurrection. Jesus gives life to whomever he wishes and executes judgment by the Father's authority. Therefore he can raise the dead both to eternal life or to a fearsome judgment.

Our minds naturally gravitate to "end time" events. But that is not necessary. Notice that there were *already* people who had passed out of death into life (v. 24). That is past and present tense, not future. When Jesus speaks of eternal life it is in the here and now. In other words, the resurrection has already begun. Those who listen to Jesus and entrust their lives to him have already experienced the essence of eternal life.

The spiritually dead will be brought to life by the preaching of Jesus. The symbol of death for sin is frequently used in Scripture (Eph 2:1,5; Col 2:13; Rev 3:1). This is the first resurrection (vv. 24-25; cf. Rev 20:4-6).

There is a second resurrection which is yet future (vv. 28-30; Rev 20:11-15). It is interesting to note that in every instance we have a picture of judgment, men are not judged on the basis of their works. We are saved by grace through faith. However, there is no practical way of observing faith outside of works, nor is there any valid faith that is not observable by works (James 2:14-26).

Jn 5:31-40

³¹"If I testify about myself, my testimony is not valid. ³²There is another who testifies in my favor, and I know that his testimony about me is valid.

³³"You have sent to John and he has testified to the truth. ³⁴Not that I accept human testimony; but I mention it that you may be saved. ³⁵John was a lamp that burned and gave light, and you chose for a time to enjoy his light.

³⁶"I have testimony weightier than that of John. For the very work that the

Father has given me to finish, and which I am doing, testifies that the Father has sent me. ³⁷And the Father who sent me has himself testified concerning me. You have never heard his voice nor seen his form, ³⁸nor does his word dwell in you, for you do not believe the one he sent. ³⁹You diligently study[a] the Scriptures because you think that by them you possess eternal life. These are the Scriptures that testify about me, ⁴⁰yet you refuse to come to me to have life."

ᵃ*39* Or *Study diligently* (the imperative)

In this final phase of Jesus' sermon, he outlines the various witnesses he has: himself (v. 31), the Father (vv. 32, 34, 37), John the Baptist (vv. 33, 35-36), his own works (v. 36), and the Scriptures (v. 39), specifically as written by Moses (vv. 45-47). This was important in the Jewish culture. No testimony could be established without two or three witnesses. Jesus outdoes himself by outlining no less than five credible sources.

First, Jesus is his own witness. However, the Jews would never accept Jesus' testimony about himself, especially if it stood alone. Thus, Jesus says, "If I alone bear witness of myself, my testimony is not true." We have to kind of fill in the blank. That is to say, his testimony would not be true insofar as the Jews perceived or accepted it, which was precisely the case in John 8:12-14. However, Jesus' testimony about himself (vv. 19-23) *is* true. He cannot lie.

Second, the Father himself testified of Jesus. We can at least assume that this has reference to the heavenly voice and endowment of the Holy Spirit at Jesus' baptism (Mt 3:17; Mk 1:11; Lk 3:22). We may also, perhaps, expand it to God's testimony of Jesus through the Scriptures (although this will be dealt with separately).

Third, John's testimony was surprisingly thorough and theologically "mature." Using the fourth Gospel alone gives us a striking picture of Jesus: (1) He is far superior to John and existed before him (1:27, 30; 3:30). (2) He is the Lamb of God who takes away the sin of the world (1:29, 36). (3) He is divinely identified as the Messiah through the Holy Spirit descending as a dove (1:31-33). (4) He is the Son of God (1:34). (5) He is the Christ/Messiah (3:28). (6) He is from heaven (3:31). (7) He reveals truths from God (3:32-34). (8) He possesses the Holy Spirit without measure (3:34). (9) He is loved by God (3:35). (10) He has all of God's authority (3:35). (11) He is the source of eternal life (3:36). Much of this testimony was given in the presence of the Sadducees and Pharisees (Jn 1:19-28). Furthermore, there was interaction between the disciples of John and the Jewish leaders (Jn 3:25). Therefore, they would have known full well what John said about Jesus.

Fourth, Jesus' works testified about him. After just one year of ministry Jesus has performed many miracles both in Judea (Jn 2:23) and

Galilee. He has turned water into wine, cleansed the temple, read people's thoughts and healed the nobleman's son at Capernaum, Peter's mother-in-law, and many others. He has cast out demons, healed paralytics and cleansed lepers. That portfolio ought to be a sufficient resumé for the Son of God.

Fifth, the Scriptures themselves testify about Jesus, not only prophetically, but typologically and analogically (Lk 24:27, 44). The KJV renders v. 39 as a command, "Search the Scriptures," which is grammatically possible but not contextually comfortable. We agree with the NIV in rendering it as a statement, "You diligently study the Scriptures." There are many, especially among conservative Christians, who live under this same illusion. Eternal life, they think, is found in the Book. Thus, if we study hard enough, we are bound to be saved and sanctified. But salvation is not in a book but in a person. There are many great Bible scholars who know all about Jesus, but have never come to know him. The Book will always point to Jesus . . . but that's all it can do. We are saved by trusting Jesus, not by gaining knowledge.

Jn 5:41-47

⁴¹"I do not accept praise from men, ⁴²but I know you. I know that you do not have the love of God in your hearts. ⁴³I have come in my Father's name, and you do not accept me; but if someone else comes in his own name, you will accept him. ⁴⁴How can you believe if you accept praise from one another, yet make no effort to obtain the praise that comes from the only God?

⁴⁵"But do not think I will accuse you before the Father. Your accuser is Moses, on whom your hopes are set. ⁴⁶If you believed Moses, you would believe me, for he wrote about me. ⁴⁷But since you do not believe what he wrote, how are you going to believe what I say?"

ª*44* Some early manuscripts *the Only One*

When all is said and done, Jesus' witnesses are all divine. The religious leaders won't accept a single one of them! Had Jesus relied on human testimony, he probably would have been welcomed into their back-slapping club. That's just the kind of thing they loved (Mt 23:5-7). But because Jesus claimed exclusive rights, they were affronted by him.

Not only were the Pharisees upset with Jesus, he was upset with them! He rebukes them harshly, not from cruelty but from clarity. He knows that the stakes are high. There will be a judgment day, and all who reject Jesus will have hell to pay. Now lest we think that Jesus is throwing a temper tantrum in self-defense, he clarifies his role. It is not Jesus who will accuse them but Moses, whom they claim to cherish. The very words of Scripture they claim to live by will be the words they die by.

**§ 50
Sabbath
Controversy:
Picking Grain**
(Mt 12:1-8;
Mk 2:23-28;
Lk 6:1-5)

In this section and the one that follows, we have back-to-back Sabbath controversies: Picking grain and healing a man with a withered hand. They illustrate how the "new" legislation of Jesus doesn't fit the "old" scheme of the Pharisees (cf. Lk 5:27-39). Jesus becomes the new rabbi for the church.[33] He gives the authoritative interpretation of the law.

The Sabbath was such an important part of Judaism that the Talmud has an entire tractate devoted to Sabbath keeping (*Shabbat*). The Mishna (*Sanh.* 7:4) records Sabbath breaking among the crimes serious enough to merit stoning. It is no small wonder, then, that Jesus' disregard for Pharisaic Sabbath traditions was particularly infuriating to the Jews.

These controversies have been brewing for some time now. We can trace the progression of the accusations against Christ: (1) Blasphemy (Healing of the Paralytic, Mt. 9:1-8); (2) Fraternizing with sinners (Banquet at Levi's House, Mt 9:9-13); (3) Neglecting Ascetic Duties (Feasting/Fasting controversy, Mt 9:14-17), and (4) Sabbath controversy (Healing Lame Man, Jn 5).

Lk 6:1-2

[1]One Sabbath Jesus was going through the grainfields, and his disciples {were hungry and[MT]} began to pick some heads of grain, rub them in their hands and eat the kernels. [2]Some of the Pharisees asked, "Why are you doing what is unlawful on the Sabbath?"

Mk 2:25-26

[25]He answered, "Have you never read what David did when he and his companions were hungry and in need? [26]In the days of Abiathar the high priest, he entered the house of God and ate the consecrated bread, which is lawful only for priests to eat. And he also gave some to his companions."

Mt 12:5-6

[5]"Or haven't you read in the Law that on the Sabbath the priests in the temple desecrate the day and yet are innocent? [6]I tell you that one[a] greater than the temple is here."

[a]6 Or *something*; also in verses 41 and 42

The Sabbath controversy, which started in Jerusalem, has now been transported to Galilee as Jesus returns from what we have assumed is the second Passover of his ministry (Jn 5). The grain fields come to maturity around April. If the textual variant in Luke 6:1 (*deuteroprōtē* = *first month, second sabbath*) is correct, then this particular grain field would have to be barley, which ripens one to three weeks before wheat.

---

[33]F.W. Beare, "The Sabbath was Made for Man," *JBL* 79 (1960): 130-136, explains how these stories may reflect the continuing controversy in the first century church about the Sabbath (cf. Gal 4:10; Col 2:16; Rom 14:5). As the church began to separate from the synagogue and as she began to include more Gentiles, the issue of Sabbath keeping would raise a number of questions for early believers.

Eating out of someone else's grainfield was permissible according to OT law (Deut 23:25). Furthermore, nothing in the OT Sabbath commands would prohibit such an innocent act. The Pharisees' complaint against Jesus' disciples was based on the Oral Law, not the written law. According to these traditions the disciples were guilty on a number of counts. By plucking the grain they were guilty of reaping; by rubbing the grain they were guilty of threshing (cf. Exod 34:21).

The Pharisees charge the disciples with breaking the Oral Law. Jesus will justify their actions through the written law. First, in the days of Abiathar, David and his men ate the shewbread reserved for the priests (cf. 1 Sam 21:1-6).[34] Jesus' snide comment, "Have you never read?" was not merely an insult. It called attention to the fact that they had superseded the Word of God with Oral Law. They knew all too well the written Word. But they were a million miles away from its intent.

Only the priests were allowed to eat this sacred Shewbread (Lev 24:5-9). But David and his companions did so without culpability. Why? Because (1) they were in need, and that superseded ritualistic regulations, and (2) under David's direction they were accomplishing God's mission. Thus, they became acceptable candidates for God's provision, even beyond the limits of the law. Typologically, Jesus is the fulfillment of David. Thus, his disciples are also appropriate candidates for God's provision through Jesus.

The comparison between Jesus and David is not about their actions but their persons. Jesus is the fulfillment of the Davidic King. Such a comparison was a bold claim for Jesus to make in the company of these Bible Scholars.

Second, the priests work on the Sabbath fulfilling their duties in the temple, but breaking the command to rest. Now, a layman would be defiled by the blood and work that Sabbath sacrifices required, but the priests were not. Why? Because they were serving in connection with the temple. Since Jesus is greater than the temple, and by extension greater also than David (cf. Mt 22:41-45), the disciples are doubly innocent because they were serving in connection with Jesus.[35]

---

[34]It is a fact that Abiathar was not the priest at Nob whom David met. It was his father Ahimelech. But then, Jesus does not say that Abiathar was priest but only, "In the days of (*epi*) Abiathar." And in fact, Abiathar was not only alive, but present at the event. Shortly afterward Saul would massacre all the priests at Nob (1 Sam 22:18-19) and Abiathar alone would escape and flee to David. Not surprisingly, David later appointed him High Priest.

[35]Jesus is using typical Jewish logic (*qal wa-homer*), arguing from the lesser to the greater. However, Rabbi D.M. Cohn-Sherbok shows why Jesus' logic would not have been acceptable to the current rabbinic lawyers ("An Analysis of Jesus' Arguments Concerning the Plucking of Grain on the Sabbath," *JSNT* 2 [1979]: 31-41).

Mt 12:7

[7]"If you had known what these words mean, 'I desire mercy, not sacrifice'[a], you would not have condemned the innocent."

Mk 2:27-28

[27]Then he said to them, "The Sabbath was made for man, not man for the Sabbath. [28]So the Son of Man is Lord even of the Sabbath."

[a]7 Hosea 6:6

Jesus draws three conclusions about the Sabbath:

(1) The quotation from Hosea 6:6 reiterates God's priority in religious duties. God is interested in love and mercy more than meticulous observations of regulations.

(2) The Sabbath was to be a blessing to God's people, not a burden. It had a two-pronged purpose: Rest and Worship. Indeed, the rest is good for our bodies, but its primary function was to provide opportunity for worship. Pharisaic Sabbath regulations were a distraction from both.

(3) All three Synoptics highlight that Jesus is in charge of the Sabbath. He gets to make and interpret the rules. Indeed, he is our Sabbath (Heb 4). Along this line, it seems significant that Matthew places these two Sabbath controversies on the heels of 11:28-30, "Come to me, all you who are weary and burdened, and I will give you rest."

We might add two other conclusions from this text:

(4) Human traditions must never supersede the Word of God. It is easy for religious communities to build ritualistic systems on human tradition and then use the Scripture to justify them. But so often, in doing so, we abrogate the spirit of the law by the letter of the law.

(5) Jesus' use of 1 Samuel 22, to some extent, validates the use of historical precedent as a support for doctrine.[36] Historical precedent can serve as a guide for contemporary behavior and ecclesiastical practice if it is based on sound logical inferences.

§ 51
Sabbath
Controversy:
Healing a
Man's Withered
Hand
(Mt 12:9-14;
Mk 3:1-6;
Lk 6:6-11)

Luke alone (6:6) tells us that these events did not occur on the same Sabbath. In the previous narrative the Pharisees harass Jesus because of the actions of his disciples. On the second occasion, Jesus initiates the controversy by placing the man with the withered hand center stage (Lk 6:8). This event takes the Sabbath controversy to a new level. Not only was the Sabbath for man's benefit; it was an opportunity to do good for other people.

---

[36]J.M. Hicks, "The Sabbath Controversy in Matthew: An Exegesis of Matthew 12:1-14," RestQ 27/2 (1984): 79-91.

Lk 6:6-8 *with*
Mt 12:10

⁶On another Sabbath he went into the synagogue and was teaching, and a man was there whose right hand was shriveled. ⁷The Pharisees and the teachers of the law were looking for a reason to accuse Jesus, {they asked him, "Is it lawful to heal on the Sabbath?"ᴹᵀ} so they watched him closely to see if he would heal on the Sabbath. ⁸But Jesus knew what they were thinking and said to the man with the shriveled hand, "Get up and stand in front of everyone." So he got up and stood there.

The Oral Law was clear in its regulations for Sabbath healing. You could provide medical attention which would save a life, but that was all. If a man fell off a cliff and cracked his head, you could stop the bleeding, but you could not set a broken leg. Since a withered hand was not life-threatening, it would be illegal to heal this fellow on the Sabbath. Jesus, perceiving their scheme, picks up the gauntlet they have thrown down and deals with their machination head-on. Jerome, commenting on this passage, says that this man was a mason. Thus, he would have been severely impaired from earning a living. Even after he's healed, he can't work until the next day. According to the Pharisees, Jesus is clearly out of bounds.

Mk 3:4-5a

⁴Then Jesus asked them, "Which is lawful on the Sabbath: to do good or to do evil, to save life or to kill?" But they remained silent.
⁵He looked around at them in anger and, deeply distressed at their stubborn hearts. . . .

Mt 12:11-12

¹¹He said to them, "If any of you has a sheep and it falls into a pit on the Sabbath, will you not take hold of it and lift it out? ¹²How much more valuable is a man than a sheep! Therefore it is lawful to do good on the Sabbath."

The answer to Jesus' question is so obvious! But religious fervor and protection of pet theologies can be blinding. Jesus gets mad. That didn't happen very often. But when people place tradition and regulation over human need his anger is predictable. How their gaze must have dropped when Jesus' angry eyes pierced deeply into their souls.

Since they won't answer his question, he will. The Oral Law made provision for rescuing animals that fell into a pit on the Sabbath (*b Sabb.* 128b). Again Jesus used typical Jewish logic — from lesser to greater. A man is more valuable than an animal. Therefore it must be lawful to do good things for people on the Sabbath beyond just saving their lives. But Jesus doesn't stop there. Not only is the Sabbath an opportunity to work for another's good; to do nothing in the face of human need is evil, paramount to murder (Mk 3:4).

Mt 12:13

¹³Then he said to the man, "Stretch out your hand." So he stretched it out and it was completely restored, just as sound as the other.

Mk 3:6 *with*
Lk 6:11

⁶Then the Pharisees went out {furious^LK} and began to plot with the Herodians how they might kill Jesus."

It appears that as the man put forth his hand, it was healed. Even the muscle atrophy from lying dormant was healed. It was as healthy as his other hand. The Pharisees start their work immediately; they were furious. In fact, the word Luke uses means "mindless anger." They plot here for the first time how they might kill Jesus. Oddly enough they pair up with the Herodians. There is no conclusive evidence to identify this group, but their political affiliation with Herod is beyond question. That would make them odd bedfellows for the Pharisees. As near as we can tell, this was the only thing these two groups ever agreed upon.

§ 52
Withdrawal
from Danger
& Crowds by
the Sea
(Mt 12:15-21;
Mk 3:7-12)

[MK 3:]⁷{Aware of this^MT} Jesus withdrew with his disciples to the lake, and a large crowd from Galilee followed. ⁸When they heard all he was doing, many people came to him from Judea, Jerusalem, Idumea, and the regions across the Jordan and around Tyre and Sidon. ⁹Because of the crowd he told his disciples to have a small boat ready for him, to keep the people from crowding him. ¹⁰For he had healed many, so that those with diseases were pushing forward to touch him. ¹¹Whenever the evil^a spirits saw him, they fell down before him and cried out, "You are the Son of God." ¹²But he gave them strict orders not to tell who he was.

^a 11 Greek *unclean*; also in verse 30

The battle lines are now clearly drawn. After the incident of healing the man's withered hand on the Sabbath, the Pharisees align with the Herodians, plotting Jesus' death. Jesus strategically removes himself from the confines of the city where such a plot could easily take place. The Sea of Galilee is the perfect spot for him to continue his preaching. The crowds love him, and in the open air it is easy to see a mob forming. If push came to shove, he could always hop in a boat and escape to any number of districts surrounding the lake.

The crowds continue to swell as rumors continue to spread about Jesus' ability to heal and cast out demons. The only area from which people did not come was, predictably, Samaria. From all directions (as the following chart shows), twisted and diseased bodies are carried to Jesus. When they come to Jesus, their anxious enterprise becomes obnoxious pushiness. They claw and clamor for Jesus to the extent that it becomes physically dangerous for him and the crowds.[37] Jesus, therefore, has to teach from a boat on the lake so that he will not be mauled.

---

[37]Mark uses a graphic word which literally rendered would read, "They fell upon him."

Place	Gospel	Distance (miles)	Direction
Syria	Mt	60	North
Galilee	Mt, Mk	20 (max)	
Decapolis	Mt	60	Southeast
Perea	Mt, Mk	30-90	Southeast
Jerusalem	Mt, Mk, Lk	75	South
Judea	Mt, Mk, Lk	65-90	South
Idumea	Mk	100-120	South
Tyre	Mk, Lk	40	Northwest
Sidon	Lk	60	Northwest

The demons have supernatural knowledge, therefore, they know who Jesus is. Jesus forbids them to declare his identity for several reasons (cf. Mk 1:34, 43-45): (1) He does not want his best testimony coming from demons. (2) The crowds are not ready to hear who he really is. Their faith is still in the seedling stage. (3) The crowds are already unwieldy. Jesus does not need *more* popularity. And (4) the antagonism against Jesus does not need to be stirred up any further.

Mt 12:17-21

[17]This was to fulfill what was spoken through the prophet Isaiah:
[18]"Here is my servant whom I have chosen,
    the one I love, in whom I delight;
I will put my Spirit on him,
    and he will proclaim justice to the nations.
[19]He will not quarrel or cry out;
    no one will hear his voice in the streets.
[20]A bruised reed he will not break,
    and a smoldering wick he will not snuff out,
till he leads justice to victory.
[21] In his name the nations will put their hope."[a]

[a]*21* Isaiah 42:1-4

This is the longest OT quote in Matthew. It is quite close to the MT but also shows familiarity with the LXX. It comes from the first suffering servant song of Isaiah 42:1-4. We have already heard this kind of Divine approval of Jesus at his baptism (Mt 3:17). This beautiful description of the Messianic ministry underscores Jesus' gentleness. He was gentle with the crowds who mobbed him for healing. He compassionately ministered to their physical needs. He was even gentle with the Pharisees who opposed him. Instead of using his popularity to lead a revolt, Jesus quieted the crowds as well as the demons.

This quote contains two striking contrasts to the popular Jewish conception of the Messiah. First, he would be gentle. He would not be the militant rebel or the aggressive chieftain they expected. To be sure, he would bring about justice, not with the sword but with two rough timbers. To say that "No one will hear his voice in the streets," does not mean that Jesus will not denounce sin (cf. Mt 12:25-45). It means that Jesus won't boisterously promote (or even defend) himself.

Second, he would be a global savior, not a national hero. The Gentiles also would call on his name. Even this thronging multitude is only a small slice of the people who will eventually be drawn to the Messiah.

§ 53
Appointment of the Twelve Apostles
(Mk 3:13-19; Lk 6:12-16; cf. Mt 10:2-4; Acts 1:13)

[LK 6:]12One of those days Jesus went out to a mountainside to pray, and spent the night praying to God. 13When morning came, he called his disciples to him and chose twelve of them, whom he also designated apostles,

[MK 3:]14that they might be with him and that he might send them out to preach 15and to have authority to drive out demons.

Although this scene encompasses only five verses, it is one of the most crucial moments in Jesus' ministry. So important, in fact, that he bathes it in prayer the entire night before. We might think it prudent to get a good night's sleep so that he could be clear headed to make these decisions. But it was in prayer that this and all other important decisions were made with Jesus.

Of all the myriads who follow Jesus, he chooses twelve in whom he can invest himself. He still teaches the crowds, but in private sessions he pours out his plans and his character to the Twelve. Even in the midst of his greatest popularity, Jesus realizes that the way to turn the world upside down is to invest heavily in a few. And it works. Eleven of these twelve men would become the foundation of the church, built on the cornerstone of Christ (Eph 2:19-20).

The word *apostolos* has a range of meaning in the NT.[38] Essentially, it indicates "a messenger sent with a commission." Furthermore, the one sent is granted the authority of the one who sends him. Thus, these chosen delegates would carry with them the authority of Christ. Here, we are specifically dealing with the group of twelve Apostles, the foundation of the church. It was their job to preach the gospel of the kingdom especially after Jesus was gone. They were sent out into all the world with the authority of Jesus to proclaim him as king. To ensure their success, Jesus endowed them with special power to cast out demons and to

---

[38]For a full discussion of the term see F.H. Agnew, "The Origin of the N.T. Apostle-Concept: A Review of Research," *JBL* 105/1 (1986): 75-96.

heal (Mt 10:1; Acts 1:8). Jesus understood what it meant to be an apostle, for he too was sent on a mission (Heb 3:1).

Mk 3:16-19

> [16]These are the twelve he appointed: Simon (to whom he gave the name Peter); [17]James son of Zebedee and his brother John (to them he gave the name Boanerges, which means Sons of Thunder); [18]Andrew, Philip, Bartholomew, Matthew, Thomas, James son of Alphaeus, Thaddaeus, Simon the Zealot [19]and Judas Iscariot, who betrayed him.

The Apostles are listed four times (Mt 10:2-4; Mk 3:16-19; Lk 6:14-16; Acts 1:13). Each list gives the names in a different order. However, all four can be divided into three sections of four names each. The three sections always begin with Peter, Philip and James. We should also note that a number of these fellows have more than one name. Simon is also called Peter;[39] Judas is also called Lebbaeus and Thaddaeus; Bartholomew is most likely the Nathanael of John 1; and Thomas (Aramaic) is called Didymus (Greek), both names meaning "twin."

Furthermore, it is likely that several of the Apostles were related to each other and possibly to Jesus as well. A comparison of Matthew 27:56, Mark 15:40, and John 19:25 suggests that James and John, the sons of Zebedee, were likely cousins of Jesus. The latter James, Simon and Judas appear to be brothers. It is also possible that they were cousins of Jesus through Joseph's brother (cf. Edersheim I:522).

Judas Iscariot is the single Apostle who was not faithful to Jesus until death. He seems to be an outsider, the only Apostle not from Galilee. His town, Kerioth, was in Judea (Josh 15:25).[40] He is always mentioned last in the list and always identified as the one who betrayed Jesus. His motives are a mystery. Suffice it to say that the only motive even hinted at in the Gospels is greed (Jn 12:4-6; Mt 26:14-15).

---

[39]C. Roth, "Simon-Peter," *HTR* 54 (1961): 91-97, observes that the name "Simon," in the first century, was studiously avoided. He lists a number of famous "Simons" of that period who were all known by their patronym. Furthermore, this phenomenon was unique to the name "Simon." Roth suggests that the name "Simon" may have been held in such patriotic honor that it seemed inappropriate to use it for just anyone. Hence, one might conclude that Jesus changed Simon's name to Peter for cultural rather than theological reasons.

[40]His town "Kerioth" is derived from his name "Iscariot." However, A. Ehrman gives etymological evidence that "Iscariot" means "dyer" not "Kerioth" ("Judas Iscariot and Abba Saqqara," *JBL* 97 [1978]: 572-573), and C.C. Torrey suggests that "Iscariot" was an approbrious appellation related to the Hebrew word *saqqar*, meaning "falsehood" ("The name 'Iscariot,'" *HTR* 36 [1993]: 51-62).

THE SERMON ON THE MOUNT

This is the greatest sermon ever given. It is also the most quoted. In it we find the epitome of Jesus' teaching — radical, sensible, spiritual, and almost vicious in its demolition of hypocrisy. It flies in the face of every culture it enters. It pierces every heart that hears it. We attempt to dissect it with an exegetical scalpel only to find that we, not the text, are under examination.

Before entering the text itself, we must ask two important questions about the sermon as a whole. The first deals with how we approach the sermon. The second deals with how to understand the differences between Matthew and Luke's use of the same material.

HOW SHALL WE APPROACH THE SERMON ON THE MOUNT?

Some of the teachings of the Sermon on the Mount are so difficult that we have a hard time handling them. Oh, they are easy enough to understand, but we are perplexed about what to do with them. This difficulty has led people to view the sermon in several different ways.[41]

(1) Interim Ethic Approach (Albert Schweitzer, Johannes Weiss) — Some suggest that Jesus thought that "the end of the age" was upon them. Thus, he advocated this radical/revolutionary ethic. It was intended to be temporary but expedient for such critical times. Because the world did not end, this "interim ethic" no longer applies. Its demands are not reasonable or possible in today's world. The problems with this view are twofold. First, we must assume that Jesus was not only mistaken, but that his ethics were driven by the exigencies of the day. Second, nowhere in the text of this sermon do we even get a hint that its ethical directives are temporary or restricted to any particular age.

(2) Existential (Demythological) Approach — This view holds that Jesus' words (if indeed they do belong to him) are not intended to formulate a specific code of ethics. Rather they are intended to create a tension in each believer between what "ought to be" and what "actually is." This tension causes self-examination which leads to individual repentance and moral improvement. The value of the sermon, then, is not in its didactic content, but in the personal change wrought in each

---

[41]D. Crump, "Applying the Sermon on the Mount: Once You Have Read It What Do You Do With It," *CTR* 61 (1992): 3-14. He asks several penetrating questions. The answer to these questions will determine which approach we take to the sermon: Does the sermon offer "entrance requirements" for the Kingdom? What is the sermon's relationship to grace and law? Is the sermon relevant to the Christian dispensation or some past or future era? Is it designed for believers only or for society at large? See also W.D. Davies and D.C. Allison, "Reflections on the Sermon on the Mount," *SJT* 44 (1991): 283-309.

individual. The problem with this approach is that it denies the value to the text/ content itself and allows for any ethical code an individual may care to adopt. It is a terrible abuse of the historical material.

There are two similar approaches, which give greater credibility to the text. First, the General Principle Approach states that Jesus was not referring to specific actions, but general ethics which would apply in a broad range of situations. Second, the Attitudes-not-Acts approach says that Jesus was not speaking of actions/deeds but the attitudes behind the deeds. Both positions have the same flaw — they diminish the power of the sermon by excusing behavior which does not live up to its standard. In proper perspective, however, they do broaden and deepen the impact of Jesus' words.

(3) Legalistic Approach — This approach takes the sermon as the constitution of the Kingdom of God. It forms the "New Law" by which Christians are to live both privately and publicly. Some would even draw a dichotomy here between Paul (Grace) and Jesus (Law). This approach does not seem to adequately consider progressive revelation. Jesus did speak as a Jew, to Jews, under the Law. That is not to say that Jesus did not go beyond the law, but it is to say that the Sermon on the Mount is not the final word on morality, war, politics, lawsuits, etc.

A similar approach is the Literal/Absolutist approach which states that each command is to be literally obeyed by all people. Such men as Augustine, Francis of Assisi and Leo Tolstoy have advocated this position to a greater or lesser degree. This position takes seriously the teaching of Jesus, but pressed to extremes it can become ridiculous and even dangerous (cf. Mt 5:29). Thus, some have taken the literalistic approach but have offered "escape hatches" for the more difficult passages (Moderationist Approach). Applying such common sense exegesis is generally advisable. However, we must be careful not to explain away Jesus' intention in favor of culturally acceptable behavior.

(4) Preparation for the Gospel (Lutheran view) — Some say the Sermon, by its impossibly high demands, shows men their sin and thus their need for the redemptive work of Christ. Thus, it prepares men to receive Jesus as Savior. The problem, however, is that this does not do justice to the exegesis of the text. It seems clear from a cursory reading of the text that its demands are intended to be obeyed, not just given to make us feel bad.

A similar approach is to say that Jesus used hyperbole to shock his audience into attention. His demands thus need to be "toned down." The danger here is the same as the Moderationist Approach above, reducing Jesus' words until they are comfortable for us.

(5) Liberal Approach — Some suggest that this sermon is the means by which mankind can save civilization. This ethical standard (not Calvary), is the key to building the Kingdom of God. It was popular before the two world wars and then again in the sixties. Its unrealistic optimism denies the fallen nature of man and places its hope in man's evolution to a kinder, self-sacrificing state. Such idealism is, perhaps, attractive but not very realistic.

(6) Dispensationalist Approach (Darby and Scofield) — According to this view Jesus outlines the constitution for the Millennial Kingdom. Because the Jews rejected Jesus as Messiah, his offer was postponed until the future. Thus, this is what Christians will live like under the literal rule of Jesus for a thousand year period on this earth (Rev 20:1-6). It is not now achievable or particularly applicable. Some of its ethical commands do "cross over" and apply to us. But as a whole it is a glimpse of "things to come." The Dispensational approach imports to this text a host of presuppositions and a prearranged theological package. Thus, it doesn't seem to do justice to the text as it stands in context.

If none of these six suggestions are adequate, how is one to approach the Sermon on the Mount? We offer these guidelines:

(1) *It calls to the church.* This is kingdom talk. It is a literal code of Christian ethics (Mt 7:24, 26). In this vein, it provides real guidelines for citizens of the kingdom to relate to citizens of this world who reject the truth (Mt 5:11-12).

(2) *It points to heaven.* It was given under the dispensation of the law, but it has the end in sight. It is an attempt to bring the ethics of the kingdom of heaven down to earth at all times. In addition, the citizens of the kingdom are in development — conformity to the image of Christ. This task will only be completed in eternity. In the meantime, there is a sense of urgency about the moral stands of Christians.

(3) *It pierces your soul.* It penetrates to the heart and attitude. This goes deeper than mere behavior or conformity to a standard. Jesus wants a changed person, not just a legalistic moralist.

(4) *It cries for Calvary.* Jesus' words create tension between what ought to be and what is. Although Calvary pays the price for this tension, it does not solve it. That is, the Christian is still called to live a life of moral excellence, diminishing, as much as possible, this gulf between the ideal and the actual.

(5) *It requires reality.* This sermon is radical and in some instances hyperbolic. Although it is intended to shock, and must be exegeted accordingly, that does not give us the right to tone it down or

explain it away. Our only goal is to understand the words and expectations of Jesus and live accordingly.

(6) *It pictures Jesus.* Here is a clear glimpse into the behavior and ethics of Jesus. The sermon is indeed a portrait of him. He alone lived it, therefore he is the true content of the Sermon on the Mount.

These six guidelines don't answer all our specific questions about approaching or applying the Sermon on the Mount. But they do put some parameters around our interpretation of the text.

HOW DOES MATTHEW COMPARE WITH LUKE'S RENDITION?

Luke uses much of the material found in Matthew's version of the Sermon on the Mount, only he places it in different contexts.[42] Take, for example, Luke's sermon on the Plain (Lk 6:17-49). D. A. Carson observes that like Matthew 5-7 it (1) begins with "Beatitudes," (2) ends with the wise and foolish builder, (3) contains the golden rule, commands to love our enemy and turn the other cheek, prohibitions against judging, and the illustrations of a log/speck in the eye and a tree and its fruit, and (4) is followed by the account of Jesus going into Capernaum.[43]

At the same time, there are marked differences. (1) Both sermons contain information the other does not have. (2) Matthew contains one hundred and seven verses whereas Luke only has thirty. (3) Luke's beatitudes are strictly physical whereas Matthew's are spiritual. (4) Matthew's was delivered on a mountain, Luke's on a plain.

How do we account for both the similarities and the differences? One solution is to say that both Luke and Matthew simply compiled a conglomeration of Jesus' sayings and packaged them as a sermon.[44] Some take it a step further and suggest that these teachings were part of the early church's catechism and not actually from Jesus at all.[45]

Both Evangelists, however, portray this as a single sermon with historic reality. For instance, both of them nail it to a specific location (Mountain/Plain) and then have Jesus leave that place and enter Caper-

---

[42]For a thorough chart of Luke and Mark's use of Mt 5-7 see J. A. Brooks, "The Unity and Structure of the Sermon on the Mount," *CTR* 6/1 (1992): 15-28.

[43]D.A. Carson, *The Sermon on the Mount*, (Grand Rapids: Baker, 1978), pp. 139-140.

[44]There is some evidence that Matthew did this with the "Sending" discourse of chapter 10. Verse 5 says not to go to the Gentiles. But verse 18 says they will witness even to the Gentiles. Unless Jesus was inconsistent, Matthew must have pulled together "sending talk" from a later discourse of Jesus.

[45]Carson contains an excellent synopsis of the issues involved in the differences between Matthew and Luke in *The Sermon on the Mount*, pp. 139-149.

naum (Mt 8:5; Lk 7:1). Matthew even records the specific reaction of the crowds — astonishment (7:28-29). Thus, we conclude that Jesus preached the same basic sermon on two different occasions. This isn't too surprising for an itinerant preacher.

This is not to say that we have the entire sermon word for word. Even Matthew's rendition would only take about fifteen minutes. Rather we have, as most every speech in the NT, an accurate summary of its content. If Jesus taught for several hours, which would be normal, we have much more left out than what is included. Furthermore, if Jesus taught in Aramaic (which is likely), then the translation into Greek could account for some of the variance between Matthew and Luke. Their variance could further be accounted for by the fact that the Evangelists do not always present a chronological biography but a theological narrative in which events and sayings are arranged topically so as to best bring out their particular emphasis. In other words, both Matthew and Luke could have incorporated later sayings of Jesus into their sermons because they fit the topic under discussion. This was not an uncommon practice in the first century. It would not be viewed as dishonest or unhistorical.

Finally, we observe that the standard mode of education in Jesus' day was rote memory. The rabbis, for instance, often memorized the entire Pentateuch as well as much of their oral traditions. Thus, it is not inconceivable that the general outlines of two different sermons could be accurately reproduced, especially with the guidance of the Holy Spirit (Jn 14:26).

§ 54a
The Setting of the Sermon
(Mt 5:1-2; Lk 6:17-19)

This sermon will deal with three things: the Torah (5:17-48), the Christian cult (6:1-18) and social issues (6:19-7:12). As Davies and Allison points out, this is strikingly similar to Simon the Just's famous saying, "Upon three things the world standeth: Upon the Torah, upon the temple service, and upon 'deeds of kindness.'"[46] Through the Sermon on the Mount, these three pillars of Judaism also become foundational for the kingdom.

Matthew has already summarized Jesus' preaching in one short sentence: "Repent, for the kingdom of heaven is near" (4:17, 23). The Sermon on the Mount will now elaborate on that summary. It is a call to a changed life. As Stott puts it: A Christian Counter-Culture.[47] In fact,

---

[46] D.C. Allison, "The Structures of the Sermon on the Mount," *JBL* 106/3 (1987): 423-445.

[47] John Stott, *Christian Counter-Culture* (Downers Grove, IL: IVP, 1978).

Stott suggests that Matthew 6:8 (cf. Lev 18:3), is the key to understanding this sermon: "Do not be like them." It will instruct kingdom citizens in appropriate behavior and attitudes amidst a worldly kingdom which rejects its precepts.

Mt 5:1-2 *with*
Lk 6:17

¹Now when he saw the crowds, he went up on a mountainside {he went down with them and stood on a level place,ᴸᴷ} and sat down. His disciples came to him, ²and he began to teach them, saying:

Jesus has to go up on a mountainside.[48] The crowds are too thick to deal with in town. Not only does Jesus preach "Good News," he also heals their diseases (Mt 4:23). As a result, his fame spreads and people come from all over Syria, Galilee, Decapolis, Jerusalem, Judea, and Perea (Mt 4:24-25; Lk 6:17-19). There are pallets and crutches, demoniacs and paralytics, disfigured and pathetic people; they moan and bleed and ooze as they painfully elbow their way toward the master. Luke (6:19) reminds us how they clamor to touch Jesus in order to be healed.

Here Jesus looks strangely like Moses (Deut 18:15).[49] While Moses went up the mountain to *get* the law, Jesus goes up the mountain to *give* it. Like Moses, Jesus is the deliverer of the New Israel and this sermon is something like the Magna Carta of the Christian Faith.

As Jesus sits down on the mountainside, his disciples come to him. This was just one of many rabbinic methods of teaching that Jesus used.[50] When a rabbi sat down, it was an indication to his students that the formal teaching was about to start. This is not just rest for the weary, it is a bell signaling the beginning of class.

---

[48]"Mountain" in Matthew's Gospel often signals a place of new revelation (Mt 4:8, temptation; 17:1, transfiguration; 21:1, triumphal entry; 24:3, Olivet discourse; 28:16, great commission). Cf. A.A. Trites, "The Blessings and Warnings of the Kingdom," *Rev & Expos* 89/2 (1992): 179-196.

[49]D.C. Allison, "Jesus and Moses (Mt 5:1-2)," *ExpT* 97/7 (1987): 203-205, suggests four ways in which Jesus reflects Moses in this passage. (1) Jesus sat, reflecting Moses dwelling (Shub) on Mt Sinai (Deut 9:9). (2) Jesus "went up" on the mountain is equivalent to the LXX description of Moses' ascent to receive the law. (3) Mt 8:1 "Jesus descended the mountain" is equivalent to Exod 34:29 LXX. (4) He suggests that Jesus' life in Mt 1-4 parallels the life of Moses and Israel.

[50]G.L. Stevens, "Understanding the Sermon on the Mount: Its Rabbinic and New Testament Context," *Theol Ed* 46 (Fall 1992): 83-95, identifies a number of rabbinic methods followed by Jesus in the Sermon on the Mount: Parable (7:24-27); Metaphor (5:13-16; 7:16-20); Antithesis (5:17-44); Logic, specifically *a minori ad maius* — from lesser to greater (6:28-30); humor (7:4); Scripture (5:27); tradition (6:1-18).

§ 54b

The Beatitudes

(Mt 5:3-12;
Lk 6:20-26)

{Looking at his disciples he said,[LK]}
[MT 5:]3"Blessed are the poor in spirit,
　for theirs is the kingdom of heaven {God[LK]}.
4Blessed are those who mourn,
　for they will be comforted {laugh[LK]}.
5Blessed are the meek,
　for they will inherit the earth.
6Blessed are those who hunger and thirst for righteousness,
　for they will be filled.
7Blessed are the merciful,
　for they will be shown mercy.
8Blessed are the pure in heart,
　for they will see God.
9Blessed are the peacemakers,
　for they will be called sons of God.
10Blessed are those who are persecuted because of righteousness,
　for theirs is the kingdom of heaven.
11"Blessed are you when people {hate you, when they exclude you and[LK]} insult you, persecute you and falsely say all kinds of evil against you because of me. 12Rejoice {in that day and leap for joy[LK]} and be glad, because great is your reward in heaven, for in the same way they {their fathers[LK]} persecuted the prophets who were before you."

Lk 6:24-26

24"But woe to you who are rich,
　for you have already received your comfort.
25Woe to you who are well fed now,
　for you will go hungry.
Woe to you who laugh now,
　for you will mourn and weep.
26Woe to you when all men speak well of you,
　for that is how their fathers treated the false prophets."

　　The beatitudes are delightful little gems that pack a powerful punch. Before we examine each beatitude individually several introductory observations need to be made.

THE COMPARISON OF THE BEATITUDES IN MATTHEW AND LUKE

　　First, Matthew's beatitudes are structured differently than Luke's. Matthew presents eight blessings. In contrast, Luke presents four blessings (similar to Mt 5:3, 6, 4, & 11), and four woes which are not included in Matthew. These four woes are the antithesis of his four blessings. In this way Luke emphasizes that the downtrodden will be blessed in the future as citizens of the kingdom. In contrast the citizens of this world are already (and only) blessed with temporal blessings. Woe to them because they opt for cheap satisfaction now, instead of greater (spiritual) blessings in the future.

A more significant difference, however, is that Luke phrases his beatitudes, not as spiritual conditions, but as physical. For instance, Matthew says, "Blessed are the poor *in spirit*." But Luke simply says, "Blessed are the poor."[51] This is also true for those who "hunger now," and "weep now;" are "rich," "well-fed now," and "laugh now." This is not surprising in that Luke typically highlights the poor and downtrodden. Some, however, use Luke as a platform for a social(istic) gospel. This simply will not stand up to careful examination. Luke does not say that Jesus promised the poor financial security. Rather, they are promised the kingdom of God.[52] This is not to say that Jesus was indifferent to the needs of the poor. Indeed he came proclaiming good news to the poor (Lk 4:18). But his primary concern was for their greater need — their citizenship in the kingdom. Furthermore, our western worldview assumes that riches are a blessing when, in fact, they are often the very thing that keeps one from entering the kingdom (Mt 19:16-24).

THE NATURE OF THE BEATITUDES

Second, the beatitudes are structured like proverbs. That is, they are short pithy statements strung together along a common theme. Each one has three parts: (1) It starts with the word "blessed," (2) then describes a particular characteristic, and (3) ends with an appropriate blessing.

Another structural device Matthew uses is to repeat the blessing, "For theirs is the kingdom of Heaven," with the first and last beatitude (vv. 3, 10). This does two things. It shows us that vv. 11-12 are explanations of the eighth and last beatitude. But more importantly, it ties the whole section together under a common theme — the kingdom of heaven.

This common theme might be stated as follows: "Reversal under Kingdom Economy." That is, in the world's system, people who are poor, persecuted, mourning, meek, etc. are viewed as unfortunate, not blessed. In God's economy, the very people who are least, lost, and last, become rich, influential and favored (Mt 19:30; 20:16; James 4:6; 1 Pet 5:6; Prov 3:34). Furthermore, these passive verbs should probably be understood as "divine passives." In other words, it is God who gives the

---

[51]However, Meadors suggests that Luke's "poor" is to be understood as "pious" against the backdrop of Ps 37 and Isa 61. Hence, both Matthew and Luke's beatitudes would be spiritually oriented. G. T. Meadors, "The 'Poor' in the Beatitudes of Matthew and Luke," *GTJ* 6/2 (1985): 305-314.

[52]This aligns with Jesus' actions throughout the gospel: (1) refusing to turn stones to bread (Lk 4:4), (2) refusing to be made king after the feeding of the 5,000 (Jn 6:15), (3) and when Pilate interrogated Jesus about his kingdom he said, "My kingdom is not of this world" (John 18:36).

blessing. Thus, "they will be comforted," should be read, "God will comfort them."

A word of caution is in order here. These statements are true within the context of the Kingdom but not necessarily in society at large. Furthermore, proverbs are general statements of truth, not absolute promises. For example, those who mourn will generally be comforted in the kingdom. This is not to say, that each time we mourn we will find immediate or complete comfort, or that we will always see God or always receive mercy. These eight blessings will have ultimate fulfillment in eternity, but not necessarily absolute fulfillment presently.

APPLICATION OF THE BEATITUDES

Third, the beatitudes do not describe eight different kinds of people. They ideally describe each citizen of the kingdom.[53] Hinckley says it well, "The beatitudes aren't isolated virtues, they're landmarks along a path of repentance that brings us near to the heart of God."[54] This not only fits well the theme of the sermon but accurately describes Jesus' preaching of repentance in conjunction with the kingdom.

Finally, our introductory word, "Blessed" (*makarios*) can also be understood as "fortunate," "lucky," or even "happy." These people are to be congratulated. We need to be careful, however, not to diminish its meaning to some transitory state of pleasure. This blessedness indicates a favorable spiritual state due to the approval of God. It is neither transitory happiness, as defined by the world, nor dependent on physical or external circumstances.

One question remains to be answered: Are these blessings present or future? Certainly they will be more fully realized in eternity, when the kingdom of heaven makes its "dwelling among men" (cf. Rev 21:3). Verse 12 is indicative of that fact. That is not to say that we receive none of these blessings now, for the kingdom of God is already present. Furthermore, vv. 3 and 10 use a present tense verb, not future. And even those future tense verbs, sandwiched in between, can emphasize certainty as much as futurity. Thus, in answer to our question, "Are these blessings present or future," we answer, "Both!"

As we turn to Matthew's beatitudes, we will notice that the first four deal with our humility before God. The last four will deal with mercy

---

[53]A kingdom citizen is today equivalent to a Christian, but to use the term Christian in relation to the Sermon on the Mount is anachronistic. With that understanding, we will use both terms interchangeably from here on.

[54]K. Hinckley, "The Journey to Freedom: A Fresh Look at the Beatitudes," *DJ* 9 (Jan 1989): 45-48.

towards men, which springs from our relationship with God. Thus, the first four beatitudes have an upward emphasis and the last four have an outward emphasis. This same kind of pattern is seen with the Ten Commandments.

HUMILITY BEFORE GOD:

Mt 5:3

³Blessed are the poor in spirit for theirs is the kingdom of heaven.

This is an appropriate introduction to the Sermon on the Mount for two reasons. First, it introduces Jesus' theme: The Kingdom of Heaven. His audience will soon become aware of the great gulf between their understanding of the kingdom and Jesus' presentation of it. Second, this first beatitude will separate Jesus' audience into two groups. Some will only accept the kingdom if it meets their preconceived ideas. Only those who recognize their own spiritual bankruptcy will be appropriate applicants for citizenship. So this first beatitude sets the tone for the entire sermon.

The theology of "Poor in Spirit" has its roots in the OT and continues to saturate the NT. The continual oppression of Israel often resulted in their material poverty which caused them to look to God for their help and sustenance. Therefore, poverty was often associated with piety — humility, contrition and dependence on God. For example, Psalm 34:6 says, "This poor man called, and the Lord heard him; he saved him out of all his troubles." Proverbs 16:19 follows, "Better to be lowly in spirit and among the oppressed than to share plunder with the proud." Isaiah 61:1-2, which is likely the basis for this beatitude, predicts that the Messiah's ministry would especially touch the poor and downtrodden.[55] Jesus has already applied that text to himself in his hometown synagogue (Lk 4:18).

So what does it mean to be poor in spirit? Well, first, it does not mean hating yourself or feeling like you have no value. It does not mean weak faith, false humility or pious asceticism. Simply put, it is the recognition of your own spiritual bankruptcy. In short, no one can participate in the kingdom who has not recognized their desperate need for God and their own inability to meet that need. Jesus said we must enter as little children. The rich and self-sufficient have a terribly difficult time entering (cf. Rev 3:17). But the poor, the sinful, the destitute see their need clearly and tend to run to God freely.

---

[55]Cf. W.R. Domeris, "Biblical Perspectives on the Poor," *JTSA* 57 (Dec. 1986): 57-61.

Mt 5:4

⁴Blessed are those who mourn, for they will be comforted.

Jesus is speaking here of the mourning of repentance, not merely the loss of a loved one. It is true that Jesus is a comfort (Isa 40:1), that he binds up the brokenhearted (Isa 61:1), but that is not the context here. Following verse 3, recognizing our poverty, verse 4 calls us to repent from our sin which caused that poverty in the first place. Such Godly sorrow is a means of great gain (2 Cor 7:8-13).

But where are the tears at the altar? Who still mourns their own sinfulness? We have ample examples in the Bible of people weeping for the sins of their people (Psa 119:136; Ezek 9:4; Mt 23:37; Phil 3:18), as well as for their own sins (Lk 5:8; 7:36-38; Rom 7:24; 1 Cor 5:2; 2 Cor 12:21). Often Evangelicals have made so much of grace that we have made too little of sin.

Mt 5:5

⁵Blessed are the meek, for they will inherit the earth.

The Greek word for meek [*praus*], also entails the idea of "gentle, courteous, considerate." It is a description of Jesus himself (Mt 11:29; 2 Cor 10:1). Sometimes, however, our culture sees meekness as weakness. That certainly is not the picture of Jesus. This word indicates power under control. It was used of war stallions who were bridled and in submission to their masters. In relation to a Christian, it involves thinking of others above yourself. It describes a gentleness and courteousness in our relationships which demonstrates that we have a realistic evaluation of ourselves. Whereas "poor in spirit" describes our personal recognition of our own bankruptcy, "meek" describes our public expression of that same sense of humility. The NT speaks highly of this characteristic (2 Cor 10:1; Gal 5:22f.; Col 3:12; 1 Pet 3:15f.; James 1:19-21).

To say, then, that the meek will inherit the earth is a laughable paradox in our materialistic, self-seeking society. How is that possibly true? Ultimately, Christians will inherit all things, because we are co-heirs with Christ (Rom 8:17). We will possess the new earth. Frankly, that sounds too "far off" for this text. It says we will inherit the earth — presumably, this one. 2 Corinthians 6:10 says that in Christ we possess everything. True, Satan is the ruler of this world (Eph 6:12), but God is still clearly the owner. As his children, then, in a spiritual sense, we too possess this world. It may be even more literal than that, however. This beatitude is essentially a quotation from Psalm 37:11. Although it is not an absolute truth, the general principle still holds that the wicked perish and the self-seeking are not trusted. Those who look out for the interests of others, who demonstrate integrity, consideration and self-control, will be entrusted with possessions and positions. There is much literal truth in this blessing, not only in the realm of the kingdom of God, but also in this present world.

⁶Blessed are those who hunger and thirst for righteousness for they will be filled.

By the time we get to the Epistles, the word "righteousness" will describe what we receive from God because of what Jesus did on the cross. In other words, God declares us righteous because our sins have been paid for. But it is too early for that definition here. The righteousness Jesus is talking about is our moral behavior (vv. 10-20) and right motives (v. 21-48). This probably reflects Isaiah 55:1 and Psalm 42:1-2. The righteous poor find their wealth and reward in God himself. So the bottom line is this: Do you crave, more than anything else, to live a life that pleases God? If you do, God will provide the means for you to achieve your goal.

It is sad that so few Christians deeply crave righteousness. We are somewhat like children who have spoiled their dinners with candies. We are satisfied with recognition, busyness, entertainment, and emotional titillation. And because we allow such things to fill us, we are distracted from this deeper desire. Because of this, we have lost our impact in our society. We are often neither salt nor light (vv. 13-16), but merely another option for benevolent work or social activities.

To truly hunger and thirst for righteousness is to have a perpetual appetite. When we eat food we are only temporarily filled; a few hours later and we are hungry again. So it is with the pursuit of righteousness. We find great satisfaction with each advance toward the character of God, but soon we are again prompted by the Holy Spirit to gain new heights. A hunger and thirst for righteousness stands firmly on the pillars of poverty in spirit, grief over sin, and meekness towards both God and man.

MERCY TOWARDS MEN:

⁷Blessed are the merciful, for they will be shown mercy.

Jesus elaborates this beatitude in the parable of the unforgiving servant (Mt 18:21-35), as well as in the Lord's Prayer (Mt 6:14). The principle is simple: God tends to treat us the way we treat others (cf. Mt 10:32-33; 25:40). Only these examples deal with grace — not getting what we do deserve. This beatitude deals with mercy — getting what we don't deserve.

The reason a Christian can show mercy is that (s)he understands how much mercy (s)he has received. We can love because we have been loved; we can forgive because we have been forgiven. When we treat others unmercifully it betrays that fact that we have not experienced or appreciated the mercy God has shown us. Thus Paul says, "Accept one another, then, just as Christ accepted you, in order to bring praise to God" (Rom 15:7).

Mt 5:8   ⁸Blessed are the pure in heart, for they will see God.

"Pure in heart" carries with it at least two connotations: cleanness and sincerity. The Pharisees were preoccupied with ceremonial cleanness (cf. Mt 23:23-27). On the outside they looked good, but there was a stench on the inside. Jesus launches a grenade into such shallow piety. He demands that our purity reach the depths of the heart. This is not new. Even in the OT it was understood: "Who may ascend the hill of the Lord? Who may stand in his holy place? He who has clean hands and a pure heart" (Psa 24:3-4).

The second connotation is sincerity. Jesus calls for hearts that are "unmixed." For instance, in Matthew 6:22-24 Jesus says, "The eye is the lamp of the body. If your eyes are good, your whole body will be full of light . . . No one can serve two masters." God expects a single-minded devotion to him. Therefore, in order to see God, we need pure hearts — hearts that are clean and sincere. This is not our ticket to see him, it is an imperative prerequisite to cleaning the clutter from our spiritual eyes. God is not hiding from us. We have put blinders on that can only be removed by purity of heart.

Mt 5:9   ⁹Blessed are the peacemakers, for they will be called sons of God.

To be called the "Son of God" is not merely a statement of relationship but of character. In Jesus' day, to call someone the son of a dog was to say they acted like a dog. To say they were a son of the Devil meant they were devilish. To say they were the son of God meant that they acted like God would.

God is a peacemaker. That is loaded with theological significance (cf. Eph 2:11-22). He reconciled man to himself, Jews to Gentiles, men to women, etc. In imitation of God, we are to make peace. It is our primary ministry (2 Cor 5:18-20). This goes beyond merely desiring peace or being peaceful, peace-loving people. We are to be agents that bring about peace in a fragmented world.

The rub comes when we enter a hostile world (vv. 10-12, 39-45). To put it bluntly, this world does not appreciate Christians. To be sure, we enjoy being a peacemaker when it involves settling a dispute for someone else, but we don't much like it when we have to turn a stinging cheek in order to make peace. To make matters worse, since Jesus is the target for much animosity (Jn 15:18-21), his mere presence will sometimes start a fight. He will even divide families, as sharply as a sword (Mt 10:34-37).

The bottom line is that we may not be at peace because of our affiliation with Jesus. Nevertheless, we are to do things that make for peace (Heb 12:14). This does not mean compromising our stand for Jesus, but it might well include listening carefully, speaking softly, setting aside personal desires, not retaliating when wronged, apologizing for offense, smiling when things get heated, putting others first, etc. When we make peace, people will recognize our affinity with the character of God.

Mt 5:10

¹⁰Blessed are those who are persecuted because of righteousness, for theirs is the kingdom of heaven.

Persecution follows immediately on the heels of the peacemakers. Why? Because our values are antithetical to the world's. When we refuse to laugh at crass jokes, approve of immorality, cheat on our taxes, or justify lies, our standards tend to incriminate those around us. That causes tension and guilt for the worldly man which often erupts in persecution against the church.

Now the Christian is not blessed for persecution caused by stupidity or abrasiveness, but persecution because of righteousness. Just as meekness, purity, and mercy are marks of every Christian, so is persecution. In other words, if we follow Christ, we should expect to be persecuted (Jn 15:18-21; 1 Pet 4:13-14; Acts 14:22; 2 Tim 3:12). If we are not, we may need to question whether we are truly demonstrating righteousness. In fact, Luke's last woe is the antithesis of this: "Woe to you when all men speak well of you."

Verses 11-12 elaborate on this final beatitude in several ways. First, Jesus moves from the third person to the second person — "Blessed are *you* . . ." That brings it a bit closer to home. Second, Jesus explains that he is not just talking about physical persecution, but includes slander and exclusion. Third, Jesus directs our response: "Rejoice, for great is your reward in heaven," ("leap for joy," Lk 6:23). We may not realize the blessings of persecution now, but we will. As Paul says, "Light and momentary troubles are achieving for them an eternal glory that far outweighs them all" (2 Cor 4:17). Fourth, Jesus clarifies "Because of Righteousness" by replacing it with "Because of Me." It is our stand for Jesus that brings beneficial persecution, not socio-religious activism.

Our response to persecution is not that of a dog, to lick our wounds.

Nor is it the response of the masochist to thrill in the pain. Nor even the response of the Stoic to refuse to acknowledge it. We rejoice for the blessings brought about by persecution. What would that be? (1) We have already mentioned a future reward (v. 12; 2 Cor 4:17). (2) It builds faith and character (1 Pet 1:6ff). (3) It validates the genuineness of our faith and witness (v. 12b; Acts 5:41).

This is the introduction to Jesus' sermon. He confronts his culture, and ours, by confuting man's most valued priorities — independence, strength, arrogance, and accomplishment. As the kingdom of God advances, it does so in the face of the kingdoms of this world. Needless to say, Jesus now has their attention.

§ 54c
Salt and Light
(Mt 5:13-16;
Lk 14:35)

¹³"You are the salt of the earth. But if the salt loses its saltiness, how can it be made salty again? It is no longer good for anything, except to be thrown out and trampled by men. {It is fit neither for the soil nor for the manure pile^{LK}}.

¹⁴"You are the light of the world. A city on a hill cannot be hidden. ¹⁵Neither do people light a lamp and put it under a bowl. Instead they put it on its stand, and it gives light to everyone in the house. ¹⁶In the same way, let your light shine before men, that they may see your good deeds and praise your Father in heaven."

The beatitudes describe the character of a Christian. We might get the impression that these kingdom citizens are monastics — some peace-loving, quiet, secluded cloister. Perhaps, because of their humble, submissive character, they could have little influence on their society. Jesus shatters these notions. These beatific citizens have, oddly enough, a worldwide impact.

Jesus illustrates Christian influence with two items found in every home in Palestine: salt and light. Both metaphors assume that there is a significant if not antithetical difference between kingdom people and citizens of this world. Both metaphors also state that this distinction can be adulterated or hidden. If this happens, the Christian loses his influence as well as his value in the world.

It may also be observed that both salt and light, although necessary, can have a stinging effect. It is no small wonder that Christians who take seriously their obligation to live out this sermon experience persecution.

Salt

Salt has a number of uses. Allison and Davies trace eleven possibilities.[56] Three are most prominent: (1) It preserves, (2) it flavors, (3) it cre-

---

[56]W.D. Davies & D.C. Allison, *Matthew*, The International Critical Commentary, Vol 1 (Edinburgh: T & T Clark, 1988), pp. 472-473.

ates thirst. Although the latter two possibilities have homiletical value, Jesus probably speaks primarily of the first. In a culture that had no refrigeration, salt was critical to preserving food (and food preserved in salt hardly needs to be further seasoned with salt). Likewise, Christians are primarily responsible for the preservation of morality, justice and social conscience. God has also instituted the state and the home for these purposes, but without the church even these lack salt and light. Historically, the church can be credited for many of the advances in science, medicine, prison reform, orphanages, abolition of slavery and child labor, education and literacy. The kingdom of God has, indeed, flavored this world in significant ways.

The problem is when salt loses its flavor. Technically, salt (i.e., sodium chloride) cannot lose its saltiness. It is an extremely resilient chemical. The word Jesus uses would be more literally translated, "is defiled." Although salt cannot become unsalty, it can be adulterated with other substances. For instance, it was likely that around the Dead Sea, the natural salt in the water dried on the ground along with other chemicals and white dust. The mixture could be scraped up and pawned off as salt. Though it contained an element of salt, it was so polluted that it lost its preserving ability. If you bought a batch of this "salt" you could do nothing with it but pitch it. The analogy to the Christian is obvious. When one becomes mixed with the world, he loses his preserving influence in the society.

Light

Even dim light in a dark place is easy to spot. What fool would want to hide it? Yet many Christians studiously avoid being recognized. They fear that darkness will overcome the light. But that is impossible. Since Jesus is the light (Jn 8:12; 9:5) and we are in him, we can shine like the stars (Phil 2:15). As he was a light to the nations, so too the church continues bearing his light (Isa 9:2; 49:6; Lk 2:32; Acts 13:47; 26:23).

"Light" is not a theological confession nor an ecclesiastical organization. It represents the good deeds of an individual Christian. It simply will not do to hide our personal responsibility behind an illumined church sign or to tuck it away in an organizational structure. Each Christian is called to move into the world and live in such a distinctly different way that the unredeemed person can catch a glimpse of God.

When we do this, the Father is praised. From the context we also understand that the world is served. And from the beatitudes we can assume that the individual Christian is blessed. These are the fruits of putting hands and feet on the beatitudes. Now that the foundation is laid with this introduction, Jesus can proceed with the meat of his message.

**§ 54d
The Law is Not
Abolished but
Fulfilled**
(Mt 5:17-20)

Just as the beatitudes were "framed" with the "Kingdom of Heaven" (vv. 3, 10) so also the main body of this sermon is "framed" with "the Law and the Prophets" (Mt 5:17, 19-20; 7:12). Thus, we understand the theme of this sermon as the application of God's word (OT) to God's Kingdom now. Jesus begins the sermon using third person (vv. 3-10, Beatitudes); he moves to second person (vv. 11-16, Christian Influence); and now uses first person (vv. 17-20), describing his own relationship to the OT.

Jesus is about to contrast his own application of the OT with the popular rabbinic interpretation (vv. 21-48). It may appear that he is contradicting the OT itself. After all, he did teach on his own authority and not that of classic Judaism (Mt 7:28-29). And he has already raised a few eyebrows by disregarding Sabbath traditions (Mk 2:23-3:6). Jesus was so radically different that the crowds attributed to him a "new teaching!" (Mk 1:27). BUT, Jesus vehemently denies contradicting any part of the OT (vv. 17-20). What he does, however, is deepen the meaning of the OT and contradict the oral traditions of the scribes.

Mt 5:17-18

[17]"Do not think that I have come to abolish the Law or the Prophets; I have not come to abolish them but to fulfill them. [18]I tell you the truth, until heaven and earth disappear, not the smallest letter, nor the least stroke of the pen, will by any means disappear from the Law until everything is accomplished."

This is a difficult text. How is it that Jesus fulfills the OT Law? One answer, which reaches as far back as Thomas Aquinas (c. 1225-74), draws a distinction between Moral, Civil and Ceremonial law. The theory goes something like this: The *ceremonial* law was abolished at Calvary and the *civil* law would no longer be in effect because the people of God are citizens of a spiritual kingdom, no longer a physical one. That would leave only the *moral* law of the OT intact for Christians.

The difficulty comes when we try to determine which OT codes are ceremonial, civil and moral. The Scriptures themselves never make these three distinctions. So we have no help from the Bible. To make matters worse, moral, civil, and ceremonial law seem to overlap. For example, the Sabbath seems to be both ceremonial and civil. Laws against divorce are both civil and moral. Laws of sacrifice are both ceremonial and moral. The bottom line is, we would not be able to discern clearly what laws we were to keep. Besides, verse 18 cannot fit into this theory. Jesus says that all the OT law is for keeps.

So how did Jesus fulfill the Law? Perhaps in several ways: (1) Predictive Prophecy — All the OT pointed to Jesus; thus, we cannot adequately understand it apart from Jesus (cf. Lk 24:27, 44; Jn 5:39). This would also include types and analogies. (2) Doctrinal Teaching — Jesus enhances the theology of the OT. His teaching brings out its richness and fullness. He adds to creation, new creation; to sacrifice, atonement; to prayer, relationship. Through Jesus we understand the Holy Spirit, resurrection, Kingdom of God, etc. (3) Obedience — Jesus alone fulfills the ethical requirements of the Law (2 Cor 5:21; Heb 4:15). (4) Redemption — Jesus pays the price for our transgressions. His death cancels our legal debt (Rom 6:23; Heb 10:11-18).

Does this mean that Christians are obligated to keep the OT law? It is clear that the Christian is no longer under the Mosaic Law. That is, we are neither judged nor condemned by it. Its penalty has been satisfied (Rom 7:4; Col 2:14; Heb 8:13; 10:8-10). We are compelled by a new law written in our hearts through the Holy Spirit (Rom 8:2-4; Gal 5:4-5, 18; Heb 8:10-11; Jer 24:7; 31:33). We have a new master, Christ, not the law (Rom 10:4; Gal 4:23-25), to whom even the OT Scriptures looked forward (Rom 3:21; Gal 3:24). To use the analogy of Seth Wilson, the apple blossom is fulfilled when it matures into the fruit. When that takes place the blossom falls off. It is not abolished, it is fulfilled.[57]

However, the fact that we are no longer controlled or judged by the OT law, does not mean that we can glibly set it aside or ignore its commands. Jesus said that it was here for keeps. Jesus wouldn't even allow a single stroke of a single letter to be ignored. The smallest letter (lit. *iota*), was equivalent to our "i." The least stroke was a minute extension at one corner of a letter which allowed the Hebrews to distinguish, for instance, between "R" and "D" in their alphabet. It is somewhat like the difference between our small "l" and "i." A mere stroke of the pen makes the difference. We might paraphrase Jesus' words: "Not even the dot over an 'i' nor the crossing of a 't' will pass away."

Jesus affirms the enduring value of the OT (not to mention his opinion of inspiration, cf. Lk 16:16-17; 2 Tim 3:16). At the same time, Jesus altered the dietary regulations of the OT (cf. Mk 7:19). It would appear that from Jesus' perspective the role of the OT law changed (cf. Mt 11:12ff). So how should a Christian today deal with the OT law? It would be naive and legalistic to keep every law. On the other hand, it would be antinomian and unscriptural to throw it all out. We need to recognize that the law was never pictured as a source of salvation in the OT.[58] Jews were saved based on the fact that God chose them, not based on their perfect obedience to the law. The purpose of the law then, was twofold. It declared the holiness of God. And it gave clear guidelines for

---

[57]Seth Wilson, *Learning From Jesus* (Joplin, MO: College Press, 1977), p. 241.

[58]J.D. Charles, "The Greatest or the Least in the Kingdom?: The Disciple's Relationship to the Law (Mt 5:17-20)," *TrinJ* 13ns (1992): 139-162.

social behavior. Since the Christian community still needs both those things, the law is relevant for the church today.[59] Therefore, all the OT is relevant for guidance and instruction (2 Tim 3:16), but not for salvation or judgment. If we trace Matthew's view of the law, we learn that it must be interpreted and applied within the parameters of love and mercy (Mt 5:43-48; 7:12; 19:19; 22:34-40; 24:12; 25:31-46).[60] In addition, the new covenant will obviously change the way we apply some of the old codes. Not all of it will apply in the Kingdom of Heaven as it did under the Mosaic covenant. Thus, we can correctly interpret the law only through Jesus' life and ministry (Lk 24:25-27). Perhaps, then, the Epistles are even more valuable than the Gospels, when it comes to a final word on a Christian's response to the Law.

Mt 5:19-20

[19]"Anyone who breaks one of the least of these commandments and teaches others to do the same will be called least in the kingdom of heaven, but whoever practices and teaches these commands will be called great in the kingdom of heaven. [20]For I tell you that unless your righteousness surpasses that of the Pharisees and the teachers of the law, you will certainly not enter the kingdom of heaven."

The Pharisees had a bad habit of dismissing texts that they felt were not applicable or were uncomfortable. Jesus is clearly digging at them. They can hardly miss his play on the words "abolish" [*katalysai*] (v. 17) and "break" [*lysē*] (v. 19). Not only did the Pharisees ignore difficult texts, but even where they did teach correctly they seldom lived accordingly (Mt 23:2-4). They feigned a reverence for the word of God, but would not submit to its demands (Jn 5:39-40).

The Pharisees were famous for their meticulous observance of religious ritual (cf. Mt 23:23-24). And even though their hearts weren't right, the people had to wonder if anyone's righteousness could surpass the persnickety compliance of the scribes and Pharisees. But what Jesus wants is not broader but deeper obedience. He is looking for hearts bent on God's priorities above lives conformed to lists of regulations. "You should practice the latter without neglecting the former" (Mt 23:23).

§ 54e
Six Contrasts:
"You have
heard . . . But I
Say."
(Mt 5:21-48)

This section is characterized by the choral refrain of Jesus, "But I say" (5:22, 28, 32, 34, 39, 44). This sets up an obvious antithesis

[59]W.C. Kaiser, "The Place of Law and Good Works in Evangelical Christianity," in *A Time to Speak: The Evangelical-Jewish Encounter*. Ed. A. James Rudin and Martin R. Wilson (Grand Rapids: Eerdmans, 1987).

[60]K.R. Snodgrass, "Matthew's Understanding of the Law," *Int* 46 (Oct 1992): 368-378.

between Jesus' words and the previous teachings. The question is, "What is the previous teaching?" If it is the OT Scripture, we see Jesus at the very least extending it and perhaps even contradicting it. Stott, however, makes a strong case for Jesus contradicting Pharisaic interpretation of the OT and not the Scripture itself.[61]

Stott supports his claim with four evidences: (1) Each of these six quotes appear to come from the law. However, when we get to the sixth, "Love your neighbor and hate your enemy," we find the first part in Leviticus 19:18, but this second half is not anywhere in the OT. In addition, v. 31 is an interpretive paraphrase of Deuteronomy 24:1, 3. (2) Jesus' introductory formula, "You have heard that it was said (vv. 27, 38, 43) to the men of old (vv. 21, 33)" aligns better with oral teaching than with the written word, which is normally introduced by the phrase, "It is written." (3) According to the context (vv. 17-20), Jesus affirms verbal inspiration of the text, while he criticizes the Pharisaic neglect of it. The following discussion, then, naturally flows from Pharisaic misinterpretation. (4) Jesus elsewhere submits to the written word (e.g., temptations, ch. 4). Thus, we can assume he does here as well.

Pharisaic interpretation tended to relax the commands of God and extend the permission of God. Thus they made God's law more "manageable." But Jesus does just the opposite. This can be clearly seen in the chart below.

LAW	TYPE	PHARISEES	JESUS
Murder (vv. 21-26)	Command	Restrict to act	Extend to thoughts
Adultery (vv. 27-30)	Command	Restrict to act	Extend to thoughts
Divorce (vv. 31-32)	Permission	Extend for nearly any cause	Restrict to adultery
Oaths (vv. 33-37)	Command	Restrict to only certain promises	Extend to yes/no
Retaliation (vv. 38-42)	Permission	Extend to "just" causes	Restrict to nothing
Love (vv. 43-48)	Command	Restrict to neighbors	Extend to enemies

The net result was that the Pharisees made God's law easier to keep whereas Jesus made it more difficult. The odd thing is that the Pharisees kept adding regulations, whereas Jesus took them away. So why were Jesus' prescriptions more difficult to follow? He internalized the law. He got, so to speak, to the heart of the matter.

1. Murder/Anger

Mt 5:21-22

[21]"You have heard that it was said to people long ago, 'Do not murder,[a] and anyone who murders will be subject to judgment.' [22]But I tell you that anyone who

---

[61]J.R. Stott, *Christian Counter-Culture* (Downers Grove, IL: IVP, 1978), pp. 76-79.

is angry with his brother[b] will be subject to judgment. Again, anyone who says to his brother, 'Raca,'[c] is answerable to the Sanhedrin. But anyone who says, 'You fool!' will be in danger of the fire of hell."

[a]*21* Exodus 20:13   [b]*22* Some manuscripts *brother without cause*   [c]*22* An Aramaic term of contempt

"Thou shalt not murder" is the 6th commandment.[62] The Pharisees stressed only the action of murder. Jesus, on the other hand, extended punishment to the motives and/or emotions behind the murder. John captured the same idea when he later said, "Anyone who hates his brother is a murderer" (1 John 3:15).

We should clarify a couple of points here. First, the progression of punishment (judgment/Sanhedrin/Hell) is probably nothing more than literary style. The Hebrews used this kind of parallelism frequently. Second, these verbal insults, "Raca" (an Aramaic insult roughly equivalent to "empty-head"), and "you fool," are not always inappropriate. After all, Jesus himself called the Pharisees fools (Mt 23:17-19; see also 1 Cor 15:36; Gal 3:1; James 2:20). They are, however, dangerous when they become seeds of "murderous" emotion. There is, in fact, a textual variant at this place with strong manuscript evidence which adds the phrase "without cause" after the word "brother." Although these words were probably not in the original, they seem to clarify Jesus' intent. And although they may soften Jesus' statement, they justify very few of us who are hair-triggered with pettiness which leads to outbursts of violent derision.

Mt 5:23-24

[23]"Therefore, if you are offering your gift at the altar and there remember that your brother has something against you, [24]leave your gift there in front of the altar. First go and be reconciled to your brother; then come and offer your gift."

Nearly every commentator transports this text into our own time by saying, "If you are at church, worshiping the Lord, and realize that someone has a grievance with you, leave the worship and first go and be reconciled to that brother." That is probably an accurate transfer to Jesus' simple principle: Correct interpersonal relationships are more important than correct ritual. This tends to grate against religious folks who say that God must be our first priority. This is true. However, our relationship with God is better gauged by our human relationships than by religious ritual. Although we cannot guarantee that the offended brother will accept us, we are obligated to make every effort "as far as it depends on" us (Rom 12:18).

---

[62]The Hebrew word "murder" does not include killing in self-defense, capital punishment, manslaughter or going to war. Those issues will have to be taken up elsewhere.

[25]"Settle matters quickly with your adversary who is taking you to court. Do it while you are still with him on the way, or he may hand you over to the judge, and the judge may hand you over to the officer, and you may be thrown into prison. [26]I tell you the truth, you will not get out until you have paid the last penny."[a]

[a]*26* Greek *kodrantes*

The previous illustration was about a friend (v. 23). This second illustration is about an enemy (v. 25). The first takes place in the temple. The second is en route to a court of law. Both, however, have a single message: The urgency of reconciliation.

There is worldly wisdom to Jesus' words. Every litigation lawyer knows how much easier it is to settle out of court. Once this issue goes to the judge, your destiny is out of your hands. As in Jesus' day, so in ours, one will be thrown in prison until the debt is paid, down to the penny.[63]

However, this metaphor is not really about earthly litigation. Contextually, it is about eternal judgment. The relationships we have in the here-and-now may determine our destiny in the hereafter.[64]

2. Adultery

[27]"You have heard that it was said, 'Do not commit adultery.'[a] [28]But I tell you that anyone who looks at a woman lustfully has already committed adultery with her in his heart."

[a]*27* Exodus 20:14

Jesus moves from the 6th to the 7th commandment: "Thou shall not commit adultery." Again, the Pharisees dealt only with the act; Jesus extends the prohibition to the motive behind the act — lust. Now Jesus is not speaking of a casual glance or an involuntary thought. The present participle "look" [*blepōn*] indicates a continued action. It describes a person who allows those initial thoughts to flourish. Jesus does not condemn looking but lusting.

It is impossible in our society, where sexual images pervade our media, to keep lustful thoughts from flickering across our mind's eye. Nor are we culpable at this point. We *are* guilty, however, even of adultery, when we fan those flickers into flame. Satan is attacking the church in its loins and gaining much ground. Often those caught in adultery say with surprise, "We just don't know how this happened." We have not listened well to Jesus. Adultery takes place long before two bodies ever touch (thus Job 31:1, 7, 9).

---

[63]This penny [*kodrantēs*] was ⅟₆₄ of a normal day's wage.

[64]It is exegetically inappropriate to allegorize this metaphor so as to import the notion of purgatory.

Mt 5:29-30

[29]"If your right eye causes you to sin, gouge it out and throw it away. It is better for you to lose one part of your body than for your whole body to be thrown into hell. [30]And if your right hand causes you to sin, cut it off and throw it away. It is better for you to lose one part of your body than for your whole body to go into hell" (cf. Mt 18:8-9).

Part of us wants to take this literally because we do want to be faithful to Jesus and we don't want to go to hell. Furthermore, we know just how sinful we can be. Then common sense takes over and we recognize that this is obvious hyperbole. Taken literally, Jesus' words would be rather gory. Besides, it would do no real good since our dominant organ of sin is our brain, not our appendages.[65]

Jesus is not speaking of literal body parts. After all, what good would it do to only gouge out one eye? We can still gawk with the other eye. What we need to do, then, is to *act* as if we cut off our hands and plucked out our eyes. That is, when we are tempted, stop looking. Get out of the places where we are tempted. Remove the company that most troubles us. These behaviors are sometimes as difficult and painful as literally cutting off a body part. But the only real solution to sin is death (Mk 8:34; Rom 6:5-7; 8:13; Gal 5:24; Col 3:5).

3. Divorce

Mt 5:31-32

[31]"It has been said, 'Anyone who divorces his wife must give her a certificate of divorce.'[a] [32]But I tell you that anyone who divorces his wife, except for marital unfaithfulness, causes her to become an adulteress, and anyone who marries the divorced woman commits adultery."

[a]*31* Deut. 24:1

The issue of divorce, which naturally follows the discussion of adultery, undoubtedly is one of the most difficult and sensitive issues the church must face. Jesus discusses divorce in more detail in Matthew 19:1-12. Thus we will deal with it more thoroughly at that time. Here, however, we want to understand how this issue of divorce fits into the message of the Sermon on the Mount.

First, we notice that Jesus restricts God's permission of divorce only to cases of adultery. The two most prominent rabbis just before Jesus' day, Hillel and Shammai, hotly debated this very issue. Based on Deuteronomy 24:1-4, it was said that a man could divorce a woman if something "improper" was discovered. Just what this "improper" thing

---

[65]Some have, in fact taken this literally and demonstrated the point just made. Probably the most famous example is Origen (c. A.D. 195-254), who castrated himself and yet continued to have lustful thoughts.

might be was the point of contention. For Shammai, it was only sexual impropriety. For Hillel, it could be something as trivial as burning her husband's dinner. Hillel's opinion generally prevailed. Again we see Jesus' interpretation contradict popular opinion.

The word Jesus used for "marital unfaithfulness" [*porneia*], is not necessarily limited to adultery but can include many forms of sexual impropriety, including fornication (sexual intercourse prior to marriage). However, *porneia* was typically used when referring to female adultery. Male adultery was called *moicheia*. Thus, we assume that Jesus is talking about some sexual infidelity during the marriage, rather than some promiscuity prior to the marriage. In Jewish law (*m. Yebam.* 2:8; *m. Sota* 5:1), a spouse was obligated to divorce an unfaithful partner. Not so for the Christian. Chrysostom rightly observed that these verses cannot be separated from the beatitudes. Even in the case of adultery, one who is meek, a peacemaker, and merciful, surely could not cast out a wife. God, as a model, has shown patience for spiritual unfaithfulness (Jer 2:1-3:1; 4:1; Hos 2:1-23).

Some, in fact, have even questioned adultery as a grounds of divorce based on the fact that Mark and Luke do not have this exception clause. But, in Jesus' day, it would be taken for granted that adultery was just grounds for divorce; even Hillel and Shammai were agreed on that. Matthew 19:9 seems to be a clear statement to that effect.

The real critical issue is "How does divorce cause one to commit adultery?" Jesus is using a metaphor, comparing divorce to adultery figuratively (Hos 2:4; Jer 5:7; Ezek 16:32). After all, you can't fairly say that a woman has committed adultery if her husband divorces her through no fault of her own. She is innocent. If she never sleeps with another man, you can't charge her with being an adulteress. Perhaps it was just assumed that a divorced woman in Jewish culture would either remarry or become a prostitute. However, this was not necessarily so. She could go live with a family member. So, Jesus is not saying that the act of divorce is equivalent to the act of adultery but that they have the same terrible consequences. In Matthew 19:1-12 Jesus describes the two pillars of marriage originating from Genesis: (1) Leaving father and mother and clinging to one's wife. That is, they make a ***commitment*** to each other. And (2) they become one flesh. That is, they pledge *faithfulness* to each other. This second pillar is epitomized, but not limited to, sexual intercourse.[66]

---

[66]C.L. Blomberg, "Marriage, Divorce, Remarriage, and Celibacy: An Exegesis of Mt 19:3-12," *TrinJ* 11ns (1990): 161-196.

When a man divorces his wife, the pillar of *commitment* is destroyed and the marriage is dissolved. When one commits adultery, the pillar of *faithfulness* is destroyed and the marriage is broken. Hence, both divorce and adultery result in a broken marriage and *to that extent they are the same*. When a third party enters the scene and marries a divorcee, (s)he participates in that brokenness and destroys practically any chance at reconciliation for the original couple. Hence, the practical result of one's involvement in a second marriage is the same as that of adultery — it seals the broken marriage.

Does that make it a sin to remarry? If all attempts at reconciliation have failed, then no, probably not. And it is certainly not perpetual adultery. Both Deuteronomy 24:1-4 and Jesus in John 4:17-18 recognize the validity of more than one marriage.[67] But just because it is not adultery does not mean that remarriage is ideal. A second marriage will always bear the burden of brokenness.

We may be facing, then, two poor options: Remarriage or celibacy. Remarriage, especially where children are involved, may be the better of the two options. But neither is ideal. This does not mean that second marriages will be poor. However, they will import past brokenness which must be dealt with. From a practical standpoint, it would be a horrible mistake to demand second marriages to be dissolved so that broken first marriages could be reinstated.

So, do remarried couples live in perpetual adultery? No. Remember, this is a metaphor. Jesus is not saying that remarriage *is* adultery, merely that it is *like* adultery in that they have similar consequences. While it is not perpetual adultery, it is perpetual brokenness. God can heal our wounds from past sins but the scars are likely permanent.

We know God hates divorce (Mal 2:16), and only allowed it because of the hardness of people's hearts (Mt 19:8; Mk 10:5). The Master's words are clear: "Don't get divorced." But what do we do after someone is already divorced? That is a difficult question. You see, nearly every Bible teaching on divorce is prescriptive (i.e., "Don't do it"). We have very few guidelines to go on after the fact. It is our arduous task to balance biblical standards with gracious reconciliation.

4. Oaths

Mt 5:33-37

[33]"Again, you have heard that it was said to the people long ago, 'Do not break your oath, but keep the oaths you have made to the Lord.' [34]But I tell you, Do not swear at all: either by heaven, for it is God's throne; [35]or by the earth, for it is his

---

[67]Marriages, in the eyes of God, can, in fact, be dissolved. Cf. M.J. Down, "The Sayings of Jesus about Marriage and Divorce," *ExpT* 95 (1984): 332-334.

footstool; or by Jerusalem, for it is the city of the Great King. ³⁶And do not swear by your head, for you cannot make even one hair white or black. ³⁷Simply let your 'Yes' be 'Yes,' and your 'No,' 'No'; anything beyond this comes from the evil one."

Jesus' words don't come straight from the OT. What we have is a summary of a number of OT injunctions on lying and oaths (Exod 20:7; Lev 19:12; Num 30:2; Deut 23:21-24). The Pharisees used oaths not to confirm another's faith, but to weasel out of promises they made. The Mishnaic tractate *Shebuoth* identifies which oath formulas were binding and which were not. It's like when children cross their fingers behind their backs. Whatever they say next doesn't really count.

According to the Pharisees, swearing by heaven or earth, God's throne or Jerusalem (vv. 34-36, cf. Mt 23:16-22), wasn't as binding as swearing by God himself. Jesus points out that all four of these things belong to God in a unique way. Even the hairs of our head have been ordained by God to be a certain color. So if God owns them all, every oath must reflect his character of truth. This logic can be extended to everything in heaven and on earth (even crossed fingers and legal fine print).

Some have taken Jesus' words overly literally and refuse to take oaths at all, even in a court of law. But in both the OT (Deut 10:20) and in the NT (Rom 1:9; 2 Cor 1:18, 23; Gal 1:20; 1 Thess 2:5, 10) there are proper examples of oaths. Jesus, at his own trial, answered the High Priest under oath (Mt 26:63-64). What Jesus was objecting to was using oaths as a form of deceit. In that case, it would be better to have no "formula" at all. Just mean what you say and say what you mean (James 5:12). The bottom line is that we are called to be honest people. If we are not, we are submitting to the influence of the evil one who is the father of lies (Jn 8:44).

5. Retaliation

Mt 5:38-42

³⁸"You have heard that it was said, 'Eye for eye, and tooth for tooth.'ᵃ ³⁹But I tell you, do not resist an evil person. If someone strikes you on the right cheek, turn to him the other also. ⁴⁰And if someone wants to sue you and take your tunic, let him have your cloak as well. ⁴¹If someone forces you to go one mile, go with him two miles. ⁴²Give to the one who asks you, and do not turn away from the one who wants to borrow from you."

ᵃ*38* Exodus 21:24; Lev. 24:20; Deut. 19:21

The OT permitted a tit-for-tat retaliation (*Lex Talionis*, Exod 21:24; Deut 19:21). The Jews, as people typically do, moved from retaliation, through courts of law,[68] to personal revenge which often far exceeded the

---

[68]S.D. Currie, "Mt 5:39a — Resistance or Protest," *HTR* 57 (1964): 140-145, calls attention to the fact that there is much "legal" talk in this context. Furthermore, the word

offense. Jesus, as he typically does, moves from retaliation to selfless sacrifice. He gives three instances in which this non-retaliation principle could be applied. All three are best understood against their Jewish background.

(1) A slap on the cheek was a common insult which would normally be returned in kind. This tit-for-tat normally escalated into a full-fledged brawl. (2) The tunic was commonly required as collateral in legal cases (Exod 22:26-27). Jesus said, "Don't just give him your inner garment, give him the more valuable outer garment as well." (3) Roman soldiers had the power to conscript common citizens to help carry their military supplies. If one demanded a mile, give him two. This has given rise to the fitting proverb, "Going the extra mile."

These three examples are illustrations (not regulations), of a single principle: Non-retaliation. It is probably neither advisable nor possible to absolutely apply any of the three illustrations. The motive to do so is, without a doubt, admirable. But the absolute application of non-retaliation, without reasonable consideration, probably honors neither Jesus nor this text.

With these words Jesus does NOT: (1) Advocate Christian submission to torture, (2) directly address pacifism or just war,[69] (3) restrict Christian intervention on behalf of an abused third party, (4) forbid self-defense, or (5) contravene retaliation by the state. Blomberg aptly summarizes Jesus' intent: "Not only must disciples reject all behavior motivated only by a desire for retaliation, but they also must positively work for the good of those with whom they would otherwise be at odds" (p. 113).

In v. 42, Jesus assumes that the needs are genuine. We are not obligated, for instance, to give a buck to a derelict to fuel his habit, or fill the tank of a panhandler. Augustine observed that Jesus said "give to everyone that asks," not "give everything to him that asks' (*De Sermone Domine en Monte*, 67). At the same time, we are not authorized to ferret out fakes. It would be better to be duped than to neglect genuine needs.

6. Love (see also Lk 6:27-30, 32-36)

Mt 5:43-48

[43]"You have heard that it was said, 'Love your neighbor[a] and hate your enemy.' [44]But I tell you: Love your enemies[b] and pray for those who persecute you, [45]that you may be sons of your father in heaven. He causes his sun to rise

---

"resist" [*anistēmi*] is often used in a judicial sense, meaning "to testify against." Thus, he suggests that Jesus means something like: "Don't 'square off' with your adversary and protest for your own rights," or "Don't make a court case out of it. Don't seek damages."

[69]Cf. J. Rausch, "The Principle of Nonresistance and Love of Enemy in Mt 5:38-48," *CBQ* 28 (1966): 31-41.

on the evil and the good, and sends rain on the righteous and the unrighteous. [46]If you love those who love you, what reward will you get? Are not even the tax collectors doing that? [47]And if you greet only your brothers, what are you doing more than others? Do not even pagans do that? [48]Be perfect, therefore, as your heavenly Father is perfect."

[a]21 Leviticus 19:18   [b]44 Some late manuscripts *enemies, bless those who curse you, do good to those who hate you*

In Leviticus 19:18 we read, "Love your neighbor." But nowhere in the OT do we read, "Hate your enemy." It is doubtful that it can be inferred even from texts such as Deuteronomy 23:3-6; 25:17-19; or Psalm 139:21. Perhaps they had read, "Love *only* your neighbor." But God has demonstrated his love for all people, even sinful people, by providing sunshine and rain (cf. Jn 3:16; Rom 5:8). If we are really sons of God, that is, if we have his character, then we will love people as radically and as inclusively as he does. In a way, this is the flip-side of non-retaliation. On the one hand, we are to be passive with an enemy, through non-retaliation. On the other hand, we are to be active with our enemies through love.

In the eyes of the Jews, there was no one more disreputable than tax collectors (v. 46), because they had sold out to Rome, and pagans (v. 47), because they served false gods. Surely these fine religious folks could do better than those heathens they despise! But that's just it! The religious elite act just like those sinners. They only care about people who are like them and who can repay them in kind. Luke 6:34-35 puts it in financial terms. If you only make a loan, knowing you'll get repaid, you have sacrificed nothing. It is only when you give of yourself, expecting nothing in return, that you have acted more nobly than the pagan.

So far we have examined six separate illustrations of how our righteousness can go deeper than the Pharisees (vv. 21-47). This is certainly not a comprehensive list, though it does paint a portrait of the kingdom citizen. If we do such things, we will move toward the character of our heavenly Father. Thus we are to "be perfect" (v. 48) as God is perfect. But this is so broad . . . so demanding. How in the world can I be like God?

The Greek word "perfect" [*teleios*] does not mean "without flaw." Rather, it means "mature, whole, complete." It is only used one other time in the Gospels (Mt 19:21). Jesus tells the rich young ruler, "If you want to be perfect, go sell your possessions and give to the poor." That fits very well our present context of radical and unconditional love (vv. 43-48). Thus, Jesus is not calling us to be morally flawless as God is. But he is calling us to love as completely and maturely as God loves. This means we love both the evil and the good, both our friends and our enemies. Luke (6:36), in his typical concern for unloved people, puts it this way, "Be merciful, just as your Father is merciful." These words are difficult, but not impossible.

This may very well echo the sentiments of Leviticus 19:2, "Be holy, because I, the Lord your God, am holy."[70] Citizens of this heavenly Kingdom, likewise are to reflect the character of the King, "Be loving, because God is love."

**§ 54f
Prohibition against Public Piety: Alms, Prayer, Fasting
(Mt 6:1-18)**

Chapter five gave six illustrations of public moral behavior (vv. 21-48). With each of the six, Jesus said, "check your motives." Chapter six is going to give three illustrations of religious duties: almsgiving (2-4), prayer (5-13), and fasting (14-18). With each of these three, Jesus will say, "check your motives." Both public morality and religious ritual are good and proper expressions of our faith in God. Yet both can be admirably practiced with hellish motives. So Jesus warns us, "Check your motives."

Another parallel between chapters five and six is Jesus' injunction: "Do not be like them." "Them" includes both the hypocritical Pharisees (Mt 5:20; 6:5), and the pagans (Mt 5:46-47; 6:7). The Sermon on the Mount continues its unequivocal call to a distinctly different lifestyle, different from religious hypocrites and different from pagans.

> The demand for genuine perfection loses itself in the lesser goal of external piety; the goal of pleasing the Father is traded for its pygmy cousin, the goal of pleasing men. It almost seems as if the greater the demand for holiness, the greater the opportunity for hypocrisy. This is why I suspect that the danger is potentially most serious among religious leaders. . . . Be perfect (5:48), but be careful (6:1)" Carson (p. 55).

Mt 6:1

[1]"Be careful not to do your 'acts of righteousness' before men, to be seen by them. If you do, you will have no reward from your Father in Heaven."

The first verse of chapter six establishes the theme of this section: Secrecy in Piety. But back in Matthew 5:16 Christians were commanded to let their lights shine. Both verses emphasize (1) before men, (2) to be seen by them, (3) to give God glory. Matthew 5:16 says to go public, while 6:1 says to keep it private. What's the deal?

The contradiction is merely verbal. When we are tempted to hide our Christian commitments, usually in the face of public opposition, we must remember the words of 5:16. When we are tempted to promote

---

[70]B.B. Thurston, "Mt 5:43-48," *Int* 41 (1987): 170-173.

ourselves through religious activity, usually in corporate church settings, we must remember 6:1.

As we have seen with other commands of this sermon, it would not be appropriate to apply these injunctions absolutely. For instance, you cannot actually hide your giving from your left hand. Moreover, there are times when public financial commitments can be of great encouragement to the body without glorifying an individual (e.g., Acts 4:36-37; 21:24; Phil 4:14-18). And who would not advocate public prayer? And does not Paul speak about mutual prayer and fasting (1 Cor 7:5)? Jesus is not primarily dictating behavior; he is dealing with the attitudes that motivate certain behaviors (cf. 5:22, 28, 44).

Alms

Mt 6:2-4

2"So when you give to the needy, do not announce it with trumpets, as the hypocrites do in the synagogues and on the streets, to be honored by men. I tell you the truth, they have received their reward in full. 3But when you give to the needy, do not let your left hand know what your right hand is doing, 4so that your giving may be in secret. Then your Father, who sees what is done in secret, will reward you."

The Jews had no governmental social security or welfare system. Thus, voluntary almsgiving was critical to the poor and disabled (Deut 15:11; Ps 41:1; Prov 19:17).[71] Often, money was given not to help the poor, nor to glorify God, but to attract attention to one's personal piety. "It is not clear whether the trumpets 'in the synagogues and on the streets' (v. 2) were literal or metaphorical, (cf. our expression 'blow your own horn'). The best guess may be that they refer to the noise and clang of throwing money into various collection receptacles" (Blomberg, p. 116).[72] Stott offers the suggestion that the trumpets were blown to call the poor to receive their dole.

Jesus is speaking against hypocrisy. This word describes Greek actors who concealed their true identity with a mask. When you go to a theater you expect the mask. No one is really fooled by it. But when you go to church, it is not supposed to be a game or an act. Thus, people are more easily taken in by the facade. Jesus is not speaking against financial accountability or keeping track of your benevolence for budgetary purposes. Perhaps closer to Jesus' words would be plaques with donors' names on them or published lists of benefactors of Christian organizations.

---

[71]Each Friday "relief officers" went door to door collecting trays of food and cash donations sufficient to supply the poor with 14 meals. D. Gaertner, *Acts* (Joplin, MO: College Press, 1993), p. 119.

[72]N.J. McElency, "Does the Trumpet Sound or Resound?" *ZNW* 76 (1985): 43-46.

We get to choose from where our reward comes (vv. 4, 6, 18). We can either receive praise from men, which the Pharisees loved (Jn 5:44; 12:43), or a reward from God. Now, God's reward is not necessarily future (e.g., heaven, crowns or "mansions"). It may be a temporal blessing, answered prayer (v. 8), the satisfaction of seeing the needs of the poor met, overcoming temptation, developing Christlike character, etc. Whatever God's reward turns out to be, you can be sure that it is better than men's fickle praise. Although the choice seems obvious, the immediate gratification of human recognition sometimes lures the best of us.

Prayer

Mt 6:5-8

⁵"And when you pray, do not be like the hypocrites, for they love to pray standing in the synagogues and on the street corners to be seen by men. I tell you the truth, they have received their reward in full. ⁶But when you pray, go into your room, close the door and pray to your Father, who is unseen. Then your Father, who sees what is done in secret, will reward you. ⁷And when you pray, do not keep on babbling like pagans, for they think they will be heard because of their many words. ⁸Do not be like them, for your Father knows what you need before you ask him."

We should pray neither like the Pharisees, for public recognition (vv. 5-6), nor like the pagans, with "vain repetitions" (KJV), (vv. 7-8). Let's first understand what Jesus does NOT mean. He is not against public prayer (cf. Acts 1:24; 3:1; 4:24ff, etc.). What he is against is prayer that preaches to the hearers; prayer that demonstrates "orthodox" vocabulary; or prayer that gains kudos from the audience, rather than prayer that genuinely talks to God.

Second, Jesus is not against repetition, for he tells us to be persistent in prayer (Mt 7:7-8; Lk 11:5-13; 18:1-8). We do not need to badger God, for he loves to give us good gifts (Mt 7:11), but he has reserved some gifts only for those who pray (James 4:2). What Jesus is against is *vain* repetitions. The word "babble" is an onomatopoeia [*battalogeō*, lit. "to say *batta*"]. This is its only known use in all Greek literature. Therefore we can't be certain of its meaning. But it seems to indicate reciting memorized prayers without thinking about what you are saying, or multiplying words, not for the sake of communicating anything thoughtful, but for lengthening the prayer in an attempt to gain God's attention. Pagan incantations, for example, often used every imaginable name for the god they were invoking, hoping at least one of them would "stick." This kind of flowery rhetoric, or even nonsense syllables, common in pagan magical incantations, doesn't impress God.

Thus, Jesus warns us against two common errors in prayer. We are not to pray so as to attract attention from a human audience. Neither are we to pray in an attempt to manipulate God into giving us what we want. We are to pray so as to genuinely communicate with God and to lay our needs before him.

A Model Prayer

This is commonly called "The Lord's Prayer" (which is a more accurate name for Jn 17). What we have here is really "The Disciples' Prayer" or "A Model Prayer." The *Didache* urged Christians to "pray thus three times a day" (8:3). It is ironic, then, that in some circles this prayer has been used mechanically (cf. vv. 7-8), while in other circles it is seldom used at all, even as a model (cf. v. 9). The operative word is "how" (v. 9). Here we have a model, not a recipe for prayer.[73] It contains the essential ingredients of prayer: Adoration, Submission, Confession, Supplication. It is not surprising that on another occasion the disciples asked Jesus to teach them to pray and he repeats these same words almost verbatim (Lk 11:2-4).

Mt 6:9

> [9]"This, then, is how you should pray,
>   'Our Father in heaven,
>   Hallowed be your name.'"

We are reminded by the very first word, "our," that prayer is a corporate enterprise. We are not mavericks, we are a body. Even when we pray individually, we pray in conjunction with the church. Thus, we also pray for *our* daily bread, *our* sins, and *our* temptations.

The second word reminds us of the intimacy we have with God. The Greek word "Father" likely translates Jesus' Aramaic "Abba" (cf. Mk 14:36; Rom 8:15; Gal 4:6), which was somewhere between our English "Father" and "Daddy." While the Jews did think and speak about God as Father, such a close relationship with Jehovah went beyond the normal bounds of Judaism.[74] Our sonship is one of the greatest privileges we have through Christ (Jn 1:12; 20:17; Rom 8:14-17; 1 John 3:1). Yet Jesus balanced it with reverence for God's name (i.e., his character and attributes), with the phrase "Hallowed be your name." Whereas Judaism, by overemphasizing God's transcendence, made God untouchable, Evangelicalism, by overemphasizing God's nearness, has permitted our

---

[73]S.J. Kistemaker, "The Lord's Prayer in the First Century," *JETS* 21/4 (1978): 323-328, shows how this prayer was used as a model in the first century church, especially with its Jewish background.

[74]D.E. Garland, "The Lord's Prayer in the Gospel of Matthew," *Rev & Expos* 89/2 (1992): 215-228.

irreverence. He has become our "buddy," "the big man upstairs," our "cosmic Santa Claus." Jesus' model prayer does not allow this.

Mt 6:10

> [10]"Your Kingdom come,
>   your will be done
>   on earth as it is in heaven.'"

This is not merely a request for Jesus' physical return.[75] It is a request that God's reign, purpose, and plans be realized as completely on earth as they are in his throne room. It is significant that prior to personal confession or supplication, Jesus directs the Christian to adoration and submission. Indeed, it is not possible to pray to our potential until we recognize who God is and who we are before him (cf. Isa 37:15-20).

Mt 6:11

> [11]"Give us today our daily bread.'"

The meaning of this rare adjective [*epiousios*], translated "daily" is uncertain.[76] Others have suggested that it means "For tomorrow." Nonetheless, the implication seems clear enough. We are to pray for God's immediate provision of our needs.[77] In Jesus' time, men were paid daily. Usually they received just enough to purchase the daily provisions for their family. Thus, if they were injured, or could not find work, they likely would not eat that day. In addition, as an agricultural society, they recognized their constant dependence on God's provision. If a crop failed or if they had a hailstorm, or locusts or any number of other disasters, they were left without food. It is hard for us to understand this. Affluent Americans can hardly ask for God's daily provision when we have a freezer full of food that would easily last a month. It creates somewhat of a tension to trust God when we have so thoroughly protected ourselves.

Mt 6:12

> [12]"Forgive us our debts,
>   as we also have forgiven our debtors.'"

What are these debts? In light of vv. 14-15 as well as Luke 11:4, we

---

[75]R.E. Brown, however, interprets this whole prayer as referring to "end time talk," rather than the Christian era, especially since these first three petitions are aorist imperative. See "The Pater Noster as an Eschatological Prayer," *TS* 22 (1961): 175-208.

[76]While there is no other clear use of *epiousios* in all of Greek literature (B.M. Metzger, "How Many Times Does 'Epiouosios' Occur Outside the Lord's Prayer," *ExpT* 69 [1957-58]: 52-54), E.M. Yamauchi, "The 'Daily Bread' Motif in Antiquity," *WTJ* 28 (1966): 145-156, cogently defends the traditional meaning of "daily bread."

[77]Many of the early church fathers allegorized this bread as the Word of God or the Lord's Supper. For them, asking for bread on the heels of such adoration was too mundane.

understand them to be sins. This is spiritual *lex talionis*. That is, we are forgiven in the same way and to the same extent that we forgive others. It is not difficult to see why. Our offense to God is so much greater than man's offense to us, it would be unreasonable for us to expect forgiveness from God and not be willing to forgive those who have offended us. "This certainly does not mean that our forgiveness of others earns us the right to be forgiven. It is rather that God forgives only the penitent and that one of the chief evidences of true penitence is a forgiving spirit" (Stott, p. 149). That is precisely the point of the parable of the unforgiving servant (Mt 18:21-35).

Mt 6:13-15

[13]"'And lead us not into temptation,
but deliver us from the evil one.[a]'
[14]"For if you forgive men when they sin against you, your heavenly Father will also forgive you. [15]But if you do not forgive men their sins, your Father will not forgive your sins."

[a]*13 Or* from evil; *some late manuscripts* one, / for yours is the kingdom and the power and the glory forever. Amen.

The second phrase of this sentence helps us understand the first. Our prayer is not, "Don't let me be tempted" but "Don't abandon me in temptation so that it overwhelms me." Several observations will help us understand Jesus' words. (1) Jesus was tempted (Mt 4:1ff); we should expect no less. (2) A single Greek word is translated both "tempt" and "test." The difference is in the motive. God does not tempt us (James 1:13), so as to cause us to fall. God does test us, to raise us to maturity (James 1:2-4; 1 Pet 1:6-9). (3) When we face tests/temptations, God provides the means by which we can endure it (1 Cor 10:13). Our prayer, then, is to be able to withstand Satan.[78]

The common ending of this prayer "For yours is the kingdom and the power and the glory forever, Amen," was almost certainly not part of the original text of Matthew, although it is found in the *Didache*.[79] Without it, the prayer has an unusually abrupt ending. So perhaps it was added, based on 1 Chronicles 29:11-13, to round out the prayer. Nevertheless, there is no need to eradicate it from the Model Prayer. It does give a nice ending to the prayer and there is certainly nothing objectionable in it.

---

[78]Whether v. 13 is translated "Evil" (KJV) or "Evil One" (NIV) is inconsequential since temptation here is understood as originating with Satan. See note in Brown, p. 207.

[79]A. Bandstra, "The Lord's Prayer and Textual Criticism: A Response," *CTJ* 17 (1982): 88-97. Although, J. Van Bruggen, "The Lord's Prayer and Textual Criticism," *CTJ* 17 (1982): 78-87, argues for the KJV text and the longer ending of the prayer.

Fasting

Mt 6:16-18

[16]"When you fast, do not look somber as the hypocrites do, for they disfigure their faces to show men they are fasting. I tell you the truth, they have received their reward in full. [17]But when you fast, put oil on your head and wash your face, [18]so that it will not be obvious to men that you are fasting, but only to your Father, who is unseen; and your Father, who sees what is done in secret, will reward you."

This is "more of the same." As with almsgiving and prayer, when we fast we must not show off our piety, otherwise, the praise of men is the only reward we will get. But if we practice our piety before God alone, he will see and reward us. So, when we fast, and Jesus assumes that we will, we are to comb our hair and wash our face as we always do, and go about business as usual. This does not mean that no one will ever know we are fasting. For instance, it would be hard to hide the fact from a spouse. What it does mean is that we don't go around announcing it. You can either impress people or God. Take your pick.

The whole of this discussion (Mt 6:1-18) can be summed up in this question: "Who's your primary audience?" It is simply not possible, nor always advisable, to practice all our piety in secret. People watch, they see what we do. But are they the ones you play for? Or do you keep practicing your piety when no human eye can see? That is the measure of a true kingdom citizen.

§ 54g
Three Prohibitions: Wealth, Worry, Judging
(Mt. 6:19-7:6)

Wealth, 6:19-24

Money consumes our time and attention to such a degree that it often displaces God as our object of worship (Eph 5:5). The church has too often cowered from teaching about money. Jesus never did. He hits it head on in our present text, understanding that our wallets are one of the best barometers of our spirits.

Earthly vs. Heavenly Wealth:

Mt 6:19-21

[19]"Do not store up for yourselves treasures on earth, where moth and rust destroy, and where thieves break in and steal. [20]But store up for yourselves treasures in heaven, where moth and rust do not destroy, and where thieves do not break in[80] and steal. [21]For where your treasure is, there your heart will be also."

It is true that "You can't take it with you." However, Jesus said you can send it on ahead. How? By using your money to help the poor (1 Tim 6:17-19). This also seems to be the implication of the parable of the

---

[80]Lit., "dig through." This was true of homes made of mud brick.

shrewd manager. In Luke 16:9 Jesus says, "I tell you, use worldly wealth to gain friends for yourselves, so that when it is gone, you will be welcomed into eternal dwellings" (cf. Mt 25:31-46).

In the first century, wealth was not accumulated in bank accounts, but in a cache of precious metals and cloth (or clothes). Thus, moths and rust (i.e., corrosion), were detrimental to wealth. Even those things that cannot be "eaten" can be stolen. What's neither eaten nor stolen will be left behind when we die (Lk 12:15-21). Thus, worldly riches are a poor investment.

Verse 21 is axiomatic. Wealth demands our time and attention, often to the exclusion of spiritual concerns. For instance, if we buy a bicycle, we then have to lock it up. When it gets a flat tire we have to fix it. We must have a place to store it. Periodically we must oil the sprockets, etc. And what's the use of having it if we can't take time to ride it or show it off? Such is the nature of worldly wealth. It is not impossible to be rich and Christian, but it is *very* difficult (Mt 19:23-26). Those who are "blessed" with wealth are frequently distracted and overpowered by it. Wealth is not antithetical to discipleship but it often stands in the way of following Jesus. When wealth becomes a ball and chain, the solution is difficult, but it may become necessary to rid ourselves of riches (Mt 19:21) in order to make more permanent investments.

Another danger of wealth is that we tend to get possessive of it rather than using it to advance the kingdom by helping the poor. Even in Christian endeavors, we protect our bank accounts for a "rainy day." Our tendency is to drastically overestimate our own needs while underestimating the plight of the poor.[81]

Light vs. Darkness:

Mt 6:22-23

[22]"The eye is the lamp of the body. If your eyes are good, your whole body will be full of light. [23]But if your eyes are bad, your whole body will be full of darkness. If then the light within you is darkness, how great is that darkness!"

D.C. Allison suggests that the eye is not what lets light into the body but what sends light forth from the body.[82] He traces how some ancients viewed both the "eye shine" of animals and human glances as actually sending light forth from the body. Thus, a body full of light would send it forth in acts of generosity [*haplous*]. A body full of darkness would

---

[81]C.L. Blomberg, "On Wealth and Worry: Matthew 6:19-34 — Meaning and Significance," *CTR* 6/1 (1992): 73-89, gives some insightful suggestions for both corporate and individual Christian financial management.

[82]D.C. Allison, "The Eye is the Lamp of the Body," *NTS* 33 (1987): 61-83.

have no light to send forth. As a result, that person would be stingy. This explanation should be commended for two things. One, it fits very nicely the context. Two, the definition of *haplous* as "generous" has strong support.[83] However, the suggestion that eye sends light rather than receives it is somewhat peculiar. Furthermore, Jesus says the light passes through the eyes into the body, not vice versa.

Perhaps a better explanation is this: The eye is the organ of light. That is, it lets light into the body. Figuratively speaking, then, the eye is the organ of moral discernment. The word "good" [*haplous*] means more specifically, "Single mindedness, undivided loyalty."[84] Applied to the context, Jesus' words mean something like this: "If you are capable of discerning between earthly and spiritual wealth, and thus devote yourself single-mindedly to attaining heavenly treasures, your whole life will be truly enlightened. If your loyalty is divided between God and money, your life will be dark."

God vs. Money:

Mt 6:24

24"No one can serve two masters. Either he will hate the one and love the other, or he will be devoted to the one and despise the other. You cannot serve both God and Money."

Three observations will help us understand Jesus' words clearly. (1) A master was a slave owner, not just a boss. These words have no bearing on "moonlighting." (2) Hate and love are comparative, not literal (cf. Lk 14:26). To put it in our vernacular, "One of the two is going to take priority." (3) The KJV borrows the Aramaic word "Mammon" which includes all of one's possessions. Many believe we can have the best of both worlds — wealth and worship. Jesus says that is simply not possible. One of the two will dominate our time and attention. Eventually both the "masters" will demand our attention at the same time. Then our true love will become obvious.

Worry, 6:25-34

"Worry" is logically connected to the previous discussion on money (with "therefore"). It is clearly the theme of this passage (vv. 25, 27, 28, 31, 34). Certainly many in the audience were thinking to themselves, "But if we don't prioritize money, how will our needs be met?" Jesus stops them short in their tracks of worry and says, "Trust God." Jesus once again turns our minds away from worldly values to a Kingdom perspective.

---

[83]H.J. Cadbury, "The Single Eye," *HTR* (1954): 69-74.

[84]T. Thiennaman, "A Comment on an Interpretation by Prof. Cadbury," *GR* 1 (1955): 9-22.

Jesus highlights two things which we worry about most: Food (vv. 26-27) and clothing (vv. 28-30). He gives three reasons why we shouldn't worry about them. (1) There are more important things in life than food and clothing (v. 25). We would do well to expend our time and energy on these rather than on worry. (2) God loves us and wants to provide for us (vv. 26, 30, 32). To illustrate his point, Jesus uses typically Jewish logic — from lesser to greater — and two very common objects, birds and grass. That is, if God will provide for birds and grass, certainly he will provide for humans who are much more valuable. (3) Worry can not actually change anything (vv. 27, 34). It's kind of like a rocking chair. It gives you something to do, but doesn't get you anywhere.

Mt 6:25-27

²⁵"Therefore I tell you, do not worry about your life, what you will eat or drink; or about your body, what you will wear. Is not life more important than food, and the body more important than clothes? ²⁶Look at the birds of the air; they do not sow or reap or store away in barns, and yet your heavenly Father feeds them. Are you not much more valuable than they? ²⁷Who of you by worrying can add a single hour to his life[a]?"

[a]27 Or *single cubit to his height*

"Look at the birds" (v. 26) implies "Look and Learn." "See how" [*katamathete*] (v. 28), is even more specific, meaning, "learn carefully from." We can learn much from these flighty little fellas. They are industrious yet carefree. Without the benefit of barns they manage to find food each day. That is God's provision for them. For us, God's provision is greater. We have been given the ability to manipulate our environment. To grow crops, raise animals, and preserve food. Not only are we more capable than the birds to provide food for ourselves, but we are also more valuable in God's eyes (Mt 10:29-31). How much less, then, we should worry.

"A single hour" (NIV) has been variously translated: "Add one cubit unto his stature" (KJV), "Make himself an inch taller" (Phillips), "Add one cubit to his span of life" (RSV), and "Add one moment to his life's course?" (Modern). Here's the problem. The Greek word *hē likian*, translated "life (span)," can mean either "length of life" or "stature" (i.e., height/size) — either a physical or a chronological measurement. A cubit was a physical measurement about eighteen inches long. But Jesus' words imply a very minute addition. Eighteen inches added to one's stature (KJV) would be a *huge* jump, thus the Phillips version pares it down to one inch. On the other hand, it seems awkward to add eighteen inches to the *chronology* of one's life. A reasonable solution seems to be to picture a man walking down the "path of life." Worry will not allow him to add even a small step (eighteen inches) to his journey. We use a similar metaphor, combining chronological and physical measurements, when we talk of "reaching a milestone" in life.

Mt 6:28-30

²⁸"And why do you worry about clothes? See how the lilies of the field grow. They do not labor or spin. ²⁹Yet I tell you that not even Solomon in all his splendor was dressed like one of these. ³⁰If that is how God clothes the grass of the field, which is here today and tomorrow is thrown into the fire, will he not much more clothe you, O you of little faith?"

"Lilies" can mean any species of wild flower. It forms a natural complement to the "birds of the air." A field of wild flowers sprinkled across a bed of fresh spring grass is a remarkable sight indeed. These little beauties don't labor or spin (probably a reference to both men's and women's work respectively). But even Solomon's wardrobe paled in comparison.

If God is so generous with something as transitory as kindling for the fire (v. 30), what do you suppose he will do for us? No wonder Jesus rebukes us, "O, you of little faith," when a mere glance out our bedroom window should teach us the futility of worry. As Mounce has said, "Worry is practical atheism and an affront to God."[85]

Mt 6:31-34

³¹"So do not worry, saying, 'What shall we eat?' or 'What shall we drink?' or 'What shall we wear?' ³²For the pagans run after all these things, and your heavenly Father knows that you need them. ³³But seek first his kingdom and his righteousness, and all these things will be given to you as well. ³⁴Therefore do not worry about tomorrow, for tomorrow will worry about itself. Each day has enough trouble of its own."

First, we are called to trust God rather than the security of riches. How can we be salt and light if we pursue the same priorities as do the pagans? Christianity will have an impact on society in proportion to its distinctiveness. Julian the Apostate, the Roman Emperor of the fourth century, said this about Christians, "We ought to be ashamed. Not a beggar is to be found among the Jews, and those godless Galileans feed not only their own people but ours as well, whereas our people receive no assistance whatever from us."

Second, God has promised to meet the needs of those who continually seek his kingdom and righteousness (v. 33). We could record multiplied testimonies of God's gracious provision. But we still have to answer the nagging question, "Why do Christians starve?" We reject the answer that they lack faith. Although we admit that v. 33 will have ultimate eschatological fulfillment, it must have immediate application or else the entire discussion of worry over temporal needs becomes irrelevant.

---

[85]R.H. Mounce, *Matthew* (Peabody, MA: Hendrickson, 1991), p. 80.

Several observations must temper our understanding of this verse. (1) Christians are not exempt from suffering, sometimes for discipline (Heb 12:7), sometimes for our testimony for Christ (Mt 5:10-12; Rom 8:17; Phil 3:10; 4:12), and sometimes simply because we live in a fallen world. There is enough food in the world to feed everyone. The problem is not with God's provision but with man's distribution. (2) Christians have the responsibility to care for the poor (Prov 22:9; 25:21f; Isa 32:6; 58:6ff; Ezek 16:49; 18:7; Mt 25:42; Mk 10:21; Lk 3:11; 12:33, 48; Acts 4:32ff.). God typically meets human needs through those who are led by his Spirit. That is an essential part of seeking God's kingdom and righteousness. The church functions as the hand of God in this world. Thus, much of the world hunger is due to greed in the church, not negligence on God's part. (3) Verse 34 seems to temper verse 33. Jesus recognizes that our days will be filled with trouble. We simply can't afford the luxury of worry, casting our eyes on future affliction. Each day will demand our best attention.

Judging, 7:1-6 (cf. Lk 6:37-42)

Mt 7:1

¹"Do not judge, or you too will be judged.

Lk 6:37-38

³⁷Do not condemn, and you will not be condemned. Forgive, and you will be forgiven. ³⁸Give, and it will be given to you. A good measure, pressed down, shaken together and running over, will be poured into your lap.

Mt 7:2

²For in the same way you judge others, you will be judged, and with the measure you use, it will be measured to you."

The word "judge" [*krinō*] can mean "to analyze" or "evaluate" or even "to condemn." Christians are expected to analyze and evaluate people and their behaviors (v. 7:5-6, 16; 1 Cor 5:5; 1 John 4:1). At the same time we have no right to condemn others. This is God's prerogative alone (Rom 14:4, 10; 1 Cor 4:4-5). Luke (6:37) clearly shows that the nature of this judging is condemnation, not evaluation. Simply put, we do not have either the ability or the authority to make pronouncements about someone's standing with God. On the other hand, the non-Christian world is all too familiar with this text. It is often used as a wild-card trump against meddling Christians who call a spade a spade (v. 6). Jesus would not support such a use of this verse torn from its context.[86] A Christian simply cannot avoid the responsibility of being a moral voice in this world (cf. 5:13-16).

---

[86]J.D.M. Derrett, "Christ and Reproof (Mt 7:1-5; Lk 6:37-42)," *NTS* 34 (1988): 271-281, shows that within Jewish culture, Jesus would not be understood as forbidding judging for reproof.

We will find ourselves on the wrong end of God's judgment if we condemn others. Luke also says that the opposite is true. If we forgive others, we will receive a whole, compact, bushel full of God's grace (Lk 6:37-38).

Mt 7:3-5   ³"Why do you look at the speck of sawdust in your brother's eye and pay no attention to the plank in your own eye? ⁴How can you say to your brother, 'Let me take the speck out of your eye,' when all the time there is a plank in your own eye? ⁵You hypocrite, first take the plank out of your own eye, and then you will see clearly to remove the speck from your brother's eye."

Jesus' incisive wit is demonstrated in this hilarious caricature. But its truth, because it is all too common, is not so funny. It is usually easier, not to mention more fun, to identify other people's faults than our own. To compound the problem, we are often most offended by character flaws in others which we ourselves have (cf. 2 Sam 12). For example, a temperamental person may be highly insulted if someone gets angry with him. Stott puts it this way, "We have a rosy view of ourselves and a jaundiced view of others. Indeed, what we are often doing is seeing our own faults in others and judging them vicariously. That way, we experience the pleasure of self-righteousness without the pain of penitence" (p. 178). Paul says essentially the same thing as Jesus:

> You, therefore, have no excuse, you who pass judgment on someone else, for at whatever point you judge the other, you are condemning yourself, because you who pass judgment do the same things. . . . So when you, a mere man, pass judgment on them and yet do the same things, do you think you will escape God's judgment? (Rom 2:1,3)

This does not alleviate our responsibility to confront erring brothers and sisters (Gal 6:1). When we do confront them, though, several principles must underlie our encounter. First, we should strive for moral purity ourselves, especially in the area in which we confront a fellow believer. This is not so that we can say, "I am above you in this," but so we can say, "I've struggled through this, and here is the way out." Second, we have a deep sense of appreciation for God's "kindness, tolerance and patience" (Rom 2:4) which led us to repentance. Third, "The Law of fair play" which is ultimately expressed in the "Golden Rule" (v. 12), calls us back to the Lord's Prayer (Mt 6:12, 14-15) and the beatitudes (Mt 5:7). Fourth, we should not pretend to be something we are not. The theme of hypocrisy once again echoes through this sermon (cf. Mt 6:2, 5, 16). Confrontation, which Jesus enjoins (v. 5), is to be punctuated with humility, admitting our own failures. Its goal is reconciliation, not pious self-aggrandizement.

Mt 7:6   [6]"Do not give dogs what is sacred; do not throw your pearls to pigs. If you do, they may trample them under their feet, and then turn and tear you to pieces."

Wild dogs and pigs were both unclean to the Jews. In a chiastic structure, the dogs tear you to pieces, while the pigs are more likely to trample something into the ground. Obviously, one would not give something sacred, such as sacrificial meat, to a dog, nor would one offer pearls to a pig. This figure is easy to exegete, but more difficult to interpret.

Jesus places it here to balance his teaching on judging. Obviously we must have some measure of evaluation of others before we can identify them as pigs or dogs. But who are these people? Jews sometimes referred to Gentiles as pigs and dogs (Mt 15:26, 27). In the kingdom, however, that distinction is erased (Gal 3:28). We conclude, then, that pigs and dogs are those who reject the truth (2 Pet 2:22) and thus become morally depraved (Rev 22:15), whether they are Gentiles or Jews (Phil 3:2).

What then are the sacred things and the pearls which we do not offer these people? The early church sometimes saw this as the Lord's Supper. For instance, the *Didache*, 9:5 said, "Let no one eat or drink of your Eucharist, but they who have been baptized into the name of the Lord; for concerning this also the Lord has said, 'Give not that which is holy to dogs.'" However, the Lord's Supper seems too early for this text. A more likely interpretation comes from the parable of the Pearl of Great Price (Mt 13:46) as well as 2 Peter 2:22, that regards these "valuables" as the preaching of the kingdom of God. The interpretation follows: "If someone rejects the truth, don't keep preaching to them." That is precisely what Jesus said when he sent out the Twelve (Mt 10:14), and that was the *modus operandi* of Paul (cf. Acts 13:44-51; 18:5-6; 28:17-28).[87]

§54h
Conclusion
(Mt 7:7-27;
cf. Lk 6:31,
43-49)

This final section of the Sermon on the Mount has several blocks of material which are only loosely connected by a common theme of "A Christian's Relationships." This has led some to say that the Sermon, as we now have it, is a collection of snippets from various times, places, and perhaps sources. That is not necessary. Considering that this is only a synopsis, one might assume that the logical transitions and connectors have been left out for the sake of brevity. Furthermore, conclusions to

---

[87]T.J. Bennett, "Mt 7:6 — A New Interpretation," *WTJ* 49 (1987): 371-386, suggests that Jesus is being sarcastic: "Don't give what *you think* is holy to what *you think* are dogs." In other words, "Don't judge at all!" This keeps Jesus from calling men dogs and avoids an apparent contradiction between vv. 1 and 6. It also explains how you could avoid the retaliation from dogs and pigs. But it does require us to add ideas (if not words) to the text which are not clearly there.

sermons lend themselves to several loosely connected implications which reach back into the body of the sermon for support.

Mt 7:7-11

7"Ask and it will be given to you; seek and you will find; knock and the door will be opened to you. 8For everyone who asks receives; he who seeks finds; and to him who knocks, the door will be opened.

9"Which of you, if his son asks for bread, will give him a stone? 10Or if he asks for a fish, will give him a snake? 11If you, then, though you are evil, know how to give good gifts to your children, how much more will your Father in heaven give good gifts to those who ask him!"

Our prayer lives are a better barometer of our belief in this text than is our confession. Do you believe that God is a good Father? Then you will pray. Certainly no human father would trick his children by giving them a rock that looked like a roll. Nor would he give them a snake or an eel that looked like a long skinny fish. God is comparable to a perfectly loving Father, a concept generally foreign to Jewish prayers. Isaiah 49:15 also compares God to a caring mother: "Can a mother forget the baby at her breast and have no compassion on the child she has borne? Though she may forget, I will not forget you!"

This implies several things. (1) He wants to give us good gifts (which Lk 11:13 identifies as the Holy Spirit). (2) We can approach him personally and persistently (as the present imperatives of "Ask, seek, knock" imply). And (3) if we ask for something harmful, or if we ask with selfish motives (James 4:2-3) or without faith (James 1:6-8), God is not bound like Aladdin's genie to grant our whimsical requests. He will grant our request as he deems best. Sometimes God's answer is "Yes," sometimes it is "No," and sometimes, "Wait."

The effectiveness of prayer is indeed a mystery. God is sovereign; his will is going to be accomplished. Furthermore, he already knows our needs. Why then should we imagine that our puny prayers would actually change anything? Precisely because the Scriptures say they do. For instance, Moses' prayer was able to avert the wrath of God on the Israelites (Exod 32:9-14). But most often what is changed is not the mind of God but the heart of man. Prayer often produces in us a perspective and a posture which enables us to receive God's intended blessing. We pray simply out of obedient faith, not because we have solved the paradox between God's sovereignty and effective prayer.

Mt 7:12

12"So in everything, do to others what you would have them do to you, for this sums up the Law and the Prophets."

This Golden Rule sums up an enormous body of material. Not only does it summarize the entire OT but also the entire Sermon on the

Mount. Its introductory "therefore" seems to take us back clear back to 5:17. As was said before, 5:17 and 7:12 bracket the body of this sermon. All of its difficult material is elucidated in one clear sentence. Well, it is clear enough to understand, but excruciatingly difficult to practice.[88]

The negative of this rule, sometimes called the Silver Rule, is frequently found in religious literature. Even Confucius supposedly said, "Do not to others what you would not wish done to yourself." Tobit 4:15 says, "Do not do to anyone what you yourself would hate." And when the great Jewish rabbi, Hillel, was asked by a would-be proselyte to expound the whole law while he stood on one leg, he replied, "What is hateful to you, do not do to anyone else. This is the whole law; all the rest is only commentary" (*Shabbath*, 31a). The difference between these negative rules and Jesus' positive one is immediately apparent. We can do nothing and still completely satisfy the demands of the Silver Rule. But the Golden Rule demands my constant and utmost action. Such is the difference between the extraneous rules of religion which men keep to the letter while weaseling their way out of love, and Jesus' clarion call to righteousness whose simplicity exposes our hypocrisy and yet stimulates our best efforts to emulate him.

Two Paths

Mt 7:13-14

[13]"Enter through the narrow gate. For wide is the gate and broad is the road that leads to destruction, and many enter through it. [14]But small is the gate and narrow the road that leads to life, and only a few find it."

"Broad" and "narrow" not only indicate the relative number of people who will become Christians, but the relative ease and difficulty that each path will bring. "Narrow" also suggests the idea of "trouble, difficulty, being hard-pressed." This does not mean, however, that the carefree, value-free, nondemanding way of the pagan is a happier life. Paradoxically, in an effort to comfort, pamper, and cater to our fleshly desires, we wreck our lives. On the other hand, when we give ourselves over to Christ, then we find true life and happiness (Mt 10:39; Jn 10:10). This path, which at first looked so constricting, we find liberating, graceful, and easy (Mt 11:28-30).

Our syncretistic society is offended by Jesus' black and white options. We demand a smorgasbord of ethical choices. We describe such

---

[88]It is exegetically irresponsible to import into this text 20th century psychosocial theories of self-esteem. True, people who don't love themselves have a difficult time loving others. But that is not what this text is talking about. Furthermore, when we follow Jesus' way of serving others, we find it terribly difficult to think too much of ourselves at all, either arrogantly or condemningly.

teaching as narrow-minded, overly simplistic, and even bigoted. Is it possible, however, that some have become so open-minded that their brains have fallen out?

Two Fruits

Mt 7:15-20

¹⁵"Watch out for false prophets. They come to you in sheep's clothing, but inwardly they are ferocious wolves. ¹⁶By their fruit you will recognize them. Do people pick grapes from thornbushes, or figs from thistles? ¹⁷Likewise every good tree bears good fruit, but a bad tree bears bad fruit. ¹⁸A good tree cannot bear bad fruit, and a bad tree cannot bear good fruit. ¹⁹Every tree that does not bear good fruit is cut down and thrown into the fire. ²⁰Thus, by their fruits you will recognize them."

Lk 6:45

⁴⁵"The good man brings good things out of the good stored up in his heart, and the evil man brings evil things out of the evil stored up in his heart. For out of the overflow of his heart his mouth speaks."

A prophet was one who received a revelation from God and spoke it to people. Sometimes these revelations dealt with future events, sometimes present and sometimes past. The definitive characteristic of a prophet is not the time period to which their words refer, but the fact that they got their message from God (Jer 23:16, 18, 22). Thus, a false prophet (cf. Mt 24:11-14; 2 Pet 2:1-3, 17-22) is one who claims, "God said to me . . ." when God did not. There are also false apostles (2 Cor 11:13-15), false teachers (2 Pet 2:1), and false Christs (Mt 24:24). The point is, some people disguise their true character (v. 15), and pretend to have a relationship with God so they can exploit God's flock. Although this text is not a license for heresy hunting, it behooves the church not to be gullible. Satan will use any means he can to destroy the flock (Jn 10:11-13). Often he uses power-hungry people (Acts 20:29-30). Jesus suggests that we balance innocence and wisdom (Mt 10:16).

How does one recognize a false prophet? First, by their fruit. There have always been Christians in name only. They walk the broad path while claiming to walk the narrow way. Some trees look surprisingly similar. They may grow for years before you can tell just what they are. But there is no disguising its fruit. We can hide our true character only so long. Our fruit (behavior) makes our affiliation obvious.

Second, we must consider the context of the narrow vs. broad way. Anyone who advocates an "easy" salvation, a syncretistic, multi-optional way to God is a false prophet. Like the false prophets of old they say, "Peace, peace when there is no peace" (Jer 6:13-15). From Jeremiah we also learn of two other common characteristics of false prophets. They are greedy for gain and they have no shame. Sexual immorality and financial mismanagement seem to attend false teaching and mercenary ministry.

Mt 7:21-23

²¹"Not everyone who says to me, 'Lord, Lord,' will enter the kingdom of heaven, but only he who does the will of my Father who is in heaven. ²²Many will say to me on that day, 'Lord, Lord, did we not prophesy in your name, and in your name drive out demons and perform many miracles?' ²³Then I will tell them plainly, 'I never knew you. Away from me, you evildoers!'"

Because people are so enamored with the spectacular rather than the spiritual, many are fooled by plastic fruit. By plastic fruit I mean the imitation of the miraculous (v. 22). Since miracles are relatively easy to manipulate or fake, they are a poor test of God's approval. Some of these miracle mongers are simply charlatans. Others are self-deluded individuals who replaced obedience to God with wooing and wowing the crowds.

We have just been told that we will "know them by their fruit." But the fact of the matter is that some people's motives will be hidden throughout their lives. But on judgment day, all the hidden things will be revealed (1 Cor 4:5).

Certainly God's priorities are less fantastic than ours, more inward. The kingdom of God is not about a big splash in bright lights; it's about a broken spirit bent on following God's ways.[89]

Two Houses

Mt 7:24-27

²⁴"Therefore everyone who hears these words of mine and puts them into practice is like a wise man who built his house on the rock. ²⁵The rain came down, the streams rose, and the winds blew and beat against that house; yet it did not fall, because it had its foundation on the rock. ²⁶But everyone who hears these words of mine and does not put them into practice is like a foolish man who built his house on sand. ²⁷The rain came down, the streams rose, and the winds blew and beat against that house, and it fell with a great crash."

"Whereas the contrast in the previous paragraph was between 'saying' and 'doing,' the contrast now is between 'hearing' and 'doing'" (Stott, p. 208). In the Palestinian desert it is much easier to build on the sandy surface than to dig down to bedrock (Lk 6:48). Likewise it is easier to listen to Jesus' words (v. 26) and profess a relationship with him (vv. 21-22), than it is to obey him (v. 24). But that is the only way to lay a lasting foundation.

These two houses will look the same to the passerby. But the difference will be obvious enough in the storm. Likewise, two professing

---

[89]In recent years, Charismatic churches have been plagued with the problems of verses 15-23, specifically false prophets and an overemphasis on the miraculous. But if we only identify these problems with charismatics perhaps we could identify ourselves with vv. 1-5.

Christians may both go to church, pray, read their Bibles, and have a Jesus bumper sticker on their car. The storm will tell the difference. We use this metaphor primarily as "the storms of life." There is truth in that. Times of tribulation often reveal the genuineness of a person's faith. The Jews, however, used this storm metaphor especially in relation to judgment (Ezek 13:10ff). Thus, contextually, our house will be tested on judgment day (1 Cor 3:12-15).

§ 54i
Response
(Mt 7:28-8:1)

[28]When Jesus had finished saying these things, the crowds were amazed at his teaching, [29]because he taught as one who had authority, and not as their teachers of the law.

[1]When he came down from the mountainside, a large crowd followed him.

This is a most austere ending to a sermon, this talk of judgment. Moreover, the whole message has incisive clarity. It is so sensible that we can't help but agree with it, and yet so radical that we are overwhelmed by it. If we try to dodge its demands, the memorable metaphors suck us back in. If we actually try to live it out, we are confronted by our blatant hypocrisy and selfish motives. It is no small wonder that this silenced crowd was amazed at his teaching. They had never heard anything like it. All their best teachers either quoted each other or the Scriptures for support of their arguments. Jesus quoted no other rabbi. And when he quoted Scriptures he felt perfectly free to go beyond them with that ostentatious phrase, "But I say!" Blomberg is correct: "Such preaching reflects either the height of presumption and heresy or the fact that he was a true spokesman for God, whom we dare not ignore" (p. 135).

The book of Matthew revolves around five speeches, each of which ends with the phrase, "When Jesus had finished saying these things" (7:28-29; 11:1; 13:53; 19:1; 26:1). This sermon then, will mark the end of the first section of Matthew's book.

§ 55
Healing the
Centurion's
Servant
(Lk 7:1-10;
Mt 8:5-13)

THE GROWING FAME OF JESUS

[1]When Jesus had finished saying all this in the hearing of the people, he entered Capernaum. [2]There a centurion's servant, whom his master valued highly, was sick {paralyzed and in terrible suffering[MT]} and about to die. [3]The centurion heard of Jesus and sent some elders of the Jews to him, asking him to come and heal his servant. [4]When they came to Jesus, they pleaded earnestly with him, "This man deserves to have you do this, [5]because he loves our nation and has built our synagogue." [6]So Jesus went with them.

After Jesus' great sermon he returns to Capernaum. While he is there, a notable centurion sends to Jesus a delegation of Jewish elders. They beg Jesus to heal the centurion's servant. Now Matthew says the centurion came himself. Does that mean that Matthew and Luke contradict each other? Not necessarily. Matthew's account is merely an abbreviation of the event. Since the centurion was responsible for the delegation he, himself, is described as coming to Jesus.[90] Besides, that fits Matthew, since he typically leaves out any positive comments about Jewish leaders.[91] In contrast, Luke gives the more detailed account which characteristically shows mercy to Gentiles. What we have, then, is not a contradiction but a variation in their presentations.

The emphasis of this passage is on the centurion, not on the sick servant. In fact, even the syntax of this sentence places the word "centurion" in a prominent position so it sticks out even though the subject of the sentence is the servant.

A centurion was a military leader in the Roman army comparable to a lieutenant.[92] As the title "centurion" suggests, he was in charge of one hundred men. The New Testament speaks of several centurions and all in favorable terms. (1) The centurion at the cross of Christ proclaimed his faith that Jesus was the Son of God or possibly a son of a god (Mt 27:54; Mk 15:39; Lk 23:47). (2) Cornelius, of Acts 10-11, demonstrated full faith in Jesus. He and his house received the Holy Spirit and were baptized. (3) Julius, in Acts 27, guarded Paul on the way to Rome. He was both reasonable and fair. (4) Only one centurion, Acts 22:25-26, may be viewed as a villain. He was about to flog Paul. But he was just doing his job and did, in fact, stop when he learned that Paul was a Roman citizen. Over all, our impression of centurions is positive. They seem to be reasonable, unbiased, and submitted to authority.

His servant is "valued highly." In several other passages this refers to positions of highest honor. In both Luke 7:7 and Matthew 8:6 he will

---

[90]Z.C. Hodges, "The Centurion's Faith in Matthew and Luke," *BibSac* 121 (Oct 1964): 321-332, suggests that the centurion did, in fact, come to Jesus, as Matthew says, but only after he had already said "I did not even consider myself worthy to come to you" (Lk 7:7). Hence the text is not in contradiction, rather the centurion is fickle. But this is unlikely since (1) the point of the story is the sterling faith of the centurion. Fickleness hardly fits that portrait. And (2) the centurion apparently sent even a second delegation (Lk 7:6) to stop Jesus from coming to his house.

[91]Furthermore, Matthew places this narrative next to the healing of the leper and highlights their similarities. Both the leper and the centurion came to Jesus, were outcasts of Israel, demonstrated great faith, and were accepted by Jesus.

[92]E. Ferguson, *Background of Early Christianity* (Grand Rapids: Eerdmans, 1987), pp. 38-42.

be referred to, not as a servant, but as a child. In other words, he is more than just a servant. He had become like a son to the centurion.

Upon hearing of Jesus' reputation for healing, this centurion sends a delegation of Jewish elders to ask Jesus for help. It was rare that Jews would go out of their way for a Gentile. But this was a rare Gentile. He had provided influence and likely much of his own money to help build the Capernaum synagogue. And now, one good deed deserves another.

Lk 7:6-8

⁶He was not far from the house when the centurion sent friends to say to him: "Lord, don't trouble yourself, for I do not deserve to have you come under my roof. ⁷That is why I did not even consider myself worthy to come to you. But say the word, and my servant will be healed. ⁸For I myself am a man under authority, with soldiers under me. I tell this one, 'Go,' and he goes; and that one, 'Come,' and he comes. I say to my servant 'Do this,' and he does it."

The delegation of Jewish elders apparently overstep their bounds, or at least the centurion's desires, when they ask Jesus to go to the man's house. Thus, a second delegation, comprised of the centurion's personal friends, is sent to keep Jesus from coming to the house.

Their message is simple: "Don't trouble yourself" (lit. "Don't be hassled"). This construction means to "stop" whatever action is in progress. The centurion either sees or hears the procession and doesn't want Jesus to bother himself further by entering his home. He is probably not just talking about the trouble of coming all the way to his house. If Jesus were to enter the house of a Gentile, he would be criticized by his own countrymen (cf. Acts 10:28). This centurion is looking out for Jesus' best interests and trying to protect his reputation.

Being a soldier, the centurion understands the power of the spoken word. Jesus doesn't need to be present or touch the servant. He simply needs to command it to be done (cf. Ps 107:20). Such is the nature of authority. Even so, there is no precedent for believing in "distance healing" save the one incident when Jesus healed the nobleman's son in Capernaum while he was twenty miles away in Cana (Jn 4:46-54). Perhaps this fellow had heard about that. Even so, his faith is astounding.

The centurion makes a keen comparison between his military position and the spiritual position of Jesus and his Father. He had superiors from whom he was given authority and subordinates to whom he gave commands. He recognizes that Jesus is granted authority from God and is authorized to give commands to his subordinates (e.g., diseases and elements).

Mt 8:10-13

¹⁰When Jesus heard this, he was astonished and said to those following him, "I tell you the truth, I have not found anyone in Israel with such great faith. ¹¹I say to you that many will come from the east and the west, and will take their places

at the feast with Abraham, Isaac and Jacob in the kingdom of heaven. [12]But the subjects of the kingdom will be thrown outside, into the darkness, where there will be weeping and gnashing of teeth."

[13]Then Jesus said to the centurion, "Go! It will be done just as you believed it would." And his servant was healed at that very hour.

Lk 7:10

[10]Then the men who had been sent returned to the house and found the servant well.

This is one of only two times that Jesus was amazed. He is amazed here at the incredible faith of a Gentile, and in Mark 6:6, in Nazareth, he was amazed at the lack of faith of his own countrymen. It is a paradox that the Jews, who had the Scriptures (Rom 3:1-2), would lack faith, while the Gentiles should demonstrate such faith.

Jesus lays out a paradox of his own. The Jews, who would expect to participate in the Messianic banquet (Isa 25:6; Mt 26:29; Lk 22:30), were kicked out. But the foreigners were allowed in. The simple lesson of this narrative is that Jesus respects faith, not ethnicity. Hence, we have a dramatized prediction of Gentile inclusion (Acts 10-11).

§ 56
Raising of the
Widow's Son at
Nain
(Lk 7:11-17)

Matthew paired the healing of the centurion's servant with the cleansing of the leper to show their similarities. Likewise, Luke pairs it with the raising of the widow's son. In both accounts a precious "child" is raised up when an unlikely candidate receives the Lord's attention.

This is the first of three people Jesus raised from the dead. The other two were Jairus' daughter (Mt 9:18-26; Mk 5:22-43; Lk 8:49-56), and Jesus' friend Lazarus (Jn 11). As Elijah raised a widow's son (1 Kgs 17:17-24; cf. Elisha 2 Kgs 4:32-37), so also does Jesus. Thus, Jesus' ministry looks like the great prophet Elijah's.[93]

Lk 7:11-13

[11]Soon afterward, Jesus went to a town called Nain, and his disciples and a large crowd went along with him. [12]As he approached the town gate, a dead person was being carried out — the only son of his mother, and she was a widow. And a large crowd from the town was with her. [13]When the Lord saw her, his heart went out to her and he said, "Don't cry."

The raising of this widow's son at Nain took place shortly after the healing of the centurion's servant, likely on the very next day.[94] The little

---

[93]C.A. Evans, "Luke's Use of the Elijah/Elisha Narratives and the Ethic of Election," *JBL* 106/1 (1987): 75-83, shows how Luke uses the Elijah/Elisha motif a number of times, especially in his central section (Lk 4:25-27; 7:11-17; 9:52-55, 61-62). When he does, he seems to be comparing Jesus to the great prophet(s) who opened God's kingdom to the Gentiles. This fits especially well here, against the backdrop of healing the centurion's servant.

[94]The word *hexēs* sometimes signifies the very next day, and never a long period of time.

village of Nain ("The Pleasant") is about twenty-five miles southeast of Capernaum just over the hill from Shunem where Elisha raised the son of the Shunammite woman. Surely this was a significant memory for the local residents. The only thing that remains of Nain today are the tombs just outside the city, cut into the sides of the hills. The people of Nain are heading toward one such tomb this particular afternoon. This poor woman has lost both her husband and her son. She is now left without adequate financial support. The whole village must feel for her. A large crowd follows the funeral procession out of the city. It is met by another large crowd going into the city. The first, according to Galilean funeral customs, was led by the woman with her outer garment torn in grief (*Jer. Moed. K.* 83 d).[95] The second crowd, having traveled all day from Capernaum, was led by Jesus. It seems somewhat awkward and almost inappropriate to have this traffic jam interfere with the funeral.

Jewish funerals were often surrounded by elaborate rituals such as a trumpet signal to announce the death, melancholy flutes, and the plaintive tinkle of cymbals. Even the poorest Jews were expected to provide at least two flute players and one mourning woman (*Kethub.* iv.4). The body would have its hair cut and nails trimmed. It would be washed, anointed and wrapped in linen. Then it would be placed face up on a wickerwork bier with the arms folded across the chest. Friends and family would carry the body through the town, taking turns so that as many people as possible could share the honor of carrying the dead. The people of Nain would have joined the procession as it passed them "for it was deemed like mocking one's Creator not to follow the dead to his last resting-place" (Edersheim, I:556). If a person was unable to follow, they would at least stand up while the procession passed. Funerals were treated with the greatest reverence partially out of reverence for God and partially due to Jewish superstitions such as the idea that "the spirit of the dead hovered about the unburied remains" (Edersheim, I:554).

Jesus experiences the human emotions of the event and was not left untouched. He hurt for the woman (*splanchnizomai*). He says to her, literally, "Stop crying." These words, in this situation, would normally be harshly insensitive. But no doubt, Jesus' tone and demeanor assure her of better things.

Lk 7:14-17   [14]Then he went up and touched the coffin, and those carrying it stood still. He said, "Young man, I say to you, get up!" [15]The dead man sat up and began to talk and Jesus gave him back to his mother.

---

[95]The Midrash explanation was that a woman introduced death, and therefore should lead the procession (*Ber. R.* 17).

¹⁶They were all filled with awe and praised God. "A great prophet has appeared among us," they said. "God has come to help his people." ¹⁷This news about Jesus spread throughout Judea[a] and the surrounding country.

ᵃ17 Or *the land of the Jews*

Under normal circumstances, no Jew would do what Jesus just did. There was no greater defilement for the Jew than touching a dead body (Num 19:11, 16). But do the rules apply when the corpse comes back to life? Needless to say, there was no rabbinic regulation to cover such a circumstance. The pallbearers are so shocked that they just stop in their tracks.

At Jesus' command, the young man sits up and begins to talk. Morticians can tell some eerie stories about a body sitting up or moving due to gases in the corpse. But none can tell of any talking. Couldn't our imaginations run wild with what he said? "Where am I? What do you guys think you're doing?!" Or perhaps he said, "Boy that was a good nap. I have never felt better!"

The crowd's reaction is classic. It is the typical response to one of Jesus' miracles. They are filled with awe, literally, "Fear seized them all." That makes sense. Now their fear gives way to praise. They realize that Jesus is a great prophet with power rivaling even Elijah. Through him God has paid them a visit. That is, God has come to care for their needs. This declaration is thick with Messianic implications (Mt 1:23; Lk 1:68, 78; 19:44; Ps 8:4; Isa 29:6; Zeph 2:7; Acts 15:14; Heb 2:6). And the news spread throughout the Jewish territory.[96]

What does a scientific society do with this passage? Can we actually accept it as a historical event? It seems that aside from a preconceived prejudice against miracles, there is no literary, historical, or theological reason to reject the reality of this event. There is good reason, however, to accept Luke's testimony of Jesus' power to raise the dead (Edersheim, I:558-560):

1. It is not reasonable to view this story as exaggeration, nor is it possible to explain it by natural causes. Thus, we are left with two options. Either it is true or it is a designed fiction.[97]

2. Although Luke alone records the raising of the widow's son at Nain, the other three Gospels also record Jesus raising someone from the dead. So Luke is not alone in his witness to Jesus' power over death.

---

[96]The term "Judea" indicates the "country of the Jews" not merely "southern Palestine" which would not fit this context since Nain is in Galilee. But it is not unreasonable to think that the news of this event spread clear to Jerusalem in southern Palestine.

[97]The fact that Philostratus (*Life of Apollonius* 4.45), records a similar kind of resuscitation does not mean that both are fictitious. Each account must be examined individually on its own merits for truthfulness and reliability.

3. There was no Jewish expectation for the Messiah to raise people from the dead. Therefore, there is no clear motive to invent such a story.

4. While this event looks a lot like Elijah and the widow of Zarephath (1 Kgs 17:8-24, esp. vv. 10 & 23 LXX),[98] there are enough differences to conclude that the account of Jesus raising the widow's son is not based on Elijah raising the widow's son.

5. Had such a story been invented, an insignificant place like Nain would probably not have been chosen as the setting for such a notable miracle.

6. The event took place in the presence of two great crowds. In Eusebius, *Hist. Eccl.* 4:3, Quadratus claims that some of these witnesses were still alive and could testify before the Emperor.

7. Raisings were not unknown to the early church, and were, in fact, an integral part of the faith for which the Apostles were willing to die (cf. Mt 10:8; Acts 9:40; 20:9-10).

§ 57
Question of
John the
Baptist
(Mt 11:2-19;
Lk 7:18-35)

This is a dark hour for John. He has been in prison in Machaerus for some ten months now (cf. Mt 4:12; 14:1-12; Lk 3:19-20). The Scriptures tell us why. John openly rebuked the adulterous and incestuous marriage of Herod. Herodias, his wife, took offense and urged her husband to shut him up (Mt 14:3-5). Thus, he was thrown into prison. There's probably more to the story than that, however. John had a tremendous following. Herod's popularity polls were way down. That combination was fertile soil for a revolt. Thus, John was likely imprisoned to squelch any kind of uprising (cf. Josephus, *Ant.* 18.5.2). Furthermore, we have our suspicions that the Jewish leaders were involved. They didn't like John any more than they liked Jesus. Perhaps their schemes were part of the equation.

Lk 7:18-20 *with*
Mt 11:2

[18]John's disciples told him {in prison[MT]} about all these things {Christ was doing.[MT]} Calling two of them, [19]he sent them to the Lord to ask, "Are you the one who was to come, or should we expect someone else?"

[20]When the men came to Jesus, they said, "John the Baptist sent us to you to ask, 'Are you the one who was to come, or should we expect someone else?'"

John has a lot of time to reflect in his cell. Death seems imminent. "Has my life been a waste? Is Jesus really the Messiah or was it my

---

[98]T.L. Brodie, "Towards Unravelling Luke's Use of the Old Testament: Lk 7:11-17 as an *IMITATIO* of 1 Kings 17:17-24," *NTS* 32 (1986): 247-267, catalogues a number of these similarities, but also shows some significant differences.

imagination running wild?" Such thoughts must have bombarded John's mind. So he sends two of his few remaining disciples to ask Jesus.

"Are you the one who was to come?"[99] It sounds strange, coming from the mouth of John, to hear his doubt expressed. After all, John was the one who first announced Jesus. Certainly his mother, Elizabeth, had related all the stories surrounding Christ's birth. He realized that both he and Jesus were fulfilling prophecy. He even saw the divine approval in the form of a dove at Jesus' baptism (Jn 1:32-34). So why doubt now?

We must remember that John has been in prison for the better part of a year. That's plenty of time for depression and doubt to set in. To make matters worse, Jesus did not fit the contemporary expectation of the Messiah. From the reports John gets, Jesus is acting weird. Why was he hobnobbing with prostitutes and tax collectors? Why was he not fasting like the rest? Why did he attend all those parties and feasts? His ministry was so unlike what John's had been. Furthermore, why had Jesus not set John free? Did not the Scriptures predict that the Messiah would release prisoners (Isa 61:1)? What's he waiting for?

John's questions are probably not so much from doubt as from impatience. Surely he believes that Jesus is the Messiah. He just wants him to get on with the program. In the following interview, Jesus not only affirms who he is but reaffirms John in such a positive light that John's dark hour becomes a shining moment.

Lk 7:21-23

[21]At that very time Jesus cured many who had diseases, sicknesses and evil spirits, and gave sight to many who were blind. [22]So he replied to the messengers, "Go back and report to John what you have seen and heard: The blind receive sight, the lame walk, those who have leprosy[a] are cured, the deaf hear, the dead are raised, and the good news is preached to the poor [Isa 35:5-6; 61:1]. [23]Blessed is the man who does not fall away on account of me."

[a]22 The Greek word was used for various diseases affecting the skin—not necessarily leprosy.

These disciples of John arrive at an opportune time. As they question Jesus' identity, he is performing a variety of miracles. Although Matthew does not mention the fact that John's disciples witnessed these miracles, he does illustrate each of the miracles mentioned in chapters 8-9. This is one of the prophetic signs of the Messiah (Isa 29:18-19; 35:5-6; 42:7; 61:1-3). Not only can they share these events with John, but there are a lot of eyewitnesses who could verify Jesus' claims, some of them, no doubt, recipients of his healing touch.

---

[99]This verb is in the present tense; it would be better rendered "Are you the one who *is* to come," rather than the NIV past tense.

Jesus mildly rebukes John (Lk 7:23) as well as the crowd around him: "Fortunate is the one who doesn't get tripped up over me." Jesus' miracles prove that he is the Messiah. Now we ought to be willing to accept him for who he is and not try to fit him into our mold. Indeed, Jesus is hard to handle. You might say, he's offensive. He was back then; he still is today. All this talk of turning the other cheek, getting logs out of your eye, selling your possessions, hating family, carrying a cross. It smacks against the core of our culture. We prefer a more domesticated Jesus, one who's a bit more bourgeois. But that is simply not an option he gives us. We either accept him for who he is or not at all.

Lk 7:24-28 *with*
Mt 11:7-11

[24]After John's messengers left {as John's disciples were leaving[MT]}, Jesus began to speak to the crowd about John: "What did you go out into the desert to see? A reed swayed by the wind? [25]If not, what did you go out to see? A man dressed in fine clothes? No, those who wear expensive clothes and indulge in luxury are in {king's[MT]} palaces. [26]But what did you go out to see? A prophet? Yes, I tell you, and more than a prophet. [27]This is the one about whom it is written:

"'I will send my messenger ahead of you,
who will prepare your way before you.'[a] [Cf. Mk 1:2; Exod 23:20]
[28]I tell you, among those born of women there is no one greater than John {the Baptist;[MT]} yet the one who is least in the kingdom of God {heaven[MT]} is greater than he."

[a]27 Mal. 3:1

After the two messengers leave to go back to John, Jesus instructs the crowd. Directly on the heels of that mild rebuke rests this encomium. Jesus offers two obviously false alternatives to this question "Who is John?" (1) A reed shaken by the wind? John was no weakling. Not only was John physically strong, growing up in the desert, but he firmly held to definite and sturdy moral convictions. (2) A man dressed in fine clothes? Hardly! Camels' hair is about as far as you can get from fine clothes.

John the Baptist was subordinate as a prophet and as a human being only to Jesus Christ. This is a powerful and somewhat surprising statement. After all, John is in a long line of great men of faith: Abraham, Moses, Elijah, David, etc. So what made John so great?

(1) John served as the forerunner of Christ (esp. Mal 3:1). None other was given the privilege and awesome responsibility of pointing out and baptizing the Messiah, the God-Man. John at no point faltered in his task. His job was great and he executed it admirably.

(2) He broke the four hundred year gap of prophetic silence. In addition he was amazingly popular. The whole country went out to hear him and to be baptized by him. A large group of personal disciples crowded around him as a testimony to his power and popularity.

(3) John portrayed divine humility. In spite of all John's popularity, he exalted Jesus. In fact, he said he was not even worthy to untie the shoes of Jesus. Then, when John's own disciples asked what to do about the decline in their ranks due to the popularity of Jesus, John immortalized these words: "He must increase but I must decrease" (Jn 3:30).

"Among those born of women" is a Semitic idiom meaning "humanity." Aside from Jesus Christ, there is no greater person in the world. Yet, astounding as it seems, even the least in the kingdom of God, is greater than John. How could the least little Christian be greater than John (and by extension Abraham, Moses, David, etc.)? (1) We are filled with the personal presence of the Holy Spirit (Jn 7:38-39; 16:7; Acts 1:7-8). (2) We are involved with a better covenant (Heb 8:8-12; 2 Cor 3:7-18), thereby (a) the Law of God is in our minds and hearts, (b) we have a personal relationship with God, (c) we have a personal knowledge of God, and (d) our sins are forgiven. (3) We are children of promise and not of will or law (Rom 9:8; Gal 4:28).

Christians have greater privileges than John and therefore greater responsibility. But Jesus is not talking about privilege but character. The privileges listed above are not just what we are given, they are what we become. We cannot separate our new nature in Christ from our gifts in Christ. I am filled with the Holy Spirit, therefore a partaker in divinity. I am forgiven from sins, therefore sinless. I know God personally, therefore I am a friend of God. Christians are greater than John, not because of what they have done for God but because of what God has done for them.

Mt 11:12-15

¹²"From the days of John the Baptist until now, the kingdom of heaven has been forcefully advancing, and forceful men lay hold of it. ¹³For all the Prophets and the Law prophesied until John. ¹⁴And if you are willing to accept it, he is the Elijah who was to come. ¹⁵He who has ears, let him hear."

Verse 12 poses a particularly difficult problem for interpreters (cf. Lk 16:16). Some view it as a positive statement. That is, men of force, with forceful faith, take the initiative to seize the opportunity to follow Christ.[100] However, the words *biazetai* and *harpazō* indicate violence and

---

[100]*Biazetai* could only be viewed as positive if it were in the middle voice, rather than the passive. But both the Syrian Peshitta and the Old Syriac translations render it as a passive. Hence, the kingdom "is suffering violence" rather than "forcefully advancing." Furthermore, the Syrian Peshitta interpretively translates the "violent men" as "Shepherd-Rulers." This, probably reflects the theology of Ezek 34, and gives credence to the idea that the Pharisees were leading this violent assault against the newly announced kingdom. E. Moore, "Violence to the Kingdom," *ExpT* 100 (1980): 174-177.

generally carry a negative connotation. In Josephus these two words are often used together, as they are here, usually in a context of war, violence and/or oppression. In fact, the phrase "seize *her* by force" (v. 12), is the phrase used to describe rape.[101] It is clear, then, that these violent men are outsiders who do not understand the kingdom and so use force rather than persuasion.[102] Furthermore, the conjunction *de*, which the NIV leaves untranslated at v. 12, seems to indicate a contrast from what precedes it. Thus, the positive nature of the kingdom, underscored in v. 11 is contrasted in verse twelve with men's violent response to it.

This also explains the historical setting. The populace eagerly awaited the Messianic kingdom. Yet, when it came, they responded violently against it: (1) John the Baptist is imprisoned and about to be beheaded. (2) The Pharisees now oppose Jesus at every turn, contradicting his teachings with their cumbersome oral traditions. (3) The populace continually attempts to thrust Jesus into a political role as the leader of a rebellion (cf. Jn 6:15). Satan's schemes against this newly proclaimed kingdom are obvious.

Jesus proclaims John to be the fulfillment of Elijah (cf. Mal 3:1; 4:6; cf. Lk 1:17); not a physical reincarnation, which John himself denied (Jn 1:21), but the spiritual harbinger of a new age.

Lk 7:29-30

[29](All the people, even the tax collectors, when they heard Jesus' words, acknowledged that God's way was right, because they had been baptized by John. [30]But the Pharisees and experts in the law rejected God's purpose for themselves, because they had not been baptized by John.)

Jesus' description of John elicits two responses from the crowd. The people, including the tax collectors, say, "Yea, that's right!" They had experienced John firsthand because they humbled themselves to be baptized by him. The Pharisees, on the other hand, have rejected John's baptism and thus Jesus too. They were not about to admit that John was right (Mt 21:23-27). Even though some Pharisees came out to John, ostensibly to be baptized (Mt 3:7; cf. Jn 1:19-27), (and some undoubtedly were), the majority of the Pharisees came to John to question him and entrap him. If the Pharisees were murderously jealous of Jesus' popularity, it is reasonable to assume they were of John's as well.

Lk 7:31-35 *with*
Mt 11:19

[31]"To what, then, can I compare the people of this generation? What are they like? [32]They are like children sitting in the marketplace and calling out to each other:

---

[101]Here the feminine pronoun *autēn* refers to the kingdom, not a woman.

[102]E. Moore, "*BIAZO, HARPAZO* and Cognates in Josephus," *NTS* 21 (1975): 519-543.

"'We played the flute for you,
    and you did not dance;
we sang a dirge,
    and you did not cry.'
33For John the Baptist came neither eating bread nor drinking wine, and you say,
'He has a demon.' 34The Son of Man came eating and drinking, and you say,
'Here is a glutton and a drunkard, a friend of tax collectors and "sinners."' 35But
wisdom is proved right by all her children {actions.MT}"

Jesus compares his contemporaries with children pretending in the marketplace. First they tried to play "wedding," but the other children wouldn't cooperate. Then they tried to play "funeral." But again, the other children refused to play their game. This was the situation with Jesus and John vs. the Pharisees and Sadducees. The religious leaders wanted to play games that Jesus and John would not play. It infuriated them. So the leaders attacked them. They said John had a demon and Jesus was a drunkard. By categorizing them, they didn't have to deal with their person and teaching. But that is not the end of the discussion. The true analysis is found at the end of verse 35.

"Wisdom is proved right . . ." The verb "proved right" [aorist passive], could be literally translated, "Wisdom has been made righteous." It may not yet be fully apprehended, but it has been fully proved by her deeds. Both Jesus and John led blameless lives. In no way could their behavior be criticized. Thus, by their lives they demonstrated their wisdom. They were right, regardless of the criticism and characterization of their opponents.

John's doubts certainly would have plagued the crowds. If John doubted, perhaps, there is room to question Jesus' identity. Added to this, the accusations of the Pharisees, coupled with Jesus' "inappropriate" behavior and preaching, would cause many in the crowd to have doubts of their own. Jesus not only fairly answers John's questions about himself, but also reaffirms John's greatness. For those who still have doubts, Jesus does not defend himself. He simply says, wait and watch, my deeds will speak for themselves.

§ 58
Woes to
Unrepentant
Cities
(Mt 11:20-30;
cf. Lk 10:13-15)

We have here a very odd text. The cities which should have responded to Jesus' miracles don't (vv. 20-24). The people who you would expect to know God are in the dark. But those you would expect to be left out are in the know (vv. 25-26). Jesus, who is clearly God's man (v. 27) turns out to be gentle and humble (v. 29, cf. Mt 3:15; 8:17; 12:19; 21:5). He puts a yoke of labor on our necks which turns out to be liberating and light (vv. 28-30).

Mt 11:20-24

²⁰Then Jesus began to denounce the cities in which most of his miracles had been performed, because they did not repent. ²¹"Woe to you, Korazin! Woe to you, Bethsaida! If the miracles that were performed in you had been performed in Tyre and Sidon, they would have repented long ago in sackcloth and ashes. ²²But I tell you, it will be more bearable for Tyre and Sidon on the day of judgment than for you. ²³And you, Capernaum, will you be lifted up to the skies? No, you will go down to the depths.ª If the miracles that were performed in you had been performed in Sodom, it would have remained to this day. ²⁴But I tell you that it will be more bearable for Sodom on the day of judgment than for you."

ª*23 Greek Hades*[103]

Korazin and Bethsaida were suburbs of Capernaum, which was the home base for Jesus' Galilean ministry. More than any other locale, they were blessed by Jesus' presence and privileged to witness his miraculous ministry. Here Jesus had healed the nobleman's son, the paralytic, a demoniac in the synagogue, Peter's mother-in-law, the centurion's servant, Jairus' daughter, the woman with a flow of blood, two blind men, a dumb-demoniac, and scads of others. The large crowds obviously enjoyed Jesus, but they did not respond appropriately with repentance.

In contrast to these cities, Jesus highlights Tyre and Sidon, the epitome of Israel's enemies (cf. Isa 23; Ezek 26-38; Amos 1:9-10), and Sodom, the epitome of sin (Gen 19). The Jews held these places in contempt, and that is the "punch" in Jesus' statement. Had Jesus gone to these pagan places they would have gladly repented even in sackcloth and ashes, the Jewish sign of deep remorse (Esther 4:1,3; Isa 58:5; Jer 6:26; Dan 9:3; Lk 10:13). The heavy coarse material made sturdy sacks, but lousy linen. The disheveled hair and an ash-smeared face was a pathetic picture of the way one felt inside.

The point is that there will be greater judgment for those who had opportunity to accept Christ, but did not, than for those who had no opportunity at all. With greater revelation comes greater accountability (cf. Rom 2:12-16). Since Jesus worked in these cities (Mt 4:15-16), they were expected to respond. Because they did not, they were doomed.[104]

Mt 11:25-27

²⁵At that time Jesus said, "I praise you, Father, Lord of heaven and earth, because you have hidden these things from the wise and learned, and revealed them to little children. ²⁶Yes, Father, for this was your good pleasure.

²⁷"All things have been committed to me by my Father. No one knows the Son

---

[103]That is, the abode of the dead. Here it symbolizes the depths, the farthest one can get from the presence of God.

[104]McGarvey notes that within thirty years all three of these cities would be destroyed (p. 288). Whereas "Tyre and Sidon received the gospel (Acts 21:3; 27:3), Tiberias became the seat of Jewish Talmudism" (pp. 286-287).

except the Father, and no one knows the Father except the Son and those to whom the Son chooses to reveal him."

Jesus adds a second paradox to this narrative: The wise, whom you would expect to be well informed, actually were not. But the children, whom you would expect to be ignorant, received special revelation. Now, it's not that the wise guys are ignorant or stupid. They know all kinds of stuff about the world, and they may even know all about God. But they don't know him personally. That kind of knowledge comes only through revelation. And such revelation had been reserved for the little ones. Jesus, the only one who really knows the Father, chooses to introduce him to the humble, lowly, least and lost. The all-powerful Son of God (Mt 28:18; Col 1:16-19) empowers the weak of this world and overpowers the strong.[105]

Mt 11:28-30

²⁸"Come to me, all you who are weary and burdened, and I will give you rest. ²⁹Take my yoke upon you and learn from me, for I am gentle and humble in heart, and you will find rest for your souls. ³⁰For my yoke is easy and my burden is light."

What a winsome invitation! For a hurried and harried people, these are refreshing words, especially when we consider that they are surrounded by controversy and rejection of Jesus. This invitation, therefore, is like the eye of the storm — calm surrounded by turmoil. Yet this text is paradoxical. In verse 28 Jesus says, "I will give you rest." Then he turns right around and says, "Take my yoke upon you." The yoke often symbolized the Law (Gal 5:1; Acts 15:10; Sirach 51:26). The Jews did not consider the Law cruel slavery but a gift. It proved they were God's special people. Therefore, the yoke of the Law was not abject oppression but voluntarily placing oneself under the direct rule of God and working for him. But the Pharisees added so many rules to God's Law that it did become a terrible burden. Jesus frees us from all that by inviting us to be yoked with him. "The yoke of Jesus as understood by Matthew was not one of fidelity to a code but of dedication to a Person who was God's representative among men."[106]

But how can Jesus say his yoke is easy and burden light when in Matthew 10:38 he called us to take up a cross and follow him? Well, the

---

[105]This is such a bold claim of Jesus' divine relationship that some scholars assert that Jesus could not have actually said this about himself. Rather, it must have been a designation of the early church. But I.H. Marshall demonstrates that this is, in fact, what Jesus thought and claimed about himself. I.H. Marshall, "The Divine Sonship of Jesus," *Int* 21 (1967): 89-103.

[106]M. Maher, "Take My Yoke Upon You," *NTS* 22 (1975): 97-103.

word *easy* does not imply "effortless," but rather "appropriate," "suitable," or even "kindly." Jesus' work is not "a breeze," but it is "fitting." Furthermore, this does not exempt Christians from difficulties or suffering. Yet, even the cross is *light* in that it is liberating. We are freed from the bondage and decay of this world (Mt 6:33), from the penalty of the law (Gal 5:1-4), and the incessant appetite for the praise of men (Jn 5:41-44). That is, indeed, good news. Matthew illustrates how this rest works by bumping it up against two Sabbath controversies (Mt 12:1-14). The first describes Jesus picking grain on the Sabbath; in the second he heals a man's withered hand. Bacchiocchi suggests that these in turn illustrate the two dominant themes of rest in Jesus: Redemption (Mt 12:1-8) and restoration (Mt 12:9-14).[107] Because Jesus saves us and restores us, we can rest in his yoke.

§ 59
Jesus Anointed
by a Sinful
Woman
(Luke 7:36-50)

This incident is similar to another recorded in Matthew 26:6-13; Mark 14:3-9 and John 12:1-8.[108] In both instances a woman enters the banquet of a man named Simon and anoints Jesus with oil from an alabaster jar. But there are some significant differences:

1. They were in two different locations: House of the Pharisee vs. house of a leper.
2. Here in Luke, only his feet were anointed. In the parallels his feet and head were anointed.
3. The tears mentioned in Luke are absent from the other accounts.
4. Luke's account takes place in the middle of Jesus' Galilean ministry. The parallels occur the week before Christ's crucifixion.
5. Two different lessons are taught. The focus of this account is the repentance of this sinful woman. The focus of the other is the large amount of money splurged on Jesus rather than the poor.

Therefore, we conclude that this is a separate anointing from the one reported in Matthew, Mark and John.[109]

---

[107]S. Bacchiocchi, "Matthew 11:28-30: Jesus' Rest and the Sabbath," *AUSS* 22/3 (1984): 289-316.

[108]Many scholars, in fact, assume that there was actually only one anointing and the other account(s) were edited for theological reasons. Cf. R. Holst, "The One Anointing of Jesus: Another Application of the Form-Critical Method" *JBL* 95/3 (1976): 435-446; and J.K. Elliott, "The Anointing of Jesus," *ExpT* 85 (1973-74): 105-107.

[109]Agreeing with this position are A. Legault, "An Application of the Form-Critique Method to the Anointings in Galilee and Bethany," *CBQ* 16 (1954): 131-145; and a number of early church fathers going back to Origen, Tatian and Chrysostom.

Lk 7:36-38

[36]Now one of the Pharisees invited Jesus to have dinner with him, so he went to the Pharisee's house and reclined at the table. [37]When a woman who had lived a sinful life in that town learned that Jesus was eating at the Pharisee's house, she brought an alabaster jar of perfume, [38]and as she stood behind him at his feet weeping, she began to wet his feet with her tears. Then she wiped them with her hair, kissed them and poured perfume on them.

Jesus, as a famed rabbi, is invited to a banquet at Simon the Pharisee's house. So far in Luke, every time Jesus encounters a Pharisee there has been trouble (Lk 5:17-20, 30; 6:2, 6-11). Now we don't want to accuse an innocent man, but we are suspicious that this dinner invitation is a setup. After all, Simon's comrades are there in typical form (v. 49). And Simon, as we shall see, neglects the normal niceties one would expect from a friend.

The Jews ate at a table which was just inches off the ground. They laid on their left side on a pillow. Each person's head would be at the table with their feet pointing away from it. As the honored guest, Jesus would likely lay at Simon's breast.

In walks this nameless woman with a reputation all over town.[110] What was her sin? We can't know for sure, but prostitution is probably the best guess.[111] That would explain why (1) she had a reputation all over town, (2) her hair was let down rather than hidden under a veil, and (3) Simon recoiled when she touched Jesus.

How does a woman of her standing get into Simon's house in the first place? During such feasts people were often allowed to observe the festivities, sometimes talk with the guests, and even receive some of the leftovers. This woman takes advantage of the custom in order to get close to Jesus. Another possibility is that she had been to the house before on business. Again, we don't want to accuse Simon unjustly, but this wouldn't be the first, or last, time a religious leader did such a thing.

She carries with her an alabaster jar of ointment. Such a jar was commonly kept on a string or chain around a woman's neck, tucked into her clothing. This was as safe a place as any for such a costly item. It was also convenient to keep this ointment on hand which was used both as a perfume and a breath freshener. (Both were important in her line of work.) Alabaster is a translucent stone which was reamed out to make a jar for such precious ointments. This is a fairly substantial gift that she is bringing. A similar gift was valued at a year's wages (Jn 12:5).

---

[110]Some have suggested that she is Mary Magdalene, from whom seven demons were cast out (Mk 16:9), since Mary is introduced in the very next pericope (Lk 8:2). But we simply can't prove that.

[111]T. Cavalcanti, "Jesus, the Penitent Woman and the Pharisee," *JHLT* 2/1 (1994): 28-40.

This gift is even more valuable considering her occupation. You see, there are no old prostitutes. As she nears retirement age, her savings are more critical. What's more, there was no social security system in Palestine. She can't rely on the state to support her, and in her occupation, she will have a difficult time attracting a husband. Contrary to popular opinion, prostitutes are not paid well. This was even more true back then.

This is a passionate scene. She comes to Jesus with the obvious intent of anointing him with the ointment. She winds up paying respect in four different ways:

1. Her tears wash his feet. The verb "wet" is translated in other places, "rain." Tears streamed down her face and fell profusely upon his feet. Enough tears, in fact, to wash them.

2. Wiped his feet with her hair. All vanity is gone (cf. 1 Cor 11:15). With the most humble act she ministers to the Lord.

3. Kissed his feet. This is a strengthened form of the verb "kiss." In other words, she kissed his feet profusely.

4. Anointed his feet with ointment. Ointment was more expensive than oil. It has a heavy, rich smell like perfume. The word used here for "anoint" is not the normal religious act ("to pour") but what we might translate as "rub" or "massage."

Lk 7:39-43

[39]When the Pharisee who had invited him saw this, he said to himself, "If this man were a prophet, he would know who is touching him and what kind of woman she is — that she is a sinner."

[40]Jesus answered him, "Simon, I have something to tell you."

"Tell me, teacher," he said.

[41]"Two men owed money to a certain moneylender. One owed him five hundred denarii,[a] and the other fifty. [42]Neither of them had the money to pay him back, so he canceled the debts of both. Now which of them will love him more?"

[43]Simon replied, "I suppose the one who had the bigger debt canceled."

"You have judged correctly," Jesus said.

[a]41 A denarius was a coin worth about a day's wages.

Simon's thoughts can be summarized in the following logical syllogism:

A: If Jesus were a prophet he would know what kind of woman she is.[112]

B: If Jesus knew what kind of woman she was he would not let her touch him.[113]

---

[112]A common characteristic of a prophet was to discern the thoughts and lifestyle of people (cf. Isa 11:2-4; 1 Kgs 14:6; 2 Kgs 1:1-3; 5:26).

[113]Jews would not even speak with respectable women in public, let alone allow a sinful woman to touch them. Likely she should have been considered unclean due to her occupational activities.

C: Jesus is letting her touch him.
THEREFORE: Jesus must not be a prophet.

The problem with this syllogism is in minor premise "B." Based on his own cultural presuppositions, the Pharisee assumes that the Messiah would not let a prostitute touch him. That is where he is mistaken.

Jesus is about to prove to Simon that he not only knows exactly who this woman is, he knows exactly what Simon is thinking. He says, "Simon, I have something to tell you." Unaware that Jesus has perceived his thoughts, in a very respectful way he says, "Tell me, teacher." What hypocrisy! What is running through his mind and running out his mouth are two different things.

Jesus responds with a simple parable about a moneylender. He's somewhere between a respectable banker and crooked loan shark. In other words, he's not going to be too generous. But let's pretend that this one just happened to release these two from their debt. It might be literally translated, "He made a gift of their debt."

A denarius represented a full day's wage for the average workman. Thus, one fellow owed about a month and a half's salary, the other guy owed ten times as much, nearly two years' salary.

So who would love the moneylender more? Simon's "I suppose" seems to have an air of supercilious indifference. He likely suspects he's about to get nailed, but can't figure out just how.

Lk 7:44-47

⁴⁴Then he turned toward the woman and said to Simon, "Do you see this woman? I came into your house. You did not give me any water for my feet, but she wet my feet with her tears and wiped them with her hair. ⁴⁵You did not give me a kiss, but this woman, from the time I entered, has not stopped kissing my feet. ⁴⁶You did not put oil on my head, but she has poured perfume on my feet. ⁴⁷Therefore, I tell you, her many sins have been forgiven — for she loved much. But he who has been forgiven little loves little."

This is a tender scene. Jesus looks at the woman but speaks to Simon. He compares the way the two have treated him:

1. Washing the feet — This was an important part of hospitality. After walking along dusty roads in sandals, a person's feet would be dirty. It was courteous to have your servant wash a guest's feet. It would save your guest the embarrassment of dirtying your carpets. Simon did not take the extra effort to get that done. This woman, however, not only washes his feet but does it with her own tears and hair.
2. Greetings of a kiss — There is nothing romantic implied in either of the kisses. Males normally greeted one another with a kiss on the cheek. Simon did not show Jesus that affection. This woman not only kissed him, but in abject humility, kissed his feet. Furthermore, she's still down at his feet fervently kissing them [*kataphileō*].

3. Anointing — This was a special sign of honor. It was often done with olive oil. That was the normal household oil. Simon does not so honor Jesus. This woman, however, not only anoints him, but does so with ointment, which was much more valuable than oil. And instead of honoring Jesus' head, she honors even his feet. That was seen as an extreme luxury (Pliny, *H.N.* 13:4).

Verse 47 continues this comparison between Simon and the prostitute. She has much to be forgiven, therefore she loves much. Simon has little to be forgiven, therefore he loves little. But the fact is that Simon is as unable to pay his debt as is this prostitute. Jesus stoops no lower in allowing this woman to touch him than when he enters Simon's house to eat with him. The bottom line is, we all need Jesus.

Lk 7:48-50

⁴⁸Then Jesus said to her, "Your sins are forgiven."

⁴⁹The other guests began to say among themselves, "Who is this who even forgives sins?"

⁵⁰Jesus said to the woman, "Your faith has saved you; go in peace."

For the second time at this meal Jesus is the subject of debate. This same debate arose many months ago in Capernaum when four men lowered their paralytic friend on a pallet. Jesus forgave his sins and then proved his power to do so by healing him (Lk 5:17-26). This time he offers no evidence, no proof. In fact, he apparently ignores the rumblings going on about the room. Instead he concentrates on this vulnerable woman.

"Your faith has saved you." This short verse is packed with meaning. First, her faith did not actually save her. Jesus did, for only he can save. But he saves those who respond to him in faith. Furthermore, her faith is not seen by a confession but by her actions of lavish worship. Indeed, our faith can only be measured by our actions.

Jesus proclaims, "You have been saved" [Gk perfect tense], so she can now "go in peace." She may not look any different, but she is because she has already been saved. She still has a lot to work out. She will still have to overcome temptation, social stigma, and poverty without this occupation. Her peace comes from within now. She is truly at peace for Jesus has forgiven her sins.

**§ 60
Support of
Jesus' Tour by
Women**
(Lk 8:1-3)

¹After this, Jesus traveled about from one town and village to another, proclaiming the good news of the kingdom of God. The Twelve were with him, ²and also some women who had been cured of evil spirits and diseases; Mary (called Magdalene) from whom seven demons had come out; ³Joanna the wife of Cuza, the manager of Herod's household; Susanna; and many others. These women were helping to support them out of their own means.

This is an interesting little section. It opens the door to Jesus' second Galilean tour, and it opens a window on Jesus' ministry. The twelve "with Jesus" (v. 1) likely begin to participate in preaching alongside the Master. They are not the only ones to accompany him. Surprisingly, there are a number of prominent women who support Jesus' ministry financially. Against social custom they continue to travel with Jesus' disciples until the very end (Lk 23:55).[114] Luke again shows consistent interest in women as did Jesus.

Mary Magdalene was often associated with Jesus. He released her from seven demons and she was one of the first witnesses to his resurrection (Mk 16:9).

Joanna was the wife of Cuza, the curator or manager of Herod's household. It was his duty to see that the funds and resources were distributed properly. This was a position of no small influence. We do not know that Cuza shared his wife's affections for Christ. If he didn't, he certainly could have stopped her. Her financial contributions were probably quite significant. Obviously Jesus' influence extended beyond the "working class."

The financial contributions of these and other women were a significant support for Jesus and the Apostles. Peter, Andrew, James, and John also likely received a stipend from their fishing business in Capernaum. These funds, placed in the care of Judas Iscariot, would go for food, taxes, supplies, clothes and even lodging if necessary.

§ 61
Blasphemy of
the Holy Spirit
(Mt 12:22-37;
Mk 3:20-30;
cf. Lk 11:14-23)

[MK 3:]20Then Jesus entered a house, and again a crowd gathered, so that he and his disciples were not even able to eat. 21When his family heard about this, they went to take charge of him, for they said, "He is out of his mind."

[MT 12:]22Then they brought him a demon-possessed man who was blind and mute, and Jesus healed him, so that he could both talk and see. 23All the people were astonished and said, "Could this be the Son of David?"

Jesus' ministry is at a critical and frenzied stage. He's trying to get the Twelve to see who he really is. At the same time he's mobbed by

---

[114]Witherington points out that while these women may have served the Apostolic band in traditional roles, the very fact that women followed a rabbi as disciples would have been scandalous in that day. (B. Witherington III, "On the Road with Mary Magdalene, Joanna, Susanna, and Other Disciples — Luke 8:1-3." *ZNW* 70 [1979]: 243-248.) Sim goes even further. He says (1) These women (mostly single, widows and a few former prostitutes) were full-fledged disciples, not mere maids. (2) Since rich disciples were made to give up other money, these women did more than make voluntary contributions. But Jesus' band was a communistic experiment like we read of in Acts. (David C. Sim, "The Women Followers of Jesus: The Implications of Luke 8:1-3." *HeyJ* 30 [1989]: 51-62.)

crowds who want to touch him for healing. He's also being interrogated by the Pharisees from Jerusalem who want to do him in. His family[115] gets wind of all this and so here they come too. They want to nab him,[116] ostensibly for his own health or safety, and whisk him away from all the commotion. He is so popular that he can't even eat!

At this time his brothers do not believe in him and are perhaps motivated by jealousy (Jn 7:1-5). One can almost hear them say, "Alright, this little charade has gone on long enough! All this activity and popularity has made him crazy. Let's take him back home and knock some sense into him." In fact, Mark lays out his narrative like a sandwich with Jesus' family on each side of this Pharisaic accusation that Jesus is empowered by Beelzebub. This narrative structure seems to suggest that Jesus' family is on a par with the Pharisees.

Jesus' deeds are defense enough for both his identity and his sanity (cf. Jn 5:36). The fact that he can cast out this demon and restore this man's sight and speech should silence all accusations against Jesus. The crowds certainly pay attention. Their question, "Could this be the Son of David?" although framed so as to expect a negative answer, clearly identifies Jesus as the Messiah.[117] This sets the stage for a showdown between the Pharisees and Jesus. They simply can't afford to let this belief in Jesus spread nor can they simply sweep him under a carpet and pretend that he doesn't exist.

Mt 12:24-28 *with*
Mk 3:22-23,
Lk 11:20

[24]But when the Pharisees {teachers of the law who came down from Jerusalem[MK]} heard this, they said, "It is only by Beelzebub,[a] the prince of demons, that this fellow drives out demons."

[25]Jesus knew their thoughts {and spoke to them in parables[MK]} and said to them, "Every kingdom divided against itself will be ruined, and every city or household divided against itself will not stand. [26]If Satan drives out Satan, he is divided against himself. How then can his kingdom stand? [27]And if I drive out demons by Beelzebub, by whom do your people[118] drive them out? So then, they

---

[115]Lit. "Those from him." It may be rendered as "family" (NIV), "relatives" (Modern), "friends" (KJV), or "own people" (NASB). It at least indicates those who were closer to Jesus than the demanding multitudes.

[116]This verb, "to take charge of" often means "to arrest" (Mk 6:17; 12:12; 14:1; etc.). Here it certainly indicates physically and perhaps forcefully grabbing hold of Jesus and taking him away.

[117]The title "Son of David" is used to identify Jesus seven times in Matthew. With the exception of the genealogy (1:1) and the triumphal entry (21:9), they are all in the context of healing (9:27; 12:23; 15:22; 20:30-31; 21:15). Thus, the people expected the Messiah, the "Son of David," to be able to heal them. D.C. Duling, "The Therapeutic Son of David: An Element in Matthew's Christological Apologetic," *NTS* 24 (1978): 392-410.

[118]Lit. "your sons" meaning those who share your character.

will be your judges. [28]But If I drive out demons by the Spirit {finger[LK]} of God, then the kingdom of God has come upon you."

[a]24 Greek *Beezeboul* or *Beelzeboul*; also in verse 27

Beelzebul was a Canaanite god whose name means *lord of the house/ temple*. He may have represented the lord of demons (cf. Mt 10:26; 12:25, 26; Mk 3:22, 27). But the Jews mocked him by changing his name ever so slightly. If you exchange the final "l" with a "b" his name becomes Beelzebub, *the lord of flies* (cf. 2 Kings 1:2-16).

The accusation against Jesus is clear. They say Jesus casts out demons, not by the power of God, but by the power of Satan. Jesus offers two logical proofs against their accusation. First, Satan would only destroy his own work if he allowed his demons to be cast out. It's not that Satan *couldn't* cast out demons, but that he *wouldn't*. Their suggestion that Jesus works for Satan is absurd.

Second, if Jesus is empowered by Satan, then who empowers the other Jewish exorcists?[119] This same accusation then applies to them. Since the Pharisees share the same character as their "sons," the Jewish exorcists, they condemn themselves as being empowered by Satan.

But what if they are wrong? What if Jesus actually does cast out demons by the Spirit of God? Then these fellows are in a heap of trouble because they are fighting against the oncoming kingdom and power of God.

Mt 12:29-32 *with*
Lk 11:21-22,
Mk 3:29-30

[29]"Or again, how can anyone enter a strong man's house and carry off his possessions unless he first ties up the strong man? Then he can rob his house. {When a strong man, fully armed, guards his own house, his possessions are safe. But when someone stronger attacks and overpowers him, he takes away the armor in which the man trusted and divides up the spoils.[LK]}

[30]"He who is not with me is against me, and he who does not gather with me scatters. [31]And so I tell you, every sin and blasphemy will be forgiven men, but the blasphemy against the Spirit will not be forgiven {he is guilty of an eternal sin.[MK]} [32]Anyone who speaks a word against the Son of Man will be forgiven, but anyone who speaks against the Holy Spirit will not be forgiven, either in this age or in the age to come." {He said this because they were saying, "He has an evil spirit."[MK]}

---

[119]R. Shirock, "Whose Exorcists Are They? The Referents of Hoi Huioi Humōn at MT 12:27 & LK 11:19," *JSNT* 46 (1992): 41-51, suggests that Jesus refers not to the Jewish exorcists but to his own disciples. (1) Jewish exorcists are nowhere supported in the NT (2) The function of judgment will later be given to the Twelve (Mt 19:28; Lk 22:30). And (3) the Apostles have just returned from a preaching/healing tour where they cast out demons. Thus, Jesus would be understood to say, "These disciples of mine are your own kinsmen and are doing the same thing. Will you accuse all of us of being in league with Satan?" Chrysostom and a number of early church fathers agreed with this interpretation.

Jesus has just explained that he is not empowered by Satan. Therefore, he has overpowered Satan by plundering his possessions. Satan is the strong man (v. 29), and Jesus is the one who has bound him (cf. Jude 6; Rev 20:2). Furthermore, those who are not plundering Satan with Jesus are against him. Now, if you have a strong man who is bound and a stronger man who tied him up, whose side do you want to be on? Jesus is drawing a line in the sand and saying, "Get on his side or mine!" Although his words are directed to the Pharisees and scribes, his entire audience now has to make a choice. They have to get on one side of the fence or the other.

During Jesus' earthly ministry he plundered Satan's domain. He bound him (Mt 12:29; cf. Rev. 20:2), disarmed him (Col 2:15), destroyed his works (1 Jn 3:8), freed his captives (Heb 2:14-15), and judged him (Jn 12:31; 16:11). Satan took a tumble (Lk 10:18). His only effective weapon now is deception (Mt 24:24; Rev 20:8). If you don't fall for it, all he can do is run (James 4:7).

These Pharisees who aligned against Jesus, by default, aligned with the Devil and were dangerously close to blasphemy against the Holy Spirit. Blasphemy is essentially reviling or criticizing another. Jesus casts out the demon by the power of the Spirit. But the Pharisees attribute it to the power of Beelzebub (Satan). Thus, they call the Holy Spirit the unholy spirit. Such an insult to the Holy Spirit is not a forgivable sin (cf. Isa 5:20).

Why could criticism against Jesus be forgiven, but not criticism against the Holy Spirit? God incarnate (in the person of Jesus) was such a radical concept that some misunderstanding or skepticism is predictable. Until sufficient evidence had been given to validate Jesus' claims, it is understandable that some would doubt. However, there is no reason to be critical of the Holy Spirit, especially his role in casting out demons. Such cynicism and unbelief is motivated by a blatant refusal to accept God's evidence. Without such evidence there can be no valid faith. Without faith there is no forgiveness of sins.

Thus, it is not the actual blasphemy that is unforgivable, but the impenetrable attitude of willful unbelief. This also appears to be the explanation of the sin that leads to death (1 Jn 5:16) as well as the point at which a person can no longer repent (Heb 6:4-6). Some worry that they have committed blasphemy against the Holy Spirit. But the fact that they are concerned seems to exclude the possibility of their having done it. Willful, high-handed rejection of God's purpose is the problem (cf. Num 15:30-31), not a particular word or deed.

There are a number of sins against the Holy Spirit: Rebellion (Isa

63:10), lying (Acts 5:3-9), resisting (Acts 7:51), using for selfish gain (Acts 8:18-22), grieving (Eph 4:30), quenching (1 Thess 5:19), disobedience (Heb 10:29). Blasphemy is the only unforgivable sin (Mt 12:31-32; Mk 3:29; Lk 12:10).

Mt 12:33-37

³³"Make a tree good and its fruit will be good, or make a tree bad and its fruit will be bad, for a tree is recognized by its fruit. ³⁴You brood of vipers, how can you who are evil say anything good? For out of the overflow of the heart the mouth speaks. ³⁵The good man brings good things out of the good stored up in him, and the evil man brings evil things out of the evil stored up in him. ³⁶But I tell you that men will have to give account on the day of judgment for every careless word they have spoken. ³⁷For by your words you will be acquitted, and by your words you will be condemned."

Our words are powerful things! As fruit displays the inner goodness of a tree, so our words display the goodness of our hearts. In fact, our words are such an accurate barometer of our thoughts, and such an accurate predictor of our actions, that we will be judged by them.

§ 62
Pharisees
Rebuked for
Seeking a Sign
(Mt 12:38-45;
cf. Lk 11:24-36)

Jesus has just claimed to cast out demons by the power of God. It is only natural that the Pharisees ask for some verification of such a bold claim. This is not a new discussion. Once already we have seen the Pharisees in Jerusalem ask for a sign (Jn 2:18-23). These two events are paralleled in several ways: (1) The unbelieving demand for a sign immediately followed a great "miracle" of Jesus (Jn 2:12-17, Jesus clears the temple; here Jesus has just healed a deaf/blind demoniac). (2) In both instances Jesus refused to perform for them but pointed to his resurrection as the ultimate evidence. (3) Jesus continues to perform miracles which served as adequate evidence for those inclined toward faith. (See Mt 16:1-4 for a similar, but shorter, incident).

Mt 12:38-42 *with*
Lk 11:16,29

³⁸Then some of the Pharisees and teachers of the law said to him, "Teacher, we want to see a miraculous sign from you {from heaven.ᴸᴷ}."
{As the crowds increasedᴸᴷ} ³⁹He answered, "A wicked and adulterous generation asks for a miraculous sign! But none will be given it except the sign of the prophet Jonah. ⁴⁰For as Jonah was three days and three nights in the belly of a huge fish, so the Son of Man will be three days and three nights in the heart of the earth. ⁴¹The men of Nineveh will stand up at the judgment with this generation and condemn it; for they repented at the preaching of Jonah, and now one greater than Jonah is here. ⁴²The Queen of the South will rise at the judgment with this generation and condemn it; for she came from the ends of the earth to listen to Solomon's wisdom, and now one greater than Solomon is here."

The crowds increase because of this hot debate, which started clear back in Matthew 12:24 (and Lk 11:14). People are crowding in to see what all the fuss was about. Voices are raising and Jesus is getting rather deliberate and direct — "Wicked and adulterous generation!" He uses the OT comparison of idolatry to adultery. The Pharisees, like their forefathers, are rejecting God's spokesman, yea, even God incarnate, to protect their own positions of power and prestige.

What was so wicked about seeking a sign? Does not God validate his messengers with signs? Yes. But Jesus has already demonstrated his claims to deity with signs. Not only had he cast out a demon from the dumb man moments before, but he has performed a slew of miracles both in Galilee and Judea: Turning water to wine, reading minds, healing all kinds of sickness, casting out demons, cleansing leprosy, paralysis, blindness, and even raising the boy at Nain. To seek a sign now, is to disbelieve what Jesus has done before. They are seeking, but not wanting to find. Unbelief like that may look noble, but is insidiously hard.

They ask for a sign from heaven, that is, from God himself (Lk 11:16; cf. Exod 19:22-24; 16:4; Josh 10:12; 1 Sam 7:9-10; 12:16-18; 1 Kgs 18:36-38; 2 Kgs 1:10; Isa 38:8). Signs were required under four circumstances: (1) to verify a prophetic utterance, (2) to justify an unusual action (cf. Jn 2:18), (3) to back up an utterance of doctrinal import (e.g., forgiveness of sins, Mk 2:6) and (4) to support a Messianic claim.[120] The sign had to correspond to the claim or action at the time. It was not about power but appropriate verification. They were not so much rejecting Jesus' previous miracles as saying "Those don't apply to your present claims." Nevertheless, they are not looking for evidence to believe in Jesus. They are looking for an excuse to criticize him and thus dissuade the crowds from following him. This is clear enough from the previous section.

The sign of Jonah is an obvious reference to the resurrection.[121] Jonah, with minimal and reluctant preaching, led the entire pagan city of Nineveh to repentance. Jesus, with many miracles, incredible sermons, and a pure life, could not lead this chosen race to repentance. The Ninevites thus displayed hearts of faith while the Jews display unbelief.

---

[120]O. Linten, "The Demand for a Sign from Heaven, *ST* 19 (1965): 12-29.

[121]E.H. Merrill asserts that Jonah's regurgitation would be particularly important to the Ninevites whose probable capital was supposedly founded by a fish god who was subsequently worshiped there. ("The Sign of Jonah," *JETS* 23/1 [Mar 1980]: 23-30.) J. Swetham, however, asserts that the sign of Jonah was his prediction of Nineveh's destruction and therefore prophetic of Jerusalem's demise. Since a wicked city repented through reluctant preaching, Jerusalem will certainly be judged for not repenting with Jesus' preaching. The resurrection talk is merely the point of comparison that justifies further comparison of the prophecy against each city (*Biblica* 68 [1987]: 74-79).

Matthew 12:40 extends the sign of Jonah to the three days and nights he spent in the belly of the fish. Likewise, Jesus' greatest sign will be the resurrection when he comes out of the belly of the earth after three days and nights.[122] But even that will not be enough to shatter such hardened unbelief (Lk 16:31).

The Queen of Sheba (1 Kgs 10:1ff) was yet another testimony against the unbelief of the Jews. Here was a pagan impressed with human wisdom. Yet God's chosen people are not even impressed with divine wisdom demonstrated in Jesus and validated through his miracles.

Both illustrations show the classic Jewish argument of lesser to greater. Jesus' spiritual wisdom is greater than Solomon's worldly wisdom. And yet the Queen of Sheba traveled far to hear Solomon. This generation rejects Jesus even though he comes to their front door. Likewise, Jonah did no miracles, but merely preached reluctantly for forty days. Jesus and his Apostles validated their forty years of preaching with great signs but were still rejected up until the destruction of Jerusalem. These pagans, therefore, rise in judgment as a reminder of the severe unbelief of the Jews. The bottom line is that the Jewish nation is going from bad to worse because of their greater rejection even with greater opportunity (cf. Mt 10:15; 11:21-24).

Mt 12:43-45

> [43]"When an evil spirit comes out of a man, it goes through arid places seeking rest and does not find it. [44]Then it says, 'I will return to the house I left.' When it arrives, it finds the house unoccupied, swept clean and put in order. [45]Then it goes and takes with it seven other spirits more wicked than itself, and they go in and live there. And the final condition of that man is worse than the first. That is how it will be with this wicked generation."

Popular Jewish wisdom at the time said that demons inhabited deserts (as well as toilets, marshes, empty houses, and the shade of certain trees). The Jews had an elaborate, superstitious system about demons. For example, they believed that although demons were invisible, if one put ashes on the floor, in the morning the footprints of the demons could be seen in the form of chicken tracks.

Jesus returns to the topic of the demoniac and uses the incident to illustrate the increasing evil of the Jewish nation. This ex-demoniac needed to fill the void in his life or else even more demons might return to enjoy the newly refurbished abode. So also, the entire Jewish nation needed to fill its spiritual void with Christ. Cleansing by moral "rightness" is not sufficient. It may only entice the demons to hide under its ostensible pharisaic purity.

---

[122]There is no need to seek three 24-hour periods. Even Jesus' language indicates this is a general time: "On the third day," "after three days," and "three days and three nights."

Mary Magdalene literally had seven demons cast from her (Lk 8:2). The Gerasene demoniac had a legion of demons in him. But the number seven here probably just represents complete wickedness. This is an analogy which should not be pressed too far.

§ 63
Jesus' True
Family
(Mt 12:46-50;
Mk 3:31-35;
Lk 8:19-21)

Mark introduced the family of Jesus earlier (Mk 3:20-21). In between this family talk, he sandwiched[123] the accusation that Jesus drove out demons by Beelzebub. We understand then that Jesus was opposed on two fronts. Both his family and the religious hierarchy misunderstood him and accused him of being out of his mind.

Mt 12:46-48 *with*
Lk 8:19, Mk 3:31

[46]While Jesus was still talking to the crowd, his mother and brothers stood outside, wanting to speak to him. {But they were not able to get near him because of the crowd[LK]} {[T]hey sent someone in to call him.[MK]} [47]Someone told him, "Your mother and brothers are standing outside, wanting to speak to you."[a]
[48]He replied to him, "Who is my mother, and who are my brothers?"

Mk 3:34a

[34]Then he looked at those seated in a circle around him . . . .

Mt 12:49

[49]Pointing to his disciples, he said, "Here are my mother and my brothers.

Lk 8:21

[21]My mother and brothers are those who hear God's word and put it into practice."

[a][Mt 12:]47 Some manuscripts do not have verse 47.

Jesus has four half-brothers: James, Joses, Judas and Simon (Mt 13:55). He also has sisters. They are concerned about Jesus. They have already appeared at the beginning of this narrative. They felt like he had pushed himself a bit too far and gone crazy because he would not take the time to rest and eat (Mk 3:20-21). Jesus' brothers, who do not believe in him yet (Jn 7:1-4; cf. 1 Cor 15:7), show up here possibly to ask Jesus to slow down and to beware of the building opposition of the Pharisees. We notice a conspicuous absence of Jesus' father. Likely, Joseph was dead by now. Even so, God alone was Jesus' father (cf. Mt 23:9). The rest of his family consisted of those faithful to God's word.

Jesus is not disregarding his own family. Jews had deep respect for their parents. Rather, he is exalting those who hear and obey the word of God. "The old adage that 'blood is thicker than water' (originally intended to advocate that family ties are stronger than the ties of baptism into the spiritual family of God) is wrong!" (Butler, p. 140).

---

[123]This is a common device Mark uses to arrange his narrative to make a particular point (cf. Mk 4:1-20; 5:21-43; 6:7-29; 11:12-25; 14:1-11; 14:53-72).

§ 64a
The Setting of
the Sermon in
Parables
(Mt 13:1-3a;
Mk 4:1-2;
Lk 8:4)

[1]That same day Jesus went out of the house and sat by the lake. [2]Such large crowds gathered around him that he got into a boat and sat in it, while all the people {from town after town[LK]} stood on the shore. [3]Then he told them many things in parables, saying:

This has been a busy day for Jesus:[124] The healing of the blind, dumb demoniac and the subsequent discussion on the blasphemy of the Holy Spirit (§ 61); the rejected request by the Pharisees that Jesus show them a sign from heaven (§ 62); Jesus' rejection of his biological mother and brothers who sought to whisk him away (§ 63); and a slew of parables spoken on the shores of Galilee (§ 64). That evening he calmed the storm (§ 65) and in the middle of the night, healed the Gerasene demoniac (§ 66).

This seashore is a familiar haunt for Jesus. Both the house and the boat were likely Peter's. As we have seen before, Jesus uses the boat as a pulpit and the shore as a natural amphitheater for teaching the crowds. What's different is Jesus preaching in parables. He has used them before (Mt 7:24-27; 9:16-17; 11:16-19; 12:29). But this time his whole sermon was simply a series of parables. This method will play a more dominant role in Jesus' teaching from here on out. His parables will polarize his audiences, confusing some and delighting others.

Wenham offers a helpful analysis of Matthew's arrangement of the parables in this sermon (Mt 13):[125]

A. Sower — parable on those who hear the word of the kingdom.
   B. Disciples' question and Jesus' answer about the purpose of parables and the interpretation of the first parable.
      C. Tares — parable of kingdom on good and evil.
         D. Mustard seed and leaven — pair of parallel kingdom parables.
            E. Conclusion of crowd section and interpretation of tares.
         D'. Treasure and pearl — pair of parallel kingdom parables.
      C'. Dragnet — parable of kingdom on good and evil.
   B'. Jesus' question and disciples' answer about understanding parables.
A'. Scribe — parable on those trained for the kingdom.

---

[124]The NIV is interpretive at this point. It inserts the word "same" in "that same day." We agree with the interpretation but question its place in a translation.

[125]D. Wenham, "The Structure of Matthew XIII," *NTS* 25 (1979): 517-518.

Before we begin an investigation of each individual parable we will examine Jesus' use and interpretation of parables:[126]

1. Jesus employed the "stock metaphors" of rabbinic parables. Masters, fathers, and kings represent God. Servants and children represent God's people or his assistants. A harvest stands for judgment. A feast pictures the messianic banquet.

2. Jesus' parables were quite unlike the other rabbis in that (a) the concepts he taught were radically different and (b) he used them both to reveal and to conceal.

3. The Greek word *parabolē* and the Hebrew word *mashal* are used to signify a number of figures of speech which are not differentiated as precisely as we do in English. They represent, for instance: Parable, similitude, allegory, fable, proverb, riddle, symbol, etc.

4. Jesus' parables were not merely for illustration, but often delivered the meat of the message.

5. Jesus' parables sprung at the audience from everyday life. In fact, Edersheim asserts that with each parable in this sermon, Jesus may well have pointed to the very objects used in the parable — a field, a woman baking, sprouting wheat, mustard plants, and dragnets.

6. There is often one main meaning given to each of the major characters or groups of characters in the parable.

7. This series of parables is "kingdom talk." The ideas are simple enough to the initiate. But to those disciples who do not grasp the spiritual nature of the kingdom, these thoughts are inscrutable.

Matthew and Mark inform us that this sermon is delivered off the shore of Galilee, likely near Capernaum. Jesus is in a boat a short distance from the shore. A large crowd stands on the bank. Where did all the people come from? Luke mentions that Jesus has just been on a tour. As a result, people from each of the towns and villages he visited have followed him back to Capernaum. They stand on the bank eager to hear still more of what this man has to say.

§ 64b
The Parable of the Soils
(Mt 13:3b-23;
Mk 4:3-25;
Lk 8:5-18)

This first parable apparently serves as an introduction to the entire sermon just as the parable of the house owner (Mt 13:51-52) summarizes the whole sermon.[127] It is different than the others in that it does not

---

[126]For a most helpful work on parables see C.L. Blomberg, *Interpreting the Parables* (Downers Grove: IVP, 1990).

[127]S.D. Toussaint, "The Introductory and Concluding Parables of Matthew Thirteen," *BibSac* 121 (1964): 351-355.

contain the phrase: "The kingdom of heaven is like." Thus, this parable sets the stage for hearing the other kingdom parables. Some, even in this crowd, are like the good soil and will be greatly blessed by this sermon. Others, for a variety of reasons, will not receive these parables. Consequently, they will wind up being confused by them.

Mt 13:3b-9 *with*
Lk 8:5-7

"A farmer went out to sow his seed. ⁴As he was scattering the seed, some fell along the path, {it was trampled on[LK]} and the birds came and ate it up. ⁵Some fell on rocky places, where it did not have much soil. It sprang up quickly, because the soil was shallow. ⁶But when the sun came up, the plants were scorched, and they withered because they had no root {no moisture[LK]}. ⁷Other seed fell among thorns, which grew up {with it[LK]} and choked the plants {so that they did not bear grain[MK]}. ⁸Still other seed fell on good soil, where it produced a crop — {multiplying[MK]} a hundred, sixty or thirty times what was sown. {When he said this, he called out:[LK]} ⁹He who has ears, let him hear."

In Jesus' agricultural society farmers would walk across their field with a sack of seed, grabbing handfuls and throwing them across the tilled ground. This was a very common picture in Palestine. While it may not be readily apparent to our Western minds, the sower was not particularly concerned with the kind of soil on which the seed fell. You see, we plow before we plant, thus we know what kind of soil we have. In Jesus' day, they often plowed after planting.[128] Thus, the road (hard soil) might become a fertile spot. And the rocky soil, which may not be visible now, would become apparent after the ground had been turned. Even if they plowed before planting, the farmer could afford to be generous in sowing seed because the more seed sown, the bigger the crop. He knows he's going to lose some seed on the edges of his field and near the rocky crags. But it's worth a handful of seed to ensure that every bit of good soil is covered.

There are four types of soils, each representing the condition of the human heart: First, the hard path. It is impenetrable. No seed can grow there, so the birds (Satan, cf. Mk 4:15) snatch it away. Second, there is shallow soil among the rocks. Matthew and Mark mention the plant's shallow roots; Luke mentions the lack of moisture. Anyone familiar with gardening realizes that there is no practical difference. It is the shallow soil which causes the lack of moisture. Third, the weeds grow up with the seed and choke it out. Fourth, there is good soil which produces an abundant crop. A good yield was tenfold. Jesus' hundredfold is a bit of an exaggeration, but by no means impossible. And it certainly grabs the attention of every gardener in the audience.

---

[128]P.B. Payne, "The Order of Sowing and Plowing in the Parable of the Sower," *NTS* 25 (1978): 123-129, explains the details of this agricultural peculiarity.

Concerning the third type of soil, it is incorrect to picture little seeds being thrown in the middle of a weed patch. The thorns, if any are left after the hot, dry summer, would be plowed under after the seed has been sown. The true picture is good seed competing with bad seed. Luke even uses the word *symphyō*, meaning "to grow up together." The implication is obvious. Our lives may look pure. Ostensibly we are in no danger of "bad weeds," but the seeds are there.

Essentially the soil is the same. The difference is what is added to the soil (i.e., weed seed, rocks, or a good trampling). How do these differences come about? Through hearing. Not the simple physiological performance of the ears, but the humble acceptance of the heart. The word of God must be obeyed and not just heard. In fact, in Hebrew culture, "to hear" also implied obedience. The soil is potentially good in each human heart. The difference is in the will. This is the meaning of the idiomatic phrase: "He who has ears to hear, let him hear."

Mt 13:10-12 *with*
Mk 4:10-11,
Lk 8:18

[10]The disciples came to him {when he was alone, the Twelve and others around him[MK]} and asked, "Why do you speak to the people in parables?"

[11]He replied, "The knowledge of the secrets of the kingdom of heaven has been given to you, but not to them. {To those on the outside everything is said in parables.[MK]} [12]Whoever has will be given more, and he will have an abundance. Whoever does not have, even what he {thinks he[LK]} has will be taken from him."

Jesus is teaching from a boat on the lake. The Twelve and a few close disciples are with him in the boat. When they see the bewildered looks among the crowds, they ask Jesus why he is confusing them with parables. This was not his normal style. They are able to ask him privately in the boat, even while Jesus is in front of a large crowd. Later he will leave the crowd and teach his disciples privately in the house (Mt 13:36).

This secret (mystery) of the kingdom is not something that needs to be figured out, it is something needing to be revealed. Once the mystery is revealed, it is easy enough to understand.

The principle of verse 12 applies to a number of areas. The more we listen, the more we are able to understand. The less we listen, the less we are able to understand. It is like money in the bank. The more money a person is able to save, the greater his ability to earn further. People go to a restaurant that is full, not one that is empty. We give responsibility to those who are responsible. Likewise, those who understand the nature and purpose of the kingdom will be instructed by these parables. But those who are not "in the know" will be further confused and disillusioned by these parables.

Mt 13:13-17 *with*
Mk 4:12, Lk 8:18

[13]"This is why I speak to them in parables:

"Though seeing, they do not see;
   though hearing, they do not hear or understand
   {otherwise they might turn and be forgiven.[a MK]}
[14]In them is fulfilled the prophecy of Isaiah:
   "'You will be ever hearing but never understanding;
      you will be ever seeing but never perceiving.
   [15]For this people's heart has become calloused;
      they hardly hear with their ears,
      and they have closed their eyes.
   Otherwise they might see with their eyes,
      hear with their ears,
      understand with their hearts
   and turn, and I would heal them.'"[b]

[16]But blessed are your eyes because they see, and your ears because they hear. [17]For I tell you the truth, many prophets and righteous men longed to see what you see but did not see it, and to hear what you hear but did not hear it."

[a]*[Mk 4:]12* Isaiah 6:9,10   [b]*[Mt 13:]15* Isaiah 6:9,10

The parable was the tool Jesus used to conceal the kingdom from many of his listeners. This quotation from Isaiah 6:9-10 is most accurately translated by the Greek in Mark 4:12. The Hebrew idiom might be rendered, "Seeing, they keep on seeing, but do not see; and hearing, they keep on hearing, but do not hear." Mark also adds the important sentence, "Otherwise they might turn and be forgiven." This doesn't mean that no one in Jesus' audience will ever come to Christ (Isa 6:13; Rom 11:25). It means for right now they are not able to accept the word of God through Jesus.

Thus, Jesus' parables kept some from seeing the kingdom and repenting and being saved. Why would Jesus do that? From the context in Isaiah, it becomes obvious that this is a response to unbelief. As an individual turns his back on Jesus, Jesus turns his back on the individual through parables. This is a fulfillment of the biblical principle that unbelief not only brings about judgment, it also destroys a person's ability to perceive truth (Jn 3:17-19; 9:39-41; Exod 8:32; 9:12; Rom 9:17-18; Acts 28:26-27; Mt 7:6; Lk 20:1-8; Jn 12:39-41; Rev 22:11).

Furthermore, this text from Isaiah 6:9-10 is used three times in the NT. Here the responsibility for their ignorance lies with the preacher. That is, Jesus hid the kingdom through parables. In John 12:40, the responsibility seems to be with God, who withdrew their opportunity for repentance. In Acts 28:26-27 the responsibility is laid at the feet of the audience. Underneath all of this is the word "hear" (used thirteen times in Mt 13:13-23). If the audience refuses to listen to God's spokesman then their opportunity is taken away.

Does God ever reject anyone? Yes. But not whimsically. God's rejection is based on a number of things: (1) Response to man's sin (Isa 6:8-13). (2) Mutual rejection between God and man (Jn 3:17-19). (3) Purging the remnant (Rom 11:5-8). (4) Opening for the Gentiles (Rom 11:9ff). (5) The closed heart and ears of unrepentant people.

Matthew adds these important words of verses 16-17 which underscore our privilege of seeing the kingdom (cf. Lk 10:23-24; Heb 11:39-40; 1 Pet 1:10-12). We may be enamored with the excitement of the OT narratives, or even those of the Gospel. We might think they were pretty lucky to live in those phenomenal times. But we are, by far, more privileged than they. We enjoy the kingdom of God, the canonical Scriptures, and the indwelling of the Holy Spirit. We are the recipients of the deepest longing of the prophets.

Mk 4:13

¹³Then Jesus said to them, "Don't you understand this parable? How then will you understand any parable?

Mt 13:18-23 *with*
Mk 4:14,
Lk 8:12-15

¹⁸"Listen then to what the parable of the sower means: {¹⁴The farmer sows the word.ᴹᴷ} ¹⁹When anyone hears the message about the kingdom and does not understand it, the evil one {Satanᴹᴷ} {the devilᴸᴷ} comes and snatches away what was sown in his heart {so that they may not believe and be savedᴸᴷ}. This is the seed sown along the path. ²⁰The one who received the seed that fell on rocky places is the man who hears the word and at once receives it with joy. ²¹But since he has no root, he lasts only a short time. When trouble or persecution {the time of testingᴸᴷ} comes because of the word, he quickly falls away. ²²The one who received the seed that fell among the thorns is the man who hears the word, but the worries of this life and the deceitfulness of wealth {and pleasuresᴸᴷ} {and the desires for other things come in andᴹᴷ} choke it {and they do not matureᴸᴷ}, making it unfruitful. ²³But the one who received the seed that fell on good soil is the man {with a noble and good heartᴸᴷ} who hears the word and understands it {[and] accept[s] it.ᴹᴷ} He {by perseveringᴸᴷ} produces a crop, yielding a hundred, sixty or thirty times what was sown."

We are fortunate that Jesus gave us his own interpretation of the parable. He will identify these four main types of people:

1. Path: People who have no desire for the word of God. It just can't penetrate. Satan snatches it away "So that they may not believe and be saved."
2. Rocks: People who fall through trouble or persecution. Matthew and Mark use the word "immediately" to describe both how this individual receives the word and how he falls away. These are flash-in-the-pan people. This individual is quickly willing to receive the word. But he is just as quick to drop it when it becomes a disadvantage to him.
3. Weeds: Choked out — Again, we remind our readers that the good seeds are in competition with the weed seeds. As they grow up

together, the weeds win out. Jesus describes three areas which are so dangerous to the Christian: life's worries, life's riches and life's pleasures.

4. Good Soil: These are people who receive the word through hearing and obedience. And they produce a bumper crop!

Jesus gives us three requirements for fruit-bearing: (1) A pure and good heart. It is this prerequisite which allows the individual to listen to the word and not just hear it. (2) We must hold on to the Word for dear life. That is exactly what it is! (3) Perseverance. No one is truly saved who does not persevere (Mt 24:13: Rev 2:10). It's kind of like riding a bull in a rodeo. First you accept the challenge. Then you get a real good grip. And for better or for worse, you hang on 'til ya hear the bell.

The Parable of The Lamp
(Mk 4:21-25;
Lk 8:16-18;
cf. Mt 5:14-16)

{He said to them,[MK]} [16]"No one lights a lamp and hides it in a jar or puts it under a bed. Instead, he puts it on a stand, so that those who come in can see the light. [17]For there is nothing hidden that will not be disclosed, and nothing concealed that will not be known or brought out into the open. {If anyone has ears to hear, let him hear.[MK]} [18]Therefore consider carefully how you listen. {With the measure you use, it will be measured to you — and even more[MK]} Whoever has will be given more; whoever does not have, even what he thinks he has will be taken from him."

[Lk 8:16 = Mt 5:14-16, see comments on § 54c]

"Consider carefully how you listen" (lit. "watch how you listen" or "keep your eyes on your ears"). This is the crux of this passage. We get our light (or "produce" as in the previous parable) from listening to the word of Jesus, not just with our ears, but with our hearts. Jesus' words shed light on our understanding of the kingdom.

§ 64c
The Parable of the Seed's Spontaneous Growth
(Mk 4:26-29)

[26]He also said, "This is what the kingdom of God is like. A man scatters seed on the ground. [27]Night and day, whether he sleeps or gets up, the seed sprouts and grows, though he does not know how. [28]All by itself the soil produces grain — first the stalk, then the head, then the full kernel in the head. [29]As soon as the grain is ripe, he puts the sickle to it, because the harvest has come."

This parable, found only in Mark, naturally follows the parable of the soils. On the one hand, the soil (man) is responsible for receiving the seed (word of God). But on the other hand, God is responsible for its mysterious growth. Man must provide a climate in which God's word can flourish. But in no way can we claim responsibility for its growth. In other words, we cultivate but God germinates. These parallel parables balance the sovereignty of God and the responsibility of man.

Furthermore, this growth is mysterious. The kingdom of God is like the vegetable kingdom. It begins with a very small seed and grows perpetually (night and day), sometimes imperceptibly, culminating in a productive harvest.

**§ 64d
The Parable of
the Weeds**
(Mt 13:24-30)

²⁴Jesus told them another parable: "The kingdom of heaven is like a man who sowed good seed in his field. ²⁵But while everyone was sleeping, his enemy came and sowed weeds among the wheat, and went away. ²⁶When the wheat sprouted and formed heads, then the weeds also appeared.

²⁷"The owner's servants came to him and said, 'Sir, didn't you sow good seed in your field? Where then did the weeds come from?'

²⁸"'An enemy did this,' he replied.

"The servants asked him, 'Do you want us to go and pull them up?'

²⁹"'No,' he answered, 'because while you are pulling the weeds, you may root up the wheat with them. ³⁰Let both grow together until the harvest. At that time I will tell the harvesters: First collect the weeds and tie them in bundles to be burned; then gather the wheat and bring it into my barn.'"

Such vicious agricultural sabotage was rare but not unrealistic. If someone did want to be so vindictive, they could have used a weed seed called darnel (Gk = *zizania*). It looked so much like wheat that you could never tell the difference until the plant was full grown and starting to "head" out. At that point it was too late to weed them out because the roots would already have intertwined. Thus, by pulling out the weeds you would also root out the wheat.

The only solution, then, was to wait until the harvest. Both plants would be cut down and then could be separated. The weeds would be bundled up and burned. The wheat would be harvested and stored in barns. Likewise, the good and evil of this world are allowed to coexist. By destroying the wicked, many good people would get caught in the crossfire.

There will come a day, however, when all the evil is rooted out. Only the good will remain. The kingdom of God will be fully manifest. But for now, we must live with this uncomfortable mix of God's kingdom in a fallen world.

Some have used this verse in relation to church discipline. That is, we should not attempt to ferret wicked people out of the church. But the field full of weeds in this parable is not the church, but the world. The New Testament is clear that the church does, in fact, have an obligation to discipline its erring members.

§ 64e
The Parable of the Mustard Tree
(Mt 13:31-32;
Mk 4:30-32;
cf. Lk 13:18-19)

[30]Again he said, "What shall we say the kingdom of God {heaven[MT]} is like, or what parable shall we use to describe it? [31]It is like a mustard seed, which is the smallest seed you plant in the ground. [32]Yet when planted, it grows and becomes the largest of all garden plants, with such big branches that the birds of the air can perch in its shade {branches[MT,LK]}."

Mark places this parable right next to the parable of the seed's spontaneous growth (§ 64c). Indeed, these two are related to one another. Not only does the seed grow spontaneously (by God's influence), but it grows tremendously large in comparison with its small beginning. Likewise, the kingdom of God, which may now look insignificant, will grow and expand. From its humble beginnings of Jesus and the Twelve, this kingdom has made an impressive impact on the globe.

The mustard seed is not actually the smallest seed in the world (that would be the black orchid).[129] But it was proverbially famous for how little it was and how tall it grew. Some mustard plants, in fact, reached ten to twelve feet. That's big enough for little birds to perch on, hence it is like a tree.[130]

Some have allegorized the birds and the shade as foreign nations resting in the kingdom of God (cf. Ezek 17:22-24; Dan 4:12).[131] While this is probably overextending the meaning of the parable, it is clear, historically, that the kingdom of God has had broad impact and benefit in this world.

§ 64f
The Parable of Leaven
(Mt 13:33-35;
Mk 4:33-34;
cf. Lk 13:20-21)

[33]He told them still another parable: "The kingdom of heaven is like yeast that a woman took and mixed into a large amount[a] of flour until it worked all through the dough."

[a]*33* Greek *three satas* (probably about ½ bushel or 22 liters)

Just as the small seed of mustard grows into a large shrub, so also the small amount of leaven permeates a large lump of dough.[132] Like leaven, the influence of the kingdom, which is now small, will soon permeate far beyond its humble beginnings. Leaven is often used in the

---

[129]J.A. Sproule, "The Problem of the Mustard Seed," *GTJ* 1 (1980): 37-42, analyzes Jesus' figurative language at this point.

[130]The word Jesus used, *laxanon*, means an edible plant or a vegetable, not actually a tree (Mt, Lk) or even a shrub. And, in fact, the mustard seed was the smallest variety of laxanon in Palestine at the time.

[131]E.g., R.W. Funk, "The Looking-Glass Tree is for the Birds," *Int* 27 (1973): 3-9.

[132]Three *satas* would come out to about 20-45 liters. That's enough bread to feed 100 people.

Scriptures to represent a negative influence, but not always (Lev 7:13-14; 23:17). In this context it certainly represents the positive influence of the kingdom.

Mk 4:33

³³With many similar parables Jesus spoke the word to them, as much as they could understand. ³⁴He did not say anything to them without using a parable. But when he was alone with his own disciples, he explained everything.

Mt 13:35

³⁵So was fulfilled what was spoken through the prophet:
"I will open my mouth in parables,
   I will utter things hidden since the creation of the world."ᵃ

ᵃ*35* Psalm 78:2

This sermon is composed entirely of parables. It leaves most of Jesus' audience bewildered (Mt 13:10-17). In fact, Jesus has to explain these parables privately to his disciples, once they get back into the house.

Matthew, characteristically, employs this OT quote from Asaph. He is not necessarily presenting Psalm 78:2 as predictive prophecy. Rather, he is saying that Jesus typifies the teachings of ancient Israel. Just as Asaph recounted the great deeds of God in cryptic language, so now Jesus reveals the great kingdom of God through veiled speech.

§ 64g
The Parable of
Weeds
Explained
(Mt 13:36-43)

³⁶Then he left the crowd and went into the house. His disciples came to him and said, "Explain to us the parable of the weeds in the field."
³⁷He answered, "The one who sowed the good seed is the Son of Man. ³⁸The field is the world, and the good seed stands for the sons of the kingdom. The weeds are the sons of the evil one, ³⁹and the enemy who sows them is the devil. The harvest is the end of the age, and the harvesters are angels.
⁴⁰"As the weeds are pulled up and burned in the fire, so it will be at the end of the age. ⁴¹The Son of Man will send out his angels, and they will weed out of his kingdom everything that causes sin and all who do evil. ⁴²They will throw them into the fiery furnace, where there will be weeping and gnashing of teeth. ⁴³Then the righteous will shine like the sun in the kingdom of their Father. He who has ears, let him hear.

Jesus leaves the crowd and goes into the house (cf. Mt 13:1). His interpretation of this parable is enlightening. Not only do we learn the meaning of the parable, but also, Jesus' method of interpretation. We notice first, that Jesus uses "harvest" as the normal Jewish metaphor for judgment. Thus, Jesus was understandable to his contemporaries through stock metaphors. Second, Jesus demonstrates a literal belief in Satan, judgment, the end of the age, and hell. Third, Jesus' interpretation is allegorical. That is, he gives a specific meaning to each of the major elements of the parable. It was neither wild nor whimsical, but it was admittedly allegorical.

§ 64h
The Parable of
the Hidden
Treasure
(Mt 13:44)

⁴⁴"The kingdom of heaven is like treasure hidden in a field. When a man found it, he hid it again, and then in his joy went and sold all he had and bought that field."

Because there were no bank vaults which could keep money safe for the general public, the rich built guarded storehouses, while the common man had to hide his wealth the best he could. If he suddenly died, then his treasure would just have to wait for someone to find it.

Strictly speaking, a hidden treasure would rightfully belong to the owner of the field. Some have called into question the morality of recovering a treasure and then buying the field. But this is not the point of the parable.[133] Jesus isn't beyond using scalawags to illustrate a valuable spiritual truth (cf. Lk 16:1-8; 18:1-8). The point is, the kingdom of heaven is of great value. Like a treasure, it's worth everything we might have to sacrifice to obtain it.

§ 64i
The Parable of
the Precious
Pearl
(Mt 13:45-46)

⁴⁵"Again, the kingdom of heaven is like a merchant looking for fine pearls. ⁴⁶When he found one of great value, he went away and sold everything he had and bought it."

The message of this parable is the same as the last — the ultimate value of the kingdom. It is worth giving up everything else to obtain. The difference is that the merchant deliberately searched for the pearl of great price. The man in the field just stumbled upon it. Whether we search for God, like Cornelius (Acts 10), or whether we stumble upon him, like the woman at the well (Jn 4), it is worth whatever we sacrifice in order to obtain its treasures. Jesus calls every disciple to rid himself of whatever stands in his way of following. Sometimes it is money (Mt 19:21), but it is always total sacrifice. "Paradoxically, salvation is free, yet costs everything."[134]

---

[133]P.S. Hawkings, "Parable as Metaphor," *CSR* 12 (1983): 226-236, says that the dishonest deal was, in fact, the crux of the parable. In his own words, the main point of the parable is this: "God works to realize his purpose even through persons and circumstances as dubious as the ones we find here." However, in response, J.W. Sider, "Interpreting the Hid Treasure," *CSR* 13 (1984): 360-372, argues persuasively that the dishonest activity of the man who found the treasure is an incidental detail and should not be factored into the interpretation. There is no such element in the parallel parable of the pearl of great price. Where ethics are central to other parables, the details are specified and dramatized.

[134]F. Stagg, *Matthew* in *The Broadman Bible Commentary*, Vol. 8 (Nashville: Broadman, 1969), p. 159.

§ 64j
**The Parable of
the Dragnet**
(Mt 13:47-50)

[47]"Once again, the kingdom of heaven is like a net that was let down into the lake and caught all kinds of fish. [48]When it was full, the fishermen pulled it up on the shore. Then they sat down and collected the good fish in baskets, but threw the bad away. [49]This is how it will be at the end of the age. The angels will come and separate the wicked from the righteous [50]and throw them into the fiery furnace, where there will be weeping and gnashing of teeth."

This net [*sagēnē*] was not the throw net normally used by fishermen. It was a dragnet that was let down in back of the boat. As it moved along, it caught all kinds[135] of fish. Only when they are back on shore will they separate the good from the bad, the big from the small.

This parable is much like the wheat and the tares. Both talk about the mixture of the righteous and the wicked and the separating judgment that will take place at the end of the age. Jesus interprets both of them for his audience and puts a P.S. on both about the nature of hell (Mt 13:42, 50). The difference is that the parable of the tares emphasizes the waiting while the parable of the dragnet emphasizes the dividing.

§ 64k
**The Parable of
New and Old
Treasure**
(Mt 13:51-53)

[51]"Have you understood all these things?" Jesus asked.
"Yes," they replied.
[52]He said to them, "Therefore every teacher of the law who has been instructed about the kingdom of heaven is like the owner of a house who brings out of his storeroom new treasures as well as old."
[53]When Jesus had finished these parables, he moved on from there.

When Jesus asks the disciples if they understand these parables, we should probably insert the word "better." It is not likely that they understand their full impact. But since they claim to understand them (better), they become responsible for teaching the truths of the kingdom. As the scribes had received pharisaic instruction, so the disciples of Jesus have been taught (lit. discipled), in the finer points of the kingdom.

As teachers of the kingdom, it is their responsibility to bring out both the new and the old. As a rich man might decorate his mansion with antiques as well as modern art, so the teacher is to explain and apply both the ancient truths and current developments. These disciples are to show how Jesus fulfilled God's ancient plan at the present time.

After a very full day of teaching, Jesus gets into a boat and leaves Capernaum, heading to the district of the Gadarenes. What have we learned, then, from these kingdom parables?

---

[135]Literally "all nationalities." This is a strange way of talking about fish, but perfectly natural in talking about men. Even this early in Jesus' ministry, he suggests that he will be a global, not a national, Messiah.

1. The kingdom is like a wheat field. Its growth is based both on the reception of man (§ 64b) and the sovereignty of God (§ 64c).
2. The division of the righteous and the wicked will not take place until the judgment (§ 64d & j).
3. The kingdom grows and influences phenomenally (§ 64e & f).
4. The kingdom is of ultimate value (§ 64h, i, k).

§ 65
Calming the
Storm
(Mt 8:18, 23-27;[136]
Mk 4:35-41;
Lk 8:22-25)

This is a powerful and important narrative. It is the first time in the Synoptics that Jesus' power acted upon the inanimate. It brought fear and astonishment, even to his closest followers. Some have tried to explain this event as coincidence or relegate it to myth or imagination. None of these, however, adequately explain such vivid eyewitness details. Furthermore, it is admitted more and more that an anti-supernatural bias is scientifically and philosophically indefensible.

At the same time, this event is more than a mere account of a historic event. Miracles are somewhat like enacted parables of the kingdom.[137] That very night, after Jesus preached a sermon on the kingdom of God, all in parables, he demonstrated two important aspects of the kingdom. First, Jesus demonstrates God's power (cf. Ps 104:7; 107:23-30).[138] In other words, the kingdom of God had broken into human history. Second, Jesus saves his people through the storm.[139]

Mk 4:35-38 *with*
Mt 8:18,24-25,
Lk 8:23-24

[35]That day when evening came, {when Jesus saw the crowds around him[MT]} he said to his disciples, "Let us go over to the other side." [36]Leaving the crowd behind, they took him along, just as he was, in the boat. There were also other boats with him. [37]{Without warning[MT]} a furious squall came up, and the waves

---

[136]Matthew takes this pericope out of its chronological order and places it in the middle of a collection of miracles in chapters 8-9. He does this for a purpose. Taken as a whole, these miracles answer a simple question: "Who is this Jesus really?" In the face of pharisaic opposition, popular misconceptions, doubt among his own family, and even ignorance of his disciples, this miracle gives us a glimpse of the true person of Jesus. Cf. P.F. Feiler, "The Stilling of the Storm in Matthew: A Response to Günther Bornkamm," *JETS* 26/4 (1983): 399-406.

[137]Cf. C.L. Blomberg, "New Testament Miracles and Higher Criticism: Climbing up the Slippery Slope," *JETS* 27/4 (1984): 425-438.

[138]P.J. Achtemeier, "Person and Deed: Jesus and the Storm Tossed Sea," *Int* 16 (1962): 169-176.

[139]This has been applied allegorically to Jesus seeing Christians through the storms of life (e.g., N. Pittenger, "Great Calm," *ExpT* 85 [1974]: 209-210). While this is not exactly what Jesus actually did, it is precisely what Jesus represents in this passage — a compassionate Lord who saves his people. Others have seen reflections in this passage of exorcism, Jonah and God's authority over the sea (Ps 104:7; 107:23-30).

broke over the boat, so that it was nearly swamped {and they were in great danger.LK} 38Jesus was in the stern, sleeping on a cushion. The disciples woke him and said to him, {LordMT} {Master, MasterLK} "Teacher, don't you care if we drown?"

Jesus has finished his sermon in parables inside the house. Apparently there are still crowds at the door waiting for him to come out and teach them. Perhaps it was apparent to the disciples that they were going to get no sleep that night unless they left town (Mk 4:35). Without taking time to change clothes or shower they hop in the boat for a quick getaway. But they aren't quick enough. The crowds attempt to follow Jesus in other boats. This is a mistake as they will discover shortly. A violent storm is brewing. Either they will be driven back to shore by the storm or dropped to the bottom of the lake.

The storm comes suddenly, as is common on the Sea of Galilee. The lake sits in a basin, 685 feet below sea level, surrounded by hills 2,000 feet high. When the winds come across those hills they sweep down quickly and with great force. This "furious squall" [*lailaps*] is the word used for a hurricane. It is a tremendously powerful storm.

Meanwhile, Jesus falls asleep in the stern on a cushion (likely made of sheepskin). This is the only place we read of Jesus sleeping, which is all the more amazing since the boat is "swamped" and "in danger." Both of these words are in the imperfect verb tense, indicating an ongoing dilemma for the disciples. In other words, the boat was being filled up with water. It is one of those sturdy, steady, but slow fishing boats. Thirteen men would certainly be a "full house." As the waves beat against the side and blow into the boat, they sink deeper and deeper into the water.

The disciples wake Jesus and say, "Master, Master we're going to drown" (Lk 8:24). This "Master," used only by Luke, means "commander." They are not only surprised that he is sleeping through all this, but also a bit peeved. By their response to the miracle, it seems obvious that they were not expecting Jesus to calm the storm. Rather, they need all hands on deck to help man the oars or bail out the boat.

Mk 4:39-41 *with*
Lk 8:25, Mt 8:27

39He got up, rebuked the wind and said to the waves, "Quiet! Be still!" Then the wind died down and it was completely calm.
40He said to his disciples, "Why are you so afraid? Do you still have no faith?"
41They were terrified and {in fear and amazementLK} asked each other, "Who is this? {What kind of man is this?MT} Even the wind and the waves obey him!"

Both the words "rebuked" (*epitiman*) and "be quiet" (*phimoun*), referring to the winds and waves, are used in narratives of casting out demons (cf. Mk 1:25). Thus, there is a strong connection between Jesus calming the sea and casting out the demons at Gerasa. Both are under his command and control. Both show Jesus' divine authority.

The elements obey Jesus' voice and there is silence on the Sea of Galilee. As co-creator (Jn 1:1-18; Col 1:16) and co-sustainer (Col 1:17; Heb 1:3), the physical universe responds to the commands of its master.

Mark alone contains Jesus' rebuke of their lack of faith (which he repeats a number of times, cf. Mk 7:18; 8:17-18, 21, 32-33; 9:19). Jesus has demonstrated power over disease, demons, and death. Now he shows that he is even master of the elements. For fishermen, this is powerful! It is not surprising that they had no faith for such a miracle. This is truly extraordinary!

In Capernaum (Mk 1:27), they asked "what is this." But now the question becomes "Who is this?" And that is the key question this miracle is designed to answer. The Pharisees oppose him, the crowds wonder at him. Why, even his closest companions don't know who he really is. But his deeds reveal the truth. Jesus is God revealed in human form.

§ 66
Healing the Gerasene Demoniac
(Mt 8:28-34; Mk 5:1-20; Lk 8:26-39)

This is a powerful and tender narrative. Jesus has just subdued the natural forces of the storm. He now subdues the spiritual forces of darkness.

[MK5:]¹They went across the lake to the region of the Gerasenes.ᵃ {which is across the lake from Galileeᴸᴷ} ²When Jesus got out of the boat, a man with an evilᵇ spirit {two demon-possessed menᴹᵀ} came from the tombs to meet him. {For a long time this man had not worn clothes or lived in a house, butᴸᴷ} ³This man lived in the tombs, and no one could bind him any more, not even with a chain. ⁴For he had often been chained hand and foot {and kept under guardᴸᴷ}, but he tore the chains apart and broke the irons on his feet {and had been driven by the demon into solitary placesᴸᴷ}. No one was strong enough to subdue him. {They were so violent that no one could pass that way.ᴹᵀ} ⁵Night and day among the tombs and in the hills he would cry out and cut himself with stones.

ᵃ1 Some manuscripts *Gadarenes*; other manuscripts *Gergesenes*   ᵇ2 Greek *unclean*; also in verses 8 and 13

If we piece together the synoptic narratives, we discover that Jesus probably left Capernaum between six and seven p.m. (cf. Mk 4:35). Because of the storm, it likely took three to four hours to go across the lake (less than five miles). Thus, it is now probably sometime between 9 p.m. and midnight. The action takes place under a starlit sky with an audience of hired hands who watch the swine.

This land is opposite Galilee, in Gentile territory, on the east bank of the lake. This holds special importance to Luke as he outlines the Gospel going to the Gentiles. Matthew labels it as Gadara rather than Gerasa. Gadara was a well-known city some sixteen miles away and seven miles back from the lake. Thus, this portion of the lake was in Gadarene territory. About half a mile from the lake was a small city named Gerasa. This is probably where Jesus landed for it is the only place on the lake where the cliff is close enough to the water for the pigs to rush down and drown. Strictly speaking, it is incorrect to speak of the area as "Gerasene." The similarities in names likely caused the confusion with the transcribers.

This area has a narrow bank, met abruptly by high limestone cliffs full of caves. Archaeologists have found tombs twenty feet square with side recesses for bodies. These were used to bury the dead. Poor indigents sometimes used the caves as shelters as well as tombs. This is not uncommon even today.

Matthew says that two demon possessed men met Jesus. Luke and Mark only concentrate on the more prominent of the two — the one who did the speaking. He comes running up to Jesus and falls at his feet. Here we have a classic description of a demoniac (Liefeld, p. 913): (1) Nakedness — disregard for personal dignity, (2) social isolation, (3) retreat to simple shelter (i.e., caves), (4) recognition of Jesus' deity, (5) demonic control of speech, (6) shouting, (7) extraordinary strength — tearing chains apart is impressive power. Besides all this he was not only homicidal but almost suicidal (Mt 8:28; Mk 5:5). He was the talk and terror of the town.

Mk 5:6-10 *with*
Lk 8:28,31,
Mt 8:29

⁶When he saw Jesus from a distance, he ran and fell on his knees in front of him. ⁷He shouted at the top of his voice, "What do you want with me, Jesus, Son of the Most High God? Swear to God {I beg you^LK} that you won't torture me! {before the appointed time^MT}" ⁸For Jesus had said to him, "Come out of this man, you evil spirit!"

⁹Then Jesus asked him, "What is your name?"

"My name is Legion," he replied, "for we are many." ¹⁰And he begged Jesus again and again not to send them out of the area {into the Abyss^LK}.

This idiomatic expression, "What do you want with me" (lit. "What to me and to you"), can be understood in a number of ways: "What do we have in common?" or "What business do you have with me?" or "Why are you interrupting my life?" He is essentially asking Jesus what is the meaning and/or significance of this encounter.

The second part of this demoniac's address, "Son of the Most High God" sounds odd coming from a demon. It is as kosher as a dill pickle. In the OT "Most High God" is an orthodox title for Jehovah (Gen 14:18-22; Num 24:16; Isa 14:14; Dan 3:26; 4:2). So why is it coming from a demon? It may be that the demon is trying to invoke the name of God before Jesus invokes the name of the demon. You see, the current practice of exorcism was to conjure up the names of powerful people and "gods" in order to overpower the demon and send him away. Whoever had the most impressive resume of names supposedly won.

This fellow had a long list of names backing him. But only one is given — Legion. This term refers to a unit of the Roman army generally consisting of 6,000 men. It is not necessary, however, to take this as a literal number. Jewish rhetoric often referred to multiple demon possession as "legion." Nonetheless, the fellow is in bad shape. He is filled with a slug of evil spirits.

The demons have Jesus way outnumbered. Still, they are petrified of him. They know he has the authority and sufficient power to punish them. They are well aware, in fact, of their impending imprisonment in the Abyss at the judgment (cf. Mt 25:41; 2 Pet 2:4; Jude 6). They beg the Master not to sentence them prematurely.

The word "Abyss" originally meant "bottomless." In general it refers to the realm of the dead. It has various specific meanings ranging from primeval chaos to the prison of evil beings (cf. Rom 10:7; Rev 9:1-3; 11:7; 17:8; 20:1-3). Matthew adds the note (8:29), "before the appointed time." Eventually Satan and all his cohorts will be punished and locked up (Rev 20:1-3, 10). They are not asking to be delivered. They know this is not possible. They are asking, however, to have their full time to wreak havoc on the earth.

Mk 5:11-13 *with*
Mt 8:30-31

{[30]Some distance from them[MT]} [11]A large herd of pigs was feeding on the nearby hillside. [12]The demons begged Jesus, "{If you drive us out[MT]} Send us among the pigs; allow us to go into them." [13]He gave them permission, and the evil spirits came out and went into the pigs. The herd, about two thousand in number, rushed down the steep bank into the lake and were drowned.

There were about 2,000 pigs in the herd. If the number of a legion and the pigs were exact, that would make three demons to one pig. No wonder they committed SUIcide. But doesn't that make Jesus guilty of destroying private property? Not at all. Jesus only permitted it, he did not cause it. Let's not blame God for Satan's work. Besides, pigs were unclean animals to the Jews. We can hardly expect Jesus to honor a herd of pigs. The bottom line is that Jesus considers the soul of one man more valuable than 2,000 pigs. And that can scarcely be criticized.

Why do the demons ask to enter the pigs and then immediately destroy their hosts? Perhaps the demons know that Jesus will be blamed for the destruction of the herd. Thus, they are trying to cause trouble for

Jesus. At the same time, demons are naturally destructive. They are doing nothing essentially different to the pigs than they did to the man. It is simply not true that Satan (and his cohorts) take care of their own. They typically destroy whatever they can get their hands on.

Mk 5:14-17 *with*
Mt 8:34, Lk 8:37

[14]Those tending the pigs ran off and reported this in the town and countryside, and the people went out to see what had happened. [15]{Then the whole town went out to meet Jesus.[MT]} When they came to Jesus, they saw the man who had been possessed by the legion of demons, sitting there {at Jesus' feet[LK]}, dressed and in his right mind; and they were afraid. [16]Those who had seen it told the people what had happened to the demon-possessed man — and told about the pigs as well. [17]Then the people began to plead with Jesus to leave their region {because they were overcome with fear[LK]}.

It must be close to midnight. As the shepherds (or pig herders) report this incident, they are waking up the owner(s) of the flock. An emergency town meeting is called in the middle of the night.

For the first time in who knows how long, this demoniac is liberated. The townspeople gather on the shore of the lake in the wee hours of the morning. There they find the ex-demoniac sitting, sane, and dressed, perhaps even in Jesus' own tunic. When they see this they are afraid. But what frightens them? They knew the power of the demoniac; they couldn't control him even with chains. But Jesus had. That kind of power was beyond them. They also know their major cash crop was just destroyed. They need a scapegoat. Jesus is available. Instead of submitting to his power, they expel him out of fear.

This is a community decision (cf. "all the people"). It is easier to ask Jesus to leave than to figure out the complexity of the situation and where they stand. Peter had asked Jesus to leave after the great catch of fish (Lk 5:8). But there was one big difference. Peter did it because he caught a glimpse of Christ's holiness and his own sinfulness. These people did it because they caught a glimpse of Jesus' power and wanted to protect themselves from it. Jesus stayed and worked with Peter. But because of the Gerasene unbelief, Jesus leaves them as they requested. He is a gentleman. He won't foist himself upon you.

Mk 5:18-20

[18]As Jesus was getting into the boat, the man who had been demon-possessed begged to go with him. [19]Jesus did not let him, but {sent him away [and][LK]} said, "Go home to your family and tell them how much the Lord has done for you, and how he has had mercy on you." [20]So the man went away and began to tell in the Decapolis[a] how much Jesus had done for him. And all the people were amazed.

[a]*20* That is, the Ten Cities

The ex-demoniac begs to go with Jesus. The imperfect verb indicates that he continues to beseech Christ. Why does he want to go? Obviously, he loves Jesus and appreciates what he has done. And he knows that if he stays close to Jesus the demons will not come back. But beyond his love for Jesus, he will always be the ex-demoniac (like an ex-con), to these Gadarenes. He will always have the scars on his body as a reminder to the community of who he was. And the town will associate him with the loss of 2,000 pigs. He wants a fresh start and a new identity. According to Jesus, however, it is more important that he witnesses in his community with his old identity.

Jesus sends him home to his family. The content of his message is simple. He is to tell two things: (a) "How much God has done for you" and (b) "How he has had mercy on you." We often make evangelism far too complex. Here we have an ex-demoniac with merely one evening of "Bible College" education. He simply goes home and tells his story. The results are phenomenal. He not only goes throughout the whole town but through the entire Decapolis, a group of ten Greek cities.[140]

But that is not the end of the story. The next time Jesus returns to that area, he has a wonderful reception and feeds 4,000. No doubt, it is largely due to the testimony of this one man.

§ 67
Healing Two
Women
(Mt 9:18-26;
Mk 5:21-43;
Lk 8:40-56)

After preaching in parables the day before, calming the storm that night, healing the demoniac and getting kicked out of town, Jesus could probably use a little rest. He returns to Capernaum from Gadara after a sleepless night, save one little catnap in the boat. The crowds line the shore in anticipation of his arrival. There will be no rest for the weary.

There is a common theme that runs through the healing of the demoniac, the woman with an issue of blood and Jairus' daughter. It is this: they were all considered ritually unclean. Demons, blood and death not only made the individual unclean but all who touched them. Among the rabbis, Jesus alone touches these and makes *them* clean.

Mk 5:21-24a *with*
Lk 8:40-42,
Mt 9:18

[21]When Jesus had again crossed over by boat to the other side of the lake, a large crowd {expecting him[LK]} gathered around him while he was by the lake. [22]Then one of the synagogue rulers, named Jairus, came there {and knelt before him.[MT]} Seeing Jesus, he fell at his feet [23]and pleaded earnestly with him, {to

---

[140]The Decapolis was originally a group of ten cities, as its name suggests. Later more cities were added. It was apparently attached to Syria but had its own system of appeal to Roman authorities. It was clearly Greek in orientation. But there is no solid evidence to suggest that it was an independent confederation as is often suggested. Cf. S.T. Parker, "The Decapolis Reviewed," *JBL* 94 (1975): 437-441.

come to his house[LK]} "My little daughter {about twelve[LK]} is dying {has just died[MT]}. Please come and put your hands on her so that she will be healed and live." [24]So Jesus went with him.

This girl is Jairus' only child [*monogenēs*, Lk 8:42], not merely his only daughter (NIV) (cf. Lk 7:12; Jn 3:16). She is about twelve years old. That's when a Jewish girl became a woman. Thus, for the last twelve years this couple has been unable to have another child. Their prospects for more children are pretty slim. Even as they speak, her young life is slipping away.[141]

Jairus, as a synagogue ruler, is a prominent member of his community. It is his job, as a layman, to direct the services and affairs of the synagogue. In the wake of Jesus' rising opposition, Jairus may be risking his position by coming to him for help. But the urgency of the situation demands that he now seek Jesus' help. Since Jesus was in Capernaum just the day before, we might assume that the girl's sickness took a drastic turn for the worse during the night. In his moment of need, Jairus humbles himself by falling at Jesus' feet (an action associated with honor and worship). Jesus responds immediately to his request and leads the urgent entourage toward Jairus' home.

Mk 5:24b-29 *with* Lk 8:42, Mt 9:20

A large crowd followed and pressed around him {almost crushed him[LK]}. [25]And a woman was there who had been subject to bleeding for twelve years. [26]She had suffered a great deal under the care of many doctors and had spent all she had, yet instead of getting better she grew worse. [27]When she heard about Jesus, she came up behind him in the crowd and touched {the edge of[MT]} his cloak, [28]because she thought, "If I just touch his clothes, I will be healed." [29]Immediately her bleeding stopped and she felt in her body that she was freed from her suffering.

The crowd is "crushing" Jesus. This is the same word used in the parable of the soils to describe how the weeds "choked out" the good seed. There are two other words also used to describe this crowding: [*synechousin*] "crowding," and [*apothlibousin*] "pressing against" or "crushing," both used in Luke 8:45. This crowd is downright rude. You can just imagine how forceful and pushy Jairus and this woman had to be to elbow their way up to Jesus. Their needs press them on.

This thronging crowd is rushing on toward Jairus' house. Time is of the essence to save this girl. But the procession is brought to a screeching

---

[141]The apparent contradiction about whether or not the girl is already dead is settled when we understand that (a) first century medicine lacked the technology to determine the exact point of death and (b) the Greek phrase of Matthew (*arti eteleutēsen*) could also be translated, "She has come to the point of death." The girl is not yet dead but is knocking on death's door.

halt by this unnamed woman. She has been bleeding for twelve years.[142] Although the bleeding is not described, it is assumed to be a gynecological problem. Edersheim notes that this must have been common:

> On one leaf of the Talmud not less than eleven different remedies are proposed of which at most only six can possibly be regarded as astringents or tonics, while the rest are merely the outcome of superstition, to which resort has had in the absence of knowledge. Such as the ashes of an Ostrich-Egg, carried in summer in a linen, in winter in a cotton rag; or a barley-corn found in the dung of a white she ass (I:620).

The law of Moses in Leviticus 15:25-33, as well as Jewish custom, would have put heavy restrictions on the social activity of this woman. She would have been excluded from temple worship, public fraternizing, and anyone she touched would subsequently become unclean (Num 19:22). This is not just a medical problem; it is a social problem as well.

Mark gives us some information that Luke, the physician, neglected to tell us for obvious reasons: "She had suffered a great deal under the care of many doctors and had spent all she had, yet instead of getting better she grew worse" (5:26).

This woman is apparently acting out of Hellenistic superstition which assumed that a healer's power was transferred to his clothes. But she gets results! Jesus respects her faith, and she is healed through her deliberate act of touching the edge of his cloak. This was most likely one of the tassels which hung from the corners of his prayer shawl (Num 15:38-39; Deut 22:12). This is, admittedly, an odd healing miracle. But it will not be the only time such a thing takes place (cf. Acts 5:15 [the shadow of Peter]; Acts 19:11-12 [the handkerchief of Paul]). God respected her faith even if it flowed from the superstitions of the day.

Mk 5:30-31 *with* Lk 8:45	[30]At once Jesus realized that power had gone out from him. He turned around in the crowd and asked, "Who touched my clothes?"

{When they all denied it, Peter said, "Master"[LK]} [31]"You see the people crowding against you," his disciples answered, "and yet you can ask, 'Who touched me?'"

Lk 8:46	[46]But Jesus said, "Someone touched me; I know that power has gone out from me."

Mk 5:32-34 *with* Lk 8:47, Mt 9:22	[32]. . . Jesus kept looking around to see who had done it. [33]Then the woman, {seeing that she could not go unnoticed,[LK]} knowing what had happened to her,

---

[142]It is probably only coincidence that the length of the woman's illness and the age of Jairus' daughter are the same. Any figurative interpretation of the twelve years is tenuous at best.

came and fell at his feet and, trembling with fear, told him the whole truth. {In the presence of all the people, she told why she had touched him and how she had been instantly healed.ᴸᴷ} ³⁴He said to her, "{Take heartᴹᵀ} Daughter, your faith has healed you. Go in peace and be freed from your suffering."

Jesus is aware that power left him. So he asks who touched his clothes. It is humorous that they all deny it when they were all over him just a moment ago! To Peter the question is unreasonable. How could Jesus possibly feel someone touch his *clothes* while he was being mauled?

Did Jesus really not know who touched him? And if not, how did this woman "sneak a healing out of him?" There are two good possibilities. First, Jesus knew the woman's faith when she touched him. So he healed her. Now, he wants to fan the flicker of her faith into a flame by pointing her out to the crowd. A second possibility, which seems more likely, is that Jesus did not know who this woman was but his Father did. God saw what was going on and allowed his power to flow through his Son and into the body of this woman. Now Jesus, using his power to see into people's hearts, is searching the crowd so that he can show this woman that while her superstition was wrong her faith was right.

This woman had not gone unnoticed.¹⁴³ This may indicate that Jesus did know who she was. He may even have been looking her right in the eyes. Or it may have been her trembling that was giving her away.

This elicits her full public confession which she wants to avoid. After all, gynecological bleeding is not the kind of thing you want to talk about. Jesus isn't trying to embarrass her by making her reveal her problem. But if her faith is to be fully developed, not to mention that of the crowd, she needs to make a public statement.

By Jesus' kind words, he not only removes her fear for having touched him, but he removes the public stigma over her problem. She has been fully healed, therefore should be fully reinstated into her community.

Here is the only place where Jesus addresses someone as "daughter." Furthermore, his words, "Go in peace" would echo the Hebrew word, "Shalom." This was more than a greeting or a wish for one's physical well-being. It was a prayer for a person's wholeness before man and God. For the first time in twelve years she can receive such a greeting.

---

¹⁴³Lk 8:47 (NIV) is translated as a present tense, "She could not go unnoticed." But it is actually a past tense, and should be read: "She had not gone unnoticed."

Mk 5:35-40a *with*
Lk 8:49-53

³⁵While Jesus was still speaking, some men came from the house of Jairus, the synagogue ruler. "Your daughter is dead," they said. "Why {Don't^LK} bother the teacher any more?"

³⁶Ignoring what they said, Jesus told the synagogue ruler, "Don't be afraid; just believe, {and she will be healed."^LK}

³⁷He did not let anyone follow him except Peter, James and John the brother of James {[and] the child's father and mother.^LK} ³⁸When they came to the home of the synagogue ruler, Jesus saw a commotion {and the flute players,^MT} with people crying and wailing loudly. ³⁹He went in and said to them, "Why all this commotion and wailing? {Stop wailing,^LK} {Go away^MT} The child is not dead but asleep." ⁴⁰But they laughed at him {knowing that she was dead.^LK}

During this delay, Jairus is no doubt a bit antsy. His frustration is worsened by the tragic news that his daughter has just died. "Death" is placed at the very beginning of the Greek sentence for emphasis. It comes out something like this: "Your daughter is DEAD!"

The servants are concerned with Jesus as well as Jairus. They don't want him needlessly bothered. But Jesus ignores their message. He quickly grabs Jairus' attention and tries to refocus it from fear to faith.

Mark makes it look like Jesus stops the crowd where they are and does not allow them to come to Jairus' house. Luke probably expresses it more clearly when he says that Jesus only allows three apostles in the house (Peter, James and John), along with the child's parents. These inner three are also given the exclusive privilege of seeing the transfiguration (Mt 17:1; Mk 9:2; Lk 9:28) and following Jesus into the garden of Gethsemane (Mt 26:37; Mk 14:33).

Outside the house there is quite a commotion. According to Jewish burial rites, a crowd would gather and make a great deal of noise. Even poor families were required to hire at least two flute players and one mourner (*m. Ketub.* 4:4). The word "mourning" involves beating the chest as a sign of sorrow. It apparently takes Jesus and Jairus long enough to get there that a funeral crowd has already gathered.

Jesus tells them to stop mourning because she is not dead but only asleep. He used that same figure of speech to describe Lazarus (Jn 11:11; cf. Mt 27:52; Acts 13:36; 1 Cor 11:30; 15:20, 51; 1 Thess 4:14). The crowd, taking his words literally, laugh at him. They know when someone has died. They are not stupid, but they think Jesus is. Then again, Peter had just committed the same error when Jesus said, "Someone touched me."

Mk 5:40b-43 *with*
Lk 8:54-56

After he put them all out, he took the child's father and mother and the disciples who were with him, and went in where the child was. ⁴¹He took her by the hand and said to her, "Talitha koum!" (which means, "Little girl {my child^LK}, I say to you, get up!"). [42]{Her spirit returned, and[LK]} Immediately the girl stood up and walked around (she was twelve years old). At this they {her parents[LK]} were completely astonished. [43]He gave strict orders not to let anyone know about this, and told them to give her something to eat.

Mt 9:26   [26]News of this spread through all that region.

When Jesus raises this little girl from the dead she is completely restored. She does not just "wake up;" she gets up and starts walking around. Furthermore, Jesus tells her parents to get her something to eat. (She must have been a typical teenager).

It is also curious that Jesus commands the parents not to tell anyone about the miracle. If Jesus ever said anything unreasonable, this was it! The crowd already knows that she is dead. It would be pretty difficult to conceal her once she is revived. Likely what Jesus means is to conceal the details of the raising. In other words, don't talk about *how* Jesus did it. We can understand why. The crowds are already oppressive. The Gerasene demoniac was commanded to go tell what had happened since that country needed to develop faith. This place is bursting with faith, curiosity, and crowds. Jesus does not need any more publicity here! In fact, in the very next chapter (Lk 9:7-9) Jesus' reputation as a miracle worker is going to lead to an official inquiry by Herod. All this attention would lead to a premature announcement and incomplete understanding of his Messiahship. The crowds have already been told that she was only sleeping. They may accept this as a resuscitation from a coma. This would still be considered a wonderful miracle but not quite as phenomenal as raising her from the dead. Despite Jesus' attempt to "play down" this miracle, news of it spreads like wildfire.[144]

This is the second of three raisings Jesus performed. The first was the widow's son at Nain (Lk 7:11ff). The third will be Jesus' personal friend Lazarus, in Bethany (Jn 11). Like his OT counterparts, Elijah and Elisha (cf. 1 Kgs 17:20-24; 2 Kgs 4:17-37), the power of God flowed through Jesus even to raise the dead.

§ 68
Healing Two
Blind Men and
a Demoniac
(Mt 9:27-34)

Both the healing of the blind men and the healing of the deaf-demoniac are paralleled by similar events later in the life of Jesus. For instance, in Matthew 20:29-34 we read of two blind men from Jericho who also cried out to Jesus, "Have mercy on us, Son of David." Some

---

[144]The following are other passages where Jesus commanded silence concerning his miracles: Mt 8:4 (Mk 1:44; Lk 5:14); Mt 9:30; 12:16; Mk 3:12; 5:43 (Lk 8:56); Mk 7:36; 8:26.

have suggested that these are the same event which Matthew edits and repeats for emphasis. A more reasonable suggestion, however, is that Matthew records two similar but different events. They were in two different locations (Capernaum and Jericho) in two different periods of Jesus' ministry. Furthermore, Matthew 9 takes place in a house while Matthew 20 takes place on a city street as Jesus passes through the town. In the first event the two men follow Jesus, in the second, they remain seated by the road. Both the vocabulary and the purpose of the two dialogues is distinctly different. Since blindness was (and is) common in Palestine (cf. Mt 11:5), we are not at all surprised to read two different accounts of blind men healed.

Matthew connects this event with the raising of Jairus' daughter as if they were simultaneous. However, elsewhere Matthew pulls together loosely connected narratives under similar themes. Thus, these events were likely in the same period of Jesus' ministry but not necessarily on the same day. They connect with the previous narrative in several ways. (1) Both demonstrate healing based on faith (i.e., woman with issue of blood). (2) Both contain injunctions for silence. (3) Both show individuals seeking Jesus' help. And (4) both show how Jesus' fame continues to spread.

These three healings conclude a series of healing stories which Matthew collects in chapters 8-9. They are brief, and somewhat repetitious. Nonetheless, they punctuate this whole series of healings by highlighting Jesus' broad fame, the inconvenience and danger that fame brought, and the tension it caused between Jesus and the religious leaders of his day (v. 34).

Mt 9:27-31

[27]As Jesus went on from there, two blind men followed him, calling out, "Have mercy on us, Son of David!"

[28]When he had gone indoors, the blind men came to him, and he asked them, "Do you believe that I am able to do this?"

"Yes, Lord," they replied.

[29]Then he touched their eyes and said, "According to your faith will it be done to you"; [30]and their sight was restored. Jesus warned them sternly, "See that no one knows about this." [31]But they went out and spread the news about him all over that region.

Considering how pushy and clamorous the crowds are (Mk 5:24), and considering that these men are blind, they must have had a lot of guts to follow Jesus to his house (either Peter's or Matthew's), and even make their way inside. They follow Jesus until he stops. All the while they have been shouting over the noisy mob, "Have mercy on us, Son of David." This was a common Messianic title of Jesus' day (Cf. Mt 15:22;

20:30; 21:9, 15; 22:42).[145] They may lack physical sight, but they clearly see who Jesus is. Isaiah 35:5-6 would sustain their hope of the Messiah healing the blind.

Jesus respects their faith and tenacity and wants to heal them but does not need any more publicity. Inside the house, Jesus has the privacy to heal these men without attracting further attention from the crowds. He again commands them to keep their mouths shut. Matthew uses a word with a stern, if not even a violent, connotation. *Embrimaomai* expresses an emotional outburst; it can even express the action of "snorting."[146] Even such a strong warning, however, does not still their tongues. As Jesus' popularity rises, so does his opposition.

Mt 9:32-34   [32]While they were going out, a man who was demon-possessed and could not talk was brought to Jesus. [33]And when the demon was driven out, the man who had been mute spoke. The crowd was amazed and said, "Nothing like this has ever been seen in Israel."
     [34]But the Pharisees said, "It is by the prince of demons that he drives out demons."

This poor man is afflicted with both demon possession and dumbness. The word (*kōphos*) can indicate deafness, dumbness or both. They are often connected. After all, when someone is born deaf, they are bound to have difficulty speaking. It would appear that the demon caused this man's physical disability. But that is not to say that all physical disabilities were caused by demons (cf. Mk 7:32-33).

Jesus doesn't respond to the Pharisees' accusation (Mt 9:34), at least not here. However, the same accusation is made against Jesus again in Matthew 12:24-37, where he responds fully. If our chronology is correct, Matthew 12:24-37 actually took place before Matthew 9:34. Thus Jesus would already have answered this accusation and doesn't waste his time rehashing an argument that he has already dealt with. Even so, the Pharisees continue (*elegon*, impf.) to bring this charge against Jesus.

In spite of the oppressive crowds and the rising opposition of the Jewish leaders, Jesus continues "teaching in their synagogues, preaching the good news of the kingdom and healing every disease and sickness" (Mt 9:35).

---

[145]Matthew uses this title, "Son of David," ten times while Mark and Luke only use it four times each. John doesn't use it at all. Furthermore, most of Matthew's uses of this title occur in the context of healing outcasts. J.D. Kingsbury, "The Title 'Son of David' in Matthew's Gospel," *JBL* 95/4 (1976): 591-602, suggests that the title is a polemic against Jewish rejection of their Messiah and king. That is, the blind outcasts "saw" their true king, while the religious leaders were blind to him.

[146]The word is only used four other times in the NT, always expressing deep emotion (Mk 1:43; 14:5; Jn 11:33, 38).

§ 69
**Jesus' Final
Visit to
Nazareth**
(Mt 13:54-58;
Mk 6:1-6a)

In this episode, Jesus is rejected by his own hometown. This is a preview of coming attractions in Jerusalem. In the capital city, Jesus, the king of the Jews, will be rejected and assassinated by his own people (Jn 1:11).

[MK 6:]1Jesus left there and went to his hometown, accompanied by his disciples. 2When the Sabbath came, he began to teach in the synagogue, and many who heard him were amazed.

"Where did this man get these things?" they asked. "What's this wisdom that has been given him, that he even does miracles! 3Isn't this the carpenter {carpenter's son?MT} Isn't this Mary's son and the brother of James, Joseph,a Judas and Simon? Aren't his sisters here with us?" And they took offense at him.

4Jesus said to them, "Only in his hometown, among his relatives and in his own house is a prophet without honor." 5He could not do any {manyMT} miracles there {because of their lack of faith,MT} except lay his hands on a few sick people and heal them. 6And he was amazed at their lack of faith.

a3 Greek *Joses*, a variant of *Joseph*

It appears that Jesus left Capernaum after healing Jairus' daughter and went straight to Nazareth.[147] From this point on, Capernaum ceases to be Jesus' headquarters. He returns "home"[148] with an entourage of disciples as a prominent rabbi. He's not there just to visit his family. Most of them have likely relocated in Capernaum (Jn 2:12). He comes as a visiting rabbi, not a local hero.

This is Jesus' second and final recorded visit to his unbelieving hometown.[149] Neither visit was very profitable. Although enamored with his teaching, bewildered by his wisdom, and amazed by his miraculous power, the synagogue congregation both times rejected Jesus' person. Why? Not because Jesus made no sense or could not back up his preaching with evidence, but because they were too familiar with him. Many of them had furniture or houses made by Jesus and/or his father.[150] They

---

[147]It is possible that sections 68 & 69 could be in reverse order. That is, that Jesus went straight from Capernaum to Nazareth and then embarked upon his third Galilean tour, in which he healed the two blind men (§ 68). Thus, we follow more closely the chronology of Mark than of Matthew.

[148]The word *patris* generally refers to "home country." But since Jesus is already in Galilee it must be more specific than that. Therefore, it is correctly translated as "hometown."

[149]Some have suggested that the two visits are actually one (e.g., Blomberg & McGarvey). If that is true, then Luke places it at the beginning of Jesus' ministry to highlight the key themes of his coming labors (cf. Lk 4:14b-15). Matthew and Mark, on the other hand, use this narrative as a summary of Jesus' ministry.

[150]The word *tektos* can also refer to a mason, but this designation is not as common as carpenter.

knew his parents[151] and helped babysit Jesus and his siblings[152] (four brothers[153] and at least two sisters).[154]

Surely this hometown boy can't think he is the Messiah. Provincial pride is an odd thing. They are proud when their children go out and make it big. But when they come home, they want to remind them that they used to change their diapers. It is as if to say, "Of course you made it big, you are one of us. Don't get cocky, though, because there are any number of us who are still better than you!"

On his first visit to Nazareth they try to kill Jesus. On this second visit, he can't heal very many people because of their rejection. Matthew clarifies Mark at this point, stating that Jesus could not do *many* miracles because of their lack of faith. (Although even Mark reports that a few sick people were healed). It is not that Jesus lost his power, but that the people didn't come to him for help. Jesus often chose to heal people in response to their faith. But here, in Nazareth, there is nothing to respond to.

§ 70a
Third Galilean
Tour
(Mt 9:35-38;
Mk 6:6b)

Matthew 9:35-11:1 is a single unit. It describes Jesus sending out the Twelve as evangelists across Galilee. This is the second of Matthew's five great speeches. Mark and Luke both contain abbreviated accounts of this "commission."[155] But they are about one eighth the length of Matthew's.[156]

---

[151]Since children were generally identified by their father, rather than by their mother, the fact that Joseph is not mentioned by name may indicate that he is now dead. (Cf. Jn 2:1-5, § 29). Others suggest that "Son of Mary" was shaped by the early church's belief in the virgin birth, or that he was illegitimate. However, H.K. McArthur argues that the phrase originated with the people of Nazareth merely as a description of Jesus, carrying no special connotation either ethically or genealogically ("Son of Mary" *NovT* 15 [1993]: 38-58).

[152]The view that these siblings were not actually Jesus' blood relatives (half-brothers/ sisters), but rather cousins (Jerome) or Joseph's children by a previous marriage (Epiphanius) is based on the Roman Catholic notion of the perpetual virginity of Mary. The Bible does not support such an idea, nor does it suggest that virgins are more spiritual than non-celibate married people. Cf. J.P. Meier, "The Brothers and Sisters of Jesus in Ecumenical Perspective," *CBQ* 54 (1992): 1-28.

[153]James, the best known of Jesus' brothers, was converted when the resurrected Jesus appeared to him (1 Cor 15:7). He was a prominent leader in the Jerusalem church (Acts 12:17; 15:13; 21:18; Gal 1:19; 2:9, 12) and likely the author of the Epistle of James. "Both Josephus (*Ant.* XX:200) and Eusebius (*Ecclesiastical History* 2.33) preserve accounts of his violent death" (Wessel, p. 665). Jude (or Judas) was also likely the author of the Epistle of Jude.

[154]Wessel suggests that, "Behind this question may be the rumor, circulated during Jesus' lifetime, that he was illegitimate (cf. Jn 4:41; 9:29; SBK, 1:39-43; Origen *Contra Celsum*, 1.28)," p. 665.

[155]R.E. Morosco, "Matthew's Formation of a Commissioning Type-Scene Out of the Story of Jesus' Commissioning of the Twelve," *JBL* 103/4 (1984): 539-556, notes that

Mt 9:35-38

³⁵Jesus went through all the towns and villages, teaching in their synagogues, preaching the good news of the kingdom and healing every disease and sickness. ³⁶When he saw the crowds, he had compassion on them, because they were harassed and helpless, like sheep without a shepherd. ³⁷Then he said to his disciples, "The harvest is plentiful but the workers are few. ³⁸Ask the Lord of the harvest, therefore, to send out workers into his harvest field."

This is Jesus' third tour of Galilee. It is the last time the Twelve get to watch Jesus work before their first solo flight. This is just typical Jesus: (1) Preaching the Kingdom in the synagogues, (2) healing all manner of sicknesses, and (3) driven by compassion for the crowds.

As Jesus moves out among the people he is overwhelmed by their many needs. He can't do it alone. He asks his apprentices to pray for workers. As is often the case, the disciples' prayer for laborers (v. 38), is answered with a personal commission by Christ (Mt 10). In this way, verses 37-38 prepare us for Matthew 10. The great need of helpless people combined with the sparse response of preachers is still the impelling force behind missions.

§ 70b
Twelve Sent
Out in Pairs
(Mt 10:1-42;
Mk 6:7-11;
Lk 9:1-5)

This is a fascinating and demanding sermon. As we process through it, we make three general observations. First, it is full of Jewish idioms and ideas. Yet, it extends far beyond any national boundary. Its starting point is clear; but it catapults the reader to the farthest reaches of the earth. Second, it is prophetic. As such, it finds initial fulfillment in the present journey but ultimate fulfillment only in global missions. Third, Matthew, characteristically synthesizes the present and the future under one theological heading: Sending out.[157] So we read this text with one eye in the present and one eye on the horizon.

Matthew's speech contains the most common elements found in the commissioning narratives of the OT (e.g., Exod 3:1-4:17): (1) Introduction, (2) Confrontation, (3) Commission, (4) Objection, (5) Reassurance, (6) Conclusion, (7) Difficulty. It is his opinion, therefore, that Matthew has edited this speech so as to show his readers how Jesus commissioned his Apostles just like Jehovah commissioned his servants in the OT, thus soliciting a powerful reader response.

[156]Mark and Luke contain much of this speech in other contexts dispersed throughout their books. For a chart of the parallel passages see R.E. Morosco, "Redaction Criticism and the Evangelical: Mt 10 A Test Case," *JETS* 22/4 (1979): 327.

[157]The content of Mt 10 suggests that Matthew had more in mind than the trip of the Twelve. The apparent inconsistencies (10:5-6 vs. 10:18 & 9:37-38 vs. 10:16-22) and the parallel passages in differing contexts (cf. Mt 10:17-22 & Mk 13:9-13), seem to suggest that Matthew has "collected" commission-type talk into one sermon (cf. R.E. Morosco, "Redaction Criticism and the Evangelical: Matthew 10 A Test Case," *JETS* 22/4 [1979]: 323-331). If this is true, then the material we read here is not just descriptive of the Twelve but prescriptive of all Christian evangelists. In other words, we need to pay attention to what Jesus is saying to *us* as well as to the Twelve.

Mt 10:1 *with*
Mk 6:7, Lk 9:1-2

¹He called his twelve disciples to him and {he sent them out two by two and^MK} gave them {power and^LK} authority to drive out evil^a spirits and to heal every disease and sickness. {And he sent them out to preach the kingdom of God and to heal the sick.^LK}

^a1 Greek *unclean*

Jesus sends his inner band of twelve disciples, also called Apostles, to the cities and villages of Galilee. They go out in pairs, likely to meet Moses' requirements of two or three witnesses. Beyond that, they would be able to protect and encourage each other, supplement each other's gifts and preaching and share a variety of responsibilities. The preachers in the book of Acts also followed this model. It seems to be a wise evangelistic principle.

Jesus empowers and commissions them to do two things: (1) Preach the kingdom of God (as did John and Jesus). (2) Heal every disease and sickness. Matthew used three separate synonyms for sickness: disease [*noson*], sickness [*malakian*], and sick (people) [*asthenountas*, lit. "weak ones," v. 8]. In other words, they can handle any physical needs they encounter whether they were congenital deformity, injury, virus, etc. Furthermore, they have authority over demons. So they can handle spiritual as well as natural ailments.

Mt 10:2-4

²These are the names of the twelve apostles: first, Simon (who is called Peter) and his brother Andrew; James son of Zebedee, and his brother John; ³Philip and Bartholomew; Thomas and Matthew the tax collector; James son of Alphaeus, and Thaddaeus; ⁴Simon the Zealot and Judas Iscariot, who betrayed him. (Cf. § 53, Mk 3:13-19; Lk 6:12-16).

It appears that Matthew lists the Apostles in the actual pairs that Jesus sent out.¹⁵⁸ So the Twelve are sent out in pairs, confronting the dark forces at both the physical and spiritual levels. An interesting aside is that Judas Iscariot was paired up with Simon the Zealot. What a spunky team they must have been. And there is no indication that Judas healed any less or preached any differently than the rest. Conclusion: It is virtually impossible to evaluate a person's true character by their religious activity.

Mt 10:5-10 *with*
Mk 6:9

⁵These twelve Jesus sent out with the following instructions: "Do not go among the Gentiles or enter any town of the Samaritans. ⁶Go rather to the lost sheep of Israel. ⁷As you go, preach this message: 'The kingdom of heaven is near.' ⁸Heal the sick, raise the dead, cleanse those who have leprosy,^a drive out

---

¹⁵⁸The use of *kai*, "and," seems to identify these pairs. The NIV also helps isolate these pairs by using a semicolon to separate them.

demons. Freely you have received, freely give. [9]Do not take along any gold or silver or copper in your belts; [10]take no bag for the journey, or extra tunic, or sandals or a staff {take nothing for your journey except a staff — no bread, no bag, no money in your belts. Wear sandals but not an extra tunic;[MK]} for the worker is worth his keep."

[a]*8* The Greek word was used for various diseases affecting the skin—not necessarily leprosy

These instructions are specifically for this local tour. Later Jesus reverses this order by telling them to take money and a bag and a sword (Lk 22:35-36). But that is when the disciples were to be sent all over the world, and to all ethnic groups (Mt 28:18-20). So what is unique about this trip that makes these instructions temporary?

(1) It is a short, quick trip. They don't need a bunch of money or extra clothes. Because the tour is short, they need to pack light and move fast. Furthermore, their hosts in each town can certainly afford to house and feed them for a few days. After all, that is the least they can do to repay the medical treatment they will receive.

(2) They are in no real danger . . . yet. There is antagonism against Jesus, but no widespread physical persecution. The disciples of Jesus are in less danger still. There is simply no need for a sword for self-protection.

(3) This is a local tour in Galilee. Jesus forbids preaching to the Gentiles and Samaritans, not because he doesn't love these people but because this trip is too early and too short. The local Jews will barely be able to understand this kingdom talk. How could foreigners possibly understand it? There will come a time, after the resurrection, when the Apostles are sent to all people (even Mt 10:18 anticipates this), but not yet.[159] We should also keep in mind that the Apostles are no strangers in these parts. Jesus has toured the area with them for about a year now. His popularity has skyrocketed; and the Twelve are known as his right-hand men. They will have no trouble gaining an audience or finding lodging.

In addition, this fits the general pattern of going to the Jews first and then to the Samaritans (Rom 1:16; Acts 13:46; 18:6; 19:9; 28:25-28).

---

[159]Mt 10:5-6 and Mt 15:21-28 restrict Jesus' ministry to the Jews. Jesus clearly had a Gentile expansion in mind for the future (Mt 21:13; Mk 1:14-15; Lk 4:16-30; Jn 10:16). Before the Gentiles could receive Jesus, however, he had to fulfill his role to the Jews first (Acts 13:46; 28:28; Rom 1:16; 11:11-12, 25-26), and that included his substitutionary death. J. J. Scott, "Gentiles and the Ministry of Jesus: Further Observations on Mt 10:5-6; 15:21-28," *JETS* 33/2 (1990): 161-169, rightly observes: "The request of the centurion — like that of the Canaanite woman — was granted only after recognition of the distinction between Israel and others. Although Jesus looked forward to the gathering of the nations in the end time, he clearly saw the cases of the Canaanite woman, the centurion's servant, and others as exceptions to what he was doing at the time."

There is an apparent contradiction between Matthew 10:10 and Mark 6:8. Matthew says, "Take no staff" while Mark says, "Take nothing for the journey except a staff." Mark uses the word *airō*, "take up." Matthew uses the word *ktaomai*, "procure." It may simply be that Matthew assumes they already have certain "travel tools" and they are not to go buy a new set of luggage for their trip. In other words, they surely already had a walking stick in their hand. They didn't need a new one for this trip.

Edersheim notes that the command to take no extra "stuff" corresponds to the rabbinic command about entering the temple for service without "staff, shoes . . . and a money-girdle." "The symbolic reasons underlying this command would, in both cases, be probably the same: to avoid even the appearance of being engaged on other business, when the whole being should be absorbed in the service of the Lord" (Edersheim, I:643).

Neither were they to take two tunics (i.e., coats). An extra tunic might be a bit bulky to carry, but if you needed to sleep outside, it would sure come in handy. Jesus urges them to trust in God's provision especially through God's people, for the worker is worthy of his wage (cf. 1 Cor 9:14; 1 Tim 5:17-18). And yet they were to offer their services without charge. In other words, they weren't expected to pay their own way for this tour, but neither were they to make a profit from it (1 Pet 5:2).

Mt 10:11-16 *with*
Mk 6:11, Lk 9:5

[11]"Whatever town or village you enter, search for some worthy person there and stay at his house until you leave. [12]As you enter the home, give it your greeting. [13]If the home is deserving, let your peace rest on it; if it is not, let your peace return to you. [14]If anyone will not welcome you or listen to your words, shake the dust off your feet when you leave that home or town {as a testimony against them.[MK,LK} [15]I tell you the truth, it will be more bearable for Sodom and Gomorrah on the day of judgment than for that town. [16]I am sending you out like sheep among wolves [cf. Lk 10:3]. Therefore be as shrewd as snakes and as innocent as doves."

Jesus discourages his disciples from moving around from house to house. Why? Well, they are going to be quite popular. Lots of people will ask them to stay at their place. The problem is that such movement eats up a lot of valuable time and creates unhealthy competition between the citizens of each town. And it may tempt the Apostles themselves to look for better accommodations instead of devoting themselves fully to the task of preaching.

When they enter a home they are to give it a greeting, which serves as a blessing. You see, the Hebrew word for peace (vv. 12-13) is more than a "hello." It is a wish for that person's "wholeness" physically, socially, and spiritually. Thus, it is tantamount to the Apostolic prayer on behalf of that home. This is a powerful blessing (Mt 18:18).

If they are rejected, rather than blessing the village, they shake the dust from their feet. Jews often shook the dust off their sandals as they reentered the Holy Land from Gentile territory. This idiomatic action for the Hebrews meant: "Even the dust you walk on is defiling and I rid myself of its uncleanness!" (cf. Acts 13:51, 18:6). This is more than a temper tantrum. It is a warning that rejection of God's program in Jesus will put you in the same boat with the Gentiles. This Apostolic rejection held sway with God. These twelve actually have the authority to curse a city. It is much like what we've read in Matthew 11:20-30 and 12:39-42. Because of their greater benefit, Galilee will be judged more harshly than even Sodom and Gomorrah.

Not everyone will welcome them with open arms. So they had better be careful. Jesus' warning (v. 16) contains four similes: sheep, wolves, snakes, and doves. The comparison of snakes and doves is stated — shrewdness and innocence. These two characteristics are often antithetical but are never mutually exclusive. Unfortunately, Christians are all too often as innocent as serpents and as shrewd as doves. The comparison of sheep and wolves,[160] although unstated is obvious — weakness and savagery. Kingdom citizens, who are often poor and powerless (1 Cor 1:26-28), live in a savage world. Our chances of survival in such an environment are pretty slim. Unless, of course, we are standing next to the Shepherd.

Mt 10:17-20

[17]"Be on your guard against men; they will hand you over to the local councils and flog you in their synagogues [cf. Mk 13:9-13; Mt 24:9-14; Lk 21:12-19]. [18]On my account you will be brought before governors and kings as witnesses to them and to the Gentiles. [19]But when they arrest you, do not worry about what to say or how to say it. At that time you will be given what to say, [20]for it will not be you speaking, but the Spirit of your Father speaking through you [cf. Lk 12:11-12; Jn 14:26]."

Verses 17-23 obviously refer to the later travels of the Twelve, since none of this stuff happened on the first journey. Perhaps Jesus spoke these words prophetically, looking for a future fulfillment. But more

---

[160]Edersheim notes that the imagery of "Sheep amid Wolves" is a "phrase which the Midrash applies to the position of Israel amidst a hostile world, adding: How great is that Shepherd Who delivers them, and vanquishes the wolves! Similarly, the admonition to 'be wise as serpents and harmless as doves' is reproduced in the Midrash, where Israel is described as harmless as the dove towards God, and wise as serpents toward the hostile Gentile nations" (I:645).

likely, Matthew compiled a number of Jesus' "travel talk" statements into one section. Much of this material is also found in the Olivet Discourse as the cross-references indicate. The fulfillment of these promises can be chronicled through the book of Acts.

The promise of vv. 19-20, while it has specific reference to the Apostles, also seems to have application to all kingdom citizens who witness for Jesus. Although a Christian may not be able to claim the promise with absolute certainty, the principle is consistent, that when we step out in faith to proclaim Jesus, the Holy Spirit steps in and speaks through us.

Mt 10:21-23

21"Brother will betray brother to death, and a father his child; children will rebel against their parents and have them put to death. 22All men will hate you because of me, but he who stands firm to the end will be saved. 23When you are persecuted in one place, flee to another. I tell you the truth, you will not finish going through the cities of Israel before the Son of Man comes."

In the Oriental mind, family, religion and politics are inseparable. Life is viewed as holistic rather than compartmentalized as it often is in the West. Consequently, betrayal in one area caused a schism in all areas. Thus, when a Jew apostatized in the faith, the family held a funeral for that individual, considering him as dead. It is not hard to see, then, why Jesus predicts such division in the family over following him.

This talk about standing firm until the end is familiar language in the NT (Mt 10:22; 24:13; Mk 13:13; 1 Cor 1:8; Heb 3:14; Rev 2:26). Clearly, salvation is not for those who begin the race but for those who cross the finish line. For some, the finish line ends in the premature death of martyrdom. For others it will be the end of their life. And for one generation it will be the glorious coming of our Lord Jesus Christ.

Yet standing firm does not mean getting trounced needlessly. Jesus tells the Twelve to flee from persecution. They're not cowards, but neither should they be fools. There is a time to stand and fight (Acts 8:1; 16:39-40; 21:13) as well as a time for flight (Acts 8:1; 13:51; 14:6, 20). There is also a time to cover as much ground as possible. Verse 23 indicates such a time. Jesus essentially says, "Don't waste time with hard hearts and closed ears. Rather, move on to more fertile soil!"

The question is, "When is the coming of the Son of Man?" (v. 23). (1) He could be speaking of the present ministry. However, this does not fit the context well. Families, by and large, are not suffering such severe division, nor are the Apostles suffering martyrdom. (2) He may be speaking of the end of time — the Second Coming of Christ. However, all of Palestine has been touched with the message of the gospel many times over in the last 2,000 years. Thus, it could hardly be said that the villages of Palestine will not be permeated with the gospel before Jesus returns. (3) He may be speaking figuratively of his coming in judgment in A.D. 70 when Jerusalem will be destroyed. This fits well both the present context as well as the parallel passages of Matthew 24 (cf. Mk 13:9-13; Dan 7:13; Jn 11:48). Thus we understand Jesus to say, "You will not finish evangelizing Palestine before it is ravaged by the Roman armies and Jerusalem itself is destroyed." How much of this the disciples understand is questionable.[161]

Mt 10:24-25
Cf. Lk 6:40,
Jn 13:16

[24]"A student is not above his teacher, nor a servant above his master. [25]It is enough for the student to be like his teacher, and the servant like his master. If the head of the house has been called Beelzebub,[a] how much more the members of his household!"

[a]25 Greek *Beezeboul* or *Beelzeboul*

We should not be overly literal with verse 24. There are times, rare though they may be, when a student excels beyond his teacher (cf. Jn 14:12). But that is not the point of this proverb. It is used in two other contexts. In Luke 6:39-40 Jesus asks, "Can a blind man lead a blind man?" Both will be equally misled. Again in John 13:16, after Jesus washes the Apostles' feet, he reminds them that he is the teacher, and they, as students are obligated to act like their teacher. In both instances the point of the proverb is clear: As goes the teacher, so goes the student. Here, it means the same thing in the context of persecution. If Jesus was persecuted, so his followers will be also. As they accused Jesus of serving Beelzebub (cf. 9:34; 12:24), so also will they accuse his disciples.

Mt 10:26-31 *with*
Lk 12:3

[26]"So do not be afraid of them. There is nothing concealed that will not be disclosed, or hidden that will not be made known. [27]What I tell you in the dark, speak in the daylight; what is whispered in your ear {in the inner rooms[LK]}, proclaim from the roofs. [28]Do not be afraid of those who kill the body but cannot kill the soul. Rather, be afraid of the One who can destroy both soul and body in hell. [29]Are not two sparrows sold for a penny[a]? Yet not one of them will fall to the ground apart from the will of your Father. [30]And even the very hairs of your head are all numbered. [31]So don't be afraid; you are worth more than many sparrows."

[a]29 Greek *an assarion*

---

[161]C.H. Giblin offers a different explanation. He suggests that we view the text paradigmatically rather than chronologically. In other words, v. 23 doesn't predict what would happen with the apostles but describes what happens whenever Christians evangelize new communities. (1) He interprets the anarthrous "Gentiles" and "Samaritans" (v. 5) as metaphors rather than literal identifications. (2) "You will not finish," he applies to the task of evangelism, not necessarily geographic expansion. (3) He applies typological hermeneutic. The bottom line is this: What we start with preaching, Jesus ends with judgment (either reward or requisition). He finishes our evangelistic work wherever we carry it out. Cf. "Theolgical Perspective and Matthew 10:23b," *TS* 29 (1968): 637-661.

This section makes three points. First, in light of the coming onslaught, the disciples will be intimidated when speaking out for Jesus. Jesus encourages them to speak out boldly in the face of opposition since the truth is destined to prevail eventually.

Second, don't fear the coming persecution. It can only touch your body, not your soul. Some read v. 28 as if it refers to Satan. It does not; it cannot. Satan cannot throw anyone into hell. He simply doesn't have the authority (or the keys, Rev 20:3)! No, we fear God. He alone has such power and authority.

Third, we shouldn't fear persecution or hell, because our loving Father sees, knows, and cares for us. Yes, we will experience persecution and troubled times. Although we may *feel* that God has forgotten us, he hasn't! Each little sparrow should remind us of God's unswerving attention to the minute details of our lives. We may not understand the perplexing problem of evil and suffering, but we know that we count with God who counts even the immeasurable hairs on our head.[162] Thus, our suffering has not escaped his watchful eye.

Mt 10:32-33 *with*
Lk 12:9

[32]"Whoever acknowledges me before men, I will also acknowledge him before my Father in heaven. [33]But whoever disowns me before men, I will disown him before my Father in heaven {the angels of God.[LK]}"

Here is yet another reason to stand fast in times of trouble. We might call it the "Law of Fair-Play." What we do for Jesus on earth, he will do for us in heavenly realms. The word "acknowledge" (*homologeō*) implies a verbal confession. Thus, while lifestyle evangelism is appropriate, it is not sufficient. We must, at some point confess Jesus with our mouths (Rom 10:9-10, Heb 3:1; 13:15). Furthermore, this needs to be done in the hearing of the world, not the church (cf. v. 27).

Mt 10:34-36 *with*
Lk 12:51-52

[34]"Do not suppose that I have come to bring peace to the earth. I did not come to bring peace, but a sword {division. [52]From now on there will be five in one family divided against each other, three against two and two against three[LK]}. [35]For I have come to turn

"'a man against his father,
    a daughter against her mother,
  a daughter-in-law against her mother-in-law —
[36]   a man's enemies will be the members of his own household.'[a]"

[a]*36* Micah 7:6

What a paradox! The Prince of Peace (Isa 9:6), who was gentle and humble (Mt 11:29), who would not even cry out on his own behalf (Isa

---

[162]D.C. Allison, "The Hairs of your Head are All Numbered," *ExpT* 101 (1990): 334-336.

53:7), will be the cause of great division (cf. Mt 10:21). Yet Jesus' word in v. 35, "Turn . . . against" (*dichazō*), is even stronger than our translations are able to tell. It suggests "inciting to revolt" or "to sow discord." Jesus' driving passion is for peace, but not at the expense of truth and discipleship.

Mt 10:37-39 *with*
Lk 9:23
Cf. Lk 14:25-27;
17:33; Jn 12:25;
also Mt 16:24-25;
Mk 8:24-35

[37]"Anyone who loves his father or mother more than me is not worthy of me; anyone who loves his son or daughter more than me is not worthy of me; [38]and anyone who does not take his cross {daily[LK]} and follow me is not worthy of me. [39]Whoever finds his life will lose it, and whoever loses his life for my sake will find it."

Salvation can never be earned . . . but it is NOT free. Jesus expects that we submit everything to him. Whatever stands in the way of our full-fledged following of Jesus, he demands that we relinquish whether it is family[163] (v. 37); money (Mt 19:21); position (Mt 19:30); power (Mt 20:27); etc.

In short, Jesus asks us to give up claim to our lives (vv. 38-39). That's clear in Jesus' "cross talk."[164] In the Roman culture, no one would ever be so crass as to turn a cross into a trinket to be worn around your neck or hung from the mirror of your car. It was an instrument of excruciating torture and death. Everyone who picked up a cross embarked on a one-way journey from which he would never return.[165] We notice too, that crucifixion was the Roman mode of execution, not the Jewish mode (which would have been stoning). Thus Jesus' words are prophetic and personal.[166]

Many who have followed Christ have marched into martyrdom. Others, however, have been called to a more difficult task than dying for him, that is, living for him. Although these two consequences are vastly different, the commitment to Christ and resignation from the world is singular.

The paradox of verse 39 is a frequent choral refrain in the Gospels. In fact, it is the most frequently quoted saying of Jesus. Truly, it is the

---

[163]Blomberg appropriately observes that this text must be balanced with such passages as Eph 6:1-4 and 1 Tim 5:8. "Devotion to family is a cardinal Christian duty but must never become absolute to the extent that devotion to God is compromised" (p. 181).

[164]D.R. Fletcher, "Condemned to Die," *Int* 18 (1964): 156-164. Based on Deut 21:22-23, "Anyone who is hung on a tree is under God's curse," Jesus' words would produce horror in his listeners.

[165]Every crucified criminal was forced to carry the patibulum (the cross beam) to the site of execution (Plutarch, *De Sera Num. Vind.* 9.554B).

[166]J.G. Griffiths, "The Disciple's Cross," *NTS* 16 (1970): 358-364, notes that besides this saying, all other references in the NT to taking up the cross relate to Jesus' own passion event. Therefore, it must be read in light of Jesus' life and our imitation of him.

lifeblood of our commitment to Christ; the promise, not only of a better future, but the reality of a better life today. It is only after a seed is buried in the ground that it springs to life. It is only after a caterpillar entombs itself in a cocoon that it can fly. And it is only after a Christian carries a cross that he finds the fullness of life (Jn 10:10).

Mt 10:40-42
Cf. Jn 13:20;
Lk 10:16; Mk 9:41

⁴⁰"He who receives you receives me, and he who receives me receives the one who sent me. ⁴¹Anyone who receives a prophet because he is a prophet will receive a prophet's reward, and anyone who receives a righteous man because he is a righteous man will receive a righteous man's reward. ⁴²And if anyone gives even a cup of cold water to one of these little ones because he is my disciple, I tell you the truth, he will certainly not lose his reward."

The idea here is simple. It is what Jesus repeats in Matthew 25:40, "Whatever you did for one of the least of these brothers of mine, you did for me." Whether it is for the Apostles, or the broader category of prophets, or broader still, the "little ones," the principle stands true: What you do for Jesus' people, he takes personally.

Another consideration is that when a prophet is blessed, the home housing the prophet is blessed as well. Those homes that supported the prophets and apostles would therefore receive God's blessing (cf. 2 Kgs 4). This may also be true of Christian workers today.

**§ 70c
The Success of
the Twelve**
(Mt 11:1;
Mk 6:12-13;
Lk 9:6)

[MK 6:]¹²They went out and preached that people should repent. ¹³They drove out many demons and anointed many sick people with oil and healed them.

After the sermon, the Twelve go out in pairs and accomplish the tasks Jesus set before them. Mark mentions the mode by which the sick were healed — anointing with oil. This is interesting in light of James 5:14.

**§ 71a
Herod Antipas'
Mistaken View
of Jesus**
(Mt 14:1-2;
Mk 6:14-16;
Lk 9:7-9)

Just before the tour of the Twelve, Jesus went to his hometown of Nazareth for the last time (§ 69). We read about their mistaken ideas of Jesus. Now we will read of Herod's.

{¹At that time^MT} [MK 6:]¹⁴King Herod {the tetrarch^MT,LK}, heard about this, for Jesus' name had become well known. {He was perplexed because^LK} Some were saying^a {he said to his attendants^MT}, "John the Baptist has been raised from the dead, and that is why miraculous powers are at work in him."
¹⁵Others said, "He is Elijah."
And still others claimed, "He is a prophet, like one of the prophets of long ago."
¹⁶But when Herod heard this, he said, "John, the man I beheaded, has been raised from the dead!" {And he tried to see him.^LK}

ª14 Some early manuscripts *He was saying*

The Jewish populace, following the Pharisees, believed in resurrection. But their theology was mixed with a good bit of superstition. For example, they believed that the spirit of a dead person could come back in another person (cf. Josephus, *Wars* 1.599). In other words, the spirit of the deceased would fill and empower a living person. That's how many accounted for Jesus' miraculous power. They assumed that the spirit of some great prophet such as Elijah, Jeremiah or John the Baptist (cf. Mt 16:14), had come upon him. Herod followed this popular superstition.

The Herod family, as a whole, was characterized by masterful political maneuvers, turbulent family relations, sexual scandal — especially through incest and divorce, and adoption of the Jewish religion (at least when it was convenient for their purposes). While the Herods adopted the politics of the Sadducees, they got their faith from the Pharisees, both for pragmatic reasons — it increased their realm of influence.

Herod the Tetrarch, also called "King," was the son of Herod the Great through his Samaritan wife Malthace. Like the other Herods, he has enough conscience to plague him with guilt for his misdeeds, but not enough to overcome his insatiable appetite for political power. He is in the uncomfortable position of a corrupt politician who dabbles in religion. His guilt causes him to ponder who this Jesus is. Yet he is not ready to become a disciple.

§ 71b
Imprisonment
and Execution
of John the
Baptist
(Mt 14:3-12;
Mk 6:17-29 [cf.
Lk 3:19-20])[167]

[MK 6:]17For Herod himself had given orders to have John arrested, and he had him bound and put in prison. He did this because of Herodias, his brother Philip's wife, whom he had married. 18For John had been saying to Herod, "It is not lawful for you to have your brother's wife." {Herod had been reproved for all the evil things that he had done.LK} 19So Herodias nursed a grudge against John and wanted to kill him. But she was not able to, 20because Herod feared John and protected him, knowing him to be a righteous and holy man. When Herod heard John, he was greatly puzzleda; yet he liked to listen to him.

[MT 14:]5Herod wanted to kill John, but he was afraid of the people, because they considered him a prophet.

a[Mk 6:]20 Some early manuscripts *he did many things*

John the Baptist was never accused of being soft-spoken (cf. Isa 40:3-5; Mt 3:7-12). He even railed against Herod's illegal and illicit marriage, as well as his other improprieties (Lk 3:19-20). The problem is described by Josephus (*Ant.*, 18.109-115). Herod's first wife was the daughter of Aretas, the king of Arabia. After they had been married for a

---

[167]The events in this section are kind of a "flashback" which help explain Herod's present misconception of Jesus.

number of years, he took a trip to Rome. While there, he stayed with his half-brother, Philip. Herod fell in love with Philip's wife, Herodias, and repaid his brother's hospitality by convincing Herodias to divorce Philip and marry him. When he got back home, Aretas' daughter caught wind of the scheme. Before Herod knew he was caught, she convinced him to let her take a little trip to Machaerus, which bordered her father's territory. From there she escaped to her father. Aretas was so angry that he declared war on Herod and eventually destroyed his army. He would have completely destroyed Herod had it not been for the intervention of the Roman General, Vitellius.

This marriage was illegal for several reasons. For one thing, Herod's first wife was still alive. In addition, Herodias belonged to Herod's brother (cf. Lev 18:16). Besides all that, Herodias was his half-niece, thus the relationship was incestuous for both brothers. John would go nuts with this!

Josephus informs us of a second reason that Herod had John arrested. As John's popularity grew, so did the unrest of the populace. This is the stuff of which rebellions are made. Thus, Herod, fearing a popular revolt, took out the key player of the opposition. Another consideration is that many of the people from Herod Philip's tetrarchy in Traconitis went over to fight with Aretas against Herod Antipas. The bulk of John's preaching was in North Judea and Perea which are dangerously close to Traconitis. Lest these people follow the lead of their northern countrymen, Herod takes out this rabble rouser.

There is possibly a third reason that Herod had John arrested. Typically, the Herods aligned themselves with the Sadducees who controlled the temple precincts. But the Pharisees continued to rise in popularity. This move to arrest John would be well received among the Pharisees who rejected John (Lk 7:30). Thus, it is an opportunity to make some very important friends.

Not only is Herod a bit miffed at John, so is Herodias. And this woman scorned is not to be taken lightly. She tries to persuade Herod to kill him, but two things stand in the way. First, Herod knows that John is a righteous man. Although his conscience is weak, it is at least enough to restrain him from whimsically killing a righteous man. Herod desires to be a just ruler. Unfortunately, his desire for justice is overwhelmed by his desire for power. Second, the populace believes John to be a prophet. They are already up in arms over John's arrest. Herod must now walk on eggshells lest he push the public over the edge into open rebellion. On the one hand, he wants to rid himself of this problem; on the other hand, he wants to be just. On the one hand, he likes to listen to John; on the other, John is a pest about his personal life. Mark thus uses the word "perplexed" to describe Herod's response to John.

According to Josephus (*Ant.* 18.119), John was held at Machaerus, a 2360-foot mountain fortress, second in strength only to Jerusalem. It was located on the northeastern shore of the Dead Sea. Josephus also says that this was the fortress to which Aretas' daughter fled when she discovered Herod's scheme with Herodias. At that time it was under Aretas' control (*Ant.* 18.112). It seems unlikely that both of these designations could be correct unless the fortress suddenly changed hands from Aretas to Herod during their little scuffle or unless Aretas did not indeed control the fortress but merely utilized it with Herod's permission while they were on friendly terms.

It is important to note that Mark devotes three verses to John's ministry but thirteen to his death. Thus, Mark seems to suggest that as John's ministry is the precursor for Jesus' ministry so also John's death was predictive of Jesus'.

Mk 6:21-25   ²¹Finally the opportune time came. On his birthday Herod gave a banquet for his high officials and military commanders and the leading men of Galilee. ²²When the daughter of Herodias came in and danced, she pleased Herod and his dinner guests.

The king said to the girl, "Ask me for anything you want, and I'll give it to you." ²³And he promised her with an oath, "Whatever you ask I will give you, up to half my kingdom."

²⁴She went out and said to her mother, "What shall I ask for?"

"The head of John the Baptist," she answered.

²⁵At once the girl hurried in to the king with the request: "I want you to give me right now the head of John the Baptist on a platter."

It has been several weeks since John's disciples returned to him from Jesus (§ 57; Mt 11:2-19; Lk 7:18-35). Herod throws himself a birthday party.[168] Part of the featured entertainment is his stepdaughter, Salome. She dances for this bunch of high-class drunks.[169] The text doesn't say that it was a sensuous dance, but the Oriental culture would suggest it. Besides, Herod doesn't offer her half of his kingdom just for good choreography. What makes this disgusting is that Salome is his stepdaughter. Furthermore, she is probably not much more than about twelve years

---

[168]Edersheim notes that this may not have been Herod's birthday, but that *genesia* may refer to Herod's accession to the Tetrarchy.

[169]Literally translated these three groups of people from verse 21 might read: (1) Magistrates — political rulers; (2) Chiliarchs — military leaders of 1,000 men each; (3) Premier (first) men of Galilee — the moguls, whether they be in business, religion, politics, etc.

old. The word Mark uses in v. 22, "girl" (*korasion*), was used in Matthew 9:24 in reference to Jairus' twelve-year-old daughter. By giving her up to half the kingdom, Herod would make her second in command only to him. This offer shows proverbial generosity but we probably should not take it too literally.

Why would a little girl do such a thing? Verse 24 hints that her mother put her up to it. As vile as that is, such was the nature of the Herod family. Their corruption is worsened by their shrewdness. Herodias hurries Salome on her way with this urgent request (v. 25): "Get the deed done before Herod sobers up."

Mk 6:26-29 *with*
Mt 14:12

²⁶The king was greatly distressed, but because of his oaths and his dinner guests, he did not want to refuse her. ²⁷So he immediately sent an executioner with orders to bring John's head. The man went, beheaded John in the prison, ²⁸and brought back his head on a platter. He presented it to the girl, and she gave it to her mother. ²⁹On hearing of this, John's disciples came and took his body and laid it in a tomb. {Then they went and told Jesus.ᴹᵀ}

Once again Herod's craving for political popularity vanquished his conscience. His greatest weakness was his fear of being considered weak. The scene is gruesome enough — John's head laying there on a silver platter. But one tradition says that Herodias took it into her bedroom, pulled out John's tongue and stuck a pin through it. So ends the life of the forerunner of Christ.

Herodias brought Herod's demise. First, the murder of John the Baptist plagued Herod personally and appalled the public. His conscience, mingled with Jewish superstition, made him think that Jesus was John come back to haunt him.[170] And of course, the people were incensed about the murder of the just man, John. Second, his marriage to Herodias was at the cost of divorce from his first wife, the daughter of Aretas, king of Arabia. As mentioned earlier, Aretas was so angry with Herod that he attacked him and destroyed his army. Herod himself was only saved by the intervention of the Roman legion under Vitellius. The people saw this as God's judgment for the murder of John (Josephus, *Ant.* 18.119). This war put Herod on the outs with Rome. Finally, Herodias, ambitious for power, cajoled Herod to go to Rome to seek greater political favor. When he did so, he was stripped of his dominion and banished to Lyons in Gaul. Herodias refused the fortunes offered to her by the emperor and chose to go to Gaul with her husband (Josephus, *Ant.* 18.254). That is the only redeeming incident of her biography.

---

[170]The word "greatly distressed" (*perilypos*, v. 26), is used to describe Jesus' agony in the garden (Mk 14:34).

With nowhere else to turn, John's disciples travel eighty to ninety miles to Jesus and deliver this sad report. Why have they held on to John so long? He told them to go to Jesus. But only now, after his death, do they let go of their beloved leader and find Jesus.

PART SEVEN
BREAKING AWAY FROM GALILEE
(Third Year of Ministry)

---

§ 72a,b
Aborted Attempt at R & R
(Mt 14:13-14;
Mk 6:30-34;
Lk 9:10-11;
Jn 6:1-3)

This is the only event prior to the last week of Jesus' life that is recorded in all four Gospels. It is the peak of Jesus' popularity. His rating in the polls will drop from here as he begins to unveil his true identity.

There are a number of elements in this feeding that have been taken as symbolic. For instance, when Jesus says to eat his flesh and drink his blood, many read into that the Lord's Supper (cf. Mt 26:20-29; Jn 6:35-59). Others see the twelve baskets as symbols of the twelve tribes/Apostles or the whole meal as a picture of the Messianic banquet. And the bread Jesus offers in a remote place is like the manna that God provided in the wilderness (cf. Jn 6:30-33).[1] The fish became one of the dominant symbols of early Christian art.[2]

No matter what we take as symbolic, Jesus is the centerpiece. Mark highlights his compassion (Mk 6:34). John highlights his power over the inanimate (cf. Jn 2:1-11) and his provision for our spiritual needs (Jn 6:26-59). And Matthew contrasts the sinfulness of Herod's drunken banquet (Mt 14:3-12) with the beauty of Jesus' simple feeding of the peasant population. Certainly the people in attendance took this to be a clear demonstration that Jesus was the Messiah (Jn 6:15; cf. 1 Kgs 17:9-16; 2 Kgs 4:42-44).

Mk 6:30-31

[30]The Apostles gathered around Jesus and reported to him all they had done and taught. [31]Then, because so many people were coming and going that they did not even have a chance to eat, he said to them, "Come with me by yourselves to a quiet place and get some rest."

The Apostles return from their first "solo flight." It had been fabulously successful. We can almost hear their excitement as they gather

---

[1]B.E. Thiering, "'Breaking of Bread' and 'Harvest" in Mark's Gospel, *NovT* 12 (1970): 1-12, is a classic example of speculative numerology applied to the feeding of the five thousand.

[2]See R. Hiers' excellent summary: "The Bread and Fish Eucharist in the Gospels and Early Christian Art," *PRS* 3 (1970): 20-47.

around the Master and recite their victories — healings, crowds, repentance, casting out demons, etc. Considering the nature of these fellows, we don't doubt for a minute that they try to top each other's stories. Jesus listens with enthusiasm and patience.

At the same time, however (in light of the previous passage), Jesus is also met by a delegation of John's disciples, who inform him of the sad news of John's death. Jesus surely feels this loss deeply and personally. John has been his relative, forerunner and friend. He was the greatest man born of woman and the last OT prophet. This puts Jesus in the difficult position of balancing opposite emotions: Joy for his Apostles and indignant sorrow over the murder of John by Herod.

It is indeed a time for retreat. Both Jesus and his Twelve need to reflect on recent events and consider where this movement is now heading. But the crowds just keep coming, so much so that Jesus can't even stop to eat. Some come because of Jesus' popularity, some because of the recent expedition of the Twelve, some in anger over John's murder. This is the peak of Jesus' popularity. The crowds are wild with expectation.

They need to find a quiet place, not only for some R. & R., but to escape the political precinct of Herod Antipas and thus avert the danger of either arrest or uprising. So they jump in the boat and cross the Sea of Galilee to the small town of Bethsaida (lit. "House of fish"), in the jurisdiction of Herod Philip. This can't be the same Bethsaida which was home to Philip, Andrew and Peter (Jn 1:44). It was common in those days to have several towns by the same name. After the miracle, they head back to Bethsaida (Mk 6:45). Besides, the home of Philip, Andrew, and Peter was not a "solitary place" nor a good getaway for Jesus and his crew.

Mk 6:32-34 *with*
Lk 9:10-11,
Jn 6:1-3

³²So they went away by themselves in a boat {to the far shore^JN} to a solitary place {to a town called Bethsaida.^LK} ³³But many who saw them leaving recognized them and ran on foot from all the towns and got there ahead of them {because they saw the miraculous signs he had performed on the sick^JN} ³⁴When Jesus landed and saw a large crowd, {he welcomed them and^LK} he had compassion on them, because they were like sheep without a shepherd. So he {went up on a mountainside and sat down with his disciples[, and]^JN} began teaching them many things {about the kingdom of God, and healed those who needed healing^LK}.

When the Apostolic band gets into the boat, the crowds watch their sail to see what direction they are headed. They run around the lake and some of them even beat Jesus to the other side.³ Jesus, so unlike us, is

---

³If we picture some of the crowd beating Jesus to the other side of the lake, and others straggling behind in what must have been a string of people over a mile long, we can solve the apparent discrepancy between Mk 6:33 and Jn 6:5 as to who arrived first.

moved by people's needs more than his own hunger and fatigue. He is moved by their ignorance and their need of *teaching*. He is moved by their sicknesses and their need of *healing*. He is moved by their hunger and their need of *feeding*. He is moved by their eagerness to follow him and their need of a Messiah. After two millennia, there is hardly a better model of ministry. We are indeed helpers of shepherdless sheep (cf. Mt 9:36, Num 27:17, Ezek 34:5, 23, 25.

About two miles north of where the Jordan enters the Sea of Galilee is a convenient place to cross the river. About a mile further, near Bethsaida Julias, is a wide, grassy plain. To the north of that plain is a hill which Jesus likely climbed to accommodate the crowds. It was quite a spectacle, 5,000 men [*andres*] plus women and children. Their numbers could easily have swelled to over 15,000.

For comments on "Sheep without a Shepherd" see § 70a.

§ 72c
Feeding the
5,000
(Mt 14:15-21;
Mk 6:35-44;
Lk 9:12-17;
Jn 6:4-13)

[JN 6:]4The Jewish Passover Feast was near.

5When Jesus looked up and saw a great crowd coming toward him, he said to Philip, "Where shall we buy bread for these people to eat?" 6He asked this only to test him, for he already had in mind what he was going to do.

7Philip answered him, "Eight months' wages[a] would not buy enough bread for each one to have a bite!"

a 7 Greek *two hundred denarii*

This Passover, likely April, A.D. 29, marks the transition between Jesus' second and third year of ministry. The Passover is more than a chronological marker. It helps explain the presence of such a large crowd, especially those who would begin their annual migration to Jerusalem. It also explains their fervor to proclaim Jesus King. Jewish religious nationalism surged during this feast. As this excited band makes its way around the lake, surely they collect an entourage from each of the towns and villages they pass. By the time the parade reaches Jesus' landing sight, it is enormous. As Jesus looks up, he sees this crowd closing in on him (cf. Jn 4:25).

Why Philip? We don't know. Perhaps Jesus has a particular lesson to teach him (cf. Jn 14:8-9); perhaps he is just the closest. Philip's precise answer indicates that he has calculated the cost. As Jesus continues to teach and heal, Philip will have ample time not only to consider his answer but to ponder the question. Obviously Jesus is not interested in Philip's answer but in his response.

Mk 6:35-38 *with*
Lk 9:12

35By this time it was late in the day, so his disciples {the TwelveLK} came to him. "This is a remote place," they said, "and it's already very late. 36Send the people away so they can go to the surrounding countryside and villages {and find food and lodging^{LK}} and buy themselves something to eat."

[37]But he answered, "You give them something to eat."

They said to him, "That would take eight months of a man's wages[a]! Are we to go and spend that much on bread and give it to them to eat?"

[38]"How many loaves do you have?" he asked. "Go and see."

When they found out, they said, "Five — and two fish."

[a]37 Greek *take two hundred denarii*

Late in the day probably indicated three to five o'clock in the afternoon.[4] Since they are in a remote place, the people will need sufficient time to get to the nearest town(s), which might be several miles away, to find a "bed and breakfast." The Apostles have learned, in some degree, to care for people as Jesus has. No doubt they are also moved by the growling of their own stomachs. Remember, they have not yet had a chance to eat.

When Jesus tells the Twelve to feed the crowd, we can just sense Iscariot getting nervous. If indeed they had that much money, which is doubtful, that would have nearly drained their reserves. That makes any accountant nervous, especially one in the habit of obfuscating funds.

Jesus sends them to scour the crowds to see what is on hand. They come back empty handed . . . almost. They commandeer a little boy's lunch: five little loaves and two small fish.[5] The loaves are not like ours. They are small, flat and round (perhaps not more than four inches in diameter). They are barley loaves, the food of the poor, but not necessarily poor food. The fish are probably pickled and used as relish for his bread, not the main part of his meal. The closest thing we have would be canned sardines. It was just enough to satisfy a little boy, but pretty pathetic in the shadow of this crowd.

Jn 6:8-11 *with*
Mt 14:18-19,
Mk 6:41, Lk 9:16

[8]Another of his disciples, Andrew, Simon Peter's brother, spoke up, [9]"Here is a boy with five small barley loaves and two small fish, but how far will they go among so many {unless we go and buy food for all this crowd^{LK}}?"

[10]Jesus said, "{Bring them here to me.^{MT}} Have the people sit down." There was plenty of grass in that place, and the men sat down {in groups of hundreds and fifties^{MK}}, about five thousand of them. [11]Jesus then took the {five^{MT,MK,LK}} loaves {and looking up to heaven, He^{MT,MK,LK}}, gave thanks {and broke the

---

[4]According to Edersheim, the Jews designated the first evening as the descent of the sun (about three to six); the second evening as the appearance of the first star, about sundown, to the appearance of the third star (about six to eight). The night would then constitute the beginning of the next day.

[5]The Synoptics use the normal word for fish [*ichthys*]. John, however uses the odd word [*opsarion*], indicating the small "relish" fish, either dried or pickled which was normally eaten with bread.

loaves,^{MT,MK,LK}} and distributed to those who were seated as much as they wanted. He did the same with the {two^{MT,MK,LK}} fish.

Three times John mentions Andrew bringing someone to Jesus: (1) Peter (1:40-41); (2) this boy (6:8-9); and (3) some Greeks (12:22). This was clearly his forte. We are impressed with the humility of a man who was one of the first two disciples, yet (seemingly willingly) takes a back-seat to his brother, Simon Peter. He was almost in the inner circle, but not quite, save Mark 13:3 during the Olivet Discourse. Andrew brings the boy with his meager meal; but still assumes that they are going to take a trip to the supermarket.

The spring grasses that accompany Passover make a welcome carpet for this company. They divide into groups of fifties and hundreds which make for easy calculation and distribution. Mark uses an interesting word to describe these groups (6:40), [*prasiai*] which literally means "garden plots." All those people laying back[6] on the grassy plain below where Jesus stood must have looked like a flower garden of God.

Jesus looks into heaven and gives thanks prior to the meal, which is the typical practice of the Jewish head of the house. He may even have recited a typical prayer of thanksgiving such as this one: "Blessed art Thou, O Lord our God, King of the Universe, who brings forth bread from the earth" (*m. Ber.* 6:1).

It is curious to note that none of the four Gospel writers even give a hint as to how this miracle took place. It is simply assumed that Jesus had regenerative powers (perhaps reminiscent of Elijah, 2 Kgs 4:42-44). As he was able to transform the water to wine in Cana, so now he reproduces *ex nihilo* barley loaves and "fishettes." Jesus has, at other times, demonstrated power over the inanimate — miraculous catch of fish (Lk 5:5-10) and the calming of the sea (Lk 8:24). But there is a qualitative difference here in his creative ability (cf. Jn 1:1-4; Col 1:16-17).

Jn 6:12-13

¹²When they had all had enough to eat, he said to his disciples, "Gather the pieces that are left over. Let nothing be wasted." ¹³So they gathered them and filled twelve baskets with the pieces of the five barley loaves left over by those who had eaten.

Mt 14:21

²¹The number of those who ate was about five thousand men, besides women and children.

Jesus was economical, not as part of his mission but as part of his nature. He never preached environmentalism or animal rights, but

---

[6][*Anepesan*] literally means to fall back. It certainly describes well the Jewish practice of reclining to eat.

simply lived a theology of man as the steward of God's creation. He viewed man as the ruler and caretaker of the earth. It was available for man to use, but not to exploit.

These sturdy wicker baskets [*kophinos*] were "a distinctively Jewish basket for carrying kosher food" (Blomberg, p. 233). The number twelve may be symbolic of the twelve tribes or even the twelve Apostles.

§ 73
Unsuccessful
Attempt to
Make Jesus
King
(Mt 14:22-23;
Mk 6:45-46;
Jn 6:14-15)

[JN 6:]14After the people saw the miraculous sign that Jesus did, they began to say, "Surely this is the Prophet who is to come into the world."

[MT 14:]22Immediately Jesus made the disciples get into the boat and go on ahead of him to the other side {to Bethsaida^MK} {Capernaum^JN}, while he dismissed the crowd.

[JN 6:]15Jesus, knowing that they intended to come and make him king by force, withdrew again to a mountain by himself {to pray^MT,MK}.

The people are convinced that Jesus is the Messiah (The Prophet, cf. Deut 18:15-18; Jn 1:21). He is finally acting like the Messiah they wanted.[7] This brash crowd, driven by the Messianic expectations of the day, fanned into flames by the recent murder of John the Baptist, are ready to inaugurate Jesus whether he wants it or not! Likely, they plan on escorting him to Jerusalem with their declaration of independence, accompanied by twelve baskets of leftovers and a train of people he has healed.

Jesus aborts their attempt with three decisive actions: (1) He sends his Apostles away. (2) He dismisses the crowd. (3) He disappears into the mountains. Finally, Jesus gets the rest for which he came. It is not rest of the body but privacy with the Father. Clearly, Jesus saw his greatest need to be prayer, not sleep. Although Matthew and Mark only represent Jesus praying at critical times (Mt 14:22-23; 26:36-39; Mk 1:35), Luke shows Jesus praying regularly (Lk 5:16; 6:12-13; 9:18; 9:28-29; 11:1).

§ 74
Walking on
Water
(Mt 14:24-33;
Mk 6:47-52;
Jn 6:16-21)

This narrative contains not one, but four miracles: (1) Walking on water, (2) causing Peter to walk on water, (3) calming of the storm, and

_____

[7]There were a number of popular movements/rebellions among the Jews in the first century which raised a humble peasant to the status of a king. Cf. R.A. Horsley, "Popular Messianic Movements Around the Time of Jesus," *CBQ* 46 (1984): 471-95. But all of these were political, militaristic, and reactionary. They were clearly designed to liberate the peasantry from Rome and the Herodian aristocracy. They can hardly be compared to Jesus' crusade, although from these popular sentiments came this attempt to make Jesus king by force.

(4) immediately arriving at land. It complements the story of the feeding of the 5,000 by highlighting the sovereignty of Jesus. Furthermore, it continues the theme that has run through this section — misunderstanding who Jesus is. He is, of course, misunderstood by the crowds. Earlier, even John the Baptist questioned who Jesus was. And even now his own disciples don't really know Jesus, even after the feeding of the 5,000 (Mk 6:52).

Mk 6:47-49 *with*
Mt 14:24,
Jn 6:19,17

⁴⁷When evening came, the boat was in the middle of the lake {a considerable distanceᵃ from land, buffeted by the wavesᴹᵀ}, and he was alone on land. ⁴⁸He saw the disciples straining at the oars, because the wind was against them {and the waters grew roughᴶᴺ}. {When they had rowed three or three and a half miles,ᵇ they saw Jesus approaching.ᴶᴺ} About the fourth watch of the night {by now it was dark, and Jesus had not yet joined themᴶᴺ} he went out to them, walking on the lake. He was about to pass by them, ⁴⁹but when they saw him walking on the lake,

Mt 14:26-27

²⁶they were terrified. "It's a ghost," they said, and cried out in fear. ²⁷But Jesus immediately said to them: "Take courage! It is I. Don't be afraid."

ᵃ*[Mt 14:]24* Greek *many stadia*   ᵇ*[Jn 6:]19* Greek *rowed twenty-five or thirty stadia* (about 5 or 6 kilometers)

Surely this party of 5,000 lasts until early evening, perhaps 9 p.m. It would not be the kind of thing one was eager to end. It will take Jesus a good little while to calm the excited crowd and dismiss both his Twelve and then the 5,000. He prays from late evening until about 3 a.m.[8] when he joins the Apostolic band.

From his mountain vantage point, Jesus can see a good distance across the lake in the light of the full moon that accompanies Passover. He can see they have been driven off course. Instead of heading toward Bethsaida on the north shore, they are approaching Genneseret on the southwest shore. They are about three or three and a half miles away, pretty close to the middle of the lake. Obviously, they have been struggling for the better part of the night against the strong head wind.

This must have been a difficult incident for the Apostles. Surely they shared the crowd's sentiments of making Jesus King. After all, they had much to gain from such a move; and such was their expectation of a political Messiah. Jesus sent them away, much to their disappointment. What's worse, they were sent into a storm. Being in the middle of the lake in the middle of this storm perhaps caused them to question the

---

[8]The night was divided into four watches, each approximately three hours long. The fourth watch was from 3-6 a.m.

Lordship of Jesus even after such an event as the feeding of the 5,000.[9] They needed the added lesson of Jesus walking on water.

John makes masterful use of the verbs in this section which give a real eyewitness flavor to his account.[10]

> He employs the imperfects "were proceeding" and "was getting rough" or "was rising" to picture the condition, respectively of the men in the boat and on the sea. But between these imperfects he makes use of the pluperfects (darkness) "had come (to be)" and (Jesus) "had not yet come," to indicate what had (or had not yet) happened before the disciples had reached the opposite shore. (Hendriksen, p. 224)

Thus, we picture two scenes. One of Jesus, praying in the calm serenity of the night. The other of the Apostles some three miles away, laboring at the oars in the middle of a storm. The Apostles are neither out of sight nor out of mind of the Master.

Jesus sets out right across the middle of the lake! He is coming to the aid of his disciples. So why does Mark say, "He was about to pass them by?" Is he just kidding around? Is he going to beat them to the other side by taking a shortcut? A simpler solution is that they are close enough to land that Jesus is simply going to meet them when they come ashore in just a little bit.[11] Perhaps they don't notice Jesus until he is parallel to the boat. Then they think he is a ghost going by. Thus, "pass them by" is the disciples' impression, not Jesus' intention.

No wonder the Apostles are frightened. Their eyes are fixed on this eerie apparition — a human-like figure emerging through the waves in the middle of a storm-tossed lake. It is natural to assume that it is a ghost (a disembodied spirit). Who today would come up with a different conclusion? Their sadness of heart and physical fatigue certainly cannot be helping their disposition.

Jesus immediately tries to calm them by identifying himself. "'It is I' reads, more literally, *I am*. This is not bad grammar but a conscious echo of the divine name of Yahweh, as in Exod 3:14. Though still some-

---

[9]We could find many allegorical parallels for the church today. The storms we find ourselves in are not the best test of the sovereignty of Jesus. As Edersheim says (I:691), "As we view it, it seems all symbolical: the night, the moonlight, the little boat, the contrary wind, and then also the lonely Savior after praying, looking across to where the boatmen vainly labour to gain the other shore."

[10]It is also interesting to note that Luke, who could not have been an eyewitness, does not include this incident in his Gospel.

[11]For these and other possible solutions, see D.F. Hill, "The Walking on the Water: A Geographical or Linguistic Answer?" *ExpT* 99 (1988): 267-269.

what veiled, this is perhaps Jesus' clearest self-revelation of his divinity to date" (Blomberg, p. 235).

Granted, this is a difficult narrative to believe . . . as was the feeding of the 5,000. Many have attempted to explain these two miracles away by naturalistic means.[12] This simply won't do. The texts clearly say what they intend. Either they are literary inventions with theological purposes, deliberate lies, or God breaking into natural law. We must accept them or reject them. But to explain them away is not intellectually honest.

Mt 14:28-33

²⁸"Lord, if it's you," Peter replied, "tell me to come to you on the water."
²⁹"Come," he said.

Then Peter got down out of the boat, walked on the water and came toward Jesus. ³⁰But when he saw the wind, he was afraid and, beginning to sink, cried out, "Lord, save me!"

³¹Immediately Jesus reached out his hand and caught him. "You of little faith," he said, "why did you doubt?"

³²And when they climbed into the boat, the wind died down. ³³Then those who were in the boat worshiped him, saying, "Truly you are the Son of God."

Mk 6:51-52

⁵¹They were completely amazed {[and] worshiped him^MT}, ⁵²for they had not understood about the loaves; their hearts were hardened.

Jn 6:21

²¹Then they were willing to take him into the boat, and immediately the boat reached the shore where they were heading.

Peter walking on the water is found only in Matthew. It tells of both the faith and failing of Peter.[13] He is impetuous, sometimes arrogant, and quick to speak before he thinks. But the bottom line is that aside from Jesus, he holds the water-walking record.

"If it is you" (v. 28) might be translated better *Since it is you* (first-

---

[12]The feeding of the 5,000 is commonly explained as a miracle of generosity. When the crowd saw the little boy offer his lunch to Jesus, they all began to open their hidden stores. D.F. Robinson (unconvincingly) argues that the feeding of the 5,000 was allegory, not history ("The Parable of the Loaves," *ATR* 39 [1957]: 107-115. The walking on water is often explained as Jesus walking along the shore and the Apostles thinking he was in the middle of the lake — they were just closer to shore than they thought. J.D.M. Derrett offers a more sophisticated naturalistic explanation. He suggests that Jesus walked on an underwater reef created by the deposits of the North Jordan River as it emptied into the sea ("Why Jesus Walked on the Sea," *NovT* 23/4 [1981]: 330-348). This is unsatisfactory, however, since it leaves the many details unexplained, such as Peter walking on the water, the ignorance of the fishermen, how they suddenly reached shore, the immediate calming of the storm, and the wind blowing from the south rather than the north as the text suggests.

[13]As Blomberg notes, this is the first of five key texts in Mt 14-18, unique to Matthew's Gospel, which highlight Peter (mostly his failings), 14:28-31; 15:15-16; 16:17-19; 17:24-27; 18:21.

class condition). Jesus bids him to come . . . and he does. Unfortunately, he is quickly distracted and begins to sink.[14]

What a stark contrast between Matthew 14:33 and Mark 6:51-52! We observe first of all that true worship is often a by-product of fear which comes from understanding who Jesus really is. Second, we see that even those who spent the most time with Jesus still did not fully know who he was. Third, we understand that being excited about Jesus' deeds (i.e., miracles) does not necessarily mean that we correctly interpret them.

Suddenly they are at the shore. This may simply mean that they are pretty close to the shore when Jesus gets into the boat. Or it may be a divine "transport" that we don't understand any better than we do water-walking. But how foolish it would be to reject the narrative because it does not submit to what we can figure out. We might find ourselves in the same categories as Jesus' unbelieving disciples (frighteningly similar to Jesus' enemies) — "their hearts were hardened."

**§ 75
Healings at
Gennesaret**
(Mt 14:34-36;
Mk 6:53-56)

[MK 6:]53When they had crossed over, they landed at Gennesaret and anchored there. 54As soon as they got out of the boat, people recognized Jesus. 55They ran throughout that whole region and carried the sick on mats to wherever they heard he was. 56And wherever he went — into villages, towns or countryside — they placed the sick in the marketplaces. They begged him to let them touch even the edge of his cloak, and all who touched him were healed.

Gennesaret is a fertile plain on the west side of the lake. Josephus says, "One may call this place the ambition of nature, where it forces those plants that are naturally enemies to one another to agree together" (*War* 3. 518). The boat was blown off course in the storm. Originally they were heading toward Capernaum (Jn 6:17), more specifically, its suburb, Bethsaida (Mk 6:45). The seasick disciples decide to walk from Gennesaret back to Capernaum. There are probably a couple of disciples assigned to sail the boat back to its home port after breakfast.

Jesus is well known, and when the people of the area hear that he is passing through, they line the streets with cots and wheelchairs, waiting for him to pass by. This event epitomizes and summarizes Jesus' healing ministry (cf. Mt 8:1-17; 9:18-34; Mk 1:32-34; 3:7-12). Matthew's extra strong word for healing [*diasozō*] indicates that the crowds were restored to complete health.

Jesus doesn't take the time to stop for a "healing service." Rather, he allows the crowds to touch him on his way through. He is in typical Palestinian garb, complete with prayer tassels at the edge of his robe (cf. Num 15:37-39; Deut 22:12). The popular belief was that power flowed

---

[14]Here again, this text is fertile soil for Christian allegories.

from the individual into his garments, especially the prayer tassels. We witnessed the same superstition with the woman with a flow of blood (§ 67, Mt 9:20-21; Mk 5:24-34). If they can touch his tassels they believe they will be healed. By the time Jesus arrives at Capernaum there must have been a massive parade left in the wake of his healings. The Capernaum synagogue is about to break their record attendance.

§ 76a
Sermon on the
Bread of Life
(Jn 6:22-59)

This is truly a unique sermon. The crowd asked several questions, some of which Jesus never answers directly. They moved from pseudo-sincerity to open hostility. By the end of this sermon, Jesus accomplished a couple of things that most preachers try desperately to avoid. He confused his unbelieving audience and alienated all but his closest comrades. On a more positive note, he (a) moved from earth to heaven, (b) made a clarion call for commitment, and (c) came closer to a clear declaration of his identity than he did in his previous two years of ministry.

The theme of this sermon is "True life in Jesus." We find here a lot of "life" talk (vv. 27, 33, 35, 40, 47, 48, 50, 51, 53, 54, 57, 58, 63). Jesus presented himself as the only true source of eternal life. And we hear the choral refrain, "I will raise him up on the last day" (v. 39, 40, 44, 54). In this passage, Jesus says six times that he came from heaven (vv. 33, 38, 41, 50, 51, 58, see also v. 62). Clearly, one of the themes of this pericope is the heavenly origin of Jesus. The Jews can hardly miss it (cf. 41-42).

Jn 6:22-24

[22]The next day the crowd that had stayed on the opposite shore of the lake realized that only one boat had been there, and that Jesus had not entered it with his disciples, but that they had gone away alone. [23]Then some boats from Tiberias landed near the place where the people had eaten the bread after the Lord had given thanks. [24]Once the crowd realized that neither Jesus nor his disciples were there, they got into the boats and went to Capernaum in search of Jesus.

After Jesus dismissed the 5,000 late last evening, they apparently did not go far. Some, perhaps found lodging in the nearby villages, others likely just camped out near the sight of the feeding. Some of these folks live as far away as Tiberias, where the whole parade began yesterday, nearly ten miles around to the opposite side of the lake.[15] There is no

---

[15]We have several indications that Jesus crossed the lake from Tiberias to Bethsaida Julias: (1) The next day boats came from Tiberias (Jn 6:23). These boats probably came to pick up family and friends of those who had followed Jesus the day before. (2) Jesus had crossed over to the "far shore" (Jn 6:1). Tiberias is on the opposite shore from Bethsaida Julias. (3) In a parenthetical note, John appends the name "Sea of Tiberias" to the normal name of the lake, "Galilee." (4) Furthermore, Tiberias is a logical place for Jesus, providing him with (a) relative privacy during the travels of the Twelve, (b) a central meeting place after their Galilean tour, and (c) a significant population which could account for the crowd once the disciples returned (Mk 6:31).

way they can get home during the night so they decide to stick around and see what festivities the morrow holds.

The next morning they are back in force. After wandering about a bit, they realize that Jesus is not there. But where could he have gone? They know he didn't cross the lake in a boat — the Apostles had taken the only boat that left the night before, and Jesus wasn't in it. With more than 5,000 people still surrounding the sight, how could he have gotten out of there without being seen? We really can't blame them for being stumped. Who would have guessed what really happened?!

Why did the boats arrive from Tiberias? Perhaps some bright-eyed, bushy-tailed teenagers from Tiberias offered to race through the night from Bethsaida to Tiberias to retrieve the boats for their tired parents. In the morning they spread the news to their neighbors that there are a number of people who need taxi service. Some industrious entrepreneurs might be happy to provide such a service.

They are not so eager to get back home. They want to see Jesus again. So instead of taking the direct route to Tiberias, across the middle of the lake, they head first for Capernaum — the known headquarters of Jesus. When they don't find him there, they hug the western shore of the lake and ask at each dock and villa if anyone has seen Jesus.

Jn 6:25-27

[25]When they found him on the other side of the lake, they asked him, "Rabbi, when did you get here?"

[26]Jesus answered, "I tell you the truth, you are looking for me, not because you saw miraculous signs but because you ate the loaves and had your fill. [27]Do not work for food that spoils, but for food that endures to eternal life, which the Son of Man will give you. On him God the Father has placed his seal of approval."

This narrative looks like a single sermon. However, it is possible that it is a summary of a full day's discussion which begins near Tiberias (v. 25) and ends in the Capernaum synagogue (v. 59).[16] We might assume then, that the feeding of the 5,000 took place on Thursday and the discussion on Friday, concluding at the regular synagogue service. However, synagogue services were also held on Mondays and Thursdays. Besides, being near Passover, there may be some kind of special synagogue service.

They ask Jesus, "When did you get here?" The answer is, "About 4-6 a.m." But we learn this from Matthew and Mark, not from Jesus. He never addresses their superficial question. Instead, he waylays their

---

[16]"It is a remarkable circumstance, that among the ruins of the Synagogue of Capernaum the lintel has been discovered, and that it bears the device of a pot of manna, ornamented with a flowing pattern of vine leaves and clusters of grapes" (Edersheim, II:29).

motive. In fact, when Jesus says, "You ate and had your fill," he uses a word normally associated with animals eating fodder (*echortasthēte*). This crowd is operating at the most carnal level — physical satisfaction and security. The paradox is that they think they are being spiritual with all this Messiah talk.

Throughout this narrative, the clear lesson is, "Look beyond the flesh." They don't get it. Even their method of interpreting Jesus' words (literal rather than figurative) misleads them.

When Jesus says, "don't work for food that spoils," he is not merely speaking of their jobs, but their present activity of seeking Jesus who fed them bread and fish. The fact is, these people are not "working." They are gallivanting all over the countryside chasing Jesus. They ran ten miles yesterday to see him, stayed all day, and camped out all night. In the morning they chase him from Bethsaida Julias to Capernaum to Tiberias. And even now they are following him back up to Capernaum. They have lost at least two full days' "work." But seeking Jesus is a "job." It is the work we are called to do. The problem with this crowd is that they are seeking Jesus for the wrong reasons. They're ready to settle for barley loaves and sardines when Jesus came to give them eternal life.

These dense Galileans (not unlike most of humanity) should have expected more from Jesus. After all, God gave Jesus his "seal of approval." In those days a seal was an impression in wax or clay made by a signet ring. It was a visible sign of ownership, especially of kings and governors. What visible signs had God granted to Jesus?

1. Miracles
2. Testimony of John the Baptist
3. The Holy Spirit in the form of a dove at Jesus' baptism
4. Messianic prophecies (as well as types and allusions)
5. The clarity and character of Jesus' teachings

Jn 6:28-29

28Then they asked him, "What must we do to do the works God requires?"
29Jesus answered, "The work of God is this: to believe in the one he has sent."

Verse 28 seems like a straightforward question — "What must we do?" But as the narrative unfolds we discover that this crowd has already turned their hearts from Jesus. When he refuses to be the king they wanted, it sends a chill across their hearts that Jesus is not able to thaw. From here to the cross, it is a sad spectacle to watch. As Jesus' self-revelation becomes clearer, the crowds become thinner.

Although their question may be based in skepticism, it is still an excellent question. I dare say, it is THE question of humanity. Jesus' answer is equally fundamental, "Your '**job**' is to believe in me." This brings up two questions. First, how is it that faith is a work? Biblical faith might better be understood as "trust." If our minds are convinced then our lives will show it. Thus, our "faith" is inevitably lived out (James 2:14-26).

The second question we ask is this: "How is it that we are saved by grace if we have to work for it?" The answer is that we don't work for it but in response to it. In no way can we earn our salvation. No matter how good we are, how nobly we live, we can neither atone for our own sins, or earn entrance into heaven. This does not mean we do nothing to receive Christ's gift. Throughout the NT there are a number of imperatives connected with salvation — repentance (Acts 17:30-31; Lk 13:3, 5), forgiveness of others (Mt 6:14-15), confessing Jesus (Mt 10:32-33; Rom 10:9-10); use of our words (Mt 12:36-37), etc. But they can all be expressed with one word: FAITH. That is, if I truly trust Jesus, these are all natural and necessary expressions of that faith.

At first it sounds so simple . . . so easy, until we realize how much that covers. True faith will rearrange every element of our lives. It demands all we possess — our time, our talents, our resources. When we first hear the requirement to do God's work, "Trust Jesus," we say, "Oh, is that all?" But after a moment's consideration we say, "Oh, that's ALL!"

Jn 6:30-33

³⁰So they asked him, "What miraculous sign then will you give that we may see it and believe you? What will you do? ³¹Our forefathers ate the manna in the desert; as it is written: 'He gave them bread from heaven to eat.'ᵃ"

³²Jesus said to them, "I tell you the truth, it is not Moses who has given you the bread from heaven, but it is my Father who gives you the true bread from heaven. ³³For the bread of God is he who comes down from heaven and gives life to the world."

ᵃ*31* Exodus 16:4; Neh. 9:15; Psalm 78:24,25 [see also Exod 16:15, Psalm 105:40]

This is, indeed a stupid question, but not a new one. Twice before, the Jews have asked Jesus for a miraculous sign (cf. Mt 12:38-45; Jn 2:18-23). Each time it immediately follows a great miracle. Each time Jesus refuses their immediate request but later continues to do miracles.

Jesus has already performed an impressive catalogue of miracles including healings, raisings, cleansings, and exorcisms, to say nothing about his power over the inanimate — wine, bread, wind, and waves. On the day following the feeding of the 5,000, how can they possibly ask for a sign?! Verse 31 offers a key to their logic, here, as well as the two previous times the Jews asked for a sign. They want a sign *from heaven,* like Moses gave them with the manna.[17] It is as if they say, "We followed you for earthly food because that is what you miraculously provided. But if you want us to follow you for heavenly food (cf. v. 27), then we will need a sign from heaven." In all three instances, the only sign Jesus promised was that of resurrection.

Their casuistry sounds good, but it is nothing more than evasion of Jesus' demands. Yesterday they were willing to inaugurate Jesus as king because he gave them what they wanted. But today, when Jesus asks for their allegiance, they reject him. They demand of Jesus, "Gimme, Gimme, Gimme . . . If not earthly bread then heavenly bread!" Jesus replied, "It is not I who give, nor was it Moses, but God. He gave manna to your forefathers; but to you he gave me. You ask me to provide heavenly bread but I am that bread!" By rejecting Jesus, they are rejecting the very thing they asked Jesus to provide.

Jn 6:34-36

³⁴"Sir," they said, "from now on give us this bread."

³⁵Then Jesus declared, "I am the bread of life. He who comes to me will never go hungry, and he who believes in me will never be thirsty. ³⁶But as I told you, you have seen me and still you do not believe."

As we read this, we can't help but think of the woman at the well (Jn 4:4-14). John surely intended this comparison. On the one hand, we have a Samaritan woman who puts her faith in Jesus, the Living Water, without so much as a single miracle. On the other hand, we have the unbelieving Jews who reject Jesus, the Bread of Life, even after a plethora of miracles.

Jesus' claim to be "The Bread of Life" is the first in a series of "I AM" statements in John's Gospel (8:12; 10:7, 11; 11:25; 14:6; 15:1). "Each represents a particular relationship of Jesus to the spiritual needs of men. . . . He desired that men should receive him, not simply for what he might give them, but for what he might be to them" (Tenney, p. 76).

Jn 6:37-40

³⁷"All that the Father gives me will come to me, and whoever comes to me I will never drive away. ³⁸For I have come down from heaven not to do my will but to do the will of him who sent me. ³⁹And this is the will of him who sent me, that I shall lose none of all that he has given me, but raise them up at the last day. ⁴⁰For my Father's will is that everyone who looks to the Son and believes in him shall have eternal life, and I will raise him up at the last day."

---

[17]"That manna, which was angels' food, distilled (as they imagined) from the upper light, 'the dew from above' [Yoma 75b] — miraculous food, of all manner of taste, and suited to every age, according to the wish or condition of him who ate it [Shem. R. 25], but bitterness to Gentiles' palates — they expected the Messiah to bring again from heaven. For, all that the first deliverer, Moses, had done, the second — Messiah — would also do [Midr. on Eccles. 1:9]" (Edersheim, II:29-30).

This text raises the difficult and sensitive issue of "Eternal Security." This, however, is probably not the best place to discuss it. After all, the speech before us is not a theological dissertation but a heated debate where Jesus speaks in enigmatic terms. This does not mean that he cannot be understood, but that he frames up his message in provocative language that causes his audience to meditate on what he says. So we will likely need to look to the Epistles for insight on this text. Besides, Jesus will make a clearer declaration of eternal security in John 10:28, and our discussion will be taken up more fully there.

In some ways, the discussion of eternal security is a moot point. If someone apostatizes, those who do not believe in eternal security will say, "He fell away from Jesus." Those who do believe in eternal security will say, "He was never saved in the first place," or "He is a prodigal who needs to be called to repentance." Notice two things. First, both theological positions would respond in the same way — call the person to repentance. Therefore, this is primarily a philosophical difference, not a practical one. Second, both positions entail a judgment about another person's position with Christ. Very few would actually say, "I am not secure." Rather, most say, "I know I'm 'O.K.,' but I really wonder about you!" This can be very dangerous. Therefore, we want to be cautious, kind, and humble.

The eternal security camp has been charged with lawlessness. Some have gotten the impression that because they once proclaimed Jesus as Lord, their lifestyles are not that important. They are saved and, accordingly, can live like they want. That is patently false (Gal 5:13, 17). On the other side of the fence, however, those who believe a person can fall away have been charged with preaching eternal INsecurity. And indeed, there are those who constantly and unnecessarily question their position in Christ (cf. 1 Jn 5:13). We want to avoid both extremes.

Before dealing with our present text, we must make one more observation about the way eternal security/apostasy texts are handled. The conclusion we come to may very well depend on our starting point. If we start by observing eternal security texts,[18] then we may end by explaining (away) the apostasy texts[19] and vice versa. Our presuppositions go farther

---

[18]E.g., Ps 89:30-35; Jn 4:14; 5:24; 6:37-40; 10:27-30; Rom 8:29-39; 11:29; 14:4; 1 Cor 1:8; 2 Cor 1:21-22; 5:4-5; Eph 1:13-14; 4:30; Phil 1:6; 1 Thess 5:23-24; 2 Tim 1:12; 2:19; 4:18; Heb 6:17; 7:25; 1 Pet 1:3-5; 1 Jn 2:18-19; 3:6; 5:12-13; Jude 24.

[19]E.g., Josh 24:19-20; Neh 1:7-9; Ps 95:7-10; Mt 10:22; 13:1-9, 18-23; 18:21-35; 24:13; Lk 12:42-46; Jn 15:1-6; Rom 11:20-22; 1 Cor 9:24-27; 10:1-13; 15:1-2; Gal 5:1-4; 6:7-9; Col 1:19-23; 1 Tim 1:18-19; 4:1; 2 Tim 2:11-13; 4:10; Heb 3:1-19; 4:1-13; 6:4-8; 10:26-31, 36-39; 12:15-17; 2 Pet 2:20-22; Jude 6; Rev 2:5, 7, 10, 11, 17, 26; 3:5, 12, 21; 21:7.

than we might like to admit in determining our conclusions. We must allow some degree of paradox here because we are dealing with the weave of God's sovereignty and man's free will, both of which are true, neither of which are fully reconcilable in the fallen mind of man. Therefore, we want to be fair-minded and let each text say what it actually says.

Now for the text at hand. Tenney has this to say about verse 37:

> "All" (*pan*) is a neuter singular rather than a masculine plural and refers to everything the Father has put under Jesus' control (cf. John 5:19-27). It includes the people who are his. The paradox latent in this text has puzzled many. How can one be sure that the Father has really given him to Christ? Will he come only to be rebuffed? Jesus made plain that human salvation is no surprise to God. He summons men to himself by his Word and by his Spirit. They can come only at his invitation. The invitation, however, is not restricted to any particular time or place, nor is it exclusively for any one nation, race, or culture. No man needs to fear that he will come in vain, for Jesus said emphatically that he would not refuse anyone (p. 76).

Verse 39 and 40 both end with the triumphant choral refrain, "And I shall raise him up at the last day." We also observe the parallelism between "I shall lose none of all that he has given me," and "Everyone who looks to the Son and believes in him shall have eternal life." Both of these are the Father's will. Verse 39 speaks of the result whereas verse 40 speaks of the means. The way we obtain security in Jesus is by looking on and believing in Jesus[20] (both of these verbs are present participles indicating continuing action). In other words, we must keep looking and believing in Jesus.

Notice that "loses none of them" in verse 39 is not a promise, but a statement of the Father's will. Does God's will always prevail? No. It didn't in the days of Eden, or Noah, or Moses, or David. It is God's will that all will come to repentance (2 Pet 3:9), but the Bible clearly states

---

[20]In numerous parallel passages, there are other imperatives connected with our salvation. "Looking on" and "believing in" Jesus are "umbrella" descriptions under which numerous specific behaviors would fall — repentance (Acts 2:38; 3:19; 17:30-31; Lk 13:5; Rev 2:16,22); confession (Mt 10:32-33; Jn 12:42; Rom 10:9-10; Jn 2:23; 4:2, 3, 15); immersion (Mk 16:15-16; Acts 2:38; Rom 6:3-5; Gal 3:27; 1 Pet 3:21); forgiveness of others (Mt 6:14-15; 18:35; Eph 4:32; James 2:13); calling on Christ's name (Acts 2:21; 22:16; Rom 10:13); obedience (Jn 3:36; Heb 5:9; 11:8; 1 Jn 5:1-3); works/fruit (Mt 7:21-23; Jn 15:2; James 2:20-26); love (Gal 5:6; 1 Jn 3:10-24; 4:7-21); benevolence (Mt 25:31-46; 1 Jn 3:17); remaining faithful unto death (Jn 15:6; Heb 3:6, 12; 10:23-31, 36-39; Rev 2:10, 26); etc.

that this is not going to happen (Mt 22:14, Lk 8:13; 13:23-24, Rev 3:4). Furthermore, we know that "Jesus losing none of them" (cf. Jn 18:9) is not an absolute statement. He did "lose" Judas Iscariot (Jn 17:12). This is not so much a statement of eternal security as it is of the hope of God. Is God's will accomplished? Yes . . . due to his sovereignty. However, in his sovereignty, he has allowed man free will. And often times men make decisions which God does not like.

Jn 6:41-47

⁴¹At this the Jews began to grumble about him because he said, "I am the bread that came down from heaven." ⁴²They said, "Is this not Jesus, the son of Joseph, whose father and mother we know? How can he now say, 'I came down from heaven'?"

⁴³"Stop grumbling among yourselves," Jesus answered. ⁴⁴"No one can come to me unless the Father who sent me draws him, and I will raise him up at the last day. ⁴⁵It is written in the Prophets: 'They will all be taught by God.'ᵃ Everyone who listens to the Father and learns from him comes to me. ⁴⁶No one has seen the Father except the one who is from God [Jn 1:18]; only he has seen the Father. ⁴⁷I tell you the truth, he who believes has everlasting life."

ᵃ45 Isaiah 54:13

Grumbling is offensive to God because it demonstrates a lack of trust. Unfortunately it is a common malpractice of his people (Exod 16:7, Num 14:27; 14:36; 16:11, Jn 6:41, 1 Cor 10:10, James 5:9). We justify it by saying, "I'm not grumbling against God but against the preacher/teacher/elder." But as these passages show, God's people have never grumbled against God per se, but against God's spokesman. Nevertheless, God took it personally. If we reject God's established authority in our lives we have rejected God, himself.

Their complaint against Jesus (like v. 28), has the form of sincerity and logic, but not the spirit. They again make the mistake of taking Jesus too literally about this "coming down from heaven" thing. Since they know his family, they know he did not come down from heaven in bodily form. They know he is part of their earthly community, not the heavenly citizenry. They never even consider the possibility of "incarnation."

Jesus, without addressing their superficial question, nails the real issue — willingness and ability to come to Jesus. We can't come to Jesus unless God draws us (v. 44). How does God draw us? Through teaching (v. 45). And how were they to be taught? Our text suggests four means:

(1) *The Knowledge of the Scriptures* — The fact that Jesus quotes Isaiah 54:13 suggests there is divine wisdom in the Scriptures. If we will learn God's written word, it will lead us to Jesus (Lk 24:25-27). Warning: This is not an academic knowledge but a heart bent on knowing God (cf. Jn 5:39-40, 45-47).

(2) *The Law of God in the Hearts of Men* — Isaiah 54:13 sounds much like Jeremiah 31:31-34. Beyond the study of God's written word, the Holy Spirit prompts our hearts (cf. 1 Cor 2:10-16; see also Jn 14:26; 15:26; 16:13-14), primarily in two areas (a) Abiding in Jesus, our source of salvation (1 John 2:27; 1 Cor 2:12), (b) learning how to express God's love in a fallen world (1 Thess 4:9).

(3) *Listening to Jesus* — Verse 46 reminds us that Jesus alone knows the nature and plan of the Father. Thus, if you want to be "taught by God" you must listen to Jesus (cf. Jn 14:26).

(4) *Hearts Bent Toward Belief* — We can't come to Jesus unless our hearts are predisposed to faith. That does not mean that we are to be gullible. But it does mean that we must have an open mind and open heart. Verse 47 (cf. v. 40) demands faith as a prerequisite to be truly taught of God.

Although our text sounds predestinarian, the deck is not stacked all on God's side. Matthew 22:14 offers a clue, "Many are called but few are chosen." Who was chosen in the parable (Mt 22:1-14)? Was it not those who responded to the invitation? Indeed, no one could come to Jesus without the call/invitation/drawing of God (cf. Acts 16:14; Isa 6:9-10). But this does not exempt man's response. We are still obligated to believe, study, listen, respond and obey. The bottom line is this: Without God's call, we have no hope of coming to Jesus. It is not we who initiated this relationship but he. At the same time, no one has ever been saved without a volitional submission of his/her will. Salvation is a partnership between the sovereignty of God and the free will of man.

Jn 6:48-59

[48]"I am the bread of life. [49]Your forefathers ate the manna in the desert, yet they died. [50]But here is the bread that comes down from heaven, which a man may eat and not die. [51]I am the living bread that came down from heaven. If anyone eats of this bread, he will live forever. This bread is my flesh, which I will give for the life of the world."

[52]Then the Jews began to argue sharply among themselves, "How can this man give us his flesh to eat?"

[53]Jesus said to them, "I tell you the truth, unless you eat the flesh of the Son of Man and drink his blood, you have no life in you. [54]Whoever eats my flesh and drinks my blood has eternal life, and I will raise him up at the last day. [55]For my flesh is real food and my blood is real drink. [56]Whoever eats my flesh and drinks my blood remains in me, and I in him. [57]Just as the living Father sent me and I live because of the Father, so the one who feeds on me will live because of me. [58]This is the bread that came down from heaven. Your forefathers ate manna and died, but he who feeds on this bread will live forever." [59]He said this while teaching in the synagogue in Capernaum.

Jesus' words are shocking, even offensive. You can almost hear them gasp as Jesus talks about drinking blood and gnawing [*trōgō*] flesh. The audience is scandalized; they begin to argue about it. Now, you might think Jesus would lighten up a bit and say, "Now don't take it literally!" But he doesn't. In fact, he presses the metaphor further.

Obviously, this is a figure of speech. Jesus is not advocating the revolting practice of cannibalism and drinking blood (cf. Gen 9:4; Lev 17:10-14; 1 Sam 14:32-35). He is talking about accepting him at the deepest levels. He is speaking of participation and incorporation of his character, purposes, and nature. But just how does one "feed on Jesus?" He has already answered that in v. 35 — by coming to Jesus and believing in him.[21]

Beyond trusting Jesus by faith, this passage speaks of Jesus' vicarious death for us (cf. Mk 10:45; Rom 3:21-26; 2 Cor 5:14-15; Col 2:13-14; 1 Pet 1:18-19; 1 John 2:2).[22] But is John also talking about the eucharist? It is anachronistic to equate John 6 with the communion, but the foreshadowing is clear.[23] John, writing in the latter years of his life, often describes the events of Jesus in theologically loaded terms. In other words, you can't help but think about the Eucharist when you read John 6:53 even though you know they symbolize Jesus himself, not the emblems of communion.[24] Thus, the language of John 6 points forward to Jesus on the cross. The symbols of the Lord's Supper look backwards to Jesus on the cross. They look so much alike because they both picture the same thing.

Through these pictures we participate in the divine activities of redemption and sanctification. But our participation is not merely in a sacramental celebration. This mystical union with Christ is only real if it permeates our tangible daily existence, how we walk and talk, live and love, work and rest.

---

[21]In verses 51 and 53, the aorist subjunctive of *esthiō*, "to eat," indicates a single decisive past action as when someone initially accepts Christ. In vv. 54 and 56, the present participle of *trōgō*, "to gnaw," indicates a continued action as in the "life practice" of the believer.

[22]The use of the word *sarx* rather than *soma* in this passage seems be an allusion to the cross. R. Bailey, "John 6," *Rev & Expos* 85 (1988): 95-98.

[23]For an excellent summary of the arguments see J.D.G. Dunn, "John 6 — A Eucharistic Discourse?" *NTS* 17 (1971): 328-338 and J.K. Howard, "Passover and Eucharist in the Fourth Gospel," *SJT* 20:1967): 329-337.

[24]John, who devotes five chapters to the Passover meal, says nothing about the Lord's Supper. This strongly suggests that the allusions to Christ's body here in chapter six are a substitution for it. John has done the same thing with baptism (Jn 3:5) and the Holy Spirit (Jn 7:38-39; 20:22). Some have even seen allusions to the sacraments in John 19:34 and 1 John 5:5-8.

**§ 76b
The Crowds
Abandon
Jesus**
(Jn 6:60-71)

[60]On hearing it, many of his disciples said, "This is a hard teaching. Who can accept it?"

[61]Aware that his disciples were grumbling about this, Jesus said to them, "Does this offend you? [62]What if you see the Son of Man ascend to where he was before! [63]The Spirit gives life; the flesh counts for nothing. The words I have spoken to you are spirit[a] and they are life. [64]Yet there are some of you who do not believe." For Jesus had known from the beginning which of them did not believe and who would betray him. [65]He went on to say, "This is why I told you that no one can come to me unless the Father has enabled him."

[a]63 Or *Spirit*

There appear to be three distinct groups in this chapter. The lines of demarcation are somewhat fuzzy. However, there are Christ's closest followers, the Twelve. This group is definite. Then there is this huge crowd, followers of Jesus, more or less adherents of his teaching, called disciples (v. 60). Also, there is this group of vocal antagonists which John calls "the Jews" (vv. 41, 52).

The Jews have already voiced their disagreement with Jesus. Now it is the disciples' turn. What they say is true. This is a tough saying. But it is not nearly as difficult as the truths they are yet to face such as the substitutionary death of Jesus, the bodily resurrection, the ascension (v. 62), the coming of the Holy Spirit, etc. If they get "tripped up"[25] on this, they have little hope of understanding the depth and breadth of Jesus' ministry! In other words, if it bothers them that Jesus said, "I came from heaven" how will they handle it if they see him ascend back to heaven? The ascension is not described in John's Gospel but it is alluded to frequently (3:13; 8:21; 14:3; 16:10; 17:11; 20:17).

Instead of back-peddling or softening the blows, Jesus forges ahead, driven by a divine agenda which he will not compromise. He now synthesizes the whole message in three verses. First, he calls them from the flesh (physical food) to spirit (heavenly fodder) found in his words. Second, he calls them to faith by challenging their unbelief. Verse 64 parallels v. 70. As Jesus knew Judas Iscariot's future betrayal, so too, he knew who would abandon ship among his broader group of disciples. Third, Jesus reminds them of God's sovereign influence in their ability to accept Jesus.

Jn 6:66-71

[66]From this time many of his disciples turned back and no longer followed him. [67]"You do not want to leave too, do you?" Jesus asked the Twelve.

[68]Simon Peter answered him, "Lord, to whom shall we go? You have the words of eternal life. [69]We believe and know that you are the Holy One of God."

---

[25]This is the literal rendering of "offend" (*skandalizō*).

⁷⁰Then Jesus replied, "Have I not chosen you, the Twelve? Yet one of you is a devil!" ⁷¹(He meant Judas, the son of Simon Iscariot, who, though one of the Twelve, was later to betray him.)

The Greek of verse 66 is much more explicit than the English translation. First, "From this time" [*ek toutou*] suggests not merely this time but this event. *As a result of this sermon* many of his disciples abandon ship. Second, the NIV translation "turned back" leaves untranslated the phrase, "unto the things *left* behind" [*eis ta opisō*]. In other words, they go back home, back to work, back to their old habits, old ways of thinking, etc. For many, this is an abdication of the movement. They not only give up following Jesus, they give up what he represents and teaches. They are not fit for the kingdom (Lk 9:62).

This is perhaps the most "unsuccessful" sermon ever preached. Jesus started with thousands and finishes with a handful. Yet it is a significant turning point in Jesus' ministry. While he moves closer to a self-revelation, he also shifts from a public ministry to thousands to a more private training of the Twelve. Jesus frames his question in v. 67 so as to expect a negative answer. This is not an invitation for them to leave, but a helpful reminder of why they have chosen to stay.

Characteristically, Peter answers for the group. "The emphatic use of the first person plural pronoun implies a contrast between the Twelve and those who had deserted Jesus" (Tenney, p. 80). And what an answer! Peter probably doesn't understand the full significance of this sermon, but he gets the main point: Life comes through incorporating Jesus' words.

Peter's magnificent confession continues (v. 69). The two verbs, "We believe and know" are translated as simple present tenses but are both perfects. They should be understood to say, "We have believed and have come to know." For Peter and the others, this is a settled conviction. They have made their decision to follow Jesus. The resilience of their faith is impervious to the ebb and flow of popularism.

Peter goes so far as to call Jesus the "Holy One" of God, a phrase familiar to Isaiah (used twenty-seven times). It is found nine times in the NT, three times in Acts (2:27; 3:14; 13:35) and once by a demon (Mk 1:24; Lk 4:34). This is one of the pinnacle confessions of Jesus, matched by Peter's other confession recorded in the Synoptics (Mt 16:16; Mk 8:29; Lk 9:20).

Not all is rosy, however, even among the Twelve. Jesus, with the foreknowledge of God, knew that Judas would betray him. Some have speculated that he felt like an outsider, being the only Apostle from

Judea (Kerioth was south of Hebron in the Negev).[26] But it is hardly thinkable that Judas, made to be the treasurer, would feel ousted by the group.

Another paradox is the comparison between Peter, the greatest Apostle, and Judas the Apostate.[27] Both are likened to Satan/Devil (Mt 16:23 and Jn 6:70; also translated "slanderers" in 2 Tim 3:3 and Titus 2:3); both are outspoken leaders (Jn 6:68, etc. and Jn 12:4-6); both betray Jesus (Jn 6:71 and Mt 26:31-35). It would hardly be fair to rob Peter of his initiative and zeal, or to absolve Judas of his responsibility. Yet who can deny that there is a line drawn between these two by the sovereign hand of God. The proud preacher ought to remember that God first chose him, before he ever made a move toward God (v. 70).

**§ 77
Conflict Over
Ceremonial
Cleanness**
(Mt 15:1-20;
Mk 7:1-23;
Jn 7:1)

[JN 7:1]After this, Jesus went around in Galilee, purposely staying away from Judea because the Jews there were waiting to take his life.

The feeding of the 5,000 and the sermon on the bread of life create quite a stir. In fact, the furor is transported to Jerusalem by the crowds Jesus fed. When they arrive in Jerusalem for the Passover, Jesus' Galilean activities become the hot topic of conversation. The Pharisees respond to these rumors by sending a delegation to "check out" what is happening with this budding "Jesus movement." They are so shocked by the blasphemous reports of Jesus' sermon, they are now prepared to kill him (cf. Mk 3:6). They come at a point of vulnerability, after the majority of Jesus' disciples have abandoned him. So Jesus takes off for one last Galilean tour (Jn 7:1), prior to escaping her borders for Phoenicia and Caesarea Philippi.

Mk 7:1-4

¹The Pharisees and some of the teachers of the law who had come from Jerusalem gathered around Jesus and ²saw some of his disciples eating food with hands that were "unclean," that is, unwashed. ³(The Pharisees and all the Jews do not eat unless they give their hands a ceremonial washing, holding to the tradition of the elders. ⁴When they come from the marketplace they do not eat unless they wash. And they observe many other traditions, such as the washing of cups, pitchers and kettles.ª)

ª4 Some early manuscripts *pitchers, kettles and dining couches*

---

[26]W.B. Smith, "Judas Iscariot," *HibJ* 9 (1911): 529-544, points out that etymologically it is questionable to associate "Iscariot" with the city of Kerioth. He suggests that the more likely meaning of "Iscariot" is "Betrayer."

[27]Judas is almost always associated with his betrayal of Christ (Cf. Mt 10:4; Mk 3:19; Lk 6:16; Jn 12:4; 18:2).

During this itinerant tour, the delegation of Jerusalem Pharisees catches up with Jesus. They attack him again because he's coloring outside the lines drawn by the oral tradition (cf. § 47-48, Mt 9:9-17; Mk 2:13-22; Lk 5:27-39). They accuse the disciples of eating with "unclean" [*koinos*] hands (cf. Mk 7:15, 18, 20, 23). This word generally means "common," but here it is correctly translated as "unclean" (cf. Acts 10:14, 28; 11:8; Rev 21:27). The issue, clearly, was not hygienic but ritualistic. Their hands had not been sanctified by this ritual washing.[28]

The Jewish Oral Law had an elaborate system of regulations about washing, perhaps based on Leviticus 15:11. In fact, there is an entire tractate of the Mishnah called *Yadim* ("Hands"), devoted to ritual cleansings. Before each meal (and some rabbis added it after the meal as well), one was required to pour a minimum of a quarter of a log — half an eggshell — of water over the hand.

Edersheim offers an extensive description of the ritual (II:11-12):

> The water was poured on both hands, which must be free of anything covering them, such as gravel, mortar, etc. The hands were lifted up, so as to make the water run to the wrist, in order to ensure that the whole hand was washed, and that the water polluted by the hand did not again run down the fingers. Similarly, each hand was rubbed with the other (the fist), provided the hand that rubbed had been affused: otherwise, the rubbing might be done against the head, or even against a wall. . . . If the hands were 'defiled,' two affusions were required: the first, or 'first waters' (*mayim rishonim*) to remove the defilement, and the 'second' or 'after waters' (*mayim sheniyim*) to wash away the waters that had contracted the defilement of the hands. Accordingly, on the affusion of the first waters the hands were elevated, and the water made to run down at the wrist, while at the second waters the hands were depressed, so that the water might run off by the finger points and tips.

Our translators have placed vv. 3-4 in parenthesis. Likely, this is an editorial comment made by Mark for the benefit of his Gentile readers. The phrase "give their hands a ceremonial washing" [*pygmē nipsōntai tas cheiras*] is somewhat difficult to translate as the following chart will show:

---

[28]*Baptizō* — lit. to immerse. "Any contact with a heathen, even the touch of his dress, might involve such defilement, that on coming from the market the orthodox Jew would have to immerse" (Edersheim, II:15).

KJV	"Wash often"
Modern	"Wash up to the elbow"[29]
NASB	"Carefully wash" with note — "with fist"
RSV & NEB	"Wash their hands" ("in a special way" = NKJV)
NIV	"Ceremonial washing"

The difficulty is with this odd little word *pygmē*, which can mean "fist"[30] or "wrist." It can indicate the thoroughness of the washing, the extent of the washing (up to the wrist), or the scrubbing action of the ball of the hand on the other hand. Nonetheless, the point is clear, these folks are meticulous with this ritual washing.

Unfortunately, the oral traditions became more important than the Word of God (*Jer. Ber.* 3 b; *Sanh.* xi. 3; *Erub* 21:b). However appalling this may seem, it is not uncommon. Religious systems often gravitate to man's interpretation above God's revelation (Papal decrees, denominational creeds, marginal notes in study Bibles, etc.). It is not motivated by a disrespect for God. Rather, we feel that if we follow the scholar's interpretation, we will, by necessity, follow God's revelation. Obviously this is not always the case.

Mk 7:5-8 *with*
Mt 15:2

[5]So the Pharisees and teachers of the law asked Jesus, "Why don't your disciples live according to the tradition of the elders instead of eating their food with 'unclean' hands?" {They don't wash their hands before they eat![MT]}

[6]He replied, "Isaiah was right when he prophesied about you hypocrites; as it is written:

"'These people honor me with their lips,
but their hearts are far from me.
[7]They worship me in vain;
their teachings are but rules taught by men.'[a]
[8]You have let go of the commands of God and are holding on to the traditions of men."

[a]*6,7* Isa. 29:13

The Pharisees hold sway over the people. These guys are the religious giants. So when they question Jesus about the behavior of his followers, the crowd is going to tune in to the controversy. His followers

---

[29]In Greek anatomy, the *pygmē* might indicate any portion of the forearm extending from the elbow to the wrist. This ceremonial washing, however, generally did not extend beyond the wrist.

[30]S.M. Reynolds, "PUGME (Mk 7:3) as 'Cupped Hand,' *JBL* 85 (1966): 87-88, argues that *pygmē* should be understood as a loose fist which shapes the hand in the form of a cup. This allows the whole hand, inside and out, to be washed with just a little bit of water. And, in fact, this form of ceremonial washing before meals can be observed in Jewish circles even today.

are going to feel quite uneasy about being the center of their attention. This is a religious heavyweight bout. Jesus is up for the challenge. Characteristically, he doesn't directly answer their question, but he gets to the real issue.

Jesus doesn't defend the disciples because they are guilty as charged in their disregard for Oral Tradition. Furthermore, they have learned it from Jesus (cf. Lk 11:38). Instead, Jesus blasts the Pharisees on two fronts. First, he calls them hypocrites. The word finds its meaning on the Greek stage. An actor would hold up a mask to conceal his real identity while he played the part of another. Essentially, Jesus is calling the Pharisees two-faced. They put on a mask of honoring God, but their true nature is self-serving. Second, Jesus quotes Isaiah 29:13 and lays it directly at their doorstep (cf. Hosea 6:6 in Mt 9:13 & 12:7). They say all the right stuff, but for all the wrong reasons. Their hearts are not bent on loving God. Therefore, their worship is worthless and their teachings are contaminated.

Mk 7:9-13 *with*
Mt 15:4-6

[9]And he said to them: "You have a fine way of setting aside the commands of God in order to observe[a] your own traditions! [10]For Moses {God[MT]} said, 'Honor your father and your mother,'[b] and, 'Anyone who curses his father or mother must be put to death.'[c] [11]But you say that if a man says to his father or mother: 'Whatever help you might otherwise have received from me is Corban' (that is, a gift devoted to God), {he is not to 'honor his father[d] with it[MT]} [12]then you no longer let him do anything for his father or mother. [13]Thus you nullify the word of God by {for the sake of[MT]} your tradition that you have handed down. And you do many things like that."

[a][Mk 7:]9 Some manuscripts *set up*   [b]10 Exodus 20:12; Deut. 5:16   [c]10 Exodus 21:17; Lev. 20:9   [d][Mt 15:]6 Some manuscripts *father or his mother*

Jesus has just accused the Pharisees of setting aside the Word of God for the traditions of men. Now he will illustrate the fact with a "case in point." The command to honor one's parents was priority for the Jews (and for God). In fact, it was such a serious obligation that it carried a death penalty for any who broke it (Deut 21:18-21).

Among the rules of the Oral Tradition was this "King's X" called Corban (e.g., *m. Ned.* 1:2-4; 9:7).[31] By labeling something as Corban, you promised to give it to God, if not sooner, then upon your death. It could be a cart, or a house, or savings, or property, etc. Since it was Corban, you could not sell it or give it to anyone, including your parents. But you, yourself, could still use it. Then, when you died, it would be given to the Lord or sold and the proceeds donated to God.

---

[31]See J.D.M. Derrett, "*KORBAN, HO ESTIN DORON*," *NTS* 16 (1969-70): 364-368 and J.A. Fitzmyer, "The Aramaic Qorban Inscription from Jebel Hallet Et-Turi and Mk 7:11/Mt 15:5," *JBL* 78 (1959): 60-65.

Corban arose out of a correct theology, that obligations to God are more important than obligations to any human, including parents. But the opportunity for abuse is all too obvious. If I have something that you want or need, I just label it as Corban. It is then off limits to you . . . but not to me.

Since we don't practice ritual washings or use the word "Corban," we feel safe to leave this text in the first century, pointing at the Pharisees. But this text is not merely about cleanliness and Corban, it is about replacing God's requirements with religious duties. This has some rather broad implications. You see, aside from the entry rite of circumcision, Jews were identified and evaluated based on three criteria: (a) Observation of the Sabbath and festivals (days), (b) Observation of clean and unclean (diet), and (c) Ritual dress. If you meticulously followed these three things, then you were considered a "good Jew." If you slacked up on one or more of these, then you weren't quite as good.

As Christians, our list of do's and don'ts is strikingly similar. We identify a "good Christian" by:

(a) **DAY**: Regular attendance and participation in church services, especially Sunday morning, but also Sunday School, Sunday evening and Wednesday night. Potluck dinners and class parties are advisable but optional.

(b) **DIET**: Avoid alcohol, nicotine, and R-rated movies. Avoiding sports cars and cable TV are advisable but optional.

(c) **DRESS**: Dressing moderately, not just to cover up skin, but avoiding black T-shirts, earrings for men, and colorful lingerie. "Jesus Slogan" T-Shirts and a suit and tie on Sunday are advisable but optional.

Now, any one of us could probably point to something on the list and say, "Oh, that doesn't bother me." But this list is more than individual items, and it is more than an individual's assessment. These are the unwritten rules (i.e., Oral Tradition), not only of the corporate church, but of our current society. This is the barometer our culture uses to identify and evaluate Christians. Jesus objects to it as much as he did to the Jewish barometer, not because the list is inherently bad, but because bad people meticulously observe this good list. The result is, bad people look good and become worse people in the process.

Why do they become worse people? Because once they have met the requirements of man's "Oral Tradition" they feel justified in neglecting God's expectations. They become experts at doing meaningless things well, all the while ignorant of their Biblical illiteracy and social irresponsibility.

Mt 15:10-14 *with*
Mk 7:14

{^{14}Again^{MK}} ^{10}Jesus called the crowd to him and said, "Listen and understand. ^{11}What goes into a man's mouth does not make him 'unclean,' but what comes out of his mouth, that is what makes him 'unclean.'" ^{12}Then the disciples came to him and asked, "Do you know that the Pharisees were offended when they heard this?" ^{13}He replied, "Every plant that my heavenly Father has not planted will be pulled up by the roots. ^{14}Leave them; they are blind guides.^{a} If a blind man leads a blind man, both will fall into a pit."

^{a}*14* Some manuscripts *guides of the blind*

Now that Jesus has critiqued the behavior of the Pharisees, he returns to the original question and critiques the behavior of his disciples. Our Lord sees no danger in becoming "defiled" by eating with unwashed hands. Hocus-pocus uncleanness, even if it should enter the body while eating, will be "flushed" out soon enough (v. 17). No, what makes a man unclean is what enters his mind and comes out his mouth via the heart. More on this later.

All their lives, these disciples have revered the Pharisees. And now, by following Jesus, they find themselves on the other side of the fence from these pillars of Judaism. More than that, they find themselves the center of this theological controversy. The Pharisees have apparently gone away in a huff (v. 12). The disciples, no doubt, are still trembling as they ask Jesus, "Do you know the Pharisees were offended?" Jesus refrains from all those clever retorts that seem so appropriate to us: "So!," "Ask someone who cares," or "If you think they are mad at me, you should see how God feels about them!" Instead Jesus employs the familiar figure from Matthew 13:28-30. Just because a plant is in the garden does not mean it is a good plant. God, like a good gardener, will weed his ground.

"Leave them," may indicate "leave them alone," which would match the parable of the weeds that are not pulled up until judgment. But we might better understand Jesus to say, "Don't follow them any longer. They are blind guides and will only lead you to destruction." This interpretation makes a lot of sense considering the internal struggle of the disciples at this point as well as the mass of disciples that have recently defected for a "safer path."

Mt 15:10-14 *with*
Mk 7:17,19

{^{17}After he had left the crowd and entered the house^{MK}} ^{15}Peter {his disciples^{MK}} said, "Explain the parable to us."

^{16}"Are you still so dull?" Jesus asked them. ^{17}"Don't you see that whatever enters the mouth goes into the stomach and then out of the body? {In saying this, Jesus declared all foods "clean."^{MK}} ^{18}But the things that come out of the mouth come from the heart, and these make a man 'unclean.'"

Mk 7:20-23 *with*
Mt 15:20

^{20}He went on: "What comes out of a man is what makes him 'unclean.' ^{21}For from within, out of men's hearts come evil thoughts, sexual immorality, theft, murder, adultery, [22]greed, malice, deceit, lewdness, envy, slander, arrogance and folly. [23]All these evils come from inside and make a man 'unclean'; {but eating with unwashed hands does not make him 'unclean.'"[MT]}

Just like the sermon in parables (Mt 13), when Jesus leaves the crowd he enters a house. This gives the disciples the opportunity to ask Jesus privately what he meant by this parable. Again we find Peter speaking for the group. Since there is no definite article with the noun "house" we have no indication that it was Peter's house in Capernaum. Since Jesus is on a tour of Galilee, this could have taken place anywhere in that region.

We should probably be thankful that v. 17 is not literally translated. "Out of the body" is a euphemistic rendering of "thrown into the toilet" [*eis aphedrōna ekballetai*]. His meaning is obvious — even if some morsel should be ceremonially defiled, it doesn't stick around to do you any harm. It just passes through. Note: Jesus is addressing the issue of ceremonial defilement, not truly harmful substances.

What does make a man defiled, however, is what comes out of his mouth. Our words express the goodness or badness of our heart (Mt 12:34; Lk 6:45). This rule is so consistent that we can even be judged by our words (Mt 12:36). This list, unusual for Jesus (but cf. Rom 1:29-31; Gal 5:19-21), illustrates the kinds of things that are talked about and practiced from the overflow of one's heart. Human behavior often moves from mind to heart to words to behavior.

Mark adds this important parenthetical comment, "In saying this Jesus declared all foods clean." The issue of "clean and unclean" will come up again in the Christian church (Acts 10:9-16; 15:20; Rom 14:13ff; 1 Cor 8). And it's not just about food; it's about people. This is the obvious lesson for Peter in Acts 10-11. The structure of this text is also suggestive. In both Matthew and Mark the very next scene is Jesus' interaction with the Syro-Phoenician woman and the healings in Decapolis. Jesus' ministry is not about sanitation but sanctification; it is not about purity but people.[32]

§ 78
Jesus and the Syro-Phoenician Woman
(Mt 15:21-28; Mk 7:24-30)

This Syro-Phoenician woman is a pathetic picture. She represents everything a good Jew wanted to avoid. She is a woman. And since there are apparently no men in her life, she is left alone to fend for herself in a

---

[32]J.E. Prelan, "The Function of Mark's Miracles," *CQ* 48 (Aug 1990): 3-14, shows how Mark's miracles support this view. Jesus continually cleanses those who are ceremonially unclean (1:25-26; 1:41; 2:5, 11, 14; 2:23-28; 5:5; 5:28-29; 5:41-42; 7:35; 8:25). Taken as a whole, these show how the Levitical holiness codes are abrogated by Jesus.

hostile environment. Worse than this, her daughter is demon-possessed. This would raise suspicions that there was some kind of sin in her life. Worse than that, she is a dirty Gentile. Yet by the end of this episode, she will be a model of faith, what every Christian wants to be. Oddly enough, however, Jesus calls her a dog. We are a bit perplexed and embarrassed by that. It cries out for some kind of explanation.

Mt 15:21

²¹Leaving that place, Jesus withdrew to the region of Tyre and Sidon.

Mk 7:24

²⁴He entered a house and did not want anyone to know it; yet he could not keep his presence secret.

Things are heating up in Galilee as a result of the recent murder of John the Baptist, feeding 5,000, sermon on the bread of life, and the investigative team from the Jerusalem Passover. In fact, things are getting a little too hot. It is time for Jesus to retire to a quieter spot. So he heads northwest to the region of Phoenicia, now called Lebanon. He doesn't have to go far. This territory borders Galilee on the northwest. Phoenicia was hostile territory. Tyre and Sidon, the major cities of Phoenicia, epitomize Israel's ancient enemies (cf. comments on § 58, Mt 11:20-30).

Here we find Jesus on the edge of "enemy territory" hunkered down in some secret hideaway. His seclusion is not long-lived because his reputation had already reached these parts a year ago (Mk 3:8; Lk 6:17). So it couldn't have been more than a few days before this "woman came out" [*exelthousa*] of Gentile territory and cornered him in his hideout.

How does this Gentile get into a Jewish home? We can only suppose that she slips in among a crowd of Jews, no doubt to the chagrin of this kosher home-owner. Also, we can't imagine that she is alone in finding out where Jesus is. So we can assume this event takes place amidst a fairly large and mongrel crowd.

Mt 15:22 *with*
Mk 7:25

{²⁵In fact^MK} ²²A Canaanite woman {a Greek, born in Syrian Phoenicia^MK} from that vicinity {as soon as she heard about him^MK} came to him, crying out, "Lord, Son of David, have mercy on me! My {little^MK} daughter is suffering terribly from demon-possession."

Nationally this woman is a Phoenician. Politically she is a Syrian.[33] Ethnically, her roots go back to the Canaanites (Mt 15:22). By using this term, Matthew takes us back to the OT and conjures up the ancient rivalries

---

[33]Mark uses the term Syro-Phoenician probably "to distinguish this woman from the Libyo-Phoenicians of North Africa" (Wessel, p. 682).

and angers that have festered for so long. Culturally and linguistically she is a Greek (probably meaning Gentile).[34]

Her trouble is simple. Her daughter is demon-possessed. She knows she has no right to petition this Jewish healer, but neither does she have much choice. Jesus is the only one who can help her. She addresses him with a most kosher Messianic title: Son of David (cf. Mt 9:27; 12:23; 15:22; 20:30-31; 21:9, 15; 22:42).[35] It is not what one expects to roll off the lips of a Syro-Phoenician woman. Why is this foreigner addressing Jesus like this? First, using the name of a powerful historical figure was a common feature in first century magic and exorcisms (cf. Acts 19:13). In this bicultural, bilingual region, it would be reasonable to assume the locals are relatively fluent in Jewish affairs. She is probably familiar with the Jewish Messianic expectations and a few of their more common titles. She may be using this title both to honor Jesus and to invoke the power of his ancestor to appropriate a healing for her daughter.

Second, the OT predicted that Jehovah, the God of the Jews, would bless the whole world through these people and specifically David's kingdom:

❖ Isaiah 9:7: Of the increase of his government and peace there will be no end. He will reign on David's throne and over his kingdom, establishing and upholding it with justice and righteousness from that time on and forever. The zeal of the LORD Almighty will accomplish this.

❖ Isaiah 11:10: In that day the Root of Jesse will stand as a banner for the peoples; the nations will rally to him, and his place of rest will be glorious.

❖ Amos 9:11: In that day I will restore David's fallen tent. I will repair its broken places, restore its ruins, and build it as it used to be, so that they may possess the remnant of Edom and all the Nations who bear my name.

(See also Gen 12:3; Deut 32:43; Ps 18:49; 67:2; 98:2; 117:1; Isa 2:2; 42:6; 49:6, 22; 51:4; 52:10; 60:3; Joel 2:28; Mal 1:11).

What this woman is asking for, as an outsider, is to be blessed by the Jewish Messiah. Jesus is wanting her to realize that she can be an insider in God's plan. Jesus is now the Jewish Messiah but soon will become the universal Lord. So Jesus rejects her request, not because he disdains

---

[34]There is no reason to believe that this conversation did not take place in Greek. Growing up in Galilee, Jesus undoubtedly was familiar with the Greek language. Cf. S.E. Porter, "Did Jesus Ever Teach in Greek?" *TB* 44/2 (1993): 199-235, and J.A. Fitzmyer, "Did Jesus Speak Greek?" *BAR* 18/5 (Sept/Oct, 1992): 58-63.

[35]See D.C. Duling, "The Therapeutic Son of David," *NTS* 24 (1978): 392-410.

Gentiles (cf. Jn 4), but because she is not ready to receive the blessing until she understands who she is in God's eyes.[36] If Jesus were now to give her what she asked for, he would be capitulating to the popular demand to become a "do-gooder." To label Jesus as a "nice guy who helps people" is to "damn him with faint praise." What she must ask for is not merely a miracle, but primarily a sign.

Mt 15:23-24   [23]Jesus did not answer a word. So his disciples came to him and urged him, "Send her away, for she keeps crying out after us." [24]He answered, "I was sent only to the lost sheep of Israel."

This does not seem like the Jesus we have imagined. He has always befriended the down and outers. You could not get much more down and out in the Jewish community than to be a Gentile woman with a demonized daughter!

The disciples are annoyed by the situation. She is a persistent pest, following them around, begging, bothering, shouting to them as they are on their way. Aside from being a woman, she is a Gentile, which irks them all the more. It's not too tough to imagine these guys asking Jesus to get rid of her (Jn 4:27; Lk 9:54). But this request may not be as harsh as it seems. The text does not say the disciples ask Jesus to send her away empty-handed, but merely that he get rid of her. In fact, v. 24 makes much more sense if we understand the disciples to say, "Give her what she wants and be done with her."

Verse 24 is clear enough to understand . . . but not in this context. We know that Jesus' earthly ministry was directed toward the Jews (Mt 10:5-6; Jn 1:11) and that it would eventually extend to all peoples (Mt 10:18; 28:18-20; Jn 10:16). We find this "Jew first" pattern consistent in the book of Acts (1:8; 10:34-35; 13:46-47; 18:6; 19:8-9; 28:28) and stated by Paul himself in Romans 1:16; 2:9-10.[37] The quandary in this context is why Jesus says, "I was sent only to Jews," then he goes ahead and helps this woman anyway.

Jesus is not only teaching her, he is also teaching the Twelve. They need to understand this terribly difficult lesson that the Kingdom of God

---

[36]"The request of the centurion — like that of the Canaanite woman — was granted only after recognition of the distinction between Israel and others" J.J. Scott, "Gentiles and the Ministry of Jesus: Further Observations on Mt 10:5-6; 15:21-28," *JETS* 33/2 (1990): 161-169. Before the Gentiles, as a whole, could become God's people, (1) Jesus had to die to establish the New Israel and (2) the Jews had to be given the first opportunity to accept it. Thus, even though it is too early for Gentile inclusion, Jesus grants this woman's individual request once she recognizes her position as a Gentile in relation to Jesus the Jewish Messiah.

[37]This "Jew first" pattern is even suggested in our present text at Mk 7:27.

is for all people. True, she is not yet a part of the chosen people,[38] but that does not mean that she has no place in the "house." Jesus' demonstration of this truth is subtle, but brilliant!

Mt 15:25-26 *with*
Mk 7:25-27

[25]The woman came and knelt before him {fell at his feet.[MK]} "Lord, help me!" she said. {[26]She begged Jesus to drive the demon out of her daughter.[MK]} [26]He replied, "{[27]First let the children eat all they want,[MK]} It is not right to take the children's bread and toss it to their dogs."

Mk 7:28-30 *with*
Mt 15:27-28

[28]"Yes, Lord," she replied, "but even the dogs under the table eat the children's crumbs {that fall from their masters' table."[MT]} [29]Then he told her, "{Woman, you have great faith! Your request is granted.[MT]} For such a reply, you may go; the demon has left your daughter." {And her daughter was healed from that very hour.[MT]} [30]She went home and found her child lying on the bed, and the demon gone.

This woman has resigned her pride; she needs help! In a society where men typically intercede for women, she oversteps her bounds out of her extreme need. Kneeling at Jesus' feet, she is the only person in Mark's Gospel to call him Lord. Jesus has already put her off with his silence and now he puts her off blatantly with his words. He does this not to kick her while she's down, but to raise her level of understanding.

To the Jews all dogs were dirty. In addition, "dog" was one of the common Jewish terms for Gentiles. So Jesus is calling this woman a dirty dog. The Greeks, on the other hand, loved dogs and commonly allowed them in their houses as pets. That's obviously how this Greek woman interprets Jesus' word here, *kynaria* (especially with its diminutive ending).[39] Even so, it was still a slam. This woman's humility is impressive. So also is her wit and persistence. She has now come to understand (a) that Jesus is her only hope, and (b) that she has a part in God's "household." She is now ready to receive God's blessing through Jesus, and he is happy to give it.

This is neither the first "long distance" miracle (Jn 4:46-54), nor the first miracle done for a Gentile (Mt 8:5-13; Lk 7:1-10). But it is the clearest statement to date of the Kingdom extending beyond the borders of Israel (cf. Mt 13:47-50). The woman returns to find her daughter

---

[38]It would be anachronistic to import here the theology of the "Israel of God." It is coming, but not yet. The true Israelite is one who is right with God (Gen 32:28; Ps 73:1; 125:5). The NT is even stronger on this point (Rom 2:28-29; 9:6-7; Gal 3:29; 6:16; Phil 3:3). Jesus looked forward to this (Mt 21:41, 43; 8:11-12; 22:1-14) and NT writers confirmed it (Gal 3:7, 29; Rom 4:11,14; Jas 2:5; Rev 21:12-14). (It was even prophesied in the OT — Isa 54:1-3; cf. Gal 4:27; Hosea 2:23; cf. Rom 9:24-26; Ezek 47; Isa 44:3; cf. Jn 7:37-39).

[39]Cf. F. Dufton, "The Syrophoenician Woman and Her Dogs," *ExpT* 100 (1989): 417.

healed but still in bed, perhaps as a result of the demon shaking the girl one last time when departing (cf. Mk 1:26; 9:26). But the greatest benefit she receives is the hope of Israel which would soon arrive at her doorstep in full fledged form (Acts 11:19; 15:3; 21:3-4; 27:3).

§ 79a
Healings in
Decapolis
(Mt 15:29-31;
Mk 7:31-37)

[MK 7:]31Then Jesus left the vicinity of Tyre and went through Sidon, down to the Sea of Galilee and into the region of the Decapolis.[a]

ᵃ31 That is, the Ten Cities

Jesus' cover has been blown in the area of Tyre, so he moves north about twenty miles into purely Gentile territory. Eventually, he winds his way back down through the Tetrarchy of Herod Philip and finds himself on the east shore of the Sea of Galilee. This too is Gentile territory, an area known as Decapolis. It literally means, "Ten Cities." However, the list of specific cities associated with Decapolis varies depending on the author and date of the list.[40] But this much is certain, it was an area dominated by Greek culture and religion.

Jesus has been in this area at least once before when he healed the Gerasene Demoniac. The last time his stay was not more than twelve hours. The locals implored Jesus to leave them. His power over the demoniac was not only frightening, but destructive. He wiped out 2,000 pigs. That's a chunk of change for these local farmers. We would like to think this massive crowd was not only attracted by Jesus' miracle working power, but by the stirring testimony of this lone ex-demoniac (Mk 5:20).

We might title § 79a & b as "More of the Same." Neither the healings nor the feeding of the 4,000 present anything new. What makes them unique, however, is that they were done for Gentiles, in Gentile territory. As we observe the ebb and flow of Jesus' ministry at this point (§ 76b-82), we will notice the consistent theme of Gentile inclusion. These specific events must be interpreted in light of this theme. In other words, we cannot correctly understand what Jesus is doing without understanding where he is going.

Mk 7:32-35 *with*
Mt 15:29

{Then he went up on a mountainside and sat down.[MT]} 32There some people brought to him a man who was deaf and could hardly talk, and they begged him to place his hand on the man.

33After he took him aside, away from the crowd, Jesus put his fingers into the man's ears. Then he spit and touched the man's tongue. 34He looked up to

---

[40]Apparently these cities, somehow connected with Syria, could appeal to Rome with certain complaints and even minted their own coins during the second century. But there was never anything like a confederation of cities with their own government, militia or commercial arrangements. S.T. Parker, "The Decapolis Reviewed," *JBL* 94 (1975): 437-441.

heaven and with a deep sigh said to him, "Ephphatha!" (which means, "Be opened!"). [35]At this, the man's ears were opened, his tongue was loosened and he began to speak plainly.

This poor fellow has a speech impediment, probably due to his hearing problem. Therefore, he is not able to ask Jesus for a healing himself, so his friends do it for him. They have heard of the power of Jesus' touch (Mt 14:36), and beg him to heal their friend.

Jesus takes this deaf-mute off to the side. It would be quieter, allowing Jesus to understand his garbled speech and/or allow this man with a hearing problem to understand Jesus. This privacy will also allow Jesus to stir the man's faith. He will be able to concentrate better without all the movement and excitement of the crowd. In addition, it will cause less commotion among the crowd (Mk 7:36). At this point in his ministry, Jesus is trying to avoid the crowds, not to "wow" them.

With his fingers in the man's ears and spittle from his tongue, Jesus mimes for this man what he is about to do. Of course, both the deaf-mute and the crowd off to the side could see Jesus better than they could hear him. Looking up to heaven, the typical posture for Jewish prayer, and with a deep sigh,[41] Jesus utters this one-word petition, "Ephphatha." Mark translates the Aramaic for his reader as he does the other two times he quotes Jesus' Aramaic speech.

If this is Greek-speaking territory, why does Jesus use Aramaic? Surely he knows a little Greek growing up in Galilee. Well, as he prays, it is natural to revert to his native tongue. Besides, the deaf guy can't hear him anyway, so it will do him no good if Jesus speaks in his native tongue. This also may be a subtle statement that Jesus' ministry does extend to the Gentiles, but it is still particularly Jewish (Jn 4:22). Jesus assents to perform the same kinds of miracles he has done for the Jews. But he must not lose the "Jewishness" of his Messiahship. It is only in connection with the prophecies, sacrifices, and promises of the OT that salvation has its full force for the Gentiles.

Mk 7:36-37

[36]Jesus commanded them not to tell anyone. But the more he did so, the more they kept talking about it. [37]People were overwhelmed with amazement. "He has done everything well," they said. "He even makes the deaf hear and the mute speak."

Same song, Gentile verse. The reasons Jesus does not want Gentile propagation of his ministry are the same as for not wanting Jewish propa-

---

[41]This word [*stenazō*] is only used here in the Gospels. In the epistles it expresses a deep pathos (Rom 8:23; 2 Cor 5:2, 4; Heb 13:17). We don't know for sure what moved Jesus so. Perhaps his deep heave was a visual demonstration of Jesus' emotional involvement with this man.

gation: (1) They are focused on miracles and not on signs. (2) They have an immature, and therefore improper, understanding of his Messiahship. (3) The religio-political scene is too hot right now. Premature propagation of this Jesus movement would only ignite a popular uprising which would destroy what Jesus was trying to do.

Mark uses the word *mogilalos*, which the NIV translates "could hardly talk." Here is the only time it is used in the NT. The LXX also only uses it once, in Isaiah 35:6. This is clearly a Messianic text. It says:

> Then will the eyes of the blind be opened and the ears of the deaf unstopped. Then will the lame leap like a deer, and the mute tongue shout for joy. Water will gush forth in the wilderness and streams in the desert. . . . And a highway will be there; it will be called the Way of Holiness. The unclean will not journey on it . . . and the ransomed of the Lord will return. They will enter Zion with singing; everlasting joy will crown their heads (Isaiah 35:5-10).

It would appear that Mark, by using this unique word, is calling our attention to the Messianic prophecy about Jesus. Moreover, Mark relates it to Jesus' dealing with a Gentile.

Mt 15:30-31

[30]Great crowds came to him, bringing the lame, the blind, the crippled, the mute and many others, and laid them at his feet; and he healed them. [31]The people were amazed when they saw the mute speaking, the crippled made well, the lame walking and the blind seeing. And they praised the God of Israel.

Here we go again! This is the typical response to Jesus — bring him your broken and he will fix them. What is unique, however, is that these Gentiles "praised the God of Israel." Hence, Jesus is successful in accenting the Jewishness of his program. We should also point out that Jesus' ministry among the Gentiles was not just in miracles, it included teaching. Matthew (15:29) says that Jesus went up on the mountainside and "sat down." When a Jewish rabbi sat, it was roughly equivalent to saying, "Class is in session" (cf. Mt 5:1; 13:1-2). But like their Jewish counterparts, these Gentiles are not so interested in what Jesus has to say, but in what he can do for them.

§ 79b
Feeding the
4000
(Mt 15:32-38;
Mk 8:1-9a)

The feeding of the four thousand looks an awful lot like the feeding of the five thousand. Some scholars think that Matthew and Mark simply repeat them as a literary doublet to emphasize a point.[42] However, there

---

[42]E.g., D.F. Robinson, "The Parable of the Loaves," *ATR* 39 (1957): 107-115. S. Masuda goes even further, arguing that both stories were redacted from a single original source ("The Good News of the Miracle of the Bread," *NTS* 28 [1982]: 191-219).

are enough differences between the two feedings that the most natural reading of the texts suggests two separate events.[43] The similarity between the events shows how Jesus ministered comparably to both the Jews and the Gentiles during this portion of his ministry.

Mk 8:1-3   ¹During those days another large crowd gathered. Since they had nothing to eat, Jesus called his disciples to him and said, ²"I have compassion for these people; they have already been with me three days and have nothing to eat. ³If I send them home hungry, they will collapse on the way, because some of them have come a long distance."

Jesus' fame spreads quickly through the Decapolis. Because he stays put for several days, the crowds begin to mushroom. After three days of healing and teaching, the crowd's backpacks and lunch-pails are empty. Instead of going home for more food, many of them fast so they can stay and hear Jesus. It's a good thing, too, for if they leave now, Jesus will be gone by the time they return.

Now it is time for Jesus to leave. But he fears that if he sends this fasting crowd away with nothing to eat they might faint before they get home. Jesus' compassion shines all the more brightly against the trivia of our daily existence.

Mk 8:4-9 *with*   ⁴His disciples answered, "But where in this remote place can anyone {we^MT}
Mt 15:33-38   get enough bread to feed them?" ⁵"How many loaves do you have?" Jesus asked. "Seven," they replied. ⁶He told the crowd to sit down on the ground. When he had taken the seven loaves and given thanks, he broke them and gave them to his disciples to set before the people, and they did so. ⁷They had a few small fish as well; he gave thanks for them also and told the disciples to distribute them. ⁸The people {all^MT} ate and were satisfied. Afterward the disciples picked up seven basketfuls of broken pieces that were left over. ⁹About four thousand men were present {besides women and children^MT}.

Are these guys dense, or what?! Have they so soon forgotten the feeding of the 5,000 (cf. Mk 6:52). Before we hang these fellows, we ought to point out a few things. First, Jesus did not always provide miracles (Jn 5:4-6; Mt 13:58). Nor is it necessarily "spiritual" to expect this (Mt 12:38-45; 16:1). Second, the disciples may not be doubting Jesus'

---

[43](1) They have different details: (a) 5,000 vs. 4,000; (b) 5 loaves vs. 7 loaves; (c) 12 small baskets (*kophinos*) vs. 7 large baskets (*spuris*, cf. Acts 9:25) of leftovers; (d) With Jesus 1 day vs. 3 days; (e) One prayer vs. two; (f) Jesus sent the Apostles away vs. leaving with them.

(2) They were at different times — They sat on grass in the first but on the ground (after the grass dried up) in the second.

(3) They were for two different people. The first feeding was for Jews, the second was primarily for Gentiles.

(4) Jesus, himself, clearly spoke of two different feedings (Mk 8:18-21).

ability, but his willingness to do for these Gentiles what he has done for the Jews. Third, Matthew's emphatic use of the word "we" (15:33) may suggest they are not doubting Jesus' ability but their own, to perform the miracles that Jesus has done. After all, Jesus empowered them to do what he did (Mt 10:1, 8). Perhaps they think he wants them to try their hand at feeding a few thousand people. Finally, an honest look at the contemporary church would hardly paint a better picture of our faith in Jesus to provide and sustain. Even though Jesus has proven trustworthy time and time again, our lives betray an embarrassing level of unbelief.

§ 80
Pharisees and Sadducees Seek a Sign at Magadan
(Mt 15:39-16:4;
Mk 8:9b-12);
[cf. § 62, 106, &
Jn 2:18-23;
6:30]

[MT 15:]39After Jesus had sent the crowd away, he got into the boat {with his disciplesMK} and went to the vicinity of Magadan {the region of Dalmanutha.MK}

1The Pharisees and Sadducees came to Jesus and tested him by asking him to show them a sign from heaven.

After the feeding of the 4,000 in Decapolis, Jesus returns to Jewish territory.[44] The Pharisees again accost Jesus (cf. Mk 7:1). This time they are accompanied by the Sadducees. These two groups generally fought with each other (cf. Acts 23:7-8), but their mortal hate for Jesus draws them together. This is the first time the Pharisees and Sadducees have gotten together since their investigation of John the Baptist (Mt 3:7; Jn 1:19, 24). It has primarily been the Pharisees alone who have pursued Jesus (Mt 9:11, 34; 12:2, 14, 24, 38; 15:1; Lk 5:17; 7:36-39), but from here to Golgotha, they will team up with the Sadducees (Mt 21:45; 22:34; 27:62), as well as with the Herodians (Mk 3:6; 12:13).

Their question is neither new nor sincere. Jesus has heard it at least three times before (Jn 2:18-23; Mt 12:38-45; Jn 6:30 — see comments on those texts, § 31, 62, & 76a). They don't really want to believe Jesus. Both Matthew and Mark capture their motive in the word "test" [*peirazō*]. Literally, they were tempting Jesus — looking for a reason to accuse him. Paul correctly assesses his compatriots when he says, "Jews demand miraculous signs and Greeks look for wisdom, but we preach Christ crucified: a stumbling block to Jews and foolishness to Gentiles, but to those whom God has called, both Jews and Greeks, Christ the power of God and the wisdom of God" (1 Cor 1:22-24).

The Judean[45] delegation conceals their insincerity. First, they ask for a sign [*semeian*] rather than a miracle. They make it look as if they are

---

[44]Both Magadan and Dalmanutha have been lost, but they were likely on the southwest coast of the Sea of Galilee, at the edge of the Decapolis.

[45]The verb *exelthen*, "came out" (8:11) indicates that they were from some other area. Based on Mk 7:1, it seems logical to assume that this delegation was also from Jerusalem.

asking for reasonable evidence as opposed to neat tricks. Second, they ask for a sign from heaven, such as was given by Elijah or Moses, as if these would be categorically different than the miracles Jesus already performed.

Mt 16:2-3 *with*
Mk 8:12

²He replied {sighed deeply[46] and said^{MK}},[a] "When evening comes, you say, 'It will be fair weather, for the sky is red,' ³and in the morning, 'Today it will be stormy, for the sky is red and overcast.' You know how to interpret the appearance of the sky, but you cannot interpret the signs of the times.

[a]*2* Some early manuscripts do not have the rest of verse 2 and all of verse 3.

Palestinian weather generally comes from the west, off the Mediterranean Sea. At dawn, the rain clouds from the west, reflect a reddish hue from the morning sun coming up over the eastern horizon. In the evening, however, that same reddish hue would indicate clear skies in the west.[47]

Jesus is visibly upset over the myopia of the Jewish leadership. They are more attentive to weather than to the Messiah. They have plenty of reason to believe in Jesus (cf. Jn 5:31-47); but have clearly refused, attributing Jesus' miraculous power to Beelzebub (Mt 9:34; 12:22-37; cf. Lk 11:14-36).

Mt 16:4

⁴A wicked and adulterous generation looks for a miraculous sign, but none will be given it except the sign of Jonah." Jesus then left them and went away.

Why is it wicked and adulterous to look for a miraculous sign? Does God expect us to believe without proof? Is faith really some leap in the dark? NO! Sign seeking is wicked for the following reasons:

(1) It ignores what Jesus has already done. It essentially says, "Jesus, we don't believe you. You must prove yourself again . . . and again . . . and again."

(2) It places us as judge over Jesus. It essentially says, "Jesus, you perform for me and I will decide whether or not you are valid."

(3) It places miracles over testimony. Miracles are used to attract our attention to valid testimony. Once the testimony has been given, the miracles have served their purpose. In addition, it often places emotions over reason. Instead of thinking through the testimony we want to feel our way along with souped up experiences.

---

[46]The NIV leaves untranslated the words "in his spirit."

[47]These verses are absent in a few of the more important manuscripts but likely belong here (see comments by Carson, p. 360). Perhaps they were eliminated from the Egyptian manuscripts because these Palestinian climatic indications do not hold true in Egypt.

(4) It places self over Jesus. Miracles used for human gratification point in the wrong direction. Instead of pointing to Jesus they point to self. They become shallow and selfish.

(5) It denigrates true faith. Instead of believing what we can't see based on true testimony, we demand validation at every point (Jn 20:29).

Again, the resurrection is promised as a sign for this generation. And even this will be concealed from unbelievers (cf. Mk 8:12; Acts 10:41). Jesus is again forced to leave the region due to the animosity of his enemies. He has been rejected and nearly ejected from Jerusalem, Nazareth, Capernaum, and now Magadan.

[Mt 16:4 = Mt 12:39. See comments on § 62, especially on the sign of Jonah.]

**§ 81a
Warnings
Against the
Leaven of the
Pharisees,
Sadducees and
Herodians**
(Mt 16:5-12;
Mk 8:13-21)

[MK 8:]¹³Then he left them, got back into the boat and crossed to the other side. ¹⁴The disciples had forgotten to bring bread, except for one loaf they had with them in the boat. ¹⁵"Be careful," Jesus warned them. "Watch out for the yeast of the Pharisees {and Sadducees^MT} and that of Herod." ¹⁶They discussed this with one another and said, "It is because we have no bread."

After another tense confrontation with the Jewish religious hierarchy, Jesus retreats with his disciples across the lake to the north shore. En route to the other side[48] Jesus warns his disciples about the leaven of the Pharisees and Sadducees. The disciples are thinking about food while Jesus is thinking about teaching (cf. Jn 4:31-34; 6:27). Jesus' words remind them that they have no lunch, save one measly loaf to split thirteen ways.

It is hard to tell how they interpret Jesus' warning. Perhaps they think he cautions them about poisoned bread. After all, the Pharisees have already expressed a desire to kill Jesus, both in Judea and Galilee (Mk 3:6; Jn 5:18; Mt 12:14). Poison was a common form of murder in those days. Perhaps their hunger hinders them from thinking much at all about what Jesus means. All they know is that it's slim pickings for dinner and they somehow connect Jesus' warning to their negligence to get groceries (v. 16).

---

[48]The aorist verb *apēlthen*, "went," used in conjunction with *peran*, "beyond" or "the other side," might imply that they had already arrived. However, grammatically, it could refer to the process of their going. In other words, this discussion might have taken place while en route to Bethsaida. This interpretation would make for a smoother transition of Mk 8:22.

The Pharisees and Herodians were strange bed-fellows. (Matthew substitutes Sadducees for Herodians, who were probably political envoys from the Saducean party. Although they did have their distinctions,[49] here the Saducean Herodians surely represent the liberal counterpart to the Pharisees.) These two groups are nearly polar opposites and yet Jesus describes their yeast as a singular evil. What error do these two groups share? The subtle but blatant rejection of Jesus. They feign a willingness to accept Jesus, by asking for a sign (Jn 2:18-23; Mt 12:38-45; 16:1-4). But there is no way they will ever accept him as leader or Lord.

Leaven is often spoken of as evil (cf. Lev 2:11; Mt 16:6; Lk 12:1; 1 Cor 5:6-8; Gal 5:9), but not always (cf. Mt 13:33; Lk 13:20-21). Some commentators suggest that the leaven removed from the Passover meal represents sin (cf. Exod 12:8 etc.). However, it could just as well represent the hurried nature of the meal. That is, they did not have time to wait for the yeast to cause the bread to "rise." In other words, "evil" is not the dominant characteristic of leaven, but rather it is "pervasive influence." With this understanding, we hear Jesus say, "Beware of the pervasive influence of unbelief of the Pharisees and Sadducees." This comes at a time of mass defection among Jesus' disciples (cf. Jn 6:60-71). They need a warning against social seduction, when Jesus' popularity wanes.

Mk 8:17-21 *with*
Mt 16:8

[17]Aware of their discussion, Jesus asked them: "{You of little faith,[MT]} Why are you talking about having no bread? Do you still not see or understand? Are your hearts hardened? [18]Do you have eyes but fail to see, and ears but fail to hear? And don't you remember? [19]When I broke the five loaves for the five thousand, how many basketfuls of pieces did you pick up?"

"Twelve," they replied.

[20]"And when I broke the seven loaves for the four thousand, how many basketfuls of pieces did you pick up?"

They answered, "Seven."

[21]He said to them, "Do you still not understand?"

Mt 16:11-12

[11]"How is it you don't understand that I was not talking to you about bread? But be on your guard against the yeast of the Pharisees and Sadducees." [12]Then they understood that he was not telling them to guard against the yeast used in bread, but against the teaching of the Pharisees and Sadducees.

Their "little faith" is lamentable (cf. Mt 6:30; 8:26; 14:31; 17:20). Not only do they fail to understand Jesus' sublime teaching on faith, they

---

[49]We are not far off in characterizing the evil of the Pharisees as Legalism, the Sadducees as Liberalism, and the Herodians as Secularism. Our modern culture and church is prone to these same errors and would likewise do well to heed Jesus' warning. All three of these share the same "leaven" of unbelief. Each, in its own way, detracts from true discipleship. Each has its unique draw, but all draw away from Jesus.

even miss the mundane meaning of food. Couched in the language of Isaiah 6:10, Jesus reminds them of his supreme ability to provide food. If five little loaves fed 5,000, with twelve baskets of leftovers, and seven loaves fed 4,000, with seven "hampers" left over, then one loaf is surely sufficient to feed thirteen men.

Having settled this little diversion about bread, Jesus gets back to the issue at hand, which is the leaven of the Pharisees and Sadducees — their teaching.[50] Now their teaching is not all bad (cf. Mt 23:3). Jesus would agree with the Sadducees in their rejection of Pharisaic oral tradition. He would agree with the Pharisees in their belief in the resurrection, etc. But Jesus warns us to watch out for their pervasive unbelief. It is especially insidious since it disguises itself in the garb of religious dialogue. While clinging to orthodox practices and espousing Biblical doctrine, their self-seeking attitudes of unbelief lead them away from God's plan. This is confusing to the populace, whose shallow evaluation never looks past the dress, talk, and public display of the clergy. So often, the *heart* of the matter is indeed the heart of the matter.

§ 81b
Two-Step
Healing of a
Blind Man
(Mk 8:22-26)

[22]They came to Bethsaida, and some people brought a blind man and begged Jesus to touch him. [23]He took the blind man by the hand and led him outside the village. When he had spit on the man's eyes and put his hands on him, Jesus asked, "Do you see anything?"

[24]He looked up[51] and said, "I see people; they look like trees walking around."

[25]Once more Jesus put his hands on the man's eyes. Then his eyes were opened, his sight was restored, and he saw everything clearly. [26]Jesus sent him home, saying, "Don't go into the village.[a]"

[a]26 Some manuscripts *Don't go and tell anyone in the village*

Likely this "Fisher-town" (Bethsaida) is the home of Peter and Co. After all, they would need to dock their boat(s) before leaving the country to travel to Caesarea Philippi. As they arrive "home," they are met by a delegation on behalf of this blind man. We can't tell his level of faith, but the faith of his friends is obvious (cf. Mk 2:3-12; 7:31-37). If he lacked faith, this might explain Jesus' odd actions as an attempt to bolster his belief.

This scene has become all too familiar. Jesus has often healed blindness (Mt 9:27-30; 11:5; 12:22; 15:31; Lk 7:21-22; Jn 5:3). It was, and is,

---

[50]Blomberg notes that "There may be an underlying Aramaic play on words in v. 12b, given the similarity between 'teaching' (*ʾamîrʾā*) and 'yeast' (*hămîrʾā*)" (p. 249).

[51]"Looked up" [*anablepō*], is better translated "regain sight," E.S. Johnson, "Mark 8:22-26: Blind Man From Bethsaida," *NTS* 25 (1979): 230-383.

a common problem in third world countries. Yet this pericope is unique. It has a number of similarities to the healing of the deaf-mute (Mk 7:31-37):[52]

(1) Both are recorded by Mark alone.

(2) Both take place in a period of retirement/retreat.

(3) Both men are taken aside.

(4) Jesus uses spittle and touch with both.

(5) Jesus tries to avoid attention with both.

What makes this healing such an oddity is that it is the only "two-step" healing Jesus ever performed. Any guess as to Jesus' motives is speculative. But Wessel (p. 691) offers a nice suggestion: "Jesus may have moved only as quickly as the man's faith would allow (in Mark's Gospel faith as a requisite for healing is emphasized). But Calvin's suggestion that Jesus was demonstrating his sovereign freedom seems more likely. One thing is certain. The early church did not make up this story!"[53]

The use of spittle aligns with the common Jewish belief in its healing properties. The fact the man sees people as if they were "walking trees" indicates he is still nearsighted and probably that he was not born blind since he has some point of reference to make such a comparison. Then, when Jesus lays his hands on him, his sight is restored. Mark uses a rare word [*telaugos*], which indicates clear sight at a distance. Not only can he see, but he can see well.

---

[52]R.A. Guelich (p. 436) suggests that Mark uses the stories of the deaf-mute (7:31-37) and the blind man (8:22-26) to bracket the disciples' spiritual deafness and blindness in the boat (8:13-21). In other words, Mark illustrates the disciples' unbelief by sandwiching it in between literal dumbness and blindness.

[53]L.W. Countryman, "How Many Baskets Full? Mark 8:14-21 and the Value of Miracles in Mark," *CBQ* 47 (1985): 643-655, suggests a partial explanation may come from the structure of Mark's book. It appears that we have two comparable cycles of Jesus' ministry here:

Cycle #1	Cycle #2
Calming the storm (4:35-41)	Walking on water (6:45-52)
Exorcism of Gerasene Demoniac (5:1-20)	Exorcism of Syrophoenician Woman's daughter (7:24-30)
Healings: Jairus' Daughter & Woman with a hemorrhage (5:21-43)	Deaf-Mute (7:31-37)
Feeding the 5,000 (6:32-44)	Feeding the 4,000 (8:1-9)

In the first cycle, Jesus' miracles flowed freely and powerfully. During the second cycle, when Jesus' ministry shifted to a more Gentile clientele, his miracles were reluctant or "strained." When he walked on the water he almost "passed them by." He argued with the Syrophoenician woman and healed the deaf-mute in two steps. And Jesus fed less people with more bread the second time around. Perhaps all of these peculiar details can be explained by Jesus' reluctance to openly minister to Gentiles without some clarification that he is, indeed, a Jewish Messiah.

Perhaps Wessel is correct in suggesting that this two-step miracle prefigures Peter's confession in the next pericope. His chart showing this comparison in Mark is insightful:

8:22	Circumstances	8:27
8:23-24	Partial Sight — Partial Understanding	8:28
8:25	Sight — Understanding	8:29
8:26	Injunction to Silence	8:30

**§ 82
Peter's Great
Confession**
(Mt 16:13-20;
Mk 8:27-30;
Lk 9:18-21)

We are now well into the third year of Jesus' ministry. To date, the disciples still do not have a clear understanding of who Jesus is. It's getting to be crunch time for such a confession.

For the last couple of months Jesus has been skirting the edges of Jewish territory. Now he abandons Galilee altogether. He travels twenty-five miles north of Capernaum into the heart of Gentile territory. At the time, this must have seemed like a crisis in Jesus' ministry. But Peter's present confession will become a centerpiece of the synoptic Gospels and a watershed for Jesus' ministry.

Mt 16:13-14 *with*
Mk 8:27, Lk 9:19

[13]When Jesus came to the region of {villages around[MK]} Caesarea Philippi, {on the way[MK]} {when Jesus was praying in private[LK]} he asked his disciples, "Who do people say the Son of Man is?"

[14]They replied, "Some say John the Baptist; others say Elijah; and still others, Jeremiah or one of the prophets {of long ago has come back to life.[LK]}"

Caesarea Philippi sits at the base of Mt. Hermon whose snowcapped peaks can be seen as far away as Nazareth on a clear day. It is a beautiful and fertile setting.[54] At 1,150 feet above sea level, it provides an impressive view of the upper Jordan. Even the scenery seems to say, "Something big is about to happen." But what that is, and whether it is good or bad, the Apostles don't yet know.

This is an important moment for Jesus. He bathes it in prayer (Lk 9:18) as he does other pivotal events (Lk 3:21; 6:12; 9:28; 22:41). There have been other confessions about Jesus (e.g., Jn 1:29-34, 49; 3:2, 36; 4:42), but none have reached such a level. None have elicited such a response from Jesus as when he plainly predicts his death for the first time (although cf. Jn 2:19; 3:14; 6:53; Mt 9:15; 10:38-39; 12:39-40).

---

[54]Caesarea Philippi is described in detail by Edersheim (II:72-74). One of his more colorful quotes comes from Tristram, *Land of Israel*, p. 586: "Everywhere there is a wild medley of cascades, mulberry trees, fig-trees, dashing torrents, festoons of vine, bubbling fountains, reeds, and ruins, and the mingled music of birds and waters."

Somewhere along the way, sometime after his prayer, Jesus turns to the Twelve and asks two carefully crafted questions. They are not designed for answers but for response. First, "Who do people say the Son of Man is?" That's an odd question for Jesus. Does he really not know? Even without his ability to read men's minds (cf. Mt 12:25; Lk 5:22; 6:8; 7:39-40; Jn 2:24-25), Jesus is not deaf. He can hear as well as the Twelve what people are saying about him. Besides, since when does Jesus really care what people think of him? He does not ask this question to get an answer, but to get his Apostles to think along with him about who he really is.

There are several opinions. Some thought Jesus was John the Baptist (cf. Mt 14:1-2). Some thought he was Elijah (Mal 3:1; 4:5-6). Others, likely based on the apocryphal books, perceived Jesus to be Jeremiah (2 Esdras 2:16-18; 2 Macc 2:1-12; 15:12-16). Now, the Jews did not believe in reincarnation. What they did believe was that departed souls might empower living men to carry out their work (cf. § 71a). Thus, Jesus either divinely resembled or was metaphysically helped by these great men.

Why does Jesus "look like" these guys? Aside from the obvious fact that all of these men were dead, they had three common characteristics that Jesus also shared. (1) They never pulled any punches. They spoke the raw truth in the face of antagonism and potential persecution. (2) They confronted the religious and political powers of their day. And (3) they all got beat up for their boisterousness. The crowds have noticed the mounting aggression against Jesus in the ranks of the religious hierarchy. All of these opinions are quite complimentary, but inadequate. To rank Jesus with the greatest teacher or the most profound prophet is to "damn him with faint praise."

Mt 16:15-16

¹⁵"But what about you?" he asked. "Who do you say I am?"
¹⁶Simon Peter answered, "You are the Christ^a, the Son of the living God."

^a*16* Or *Messiah*; also in verse 20

Now comes the real question . . . the only one that really matters: "Who do *YOU* say that I am?" The NIV properly stresses the "you" by repeating it. Although Jesus addresses the whole group, Peter characteristically answers for all of them. Sometimes he says some really stupid things (Mt 16:22-23; 26:31-35; Jn 13:6-11). At other times he speaks brilliantly (Mt 14:28-31; 16:16-18; Jn 6:68-69; Acts 2:14ff). But never does Peter shine more brightly than he does right here. He has already made a preliminary confession (Jn 6:69), and he obviously has much ground to cover in his Messianic understanding (vv. 22-23). But who could deny, especially in light of Jesus' response, the majesty of this simple statement of faith.

"Christ" is the Greek equivalent of the Hebrew "Messiah." Both words mean, "The anointed one." In Hebrew culture, this represents "one set apart" for the work of God and endowed with the power of God. The practice of pouring oil over one's head was primarily reserved for the consecration of prophets, priests, and kings (Exod 29:7, 21; 1 Sam 10:1, 6; 16:13; 2 Sam 1:14, 16). These three positions, of course, describe Jesus' ministry for the Christian. We gladly accept Jesus as prophet and priest, but unfortunately too many professing Christians reject His Majesty's reign in their life. We are simply not given the option of selecting two out of three. "Christ," then, became an official title of the Jewish Messiah. This single individual was to liberate Israel from all bonds and extend her rule over all the earth (cf. Dan 9:25-27).[55]

"Son of the living God" was as kosher a title as "Christ." It comes from the Hebrew idea that God is "living" as opposed to the dead idols of pagans. Hence, Peter is speaking not only for the Twelve but for the Jewish populace as well.

Mt 16:17-18

[17]Jesus replied, "Blessed are you, Simon son of Jonah, for this was not revealed to you by man, but by my Father in heaven. [18]And I tell you that you are Peter,[a] and on this rock I will build my church, and the gates of Hades[b] will not overcome it.[c]

[a]*18* Peter means *rock*.   [b]*18* Or *hell*   [c]*18* Or *not prove stronger than it*

Jesus' response parallels Peter's. Peter identifies Jesus as the Son of God; Jesus identifies Peter as the son of Jonah (Jn 21:15 has "of John"). Peter identifies Jesus' position as Messiah; Jesus identifies Peter's position as the foundation of the church.

That much is simple. But verse 18 complicates things a bit. What exactly is Peter's position as the "rock" of the church? Does this mean that Peter was the first pope with the power of Apostolic succession? That is the traditional Catholic response. Protestants have protested, however. They suggest that it is not Peter, but his confession that is the foundation of the church. They base this on the fact that Jesus' play on words changes from masculine [*Petros* = Peter] to feminine [*Petra* =

---

[55]The Jewish hope of a liberator Messiah was primarily found among the populace, not Israel's leaders. There were a number of Messianic movements in Jesus' day, where some peasant would be proclaimed "King of the Jews." (See R.A. Horsley, "Like One of the Prophets of Old": Two Types of Popular Prophets at the Time of Jesus," *CBQ* 47 [1985]: 435-463). However, the "Jesus movement" was clearly unique. He was both a peaceful and an eschatological leader.

rock]. Furthermore, they claim that a *petros* was a small throwing stone, but that *petra* was a huge rock. Thus, they hear Jesus say, "Peter, you are a little rock (cf. Jn 1:42; also 1 Cor 15:5; Gal 1:18), but the confession you have made is great enough to build a church upon," or "I, Jesus am the true bedrock of the church" (cf. 1 Pet 2:5-8).

However, this subtle distinction between *petros* and *petra* is found only in Greek poetry. Its application here is questionable. Besides, Jesus was probably speaking in Aramaic. At least he does when he addresses Peter as "Bar Jonah." And Aramaic does not have the subtle distinction between the Greek words for "rock." It simply uses *kepha*. Furthermore, even if Peter is not the "rock" (v. 18), he still has the "Keys of the Kingdom" (v. 19). That also must be explained.

On the other hand, the whole concept of the primacy of Peter as the first pope is objectionable. In the book of Acts, Peter is not portrayed as having papal authority (11:2; 15:13-21; 21:18; see also Gal 2:14). And Apostolic succession would require that Peter overlooked John, a living Apostle, and passed the command on to another disciple. There is simply no NT text, including this one, which can adequately support such a doctrine.

We conclude, therefore, that Peter is the rock, but not the first pope. Peter's specific function will be explained below. Suffice to say here that the church is built on Peter, a representative figure of the Twelve (cf. Eph. 2:20).

The word "church" [*ekklēsia*] is a compound word whose roots literally mean "called out." It is only used three times in the Gospels (Mt 16:18; 18:17 [twice]). Some have overemphasized this etymology and stressed that the church is "called out of darkness" and/or is to be "separate" from the world. But the word merely meant an assembly, sometimes pagan (Acts 19:32), sometimes Christian. A more important background than its Greek etymology, is its Hebrew counterpart, the word *qahal* — an assembly of God's people. "The Assembly" or "church" represents the citizenry of God's kingdom — those who share God's purpose, program, and authority.

The bad news is that this "assembly of God's people" will soon have to confront the "gates of Hades." The good news is that the church wins the contest. The question is, what in the world is Jesus talking about? There are a number of possibilities.[56] But we should recognize at least

---

[56]Some of the most popular suggestions include: (1) The death of Jesus Christ will not demolish the establishment of the church (the gates are offensive). Jesus' resurrection will destroy the power of the devil — death, Rev 1:18 (defensive). (2) The death of the saints will not destroy the church because the resurrection of the last day will revive them to the kingdom (offensive). (3) Martyrdom will not destroy the church. As Ambrose

this much: (1) "Gates" are normally located at the fortress being defended. But this metaphor also symbolized "power." Thus, the gates of Hades might be either offensive or defensive. (2) "Hades" is not necessarily equivalent to hell. Properly, it signifies the abode of the dead, and by extension, death itself (Job 17:16; 38:17; Ps 9:13; 107:18; Isa 38:10). And (3) it is the church as a whole, not Jesus or Peter, which confronts the Gates of Hades. So we wind up with something like this: The church is not overpowered by death. Neither the cross nor martyrdom can stifle the progress of the church.

Mt 16:19-20

[19]I will give you the keys of the kingdom of heaven; whatever you bind on earth will be[a] bound in heaven, and whatever you loose on earth will be[a] loosed in heaven." [20]Then he {strictly[LK]} warned his disciples not to tell anyone that he was the Christ.

[a]*19* Or *have been*[57]

These "keys" obviously represent some kind of authority, but authority to do what? Hiers[58] offers a number suggestions including:
(1) Rabbinic absolution of a vow (but cf. Mt 5:33-37).
(2) Rabbinic ratification of forbidden/permitted practices (but cf. Mt 23:8).
(3) Excommunication (Mt 18:18; 1 Cor 5).
(4) Forgiveness of sins in the present (Jn 20:23; however, cf. Mt 5:23-26; 6:12-15; 18:21-35), or at the judgment (Mt 10:23; 11:20-24; 19:28)
(5) Exorcism, based on the intertestamental usage of the words "bind" and "loose" (Tobit 3:17; 8:3; Josephus, *Ant.* 8.2.5).

One option that Hiers does not mention, which seems to best fit the body of evidence from the book of Acts, is Peter's preaching of the gospel (cf. Lk 11:52). It was Peter who "opened the door" for both the Jewish church (Acts 2) and the Gentile church (Acts 10; cf. 15:7). This may not account for all the implications of binding and loosing, but it goes a long way. Option #2 (above) probably covers the bulk of the

---

said, "The blood of the saints is the seed of the church" (offensive). (4) Satan can't stop the progress of the church. She continues to grow and establish God's kingdom on earth (defensive). (5) Christians, especially through "Power Encounters," can dominate Satanic and demonic activity (defensive).

[57]J.R. Mantey, "Evidence that the Perfect Tense in John 20:23 and Mt 16:19 is Mistranslated," *JETS* 16 (1973), suggests that the perfect tense here is the most accurate translation and that this binding/loosing is carried out through the three-step process of inspiration, declaration, and divine substantiation.

[58]R.H. Hiers, "Binding and Loosing: The Matthean Authorizations," *JBL* 104 (1985): 233-250.

remaining ground, especially in light of canonical writing. And option #3 may also play a part in Apostolic "binding" in such passages as Acts 4:11-12; 5:3-10; 8:20-21; 13:51-52; 28:28.

Furthermore, we need not assume that Peter was the only one with the keys. He is the spokesman for the Apostolic band here (cf. Mt 15:15-16; 19:25-29; 26:40; Mk 11:20-22; Lk 12:41; Jn 6:67-70). He is also center stage in Acts 2 and 10. Chrysostom calls Peter "the mouth of the Apostles." But his primacy is chronological, not hierarchical.[59] The other Apostles will help shoulder the burden for evangelism (Acts 2:4, 14), persecution (Acts 5:18), establishing policy (Acts 6:2), doctrine (Acts 2:42; 8:14; 15:10, 22-28), etc. (Eph 2:20).

Again Jesus calls for silence, but not because he shrinks from this overpowering Messianic revelation. This confession of Christ is not too strong, just too early for the general populace to accept it.

§ 83
Jesus' First
Clear
Prediction of
His Death
(Mt 16:21-23;
Mk 8:31-33;
Lk 9:22)

Jesus has already alluded to his death a number of times (Jn 1:29; 2:19; 3:14; Mt 9:15; 10:38-39; 12:39-40). The disciples didn't get the hint. But now that they have come to understand who Jesus really is, he must tell them clearly what their Messiah will do for them.

[MT 16:]21From that time on Jesus began to explain to his disciples that he {the Son of Man[MK]} must go to Jerusalem and suffer many things {and be rejected[MK]} at the hands of the elders, chief priests and teachers of the law, and that he must be killed and on {after[MK]} the third day be raised to life. {He spoke plainly about this.[MK]}

This event marks a turning point in the teaching of the Twelve. "From that time on" Jesus speaks openly about his impending death. Since the Apostles, as articulated by Peter, have now come to an open understanding of Jesus as Messiah, Jesus must now begin to reorder their thinking about the nature and work of the Messiah. They expect an earthly kingdom with a human army. They will get a spiritual kingdom with a heavenly army. They expect liberation from Rome through a conquering king. They will get liberation from sin through a risen Lord. It is a much better deal than they had hoped for, but all this will take time to learn. It must begin in earnest here.

The term "Son of Man" is used 81 times throughout the Gospels, but only by Jesus to refer to himself. "Son of Man" is used a lot in the

---

[59]According to Matthew, Peter was the first called (4:18-20), and is always listed first among the Apostles (10:2-4). Galatians 2:11 lists him as a "pillar" of the church along with James and John.

OT,[60] but not as a compliment. It highlights the "humanness" of a man, that is, the limitations of body, time, and mind (Num 23:19; Job 25:6; Ps 8:4; 144:3). That's why Daniel 7:13-14 is such an oddity:

> In my vision at night I looked, and there before me was one like a *son of man*, coming with the clouds of heaven. He approached the Ancient of Days and was led into his presence. He was given authority, glory and sovereign power; all peoples, nations and men of every language worshiped him. His dominion is an everlasting dominion that will not pass away, and his kingdom is one that will never be destroyed [emphasis added].

Here we have this "human-like" figure doing what only God could do (i.e., riding on the clouds). This commingling of human/divine attributes is an allusion to the incarnation. For this same reason, Jesus uses the title for himself. He is this "Son of Man" from Daniel 7:13. But this title is more than an indication of Jesus' divine attributes. It also serves to remind us of Jesus' "very humanness." Due to the fact that Jesus has felt what we feel — pain, loneliness, betrayal, temptation, limitation — he truly understands. Because he sympathizes with our weakness (Heb 4:14-16) he is an undaunted advocate (Rom 8:31-35).

Both Matthew and Mark tell how clearly Jesus spoke. Matthew uses a word for "explain" [*deiknymi*] which means "to point out, to demonstrate with evidence." Mark says Jesus spoke "plainly" or "boldly" [*parrēsia*] (8:32). Jesus identifies the place (Jerusalem, known for killing prophets, Mt 23:37), the persecution, (rejection, execution, resurrection), and the people (Sanhedrin), that he is about to encounter. The three groups listed make up the body of the Sanhedrin. The elders are lay leaders from the community. The Chief Priests are the professional "administrators" of the temple, roughly equivalent to the Sadducees. And the Scribes are the lawyers and teachers of the community, roughly equivalent to the Pharisees.

Jesus' death was necessary [*dei*], not only to fulfill God's plan but to pay for our sin.[61] It was also the inevitable result of the rising hostility against Jesus' claims. As one might suspect, such an important issue is predicted in both testaments.[62] The Jewish leaders never suspected sub-

---

[60]"Son of Man" is used one hundred times in the OT, ninety-three of which are found in Ezekiel. It serves as a title for Ezekiel by which God contrasts his own deity with Ezekiel's humanity.

[61]See comments on John 6:48-51 from sec. 76a, for a discussion of the substitutionary atonement of Christ's death.

[62]Gen 3:15; Ps 22:1ff; Isa 53:7-12; 63:1-6; Zech 13:6-7; Mt 9:15; 10:38-39; 12:39-40 [& Lk 11:30]; 16:21 [& Lk 9:22]; 20:18-19 [& Mk 10:33-34; Lk 18:31-33]; 26:2; Mk 8:31;

stitutionary atonement, even with passages like Isaiah 53:7-12; Psalm 22; and Zechariah 13:6-7. On the other hand, the Apostles were caught off-guard, even with Jesus' clear predictions of his own death (Mt 12:40; 16:4,21; 17:11-13, 22; 20:17; 21:33-39; 26:2).

Now, one might think that the Twelve, after Jesus died, would remember these words and expect a resurrection. That was not the case. Some critics will assert that these predictions are editorial insertions decades after the event. Indeed, that would explain the Apostles' lack of expectancy. But it also denies (1) Jesus' ability to predict the future, (2) the ability of the Holy Spirit to remind the Evangelists of these statements, and (3) the credibility and honesty of the four authors of the Gospels. Such presuppositions are unnecessary and they have monumental consequences.

Assuming Jesus really did make these statements (and we do), how can we account for the Apostles' lack of expectancy at the resurrection? First, there are numerous examples of Jesus' audiences, including the Apostles, interpreting him figuratively when he spoke literally and literally when he spoke figuratively (e.g., Jn 2:19-20; 3:3-4; 6:51-52; 7:34-35; 8:51-52; 11:11-12, 23-24; 14:4-5). These stark words may appear to them as some kind of cryptic revelation which they passed off as a figure of speech. Second, just because the Apostles heard these words, does not mean that they sunk in. Once Jesus mentioned his own death, the rest of what he said was surely just a blur. It might be like a teenage girl coming home and saying, "Dad, I'm pregnant, and Sally and I are going shopping tonight, and then out for pizza." Poor Dad is still stuck on the first two words. The Twelve may have locked in on Jesus' statement about death and never made it to the resurrection until after the fact.

Mt 16:22-23 *with*
Mk 8:33

²²Peter took him aside and began to rebuke him. "Never, Lord!" he said. "This shall never happen to you!"

²³Jesus turned {and looked at his disciples^MK} and said to {rebuked^MK} Peter, "Get behind me, Satan! You are a stumbling block to me; you do not have in mind the things of God, but the things of men."

Peter, still a bit puffed from Jesus' acclamation, confronts him with the strongest of terms. "Never, Lord" [*hileos soi, kyrie*], literally means, "God be merciful to you." But it came to mean, "God forbid!" Carson calls this a "vehement Septuagintalism" (p. 377). Impetuous Peter is going to take things in hand before they get out of control. After all, he knows who Jesus is . . . he thinks! We must remember that Peter's

9:9, 31; 10:38-39; Lk 2:34; 5:35; 12:50; 17:25; 22:15, 37; Jn 2:19; 3:14; 6:53; 10:11; 12:7, 32-33; 14:19; 15:13; 16:20.

motives are pure. His foolishness is prompted by love . . . often the most egregious errors are.

As Peter's praise is in public, so is his rebuke. Jesus turns, catches the eyes of the Twelve, and says to Peter (essentially), "Get out of my way!"[63] The word "Satan" means "adversary." Jesus did not necessarily call Peter the Devil, but the comparison is clear. In his wilderness temptation, Satan offered Jesus the easy way out, the quick road to fame and fortune. Peter is saying the same thing to Jesus, "You don't have to die, that surely is not God's will for you!" There can be but one Lord. Anyone who goes nose to nose with the master will soon enough find himself face down. Our Lord Jesus knows God's will. If his words sound strange, or even horrible, it is due to our short-sightedness or misunderstanding, not to his folly.

Peter, the rock foundation of the church, quickly becomes the stone of stumbling. He who received a great revelation from God about the person of Jesus, now confuses his own thinking with the mind of "man." Perhaps part of Peter's attraction is his likeness to most of us. This spokesman of the Twelve is often typical of the church.

§ 84
Some
Implications of
Discipleship
(Mk 8:34-9:1;
Mt 16:24-28;
Lk 9:23-27)

[MK 8:]34Then he called the crowd to him along with his disciples and said: "If anyone would come after me, he must deny himself and take up his cross {daily[LK]} and follow me. 35For whoever wants to save his life[a] will lose it, but whoever loses his life for me and for the gospel will save it. 36What good is it for a man to gain the whole world, yet forfeit his soul? 37Or what can a man give in exchange for his soul?

[a]35 The Greek word means either *life* or *soul*; also in verse 36.

Everywhere Jesus goes he attracts attention. He probably intends this trip to provide private training of the Twelve. But like his trip to Tyre and Sidon (Mk 7:24), and his trip through the Decapolis (Mk 8:1), the crowds again find Jesus (Mk 8:34; 9:14).

Mark 8:34-35 (and Mt 16:24-25) echo Matthew 10:38-39 (see comments on § 70b). Luke's addition of "daily" taking up the cross has significant ramifications. No matter how you reckon vv. 36-37, it is still a bad investment to sell your soul for the temporary, albeit present, pleasures of this world.

Mk 8:38-9:1 *with*
Mt 16:27-28

38"If anyone is ashamed of me and my words in this adulterous and sinful generation, the Son of Man will be ashamed of him when he comes in his Father's

---

[63]Jesus uses this same verb in Mt 4:10 to tell Satan "Get away from me." The implication here is not for Peter to leave but to step aside.

glory with the holy angels {and then he will reward each person according to what he has done."^MT} ^9:1And he said to them, "I tell you the truth, some who are standing here will not taste death before they see {the Son of Man coming in his^MT} the kingdom of God come with power."

Mark 8:38 also takes us back to Matthew 10 (vv. 32-33) and specifically, "the law of fair-play." If you stand with Jesus now, you can stand with him in judgment. Although it has its price, discipleship is a good investment. Verse 38 also alludes to Daniel 7:13-14, as cited above, but this time with particular emphasis on Jesus' deity (e.g., his coming with the angels, cf. Mk 13:26; 14:62). Matthew's addition, about rewards according to deeds, is not salvation by works, but evaluation of faith based on what it does. The NT consistently portrays judgment as based on works (Mt 25:31-36; Jn 5:28-29; Rom 2:6-8; 2 Cor 5:10; 1 Pet 1:17; Rev 20:12-13).

The sticky question of this text is, "When is the kingdom coming?" Some of Jesus' audience would be alive to see it. Several options have been suggested:

(1) The Transfiguration — the very next event mentioned (cf. 2 Pet 1:16-18). This event, however, took place only six days later. It would be strange to talk about some not dying in a mere six days. We might understand the phrase to signify, "in the course of your lifetime some of you will see the kingdom manifest." But, the Transfiguration, as glorious as it was, was not necessarily a manifestation of the kingdom, nor did it offer "rewards according to what each person did."

(2) The events surrounding the death, burial and resurrection of Jesus as just mentioned. This might also include the Ascension and Pentecost. Even these events, however, are close enough so as to strain the phrase, "will not taste death . . ." Here again "reward" is not immediately conspicuous in these events.

(3) The destruction of Jerusalem in A.D. 70. This would align with Matthew 10:23 and according to some commentators Matthew 24:27, 30. Although it fits well with the phrase "will not taste death . . ." and does explain at least the negative side of the rewards, it does not fit as well this context which seems to imply the parousia (cf. 2 Thess 1:7). Because of this, however, some people believe that Jesus did, indeed, return in A.D. 70 but we either missed it or he somehow continued his eschatological plan after his return. This is questionable at best.

(4) Some have suggested that this refers to the Second Coming, but that "some who are standing here" does not refer to Jesus'

immediate audience, but to the final generation, heirs of these present disciples. An alternate theory, by the radical fringe, suggests that Jesus, rather than referring to distant disciples, mistakenly believed in his own imminent return.

(5) A combination of two or three above. This may sound "wimpy," but considering the nature of the kingdom as it comes in stages, this is likely what Jesus had in mind.

§ 85
The
Transfiguration
(Mt 17:1-8;
Mk 9:2-8;
Lk 9:28-36)

The Transfiguration was the pinnacle of Jesus' earthly ministry.[64] It is, as Liefeld says, "the most significant event between his birth and passion" (p. 925). Jesus was never closer to his divinity prior to the resurrection. What's more, the Transfiguration was a microcosm of the gospel. As Caird suggests, "A satisfactory explanation of the Transfiguration must do justice to its connection with the Baptism, Caesarea Philippi, Gethsemane, the Crucifixion, the Resurrection, the Ascension, and the Parousia."[65]

The three themes of the previous pericope return here in reverse (chiastic) order: (a) Jesus' identity as Messiah, (b) prediction of Jesus' Passion, and (c) his coming glory. This event was indelibly etched into Peter's mind who later recounts it as evidence of Jesus' divinity (2 Pet 1:16-18).

Lk 9:28 *with*
Mt 17:1, Mk 9:2

[28]About eight {six^MT,MK} days after Jesus said this, he took Peter, John and James with him and went up onto a {high^MT,MK} mountain to pray {where they were all alone^MK}.

About a week[66] after Peter's great confession, the "inner three" (cf. Mk 5:37; 9:2; 13:3; 14:33) are taken aside for this momentous revelation. Luke is careful to connect Jesus' self-revelation of a week ago (9:22-27) with the Transfiguration which is about to take place. The two must stand together. Like many modern Christians, the disciples have

---

[64]A number of source critics have suggested that the transfiguration is a misplaced and radically altered resurrection account. As Stein shows, that theory is hardly tenable (cf. R.H. Stein, "Is the Transfiguration (Mk 9:2-8) A Misplaced Resurrection-Account?" *JBL* 95 [1976]: 76-96).

[65]G.B. Caird, "The Transfiguration," *ExpT* 67 (1955-56): 292.

[66]The difference between Matthew and Mark's "six days" and Luke's "eight days" is negligible. They both mean to indicate a period of about a week. It may also allude to the period Moses waited on Mt. Sinai for the giving of the law (Exod 24:15-16). Furthermore, "six days" in Semitic literature was often used as a device to lead up to a climax on the seventh day (cf. F.R. McCurley, "'And After Six Days' (Mk 9:2): A Semitic Literary Device," *JBL* 93 [1974]: 67-81). Thus, Matthew and Mark would signal their readers to expect something big.

been raised to believe in triumphalism — the Messiah will come and conquer. The truth is that suffering is often a prerequisite of, or even the passage to, victory. Jesus will not avoid death, but conquer through death. The Transfiguration, then, is a reminder of Jesus' future glory, at a time when the disciples are discouraged by Jesus' imminent suffering.

The traditional location of the Transfiguration is Mt. Tabor (1,929'), which can hardly be called a high mountain. There are reports of a Roman fortress there just a few years later (Josephus, *War* II, 20.6), which possibly existed at this time as well. More recently, scholars have looked to Mt. Hermon (9,232') as the site. There is some question, however, whether Jesus and the three would have expended the energy on the arduous hike to the summit of Hermon or spent the night on her frigid heights (cf. Lk 9:37). Furthermore, Liefeld notes that their return trip from Mt. Hermon would not have been "through Galilee" (Mk 9:30). But there is nothing in the text to suggest they went all the way to the top. A more serious objection, though, is that when Jesus and Co. come down, they encounter a large crowd including teachers of the law (Mk 9:14). This does not seem likely in such a secluded Gentile territory. Therefore, Mt. Miron (3,926') is perhaps a more reasonable suggestion. It is the highest mountain in Palestine, located just to the northwest of Capernaum. It would provide privacy at the top and Scribes at its base. And when they returned to Capernaum they would, indeed, pass "through Galilee."

As in the Garden of Gethsemane, this privacy with the three provides an appropriate setting for prayer. We are not told what time this took place, but late evening would explain a number of things: (1) The time it took them to climb the mountain, (2) why they are alone, (3) why the disciples are tired, (4) the extraordinary brilliance of the light, and (5) why they spend the night on the mountain. If this is the case, then we might picture all four praying and one by one the three give out until Jesus alone is left alert.

Lk 9:29-32 *with*
Mt 17:2, Mk 9:2-3

[29]As he was praying, {he was transfigured before them,[MT,MK]} the appearance of his face changed {shone like the sun[MT]}, and his clothes became as bright as a flash of lightning {as white as the light,[MT]} {dazzling white, whiter than anyone in the world could bleach them[MK]}. [30]Two men, Moses and Elijah, [31]appeared in glorious splendor, talking with Jesus. They spoke about his departure, which he was about to bring to fulfillment at Jerusalem. [32]Peter and his companions were very sleepy, but when they became fully awake, they saw his glory and the two men standing with him.

We picture Jesus praying deep into the night (cf. Mk 1:35, Lk 5:16; 6:12; 22:44-46), while his best friends sleep. His appearance changes.

That is, it undergoes a radical transformation [*metamorphaō*, cf. Rom. 12:2; 2 Cor 3:18]. Each of the Synoptics use different descriptions, but all three indicate that his clothes and his face become white like light. Moses had a similar experience coming off Mt. Sinai (Ex 34:29; 2 Cor 3:7).

Moses and Elijah appear, talking with Jesus. Both are strongly tied to miracles and Messianic expectations. Moses, the ideal prophet (Deut 18:16-18), represents all the law. Elijah, the forerunner of the Messiah (Mal 4:5,6), represents all the prophets. Jesus embodies both men, the fulfillment of Israel's past and the hope of her future. In addition, both men came to an odd end. Moses was buried by the Lord[67] (Deut 34:1, 6); Elijah was taken up in a whirlwind (2 Kgs 2:11). More than this, both Moses and Elijah had been rejected by their own people but vindicated by God. The Transfiguration, sandwiched between two passion predictions, shows that Jesus will experience the same thing.[68]

The focus of their discussion is Jesus' departure [*exodos*]. This has obvious typological connection to Moses' liberating Israel from Egyptian bondage, particularly the Passover lamb. Jesus' last Passover is probably about seven to nine months away. In addition to fulfilling the Passover, Jesus will fulfill the law (Mt 5:17; Rom 10:4; Col 2:14). Like Moses, Jesus will institute a new law (Rom 13:10; Gal 6:2; James 2:8; 1 Jn 3:23-24).

Perhaps it is their conversation, or perhaps it is the light that wakes the sleepy Apostles.[69] No doubt they pinch themselves to see if they are dreaming. We have not a clue how Peter knows it was Moses and Elijah. We can only assume that they call each other by name or make some reference to their own ministry as it relates to Jesus.

Mt 17:4-8 *with*
Lk 9:33-35,
Mk 9:5-8

{[33]As the men were leaving,[LK]} [4]Peter said to Jesus, "Lord {Rabbi,[MK]} {Master[LK]}, it is good for us to be here. If you wish {let us,[MK,LK]} I will put up three shelters — one for you, one for Moses and one for Elijah." {[6](He did not know what to say, they were so frightened.)[MK]}

[5]While he was still speaking, a bright cloud enveloped them, and a voice from the cloud said, "This is my Son, whom I love {whom I have chosen;[LK]} with him I am well pleased. Listen to him!"

---

[67]Based on the *Assumption of Moses*, written in the intertestamental period, many Jews believed that Moses didn't actually die.

[68]M. Pamment, "Moses and Elijah in the Story of the Transfiguration," *ExpT* 92 (1980-81): 338-339.

[69]From the Greek we can't tell whether they were fully asleep or just "nodding off." Nonetheless, the vision catapulted them into full consciousness. Furthermore, had this story been an invention or legend it hardly seems possible that the Apostles would have been pictured as drowsing.

[6]When the disciples heard this, they fell facedown to the ground, terrified. [7]But Jesus came and touched them. "Get up," he said. "Don't be afraid." {[8]Suddenly,[MK]} [8]When they looked up, they saw no one except Jesus.

As the men are leaving, Peter, in classic form, attempts to hold onto this golden moment. He suggests to Jesus[70] that they make three "tabernacles," what we might call a "lean-to." It would be reminiscent of the forty years of wilderness wanderings. It is a bad suggestion based in fear (Mk 9:6). Not only would that ignore the supremacy of Jesus, it would also prolong the moment, hindering the progress of Jesus' mission. Peter is making essentially the same mistake he made near Caesarea Philippi a week earlier. There he was rebuked by Jesus. Here he will be rebuked by the Father.

Peter is interrupted by a cloud and a voice. The cloud serves its immediate purpose to conceal and perhaps convey Moses and Elijah. It may also be symbolic of (a) the cloud that led the Israelites by day (Exod 13:21-22), (b) the presence of God in his Shekinah[71] Glory (Exod 19:16), and (c) the future coming of the Son of Man (Dan 7:13; Mk 14:62; 1 Thess 4:17). Then comes the voice of God, repeating verbatim what he had said at Jesus' baptism (Mt 3:17; see also Jn 12:28), with this addition: "Listen to him." Both are likely based on Psalm 2:7 and Isaiah 42:1. "Listen" is a plural imperative so that Peter is not singled out. The message is clear: Jesus is superior to Moses and Elijah.

Peter and John respond in the only way anyone ever responded to a "Christophany" (i.e., an appearance of the non-incarnate Christ). They fall facedown to the ground (cf. Ezek 1:28; Dan 8:17; Rev 1:17). Jesus responds with a strange mixture of his humanity and divinity. The humanity of Jesus reached down and touched them. His divinity spoke the words so common from angelic messengers, "Stop being afraid."

When they lift their eyes from the dust, all is back to normal. Moses, Elijah and the cloud have vanished. Jesus alone is standing there, all the glowing gone, except perhaps for a shining smile and a sparkle in his eye.

§ 86
Discussion of
the Coming of
Elijah
(Mt 17:9-13;
Mk 9:9-13;
Lk 9:36b)

[9]As they were coming down the mountain, Jesus instructed them {gave them orders[MK]}, "Don't tell anyone what you have seen, until the Son of Man has been raised from the dead." {[10]They kept the matter to themselves[MK]} {and told no one at that time what they had seen,[LK]} {discussing what "rising from the dead" meant.[MK]}

---

[70]Each of the Synoptics use a different title for Jesus with little or no difference in meaning. Mark's "Rabbi" is likely the original since it probably came from Peter himself.

[71]The Greek word *episkiazō* ("overshadow") was the word used to translate the Hebrew "Shekinah" in the LXX at Exodus 40:35 (Liefeld, p. 928). Thus, the suggested connection is strong.

¹⁰The disciples asked him, "Why then do the teachers of the law say that Elijah must come first?"

¹¹Jesus replied, "To be sure, Elijah comes and will restore all things. ¹²But I tell you, Elijah has already come, and they did not recognize him, but have done to him everything they wished. {Why then is it written that the Son of Man must suffer much and be rejected?ᴹᴷ} In the same way the Son of Man is going to suffer at their hands." ¹³Then the disciples understood that he was talking to them about John the Baptist.

This is the final injunction to silence.[72] But this time Jesus puts some parameters on it: "Until the Son of Man has been raised from the dead." There will come a time when they can spill the beans. However, it will only be after "all has been accomplished," and when the crowds have been properly prepared for the news. This particular secret is going to be especially hard to keep, however. This is the very thing the other nine should know about. It is what Thomas needed to know to allay his doubts. It is the answer to all of Andrew's questions. It is the explanation to Simon's Messianic expectation. Besides, they will all soon argue about who is the greatest (§ 90). Such ammunition would almost be irresistible for the inner three. But apparently they do keep quiet. And as near as we can tell, they were the only ones who ever obeyed Jesus' command to keep quiet.

The disciples still don't know what Jesus means by "rising from the dead." And they are too chicken to ask. Perhaps they are afraid of what he might say. Perhaps they are afraid of sounding stupid. This much is almost certain, they could not imagine a literal death for Jesus. For them, a suffering Messiah is unthinkable. Perhaps they think "rising from the dead" means: (a) Jesus would regain his lost popularity. (b) Jesus would avoid the death-plots of the Jews. Or (c) the crowds at the base of the mountain might assume Jesus was dead, as the Israelites did with Moses at the base of Mt. Sinai. Thus when he reappeared he would inaugurate his kingdom.

Even more perplexing than "rising from the dead" was this "coming of Elijah." Based on Malachi 4:5-6, the Scribes taught that Elijah would be the forerunner of the Messiah.[73] That was correct. But Jesus said that

---

[72]See Matthew 8:4; 9:30; 12:16; 16:20; 17:9; Mark 1:44; 3:12; 5:43; 7:36; 8:26, 30; 9:9; Luke 8:56; 9:21. This includes eight different incidents (§ 45, 52, 67, 68, 79a, 81b, 82, 86), of which only § 68 is not mentioned in Mark. For a discussion of injunctions to silence, see notes on § 52.

[73]Because Elijah did not officially die, the Jews expected him to return to earth. Even today some Bible scholars believe Elijah will return as one of the two witnesses (Rev. 11:3-6) just prior to Christ's Second Coming. Cf. C. Blomberg, "Elijah, Election, and the Use of Malachi in the New Testament," *CTR* 2 (1987): 100-108.

this prophecy was figuratively fulfilled in John, not literally to be fulfilled by Elijah. The three don't yet understand that, even though Jesus clearly tells them (Mt 11:14; cf. Lk 1:17). Sometimes it takes us all two or three times to grasp a difficult concept.

If John is the Elijah of Malachi 4:5-6, how did he "turn the hearts of their children back to their fathers?" In the Jewish mind, this is seen not so much in family relationships as in ancestral relationships. That is, many Jews who heard John repented and remembered the ways of their forefathers and were thus prepared to receive their Messiah. But who can deny the fact that the vast majority of the Jews were not prepared to accept Jesus as Messiah. (That is why, in fact, Jesus is now in seclusion with the Twelve, telling them to keep quiet.) So we are forced to admit that John's mission as forerunner, by and large, failed, through no fault of his own. Turning back to Malachi 4:5-6, we find that possibility predicted in the text: ". . . the hearts of the children to their fathers; or else I will come and strike the land with a curse." John did his part, but the people did not do their part. As a result, they would suffer the curse of God on their land (cf. Mt 24).

Furthermore, the fact that John was Elijah and that Jesus was Messiah, did not exempt them from suffering. Jesus claimed that such suffering was even predicted (Mk 9:12). We presume he was speaking of Isaiah 53. Thus, Jesus answers their question about John. He is Elijah (figuratively), and as for his rejection, the Scriptures themselves suggest the possibility of an "unsuccessful" mission. Jesus also answers their unstated question. They can't imagine a suffering Messiah. As Jesus has shown, they got a suffering forerunner. Why would they expect any less from the Messiah? If the forerunner was rejected and killed, how much more the Messiah?

§ 87
Healing the
Demonized
Boy
(Mt 17:14-20;
Mk 9:14-29;
Lk 9:37-43a)

This section might be titled, "From the Divine to the Mundane." Jesus, and the three, have just had the most incredible spiritual experience of their lives. Then while coming down the mountain, Jesus is confronted by this quarrelsome, faithless mob, and impotent Apostles. It is a powerful reminder that we live in a real world, filled with unbelief, immaturity, and quarrels. Yet, this is the world that needs the divine experience related to it. This is where religion belongs, not up on the mountain.

Mk 9:14-16 *with*
Lk 9:37

¹⁴{The next day, when they came down from the mountain [and]ᴸᴷ} came to the other disciples, they saw a large crowd around them and the teachers of the law arguing with them. ¹⁵As soon as all the people saw Jesus, they were overwhelmed with wonder and ran to greet him.

¹⁶"What are you arguing with them about?" he asked.

As Jesus descends from the mountain he begins to hear the din of the quarrelsome crowds. The fray is fueled by the Scribes who constantly lie in wait for Jesus to do or say something objectionable. While Jesus is away, they seize the opportunity to discredit the remaining nine disciples who have failed in a basic exorcism. We are not given the specifics of the argument, but surely it centered on their authority to cast out demons and Jesus' relation to the spirit world (cf. Mt 9:34; 12:22-37; Mk 3:20-30).

The people were amazed when Jesus arrives "just on time." Some have suggested that they were surprised by Jesus' glowing countenance (cf. Moses, Exod 34:29-35). But that hardly fits Jesus' previous injunction of silence. It seems more likely that his presence alone startles them like children caught with their hand in the cookie jar. The Scribes realize their "bullying" is about to come to an abrupt and premature end. The nine disciples realize they are "caught with their pants down," having failed in this basic healing. The crowds realize Jesus can do what his disciples could not and that it is now "show time!"

Jesus' question, "What are you arguing about?" is met with silence by all involved. This poor father, the only one no longer self-conscious, breaks the silence. He kneels at Jesus' feet, not so much in worship as in entreaty. His request is simple, but passionate. After all, this is his only child (like Jairus and the widow at Nain).

Mk 9:17-19 *with*
Mt 17:14-17,
Lk 9:37

[17]A man in the crowd {approached Jesus and knelt before him[MT]} answered {called out,[LK]} "{Lord, have mercy on my son.[MT]} Teacher, I brought you my son {for he is my only child,[LK]} {he has seizures and is suffering greatly[MT]} who is possessed by a spirit that has robbed him of speech. [18]Whenever it seizes him, {he suddenly screams,[LK]} it throws him to the ground {into convulsions.[LK]} He foams at the mouth, gnashes his teeth and becomes rigid. {It scarcely ever leaves him and is destroying him.[LK]} I asked your disciples to drive out the spirit {heal him,[MT]} but they could not."

[19]"O unbelieving {and perverse[MT,LK]} generation," Jesus replied, "how long shall I stay with you? How long shall I put up with you? Bring the boy to me."

The description of this boy is pathetic. Matthew identifies his ailment as epilepsy (Gk. *selēniazō*).[74] It is interesting that Luke, the physician, bypasses any medical description in order to deal with the issue at hand — demon possession. His physical problems, induced by the demon, include the following:

1. Dumbness — except for occasional and sporadic screams.
2. Seizures — which throw him to the ground, into fire and water.

---

[74]The KJV "lunatic" is misleading and inaccurate. Although the thought of the influence of the moon (Greek, *selēnē*, Latin, *luna*) is inherent in both words, there is otherwise no connection between them.

3. Loss of oral control — including foaming at the mouth and grinding his teeth.

4. Rigidity — The word [*xēraino*] more properly indicates "withering" or "dehydration." Probably not indicative of "stiffness" (i.e., muscle cramps), but "weakness" (i.e., atrophy).

Demons often attacked a person's body through sickness.[75] Thus exorcism is also called healing (cf. Mt 15:28; 17:16, 18; Mk 9:18; also Lk 9:42). Perhaps that's why demon possession is often included in the lists of ailments Jesus cured (Mt 4:24; 8:16; 10:8; Mk 1:32-34, 39; Lk 4:41; 13:32). This is not to say sickness is always demon induced or that certain demons specialize in certain sicknesses. The Gospels clearly differentiate between sickness and demons. But part of the nature of demons is the love for destruction (e.g., Gerasene pigs). So it would appear that whenever they can, demons attack and destroy the bodies they possess and oppress.

The Apostles had been unable to drive out this demon. By now they should have been masters at it (Mk 3:15; 6:13). That is certainly part of Jesus' disappointment when he utters a sigh of disgust, "O unbelieving and perverse generation . . ." (reminiscent of Deut 32:5, 20). After coming off the Mount of Transfiguration he is immediately confronted with the petty jealousy of the Scribes, the quarrelsome and curious crowds, and the impotent faith of his own inner band. Now even his Apostles share the faithlessness resulting from their sinful society (cf. Mt 11:16; 12:39). In short, the mountain made Jesus homesick and the valley reminds him how far he yet had to go.

Mk 9:20-24 *with* Lk 9:42

[20]So they brought him. When the spirit {demon[LK]} saw Jesus, it immediately threw the boy into a convulsion. He fell to the ground and rolled around, foaming at the mouth.

[21]Jesus asked the boy's father, "How long has he been like this?"

"From childhood," he answered. [22]"It has often thrown him into fire or water to kill him. But if you can do anything, take pity on us and help us."

[23]"'If you can'?" said Jesus. "Everything is possible for him who believes."

[24]Immediately the boy's father exclaimed, "I do believe; help me overcome my unbelief!"

The demon knows its moments are numbered. So it gets in one last hurrah by throwing the child to the ground. It has often done much worse, trying to drown the child or burn him to death. This distraught

---

[75]Of the six descriptions of Jesus casting out a demon (§ 42, 61, 66, 68 78, 87), three clearly indicate a physical ailment (blindness, deaf/mute, epilepsy), and one suggests some sort of sickness (Mt 15:22; Mk 7:30). See also Lk 13:11 for a non-possessed, spirit induced ailment.

father is, indeed, a pathetic picture. That may account for part of his error in laying the difficulty at Jesus' feet rather than his own. His actions speak of faith, but his words resound doubt — "If you can . . ."

Here is one of those passages where vocal inflection determines the meaning. When Jesus responds, does he say, "If you CAN?," meaning "You doubt my ability?!" Or does he say, "If YOU can!," meaning, "I can do it. But the real question is whether you have the faith to receive it!" Here is one of the times when healing is contingent upon the recipient's faith.[76] This man's cry is echoed in the heart of every Christian. Who has not felt it? "I do believe; help me overcome my unbelief!" In order to come to Jesus we must have some level of faith. But so often it is weak and insufficient for the task before us. We need Jesus to rise in our hearts and supply the faith we lack.

Mk 9:25-29 *with*
Mt 17:18,20,
Lk 9:42b-43

[25]When Jesus saw that a crowd was running to the scene, he rebuked the evil spirit. "You deaf and mute spirit," he said, "I command you, come out of him and never enter him again."

[26]The spirit shrieked, convulsed him violently and came out. The boy looked so much like a corpse that many said, "He's dead." [27]But Jesus took him by the hand and lifted him to his feet, and he stood up. {[H]e was healed from that moment[MT]} {and [Jesus] gave him back to his father. [43]And they were all amazed at the greatness of God.[LK]}

[28]After Jesus had gone indoors, his disciples asked him privately, "Why couldn't we drive it out?"

[29]He replied, "{Because you have so little faith. I tell you the truth, if you have faith as small as a mustard seed, you can say to this mountain, 'Move from here to there' and it will move. Nothing will be impossible for you."[MT]} This kind can come out only by prayer.[a]"

[a]29 Some manuscripts *prayer and fasting*

There is already a crowd around Jesus. Even more people continue to stream from their shops and the marketplace. Crowds tend to reproduce themselves. As their numbers swell with cricked necks and bugged eyes, Jesus wants to quickly close this incident before it causes any more of a stir. Jesus identifies the spirit by what it was causing and ordered it out. The demon has no alternative but to obey. The crowds are amazed at the power of God. The argument initiated by the Scribes is obviously

---

[76]Faith is often essential to receive a healing or even an answer to prayer (Mt 9:22; 21:22; Mk 6:5-6; 10:52; Lk 7:36-50; 17:19; Acts 14:8-9; James 1:6-8). At other times, however, it is the faith of a friend or family member that effectively brings healing to a loved one (Mt 8:5-13; 15:28; Mk 2:5; 9:22-24; Lk 8:40-42, 49-56; James 5:15). And sometimes the healing is based solely on the faith of the healer, not the healed (Lk 7:11-16; 8:26-33; Jn 5:1-9; 11; Acts 3:1-8; 9:36-43; 20:1-12).

over. We assume that they slip off into the crowd with their tails between their legs.

The Scribes aren't the only losers this day. The nine Apostles have been badly beaten. We might think the other three would rub it in a bit. But they, too, have come off the mountain feeling somewhat spanked. Not only had they not been able to answer the basic questions about Jesus' death and Elijah, but even the heavenly voice had rebuked them.[77]

In the privacy of a house (cf. Mt 13:36; 15:12) they are eager to ask, "What went wrong? Why couldn't we drive out that demon?" Was it some methodological error? Were they supposed to identify the nature of the demon as Jesus had? Was this an especially difficult demon that required extra wrestling? Was there some kind of incantation with the name of Jesus that would have worked? NO! Their problem was not methodology. It was the littleness of their faith. We might assume that Jesus' absence, and perhaps even their own self-reliance, caused the disciples to weaken in faith. Even the barest minimum of faith ("mustard seed" was parabolic for littleness) would overcome the big problems (i.e., "mountains"). Jesus was speaking figuratively here. Moving mountains would be a great trick, but not a very productive one. Thus, no one ever did it, including God. But standing in the shadow of the Mount of Transfiguration his words would have great visual impact.

Jesus' promise, "Nothing will be impossible for you" is not absolute. It is not like Aladdin's lamp. It is limited by its contextual parameters. It must be determined by (1) what Jesus has authorized us to do, and (2) by other passages with similar statements (e.g., 1 Cor 6:12; Phil 4:12-13).

What would have helped the nine was prayer,[78] not so much as part and parcel of the exorcism rite, but as a regular practice in preparation for spiritual warfare. In other words, Jesus may not be directing them so much to "pray out" the demon as to "pray up" the disciple. Many Christians fail in spiritual warfare, not because they are unfamiliar with the armament or battle tactics, but because they are fat, lazy and undisciplined.

§ 88
Second
Prediction of
Jesus' Passion
(Mt 17:22-23;
Mk 9:30-32;
Lk 9:43b-45)
[cf. § 83 & 86]

[30]They left that place and passed through Galilee. Jesus did not want anyone to know where they were, [31]because he was teaching his disciples. He said to them, "The Son of Man is going to be betrayed into the hands of men. They will kill him, and after {on^MT} three days he will rise." [32]But they did not understand

---

[77]Carson (p. 390) notes that "the disciples' failures are a recurring theme throughout this section (Mt 14:16-21, 26-27, 28-31; 15:16, 23, 33; 16:5, 22; 17:4, 10-11)."

[78]The inclusion of "fasting" is likely a scribal addition. It has late manuscript attestation. And Jesus said the disciples wouldn't fast until after his death (Mt 9:15). The early church's penchant for fasting is likely the impetus for including it here.

what he meant {it was hidden from them, so that they did not grasp it,ᴸᴷ} and were afraid to ask him about it. {And the disciples were filled with grief.ᴹᵀ}

The dramatic effect of Jesus healing the demonized boy makes it difficult for him to continue the private training of the Twelve. The presence of the Scribes makes matters worse. They head back to Capernaum, presumably to Peter's house, where they can at least shut the door behind them. This is a critical period for the Apostles. Jesus has revealed, as never before, both his glory and his impending passion. It is clear that the Twelve have not assimilated this new revelation and it is imperative that they do. Thus, their privacy is all the more important as Jesus makes a beeline to the cross.

We now hear the second clear prediction of Jesus' death. Although there is nothing radically new in this passage, we do notice several things. First, as in the first prediction, Matthew says "on the third day" whereas Mark says "*after* the third day." It becomes clear that three days is not intended to be an exact measurement but a general period of time.

Second, Luke alone ties this passage to the previous miracle (Lk 9:43). It would probably be a mistake to view this second prediction as a public one (cf. Mk 9:30-31), which is the impression Luke gives. At the same time, it would be a mistake to separate it from the previous narrative. The first prediction immediately followed Peter's great confession and served as a "corrective" for their mistaken notion of Jesus' Messianic functions. Likewise, this second prediction immediately follows the Transfiguration and victorious confrontation of demonic forces as a second "corrective."

Third, this second prediction reveals that Jesus would be betrayed before he suffered. The word [*paradidomi*], is somewhat ambiguous. NIV translates it "betrayed," which would suggest Judas' role in Jesus' death. But the word may also mean, "delivered up" or "handed over," which would suggest God's role in Jesus' death. It would not be surprising if both elements were involved (cf. Acts 2:23). But as Origen suggested, the phrase "into the hands of men" would seem to describe God's role more than Judas'.

Fourth, the disciples still do not catch the full meaning of Jesus' prediction. Luke is most emphatic about their bewilderment (9:45). He also indicates that it is not completely their fault. There seems to be some divine concealment in the phrase, "It was hidden from them, so that they did not grasp it." Furthermore, they are afraid to ask Jesus about it. Perhaps they think that after two explanations, Jesus will rebuke them for their dullness if they ask him about it. Or maybe they are afraid to hear any explanation that might point to a literal fulfillment. Yet they have made some progress since the first prediction. Matthew says they are filled with grief (17:23). They know enough to realize that trouble is coming, even if they don't know all the details.

§ 89
Peter's
Payment of the
Temple Tax
(Mt 17:24-27)

[24]After Jesus and his disciples arrived in Capernaum, the collectors of the two-drachma tax came to Peter and asked, "Doesn't your teacher pay the temple tax[a]?"

[a]*24 Greek* the two drachmas

It's not too surprising that Levi, the tax collector, is the only Evangelist to record this odd event. Aside from his interest in this unique method of collecting revenue, why does he include it? After all, it appears to interrupt the story line. But upon closer examination, it actually continues the trend that began in Caesarea Philippi. That is, Jesus is exalted by others but humbles himself. No one reading this story would really expect Jesus to pay temple taxes when he was the Son of God. But he does. This sets up a contrast between Jesus' self-humiliation and the disciples' self-aggrandizement in the following verses.

This particular tax was not a legal Roman tax. The Jews, however, expected that each male, between ages twenty and fifty would support the temple each year with two drachma (cf. Josephus, *Ant.* III. 8.2; XVIII, 9.1). This was based on Exodus 30:11-16; 38:25-26, where God commanded support for the tabernacle. The cost was equivalent to about two day's wages. Why do they ask for it now? We can only guess that since Jesus missed the last Passover, there was some question about him fulfilling his financial obligation as a Jew. The tax collectors question Peter, who apparently has distinguished himself as the spokesman of the group. Their question is framed so as to expect a positive reply. It might be better translated, "Your teacher pays the temple tax, doesn't he?" It is of interest that officially ordained rabbis were exempt from this tax. Since Jesus had not attended their schools, he could not rightly claim this advantage.

Mt 17:25-27

[25]"Yes, he does," he replied.

When Peter came into the house, Jesus was the first to speak. "What do you think, Simon?" he asked. "From whom do the kings of the earth collect duty and taxes — from their own sons or from others?"

[26]"From others," Peter answered.

"Then the sons are exempt," Jesus said to him. [27]"But so that we may not offend them, go to the lake and throw out your line. Take the first fish you catch; open its mouth and you will find a four-drachma coin. Take it and give it to them for my tax and yours."

We assume Peter's reply is without Christ's consent, though we don't know for sure. Peter may know that Jesus did, in fact, pay this tax before. When Peter goes back into the house Jesus is the first to speak. Matthew probably wants us to see that Jesus reads Peter's mind. He questions Peter with the use of this brief parable which suggests that because of Jesus' relationship with God, he is rightly exempt from paying the temple tax. But so that he might not offend the Jewish rulers he goes ahead and pays. Not only is Jesus exempt, but so is Peter because he is a disciple of Jesus. But he, too, is to pay the tax. Notice that the coin Peter is to get would pay for both of them.

The lesson is clear. Christians ought to be in submission to governing authorities, not because we are in agreement, nor because we are ultimately obligated to them, but so that we will not cause an offense. Such offense would sully the good name of the church and cause unnecessary friction with rulers. We find this principle repeated in Romans 13 with specific reference to civil, rather than religious, government (see also Mt 22:15-22). Recently, some Christians have objected to the Federal Government's use of tax dollars to fund questionable or even immoral practices. Therefore, some have questioned whether they could, in good conscience, pay their taxes. Both Paul and Jesus paid their taxes to both civil and religious authorities. Both could have strenuously objected to a number of practices of both religious and civil leaders. The argument does not seem to hold that if rulers are using Federal funds for immoral practices that Christians should stop paying taxes or reduce the amount sent in.

Furthermore, it would be difficult to biblically support a position of Christian intervention which forces unbelievers to stop their wicked practices. In fact, Paul refused to speak against pagan worship (Acts 19:37). Such aggressive and illegal intervention is unwise for several reasons: (a) The surrounding culture can then argue the illegality of Christianity. (b) It forces a Christian ethic on those who have no basis to receive it. (c) It often confuses a spiritual enemy for a physical one.

Here are some responses that would seem to be more appropriate:

(1) Benevolence to the needy in the community (e.g., crisis pregnancy centers, food banks, counseling centers, literacy programs).

(2) Continued proclamation of the gospel of Jesus Christ (television, radio, Bible distribution, billboards, magazines, tracts).

(3) A coalition of Christian churches which could speak with an organized voice and political clout to governing officials (Christian lobbyists, letter writing campaigns, voter education).

(4) Legal public protests and advertising which promote positive

alternatives. The world knows all too well what Christians hate, but they often have no idea of the one whom we love.

(5) Financial boycott of organizations which promote anti-Christian values.

Civil disobedience for the Christian should be reserved for when the individual is asked to disobey a direct command of God (Exod 1:15ff; Dan 3:1ff; 6:10ff; Acts 4:19; 5:29).

Back to the text. Matthew stops short of telling us that Peter goes out and catches the fish. Perhaps we are to understand that he did go catch a fish that had a coin (lit. *statēra,* = four drachma) in its mouth. Fish are often attracted to shiny objects. And there have been accounts of fish caught in the Sea of Galilee that have swallowed coins. Thus, perhaps Jesus "saw" the fish before Peter caught it and brought the two together.[79]

---

§ 90
Discussions
About Who is
the Greatest
(Mt 18:1-5;
Mk 9:33-37;
Lk 9:46-48)

Jesus and his disciples return to Capernaum from the Mount of Transfiguration. On the way, the disciples debate about which one of them was the greatest. How crass! We're shocked that the future leaders of the church would act so unchristian. But this is only the first of three times they have this argument (cf. § 125b and 144). What makes matters worse, is that each time it follows on the heels of a significant prediction of Jesus' suffering. So while Jesus is talking about laying down his life, these guys are promoting theirs.

Mk 9:33-35 *with*
Mt 18:1, Lk 9:47

[33]They came to Capernaum. When he was in the house, {the disciples came to Jesus and asked, "Who is greatest in the kingdom of heaven?"[MT]} he asked them, "What were you arguing about on the road? [34]But they kept quiet because on the way they had argued about who was the greatest.

[35]Sitting down {knowing their thoughts,[LK]} Jesus called the Twelve and said, "If anyone wants to be first, he must be the very last, and the servant of all."

Matthew makes it look like the disciples initiate this conversation. But Mark says that Jesus did. We might reconstruct the scene as follows: Jesus, knowing their thoughts (Luke), asks them what they were discussing on the way into town. They are embarrassed by their crass self-seeking competitiveness, so they just stand there silently (Mark). Finally, one of the Twelve breaks the silence with this question: Who is the

---

[79]A second alternative is that Jesus was speaking figuratively to Peter, saying, "Go catch some fish and sell them to gain the money to pay our taxes." Against this theory, however, is the fact that Jesus told him to catch it with a hook, rather than with a net. (This is the only time in the NT where a hook was used.) One good net full of fish would have done the trick (cf. Lk 5:1-11). But he could fish all day with a hook and still come up short.

greatest in the kingdom of heaven? (Matthew; cf. 5:19; 11:11). This question will become increasingly important to the Twelve the nearer Jesus comes to inaugurating his Kingdom.

This was a common discussion among the rabbis. The attitude that lies behind it, however, is certainly not unique to Judaism. Egoism is natural to most people. It drives us to the front of the line, to the best seat in the house, and to the biggest piece of cake. It is seen as innocuous and natural in ourselves but somewhat irritating in others. In fact, it is even encouraged by parents and teachers. Jesus sees beyond this facade. This egoism is the cause of arrogance, selfishness, war, greed, corporate takeovers, jealousy, rape, etc. It is even the cause of low self-esteem. The problem with a low self-esteem is not that a person thinks too lowly of himself but that he thinks too much of himself. When our eyes are outward, serving others, it is impossible to be plagued with self-pity or self-abasement.

Egoism was even the cause of Eve's demise. It was not the beauty or nutritional value of the fruit that allured her. It was the idea that she could be "like God." She could be independent, in control, calling the shots, determining her own destiny. Much of modern advertising appeals to that same vanity: "It's expensive, but I'm worth it;" "You deserve a break today;" "Have it your way!" It would appear that egoism is the common thread through all sin. But the base evil of egoism remains disguised because of our cultural acceptance of it and its sheer pervasiveness.

These twelve men, chosen by Jesus, are really no better than the clamoring crowds that they often shun. They are arguing about who is the greatest. Who will it be that gets to sit on Jesus' right and left hand? No doubt Peter can make a good case for himself. After all, he's the one with the keys of the kingdom; he is the one who walked on water; he is the one who said, "Lord, to whom shall we go? You have the words of eternal life." In response, the others would say, "Yes, but you are also the one Jesus called 'Satan.' You are the one that nearly drowned with your stupid trick of walking on the water. And you are the one that made the idiotic suggestion of building three tabernacles on the Mount of Transfiguration." John and James no doubt stake their claim to prominence. In fact, in the near future, they will employ their mother to help them gain the upper hand among the Twelve (Mt 20:20-24). After all, they have more corporate shares in the "Inner Three" than anyone. And Judas Iscariot, no doubt, put in his two cents.

Jesus introduces here a new theology that he will reiterate time and again. It could be called "The Theology of Humility." It is captured in phrases like, "The first shall be last and the last shall be first" (Mt 19:30; 20:8, 16, 27; Mk 9:35; 10:31, 44; Lk 13:30; 22:26). "The greatest among you will be the servant of all" (Mt 20:26; 23:11; Mk 10:43; Lk 9:48; 22:26-27; 1 Tim 3:13). "Humble yourselves before the mighty hand of God and he will exalt you" (Mt 23:12; Lk 14:11; 18:14; James 4:10; 1 Pet 5:5, 6).[80] It is through this theology that Jesus sees the incredible value of people. All people are precious to Jesus, even the least and the lost: Prostitutes, children, women, crippled, lepers, tax collectors, Samaritans, and foreigners. This "theology of humility" is easy to understand, couched in such simple phrases. But it is deceivingly difficult to practice. It matters little what our level of cognitive understanding is. If we don't have a practical handle on the theology of humility it will be nearly impossible to understand even the simplest theological truths, such as John 3:16. Most people can accept the fact that God loves us. It is inconceivable, though, that he loves our surly neighbor. Homogeneous, money myopic churches, with a thin band of social strata, betray our woeful ignorance of the theology of humility. Like the Twelve, we have miles to go in understanding Jesus' call to the cross.

Mt 18:2-4 *with*
Mk 9:36-37

Lk 9:48

²He called a little child and had him stand among them {taking him in his arms.ᴹᴷ} ³And he said: "I tell you the truth, unless you change and become like little children, you will never enter the kingdom of heaven. ⁴Therefore, whoever humbles himself like this child is the greatest in the kingdom of heaven.

⁴⁸Whoever welcomes this child {one of these little childrenᴹᴷ} in my name welcomes me; and whoever welcomes me welcomes the one who sent me. For he who is least among you all — he is the greatest."

Jesus pulls a child into the discussion as a visual aid. He embraces him, probably even pulling him onto his lap (cf. Mk 10:16). He then gives his famous quote about becoming like a child to enter the kingdom of heaven. This is surprising since children in Jesus' day held little esteem. In fact, in Aramaic the same word is used for both "children" and "servants." We mustn't allow the tenderness of the moment to hide its severity. Jesus is warning the Twelve. Unless they change their attitude, even they might not make it into the Kingdom of Heaven. And in fact, one of them does not!

Jesus calls us to be child-like, not childish. We are to be shrewd (Mt 10:16), even cunning (Lk 16:1-9). Yet like children we are to be totally dependent upon our Father. But our text means more than that. Though children are selfish and competitive (like the disciples), they care little about status (unlike the disciples). They are not put off by clothes, or

---

[80]This theology is also taught in passages like Mt 11:29; Rom 12:16; Eph 4:2; Phil 2:3-11; Col 3:12. It is even found in the OT (Ps 18:27; 147:6; Prov 16:18-19; 18:22; 29:23; Isa 2:11-17; 53:10-12; 57:15; Ezek 17:24; 21:26).

dirt, or color of skin. Because they are not judgmental, they are often excellent judges of character. Furthermore, the approval they desire is primarily from their parents. If we will act only for the approval and recognition of our Heavenly Father, how much different our homes and ministries would be! Indeed, with such behavior we can find ourselves in the center of the Kingdom of Heaven.

§ 91a
Hindering
Other Workers
in the Kingdom
(Mk 9:38-41;
Lk 9:49-50)

Section 91 has been divided here into three parts that are held together by this common theme: The importance of the "little ones" and the danger of causing them to stumble. Each of the Synoptics have a unique emphasis at this point and must be read in their own context. Yet all three story lines emphasize humility in dealing with others, especially those who are belittled or struggling. Thus, section 91 illustrates the theology of humility in three tangible ways.

Mk 9:38-41 *with*
Lk 9:49

³⁸"Teacher, {Master^LK}" said John, "we saw a man driving out demons in your name and we told him to stop, because he was not one of us."
³⁹"Do not stop him," Jesus said. "No one who does a miracle in my name can in the next moment say anything bad about me, ⁴⁰for whoever is not against us is for us. ⁴¹I tell you the truth, anyone who gives you a cup of water in my name because you belong to Christ will certainly not lose his reward."

Jewish exorcists were not uncommon (Mt 12:27; Lk 11:19; Acts 19:13-14). They were always on the lookout for powerful incantations by which they could drive out demons. Frequently they would invoke the name of a powerful magician or miracle worker as an authority over the demon(s). It is not surprising this Jewish exorcist used Jesus' name to drive out demons. What is surprising, however, is that it worked (cf. Acts 19:13-16). This probably indicates he is not merely using Jesus' name as a formula, but he truly believes in Jesus and is on the verge of discipleship. Thus, his work should not be hindered even if he is not a direct disciple of Jesus.

The point of this passage is not about denominations, but the application seems inevitable. The fact that someone doesn't adhere to my little band or confess my creedal idiosyncrasies doesn't necessarily make him an enemy. This is not a call to ignorant ecumenicalism. After all, allegiance to Jesus is essential to fellowship. It is a call, however, to cooperation for the proclamation of Jesus and the alleviation of human suffering. Most denominations can't cooperate precisely because they are like John at this point. Their focus is inward rather than outward. They are trying to establish "Who is the greatest" (Mk 9:33-37). John's response is all the more repulsive when we realize that it follows on the heels of Jesus' statement, "Whoever welcomes one of these little children in my name welcomes me; and whoever welcomes me does not welcome me but the one who sent me" (Mk 9:37). If all those who are truly disciples of Jesus would band together, despite their varied-colored stripes, the church could have a powerful impact on world hunger, global evangelism, politics, media, medicine, etc.

Jesus tells John not to hinder this fellow's work. First, if he is performing miracles with Jesus' name, he could not soon turn against Jesus (v. 39). Second, he is not opposed to Jesus. Therefore, his work in casting out demons actually promotes Jesus (v. 40). Third, his work is alleviating human suffering in the name of Jesus. Thus, he earns a reward from God (v. 41; cf. Mt 10:42). We notice too that the discussion about "little ones" has changed from children (Mt 18:5; Mk 9:37) to disciples (Mk 9:41; Mt 18:6).

Back in Matthew 12:30, Jesus said, "Anyone who isn't for me is against me." Doesn't that contradict Mark 9:40? No. These are two different situations. Here, this fellow is on the road to discipleship. He is going in the right direction. Thus, he is not against Jesus. Therefore, "don't hinder his work." In Matthew 12:30, the Pharisees have already been faced with the call to follow Jesus. But they refused, trying to make themselves look impartial and noncommitted. But once you have come face to face with Jesus, there can be no middle ground. Either you are openly and vocally for him, or you are against him.

§ 91b
Causing a
Little One to
Stumble
(Mt 18:6-11;
Mk 9:42-50)

[MT 18:]6"But if anyone causes one of these little ones who believe in me to sin, it would be better for him to have a large millstone hung around his neck and to be drowned in the depths of the sea.

7Woe to the world because of the things that cause people to sin! Such things must come, but woe to the man through whom they come! 8If your hand or your foot causes you to sin cut it off and throw it away. It is better for you to enter life maimed or crippled than to have two hands or two feet and be thrown into eternal fire {hell, where the fire never goes out.ᵃ ᴹᴷ} 9And if your eye causes you to sin, gouge it out and throw it away. It is better for you to enter life {the kingdom of Godᴹᴷ} with one eye than to have two eyes and be thrown into the fire of hell

[MK 9:]48where

"'their worm does not die,
and the fire is not quenched.'ᵇ

49Everyone will be salted with fire.

50"Salt is good, but if it loses its saltiness, how can you make it salty again? Have salt in yourselves, and be at peace with each other."

ᵃ[Mk 9:]43 Some manuscripts *out, "where / "'their worm does not die, / and the fire is not quenched.'*   ᵇ48 Isaiah 66:24

Matthew moves directly from the literal child to the disciples. By doing so, he keeps us thinking about these little ones who are precious in God's sight and relatively defenseless. God takes extra care over such individuals. Anyone who "trips up" one of these little guys will be in a heap of trouble. Jesus' word picture is grave. This millstone is not the normal hand-held grinder. It is one of those huge round stones which are turned by donkeys to grind large quantities of grain. In other words, with one of these tied around your neck, you are going to sink fast into the deepest part of the sea.

Mark connects this pericope with John's resistance to the unknown exorcist. We understand then, that the stumbling blocks to these little ones often come from within the circle of Jesus' own disciples. Verse 7 states that they may also originate from the world. Romans 5:12, on the other hand, suggests that sin springs from the individual himself. Thus, there may be three responsible parties for a particular sin: (1) The world, (2) the one who tempts, and (3) the one who falls. Living in this world, we simply can't avoid temptations to sin. But neither can we avoid personal responsibility when we are the cause of another person's stumbling. Nor can we say, "The Devil made me do it." We are each responsible for our own sin (vv. 8-9; cf. Mt 26:24).

Verses 8-9 echo Jesus' words from the Sermon on the Mount (Mt 5:29-30), with two noticeable differences. First, Matthew 5:29-30 has specific reference to looking lustfully at a woman. Here they refer to any kind of sin. Second, the descriptions of punishment are more vivid here: "Hell, where the fire never goes out" (Mk 9:43), "Where their worm does not die and the fire is not quenched" (Mk 9:48, cf. Isa 66:24). This last verse, which concludes the book of Isaiah, paints a frightening picture of eternal punishment in contrast to the joys of the new heaven and earth.

The word "hell" [gehenna] was the name of a valley south of Jerusalem. It was the center of idol worship which included human sacrifice (Jer 7:31; 19:5-6; 32:35). King Josiah's reforms turned it into a city dump where trash was burned, including human excrement and animal carcasses (2 Kgs 23:10). Its stench was no doubt repulsive. Its fire never went out and there were always worms there. Thus, it became a picture of the place of God's punishment.

The main point is simple enough: Hell is hot and it is for a very long time. Nothing in this world, not even physical wholeness, is worth that kind of suffering. Jesus is not advocating actual physical mutilation (see notes on Mt 5:29-30). Rather, he is suggesting to act as if your eyes, hands, or feet were cut off. This is simply a call to radical repentance.

Mark 9:49 is clearly a difficult saying of Jesus. It has resulted in more than a dozen different interpretations and a number of textual variants. So we humbly, and tentatively offer this suggestion. In Jesus' day, when you salted something, you didn't sprinkle it, you covered it. So the picture is one of being covered with fire, a clear allusion to suffering.[81] The question is, "Who gets covered with fire?" If we look back at Mark 9:48, we see a picture of hell. Thus, we might conclude that those bad people who cause little ones to stumble will be utterly destroyed.[82] On the other hand, if we look forward to Mark 9:50, it looks like it is Jesus' disciples who will be "salted with fire." If that's the case, then this fire of suffering is equivalent to purification (cf. Mt 5:10-12). Indeed, the combination of fire and salt may refer to the salting of Levitical sacrifices for purification (Lev 2:13). Such a thought would have given great comfort to the Christians of Rome who received Mark's letter. There is a contrast then, between vv. 48 & 49: You can suffer now for following Jesus or suffer later if you don't.

Mt 18:10

[10]"See that you do not look down on one of these little ones. For I tell you that their angels in heaven always see the face of my Father in heaven.[a]

[a]10 Some manuscripts *heaven.* "*The Son of Man came to save what was lost.*

This verse, along with Hebrews 1:14 and Psalm 91:11, has led some to suggest that each individual has a "guardian angel" who is assigned by God to their personal care. The Jews believed something like that (*b. Sabb.* 119b). But there is nothing in these verses to either prove or disprove their existence.

Wessel makes a reasonable suggestion that these are not guardian angels but the spirits of the deceased "little ones" who are so precious to God that they are privileged to live continually in his presence. After all, how could these angels both be in the presence of God and watch over their assigned person on earth?

§ 91c
One Lost
Sheep
(Mt 18:12-14;
cf. Lk 15:3-7)

This parable is repeated in Luke 15:3-7 but in an entirely different context. Here the lost sheep represents a "fallen" disciple. In Luke the lost sheep represents a lost sinner. Furthermore, most of the major words

---

[81]Fire is sometimes associated with the Holy Spirit. Thus some have suggested that "salted with fire" is the baptism of the Holy Spirit. However, the context refers to suffering (v. 48) and an influence that can be lost (v. 50). That can't be the Holy Spirit. Besides, not "everyone" will receive the baptism of the Holy Spirit.

[82]W.W. Fields, "Everyone Will Be Salted with Fire," *GTJ* 6/2 (1985): 299-304, shows that by translating Mark 9:49 back into Hebrew, the word "salted" could also be rendered "destroyed."

in the Greek text are different. It would not appear, as the source critics allege, that this parable is adapted by Matthew and Luke from a third source. Rather, it appears that Jesus used a similar parable on two different occasions, in two different contexts, to make two different (albeit similar), points.

Mt 18:12-14

¹²"What do you think? If a man owns a hundred sheep, and one of them wanders away, will he not leave the ninety-nine on the hills and go to look for the one that wandered off? ¹³And if he finds it, I tell you the truth, he is happier about that one sheep than about the ninety-nine that did not wander off. ¹⁴In the same way your Father in heaven is not willing that any of these little ones should be lost.

The point of the parable is simple: God loves people, especially those who are lost and helpless.[83] He is absolutely ecstatic when a sinner is saved. He does not want any to perish, but all to come to repentance (2 Pet 3:9).

The parable says that the shepherd leaves the ninety-nine in the open field. In real life, no shepherd would actually do that. There would be other shepherds to watch them. Certainly, God is able to both watch the ninety-nine and seek the one. But since the parable is silent at this point, we should probably not allegorize that particular detail.

The "if" of verse 13 opens the possibility that the one could be lost from the fold. Shepherds of Palestine did frequently lose sheep that stupidly wandered off. That does not mean the shepherd was a bad shepherd. Even Jesus lost one of his twelve (Jn 17:12; 18:9). This is an important balance to John 10:27-28.

§ 92a
Discipline and
Forgiveness
(Mt 18:15-22)

This is a difficult passage, not because it is hard to understand, but because we live in a society that prizes rugged individualism. We actually honor statements like, "Mind your own business," and "I'll do it myself." We almost invariably answer "No" when asked, "Am I my brother's keeper" (Gen 4:9), when the correct answer is "Yes, I am responsible for the spiritual welfare of others." True enough, we must first remove the plank from our own eye (Mt 7:3-4), but we are also charged to remove the speck from our brother's eye (Mt 7:5). And although we must never condemn (Mt 7:1-2), we are given charge to judge/evaluate other believers (1 Cor 6:4-5). True, we are not to judge brothers hypocritically (Rom 2:1) or in matters of opinion or conscience (Rom 14:4, 10; 1 Cor 4:3-5; 10:29; Col 2:16). Nonetheless, we do have the responsibility to both judge and discipline in the church.

---

[83]The Bible doesn't teach that "God helps those who help themselves." Rather, this passage seems to say that God helps the helpless.

Mt 18:15-17

¹⁵"If your brother sins against you,ᵃ go and show him his fault, just between the two of you. If he listens to you, you have won your brother over. ¹⁶But if he will not listen, take one or two others along, so that 'every matter may be established by the testimony of two or three witnesses.'ᵇ ¹⁷If he refuses to listen to them, tell it to the church; and if he refuses to listen even to the church, treat him as you would a pagan or a tax collector.

ᵃ15 Some manuscripts do not have *against you*   ᵇ16 Deut 19:15

The first difficulty in personal confrontation is the attitude of the recipient. But equally difficult is the attitude of the one confronting. It is relatively easy to point out other people's sins, especially when they are absent. Much more difficult, however, is to do it in love (Lev 19:17-18), and humility (Gal 6:1), with an eye to reconciliation (Lk 17:3-4; James 5:19-20).

There are three steps in this process. First, one on one confrontation. This privacy allows the individual to be less defensive and shuts down gossip before it ever gets started. Most of the time, if step number one is done in love, with humility, aimed at reconciliation, it will go no further. Most problems occur because step #1 is either done out of order or not at all.[84]

The second step involves two or three witnesses (cf. Deut 19:15). This is not a "ganging up" on the "sinner" but a legal and judicious witness to the confrontation. It served at least two purposes. First, it would verify the stories of both parties should the matter come before the whole church. Second, it would "civilize" the confrontation and assure a fair hearing for both parties. Furthermore, according to Jewish jurisprudence, one of the witnesses might even represent the side of the "sinner." There is no indication that these witnesses are church administrators (e.g., elders, deacons, pastors). But it is a logical necessity that they be mature, spiritual and impartial.

The third step involves what came to be called "excommunication." Although what Jesus commands here is not nearly as ecclesiastical as is practiced in the Catholic church, it is a scriptural mandate (cf. 2 Thess 3:14-15), which is often ignored by Protestant churches. If the erring brother refuses both a private confrontation and the one involving a few witnesses, he is to be taken before the church. For Matthew's Jewish audience, treating someone as a tax collector or a sinner would mean exclusion from worship and social interaction (e.g., Gen 17:14; Exod

---

[84]Paul's public confrontation of Peter (Gal 2:11-14) was a notable exception, but then so was Peter's sin. It was not a private offense between Paul and Peter. And Peter was a public figure. His actions had caused many to follow his hypocrisy. Such a public and influencing sin merited Paul's public confrontation of it.

12:15, 19). In other words, they are out of fellowship. 1 Corinthians 5:1-5 and 2 Corinthians 2:5-11 probably provide the only actual example of this in the NT. It describes both the excommunication (1 Cor 5) and the resulting reconciliation (2 Cor 2).

There are two further difficulties in this whole process of confrontation. First, churches without careful guidelines and documentation may be liable to lawsuits if they carry out this scriptural mandate. We cannot afford to be careless with this process in an institutional church.[85] But neither can we afford to ignore Jesus' teaching. If there were ever a time to be shrewd as snakes and innocent as doves, it is here (Mt 10:16). Finally, with a church on every corner, and with numbers as a barometer of successful ministry, it is difficult to solicit cooperation between churches in this issue of excommunication. It is even more difficult when crossing denominational lines.

Mt 18:18-20

¹⁸"I tell you the truth, whatever you bind on earth will be^a bound in heaven, and whatever you loose on earth will be^a loosed in heaven.

¹⁹"Again, I tell you that if two of you on earth agree about anything you ask for, it will be done for you by my Father in heaven. ²⁰For where two or three come together in my name, there am I with them."

^a18 Or have been

Verse 18 repeats almost verbatim what Jesus already promised to Peter in Matthew 16:19 (see comments there). Now it appears that this promise is extended to all disciples, but not in all situations. We must keep two things in mind: (1) This context is dealing specifically with two brothers who are at odds. The two who agree may either be the witnesses against the erring brother, thus executing divine exclusion of the sinner. Or the two may be the two brothers who were at odds and have now been reconciled, perhaps with the help of a third-party arbitrator. (2) The reason the agreement between the two is recognized in heaven is because Jesus' presence validates the decision. The incarnation of Christ continues in the local church. His presence authorizes the judicial decisions of the body.

The prayer of verse 19 is not for "anything" we might plan or desire, but any judicial matter. The word *pragma* often indicates financial matters or legal decisions (cf. 1 Cor 6:1). And the "two or three brought together" in verse 20 is not talking about worship services. (The omnipresence of God and the indwelling of the Holy Spirit assure Jesus'

---

[85]For helpful guides one might consult Marlin Jeschke, *Discipling in the Church*, (Scottdale, PA: Herald Press, 1988) or John White and Ken Blue, *Healing the Wounded: The Costly Love of Church Discipline*, (Downers Grove, IL: InterVarsity, 1985).

presence even where a Christian is alone.) The word "come together" [*synegmenoi*] means "united," not merely "gathered." So what this text promises is that God will put his stamp of approval on judicial decisions among church members who come to a mutual agreement (cf. Ps 82:1). Thus "peacemakers perform a divine function."[86]

Mt 18:21-22

[21]Then Peter came to Jesus and asked, "Lord, how many times shall I forgive my brother when he sins against me? Up to seven times?"

[22]Jesus answered, "I tell you, not seven times, but seventy-seven times.[a]"

[a]22 Or *seventy times seven*

Peter is being more than generous according to rabbinic law. The current maximum required forgiveness was three times (*b. Yoma* 86b, 87a). Jesus shocks Peter by multiplying his "generous" seven by eleven.[87] He sets up what is likely an intentional contrast to Lamech in Genesis 4:24, "If Cain is avenged seven times, then Lamech seventy-seven times." The point of both passages is not the number itself, but the exaggeration of the number. In other words, Jesus is not saying, "Don't forgive on the seventy-eighth time;" but "Forgive indefinitely."

§ 92b
The Parable of
the Unforgiving
Servant
(Mt 18:23-35)

Jesus has just told Peter to forgive, not seven times, but however many times it takes. Now, he illustrates the point with a parable. This is essentially the same sentiment expressed in the Lord's Prayer (Mt 6:12-15 & Lk 17:3-5). That is, our forgiveness by God is based on our forgiveness of others (Lk 6:37). Jesus can expect us to forgive freely because that's how he forgave us (Lk 23:34; 1 Jn 1:9). Paul puts it this way: "forgive one another as Christ has forgiven you" (Eph 4:32; Col 3:13).

[23]"Therefore, the kingdom of heaven is like a king who wanted to settle accounts with his servants. [24]As he began the settlement, a man who owed him ten thousand talents[a] was brought to him. [25]Since he was not able to pay, the master ordered that he and his wife and his children and all that he had be sold to repay the debt.

[26]"The servant fell on his knees before him. 'Be patient with me,' he begged, 'and I will pay back everything.' [27]The servant's master took pity on him, canceled the debt and let him go.

[28]"But when that servant went out, he found one of his fellow servants who owed him a hundred denarii.[b] He grabbed him and began to choke him. 'Pay back what you owe me!' he demanded.

---

[86]Cf. J.D.M. Derrett, "'Where Two or Three Are Convened In My Name . . .': A Sad Misunderstanding," *ExpT* 91 (1979-80): 83-86.

[87]The NIV is probably correct in its rendering of "seventy-seven" rather than "seventy times seven."

²⁹"His fellow servant fell to his knees and begged him, 'Be patient with me, and I will pay you back.'

³⁰"But he refused. Instead, he went off and had the man thrown into prison until he could pay the debt. ³¹When the other servants saw what had happened, they were greatly distressed and went and told their master everything that had happened.

³²"Then the master called the servant in. 'You wicked servant,' he said, 'I canceled all that debt of yours because you begged me to. ³³Shouldn't you have had mercy on your fellow servant just as I had on you?' ³⁴In anger his master turned him over to the jailers to be tortured, until he should pay back all he owed.

³⁵"This is how my heavenly Father will treat each of you unless you forgive your brother from your heart."

ᵃ22 That is, millions of dollars   ᵇ28 That is, a few dollars

This unforgiving servant, obviously some kind of governor, has racked up a debt of ten thousand talents. That was huge! For the Romans, ten thousand was the largest number in their vocabulary. A talent was the largest monetary unit available. In today's terms ten thousand talents may vary from several million, to a trillion dollars. (It depends on whether you're talking about a talent of gold, silver, or some cheaper metal). But that's beside the point. This guy owed as much as the first century mind could comprehend.

The king wants his money back. So he threatens to sell this guy and his family into slavery. That was a legal Jewish practice (Lev 25:39; 2 Kgs 4:1). But the maximum price of a slave would only fetch five hundred day's wages (Carson, p. 407). Thus, selling his property and his family into slavery would not even make a dent in his debt. The point is punishment, not repayment. The servant's promise to repay his debt is mere stalling. He is hopelessly unable to pay back the money. The king knows it and takes pity on this groveling governor. His debt is canceled.

No sooner has the servant left than he does a little debt collection of his own. Perhaps he wants to make a token payment to the king as a gesture of goodwill. He grabs one of his fellow servants by the neck who owes him one hundred denarii. A denarii was the daily wage of a common worker. Thus, this represents less than five months wages. A substantial debt, true, but a pittance compared to what the governor owed. A talent has been estimated anywhere between sixty to ten thousand denarii (Blomberg, p. 284). Thus the difference between the two debts could be as great as a million to one.

The other servants are appalled at this hypocrisy and report it to the king. The king is furious. He does to the governor what the governor has threatened to do to his fellow servant. He throws him in prison to be tortured until he can repay his debt. But the fact is, you can't earn any money in prison. Thus, it was a life sentence.

Jesus' conclusion in verse 35 is simple yet startling. If we don't forgive our fellow servants their puny little offenses against us, God won't forgive our huge offenses against him. God's actions are both severe and fair. Those in the church who bear grudges against brothers, or spouses, or parents must pay attention to this teaching. Forgiveness of others is essential to our own salvation (see Mt 6:14-15; 18:21-35; Mk 11:25; Lk 6:37).

> Jesus sees no incongruity in the actions of a heavenly Father who forgives so bountifully and punishes so ruthlessly, and neither should we. Indeed, it is precisely because he is a God of such compassion and mercy that he cannot possibly accept as his those devoid of compassion and mercy (Carson, p. 407).

§ 93 —
(See after § 101)
§ 94
Jesus' Half-brothers Prod Him to Go to the Feast of Tabernacles
(Jn 7:2-9)

It is now October of A.D. 29.[88] John captures the last six months of Jesus' itinerant ministry with a single verse (7:1), "After this, Jesus went around in Galilee, purposely staying away from Judea because the Jews there were waiting to take his life." It was a period of retirement and training of the Twelve which included their travels to the area of Tyre and Sidon, Decapolis, Caesarea Philippi, and Galilee.

The next six months, however, will be marked by Jesus' deliberate advance to the cross. The chronology of this period is perhaps the most difficult of the Gospels for a number of reasons. (1) Matthew and Mark have little to say about this period. (2) Luke's extensive narrative (9:51-19:44), lacks his usual chronological markers. And (3) John kicks in and tells us about three feasts, two of which are not mentioned in the Synoptics at all.

Jn 7:2-5

²But when the Jewish Feast of Tabernacles was near, ³Jesus' brothers said to him, "You ought to leave here and go to Judea, so that your disciples may see the miracles you do. ⁴No one who wants to become a public figure acts in secret. Since you are doing these things, show yourself to the world." ⁵For even his own brothers did not believe in him.

The fall Feast of Tabernacles, along with Passover and Pentecost, were the major feasts which Jewish men were expected to attend (Deut 16:16). Tabernacles was a delightful eight-day festival (Deut 16:13-17) that celebrated two things: The fall harvest, much like our Thanksgiving, and the Exodus from Egyptian slavery. Along with the seventy sacrificed

---

[88]Tabernacles took place on the fifteenth day of the seventh month (Lev 23:34), which is about the second week of October.

bulls and the daily sounding of the temple trumpets, there were several symbols incorporated into the feast which reminded the Jews of their wilderness wanderings. Booths (i.e., tabernacles) were erected all over the city, where families would eat and sleep as a reminder of their wilderness dwellings (Lev 23:43). The holy candelabra and a parade of torches reminded them of the pillar of fire that led them by night (Num 14:14; Jn 8:12). Water from the pool of Siloam reminded them of God's provision of water from the rock at Meribah (Exod 17:1-7; cf. Jn 7:37). Not only will Jesus attend this feast, he will use these symbols as a platform for his preaching (Jn 7:37; 8:12).

It's time to begin their pilgrimage to Jerusalem. Jesus' brothers, James, Joses, Judas, and Simon (Mt 13:55), accost him. They suggest that Jesus go to the feast to prove he is the Messiah. But they don't believe in him. No, they're throwing down a gauntlet. For the last six months, Jesus has been running around the borders of Jewish territory, hiding. To make matters worse, Jesus missed the last Passover. So it's been eighteen months since he last went to Jerusalem. Any "good" Jew would now feel obligated to fulfill his religious duty to worship in the Holy city. The last time Jesus was there, however, the ruling council decided to kill him (Jn 5:18). It's not a safe place for Jesus. And now his brothers are essentially saying, "Put up, or shut up! If you can't do it in Jerusalem, then you're a fraud."

Jn 7:6-9

⁶Therefore Jesus told them, "The right time for me has not yet come; for you any time is right. ⁷The world cannot hate you, but it hates me because I testify that what it does is evil. ⁸You go to the Feast. I am not yetª going up to this Feast, because for me the right time has not yet come." ⁹Having said this, he stayed in Galilee.

ª8 Some early manuscripts do not have *yet*

Jesus and his half-brothers look a lot alike socially and culturally. But spiritually they are worlds apart. Jesus highlights two differences here. First, Jesus is on God's divine timetable. He will go to Jerusalem and die, but not yet. He will even go up to this feast and confront the crowds and their rulers, but not yet. Jesus' brothers are under no such divine chronology. They can come and go as they please. Jesus, on the other hand, can't. His whole life is meticulously timed and choreographed under God's direction (cf. Jn 2:4).

The second major difference is Jesus' relationship with the world. He is not saying that James, Joses, Judas and Simon have no enemies, but that they are part and parcel of the world's system, specifically the Jewish culture. They may ruffle some individuals' feathers, but they don't rock the societal boat. Jesus, on the other hand, stands in opposition to the world's ideology, theology, and culture (cf. Jn 2:14-16; 3:19-20; 5:30-47). Since he is not part of the world, Jesus is a major threat to the powers that be. Thus, the world hates Jesus (Jn 15:18, 19; 17:14).

**§ 95
Journey
Through
Samaria**
(Lk 9:51-56;
John 7:10)[89]

This passage opens Luke's carefully crafted central section (Lk 9:51-19:44).[90] He does a couple of things through this portion of his book. First, he takes many of the words and deeds of Jesus that Matthew records in the Galilean ministry, and places them in Jesus' tour of Judea and Perea. Thereby, Luke shows that what Jesus did and said in Galilee, he later repeated in the southern parts of Palestine as well. Second, Luke's central section highlights the conflicting worldviews of Jesus and his enemies.[91] This prepares us for the great conflict of the cross.

Jn 7:10

[10]However, after his brothers had left for the Feast, he went also, not publicly, but in secret.

Lk 9:51

[51]As the time approached for him to be taken up to heaven, Jesus resolutely set out for Jerusalem.

Jesus leaves late so as to arrive at the feast halfway through it (Jn 7:14). He takes the direct route from Galilee to Judea, through the heart of Samaria. Most Jews crossed over to the east bank of the Jordan to travel south. Then they would come back across the Jordan and arrive at Jerusalem via Jericho. It was a longer route, but it allowed them to avoid Samaritan territory. They did so for two reasons. First, they considered these "half-breed" Samaritans as unclean. Even the dust from Samaria's roads might defile a worshiper going up to Jerusalem. Second, travelling through "enemy territory" can be dangerous. The tensions between the Jews and Samaritans were significant and well documented (see notes on § 35a). Jesus chooses this route anyway because he can make better time and he can travel incognito.

Jesus marches to Jerusalem with a vengeance. (The Greek idiom, "Set his face toward" [v. 51] indicates Jesus' dogged determination.) Furthermore, Luke isn't just referring to this one trip. Luke 9:51 opens a new section of Luke (9:51-19:44), which stresses Jesus' determined

---

[89]See notes on J.M. Dawsey, "Jesus' Pilgrimage to Jerusalem," *PRS* 14 (1987): 217-232 (esp. nn. 1 and 2, p. 217).

[90]H.K. Farrell, "The Structure and Theology of Luke's Central Section," *TrinJ* 7 ns (1986): 33-54.

[91]J.L. Resseguie, "Point of View in the Central Section of Luke (9:51-19:44)," *JETS* 25/1 (1982): 41-47.

course for the cross (Lk 9:51; 10:38; 13:22, 32-33; 17:11; 18:31, 35; 19:1, 28-29). He compresses John's three trips to Jerusalem (Jn 7:10; 10:22; 12:12) into one movement. Like John in the previous section, Luke recognizes God's schedule in all this. His word "approached" (*sympleroō*, v. 51), indicates a sense of destiny — a divine appointment (cf. Lk 1:1; 4:21; 9:31; 22:16; 24:44). While there are still six months until the cross, the hourglass of Jesus' ministry is getting thinner.

The phrase "to heaven" (v. 51) is not in the Greek, but the NIV is surely correct in adding it to the words "taken up." A cognate of the word *analēmpseos* "taken up," is found in Acts 1:2 & 11 with specific reference to the ascension. Although *analēmpseos* does not directly describe the crucifixion, it seems to include the death, burial, and resurrection of Jesus with the ascension as the culmination of Jesus' life.

Lk 9:52-56

[52]And he sent messengers on ahead, who went into a Samaritan village to get things ready for him; [53]but the people there did not welcome him, because he was heading for Jerusalem. [54]When the disciples James and John saw this, they asked, "Lord, do you want us to call fire down from heaven to destroy them[a]?" [55]But Jesus turned and rebuked them, [56]and[b] they went to another village.

[a]*54 Some manuscripts them, even as Elijah did*   [b]*55,56 Some manuscripts them. And he said, "You do not know what kind of spirit you are of, for the Son of Man did not come to destroy men's lives, but to save them." *[56]*And*

The first time Jesus passed through Samaria he was accepted as Messiah, even "the savior of the world" (Jn 4:39-42). Why then do they reject him now, some 21 months later? They probably are not rejecting the person of Jesus as much as this band of Jews heading to Jerusalem, the rival temple of worship (cf. Jn 4:20-24).

James and John, living up to their nickname, "Sons of Thunder" (*Boanerges*, Mk 3:17), kindly offer to take care of the situation for Jesus. Their impetuousness and arrogance is appalling. First, where do they think they are going to get that kind of power? Sure, they have performed many miracles, cast out demons, and perhaps even raised people from the dead (Mt 10:1, 8). But commanding the forces of nature is something else. Second, in one textual variant, reflected in the KJV, they compare themselves to Elijah (cf. 2 Kings 1:9-12). That is a bit presumptuous. Third, why do they think they need to stick up for Jesus anyway? Like preachers who feel that they need to defend God in the face of a hostile society, James and John have stepped out of bounds when they try to take matters into their own hands. Worse than all this, they have missed Jesus' last two lessons on humility and forgiveness (§ 90-92).

Again, the Master models for us a life of humility and peace. Instead of rebuking the hostile Samaritans, he reprimands his disciples who should have known better. In fact, one interesting variation of v. 55 reads, "You do not know what kind of spirit you are; for the Son of Man did not come to destroy the souls of men but to save them." Then Jesus just picks up his bags and quietly moves on.

PART EIGHT
THE LATER JUDEAN MINISTRY OF CHRIST

§ 96a
Jesus' Arrival at the Feast of Tabernacles
(Jn 7:11-31)

John 7 takes up where John 5 left off eighteen months earlier. Both take place at a feast in Jerusalem. In both chapters the Sanhedrin is determined to kill Jesus (5:18; 7:1, 19-20, 25, 30, 32, 44-45, cf. also 8:59; 9:22; 10:31, 39; 11:8, 53). In both chapters Jesus testifies about himself and against the leaders. And in both chapters the Sabbath controversy rears its ugly head (5:1-17; 7:21-24), as well as the question of Jesus' authority (5:30-49; 7:18-19). This is the same song . . . second verse.

Jn 7:11-13

¹¹Now at the Feast the Jews were watching for him and asking, "Where is that man?"
¹²Among the crowds there was widespread whispering about him. Some said, "He is a good man."
Others replied, "No, he deceives the people." ¹³But no one would say anything publicly about him for fear of the Jews.

The Feast of Tabernacles drew crowds from all over the Roman world. These pilgrims (v. 20, 31-32), the Sanhedrin (v. 15, 32, 35), and the residents of Jerusalem (v. 25) make up the three distinct groups at this feast. Within each group there are mixed opinions about Jesus, but by and large, the religious leaders hate him. The Jerusalemites are skeptical while the pilgrims love him (although the sermon on the Bread of Life soured many of Jesus' supporters).

The religious hierarchy, which John labels "the Jews," is on the lookout for Jesus. They decided a year and a half ago that he must be executed (Jn 5:18; 7:1). But because of his popularity, they couldn't touch him. Since that time, they have sent detectives from Jerusalem to scrutinize his every move (Mk 7:1; 8:15; 9:14; Mt 16:1, 6; 17:24). Six months ago they brought back a good report. The crowds at Capernaum abandoned Jesus after his sermon on the Bread of Life (6:41, 52). Jesus has been laying low ever since. But here's their big chance. They've had plenty of time to plot. The crowds are divided over him. And Jesus is on their turf. This is the feast where they get their man. Problem: Jesus hasn't shown up yet.

The crowds are as eager as the Sanhedrin to see Jesus. Some were for him, others against. This they can agree on, however: Whenever Jesus turns up, it makes for an exciting show. The crowds debate in a whisper, fearing what the Sanhedrin might do to any of Jesus' supporters. Their plot to kill Jesus is not yet public (Jn 7:20), but their desire is obvious to those who live in Jerusalem (Jn 7:25). The Sanhedrin's dislike for Jesus is clear enough to all to deter them from speaking out for him. They have the power to excommunicate people from the synagogue (cf. Jn 9:22, 34; 12:42). That is a frightening punishment to a people whose religious, social, and economic life are wrapped up in the fellowship of the synagogue.

Jn 7:14-18

¹⁴Not until halfway through the Feast did Jesus go up to the temple courts and begin to teach. ¹⁵The Jews were amazed and asked, "How did this man get such learning without having studied?"

¹⁶Jesus answered, "My teaching is not my own. It comes from him who sent me. ¹⁷If anyone chooses to do God's will, he will find out whether my teaching comes from God or whether I speak on my own. ¹⁸He who speaks on his own does so to gain honor for himself, but he who works for the honor of the one who sent him is a man of truth; there is nothing false about him."

About the third or fourth day of the feast, Jesus finally arrives. The leaders are surely surprised that he has actually shown up. More surprising still is Jesus' extraordinary teaching (Mt 7:28-29; Mk 1:22; Lk 2:46-47). All the more remarkable, since he has no degree.[1] Their subtle suggestion is that you can't really trust a self-taught man since he has no guides to insure his orthodoxy. Jesus counters by saying, "I'm not self-taught. God has been my guide!" There is no comparison between the teaching of God and the erudition of men.

Verse 17 suggests that those who obey God will understand the truth. It's as if Jesus is saying, "Test my teaching. See if it doesn't work in real life!" When we try the "nonsense" of Jesus (like turning the other cheek, or seeking to be last), we discover, to our delight, that it works. It is like trying to focus a telescope with dozens of knobs on it. When you finally turn the right one, no one has to tell you it is right. You know it when all comes into focus. So it is with following Jesus' teaching.

The leaders perceive Jesus as a self-taught man. He speaks with independent authority (Mt 7:28-29), without quoting famed rabbis.

---

[1]Lit. "How does this man know *letters*" [*grammata*]. Aside from meaning actual letters (Gal 6:11), epistles (Acts 28:21), or even the Scriptures (2 Tim 3:15), it indicates the entire educational system.

Therefore, he is accused of being a misguided maverick. Here in verse 18, Jesus attempts to diffuse that accusation. We are taken back to John 5:30-47 and Jesus' impressive list of supporting witnesses (God, John the Baptist, his deeds, Scriptures, and Moses). Jesus doesn't bother to retrace his steps, but does recall the first and last witnesses of John 5 — God and Moses. The implication is the same — You guys aren't listening to either God or Moses! Since Jesus speaks on behalf of God, to reject Jesus is to reject the Father (Jn 5:23-24, 30; Mt 10:40).

Jn 7:19-24

[19]"Has not Moses given you the law? Yet not one of you keeps the law. Why are you trying to kill me?"

[20]"You are demon-possessed," the crowd answered. "Who is trying to kill you?"

[21]Jesus said to them, "I did one miracle, and you are all astonished. [22]Yet, because Moses gave you circumcision (though actually it did not come from Moses, but from the patriarchs), you circumcise a child on the Sabbath. [23]Now if a child can be circumcised on the Sabbath so that the law of Moses may not be broken, why are you angry with me for healing the whole man on the Sabbath? [24]Stop judging by mere appearances, and make a right judgment."

Jesus' accusation is blatant and offensive. To tell a rabbi that he doesn't keep the law of Moses is a quick way to a quarrel. But it was true. Without legal justification, and ignoring proper jurisprudence, the Sanhedrin is plotting Jesus' murder. This is an especially strong accusation in light of Jesus' teaching about murderous desires (Mt 5:21-22). The crowds are ignorant of that fact, so they call Jesus crazy (i.e., demon-possessed).[2] The crowd may be imagining that Jesus is talking about them and not specifically the Sanhedrin. Even so, in six short months, many of them will reconvene in Jerusalem and shout with the Sanhedrin, "Crucify him!"

In answer to the crowd's question (v. 20), Jesus takes them back to the Passover (Jn 5). The "one miracle" was a lame man healed on the Sabbath. He can cite many others (2:23; 3:2), but that one sparked their murderous motives (5:18). They weren't upset about the miracle per se. They were mad because he did it on the Sabbath. Sabbath healing is strictly forbidden by their oral traditions (see notes on § 51). Now Jesus will demonstrate the foolishness of those man-made rules (cf. § 50).

Circumcision was as sacred to a Jew as anything. It was what identified a male as being Jewish. (Although, as Jesus pointed out, it preceded Jewish nationality, going back to Abraham, Gen 17:9-14). It was so sacred that even the Sabbath could be broken so that circumcision could

---

[2]Every reference to demon possession in John's Gospel equates it with insanity in reference to Jesus (cf. 8:48-52; 10:20-21).

be performed at its appointed time on the eighth day. The logic is obvious. People are more valuable to God than ritual. The Sabbath can be broken so that the ritual law of Moses will not be. Why, then, should the Sabbath not again be broken so that a human being might not be. The reprimand of verse 24 may be as heavy against the Christian church as it was against the Sanhedrin (cf. 1 Sam 16:7). Whenever religious ritual takes precedence over human need, God is dishonored. Whether the issue is divorce, AIDS, war, homelessness, education, or racial tensions, human need is more important to God than religious ritual.

Jn 7:25-31

[25]At that point some of the people of Jerusalem began to ask, "Isn't this the man they are trying to kill? [26]Here he is, speaking publicly, and they are not saying a word to him. Have the authorities really concluded that he is the Christ[a]? [27]But we know where this man is from; when the Christ comes, no one will know where he is from."

[28]Then Jesus, still teaching in the temple courts, cried out, "Yes, you know me, and you know where I am from. I am not here on my own, but he who sent me is true. You do not know him, [29]but I know him because I am from him and he sent me."

[30]At this they tried to seize him, but no one laid a hand on him, because his time had not yet come. [31]Still, many in the crowd put their faith in him. They said, "When the Christ comes, will he do more miraculous signs than this man?"

[a]26 Or Messiah; also in verses 27, 31, 41 and 42

Although the pilgrims are ignorant of the plot of the Jews, the locals are not. They have heard the rumblings of the Sanhedrin. They are shocked that Jesus is getting away with speaking so forthrightly [*parrēsia*, cf. Heb 4:16] in public. They even ask, expecting a negative answer, "Could the leaders have concluded that this is the Messiah?" But what could the leaders do? If they let the cat out of the bag about their plot against Jesus, the pilgrims could easily turn against them. After all, that would prove that Jesus was right (v. 19). And this fickle crowd might just decide to support the underdog.

As for the Jerusalem residents, they have concluded, by and large, that Jesus is not the Messiah. Their reasons for this are both misguided and misinformed. They are misguided because they seem to think the Messiah is going to appear miraculously from heaven, without human origin. They are misinformed because they think Jesus is from Galilee (v. 41; cf. 6:42).

Jesus responds with what we interpret as biting sarcasm.[3] "Yes, you

---

[3]Our reasons for viewing this as sarcasm are these: (1) The Sanhedrin tried to seize him afterward (v. 30). (2) Jesus could not truthfully affirm their error about his origin. (3) Jesus often used sarcasm in similar situations of ignorant antagonism.

think you know where I'm from! But you don't know where I am from because you don't even know the One who sent me! If you would just listen to me I would tell you all about him" (cf. Jn 8:42-43, 55-59). With this, Jesus draws a line in the sand and asks the crowd to choose sides. There is both open antagonism and acceptance. The crowds have seen what Jesus can do. That got their attention. Now they have heard how he deals with the Jewish leaders. His clarity of thought, purity of priorities, boldness, independent authority, and perceptive preaching has won them over. Even if he is not their Messiah, surely he will not be outdone in the number or significance of his miracles. Thus they align with the Master.

§ 96b
Failed Attempt
to Arrest Jesus
(Jn 7:32-52)

[32]The Pharisees heard the crowd whispering such things about him. Then the chief priests and the Pharisees sent temple guards to arrest him.

[33]Jesus said, "I am with you for only a short time, and then I go to the one who sent me. [34]You will look for me, but you will not find me; and where I am, you cannot come."

[35]The Jews said to one another, "Where does this man intend to go that we cannot find him? Will he go where our people live scattered among the Greeks, and teach the Greeks? [36]What did he mean when he said, 'You will look for me, but you will not find me,' and 'Where I am, you cannot come'?"

The Pharisees and Sadducees don't usually team up (cf. Acts 23:6-8). But here they have a common enemy. They send their guards to arrest Jesus. But they couldn't get past the force of his teaching.

They are struck with his talk about the ascension (vv 33-34). Unlike Christians, they have no reference point to understand this. All they can think of is that Jesus will slip away into the diaspora of the Hellenistic world. If Jesus runs away into the far reaches of Gentile territory, he will be safe from the attacks of the Sanhedrin. But as far as the diaspora is from Jerusalem, so far are they from understanding what Jesus means. Yet even this derision of Jesus is prophetic of the victorious spread of the Kingdom of God.

Jesus returns their mockery tit for tat. There will come a time when they will turn to look for Jesus only to find that he is gone (v. 34). Amos 8:11-12 has a similar thought:

> "The days are coming," declares the Sovereign LORD, "when I will send a famine through the land — not a famine of food or a thirst for water, but a famine of hearing the words of the LORD. Men will stagger from sea to sea and wander from north to east, searching for the word of the LORD, but they will not find it."

Jn 7:37-39

[37]On the last and greatest day of the Feast, Jesus stood and said in a loud

voice, "If anyone is thirsty, let him come to me and drink. [38]Whoever believes in me, as[a] the Scripture has said, streams of living water will flow from within him." [39]By this he meant the Spirit, whom those who believed in him were later to receive. Up to that time the Spirit had not been given, since Jesus had not yet been glorified.

[a]*37,38 Or / If anyone is thirsty, let him come to me. / And let him drink, [38]who believes in me. / As*

The last day of the feast could either be the seventh day, which officially concluded the festival, or the eighth day, which was appended to the feast as a solemn day of teaching.[4] But because the eighth day would not be a regular part of the feast, and certainly would not be the "greatest day" of the feast, we will assume that John speaks here of the seventh day.[5]

For the past seven days a priest has gone to the pool of Siloam and filled up a golden pitcher with water. The crowds have followed as he carried it to the temple. They have watched as he poured this libation offering into a bowl which drains into the base of the altar. Wine was likewise poured into a similar bowl, filling up the other side of the altar. This was done while reciting Isaiah 12:3, "With joy you will draw water from the wells of salvation." The ceremony remembers God's divine provision of water from a rock in the wilderness. Playing off this public celebration, Jesus stands and shouts about living water. In essence, he claims to be the rock of divine provision (1 Cor 10:4).

In a parenthetical note,[6] John informs his reader what Jesus really had in mind. After the ascension, Jesus promises the Holy Spirit will come as a permanent partner of the Christian (Jn 14:16-19; 16:5-7).[7] The OT long before had promised his coming, often with the figure of water (Ps 46:4-5; Isa 32:15; 44:3; 55:1; 58:11; Ezek 39:29; Joel 2:28). But just

---

[4]Lev 23:34-36 "Say to the Israelites: 'On the fifteenth day of the seventh month the LORD's Feast of Tabernacles begins, and it lasts for seven days. The first day is a sacred assembly; do no regular work. For seven days present offerings made to the LORD by fire, and on the eighth day hold a sacred assembly and present an offering made to the LORD by fire. It is the closing assembly; do no regular work."

[5]It was on this very day some five centuries earlier that Haggai, not far from this very spot prophesied the following: "This is what the LORD Almighty says: 'In a little while I will once more shake the heavens and the earth, the sea and the dry land. I will shake all nations, and the desired of all nations will come, and I will fill this house with glory,' says the LORD Almighty. 'The silver is mine and the gold is mine,' declares the LORD Almighty. 'The glory of this present house will be greater than the glory of the former house,' says the LORD Almighty. 'And in this place I will grant peace,' declares the LORD Almighty" (Haggai 2:6-9).

[6]For other parenthetical notes in John see 2:21; 6:6, 71; 11:51; 12:6, 33; 21:19.

[7]Another possible interpretation is that the "water" issues forth from Jesus rather than the Christian. But that is less likely. G. Fee, "Once More — Jn 7:37-39," *ExpT* 89 (1978): 116-118.

what passage does Jesus have in mind in v. 38? There have been more than a few suggestions (e.g., Exod 17:5-6; Num 20:7-11; Ps 78:15-16; Prov 5:15; 18:4; Isa 12:3; 58:11; Zech 13:1; etc.). Dodd observes that Isaiah 12:3; Ezekiel 47:1-10 and Zechariah 14:8 were all read publicly during the Feast of Tabernacles.[8] Ezekiel 47:1-10, in particular, seems appropriate. It describes water flowing from the millennial temple. This is a striking picture of the Christian, who becomes the temple of God through the indwelling of the Holy Spirit (1 Cor 6:19-20).[9]

Water is an important symbol.[10] In Palestine, it is not just refreshment, it is life! Likewise, the Holy Spirit is not merely nice to have around. He gives us life, even to our bodies according to Romans 8:10-11 (cf. Ezek 47:9). It is as if our spirits were lying dormant (i.e., dead), because of the curse of death from Eden. But after Christ's death paid the penalty of sin, Eden's curse is removed and we can once again walk with God in the cool of the day (Gen 3:8), through the indwelling of the Holy Spirit (cf. Rev 22:17).

Jn 7:40-44

[40]On hearing his words, some of the people said, "Surely this man is the Prophet."
[41]Others said, "He is the Christ."
Still others asked, "How can the Christ come from Galilee? [42]Does not the Scripture say that the Christ will come from David's family[a] and from Bethlehem, the town where David lived?" [43]Thus the people were divided because of Jesus. [44]Some wanted to seize him, but no one laid a hand on him.

[a]*42* Greek *seed*

This difficult teaching divides the crowds into three opinions. Some think he is "The Prophet." This is not far from a declaration that Jesus is the Messiah. They likely have Deuteronomy 16:15-18 in mind (cf. Jn 1:20-21). Others are willing to make their confession in kosher terms, "He is the Messiah." The third group denies that Jesus could be the Messiah because he is from Galilee and not from Bethlehem. Although their understanding of the OT is more accurate than those of v. 27 (cf. Micah 5:2; Mt 2:5-6), they are just as ignorant about Jesus' history. We wonder why Jesus did not explain to the crowds that he was, in fact, born in Bethlehem. Perhaps he wanted to avoid the ugly accusation that

---

[8]C.H. Dodd, *The Interpretation of the Fourth Gospel*, (Cambridge: University Press, 1953), p. 349.

[9]Z.C. Hodges, "Rivers of Living Water," *BibSac* 136 (1979): 239-248.

[10]S.H. Hooke, "'The Spirit Was Not Yet,'" *NTS* 9 (1962-63): 372-380, suggests that most of the water talk in John is symbolic (cf. Jn 2:9; 3:5; 4:10-15; 5:7; 6:35; 7:37-38; 19:34).

he was illegitimate. Or perhaps he did try to explain it, but the tumult of the crowd drowned him out. After all, he did have to shout (v. 37) to get this discussion started in the first place.

The division of the crowd is no mere civil dispute. There are guards ready to arrest Jesus, backed by a certain sector of the crowd. An opposing sector stands just as vehemently for Jesus. And no doubt, many, especially the devout pilgrims, stand neutral, stunned by the impiety of the whole nasty business. We would probably not be wrong for importing here our image the stereotypical middle-eastern passion for controversy. But Jesus stands above the schemes of men in the chronology of God (Jn 2:4; 7:30; 7:44).

Jn 7:45-52

45Finally the temple guards went back to the chief priests and Pharisees, who asked them, "Why didn't you bring him in?"

46"No one ever spoke the way this man does," the guards declared.

47"You mean he has deceived you also?" the Pharisees retorted. 48"Has any of the rulers or of the Pharisees believed in him? 49No! But this mob that knows nothing of the law — there is a curse on them."

50Nicodemus, who had gone to Jesus earlier and who was one of their own number, asked, 51"Does our law condemn anyone without first hearing him to find out what he is doing?"

52They replied, "Are you from Galilee, too? Look into it, and you will find that a prophet[a] does not come out of Galilee."

[a]52 Two early manuscripts the Prophet

When the guards return empty-handed, both the Pharisees and chief priests pounce on them. They are smarting from yet another failure to apprehend their archenemy who keeps beating them at public debate. All their years of training and they still can't take this hillbilly from Galilee! Wounded, they are going to strike at anything that moves. The guards simply state that the force of his speech kept them at bay. The leaders extend the guard's statement, which they themselves could scarcely deny, to a full-blown confession of Christ. However, the word "man" [anthrōpos] stands in an emphatic position at the end of the sentence. This may suggest the guards believe that Jesus is more than a mere man.

The Pharisees are skillful orators. Here they use their ability to attack the guards. Essentially, they say, "The crowds (Am ha-aretz) are a bunch of ignorant buffoons. They are easily deceived. And you are acting like these vulgar commoners. Not only are they stupid, they are cursed!" In a moment of frustration, these Pharisees show their true colors. They are arrogant and vicious to all who do not cower to their status and opinions.

Although they claim that no Pharisee has believed in Jesus,

Nicodemus is in the crowd. Not only did he believe in Jesus, but he clearly indicated that there were others also (Jn 3:1-2). Nicodemus speaks with civility and reason. He does not spout out his opinion. Rather, he gently couches it in a question. Any impartial observer has to agree with the judicial question that he raised (Deut 1:16-17). The Sanhedrin is on the verge of a serious breach in the judicial process. But Nicodemus' compatriots are not in the mood for listening, but for murdering. They attack their comrade as they had the guards. Their vicious accusation not only goes beyond what Nicodemus said, but it ignores the truth of his question.

They state that a prophet does not come out of Galilee. This is patently false. Jonah came from Galilee (2 Kgs 14:25), and possibly Hosea and Nahum as well. We might, however, give them the benefit of the doubt and add an article to their statement (as does one of the oldest manuscripts, $\mathfrak{P}^{66}$). "*The* prophet" does not come out of Galilee. That is to say, "The Messiah" will not come from Galilee. This probably makes more sense in light of their great knowledge of the OT.

§ 97
Woman Caught
in Adultery
(Jn 7:53-8:11)

Before we even read this passage we notice that the NIV has set it off in brackets. Their note says, "The earliest and most reliable manuscripts and other ancient witnesses do not have John 7:53-8:11." That's true. In fact, its not found in any manuscript before the sixth century. In addition, there are a number of other reasons to suspect that this was not written by John but added later by some well-meaning scribe. (1) Even when it is included, there are substantial textual variants as well as differences as to where it is placed. Some manuscripts put it after 7:36, some at the end of John, others after Luke 21:38. Several include it here but mark it with an obelisk indicating that there is something fishy about it. "No early commentator contains it, nor is it quoted in any of the church fathers before Irenaeus . . . The multiplicity of small variants within this pericope indicate that it may have had a checkered literary history" (Tenney, p. 91). (2) Its inclusion breaks the natural flow between 7:52 and 8:12.[11] And 7:53 makes an abrupt switch between the private meeting of the Sanhedrin to the public dispersion of the crowd. (3) If it is authentic, it is the only place that John mentions scribes and

---

[11]The allusion to water (Jn 7:38-39) and light (8:12), two dominant symbols of the Feast of Tabernacles, both belong together on the last day of the feast (Jn 7:37). The woman caught in adultery would push Jn 8:12 to the next day when the feast was actually over. Furthermore, Jn 8:12 answers the question of 7:52 with an allusion to Isa 9:1-2 (cf. P. Comfort, "The Pericope of the Adulteress," *BT* 40/1 [1989]: 145-147).

the only place in the Gospels where Jesus writes. (4) There are a couple of things in the narrative which are difficult to explain: Why is Jesus given the authority of a judge? And why did they bring the woman to Jesus but not the man she slept with? All of this suggests that John 7:53-8:11 was most probably not part of John's original text.[12]

To say this text is unauthentic is not to say it is unhistoric. In other words, it probably was not part of John's original Gospel. But it was probably based on a true oral tradition from the life of Jesus. Papias, John's disciple, was apparently familiar with the story. Eusebius explains: Papias "has expounded another story about a woman who was accused before the Lord of many sins, which the Gospel according to the Hebrews contains" (*Ecclesiastical History* III, 39.17). Augustine (*De adulterinis conjugiis* II, 7) stated that this story was removed from some manuscripts lest it be appealed to by would-be adulteresses. This would be understandable as well amidst the rise of asceticism. Therefore, we will treat this text as a useful vignette from Jesus' life. But we hold it lightly since its inclusion in John's Gospel is dubious.

Jn 7:53-8:5

⁵³Then each went to his own home.

¹But Jesus went to the Mount of Olives. ²At dawn he appeared again in the temple courts, where all the people gathered around him, and he sat down to teach them. ³The teachers of the law and the Pharisees brought in a woman caught in adultery. They made her stand before the group ⁴and said to Jesus, "Teacher, this woman was caught in the act of adultery. ⁵In the Law Moses commanded us to stone such women. Now what do you say?"

Everyone went home for the night after a day of heated debates. Since the feast is now over, they all dismantle their "tents" and go back to their beds. But Jesus is still camping out at one of his favorite haunts, the Mount of Olives. The following morning, just after sunrise, Jesus is again in the midst of the temple with an eager audience around him. This would be the eighth day of the feast, the solemn assembly.

The educated religious right (i.e., Pharisees and scribes) present Jesus with a dilemma. Here is a woman caught in the act. She stands in the midst of a murderous mob with her heart pounding and her palms sweating. She wonders if she will survive the incident. This all happened so suddenly. The sinners' sheets haven't even cooled.

Perhaps the joyous celebration and its delicious wine during the last

---

[12]For more details see G.M. Burge, "A Specific Problem in the N.T. text and Canon: The Woman Caught in Adultery (Jn 7:53-8:11)" *JETS* 27/2 (1984): 141-148. However, for a defense of its authenticity, see Z. Hodges, "The Woman Taken in Adultery (Jn 7:53-8:11): The Text," *BibSac* 137 (1979): 318-332.

seven days seduced her into sin. Now, here she is in the temple of God, exposed. The very stones of this holy place seem to condemn the sin in its midst. The crowd, while peeved at the interruption, are yet sadistically curious of the spectacle, and speak volumes with their eyes. She is publicly disgraced and standing alone without so much as the support of her lover. By the way, where is he? If they were caught in the act, why is he not here to receive his just punishment of stoning (Lev 20:10)? Their hypocrisy is blatant. Not only is the man's absence a glaring inconsistency, so is the Pharisaic presence when this act took place. How could this woman be caught in the act without a malicious trap? They care neither for the sin nor the woman. She is merely a tool to get at Jesus.

So Jesus is presented with this dilemma. They ask him emphatically, "What do YOU say?" If he condemns the woman he may risk the wrath of Rome for pronouncing capital punishment. He may also lose face with the crowds who have followed him partially because of his compassion. But on the other hand, if he excuses this woman, he could rightly be accused of contradicting the law of Moses which demands the stoning of an adulteress (Deut 22:22-24). But Jesus will not be trapped in a catch-22 (cf. Mt 22:15-40). Nor will he allow such flagrant hypocrisy to go undetected.

Jn 8:6-11

⁶They were using this question as a trap, in order to have a basis for accusing him.

But Jesus bent down and started to write on the ground with his finger. ⁷When they kept on questioning him, he straightened up and said to them, "If any one of you is without sin, let him be the first to throw a stone at her." ⁸Again he stooped down and wrote on the ground.

⁹At this, those who heard began to go away one at a time, the older ones first, until only Jesus was left, with the woman still standing there. ¹⁰Jesus straightened up and asked her, "Woman, where are they? Has no one condemned you?"

¹¹"No one, sir," she said.

"Then neither do I condemn you," Jesus declared. "Go now and leave your life of sin."

Jesus, as if disinterested in the whole question, stoops down and starts to write on the ground. There have been many speculations as to what he wrote. One attractive suggestion is that he wrote accusations against the various Sanhedrin members. Another says he wrote a list of their names. Still another supposes that he just doodled to show his disinterest. We're curious about what he wrote. But apparently it doesn't matter. The emphasis is on the act of writing, not what was written. While Jesus scribbles in the sand they keep pressing him for an answer. They get more of an answer than they bargain for.

Jesus stands up, adding force to his response. Without disregarding either the law of Moses or this precious person, he simply says, "If any one of you is without sin, let him be the first to throw a stone at her." Jesus is not saying that her accusers have to be sinless. That would spell the demise of all legal proceedings. He is merely suggesting that they be adequate witnesses.[13] According to Deuteronomy 19:16-19 (cf. Exod 23:1-3, 6-8), this means that they must not be malicious or deceitful. Jesus exposes their devious sting operation. They're trying to nail Jesus, not this woman. Now they, along with this woman, have been caught in the act. Furthermore, those who would throw the first stone, according to Jewish jurisprudence, must be witnesses of the crime. These guys are at the center of this vicious trap. Bull's-eye! Jesus, with one sentence identifies, criticizes, and dismantles this whole dirty business. He then stoops down and continues to doodle in the dust.

The older ones leave first, their wisdom and moderation having been forged by time. The others follow reluctantly. By and by this whole inner band of accusers disappears, leaving this woman alone with Jesus in the center [Gk = *en mesō ausa*]. But in the center of what? The original crowd of disciples whose class was broken up by this charade.

All the woman's accusers are gone. Jesus alone is left. But a single witness isn't sufficient for capital punishment.[14] Nor does Jesus desire to condemn her (Rom 8:31-34). He treats her with gentleness and respect (cf. Jn 2:4; 20:13). She is forgiven; she is free. Now, Christ's forgiveness is freely given, but it is not cheap. With grace comes the expectation of godliness. Jesus sends her away with a commission to purity. If this story is not true, it at least truly reflects the character and beauty of our Lord's love for broken people.

§ 98
I Am the Light
of the World
(Jn 8:12-20)

In John 8 Jesus moves about the temple preaching. His message(s) expands the discussion in chapter 7. We find him first in the court of the women where thirteen trumpet-shaped vessels lined one wall. On the other side of the wall was the meeting room of the Sanhedrin. This court was reserved for the Pharisees. Here they taught their disciples. Jesus took over their spot. Yet no one stopped him even though he was within

---

[13]C.P. Baylis, "The Woman Caught in Adultery: A Test of Jesus as the Greater Prophet," *BibSac* 146 (1989): 171-184.

[14]S.A. James, "The Adulteress and the Death Penalty," *JETS* 22/1 (1979): 45-53, rightly concludes that this text does not abrogate capital punishment. According to Jewish jurisprudence, the Pharisees were illegal witnesses. Jesus, as a single witness, was insufficient to support a capital sentence.

earshot of the Sanhedrin. Oh, they wanted to, but his time had not yet come (cf. Jn 2:4; 7:6, 30; 12:23, 27; 17:1). From here Jesus moves out to the porches of the temple. Outside the sanctuary the crowds would be free to ask questions and enter into the conversation. Unfortunately they didn't much like what he said out there. In fact, they picked up stones from the construction site to kill him (Jn 8:59).

Jn 8:12-20

[12]When Jesus spoke again to the people, he said, "I am the light of the world. Whoever follows me will never walk in darkness, but will have the light of life."

[13]The Pharisees challenged him, "Here you are, appearing as your own witness; your testimony is not valid."

[14]Jesus answered, "Even if I testify on my own behalf, my testimony is valid, for I know where I came from and where I am going. But you have no idea where I come from or where I am going. [15]You judge by human standards; I pass judgment on no one. [16]But if I do judge, my decisions are right, because I am not alone. I stand with the Father, who sent me. [17]In your own Law it is written that the testimony of two men is valid. [18]I am one who testifies for myself; my other witness is the Father, who sent me."

[19]Then they asked him, "Where is your father?"

"You do not know me or my Father," Jesus replied. "If you knew me, you would know my Father also." [20]He spoke these words while teaching in the temple area near the place where the offerings were put. Yet no one seized him, because his time had not yet come.

This is the second of Jesus' "I AM" statements (cf. Jn 6:35; 8:12; 10:7, 9, 11, 14; 11:25; 14:6; 15:1, 5). Perhaps it is the richest. Light is used to represent *truth* because it exposes what is actually there, and purity because of its own essence. In the NT these two qualities of light are personified in: (1) God (1 Tim 6:16; 1 John 1:5). (2) Jesus — God's envoy (Mt 4:16 [Isa 9:1-2]; Lk 2:32; Jn 1:4-5, 9; 3:19; 8:12; 9:5; 12:36, 46-47). (3) Christians — as envoys of Jesus (Mt 5:14; Lk 16:8; Jn 12:36; 1 Thess 5:5). (4) The gospel — as proclaimed by Christians (Acts 26:23; 2 Cor 4:4; Titus 1:3; 2 Pet 1:19). There is a fierce conflict between light and darkness (Jn 1:5; 3:19-21; 12:35; Acts 26:18; Rom 13:12; 2 Cor 6:14; Eph 5:8; 1 Thess 5:5; 1 Pet 2:9; 1 John 2:9). Darkness hates the light because it exposes and thereby judges its evil deeds (Jn 3:19-21; 1 Cor 3:13; 4:5; Eph 5:13-14). This competition between darkness and light (i.e., God and Satan) will end with the consummation of the kingdom (Col 1:12; 1 John 2:8). Finally, all this "light" theology is embodied in the New Jerusalem which will have as its light the Lord Jesus (Rev 21:23-24; 22:5).

The light of the menorah (candlestick) played a prominent role in the Feast of Tabernacles. Its light spreads across the court of women where Jesus is presently teaching. Perhaps this allusion connects directly with God's light of the tabernacle. Nonetheless, when Jesus applies to himself the metaphor of "light," the Pharisees can hardly miss its Messianic implication. They challenge him on such an audacious claim. Again they call him a misguided maverick, speaking on his own behalf. According to the Mosaic law of testimony, any statement required at least two or three witnesses. Twice already Jesus has delineated his supporting witnesses (Jn 5:30-47; 7:16-19). He hardly needs to cover that ground again here.

It may sound like Jesus is contradicting himself in v. 14 (cf. Jn 5:31, and notes). But since the Pharisees have rejected or ignored all of Jesus' supporting witnesses, what can he do but simply verify his own testimony? Truly, he is the only one who can testify about his heavenly origin (v. 14), his unity with the Father (vv. 15-16), and the consistency between what he says and what God says (vv. 17-18). No one else has been to heaven and back who can verify the truth of what Jesus says. John and Moses received divine revelation about Jesus, but the Pharisees have rejected their testimony. Jesus' miracles indicate supernatural power, but the Pharisees have relegated them to a demonic power. The only two witnesses left are Jesus and the Father. The Pharisees have demonstrated a resolute refusal to listen to Jesus. And since they know not the Father, they have no way to receive his testimony. Sadly, Jesus is their only way to the Father, but they have cut him off. They have now burned every bridge out of the valley of the shadow of death.

All that is left is judgment and certain death. Jesus came not to judge the world but to save it (Jn 3:16-17). However, in the process of preaching the gospel of salvation, his words set some parameters around who would and who would not be saved (Jn 5:24). In this slice of time we call the incarnation, it is not the Son of Man who judges, but his words most certainly do. The future nonincarnate Christ will, indeed, pass judgment on this world and all evil men who refuse to accept God's messenger (Jn 5:26-30).

§ 99a
I Am Returning
to My Father
(Jn 8:21-30)

[21]Once more Jesus said to them, "I am going away, and you will look for me, and you will die in your sin. Where I go, you cannot come."

[22]This made the Jews ask, "Will he kill himself? Is that why he says, 'Where I go, you cannot come'?"

[23]But he continued, "You are from below; I am from above. You are of this world; I am not of this world. [24]I told you that you would die in your sins; if you do not believe that I am the one I claim to be,[a] you will indeed die in your sins."

[25]"Who are you?" they asked.

"Just what I have been claiming all along," Jesus replied. [26]"I have much to say in judgment of you. But he who sent me is reliable, and what I have heard from him I tell the world."

[a]24 Or I am he; also in verse 28

The last time Jesus said he was going away the Jews assumed he was going into the dispersion (7:33-36). Now, perhaps in ridicule, they wonder if he is going to commit suicide. Certainly they would not follow Jesus into death. As Jesus said, "You are going to die in your sins," they respond, "No, you are going to die through suicide!" Strangely enough, they are not far from the truth. Jesus will lay down his life for our sins (Jn 10:18; Mt 20:28), a voluntary and substitutionary death.

How is it that they would look for Jesus and not find him? There are several possibilities. Hendriksen thinks that on their deathbed, they would finally seek Jesus but it would be too late and they would die in their sin. It may also refer to the punishment of Jerusalem (A.D. 70). They would look for their Messiah to deliver the city (Mt 24:4-5, 23-26), but he would not be found because he had already come and gone. Or, it may be that they would look for a Messiah of their own making and never find him because the true Messiah, Jesus, had already been offered and rejected. Yet another possibility, and even more frightening, is that their days of opportunity to repent are over. God hardened Israel as a nation until the Gentiles had full opportunity to accept the gospel (Rom 11:25). Thus, those that don't accept Jesus now would lose the chance (cf. Jn 8:43; Mt 13:13-15; Acts 28:25-28; Heb 6:6; Isa 55:6).

The crowds have just suggested that they would not be able to find Jesus because he will commit suicide. Jesus responds, "Suicide has nothing to do with it. You won't find me because we are from two different worlds." Even though Jesus came to earth — out of his world into ours — the Jews still miss the point because they keep thinking with earthly minds instead of being raised to God's thoughts. We could never have come to know God except through Jesus coming to earth in bodily form. But neither can we know God except by our minds ascending to heavenly realms. It requires both the incarnation of God in a human body and the renewing of the human mind to divine thinking.

The time for mincing words is over. Jesus is as clear as he can be: "You either believe me, that I am the Messiah, or you will go to hell" (cf. 3:36). They ask emphatically, "You, who are you?!" [*su tis ei*]. Perhaps they are patronizing him; perhaps they are sobered by such a serious statement. As we shall see, there are mixed emotions in the crowd (Jn 8:30-31). Nevertheless, their question betrays their deafness. For the last two days he has been teaching in the temple exactly that: Who he is! Jesus is not going to retrace his steps now. Nor is he going to spin off into a judgmental diatribe, although he has both the material and the authority. He will leave that up to the Father and the logical force of his teaching. These alone will be enough to convict or condemn the crowds, and not these Jews alone, but the whole world as well (v. 26).

Jn 8:27-30

²⁷They did not understand that he was telling them about his Father. ²⁸So Jesus said, "When you have lifted up the Son of Man, then you will know that I am the one I claim to be and that I do nothing on my own but speak just what the Father has taught me. ²⁹The one who sent me is with me; he has not left me alone, for I always do what pleases him." ³⁰Even as he spoke, many put their faith in him.

Again Jesus' words are cryptic to his unbelieving audience. Instead of catering to their questions, he adds yet another enigma. We are reminded again (cf. Mt 13:10-17) that Jesus does not teach for clarity but for disciples. If his students are predisposed to unbelief, Jesus has no qualms about confusing them further. But those who have a bent toward belief are drawn closer to him.

As in 3:14, being "lifted up" begins at the cross (cf. 12:32). How is it that these Jews will suddenly know who Jesus is? After all, there will be no great conversions at Golgotha. For most of the Jews, the crucifixion does not convince them that Jesus is the Christ. Yet after the resurrection and ascension, also part of the "lifting up," the remnant of Israel is saved. We can hardly help but think of Pentecost, when Peter's preaching about the death, resurrection, and ascension of Jesus prompted the question, "Brothers, what shall we do?"

Furthermore, Jesus' submission to the cross will be the ultimate demonstration of his obedience and unity with the Father. Not only will that demonstration bear fruit in the future, but even here it convinces many to put their trust in him. This "belief" may not go as far as "saving" faith (cf. Jn 2:23; 12:42), yet it is a step in the right direction.

§ 99b
Before
Abraham Was,
I Am
(Jn 8:31-59)

³¹To the Jews who had believed him, Jesus said, "If you hold to my teaching, you are really my disciples. ³²Then you will know the truth, and the truth will set you free."

³³They answered him, "We are Abraham's descendants^a and have never been slaves of anyone. How can you say that we shall be set free?"

³⁴Jesus replied, "I tell you the truth, everyone who sins is a slave to sin. ³⁵Now a slave has no permanent place in the family, but a son belongs to it forever. ³⁶So if the Son sets you free, you will be free indeed.

^a*33* Greek *seed*; also in verse 37

During this discussion, Jesus speaks to both believers and unbelievers with little or no distinction between the two. That's because his audience is divided. Some are determined to kill him; others are beginning to believe in him. Yet even these "believers" may be vacillating between faith and doubt. After all, they are only "baby" believers and Jesus' claims are extraordinary.

As Jesus nurtures their nascent faith he lays out both the responsibility and the privilege of being his disciple. Their responsibility is to continue to hold (accept and obey) his teaching. It is not enough to talk the talk, they must walk the walk, even in the face of the imminent opposition. Their privilege is freedom. This is not freedom to do what they please, but the power and desire to do what they ought to do.

The crowd objects to the insinuation that they are slaves. They are, after all, God's privileged people. They are children of Abraham! Certainly they cannot have forgotten their political slavery to Egypt, Babylon, Syria, and now Rome. Nor could they deny the fact that many Jews had been socially enslaved. The Mosaic law, in fact, legislated temporary slavery of Jews to Jews. What they must mean is that spiritually they are slaves to no one, nor had they ever been. They are not subject to the idols of pagan polytheistic peoples all around them. Nor are they indentured to the dark doctrine of demons inherent in idolatry. They are the pure monotheists of Jehovah. They need no spiritual liberation . . . so they think.

Jesus explains that adopting the right religion is not what makes you free any more than living in the house makes you a son. Yes, they have the right religion but they do not have the right lifestyles. They are sinners (the present participle indicates a continued lifestyle of sin, cf. 1 John 3:4). Anyone in bondage to sin is a slave (Rom 6:16; 11:32; 2 Pet 2:19). Verse 36 is our "Proclamation of Emancipation" (2 Cor 3:17; Gal 4:6-7). Jesus, as the Son of God, has the legal right to emancipate his slaves and adopt them as sons into the family. Our freedom in Christ is freedom from sin: (1) From its *penalty* — our debt has been canceled (Isa 53:5); (2) from its *practice* — we can overcome our habits of sin; and (3) from its *power* — we are given new hearts so that we no longer desire the things we used to.

Furthermore, in Christ, we are free from men's judgments (Rom 14:4), from guilt (Rom 8:1-2), from the constraints and philosophies of this world (Jn 3:8). We are free from worry over material possession (Mt 6:25-34), free from fear of judgment (1 Jn 4:18), free from ourselves and our ominous egos (Gal 2:20), free from death (Rom 6:5-6). When Jesus sets us free we are free indeed!

Jn 8:37-41

[37]"I know you are Abraham's descendants. Yet you are ready to kill me, because you have no room for my word. [38]I am telling you what I have seen in the Father's presence, and you do what you have heard from your father.ᵃ"

[39]"Abraham is our father," they answered.

"If you were Abraham's children," said Jesus, "then you wouldᵇ do the things Abraham did. [40]As it is, you are determined to kill me, a man who has told you the truth that I heard from God. Abraham did not do such things. [41]You are doing the things your own father does."

"We are not illegitimate children," they protested. "The only Father we have is God himself."

[a]*38* Or *presence. Therefore do what you have heard from the Father.*   [b]*39* Some early manuscripts *"if you are Abraham's children," said Jesus, "then*

Being a child of Abraham carried numerous blessings according to Jewish theology: Covenant relationship with God, participation in the Messianic banquet, the trust of the oracles of God (cf. Rom 3:1-2; 9:4-5), etc. But there is a difference between being Abraham's descendants (v. 37), and being his children (v. 39). To be Abraham's descendant was merely a biological matter. Being his child required living as he lived (Rom 2:28-29; 4:12-13, 16, 18; 9:7-8; Gal 3:6-9, 14, 29; 4:22-28, Rev 2:9; 3:9). Jesus does not deny their genealogy but their Jewishness. To say that they were acting in a characteristically un-Jewish way was a serious insult. Jesus was casting aspersion on their total identity as Jews. It would not have been so bad if Jesus said they did not listen to Moses (7:19-23), Elijah, or even Hillel. But Abraham, as the father of the Jewish nation, represented all their leaders, promises, and practices.

Jesus' accusation is harsh, but it is also justified. By seeking to kill Jesus, they are trying to destroy the very thing that Abraham was looking for (Gen 12:1-3; Gal 3:16-29). They seek to destroy the key to all Abraham's life and calling — the promised Messiah. Thus, they can hardly claim to be Abraham's descendants. Furthermore, faith was the dominant characteristic of Abraham. It was a faith that came from hearing God and doing what he said (cf. Gen 18:1-8). Jesus' present audience is not listening to God's messenger. Therefore they don't have faith, the mark of Abraham.

Their actions speak of a different father. They are murderers. They reject God's message and messenger. They are arrogant even to the extent of usurping God's authority. Those are Satanic characteristics. Their deeds betray their commitment to the Devil rather than to Abraham. They react strongly to such a flagrant insult. "We are God's children," they protest. No doubt they are convinced of it. But they are wrong. So it is with many who think they are in good standing with God but are as lost as they can be (cf. Mt 7:21-23; 25:41-46). But this is not to say that we cannot be sure of our salvation (cf. 1 John 5:13). Our assurance, however, must come through listening to Jesus, God's messenger.

They object strenuously to being called spiritual bastards. In so doing, they may be casting subtle aspersion on Jesus' own birth. This was not an uncommon accusation against Mary and Joseph. Rumor had it that Jesus was physically what he was accusing them of being spiritually.

Jn 8:42-47

[42]Jesus said to them, "If God were your Father, you would love me, for I came from God and now am here. I have not come on my own; but he sent me. [43]Why is my language not clear to you? Because you are unable to hear what I say. [44]You belong to your father, the devil, and you want to carry out your father's desire. He was a murderer from the beginning, not holding to the truth, for there is no truth in him. When he lies, he speaks his native language, for he is a liar and the father of lies. [45]Yet because I tell the truth, you do not believe me! [46]Can any of you prove me guilty of sin? If I am telling the truth, why don't you believe me? [47]He who belongs to God hears what God says. The reason you do not hear is that you do not belong to God."

The Jews are hearing two conflicting voices, one from God (through Jesus), the other from Satan. The voice they will listen to is the one that is familiar (1 John 4:5-6). Like children who believe whatever their dad says, these Jews are listening to their father, the Devil. Listening is not merely a matter of truth and logic. It is an issue of love (v. 42; cf. 1 John 3:10; 5:1-2). They are obtuse to Jesus' words, not because they are stupid, nor because Jesus is confusing. They refuse to listen (cf. Jn 8:19, 22, 25, 27, 33) because they don't love Jesus. And they don't love Jesus because they don't love his Father.

Unlike natural children who cannot choose their parents, the Jews became children of the Devil by doing what he does (Mt 13:38; 23:15; 1 John 3:8; Rev 12:9). The bottom line is that we choose who we will listen to. We choose who our father will be. There comes a point when we listen to the lies so long that we are no longer able to believe the truth (v. 43).

Satan is a liar (Gen 3:1,4; Job 1:9, 10, 11; Mt 4:6, 9; Acts 5:3; 2 Thess 2:9, 10, 11). But even more, he is a master of half-truths (Gen 3:4), and Scripture twisting (Mt 4:6). He accomplishes his objectives not merely by lies, but by substituting the mind of God with the mind of "man" (Isa 55:6-9). In our Western world we have assumed that truth will conquer; that reason, by its logical force, will ultimately convince. But what we accept as "fact" or "truth" will largely depend on our prior commitments. Put simply, Satan does not necessarily need to deprive us of information. If he can get us to view the information through the lens of this world, even the cross looks foolish (1 Cor 1:18-25). That is why these Jews, who knew the facts about Jesus, could reject him. Jesus did not fit their philosophy so his "voice" was discarded.

There does come a time when a faulty philosophy is unable to account for certain truths. At that point, the honest individual must abandon his "way of thinking" and adopt another system which can better account for all the facts. Verse 46 is designed to destroy their faulty philosophy by inviting them to identify[15] any moral flaw in Jesus. That's a dangerous invitation! If political campaigns have taught us anything, it is that no one is perfect. Yet Jesus' accusers are stymied. They have nothing to say. This is perhaps the most powerful indication of the sinlessness of Jesus (cf. 2 Cor 5:21; Heb 4:15).

Jn 8:48-53   [48]The Jews answered him, "Aren't we right in saying that you are a Samaritan and demon-possessed?"

[49]"I am not possessed by a demon," said Jesus, "but I honor my Father and you dishonor me. [50]I am not seeking glory for myself; but there is one who seeks it, and he is the judge. [51]I tell you the truth, if anyone keeps my word, he will never see death."

[52]At this the Jews exclaimed, "Now we know that you are demon-possessed! Abraham died and so did the prophets, yet you say that if anyone keeps your word, he will never taste death. [53]Are you greater than our father Abraham? He died, and so did the prophets. Who do you think you are?"

Now this crowd returns tit for tat the insults of Jesus. He says they are doctrinally deceived. They say he follows the deviant teachings of the Samaritans (see on Jn 4:9). He says they are children of the Devil. They say he is demon-possessed (see on 7:20). There could scarcely be greater insults exchanged than these. Rather than defend himself or retaliate (God will do that, v. 50), he simply offers life (v. 51). For that was his mission (Jn 10:10).

The offer of eternal life is a bodacious claim. Who does Jesus think he is? . . . If they only knew! As unimaginable as it is to these Jews, yes, Jesus is greater than Abraham (cf. Jn 5:18; 10:33; 19:7). The Messiah, by necessity, must be if he is to bless the whole world (Gen 12:3). And although the three most prominent religions of the world (Jewish, Christian, and Muslim) are all based on Abraham, history has demonstrated that Jesus has had much more influence on our globe than Abraham. The unmistakable lesson of history, sociology, philosophy, and theology is that Jesus is indeed greater than Abraham. And that says nothing about his identity as God's Son and the second person of the Trinity.

If they would only listen to Jesus they would understand that the Messiah is so much more than they ever dreamed. He brings liberation

---

[15]The word "prove" [*elenchei*] (v. 46) means both to prove and convict on the basis of adequate evidence. It must be more than a mere accusation.

from death (1 Cor 15:54-57), not some petty human government. His is the power of life and eternity for those who hear and obey his word (Mt 7:24-27).

Jn 8:54-59

[54]Jesus replied, "If I glorify myself, my glory means nothing. My Father, whom you claim as your God, is the one who glorifies me. [55]Though you do not know him, I know him. If I said I did not, I would be a liar like you, but I do know him and keep his word. [56]Your father Abraham rejoiced at the thought of seeing my day; he saw it and was glad."

[57]"You are not yet fifty years old," the Jews said to him, "and you have seen Abraham!"

[58]"I tell you the truth," Jesus answered, "before Abraham was born, I am!" [59]At this, they picked up stones to stone him, but Jesus hid himself, slipping away from the temple grounds.

The brazen claim to give eternal life is not mere boasting. Jesus does not defend the claim, he just makes it. Only time can prove it. And only the Father needs to defend Jesus. The remainder of the NT is a record of both the life-giving power of Jesus and God's glorification of his Son. Here, however, we have neither a debate nor a defense but a simple statement of fact.

Abraham was pleased to see Jesus' day. But when did Abraham see Jesus' day? Does this mean that he was happy to see the incarnation from heaven? Or that Jesus was one of the three visitors who announced the birth of Isaac (Gen 18:1-2)? More likely it means that Abraham rejoiced at the initial fulfillment of the Messianic promise (Gen 12:1-3), when his own son Isaac was born. His name, after all, does mean "laughter" (Gen 21:3-6). This was the first fruits of God's promise which some 2,000 years later is now culminated in their presence.

They obviously misunderstand Jesus. They assume that Jesus is claiming to be a contemporary of Abraham. But Jesus isn't 2,000 years old. Even stretching it, he is not even fifty, that is, in his incarnate state. The fact of the matter is that Jesus was alive when Abraham was, and even long before that. Jesus was coexistent and coeternal with the Father (Jn 1:1-2; Col 1:15-17).

While they misunderstand Jesus' chronology, they don't miss his claim. When he says, "Before Abraham was, I AM," they know he is equating himself with God. Whether Jesus says this in Greek, or more likely, Aramaic, the translation of the Tetragrammaton, is clear. This ineffable name for God, "Jehovah," Jesus applies to himself. It was with this title that God identified himself. He told Moses that he was the "Ever Existing One" (Exod 3:14). This is perhaps Jesus' clearest claim to deity. And it is not wasted on the Jews. They understand precisely what Jesus means and they are prepared to kill him for blasphemy. If what Jesus claims is a lie, then he deserves to die according to the law of Moses (Lev 24:16). But if what he says is true, then they are about to kill the Author of Life incarnate (Acts 2:36; 3:15). They collect stones from the rubble of the continuing temple construction (cf. Jn 2:20). They are now poised for the greatest travesty of human history.

§ 100a
The Blind Man
Healed by
Jesus
(Jn 9:1-7)

This miracle resembles the healing of the lame man in chapter 5. Both occurred on the Sabbath, both involved a pool of water, and both spawned a major debate with the religious leaders. It is also quite similar to the healing of the lame man by Peter and John (Acts 3). That too stirred up a good bit of controversy and created a considerable opportunity for evangelism.

Jn 9:1-3

¹As he went along, he saw a man blind from birth. ²His disciples asked him, "Rabbi, who sinned, this man or his parents, that he was born blind?"

³"Neither this man nor his parents sinned," said Jesus, "but this happened so that the work of God might be displayed in his life.

It is unlikely that this healing takes place on the same day as their attempt to stone Jesus (Jn 8:59) since Jesus slips out of the temple and hides. But surely it takes place soon afterward, probably the very next day. The text does not tell us where the man is, but it would be most common for a blind beggar (Jn 9:8) to sit at one of the gates of the temple and ask for alms (cf. Acts 3:2). He is afflicted with congenital blindness, a common problem in third world countries which lack proper hygiene during birth and proper vitamins for children.

Both the Jews (cf. Job 4:7; 8:20; but see Lk 13:2-5) and Gentiles of the day (cf. Acts 28:4) believed that divine punishment for sins would be meted out through physical suffering. Thus, this pathetic sight prompted a question among the disciples: "Whose fault is this?" They can only imagine two options.

First, they ask if this man sinned, causing his own blindness as punishment from God. Since he had been blind from birth, his sin would have been in utero. Surprisingly, that was not an uncommon belief of the day. Based on Genesis 25:22-26, the rabbis taught that Esau attempted to murder Jacob in the womb (cf. Ps 51:5; 58:3).

A second option is that this man's parents had sinned and God was visiting the sin of the parents on the next generation (Exod 20:5; however, cf. Jer 31:29-30; Ezek 18:1-4). God did that because under the Old Covenant salvation was through a mediator, both the priests and the fathers. Salvation of the family was dependent upon the father, thus the consequences of his actions were not only individual, but affected his family as well. The New Covenant changed all that (Jer 31:29-34). However, even today, in a physical and social sense, the sins of the fathers are visited on their children. Physically, for example, if the father is unfaithful, children may suffer from syphilis or AIDS. Socially, children who were beaten or molested often inflict the same curse on their own children. Not only do we inherit the physical traits of our parents but often their sins are passed on as well.

Third (an option not expressed by the disciples), this sin may be caused by Adam's inheritance (cf. Rom 5:12-21). One does not have to believe in original sin to understand that this world was vastly changed by Adam's sin. Not only are men and women under a curse (Gen 3:16-19), the earth itself is under a curse (Gen 3:18; Rom 8:19-22). Because of this curse on the earth, combined with men's sinful lifestyles, we have all sorts of diseases, sicknesses, and ailments that God did not intend.[16]

Fourth, Jesus suggests that this sickness is for the glory of God. It may sound cruel to us that God would permit a man to be blind for decades in order that he could be glorified by his healing. Yet according to Romans 9:20-23, it is well within his sovereign jurisdiction. Even so, the phrase "in order that" (v. 3) does not necessarily mean that this sickness was ordained by God.[17] Jesus may, in fact, be ignoring any speculation as to the cause of this sickness, and simply stating its positive result. It is as if he says, "I don't care how he got this way, but I am pleased that God is about to be glorified through his healing." This suggestion makes a lot of sense. Jesus typically operates on a higher plane of priorities than his disciples. Enamored with the whole temple scene, they begin to emulate the theological speculations of the rabbis. Jesus calls them to a more pragmatic compassion. They ask, "How did he get this way?" Jesus asks, "What can we do for him?"

Jn 9:4-7

[4]"As long as it is day, we must do the work of him who sent me. Night is coming, when no one can work. [5]While I am in the world, I am the light of the world."

[6]Having said this, he spit on the ground, made some mud with the saliva, and put it on the man's eyes. [7]"Go," he told him, "wash in the Pool of Siloam" (this word means Sent). So the man went and washed, and came home seeing.

Verses 4 and 5 must be read together. "Day" is equivalent to "While

---

[16]These would include things like AIDS, syphilis, gonorrhea, many cancers, ulcers, mental illnesses, diseases caused by lack of nutrients, lung/liver/heart disease, etc.

[17]The *hina* clause can indicate result but most often indicates purpose.

I am in the world." Jesus is conscious of his impending passion. The closer it gets, the more keenly he is focused on his own mission as well as the training of the Twelve. Night is coming when Jesus will leave and his work will be over. But for his Twelve it will still be day. Their work will continue. This transition, the passing of the mantle, is critical. So here, with the use of a small pronoun "we," Jesus pulls them closer to the center of his mission. "*We* must work," says Jesus.

This is the first mention of the disciples since John 7:3. But they have been with Jesus the whole time. They have been silent observers to the dangerous confrontations that have taken place. Now Jesus hearkens back to his previous Messianic claim. He repeats it word for word, "I am the light of the world," as if to say, "Gentlemen, in spite of powerful opposition, I am the Messiah. And I won't, indeed I can't, back off from the truth, and neither must you. Forward!"

This claim to be the light of the world not only strikes the hearts of the disciples; it must also have struck the blind man. As a Jerusalem resident he must have heard the passing uproar as the Tabernacle crowds filed out of the temple just yesterday. As a beggar at the temple gate, he probably recognizes Jesus' voice. He has no sight; but surely good ears. And as the text will show, he has a keen mind. When Jesus claims to be the light of the world, he likely knows not only who stands before him (cf. v. 11), but what an uproar this man has caused.

Mixing spittle and mud sounds like odd medicine to us. But it was a clear sign to the blind man. As Edersheim has shown (II:48), the Jews believed that saliva had certain medicinal value. Jesus never has to tell the man that he is about to heal him. The mud patches on his eyes and Jesus' reputation as a healer speak for themselves (Jn 7:31; also Jn 5:1-9 & 7:23). So when Jesus sends him to Siloam (meaning "sent"), he goes without hesitation.

There is much possible symbolism here. Jesus, the light of the world (Jn 8:12; 9:5), brings light to this blind man.[18] Jesus, as the one sent from God (Jn 7:16, 18, 28-29, 33; 8:14, 16, 18, 26, 29, 42), sends the blind man to the pool "Sent" (Siloam) to wash. Siloam was where the waters were drawn for the Feast of Tabernacles. It was here that Jesus said, "If any man is thirsty, let him come to me and drink" (Jn 7:37). This healing embodies the last few days of the feast and Jesus' bold claims. They may be able to deny Jesus' words but let's see what they do with his works. After all, they both say the same thing.

---

[18]Blindness in Johannine writings appears to be symbolic of unbelief (Jn 9:39-41; 12:40; 1 Jn 2:11). Thus, the story of this blind man illustrates Israel's spiritual condition. Cf. J.M. Lieu, "Blindness in the Johannine Tradition," *NTS*, 34 (1988): 83-95.

⁸His neighbors and those who had formerly seen him begging asked, "Isn't this the same man who used to sit and beg?" ⁹Some claimed that he was.

Others said, "No, he only looks like him."

But he himself insisted, "I am the man."

¹⁰"How then were your eyes opened?" they demanded.

¹¹He replied, "The man they call Jesus made some mud and put it on my eyes. He told me to go to Siloam and wash. So I went and washed, and then I could see."

¹²"Where is this man?" they asked him.

"I don't know," he said.

As one would expect, the man makes a beeline for home after being healed (v. 7). His neighbors can scarcely believe their eyes. It looks like him and it sounds like him. But nothing like this has ever happened before (v. 32). How can a man who was born blind be healed? Like the crowds in the temple, this neighborhood is divided between two different opinions. Some are certain that it is the man. Others believed it is a "look-alike" imposter. The ex-blind man simply insists, "It's me!"

The crowd begins their investigation. Question #1: What happened? The man recounts in simple but clear terms what took place. In the midst of his explanation, he makes a statement which raises red flags among these Jerusalemites. He says, "The man they call Jesus . . ." Wait a minute! This is the Galilean troublemaker of the temple. These Jerusalemites are much less sympathetic to Jesus' claims than the simple pilgrims who came to the feast. They know that even prior to the feast, the Sanhedrin had it in for Jesus (Jn 7:25). And during the feast there were several attempts to arrest him (Jn 7:30, 32, 44), and even one attempt to stone him (Jn 8:59). They also know that any sympathizers of Jesus are to be excommunicated (Jn 9:22). This is a matter that the officials would need to know about. Thus, they ask question #2: Where is Jesus? Well, how should the blind man know? Once he left Jesus there was no way to track him. He was still blind until he washed at the pool. And he came straight from the pool of Siloam to home.

¹³They brought to the Pharisees the man who had been blind. ¹⁴Now the day on which Jesus had made the mud and opened the man's eyes was a Sabbath. ¹⁵Therefore the Pharisees also asked him how he had received his sight. "He put mud on my eyes," the man replied, "and I washed, and now I see."

¹⁶Some of the Pharisees said, "This man is not from God, for he does not keep the Sabbath."

But others asked, "How can a sinner do such miraculous signs?" So they were divided.

¹⁷Finally they turned again to the blind man, "What have you to say about him? It was your eyes he opened."

The man replied, "He is a prophet."

Since this was a Sabbath, this gathering of Pharisees does not represent any official meeting of the Sanhedrin. In other words, they don't have official authority to hold a trial against Jesus or to excommunicate this ex-blind man (v. 34). However, it is clear that these Pharisees are powerful enough to get their way. They seem confident that the Sanhedrin will uphold their decisions, not only because the Pharisaic party held sway over the populace, but because when it comes to Jesus, the Sadducees and Pharisees agree that he is bad news.

The ex-blind man is brought to the Pharisees. Either his neighbors escort him or he is summoned by the Pharisees after they catch wind of the situation. When he gets there, the Pharisees open the investigation with the same question as the man's neighbors had asked, "How did you receive your sight?" The man's answer is even more concise but just as clear as the first time: "He put mud on my eyes and I washed, and now I see." The Pharisees are appalled (and probably secretly pleased) to learn that Jesus has now broken the Sabbath, not once, but twice! First, he made mud and placed it on the man's eyes. Second, he healed someone on the Sabbath. Both are expressly forbidden according to their oral tradition.

This whole debate about Sabbath healing is old hat to Jesus. Both in Jerusalem (Jn 5:10-18) and in Galilee (Mt 12:1-14) some eighteen months earlier, Jesus demolished their defense for the Sabbath regulations (cf. § 49b, 50, 51). As we have seen before, once Jesus wins an argument, he tends to ignore it the second time (e.g., Lk 7:49). But the Pharisees are not about to ignore it. This is just the kind of ritual *faux pas* they have been looking for. But as we shall see, it will be better for them to leave this one alone.

Part of the problem in dealing with this Sabbath breach is that a notable miracle had taken place. (The use of the plural "signs" in verse 16 may suggest that they were familiar with other miracles of Jesus as well). To heal congenital blindness is admittedly impressive. In fact, it was unheard of. This fact did not escape some of the Pharisees who ask, "How can a sinner do such miraculous signs?" The current Pharisaic theology stated clearly that God did not listen to sinners (cf. Ps 34:15f; 66:18; Prov 15:29; 28:9; Isa 1:15; 59:2; Micah 3:4; James 5:16ff).[19] That

---

[19]The fact that the Pharisees attributed Jesus' power to cast out demons to Beelzebub does not contradict their belief that God does not listen to sinners. It would be logical for Satan to have power over demons and thus be able to control them. Hence Jesus' power to exorcise demons could be Satanic rather than divine. But it would not necessarily be logical for Satan to have power over congenital blindness. This is clearly a qualitatively different miracle.

being the case, a sinner could never perform this kind of a miracle.[20] Thus the quandary. On the one hand, Jesus clearly broke the oral traditions. These were considered as important as the Scripture itself. That would make him a sinner. On the other hand, such a miracle would indicate that he is God's man. That would mean he is not a sinner. Therefore, one of two things must be true: Either this miracle did not actually happen (which they will go to great lengths to prove). Or, as God's prophet, Jesus is not bound by the oral tradition. And that they do not want to admit. Even so, there they are, a few noble-minded Pharisees in their midst who are willing to honestly face the problem. Again Jesus divides . . . even the solidarity of the Pharisees.

Turning away from the miracle to the man, Jesus (for that is always the real issue), they asked the healed man, "What do you have to say about him?" His answer will help the Pharisees assess the damage. It will help them determine the true effects of this miracle. But what did they expect him to say? Jesus gave sight to a blind man. This blind beggar cares little for hair-splitting traditions. He was blind and now he sees. This healer can be none other than a prophet of God!

Jn 9:18-23

[18]The Jews still did not believe that he had been blind and had received his sight until they sent for the man's parents. [19]"Is this your son?" they asked. "Is this the one you say was born blind? How is it that now he can see?"

[20]"We know he is our son," the parents answered, "and we know he was born blind. [21]But how he can see now, or who opened his eyes, we don't know. Ask him. He is of age; he will speak for himself." [22]His parents said this because they were afraid of the Jews, for already the Jews had decided that anyone who acknowledged that Jesus was the Christ[a] would be put out of the synagogue. [23]That was why his parents said, "He is of age; ask him."

[a]22 Or *Messiah*

The first investigation was a flop. Instead of an opportunity to condemn Jesus, it caused some of the Pharisees themselves to question their stance against him. So, they take another route. They call in the parents of the blind man. This second investigation leads to even further failure. The parents are able to confirm their worst fears: "Yes, he is our son and yes he was born blind." But that is all they are willing to say. They don't want to be excommunicated [lit. "exsynagogued," *aposynagōgos*]. The fact is, they lie about not knowing how their son was healed. They know Jesus did it (v. 22). Besides, it is unimaginable that all the neighbors know how it happened but his parents don't.

---

[20]This, however, is a questionable conclusion. God's is not the only power able to perform miracles (Mt 7:22; 2 Cor 11:14; 2 Thess 2:9).

We shouldn't be too hard on these folks. Excommunication was a fearful thing (cf. Lk 6:22; Jn 12:42; 16:2). Because Jewish society was holistic, when someone was kicked out of the synagogue, they lost their religious, family, social and economic ties as well. It was a frightening possibility. In addition, the blind man is a beggar (v. 8). That would indicate the lower economic status of this family. They simply could not survive as outcasts from the community. Besides, the wit and intelligence of their son is considerable, as we shall see. They can hardly give a better defense than he. Although it may look like they are abandoning their son, this may be the wisest action for the whole family.

Jn 9:24-27

²⁴A second time they summoned the man who had been blind. "Give glory to God,ᵃ" they said. "We know this man is a sinner."

²⁵He replied, "Whether he is a sinner or not, I don't know. One thing I do know. I was blind but now I see!"

²⁶Then they asked him, "What did he do to you? How did he open your eyes?"

²⁷He answered, "I have told you already and you did not listen. Why do you want to hear it again? Do you want to become his disciples, too?"

ᵃ*24* A solemn charge to tell the truth (see Joshua 7:19)

The Pharisees are just having a bad day! It is now obvious that a miracle in fact did take place. If they attribute it to Jesus, then they must also admit that they are wrong in opposing God's prophet. Their only recourse is to admit the miracle but rob Jesus of it. That is to say, "Yes you were healed of blindness, but Jesus' role was only coincidental. You were healed by God and God alone!" Thus, they ask him to "Give glory to God." Now to a Jewish ear, this is not merely a statement of praise, but also of confession (cf. Josh 7:19). In so many words, they are asking the ex-blind man to confess his error, and possible sin, in exalting Jesus by attributing this miracle to him.

This healed man is nobody's fool. His answer is incisive. He says (essentially): "You Pharisees claim to know all about Jesus. But I'm not convinced. I don't care about your theological debate. All I know is that I was blind and now I see! That settles it for me."

The Pharisees respond, "What did he do to you?" It's like they ask him to prove that Jesus really did cause the healing. But again, the healed man refuses to fall into their trap. He points out that they have come full circle by asking again the same question which opened their proceedings. He simply refuses to get on the merry-go-round or to beat around the bush. He ends the cycle by asking the Pharisees if they want to become Jesus' disciples too.

Now this man is blind, not deaf. Surely he has heard the debates in the temple. Surely he understands that such biting sarcasm can only isolate him from the Pharisees. He apparently doesn't care. He is already an outcast, a beggar shunned by society. He has never known what it is like to be on the "inside." So to be kicked out is not a perceptible loss for him. In addition, a blind beggar with a keen mind would have a lot of time on his hands to sit and meditate at the temple gate. This is surely not the first time that he has analyzed the Pharisees' words and motives. He sees past the facade of the Pharisees. He sees in them what Jesus saw, a squabbling, arrogant, ambitious bunch. He has meditated on what is truly important and beautiful in life. And he hasn't found it here. The bottom line is simple: Jesus gave him this incredible gift of sight. In so doing, he proved that he is no mere man. Thus, to turn his back on Jesus would not only be the height of ingratitude, it would be downright dumb. He is the hope of Israel — the Messiah!

Jn 9:28-34

> [28]Then they hurled insults at him and said, "You are this fellow's disciple! We are disciples of Moses! [29]We know that God spoke to Moses, but as for this fellow, we don't even know where he comes from."
>
> [30]The man answered, "Now that is remarkable! You don't know where he comes from, yet he opened my eyes. [31]We know that God does not listen to sinners. He listens to the godly man who does his will. [32]Nobody has ever heard of opening the eyes of a man born blind. [33]If this man were not from God, he could do nothing."
>
> [34]To this they replied, "You were steeped in sin at birth; how dare you lecture us!" And they threw him out.

The very thought of a Pharisee becoming a disciple was ridiculous! Or was it (cf. Jn 3:1-2; 7:50-52; 8:30; 19:39; Mt 27:57; Acts 15:5)? As Shakespeare said in Hamlet, "The lady doth protest too much, methinks." Their insults seem to be a sign of their insecurity. They loudly proclaim their allegiance to Moses. "But this Jesus fellow," they say, "is spurious."

We can't help but wonder at the abrasive boldness of the blind man. His intrepid tenacity, combined with his impeccable logic is too much for these Pharisees to bear. Improving on the Pharisees' own syllogism (v. 16), he presents evidence for Jesus to which they are unable to respond. The Pharisees are forced to resort to one of the oldest rules of argumentation: When reason fails, attack the man. They accuse him of being a sinner at birth. He has heard that before from Jesus' own disciples (Jn 9:2). But again the "Light of the World," this "sight-giver," Jesus, has already given the correct answer: "Neither this man nor his parents sinned, but this happened so that the work of God might be displayed in his life." Their accusation can't "stick." The healed man already knows that it is not true.

The Pharisees won't be lectured by this plebeian. But his very presence condemns them. He is a living reminder of Jesus. So they cast him out. Although the word [*exebalon*] is different than in v. 22, it looks very much like he has been "exsynagogued." It is no big loss. They have taken nothing away from him, especially his sight.

§ 100d
Jesus Calls the
Blind Man to
Belief
(Jn 9:35-38)

[35]Jesus heard that they had thrown him out, and when he found him, he said, "Do you believe in the Son of Man?"

[36]"Who is he, sir?" the man asked. "Tell me so that I may believe in him."

[37]Jesus said, "You have now seen him; in fact, he is the one speaking with you."

[38]Then the man said, "Lord, I believe," and he worshiped him.

In his compassion, Jesus searches out this "cast off." He is followed by a meddling delegation of Pharisees (v. 40), and probably a crowd of disciples. This is the first time the ex-blind man has actually seen Jesus. But his voice and his entourage give him away.

Some texts replace "Son of Man" with "Son of God" (v. 35). It makes little difference since John uses both as Messianic titles. We might, therefore, paraphrase the question to the blind man, "Do you believe in the Messiah?" And we might paraphrase the blind man's answer, "You tell me who he is and I'll believe in him." The man has already stood by Jesus in the face of the fiercest opposition and most dire consequences. He has demonstrated his firm resolve to be a disciple of Jesus (v. 28). Now it is simply a matter of full instruction.

"Who is the Messiah?" asks the man. "I am," responded Jesus. So the conclusion is predictable, "Lord, I believe!" And he worships Jesus. How far he has come in his understanding of Jesus. In verse 11, he calls him, "The man they call Jesus." By verse 17, he acknowledges Jesus as "a prophet." Then, in verse 33 he recognizes Jesus was "from God." And finally, in verse 38, he proclaims him "Lord." There is much left to teach and much left to do. But he has completed his induction into Jesus' band of disciples. In a dramatic fashion he has fulfilled Jesus' requirement for abandonment (Mt 10:34-39; Lk 14:26-33).

§ 100e
Jesus
Condemns the
Pharisees'
Blindness
(Jn 9:39-41)

[39]Jesus said, "For judgment I have come into this world, so that the blind will see and those who see will become blind."

[40]Some Pharisees who were with him heard him say this and asked, "What? Are we blind too?"

[41]Jesus said, "If you were blind, you would not be guilty of sin; but now that you claim you can see, your guilt remains.

Sometimes Jesus says that he did not come to judge (Jn 8:15) but other times he says he did come to judge (Jn 5:27). What's the deal?

There is no question the Father has given all judgment to the Son (Jn 5:22). But his purpose in coming to earth was not to execute judgment but to save the world (Jn 3:17). At the same time, Jesus' word (Jn 8:26), brings judgment on those who reject him (Jn 12:31). This is best expressed in John 12:47-48, *"As for the person who hears my words but does not keep them, I do not judge him. For I did not come to judge the world, but to save it. There is a judge for the one who rejects me and does not accept my words; that very word which I spoke will condemn him at the last day."*

You just have to love the way that Jesus lifts up the lowly while humbling the mighty (Mt 11:25). In Matthew 13:13-17, in reference to his parables, Jesus said that many people have ears but cannot hear. Here he says they have eyes but cannot see. Playing off the healing of the blind man as a physical example, he speaks of spiritual sight.

The Pharisees react quickly with a question expecting a negative answer: "You aren't saying that we are blind too, are you?" With a surprising and delightful twist, Jesus says, "No, you aren't blind. You see quite well. And that is why you are guilty of sin." If they were ignorant, if they lacked God's word through Moses, if they didn't know the right theological answers, then they would not be guilty of rejecting Jesus. As it is, they know better (Jn 15:24).

In God's reversal of the human economy, the first will be last and the last will be first. The greatest will be least and the least will be greatest. Those who admit their blind ignorance, come to Jesus and receive spiritual sight. But those who rely on their own arrogant erudition are blinded by God from seeing the truth.

§ 101a
Allegory of the
Good
Shepherd and
the Thief
(Jn 10:1-18)

Jesus' teaching style changes here. In chapters 7-9 he used straight polemic. Suddenly he shifts into allegory. And in three months, at the Feast of Dedication (Jn 10:27-29), he'll continue to talk about the shepherd and his sheep. This has led some to say that John 10:1-18 is connected with the Feast of Dedication which follows (Jn 10:22ff), not the Feast of Tabernacles which preceded it. But this text probably belongs at the tail end of Tabernacles rather than the front side of Dedication. It continues the (1) opposition of the leaders (Jn 10:19-21); (2) division of opinion about Jesus (Jn 10:19); (3) accusation that Jesus had a demon (Jn 10:20); and (4) mention of the healing of the blind man (Jn 10:21). Again, in three months, at the Feast of Dedication, Jesus will pick up where he left off. That's exactly what he did at the Feast of Tabernacles (cf. Jn 7:21-24 & 5:1-18).

Jn 10:1-6

¹"I tell you the truth, the man who does not enter the sheep pen by the gate, but climbs in by some other way, is a thief and a robber. ²The man who enters by the gate is the shepherd of his sheep. ³The watchman opens the gate for him, and the sheep listen to his voice. He calls his own sheep by name and leads them out. ⁴When he has brought out all his own, he goes on ahead of them, and his sheep follow him because they know his voice. ⁵But they will never follow a stranger; in fact, they will run away from him because they do not recognize a stranger's voice." ⁶Jesus used this figure of speech, but they did not understand what he was telling them.

Jesus' allegory plays off of shepherding, one of the three major occupations of Palestine along with fishing and farming. Shepherding is deeply imbedded into the Middle Eastern culture. And it is also a frequent metaphor in the OT. Both of these facts make Jesus' words particularly poignant. He says a lot with just a few words. To fully appreciate Jesus' allegory we must understand a little bit about both Palestinian shepherding and about sheep themselves.

After a long day of grazing, the sheep were kept in caves or pens with only one opening. Sometimes it had an actual door on it (v. 3), but often it was simply a hole in the rock wall and the shepherd would lay himself down across the opening. Several flocks could be kept together in one pen. In the morning, when the shepherds called them, each sheep would recognize his own shepherd's voice and follow (v. 3). The oriental relationship between a shepherd and his sheep was personal. He knew all his sheep by name and they knew his voice (v. 5). Even if someone dressed themselves like the shepherd and imitated his voice, the sheep would not be fooled (v. 5). If they were in the pen they would stay put. If they were in the field, they would scatter with fear.

If the shepherd could afford hired help, he might employ a night watchman. His job was simply to guard the door of the pen against intruders, wild animals and stupid sheep who wanted to wander off. Only the chief shepherd could gain access through the watchman (v. 3). That is important because the sheep were a valuable commodity and easily stolen. Palestine was full of both thieves (*kleptēs*), who snuck in to steal, and bandits (*lēstēs*), who used violent force rather than stealth (v. 1). Another peculiarity of Oriental shepherds is that they led their sheep (v. 4). In other parts of the world, sheep are driven. This is another indication of the kind care Palestinian shepherds took with their sheep.

Now, for the interpretation of this allegory (lit. *paroimia* — a figure of speech which conceals lofty information, v. 6). We must weave together both the cultural symbols and the OT theology behind these symbols. Jesus is clearly the Good Shepherd. But that was a position occupied by God in the OT (Ps 23; 79:13; 95:7). It was also promised to the Messiah, as God's delegate (Ezek 34:23). This is yet another bold claim of Jesus to be the Messiah. We also have thieves and robbers who steal and kill the sheep for their own advantage. Certainly Jesus has in mind the leaders of the Jews who were part of his present audience (Jn 9:40; 10:19). By rejecting Jesus, they refused most adamantly to enter the fold through the gate. Yet they want access to the sheep. They plunder avariciously without concern for the sheep's welfare (e.g., Mt 23:14-15; Ezek 34:1-6).

Nothing in this *paroimia* is difficult to understand, especially against the background of OT shepherding imagery (esp. Jer 23:3; Amos 3:12; Micah 2:12; 5:7-8). This makes verse six somewhat surprising. We might well assume their inability to understand was part of God's hardening (Mt 13:13-16; Rom 11:25).

Jn 10:7-13

[7]Therefore Jesus said again, "I tell you the truth, I am the gate for the sheep. [8]All who ever came before me were thieves and robbers, but the sheep did not listen to them. [9]I am the gate; whoever enters through me will be saved.[a] He will come in and go out, and find pasture. [10]The thief comes only to steal and kill and destroy; I have come that they may have life, and have it to the full.

[11]"I am the good shepherd. The good shepherd lays down his life for the sheep. [12]The hired hand is not the shepherd who owns the sheep. So when he sees the wolf coming, he abandons the sheep and runs away. Then the wolf attacks the flock and scatters it. [13]The man runs away because he is a hired hand and cares nothing for the sheep.

[a]9 Or *kept safe*

The metaphor for Jesus now changes from a shepherd to a door. The fact is, shepherds often functioned as a door to the sheep pen. When the sheep came in the fold at night they would pass the shepherd one at a time. He would examine them for cuts and abrasions. If necessary he would treat them with oil to avoid infection. Then, when the whole flock was in, he would lay himself in front of the opening of the pen.

Jesus is the *Good* Shepherd (*kalos*, not *agathos*) (cf. Heb 13:20; 1 Pet 2:25; 5:4). That is, he is beautiful, excellent, and kind. Whoever knows and is known by Jesus is part of the fold. And being in the fold brings certain privileges:

- ❖ Salvation, v. 9 — Lk 19:10; Jn 3:17; Acts 4:12; Rom 5:9; 10:9-10; Eph 2:5-8; 2 Thess 2:13; Titus 3:5; 2 Pet 1:11.
- ❖ Provision, "come in and go out and find pasture," v. 9 — Mt 5:6; Rom 5:5; 12:6; 1 Cor 2:12; 2 Cor 5:5; 2 Pet 1:3-4.
- ❖ Life, "in abundance," v. 10 — Jn 1:16; Rom 6:4, 23; 8:2, 6, 11; 1 Cor 15:45; Gal 2:20; Eph 1:7-8; 2 Tim 1:10; 1 Jn 3:14; 5:11-13; Rev 22:1-2, 14, 17.

❖ Redemption, "lays down his life for the sheep," v. 11 — Isa 53:3-6; Mt 20:28; Acts 20:28; 2 Cor 5:14-15, 21; Gal 3:13-14; Eph 5:25-27; 1 John 2:2; 1 Pet 1:18-19.

❖ Protection, v. 12-13 (by contrast) — Rom 8:31-39; Heb 13:5.

Each of these, mentioned here so briefly, is of inestimable value, and certainly good grist for the devotional mill.

Jesus applies to himself two metaphors — shepherd and door. He applies to the Jewish leaders four metaphors — thief, robber, stranger and hireling. These don't represent four different types of Jews. Rather, each of the four identifies a particular trait. These four traits may not be applicable to every Pharisee and Sadducee. But they paint an accurate portrait of the group as a whole.

Jesus says the robbers and thieves were "all who came before me." He never comes out and says, in so many words, "The Pharisees and Sadducees are the bad guys." But who else could he intend? Certainly, he doesn't mean that John the Baptist and the other preceding prophets were the false shepherds. And it is somewhat of a leap to import false Messiahs into the context, although there were plenty around at this time.[21] The present and past Jewish leaders fit the bill. During this feast, the Jews have clearly expressed their murderous desires against Jesus (7:19, 25; 8:59). Because they hate him, they have been ruthless with some defenseless sheep. They didn't care for the lame man of chapter 5 or the blind man of chapter 9. They didn't rejoice with their healing but grilled them for this Sabbath breach. As for the supposed woman who was caught in adultery, they baited a trap with her for Jesus with no apparent concern for her dignity or redemption. They even nipped at their own people who had the gall to question their hateful schemes (Jn 7:46-52).

Such behavior from the Jewish leaders is nothing new. The prophets of old also criticized their leaders as bad shepherds (Jer 23:1-2; Ezek 34:1-10). Both past and present leaders were characterized by (a) rejection of God's men, (b) selfish desire for gain, (c) the use of intimidation or even violence to get their way, and (d) neglect to feed the hungry and nurse the sick. The result then, as now, is a scattered and frightened flock.

Why do these false shepherds not care for the flock? Because they don't own them and have no stock in them. They are like hirelings who are only among the flock for what they can get out of the flock. So when danger presents itself, they run. They lack commitment because they lack investment. This is an age old problem with contemporary counterparts. These are mercenary clergy who feed off the fat of the flock and when

---

[21]Cf. Josephus, *Ant*, 17.10.4-8; also Acts 5:36-37.

danger or opposition presents itself, they move on to greener pastures. They are so unlike the Good Shepherd who lays his life down for the sheep and calls us to the same commitment (1 Jn 3:16; 1 Pet 5:2-3).

This poor flock not only endures mercenary hirelings, but robbers and wolves as well. These outside enemies likely symbolize Satan and his cohorts. They steal, kill and destroy. That's what Satan specializes in. So, God's people are abused by corrupt leaders from within and hounded by Satanic forces from without. The irony of it all is that the hirelings do as much damage as the wolves and robbers. Perhaps we should turn back to John 8:44. The hirelings are related to the robber.

Jn 10:14-18

[14]"I am the good shepherd; I know my sheep and my sheep know me — [15]just as the Father knows me and I know the Father — and I lay down my life for the sheep. [16]I have other sheep that are not of this sheep pen. I must bring them also. They too will listen to my voice, and there shall be one flock and one shepherd. [17]The reason my Father loves me is that I lay down my life — only to take it up again. [18]No one takes it from me, but I lay it down of my own accord. I have authority to lay it down and authority to take it up again. This command I received from my Father."

As the allegory winds down, Jesus again emphasizes three familiar themes: "I am the good shepherd" (cf. v. 11), "I know my sheep and they know me" (cf. v. 3), and "I lay down my life for the sheep" (cf. v. 11). But some new information is added. First, Jesus says that his knowledge of the sheep is connected to the Father. He is the chief shepherd of the Father's flock.

Next, we learn that the flock is bigger than the present audience. From this one sheep pen (the Jews), Jesus draws out only a remnant — the true sheep (Jer 23:3; Eze 34:11-13). In other words, not all the Jews are part of God's flock. Then Jesus goes on to other "folds" (i.e., the Gentiles, cf. Jn 17:20 & Mt 28:19), and draws from different nations those who, by faith, belong to God's fold (Gen 12:3; Ps 87:4-6; Isa 54:2-3; 60:3; Joel 2:28; Mic 4:1-2; Mal 1:11; Eph 1:9-10; 3:6).

Finally, we read that Jesus' death for the flock was voluntary and temporary. Any other shepherd must preserve his own life to save the flock. Once the shepherd dies the flock is scattered and destroyed. And that is what happened to the disciples at Jesus' death. But because he also "took up" his life again, the flock was then gathered and restored.

§ 101b
Division Over
Jesus
(Jn 10:19-21)

[19]At these words the Jews were again divided. [20]Many of them said, "He is demon-possessed and raving mad. Why listen to him?"

[21]But others said, "These are not the sayings of a man possessed by a demon. Can a demon open the eyes of the blind?"

Once more the crowds are divided over Jesus (Jn 6:52; 7:12, 30-31, 43; 8:30; 8:30; 9:16). Many say, "He's crazy" (demon-possessed). They haven't changed their tune since John 7:20 (cf. Jn 8:48). But others say he can't be crazy. His words are not those of a raving lunatic. They are not normal, but neither are they nonsense. They carry their own force, authority and sanity. And his deeds are not those of a demon-possessed person. He is not convulsing about in the dust, drooling on himself. He is mixing his saliva with dust and healing blind eyes. That is neither natural nor demonic. This man at least deserves a hearing.

§ 93
Not All Can
Follow
(Mt 8:19-22;
Lk 9:57-62)[22]

Matthew places this event in the first year of Jesus' ministry even before he appointed the Apostles. Luke, however, puts it in the third year of ministry, as Jesus heads to Jerusalem. It is such a specific story that it's unlikely this same thing happened twice. So we must choose. Do we follow Matthew's order? Or Luke's? Or neither?[23]

If we follow Matthew, two guys come up to Jesus just as he was trying to escape from the crowds. He's about to cross the sea over to the area of the Gadarenes. They want to follow him but he says, "No." Matthew's placement fits the context well. It explains why Jesus would not have wanted them to tag along. It also explains Mark's additional comment that other boats tried to follow Jesus across the sea (4:36). However, Matthew 8 and 9 are notoriously topical, not chronological. Furthermore, how can Jesus say that he doesn't have a house in Capernaum? He has just come out of Peter's house (Mt 8:14) and his own family had apparently moved to that city (Jn 2:12).

Luke's chronology makes more sense. Jesus' ministry turns toward Jerusalem (Lk 9:51). On the way there he is rejected in Samaria (Lk 9:52-56). Once he gets there, he is rejected by the Jews (Jn 7-9). In fact, they even try to assassinate him. That sets the stage for this event. Anyone who wishes to follow Jesus had better not waver. He is an itinerant preacher in Judea, a place particularly bitter towards him right now. It does seem strange that a scribe would want to follow Jesus in such a hostile environment. But opinions were mixed about this phenomenal teacher (Jn 10:21), and this scribe's wavering faith betrays his struggle.

---

[22]We have kept Thomas & Gundry's section number, but have reordered the events to follow Luke's presentation.

[23]This work will follow Luke's order. R.C. Foster follows Matthew's. And Thomas and Gundry follow neither.

Lk 9:57-62 *with*
Mt 8:19-22

[57]As they were walking along the road, a man {a teacher of the law[MT]} said to him, "{Teacher,[MT]} I will follow you wherever you go."

[58]Jesus replied, "Foxes have holes and birds of the air have nests, but the Son of Man has no place to lay his head."

[59]He said to another man {disciple,[MT]} "Follow me."

But the man replied, "Lord, first let me go and bury my father."

[60]Jesus said to him, "{Follow me, and[MT]} Let the dead bury their own dead, but you go and proclaim the kingdom of God."

[61]Still another said, "I will follow you, Lord; but first let me go back and say good-by to my family."

[62]Jesus replied, "No one who puts his hand to the plow and looks back is fit for service in the kingdom of God."

Jesus has created quite a stir at Tabernacles (Jn 7-9). Some people loved him; some hated him (Jn 10:20). As he leaves the city for an itinerant tour of Judea a number of folk follow him. Three individuals in particular seek to follow Jesus, but with "riders" attached. Jesus rejects all three excuses and demands total resignation from these would-be disciples.

First comes a teacher of the law, likely a Pharisee. He is an outsider wanting in. He promises to go anywhere with Jesus. Jesus reminds him that discipleship promises none of the "creature comforts" to which a man in his position is undoubtedly accustomed. That is not to say that Jesus is penniless, but that his itinerant ministry guarantees no security. The text doesn't say for sure whether or not the scribe follows, but it strongly suggests that he does not. No one in Matthew who addresses Jesus as "Teacher" fully believes in him (cf. 12:38; 19:16; 22:16, 24, 36).[24] And elsewhere Pharisees and teachers of the law lack sincerity in dealing with Jesus.

Second comes a disciple. He is an insider wanting out temporarily. He wants to postpone his appointment until after his father's funeral. He may be asking Jesus leave for the normal period of mourning, which may last for months. More likely, his father is not even dead yet. Since Palestinian funerals were typically performed on the day of death, it is not likely that this fellow would be hanging out with Jesus if his dad just died. There would be funeral duties to perform.[25] Therefore, we suggest that this fellow's father was on his deathbed and that after his passing the

---

[24]In Matthew, true believers address Jesus as Lord (Mt 8:2, 6, 8, 21, 25; 9:28; 14:28, 30; 15:22, 25, 27; 16:22; 17:4, 15; 18:21; 20:30-31, 33; 26:22). Furthermore, Jesus calls himself "Son of Man" with outsiders (Mt 9:6; 11:19; 12:8, 32; 16:13), except when he is speaking eschatologically. J.D. Kingsbury, "On Following Jesus: The 'Eager' Scribe and the 'Reluctant' Disciple (Mt 8:18-22)," *NTS* 34 (1988): 45-59.

[25]Some have made the unlikely suggestion that Jesus was granting his disciples the same exemption from funeral duties that the Nazirites and priests had (Lev 21:1-12; Num 6:7).

son would resume following Jesus. Jesus' cryptic saying, "Let the dead bury their own dead" may be severe sarcasm but more likely he means, "Let the spiritually dead take care of the mundane affairs; you have more important business to attend to."

B.R. McCane offers another attractive solution to this cryptic passage.[26] About a year after burial, when nothing was left but bones, Jewish families would reenter the tomb and collect the bones into a stone box called an ossuary. Thus the whole family could be buried together. This act completed the mourning process and was so sacred as to be compared with the rites of weddings and circumcisions (*Semahot* 12.5). Thus, "Let the dead bury the dead," would mean, "Let the other bones in the ossuary collect these bones for themselves." Either way, Jesus' words are so insightful and incisive that his hearers would have to have said, "Ouch!" with a smile on their faces.

Here comes a third disciple. He asks for leave to say good-bye to his family. But Jesus has already demanded total allegiance above family (cf. Mt 10:37; Lk 14:26). Any good farmer knows that looking backwards at the plow causes crooked furrows. Any good follower of Jesus knows that dual devotion is devastating to productivity in the kingdom (Mt 6:24).

Jesus allows no excuses for not following: Desire for security; secular duties; or even family ties. Jesus does not want to be number one, he wants to be the *only* one!

§ 102a
Sending Out
the "Seventy"
(Lk 10:1-16)

As Jesus sent out the Twelve (Lk 9:1-6; Mt 10), he now sends out seventy-two. In fact, much of this section is word for word what we find in Matthew 10-11. Because they are such similar settings, the same words apply to both situations. Edersheim notes (II:138), however, that the mission of the seventy-two was temporary as compared to the lifetime mission of the Twelve. That becomes clear when we observe what was left out of Jesus' commission to the seventy-two (Lk 10) as compared to the Twelve (Mt 10).

During the Feast of Tabernacles, Jesus regained much of the popularity he lost during the last six months of secrecy (Jn 7:31, 40-41, 45-51; 9:16, 38; 10:21). That made for a ready militia of preachers to do in Judea what the Twelve did nearly a year earlier in Galilee. Jesus is about to tour Judea. These men were sent ahead to prepare for his arrival in each town and village.

---

[26]B.R. McCane, "'Let the Dead Bury Their Own Dead': Secondary Burial and Matt 8:21-22," *HTR* 83/1 (1990): 31-43.

Lk 10:1-4

[1]After this the Lord appointed seventy-two[a] others and sent them two by two ahead of him to every town and place where he was about to go. [2]He told them, "The harvest is plentiful, but the workers are few. Ask the Lord of the harvest, therefore, to send out workers into his harvest field. [3]Go! I am sending you out like lambs among wolves. [4]Do not take a purse or bag or sandals; and do not greet anyone on the road."

[a]*1 Some manuscripts* seventy*, also in verse 17*

Jesus has just rejected three "would-be" followers (Lk 9:57-62). Because they have their own conditions, they are not worthy of discipleship. Just when we think that following Jesus is too difficult, we find seventy-two who rise to the challenge. They are prepared to give him their undivided loyalty.

There is strong manuscript support for both the number seventy and seventy-two. Interestingly, there is also a good bit of confusion about the number of Sanhedrin members. Some say there were seventy, some seventy-two. Perhaps this suggests that this group of preachers somehow represented an authoritative, legislative body of the Kingdom of God (cf. Num 11:16). That is not to say that this is not literally the number of preachers sent out. It is to suggest, however, that this band of itinerant preachers was an official delegation of Jesus as were the Twelve earlier.[27]

Like the Twelve, the seventy-two were: (1) Sent out in pairs (cf. Mk 6:7; compare Lk 7:18-19; Acts 13:2; 15:27, 39-40; 17:14; 19:22), (2) sent as precursors of Jesus' visit, (3) sent like lambs[28] among wolves, (4) not to take extra provisions, (5) to graciously accept hospitality without taking advantage of it by moving from house to house, (6) to bless homes with peace or curse towns by shaking dust, (7) granted supernatural power (compare Lk 10:17-19 with Mt 10:1, 8), and (8) to announce the presence of the Kingdom of God/Heaven. These similarities are further evidence that the seventy-two, like the Twelve, are an authoritative group. It would be hard for the locals of Judea not to compare them with the Sanhedrin, which Jesus has just confronted and confounded at the last feast.

Their journey is to be light and fast. Jesus orders them not to take any extra "stuff" and not even to stop and greet people along the road

---

[27]Liefeld (p. 940), observes that there is a manuscript variant at Genesis 10. The MT has seventy nations, the LXX has seventy-two. Thus, this might suggest that the number of evangelists has reference to the number of nations. As the twelve Apostles represent each of the twelve Jewish tribes, the seventy-two represent each of the known nations. Of course that fits the numbers well, but is foreign to this context. It is still a bit early to speak about salvation going to the Gentiles.

[28]Mt 10:16 reads "sheep." Luke paints an even more pathetic picture than Matthew.

(cf. 2 Kgs 4:29). Oriental customs of greeting are elaborate and time-consuming. They may appear impolite as they snub the strangers they meet along the way. But they simply don't have the time to spend on the luxury of social niceties. There are only two months between the feasts of Tabernacles and Dedication. That is all the time Jesus has to cover the large territory of Judea. Thus, even seventy-two will have to hustle to accomplish in Judea what Jesus and the Twelve have accomplished in Galilee.

[Verse 2 = Mt 9:37-38, see comments in § 70a]
[Verse 3 = Mt 10:16a, see comments in § 70b]
[Verse 4 = Mt 10:9-10a, see comments in § 70b]

Lk 10:5-8

⁵"When you enter a house, first say, 'Peace to this house.' ⁶If a man of peace is there, your peace will rest on him; if not, it will return to you. ⁷Stay in that house, eating and drinking whatever they give you, for the worker deserves his wages. Do not move around from house to house.
⁸"When you enter a town and are welcomed, eat what is set before you."

This blessing of "peace" [Heb. *shalom*] was the normal Hebrew greeting. But it was deeper than a "How do you do?" It was almost equivalent to a prayer for the person's wholeness. As we saw in Matthew 10:12-13, the Apostles have Jesus' delegated authority for preaching, healing, and this blessing. Likewise, the seventy-two, as representatives of Jesus, also have his access to the Father. When they bless a home with "Peace," it is an effectual prayer for the welfare of that home. Likewise, in the next section, when they curse a town by shaking off its dust, that is no mere symbol. It is an effectual imprecation against that town.

The instruction of verses 7-8 is not intended to be ammunition for parents to command their children to eat all their peas. Rather, these commissioned preachers are not to be shy about eating off someone else's table. They have earned it by their preaching (cf. 1 Cor 9:3-18; 3 John 5-8).

[Verses 5-8 = Mt 10b-13, see comments in § 70b]

Lk 10:9-12

⁹"Heal the sick who are there and tell them, 'The kingdom of God is near you.' ¹⁰But when you enter a town and are not welcomed, go into its streets and say, ¹¹"Even the dust of your town that sticks to our feet we wipe off against you. Yet be sure of this: The kingdom of God is near.' ¹²I tell you, it will be more bearable on that day for Sodom than for that town."

The message is the same for those who accept and those who reject: "The kingdom of God is near." The reception a preacher gets must not change his messages. Furthermore, the verb "is near" is in the perfect tense. That is, the kingdom of God *has come near* — it is near *now*! That makes verse 12 all the more frightening. If you reject Jesus, there will be hell to pay (cf. Rom 9:29; 2 Pet 2:6; Jude 7).

[Verses 9 = Mt 10:7-8, see comments in § 70b]
[Verses 10-12 = Mt 10:14-15, see comments in § 70b]

Lk 10:13-16

¹³"Woe to you, Korazin! Woe to you, Bethsaida! For if the miracles that were performed in you had been performed in Tyre and Sidon, they would have repented long ago, sitting in sackcloth and ashes. ¹⁴But it will be more bearable for Tyre and Sidon at the judgment than for you. ¹⁵And you, Capernaum, will you be lifted up to the skies? No, you will go down to the depths.ª

¹⁶"He who listens to you listens to me; he who rejects you rejects me; but he who rejects me rejects him who sent me."

ª*15* Greek *Hades*

The mention of Korazin, Bethsaida and Capernaum seems out of place here in Judea. Luke likely incorporates this saying of Jesus here because it fits so well with the mention of Sodom in verse twelve. Nonetheless, the meaning is hard to miss. Had Jesus done his great miracles on these enemies of Israel, they surely would have repented. Yet God's people continue to reject God's messenger.

[Verses 13-15 = Mt 11:21-23, see comments in § 58]
[Verse 16 = Mt 10:40, see comments in § 70b]

§ 102b
Return of the "Seventy"
(Lk 10:17-24)

¹⁷The seventy-two returned with joy and said, "Lord, even the demons submit to us in your name."

¹⁸He replied, "I saw Satan fall like lightning from heaven. ¹⁹I have given you authority to trample on snakes and scorpions and to overcome all the power of the enemy; nothing will harm you. ²⁰However, do not rejoice that the spirits submit to you, but rejoice that your names are written in heaven."

The tour was exhilarating to the "seventy." No doubt they enjoyed the power of Jesus flowing through them to the benefit of the crowds. Jesus enjoyed it too. We can almost see him laugh with the seventy-two as they top each others' stories with accounts of healings and "power encounters." Jesus sees all this from a different vantage point.[29] His

---

[29]J.V. Hills, "Luke 10:18 — Who Saw Satan Fall?" *JSNT* 46 (1992): 25-40, proposes that *etheōroun* should be translated "they saw" rather than "I saw." Thus, it would not be Jesus who watched Satan's demise but the demons of v. 17 who saw their leader fall. Hence "Jesus' response to the disciples is an explanation of their successful exorcism: the demons became subject to the disciples because they had seen their leader, Satan, dethroned."

spiritual perspective reveals Satan's demise (cf. Isa 14:4-11; Rev 12:9). It looked like lightning. Does that mean that Satan fell with great speed? Or that his fall was dazzling? More likely, it means that Satan's fall was seen all over the place. After all, the verb "saw" is in the imperfect tense, indicating that Jesus "was seeing" Satan fall. In other words, Jesus saw Satan falling all over the place. This is how the simile of lightning is used with reference to Jesus' return (Mt 24:27; Lk 17:24).

Like Mark 16:18 (a disputed text), verse 19 mentions a couple of peculiar powers. The ability to trample on snakes and scorpions would actually be more helpful to back-packers than urban preachers. It is probably more reasonable to view these abilities figuratively. That is, the snakes and scorpions likely represent the demons these men cast out (cf. Gen 3:15). After all, the context here is about power over Satan's forces, not natural forces. Even so, Jesus urges them to celebrate their greater blessings. Supernatural powers pale in significance when placed beside salvation.

Lk 10:21-22

²¹At that time Jesus, full of joy through the Holy Spirit, said, "I praise you, Father, Lord of heaven and earth, because you have hidden these things from the wise and learned, and revealed them to little children. Yes, Father, for this was your good pleasure.

²²"All things have been committed to me by my Father. No one knows who the Son is except the Father, and no one knows who the Father is except the Son and those to whom the Son chooses to reveal him."

This is a unique statement about the Holy Spirit giving Jesus joy. Matthew doesn't even contain it. To complicate things further, there is a textual variant here in Luke which leaves out "holy." But the Holy Spirit is one of Luke's favorite themes. It is not altogether surprising that he includes this saying which Matthew doesn't. And Jesus did live in full fellowship with the Holy Spirit (Lk 4:14, Jn 3:34).

[Verses 21-22 = Mt 11:25-27, see comments in § 58]

Lk 10:23-24

²³Then he turned to his disciples and said privately, "Blessed are the eyes that see what you see. ²⁴For I tell you that many prophets and kings {righteous men^MT} wanted {longed^MT} to see what you see but did not see it, and to hear what you hear but did not hear it."

These verses were likely snatched from the sermon in parables. Matthew places them within the private training of the Twelve (Mt 13:10; Mk 4:10). Luke, on the other hand, places them within the private training of the seventy-two. Again we see the privileged position Jesus granted this group.

To say that Luke "borrowed" these words, is not to say that they are unauthentic. Luke, writing from the research of eyewitnesses, uses a quote which Matthew places with another event, but which aptly summarizes the content of this event as well.

[Verses 23-24 = Mt 13:16-17, see comments in § 64b]

§ 103
The Good
Samaritan
(Lk 10:25-37)

This is one of the most powerful stories ever told.[30] An expert in Mosaic law tests Jesus' wits with a complex theological question about eternal life. Jesus, in response, rocks his world with a simple story about living life in the here and now. In this story, we encounter three philosophies of life. The thieves selfishly say, "What's yours is mine." These clergymen, with dreadful justification, say, "What's mine is mine." This Samaritan surprisingly says, "What's mine is yours." He alone is worthy to inherit eternal life. It's not an issue of what he does, but what he is.

Lk 10:25-29

[25]On one occasion an expert in the law stood up to test Jesus. "Teacher," he asked, "what must I do to inherit eternal life?"
[26]"What is written in the Law?" he replied. "How do you read it?"
[27]He answered: "'Love the Lord your God with all your heart and with all your soul and with all your strength and with all your mind'[a]; and, 'Love your neighbor as yourself.'[b]"
[28]"You have answered correctly," Jesus replied. "Do this and you will live."
[29]But he wanted to justify himself, so he asked Jesus, "And who is my neighbor?"

[a]27 Deut. 6:5   [b]27 Lev. 19:18

In Galilee Jesus had been hounded by lawyers from Jerusalem. Here in Judea his movements would certainly be monitored even more closely. We don't know that this guy is a spy, but he looks suspicious. He comes to question Jesus. It's more than a quiz; it's a potential trap (*ekpeirazō*). His question is reasonable and important, but not easy. With the hundreds of laws in the OT and the thousands of oral traditions, how's a fellow to know which ones are essential for gaining eternal life? It's not always easy, you see, to weed out the wheat from the chaff.

My, how well Jesus understands people! He knows this lawyer would rather talk than listen. So he invites him to give his own professional interpretation of the law. After all, that was his field. His answer

---

[30]F.S. Spencer, "2 Chronicles 28:5-15 and the Parable of the Good Samaritan," *WTJ* 46 (1984): 317-349, persuasively suggests that this story is based on the framework found in 2 Chron 28:5-15.

was excellent! It was, in fact, exactly what Jesus would say (cf. Mt 22:37-40; Mk 12:29-31). Being God's child all boils down to this: Love God and love his other children.

This first and greatest command is what the Jews called the *shema*. It is found in Deuteronomy 6:5 where it says to love God with three things: Heart, soul, and "everything." But here, because there is no equivalent Greek word for the Hebrew "everything" [*moed*], two words are used in the place of the one: strength and mind. Thus we love God with our heart, soul, strength and mind.

The second commandment, from Leviticus 19:18, is crucial to understanding the first. How can we show love to God? Sure, there are certain rituals we can perform. But they can be done rather emptily. We can go to church, read our Bibles, give offerings, etc. for a number of reasons *besides* the love of God. The only practical way we can demonstrate love to God is by loving our neighbor (cf. 1 Jn 4:20-21).[31]

Jesus congratulates the lawyer for answering well. But then, with a gentle nudge, he says, "You know what is right, now just do it." This lawyer is sharp. He hears what Jesus means: "Your answer is excellent, but your behavior needs improvement." Instead of repenting, he does what any good hypocrite would do . . . he tries to justify himself. But the only way to justify oneself is to diminish the demands of the law. Since we can't live up to the law, we must cut it down to our size. If we rationalize, justify, modify, or explain away the demands of the law, then maybe we have a chance. If I can just narrow the field enough, then I can claim to love my neighbor. This question, "Who is my neighbor?" is designed to do just that. The power of this parable is that it explodes the parameters of "neighborness" far beyond what this lawyer, or most of us, would ever imagine.

Lk 10:30-35

[30]In reply Jesus said: "A man was going down from Jerusalem to Jericho, when he fell into the hands of robbers. They stripped him of his clothes, beat him and went away, leaving him half dead. [31]A priest happened to be going down the same road, and when he saw the man, he passed by on the other side. [32]So too, a Levite, when he came to the place and saw him, passed by on the other side. [33]But a Samaritan, as he traveled, came where the man was; and when he saw him, he took pity on him. [34]He went to him and bandaged his wounds, pouring on oil and wine. Then he put the man on his own donkey, took him to an inn and took care of him. [35]The next day he took out two silver coins[a] and gave them to

---

[31]J. Piper, "Is Self-Love Biblical?" *CT* 21 (1977): 1150-1153, points out that this text says nothing about the current interest in a healthy self-esteem. In fact, he suggests that while the ancient error was loving others too little, the modern error is narcissistic self-engrossment.

the innkeeper. 'Look after him,' he said, 'and when I return, I will reimburse you for any extra expense you may have.'"

ª35 Greek *two denarii*

Verse 30 begins with an interesting word [*hypolabōn*], which the NIV leaves untranslated. In effect, it means that Jesus "took up" the debate with this guy. The gauntlet has been thrown down and Jesus picks it up and rises to the verbal contest. This parable is not just in response to the lawyer's second question, "Who is my neighbor," but to his first, "What must I do to be saved?"

This road from Jerusalem to Jericho was especially dangerous. Robbers loved it because there were lots of curves, caves and cliffs to hide in. It was nicknamed Adummim (Josh 15:7; 18:17), which means "The Pass of Blood." So no one was surprised to hear in this story that the traveler was brutalized and abandoned.

The first two people to pass his way were both clergymen. The primary job of priests was to officiate at the temple sacrifices. Levites, on the other hand, helped maintain the temple and its services. Both were obligated to remain ceremonially clean while on duty, about four weeks out of the year. The man appears to be dead. And touching a dead body would disqualify them from their sacred duties. Is that why they passed him by? It is, of course, questionable whether ceremonial defilement was a proper excuse for passing by a person in need. This is especially true in light of Jesus' teachings on Sabbath observance (Mt 12:7; Mk 3:4-5). But even this excuse is not applicable to these two. The priest was going down, that is, away from Jerusalem, not toward it. In addition, when going up to Jerusalem for service, priests and Levites traveled in groups, not alone as these two. The bottom line: These guys have no excuse but selfish fear for passing him by.[32]

The next person to pass by was a Samaritan. Now to this Jewish lawyer, the term "Good Samaritan" would be an oxymoron. Samaritans were the hated half-Jews whose rivalry and antagonism was often violent and sometimes deadly (cf. Jn 4:5-26, § 35a). But this unclean Samaritan took pity on this victim. Seeing the man bloodied and beaten

---

[32]It may be somewhat surprising that men of the cloth would be so heartless. But that's nothing new. Darley and Bateson recreated this parable. In their study, forty seminary students were asked to give a talk on the topic of vocational careers of seminarians. They were sent to a nearby building to record their talks. On the way a "victim" was planted to see how these students would react. Twenty-four (60%) of the students walked past the victim, some of them even stepped right over him to get to the recording studio. (Darley, J.M., & Bateson, C.D. "'From Jerusalem to Jericho': A Study of Situational Variables in Helping Behaviour," *JPSP* 27 (1973): 100-108).

broke down the walls of his deep-seated prejudice. There was no natural affinity between these two, only a need.

He bound up his wounds, perhaps making bandages with his own clothes. He poured his own wine on his wounds as a disinfectant. He poured his own oil on his wounds to soothe the pain. He then put the man on his own donkey.[33] He spent his own money for the man's lodging and food. It was not that he liked the man, but the man had a need. He loved in deed.

Lk 10:36-37

[36]"Which of these three do you think was a neighbor to the man who fell into the hands of robbers?"
[37]The expert in the law replied, "The one who had mercy on him."
Jesus told him, "Go and do likewise."

The phrase "was a neighbor" could be translated more literally "became a neighbor." "Neighborness" is not a characteristic inherent in an individual or a location. It is a way of behaving toward any person with whom we come in contact.

There is a striking reversal here. The lawyer has concentrated on the object of love (i.e., God and neighbor). But Jesus concentrates on the subject of love (i.e., the lawyer or me!). We can comfortably theologize about the objects of love. But in order to become the subject, the love-giver, it requires our personal commitment. And if we are like the Samaritan, it will also require a substantial amount of our cash flow.

In answer to Jesus' question, the lawyer could not bring himself to even speak the word "Samaritan." But he could not ignore the obvious thrust of the parable. Jesus has answered both questions, "Who is my neighbor?" and "What must I do to inherit eternal life?"

Jesus' final words are pragmatic and persistent. Persistent because he has already urged the lawyer to *do* what he *knows* is right (v. 28). As if driving the point home, he repeats it again here. His words are pragmatic, because he reminds the lawyer (and the reader), that correct theology is insufficient for inheriting eternal life. If we don't *do* what we know is right, then all our correct answers to Bible questions won't get us one step closer to the Kingdom of God.

---

[33]The word could be used for any pack-animal: Donkey, camel, horse, or ox. It is translated donkey because that was the most commonly used pack animal.

BIBLIOGRAPHY OF CITED SOURCES

Alford, Henry. *The Greek Testament.* Vol. 1. Chicago: Moody, 1958.

Ash, Anthony L. *The Gospel According to Luke.* 2 Vols. Austin, TX: Sweet, 1972.

Barclay, William. *The Gospel of Matthew.* 2 Vols. Philadelphia: Westminster, 1975.

Beasley-Murray, George R. *John.* Vol. 36: *Word Biblical Commentary.* Dallas: Word, 1987.

Blomberg, Craig L. *Matthew.* Vol 22: *The New American Commentary: An Exegetical and Theological Exposition of Holy Scripture.* Ed. by David S. Dockery, et al. Nashville: Broadman, 1992.

Brooks, James A. *The New American Commentary: Mark.* Nashville: Broadman, 1991.

Brown, Raymond E. *The Gospel According to John XII-XXI.* New York: Doubleday, 1970.

Bruce, F.F. *The Hard Sayings of Jesus.* Downers Grove: InterVarsity, 1983.

Butler, Paul T. *The Gospel of John,* Vol. 1. Joplin, MO: College Press, 1961.

_____. *The Gospel of Luke.* Joplin, MO: College Press, 1981.

Carson, D.A. *Matthew.* Vol. 8: *The Expositor's Bible Commentary.* Ed. by Frank E. Gaebelein. Grand Rapids: Zondervan, 1984.

_____. *Sermon on the Mount: An Evangelical Exposition of Matthew 5-7.* Grand Rapids: Baker, 1978.

Crowther, Duane S. *Atlas and Outline of the Life of Christ.* Bountiful, UT: Horizon Publishers & Distributors, 1982.

Dodd, C.H. *Interpretation of the Fourth Gospel.* Cambridge: University Press, 1955.

Edersheim, Alfred. *The Life and Times of Jesus the Messiah.* Peabody, MA: Hendrickson, 1993.

Evans, Craig A. *Luke.* Peabody, MA: Hendricksen, 1990.

Ferguson, Everett. *Backgrounds of Early Christianity.* Grand Rapids: Eerdmans, 1987.

Foreman, Dale. *Crucify Him: A Lawyer Looks at the Trial of Jesus.* Grand Rapids: Zondervan, 1990.

Foster, R.C. *Studies in the Life of Christ.* Joplin, MO: College Press, 1995.

Green, Joel B., Scot McKnight, and I. Howard Marshall, eds. *Dictionary of Jesus and the Gospels.* Downers Grove: InterVarsity, 1992.

Guelich, Robert A. *Mark 1-8:26.* Vol. 34A: *Word Biblical Commentary.* Ed. by David A. Hubbard, Glenn W. Barker, John D.W. Watts, and Ralph P. Martin. Dallas: Word, 1989.

Gundry, Robert H. *Matthew: A Commentary on His Handbook for a Mixed Church Under Persecution.* Grand Rapids: Eerdmans, 1994.

Hendriksen, William. *New Testament Commentary: Exposition of the Gospel According to John.* Grand Rapids: Baker, 1953.

Johnson, Luke Timothy. *The Gospel of Luke*. Ed. by Daniel J. Harrington. Collegeville, MN: Liturgical Press, 1991.

Lane, William L. *The Gospel According to Mark*. Grand Rapids: Eerdmans, 1974.

Lewis, Jack P. *The Gospel According to Matthew*. 2 Vols. Austin, TX: Sweet, 1976.

Liefeld, Walter L. *Luke*. Vol. 8: *The Expositor's Bible Commentary*. Ed. by Frank E. Gaebelein. Grand Rapids: Zondervan, 1984.

Linnemann, Eta. *Is There a Synoptic Problem?* Grand Rapids: Baker Books, 1992.

Longenecker, Richard N. *Acts*. Vol. 9: *The Expositor's Bible Commentary*. Ed. by Frank E. Gaebelein. Grand Rapids: Zondervan, 1981.

The Lost Books of the Bible. New York: Bell Publishing, 1979.

MacArthur, John. *The MacArthur New Testament Commentary: Matthew 16-23*. Chicago: Moody, 1988.

Matthew-Mark. Vol. 8. *The Broadman Bible Commentary*. Ed. by Clifton J. Allen, et al. Nashville: Broadman, 1969.

McGarvey, J.W. and Philip Y. Pendleton. *The Fourfold Gospel: Or A Harmony of the Four Gospels*. Cincinnati: Standard, 1914.

Meserve, Albert D. *The Olivet Discourse: A Study of Matthew 24*. San Jose, CA: San Jose Bible College, 1970.

Morris, Leon. *Expository Reflections on the Gospel of John*. Grand Rapids: Baker, 1988.

Mounce, Robert H. *New International Biblical Commentary: Matthew*. Peabody, MA: Hendrickson Publishers, 1991.

Nolland, John. *Luke 1-9:20*. Vol. 35A: *Word Biblical Commentary*. Ed. by David A. Hubbard, Glenn W. Barker, John D.W. Watts, and Ralph P. Martin. Dallas: Word, 1989.

_____. *Luke 18:35-24:53*. Vol. 35C: *Word Biblical Commentary*. Ed. by David A. Hubbard, Glenn W. Barder, John D.W. Watts, and Ralph P. Martin. Dallas: Word, 1993.

Rogers, Cleon L., Jr. *The Topical Josephus: Historical Accounts that Shed Light on the Bible*. Grand Rapids: Zondervan, 1992.

Rudin, A. James and Marvin R. Wilson. *A Time to Speak: The Evangelical-Jewish Encounter*. Grand Rapids: Eerdmans, 1987.

Ryle, John C. *Expository Thoughts on the Gospels: St. Matthew*. Greenwood, SC: Attic Press, 1974.

Shepard, J.W. *The Christ of the Gospels*. Grand Rapids: Eerdmans, 1939.

Stott, John R.W. *Christian Counter-Culture: The Message of the Sermon on the Mount*. Downers Grove: InterVarsity, 1978.

Tenney, Merrill C. *John*. Vol. 9: *The Expositor's Bible Commentary*. Ed. by Frank E. Gaebelein. Grand Rapids: Zondervan, 1981.

Walvoord, John F. *Matthew: Thy Kingdom Come*. Chicago: Moody, 1974.

Wenham, John. *Easter Enigma: Are the Resurrection Accounts in Conflict?* Grand Rapids: Baker, 1992.

Wessel, Walter W. *Mark.* Vol. 8: *The Expositor's Bible Commentary.* Ed. by Frank E. Gaebelein. Grand Rapids: Zondervan, 1984.

Westcott, Brooke F. *The Gospel According to St. John.* Grand Rapids: Eerdmans, 1950.

Wieand, A. *A New Harmony of the Gospels.* Grand Rapids: Eerdmans, 1947.

The Works of Flavius Josephus, Tr. William Whiston, four volumes. Grand Rapids: Baker, 1974.

TABLES FOR FINDING PASSAGES IN THE *HARMONY*

SUBJECT INDEX